CANADIAN ENVIRONMENTAL POLICY AND POLITICS

The Challenges of Austerity and Ambivalence

Fourth Edition | Debora L. VanNijnatten

OXFORD
UNIVERSITY PRESS

OXFORD
UNIVERSITY PRESS

Oxford University Press is a department of the University of Oxford.
It furthers the University's objective of excellence in research, scholarship,
and education by publishing worldwide. Oxford is a registered trade mark of
Oxford University Press in the UK and in certain other countries.

Published in Canada by
Oxford University Press
8 Sampson Mews, Suite 204,
Don Mills, Ontario M3C 0H5 Canada

www.oupcanada.com

First Edition published in 1992
Second Edition published in 2002
Third Edition published in 2009

Library and Archives Canada Cataloguing in Publication

Canadian environmental policy
Canadian environmental policy and politics: the challenges
of austerity and ambivalence/edited by Debora L. VanNijnatten.

Revision of: Canadian environmental policy: ecosystems, politics,
and process/edited by Robert Boardman.—Toronto: Oxford University Press, 1992.
Includes bibliographical references and index.

ISBN 978–0–19–900542–0 (paperback)

1. Environmental policy—Canada. 2. Environmental policy—Canada—
Case studies. 3. Environmental protection—Canada. I. VanNijnatten, Debora,
1967–, author, editor II. Title.

HC120.E5C355 2015   363.700971   C2015-906384-1

Cover image: The vast Faro Mine Complex in the Yukon,
one of the worlds largest open-pit lead-zinc mines. Paul Nicklen/Getty Images

Oxford University Press is committed to our environment.
This book is printed on Forest Stewardship Council® certified paper
and comes from responsible sources.

FSC
www.fsc.org

MIX
Paper from
responsible sources
FSC® C014174

Printed and bound in the United States of America

1 2 3 4 — 19 18 17 16

Contents

For my mother
Marjorie Eileen VanNynatten

Acknowledgements

With large projects such as this, even the best-laid production plans are sometimes thrown into disarray by life's unexpected difficulties. This book was delayed by such difficulties, and I want to sincerely thank all of the contributors for their patience during a long period of silence, as well as for their responsiveness when work on the volume resumed. I am also very grateful to Kate Skene and Meg Patterson for their commitment to this project and their support throughout. Richard Tallman was an exceptional copy editor, who provided critical advice and encouragement during the fits and starts of the manuscript process.

And, with large projects such as this, it is families who are most disadvantaged by the process of writing and editing. For all the absences on evenings and weekends when I was trying to catch up on things, I apologize to my three children and my husband, Gerry Boychuk. As with all of my other projects, Gerry gave me critical support throughout—and especially at the end, when I was trying to finish what I had started. This is my fifth book, and there is a piece of him in all of them.

I also want to thank my sister, Barbra Dimen, and my father, Jack VanNynatten, for helping me to get back on track after a particularly trying time.

Debora L. VanNijnatten
October 2015
Waterloo, Ontario

Contributors

Cameron D. Anderson is an associate professor in the Department of Political Science at the University of Western Ontario.

Stephen Bocking is a professor in and the chair of the Environmental and Resource Science/Studies Program at Trent University.

Angela V. Carter is an assistant professor in the Department of Political Science at the University of Waterloo.

David Cherniak is a research associate in the School of Public Policy and Administration at Carleton University.

Neil Craik is an associate professor and Director of the School of Environment, Enterprise and Development at the University of Waterloo.

Clare Demerse is a senior policy adviser at Clean Energy Canada.

Timothy Heinmiller is an associate professor in the Department of Political Science at Brock University.

Michael Howlett is Burnaby Mountain Professor in the Department of Political Science at Simon Fraser University.

Carolyn Johns is an associate professor in the Department of Politics and Public Administration at Ryerson University.

Nigel Kinney is a Ph.D. candidate in the Department of Political Science at Simon Fraser University.

Christopher J. Lemieux is an assistant professor in the Department of Geography and Environmental Studies at Wilfrid Laurier University.

Nathan Lemphers is a Trudeau Scholar and Ph.D. student in the Department of Political Science at the University of Toronto.

Douglas Macdonald is a senior lecturer and associate member of graduate faculty in the School of the Environment at the University of Toronto.

Mary Louise McAllister is an associate professor and teaching fellow in the Department of Environment and Resource Studies in the Faculty of Environment at the University of Waterloo.

James Meadowcroft is a professor in both the School of Public Policy and Administration and the Department of Political Science at Carleton University. He holds the Canada Research Chair in Governance for Sustainable Development.

Don Munton is a professor of International Studies, University of North British Columbia.

Tahnee Prior is a Ph.D. candidate at the Balsillie School of International Affairs and the University of Waterloo.

Ian H. Rowlands is a professor in the Department of Environment and Resource Studies in the Faculty of Environment at the University of Waterloo.

Julie M. Simmons is an associate professor in the Department of Political Science at the University of Guelph.

Mark Sproule-Jones is an emeritus professor in the Department of Political Science and Copps Chair in Urban Studies at McMaster University.

Laura B. Stephenson is an associate professor in the Department of Political Science at the University of Western Ontario.

Owen Temby is an assistant professor in the Department of Political Science at the University of Texas Rio Grande Valley.

Glen Toner is a professor in the School of Public Policy and Administration at Carleton University.

Marcia Valiante is a professor in the Faculty of Law at the University of Windsor.

Debora L. VanNijnatten is an associate professor and chair of the Department of Political Science and North American Studies Program at Wilfrid Laurier University.

Inger Weibust is an assistant professor of international affairs, Norman Paterson School of International Affairs, at Carleton University.

Graham White is a professor emeritus in the Department of Political Science at the University of Toronto Mississauga.

Mark Winfield is an associate professor in Environmental Studies at York University, co-chair of the Faculty of Environmental Studies Sustainable Energy Initiative, and co-ordinator of the Master in Environmental Studies/Juris Doctor joint program.

Introduction

Debora L. VanNijnatten[1]

This fourth edition of *Canadian Environmental Policy and Politics* was just supposed to be an "update." Our colleagues at Oxford wanted a relatively straightforward revision to reflect recent changes, keeping for the most part to the third edition's form and function. This proved impossible—which should come as no surprise to students of Canadian environmental policy. Since the third edition was published in 2010, the political and policy landscape has been altered deeply and dramatically. The primary aim of this fourth edition is to examine the nature and extent of these changes, and understand the impact they have had on the existing policy regime, on opportunities for policy progress and innovation, and on the longer-term resilience of that regime.

The phrasing "has been altered" is most deliberate; the changes are neither spontaneous nor primarily external. Broader forces—the global financial crisis comes to mind here—have certainly played a role in setting the domestic scene. In addition, Canada's particular constellation of institutions, featuring a decentralized federation and strong executive control over policy-making, continues to shape the opportunities and constraints that environmental policy actors face. Yet, the most important changes explored in this edition of *Canadian Environmental Policy and Politics* reflect actions taken by our own political and bureaucratic architects in terms of policies and programs. The election of the Harper government with a majority in 2011 presented Conservative policy-makers with an opportunity to superintend the redesign or removal of program structures, including those relating to environmental protection and sustainability, and to construct new policy planking that undergirded a central aim—an economy, and indeed an economic future, based primarily on natural resource development, especially oil and gas. Canada, as Stephen Harper famously stated, should be an "energy superpower."[2] Our policy infrastructure was remade to more directly address this aim, with consequences for environmental protection and sustainability programming.

Certainly, there were many and varied signs in the third edition of *Canadian Environmental Policy and Politics* that all was not well. In the last edition, our authors pointed to a decided lack of environmental policy leadership and an ongoing unwillingness to engage in policy innovation, particularly in terms of instrument choice—despite a context that was somewhat more amenable to such actions in terms of trends in public opinion, the evolving constellation of legislative and political actors, and Canada–US dynamics.[3] Indeed, looking across all editions of this volume, one comes away with the impression that the Canadian environmental policy regime has not become "rock solid" over time. Instead, the collective wisdom presented by this ongoing enterprise indicates a policy regime that has matured in fits and starts, with a gradual strengthening in some areas (such as air pollutant regulation, protected areas, and species at risk), a "yo-yoing" between progress and decline in others (e.g., environmental assessment, water quality, greening of government), and in still other areas, such as climate change, a stubborn lack of progress. Yet, although observers of environmental policy might understand the relatively precarious nature of environmental protection and sustainability in Canada, developments over the past few years have never-theless taken us all by surprise. The differences we see in this fourth edition are more than ones of degree. Rather, they are the equivalent of turning the steering wheel hard to the right (pun intended) and turning onto a new road, one that involves some choices that may be difficult to "unmake" and others that can be rectified only over long periods of time. As this edition goes to press, the October 2015 federal election has—in a result that surprised most observers—brought a majority Liberal government to power. Undoing the many and varied Conservative changes to the environmental policy regime, should the new government wish to undertake this, will be an immense task.

To some considerable extent, these changes were encouraged by both the fiscal and the budgetary context, but the ambivalence towards environmental protection and sustainabil-ity in Canada also has played a role. In this fourth edition, we have organized our exploration under the twin themes of "austerity" and "ambivalence." Austerity, in the most immediate sense, refers to the policies used by governments to reduce budget deficits during adverse economic conditions, and we have seen deep budget cuts at the federal level, as well as across the provinces. Ambivalence, for its part, is a term used to convey "mixed" impulses of a more general sort, by a simultaneous desire to say or do two opposite or conflicting things, resulting in uncertainty or indecisiveness. The themes of "austerity" and "ambivalence" are not intended to be conceptual but rather substantive. In this Introduction, we highlight the cumulative evidence of a deeply rooted ambivalence in the Canadian environmental policy regime compounded by the impacts of austerity, and we reflect more broadly on the kind of environmental policy regime that has been (re)fashioned. We also reflect on the challenges that confront the Liberals under Justin Trudeau, given that they have resolved to take quick action to restore environmental safeguards and pursue sustainability.

The Context at Home and Abroad

In retrospect, it may be that the contributions to the third edition underestimated the impact of the global financial crisis on Canada more generally, and on the environmental policy and political context more specifically. Or, to be fair, one might argue that its impacts had simply not yet become manifest. In an overview of the causes and impacts of the global financial crisis written for the Parliament of Canada in December of 2008, Philippe Bergevin explained that Canada's financial system "has been relatively less affected by the global financial crisis than those of other industrialized countries such as the United States and Great Britain."[4] He attributed the low level of impact to the stable, well-capitalized (and concentrated) bank-ing sector and to Canada's "more prudent" regulatory framework, particularly vis-à-vis the "securitization" of mortgages and other assets into tradable financial instruments. Where Bergevin saw cause for worry was in weaker demand for Canadian exports to the US, which meant further problems for the already weak manufacturing sector and lower demand for energy and natural resources.[5]

By the end of 2009, amid warnings by international organizations such as the IMF and OECD about "worrisome parallels" between 2009 economic vitals and those during the Great Depression of the 1930s,[6] signs that the Canadian economy was weakening grew: exports shrank by a third over 2008–9; the economy contracted swiftly (5.4 per cent in the first quar-ter of 2009); and the official unemployment rate had risen to 8.4 per cent.[7] The federal govern-ment, though it was initially very reluctant to do so, responded with an impressive stimulus package worth $47 billion over two years, which provided huge monies for infrastructure funding, a bailout for automakers (on the order of $13.7 billion), and a wide array of credits to homeowners and parents.[8] At the same time, however, the government promised that the books would once again be balanced by 2015. Given that this was the first deficit announced since the 1996–7 fiscal year, and that larger deficits were predicted, it was clear that program cuts were on the horizon.

The economic situation certainly changed the rules of the game. It provided the Conservatives, who gained majority government status in the May 2011 federal election, with a clear lens for framing their domestic policy activities, one that emphasized the economic vulnerability of Canadians, the importance of financial stability, and Canada's leadership role internationally in addressing the crisis. All of these, as Cameron Anderson and Laura Stephenson point out in Chapter 1, were a good sell with Canadian voters. This crisis, so framed, ushered in and legitimized a series of belt-tightening measures and program changes deemed "necessary" to achieve the all-important goal of a balanced budget, portrayed as the centrepiece of financial stability. Indeed, by February 2014, then Finance Minister Jim Flaherty had released an update on the Economic Action Plan indicating that the government was on track to deliver on the balanced budget commitment, and even predicted a surplus of $6.4 billion by 2015–16.[9]

This emphasis on getting Canada's finances in order to address the crisis fit nicely with the Harper government's other major aim: growing the economy through aggressive expansion of the oil and gas sector. Our readers will immediately notice that this volume is overwhelmingly focused on the energy–climate policy nexus. This is simply unavoidable in the current context. As Clare Demerse and Nathan Lemphers argue in Chapter 2, "Responsible Resource Development" became the mantra of the day. As the authors explain, Canada's natural resources include mineral riches and forests, but the sector with the most ambitious growth plans is oil and gas. Canada has the world's third largest proven oil reserves, and the overwhelming majority of those reserves are in the tar sands—where deposits of bitumen are found mixed with sand, silt, and water, and require considerable energy- and water-intensive refining and processing.[10] In the Harper government's Economic Action Plan, natural resource development was described as "the backbone of our economy" and was equated with "jobs, long-term growth and prosperity for all Canadians—both today and for generations to come."[11] Citing the natural resources sector as accounting for 50 per cent of exports, 10 per cent of jobs and 20 per cent of gross domestic product (GDP), the Responsible Resource Development policy aimed to "seize this opportunity" to unleash the "potential for massive investments in resource sectors in every region."[12]

Taken together, the need to respond to financial crisis and the portrayal of energy development as the economic panacea provided the government with a firm rationale for remaking federal policy. Indeed, the introduction of the Conservatives' focus on resource development and energy policy came with overhauls of the Canadian Environmental Assessment Act, the Navigable Waters Protection Act, the National Energy Board Act, and the Fisheries Act, among others, as analyzed in detail by Marcia Valiante in Chapter 4 and Mark Winfield in Chapter 5. To maximize the value that Canada draws from natural resources, significant system-wide changes were introduced to decrease the regulatory burden associated with assessing the environmental impacts of new development projects, to "achieve the goal of one project, one review in a clearly defined time period, and streamline the review process for major economic projects." As Valiante explains, the number and type of projects that must undergo environmental assessment, the privileging of the project proponent in the provision of information on which screening decisions are based, new (and significant) restrictions placed on the role of the "interested public" in the assessment process, and a greater ability to "substitute" provincial assessments for federal ones are all features of the new regime. Other noteworthy changes to the environmental protection regime include a narrowing of what was formerly a broad-based federal authority to protect aquatic eco-systems and restore or maintain fish habitats, and an off-loading of federal regulatory duties in other areas to provinces under designated "equivalencies." Quite concerning, as Graham White points out in Chapter 10, is the amalgamation of multiple assessment authorities and bodies originally created under the terms of agreements with Aboriginal groups in order—again—to streamline the approval process for natural resource developments.

These thoroughgoing substantive and procedural changes to the legal and policy frame-work governing environmental policy were accompanied by significant changes to how policy discussions were taking place at the federal level. The election of a Harper majority government in 2011 altered both the possibilities and the pathways for dissent across the political system. Certainly, in a majority Parliament, government MPs can set the agenda and ensure passage of government legislation relatively easily. The majority Parliament, however, seemed even more inaccessible to members of the opposition parties. The legisla-tive agenda, committee deliberations, the rights of parliamentary officers to testify before legislative bodies, and even resources for the offices of opposition members all came under the tight control of the governing party.[13] Parliament was prorogued three times in order to block opposition motions to defeat the government (as in 2008), to question government actions (the Afghan detainee issue in 2009), or to delay the legislative start (and avoid ques-tions about the Senate spending scandal).[14] Opposition party questions about environ-mental issues in Question Period could still theoretically generate media attention, as could critiques of government performance through statements or reports by the federal Commis-sioner of the Environment and Sustainable Development (see Chapter 7 for an explanation of this important role), but it might be fair to say that the lack of Conservative concern for the environment became "old news," rarely producing sustained coverage.

The Conservative fondness for "omnibus" (derived from the Latin term for "everything") legislation allowed the government to pass far-reaching and often controversial changes to diverse pieces of legislation in one fell swoop, wherein debate was limited and voting strictly controlled by the governing party. In June 2012, the omnibus budget bill C-38 was passed. Entitled the Jobs, Growth and Long-term Prosperity Act, this legislation repealed, amended, or overhauled no less than 70 existing pieces of legislation, including (among many others) the Canadian Environmental Assessment Act (totally overhauled), the Canadian Environmental Protection Act (waste disposal limits weakened), the Kyoto Protocol Implementation Act (repealed), the Navigable Waters Protection Act (pipelines and power lines exempted from its provisions), the Energy Board Act (reviews limited), the Species at Risk Act (critical habitat protections weakened, especially in regard to pipeline development), the Coasting Trade Act (changes made to facilitate offshore drilling), and the Nuclear Safety Control Act (assessment moved to the licensing body, the Canadian Nuclear Control Commission).[15] C-38 also termin-ated the National Round Table on the Environment and the Economy, a highly respected (and sometimes critical) voice on environmental and sustainable development policy.[16] Funding for a wide range of departments and programs supporting environmental program imple-mentation, monitoring, and research was ended or reduced (see examples below). Later that year, in December 2012, another 457-page omnibus budget bill, C-45, called the Jobs and Growth Act, amended 64 different Acts or regulations, making additional changes to the Navigation Protection Act, the Fisheries Act, and the Canadian Environmental Assessment Act in order to further widen the applicability of restrictions on project assessments.[17]

Inside the policy-making machinery of the federal bureaucracy, the Prime Minister's Office maintained firm control over the provision and processing of information, the making of policy, and communications to the public. As Donald Savoie has observed more generally, public servants have lost much of the power they once held over the formation of public policy to a tight-knit group that revolves around the Prime Minister, including political insiders, pollsters, lobbyists, and consultants.[18] This trend started long before Harper, but undergirding this dynamic under the former governing party was its deep mistrust of even the most competent and highly placed public servants.[19] On this issue, the Professional Institute of the Public Service of Canada (PIPSC) conducted a survey of public servants in an attempt to gauge the impact of requirements introduced by the Harper government that they seek approval before being interviewed by journalists. The 2013 report revealed that large majorities (on the order of 80–90 per cent) of those surveyed felt that they were not allowed to speak freely, to share their concerns with the public, or to develop objective policies, and they admitted that they had witnessed political interference and the withholding of information important to public health or the environment. Such a context of strict control over policy-relevant information has very clear impacts, as Stephen Bocking argues in Chapter 6, impairing our ability to manage our resources sustainably, to adjudicate among conflicting uses or values regarding the environment, and to anticipate new environmental problems.

Public interest groups outside of government were also effectively shut out of the policy process. As Demerse and Lemphers explain in Chapter 2, the corridors of Parliament and its offices were all but closed to environmental groups intent on reminding ministers of their statutory and international responsibilities, to the point that ENGOs pulled up stakes in federal politics and focused their efforts in other venues, particularly at the provincial and local levels. It is fair to say that the levels of animosity directed at ENGOs had not been seen for decades (if ever). To provide but one clear example of this, in 2012 Joe Oliver, then Minister of Natural Resources, stated in no uncertain terms that the Conservative government viewed "environmental and other radical groups" as an obstacle to natural resource development, "hijacking" the regulatory system to "achieve their ultimate objective: delay a project to the point it becomes economically unviable."[20] Industry groups, however, received ongoing government support. As Angela Carter notes in Chapter 17, the federal government and many provincial governments have actively facilitated the growth of Canada's oil industry, providing a variety of direct and indirect subsidies as well as privileged access to decision-makers, and creating lobbying campaigns to defend it at home and abroad.

In earlier editions of *Canadian Environmental Policy and Politics*, it has been argued that the United States can be a positive influence on Canadian environmental policy-making, through such mechanisms as diplomatic pressure, the "California effect," or cross-border co-operation on pollution problems.[21] Yet, the Harper government's approach to resource development and environmental policy has not sat well with the US Democratic administration—although there are certainly admirers among Republicans in Congress. While Harper has made concerted efforts to keep American and Canadian trade interests in line (given Canada's clear economic vulnerability here), his aggressive stance on the

Keystone XL pipeline expansion into the US and his lack of interest in domestic and international climate change efforts were clearly at odds with efforts by the Obama administration to leave a climate change regulatory "legacy." In this regard, as Debora VanNijnatten discusses in Chapter 11, Canada–United States relations have long passed the point of "unconstructive." Yet, thinly veiled comments made by Obama, or by the US Ambassador to Canada, apparently had little impact on the Harper government.[22]

It is also unfortunately the case that, during this same period when Harper was refining and underscoring his commitment to resource development, environmental policy discussions at the international level made little progress, particularly with respect to climate change. Indeed, as with US–Canada relations, pressures from international institutions and actors failed to temper the Harper government's aggressively pro–natural resource policy stance. Successive United Nations Framework Convention on Climate Change (UNFCCC) Conference of Parties (COP) meetings over 2009–14 remained mired in long-running disagreements between developing nations, such as China, Brazil, and India, and OECD countries on the relative burden for greenhouse gas (GHG) emission reduction as well as where the financing for reduction projects should come from. The Harper government's position in successive COP meetings was that Canada would move on climate change only when there was a commitment from "all major emitters" to reduce emissions.[23] As Neil Craik and Tahnee Prior suggest in Chapter 12, the Conservatives took this stance as part of a broader "interest-based" approach to engagement in international environmental discussions, one that adopted a nuanced, non-interventionist, and narrow perspective on global environmental co-operation in order to safeguard Canada's economic interests.

Understanding the Impacts of Ambivalence and Austerity

As Mark Winfield notes in Chapter 5, "[t]he period following the 2008 economic downturn and federal election has been one of profound retrenchment." Austerity has been the hallmark of all three Harper administrations. While it is impossible here to provide an exhaustive list of all of the cuts relating to environmental protection and sustainability policy, we can provide a few highlights that convey the scope and depth of the reductions.

There have been significant reductions to the budgets of Environment Canada, the Department of Fisheries and Oceans (DFO), Parks Canada, and the Canadian Environmental Assessment Agency, which have resulted in staff losses, for example, in regard to research capabilities, libraries, and data collection (loss of baseline information), diminished core programs, and weaker enforcement.[24] And more were planned to come. If we look at Environment Canada alone, the planned cuts to program funding and staff over the 2014–15 to 2016–17 period would have been considerable, as shown in Table I.1.

If we take a somewhat longer view, projected total program spending cuts over 2011–12 to 2016–17 would have amounted to approximately 31 per cent.[25] Projected decreases over

TABLE I.1 Environment Canada Budgetary Financial Resources (Planned Spending)

2014–15 Planned Spending	2015–16 Planned Spending	2016–17 Planned Spending
$1,011,506,073	$861,462,657	$698,817,787

Source: Environment Canada, *Report on Plans and Priorities*, https://www.ec.gc.ca/default.asp?lang=En&n=024B8406-1&offset=3&toc=show.

2014–15 to 2016–17 in full-time equivalent (FTE) staff were close to 20 per cent. To provide a few examples of how the cuts were allocated, funding for climate change and clean air programs would fall to $55 million from $118 million, while the enforcement budget would drop to $29 million from $41 million by 2017.[26] Cuts of this magnitude were replicated across departments with environmental protection functions, and also occurred at the provincial level. Alberta and Ontario, at the time of writing, are embarking on serious budgetary restructuring and cuts to environment protection functions.

For our students, ambivalence may be more difficult to understand, but the term is an accurate descriptor of the broader context. Ambivalence is a state of having both positive and negative attraction towards someone or something, situations where "mixed feelings" of a more general sort are experienced, or where a person experiences uncertainty or indecisiveness. The ambivalence theme comes from different directions at the decidedly uncertain place of environmental policy and politics in Canada: for example, understanding the role of public concern (as Chapter 1 shows, the public supports environmental protection but won't choose it over economic growth policies); of political parties and especially the governing party (as Chapters 5 and 7 show, there are few incentives in the political system to reward parties that highlight environmental protection); and of ENGOs (as Chapter 2 queries: how do ENGOs design issue campaigns when their product is not clearly of interest to any policy communities?).

Similarly (and relatedly), evidence of ambivalence in our environmental policy architecture is seen by authors throughout this volume in attempts to graft more environmentally friendly policy tools onto regimes fundamentally favouring extractive and other economic activities. Michael Howlett and Nigel Kinney, in Chapter 3, show how this ambivalence is reflected in the ways that federal and provincial governments try to balance environmental policies of conservation against the entrenched staples economic policies that underlie their large but fragile resource sectors. They argue that even those sectors heading into a post-staples reality pose serious challenges to those who want to expand the environmental policy regime, given the subsidies and infrastructure that are firmly in place. Douglas Macdonald in Chapter 13 demonstrates the failure of both federal and provincial governments to this point to seriously grapple with the trade-offs that must be made in order to require emissions reductions from the highest-emitting provinces but also to support these reduction efforts. In Chapter 16, Tim Heinmiller details the attempts made in western provinces to decrease overall water allocations to stakeholders while leaving the existing—clearly unsustainable—allocation regime in place. Owen Temby, Don Munton, and Inger Weibust, in Chapter 19, highlight the superficial nature of the new federal coal regulations, which, in their final form, do not truly accelerate the rate of retirement of old, more polluting plants. So deeply entrenched is this ambivalence in our environmental policy regime, that even the most well-intended government (e.g., the Trudeau Liberals) will face immense difficulties trying to overcome this tendency.

The problem—again, as our chapters highlight—is that when "austerity" hits and budgets/programs get cut, environmental policies are not rooted firmly enough to survive, and they get stripped away or are left untended/unenforced/unimplemented. This pattern certainly predates Stephen Harper, but it has become decidedly more pronounced in recent years, as Winfield argues in Chapter 5. Ian Rowlands provides a fitting example of this dynamic in Chapter 14 in his analysis of renewable electricity policies. Against a backdrop of widely differing levels of support for renewables within single communities (some supporting, others opposing), he finds that transformational energy options, which tend to be more costly than conventional sources, are quite vulnerable to the opposition of "cost-conscious consumers." The impact of austerity here is that renewables attract "scrutiny and disdain" while those energy options that do "more of the same," regardless of their environmental cost, seem to have an easier time. In Chapter 15, Carolyn Johns and Mark Sproule-Jones demonstrate how the "myth of abundance" underpins a longstanding ambivalence in water and environmental policy in the Great Lakes, making it vulnerable over the past several decades to successive cycles of fiscal restraint and budget cuts. Even heightened public awareness, concerted action on the part of policy communities, and international commitments have been unable to sustain appropriate support over time. And, even in those policy areas, such as air quality, which at first blush appear to be an exception to this broader ambivalence in the environmental policy architecture, the commitments made by the Harper government were more akin to "smoke and mirrors," as suggested by Temby, Munton, and Weibust.

Resilience and Our Environmental Policy Future

In Chapter 7, Glen Toner, James Meadowcroft, and David Cherniak, in speaking of sustainable development (SD), explain that:

> SD is often described in terms of three "pillars"—the economic, social, and environmental. Yet, in a rich country like Canada the environmental pillar has been systematically neglected, and the integration of the environmental dimension into development decision-making is both critical and often contested. Environmental integration requires a reconceptualization of what "growth," "development," and "the public good" imply. And it points towards a dramatic transformation of key economic sectors (energy, transport, agriculture, construction, and so on) to reduce the environmental impacts of production and consumption.

The link between the existing and increasing ambivalence in the Canadian environmental policy regime and the resilience of that regime is most worrying. It is no secret that those working in the environmental policy sphere are, for the most part, interested in building and maintaining a policy and program regime that is, to the greatest extent possible, "bulletproof" in the face of political, economic, and social change. What we want is a regime that puts in place a framework for environmental protection and sustainability that can withstand the winds of change—changes in government and leadership, economic highs and lows, alterations in societal trends. This we do not have. The mixed impulses in our regime provide a few foundation blocks, but the architecture is clearly not able to withstand the political damage that has been done. The increasing extent of ambivalence in the regime, coupled with the austerity legacy, will have long-lasting consequences for our ability to respond to current and future environmental challenges.

A clear concern, which wends its way across all the chapters in this volume, is the decline of environmental policy capacity in Canada, particularly at the federal level but also at the provincial level. The deterioration of scientific capacity, discussed by Bocking in Chapter 6, is acute; in the PIPSC report, "91 per cent of federal scientists have concluded that these budget cutbacks are bound to restrict the government's ability to serve the public adequately" and "51 per cent of these scientists believe that the cutbacks have already had a negative impact."

The ability of Environment Canada to enforce its own air pollutant regulations,[27] to perform its roles in freshwater and fisheries management,[28] and to implement marine pollution and emergency response requirements,[29] among other areas, is in serious question. Carter in Chapter 17 provides a long list of concerns regarding the management of oil sands development by federal and provincial environmental agencies—missing ecosystem baseline data, a poor understanding of cumulative environmental impacts, and inadequate monitoring associated with water pollution and withdrawal rates, air pollution, and wildlife and fish. In fact, as Carter notes, the Commissioner of the Environment and Sustainable Development reported that federal government departments were simply unable to assess cumulative impacts of tar sands projects due to "incomplete environmental baselines and environmental data monitoring systems." In the area of biodiversity management, Christopher Lemieux presents evidence in Chapter 18 of inadequate human and financial resources to meet legal requirements for establishing species-at-risk strategies across agencies. To provide but one example, Parks Canada—where staffing for conservation has declined by 23 per cent and the scientific staff complement has been reduced by more than one-third—faces severe capacity challenges associated with implementing biodiversity conservation-related policies and programs. Similar capacity limitations, Lemieux notes, have been observed at the provincial level by the Environmental Commissioner of Ontario and the BC Auditor General.

How, then, might we shore up this architecture? Where should we focus our efforts? Since its first iteration, this volume—explicitly and implicitly—has been organized around "veto points," that is, how do institutions provide constraints and opportunities for actors to push for "better" environmental policy? In reviewing the discussion above, if we use the analogy of a hardening of the arteries, we might argue that the participatory channels leading to central decision-making points have been markedly narrowed, as constraints are placed on these channels and fresh ideas and different viewpoints are unable to circulate around the system. Over time, these constraints become calcified, permanently blocking participation and reinforcing the status quo. This state of affairs greatly complicates the already difficult task in Canada of building the comprehensive and integrated regime necessary to meet the challenge of sustainability. One of the messages conveyed by our authors is that it is critical to focus on keeping these arteries open, so that when interest constellations shift, opportunities for policy change might be pursued. As Mary Louise McAllister notes in Chapter 9, "despite numerous constraints at work in public institutions, the functions and practices of . . . governments are dynamic; as institutions, they do learn and evolve. Possibilities do exist, opportunities arise, and the collective environmental costs of retaining the status quo are becoming painfully apparent." Outside of government, public interest groups are also adapting; both Chapters 2 and 17 highlight the ways in which environmental groups are exploring alternative avenues of protest and dissent.

Another lesson is that national leadership—no matter how strong the provinces are—is required if we are to co-ordinate our environmental protection and sustainability efforts. The current dynamics make a national approach very difficult. Across the chapters in this volume there is some hope that certain provinces—particularly Ontario, British Columbia, and Quebec—would keep the environmental policy fires burning, continuing to prioritize sustainability and experimenting with innovative instruments. Indeed, when majority governments dominate in Ottawa, the most powerful resistance has often come from the provinces. Environmental policy-making in Canada, as Julie Simmons explains in Chapter 8, features a federal government, by decision as well as by design, forced to bargain with muscular provinces. Though the Canadian federal government has the constitutional jurisdiction to address transboundary pollution problems, through such means as the negotiation of international agreements (e.g., the Kyoto Protocol), in most cases the federal government treads lightly. Under the Harper Conservatives, the federal government actually vacated environmental platforms in favour of provincial regulations and, as Simmons so aptly shows, also abandoned any effort to create a co-ordinated federal and provincial environmental policy through the Canadian Council of Ministers of the Environment (CCME). The problem, of course, is that a strategy relying on the provinces to maintain environmental commitments during political transitions and through economic cycles is difficult, particularly when we understand the key role that natural resource development plays in most provinces. And as Macdonald shows in the climate change policy case, there is no substitute for national engagement to bring about the necessary trade-offs across the country to achieve GHG reductions.

One of the clearest weaknesses in our environmental policy architecture is an inability to integrate and co-ordinate—across issues, functions, and instruments. Quite aside from our failure to co-ordinate efforts across federal, provincial, and local jurisdictions, the chapters in this volume highlight the narrow, highly focused lens often applied to policy-making and implementation, and the need to resist this tendency. At the most basic levels, we fail to integrate sustainable development into government planning and programming. We fail to think broadly about policy instrument choice, in terms of how different combinations of instruments can achieve our goals. We fail to think about how incentive structures might be strategically inserted into programs, in more holistic ways. Without a more integrative policy perspective, we are unable to understand the complexities of environmental problems, to co-ordinate our efforts in such a way that we can deliver cobenefits in terms of addressing more than one environmental problem, or to assess adequately where we are succeeding or failing with our chosen policy instruments. In fact, without an integrative perspective, it is difficult even to assess the cumulative impact of austerity programming on the policy and operational capacity of environmental agencies.

Adopting a more inclusive, integrative lens also encourages us to think about broader economic forces on environmental policy. As Howlett and Kinney note in Chapter 3, the very high oil prices during the run-up to the global financial collapse of 2007–8 benefited many governments and companies with windfall revenues and profits. However, oil prices dropped shortly thereafter and again starting in late 2014 as US shale gas and fracking activities increased supplies in that country dramatically. As this book goes to print, oil is trading well below the threshold of profitability for much of the oil sands, and there have been a series of major project cancellations (e.g., Total's Joslyn mine, Shell's at Pierre River, and Statoil's Corner oil sands venture), while others have been indefinitely postponed; such projects no longer make sense in the current marketplace.[30] Thus, even before the defeat of the Harper Conservatives in the October 2015 federal election, it was becoming clear that we were unlikely to see the kind of massive expansion of oil sands production that would undergird the activities of a purported "energy superpower," one whose grand vision included a doubling of oil sands production over the next 20 years. The length of the slump in prices, as well as the turnover in governments in 2015, could lead to a re-evaluation of energy policy; it also places a rather large question mark beside the highly contentious proposed Keystone XL and Northern Gateway pipelines to US and Asian markets. Of further note, the impacts of the oil slump are not being felt uniformly across the country. Ontario, for example, benefits in myriad ways from lower energy prices, and as one commentator put it, the engine of Ontario's economy "is just beginning to rev up,"[31] buoyed by a lower Canadian dollar, greater trading leverage with the US, and a more attractive manufacturing context.

In these altered circumstances, a window (or multiple windows) of opportunity for environmental policy is opening up. At the centre, of course, is the prospect of a new Liberal government, which has declared that "you cannot build a strong economy without protecting and preserving our environment."[32] Initial statements and policy positions are promising. Trudeau has made immediate overtures towards the provinces (most notably on getting a national climate change framework together), towards the environmental movement (promising to restore environmental assessment processes), and towards the opposition parties (inviting opposition leaders and also the sole Green Party Member of Parliament, Elizabeth May, to accompany the government to the UNFCCC COP 21 meeting in Paris in December 2015). The Liberal platform commits the new government to pursuing evidence-based policy, appointing a chief science officer, allowing scientists to speak freely about their work, and ensuring the proper consideration of scientific analyses in decision-making.[33] This new government is very likely to be more open and more consultative.

Trudeau has promised "positive" leadership, particularly on the environmental file. However, exercising leadership—particularly in terms of climate change—will not be easy. On the one hand, given the environmental policy orientation of current governments in British Columbia, Ontario, and Quebec, conditions seem favourable for a productive national policy discussion. In addition, Alberta's recently elected New Democratic government is fostering a new (and more activist) brand of climate policy discussions. However, setting a national target that incorporates (probably) differential targets across provinces will require strength yet flexibility, finely honed diplomatic skills, and—perhaps most importantly—political luck. Further, it is not entirely clear how the Trudeau Liberals will balance their environmental policy efforts with their energy policy; in pre-election media statements, Trudeau declared support for pipelines (rather than trains) in getting oil to market, supporting the Keystone XL pipeline extension but not new pipelines running through BC's wilderness (e.g., the Northern Gateway pipeline proposal). Much also depends on the proclivities and ambitions of the new Minister of the Environment, as yet unknown.

Media coverage directly after the election indicates that those orchestrating the transition to the new Liberal government in Ottawa are determined to put "delivery units" in place such that the bureaucracy is encouraged to meet the new government's ambitious policy goals in a coherent manner. While such top-level machinery may enhance the prospects for integration of policy (i.e., climate and energy priorities), it will be difficult to ensure that centralizing policy infrastructure does not continue to cut off meaningful participation in policy-making by an already demoralized public service.[34]

The collective wisdom provided by this fourth edition of *Canadian Environmental Policy and Politics* indicates that job number one for our new Liberal government will be to quickly identify the most significant gaps in capacity and knowledge; these gaps need to be addressed so that problems can be properly diagnosed and meaningful action can be taken. The cuts that have been made—to people, to science, and to infrastructure—have put us far behind in realizing our ultimate aim, namely a strong policy framework for environmental protection and sustainability.

Notes

1. Many and heartfelt thanks to the authors in this volume who provided the insights on which this Introduction is based. Also, thanks to my research assistant, Nick Zebryk, who provided considerable support for my work on the volume.

2. "Notes for an Address by the Right Honourable Stephen Harper, Prime Minister of Canada, to the UK Chamber of Commerce, 14 July 2006," accessed 17 May 2014, http://pm.gc.ca/eng/news/2006/07/14/address-prime-minister-canada-uk-chamber-commerce.

3. Debora L. VanNijnatten and Robert Boardman, "Introduction," in VanNijnatten and Boardman, eds, *Canadian Environmental Policy and Politics: Prospects for Leadership and Innovation*, 3rd edn (Toronto: Oxford University Press, 2010), ix–xxvii.

4. Philippe Bergevin, "Canada and the United States: The Global Financial Crisis and Its Impact on Canada," in Library of Parliament, *Canada and the United States: Shared Interests and Concerns*, Jan. 2009, accessed 25 Apr. 2014, http://www.parl.gc.ca/content/lop/researchpublications/prb0834-e.pdf.

5. Ibid.

6. Marco Terrones, Prakash Kannan, and Alasdair Scott, "From Recession to Recovery: How Soon and How Strong?" *World Economic Outlook* (Apr. 2009): 103–38.

7. See, e.g., *The Economist*, "Poll of Forecasters," January through December 2009.

8. Bill Curry and Barrie McKenna, "Stimulus Gamble: How Ottawa Saved the Economy—and Wasted Billions," *Globe and Mail*, 8 Feb. 2014, accessed 26 Apr. 2014, http://www.theglobeandmail.com/report-on-business/stimulus-gamble-how-ottawa-saved-the-economy-and-wasted-billions/article16760149/?page=3.

9. Department of Finance, "Minister of Finance Confirms Return to Balanced Budgets in 2015," news release, 11 Feb. 2014, http://www.budget.gc.ca/2014/docs/nrc/pdf/EN.pdf.

10. Over the lifecycle of the fuel—extraction, processing, and then combustion—tar sands oil leaves a much larger environmental footprint than conventional sources. The tar sands are Canada's fastest-growing source of GHG emissions.

11. Government of Canada, "Canada's Economic Action Plan: Responsible Resource Development," http://actionplan.gc.ca/en/content/r2d-dr2.

12. Government of Canada, "Canada's Economic Action Plan: Responsible Resource Development and Jobs," http://actionplan.gc.ca/en/backgrounder/r2d-dr2/responsible-resource-development-and-jobs.

13. See Brent Rathgeber, *Irresponsible Government: The Decline of Parliamentary Democracy in Canada* (Toronto: Dundurn Press, 2014; Alison Loat and Michael MacMillan, *Tragedy in the Commons: Former Members of Parliament Speak Out about Canada's Failing Democracy* (Toronto: Random House, 2014).

14. Duff Conacher, "Proroguing Parliament without Cause? Canadians Want It Banned," *Globe and Mail*, 23 Aug. 2013, http://www.theglobeandmail.com/globe-debate/proroguing-parliament-without-cause-canadians-want-it-banned/article13935119.

15. Parliament of Canada, Bill C-38: Table of Contents and Summary, http://www.parl.gc.ca/HousePublications/Publication.aspx?DocId=5697420.

16. Brenda Heelan Powell, Staff Counsel, Environmental Law Centre, "An Overview of Bill C-38: The Budget Bill That Transformed Canada's Federal Environmental Laws," http://www.elc.ab.ca/Content_Files/Files/Bill38AnalysisArticlefinal.pdf.

17. Brenda Heelan Powell, Staff Counsel, Environmental Law Centre, "Back on the Omnibus with Bill C-45: Another Omnibus Budget Bill Drives More Change to Federal Environmental Law," https://environmentallawcentre.wordpress.com/2012/11/06/back-on-the-omnibus-with-bill-c-45-another-omnibus-budget-bill-drives-more-change-to-federal-environmental-law/.

18. Donald Savoie, *Power: Where Is It?* (Montreal and Kingston: McGill-Queen's University Press, 2010).

19. Professional Institute of the Public Service of Canada, "The Big Chill: Silencing Public Interest Science," *Communications Magazine* 39, 3 (2013), http://www.pipsc.ca/portal/page/portal/website/issues/science/bigchill.

20. "An open letter from the Honourable Joe Oliver, Minister of Natural Resources, on Canada's commitment to diversify our energy markets and the need to streamline the regulatory process in order to advance Canada's national economic interest," 9 Jan. 2012, www.nrcan.gc.ca/media-room/news-release/2012/1/1909.

21. See Debora L. VanNijnatten, "The North American Context: Canadian Environmental Policy and the Continental Push," in Debora L. VanNijnatten and Robert Boardman, eds, *Canadian Environmental Policy and Politics: Prospects for Leadership and Innovation*, 3rd edn (Toronto: Oxford University Press, 2010); George Hoberg, "Canadian–American Environmental Relations: A Strategic Framework," in Robert Boardman and Debora L. VanNijnatten, eds, *Canadian Environmental Policy: Context and Cases* (Toronto: Oxford University Press, 2002), 171–89.

22. See, e.g., Canadian Press, "U.S. Ambassador Tells Canada 'Climate Change Is Real,'" 26 Feb. 2015, http://newsalberta.ca/2015/02/26/u-s-ambassador-tells-canada-climate-change-is-real/; Canadian Press, "Canadian Oil Extraction Is 'Extraordinarily Dirty' Process, Obama Says," 6 Mar. 2015, http://calgaryherald.com/business/energy/obama-canadian-oil-extraction-is-extraordinarily-dirty.

23. Emily Chung, "Canada's Climate Inaction Leaves It 'Increasingly Isolated' ahead of COP 20," CBC News, 3 Dec. 2014, http://www.cbc.ca/news/technology/canada-s-climate-inaction-leaves-it-increasingly-isolated-ahead-of-cop-20-1.2853774.

24. See, e.g., Cindy Harnett, "Another Round of Cuts Planned for Fisheries and Oceans Canada," *Victoria Times Colonist*, 12 Mar. 2013; Paul Withers, "DFO at Risk from Budget Cuts, Change: Internal Report," CBC News, 8 Nov. 2013; Mike DeSouza, "Federal Budget Cuts Undermine Environment Canada's Mandate to Enforce Clean Air Regulations: Emails," *National Post*, 17 Mar. 2013; Alex Boutilier, "Environment Canada Braces for Cuts to Climate Programs," *Toronto Star*, 12 Mar. 2014. Annual reports on plans and priorities for Environment Canada are found at www.ec.gc.ca.

25. See Environment Canada, "Report on Plans and Priorities 2014. Budgetary Planning Summary for All Programs (dollars)," https://www.ec.gc.ca/default.asp?lang=En&n=024B8406-1&offset=3&toc=show.

26. Andrew Nikiforuk, "Facing Millions in Cuts, Environment Canada Prepares to Get Lean: Harper Gov't Releases a Trim Three-Year Budget for the Department," *TheTyee.ca*, 15 Mar. 2014, http://thetyee.ca/News/2014/03/15/Environment-Canada-Cuts/.

27. See, e.g., Mike De Souza, "Federal Budget Cuts Undermine Environment Canada's Mandate to Enforce Clean Air Regulations," *National Post*, 17 Mar. 2013, http://news.nationalpost.com/news/canada/canadian-politics/federal-budget-cuts-undermine-environment-canadas-mandate-to-enforce-clean-air-regulations-emails.

28. Council of Canadians, "Prominent Scientists, Environmentalists Decry Cuts to Public Sector and Their Effect on Canada's Freshwater Heritage," media release, 4 July 2011, http://www.canadians.org/media/water/2011/04-Jul-11.html.

29. Northwest Coast Energy News, "Environment Canada Cuts Enforcement, Marine Pollution and Emergency Budget," 14 Mar. 2014, http://nwcoastenergynews.com/2014/03/14/5964/enviroment-canada-cuts-enforcement-marine-pollution-emergency-budgets/.

30. Jeff Rubin, "How $40 Oil Would Impact Canada's Provinces," *Globe and Mail*, 5 Jan. 2015, http://www.theglobeandmail.com/report-on-business/industry-news/energy-and-resources/how-40-oil-would-impact-canadas-provinces/article22288570/.

31. Ibid.

32. Daniel LeBlanc and Andrea Woo, "Trudeau Vows Liberal Environment Plan Will 'Be Putting a Price on Carbon,'" *Globe and Mail*, 29 June 2015, http://www.theglobeandmail.com/news/politics/trudeau-unveils-liberal-environment-plan-including-green-bonds/article25176587/.

33. The Liberal Party of Canada, "Science and Scientists," https://www.liberal.ca/realchange/science-and-scientists/

34. Doug Saunders, "How the Liberal Dream Machine Will Work," *Globe and Mail*, 24 Oct. 2015, http://www.theglobeandmail.com/news/politics/crafting-a-blueprint-that-aims-to-transform-liberal-promises-into-real-lifepolicy/article26950746/

PART I
The Context for Environmental Action

The chapters in this section provide an encompassing yet in-depth understanding of the conditions underlying and the constraints on current environmental policy-making in Canada. The picture they paint is not particularly pretty; instead, the policy context is rather gloomy, with a wide array of limitations facing those who wish to take action to address environmental degradation and pursue sustainability. There is also considerable evidence that we have lost ground in terms of putting in place a firm foundation for nationwide environmental protection.

All of the contributors in Part I proceed from the starting point that the current context is markedly different from the 2003–8 period, when public concern about the environment had hit new highs, economic circumstances were more stable, and real pressures for action emanated from abroad. After the US economic collapse in the fall of 2008 began to reverberate on this side of the border, the Canadian unemployment rate increased substantially and politics became more clearly (for it always is) about economic stability and growth. The 2008 election of a second Harper minority government meant the continuation of the minimalist federal approach to environmental policy, noted in the third edition of *Canadian Environmental Policy and Politics*. However, the majority win by the Conservatives in 2011 signalled a highly visible shift in the rules and focus of the game, with a narrow view of Canada's economic future as dominated by resource development. Policy initiatives to hasten the realization of this vision—under the umbrella of "Responsible Resource Development"—were lined up accordingly.

Taken together, the chapters in this section raise the critical question of what the "winning conditions" might be for pursuing ambitious environmental policy, given this rather difficult set of circumstances. Anderson and Stephenson's analysis of public opinion in Chapter 1 points to a deep ambivalence in how Canadians view environmental threats; while a respectable number of Canadians believe that environment is the most important issue and a clear majority favour increased spending on the environment, the perceived "environment–economy trade-off" still permeates the public consciousness such that support for environmental action decreases as concern about the economy (and particularly unemployment) increases. This suggests several strategic directions: first, finding new and innovative means to highlight positive environment–economy linkages (the proverbial golden egg); second, emphasizing perceptions of "threat" to the environment, which Cameron Anderson and Laura Stephenson suggest may increase support for environmental protection; and, third, given the support for environmental spending, making much of the real-world impacts of recent, deep budget cuts.

These findings are echoed in Chapter 2, by Clare Demerse and Nathan Lemphers, particularly the importance of making the link between economic activities and environmental impacts in the minds of voters. Demerse and Lemphers trace the reorientation of environmental non-governmental organization (ENGO) activism, away from the corridors of Ottawa's political institutions (now much less open to ENGO influence) and towards public mobilization campaigns targeting issues of direct relevance to local communities. The authors offer a potential answer to Anderson and Stephenson's conundrum—the ambivalence in public attitudes might be overcome by taking the political focus down, targeting issues closer to voters. Though not without costs, Demerse and Lemphers indicate that this tactic may have tangible political impacts.

In Chapter 3, Michael Howlett and Nigel Kinney provide us with a multi-faceted understanding of the ways in which our reliance on natural resource (staples) development—particularly agriculture, fisheries, forestry, mining, and oil and gas—has shaped the nature of our national and regional economies as well as our policy responses. These responses might also be characterized as ambivalent. They argue that sectors such as forestry, which have been forced into a "post-staples" state through management schemes (among other factors) that take environmental protection into account, can help us to break away from an addictive economy reliant on large-scale resource exploitation. On the other hand, the oil and gas sector, which has not been subject to serious environmental regulation, appears to be heading towards a degenerative mature state, whereby the increasing capital- and technology-intensiveness of activities is actually accompanied by declining employment, the deterioration of communities, and high vulnerability to global boom–bust cycles. This provides fodder for arguing more forcefully that, in actuality, a natural resource economy focused on fossil fuel development poses economic costs.

But what are the implications of this overwhelming focus on natural resource development on our environmental legal and policy framework? In Chapter 4, Marcia Valiante takes the reader through the sweeping changes to Canada's federal environmental laws made by the Harper Conservatives as part of their "Responsible Resource Development" agenda. The changes have resulted in reductions of the federal role in the protection of aquatic habitat, fish, and navigable waterways, in the types of projects subject to environmental assessment, in opportunities for public participation in related federal processes, and of oversight mechanisms. There remain, Valiante argues, relatively few avenues for supporters of environmental protection to oppose the changes or force government action through legal processes.

Chapter 5 shifts the analysis to environmental policy implementation, where the commitment to the natural resource economy is realized in very concrete ways through the policy tools used by the Harper administration and certain provinces. Here, Mark Winfield traces the shift away from procedural and institutional mechanisms, which in the past have served to strengthen consideration of environment in decision-making (e.g., environmental assessment) and open the doors of policy processes to the public. In addition, Winfield highlights a retreat away from substantive instruments, such as regulatory tools, which are intended to change behaviour away from polluting activities, and towards a form of "smart" regulation reliant on partnering with the regulated industry. While considerations of effectiveness and efficiency partly explain these developments, political and policy factors figure prominently in decision-making. The long-term impact of these shifts is unknown at the present time, but there are clear potential concerns in terms of the legitimacy of government activities, public health, and safety risks, and a loss of capacity to respond to emerging problems.

In the final contribution to this section, Stephen Bocking adjusts our lens in Chapter 6 to analyze the role that science has played, and is currently playing, in environmental policy-making.

Bocking provides a nuanced understanding of the "uses" and "abuses" of science through reference to four models of science—basic, regulatory, activist, and innovative—that incorporate distinctive purposes, institutions, and governance arrangements. Good environmental policy-making requires components of all of these models, plus clear communication channels and strategies that promote credibility, policy, relevance, and legitimacy—all wrapped up in a new model of "modest science." The problem, under the current federal administration, is that we are moving in the opposite direction, with cutbacks to research funding, the closing of laboratories, the muzzling of government scientists, and a closing off of other science–policy communication channels in Canada.

1 Environmentalism and Austerity in Canada: Electoral Effects

Cameron D. Anderson and Laura B. Stephenson

Chapter Summary

This chapter considers why the Conservative Party, widely seen as Canada's least environmentally friendly political party, was able to win a majority government in 2011 despite the acknowledged importance of protecting the environment for Canadians. This electoral puzzle can be understood in terms of competing pressures and issue salience. The environment, while important and supported by a majority of Canadians, was not the most important electoral issue in 2008 and 2011. The economy was a more salient, demanding, and pressing issue for voters. The Conservative Party is widely seen as the party best able to deal with economic issues. The party was thus privileged by the relative importance of these two issues to voters in these recent Canadian elections.

Chapter Outline

- Public opinion and the environment
  - Perceptions of environmental threat
  - Support for environmental spending
- Political implications of environmental concern
  - Party ratings and environmental concern/spending
- Environmental support in times of economic stress
  - The relationship between environmental concern and unemployment
  - The 2008 federal election
  - The 2011 federal election
- Is there any incentive for the Conservatives to do better on the environment? No!

Introduction

Protecting the environment is an important concern for Canadians. Consider, for example, the number of Canadians who shun disposable water bottles in favour of reusable ones, compost their food scraps, use their blue bins, and turn off their lights when they leave a room. Many of the practices that would have been unheard of a generation ago are now common, expected, and part of everyday life. Even the emergence of the Green Party of Canada as a stable electoral competitor demonstrates that Canadians are attuned to the need to protect our environment for future generations. Although national support for the party has not exceeded 6.8 per cent since it began contesting elections in 1984, the inclusion of Green Party leader Elizabeth May in the 2008 leaders' debate and the uproar over her exclusion in 2011 demonstrate the degree to which the party (and the main issue it represents) has been adopted into the mainstream of Canadian political life.

Since 2006, however, Canadian electoral outcomes seem contrary to these trends. Of all the political parties, the Conservative Party of Canada is seen as the least environmentally friendly—in 2004 and 2006 it was named by the fewest respondents (8.6 per cent and 7.8 per cent, respectively) in our study as the party best able to deal with the environment.[1] In 2008 only 12 per cent thought it was the political party most able to deal with the issue, compared to 48 per cent for the Green Party. Our study also showed that support for the Conservative Party, the only federal party on the ideological right of the political spectrum, declined as environmental concern increased.

This creates a puzzle. How should we interpret the electoral success of the Conservative Party, especially in 2008 and 2011, in light of the generally high level of environmental concern in Canada? Has there been a sharp decline in support for the environment? Has the relationship between the views of the Conservative Party and environmental concern changed?

This chapter aims to understand the 2008 and 2011 Conservative election wins in terms of two competing trends in public opinion—support for the environment and concern about the economy. We argue that, despite relatively high levels of support for the environment among Canadians, the **salience** of the environment as an electoral issue has not been high in recent federal elections. This was true even in 2008 when the Liberal Party staked its electoral fortunes on the "Green Shift," a plan to use policy instruments, including tax credits, to encourage environment-friendly behaviour. The importance of other issues, such as the economy, worked in favour of the Conservative Party, which campaigned on proven leadership and economic management.

This chapter presents empirical evidence to support our argument. We begin by documenting Canadian public opinion on the environmental issue and then assess the relationship between environmental attitudes and political party preferences. Having established that a strong degree of support for the environmental issue exists among Canadians and that this issue is consistently related to party support, we then consider the relationship between environmental attitudes and economic concerns. Finally, we consider the 2008 and 2011 elections in specific detail using data from the Canadian Election Studies in those years. We show that Canadians have not ceased to care about the environment, but the imperative of dealing with the economy since the economic downturn in 2008 has privileged the Conservative Party in federal elections. In future federal elections, should the salience of the economy decrease, environmental concerns may play a greater role in the electoral decisions of Canadians and lead to a more environment-friendly party being elected to office.

Public Opinion about the Environment

To begin, we first need to review broader understandings about the relationship of public opinion and the environment. Research into environmental attitudes has revealed two sources of environmental concern. The first is actual environmental decline. When the environment is at risk and/or there is the perception of environmental threat, support for environmental protection increases.[2] The second is the rise of post-materialist values in society. The concept of **post-materialist values** rests on the idea that an individual's priorities and concerns are intimately related to their material well-being. In circumstances of relative scarcity, the prevalence of material concerns (such as food, clothing, housing, employment security) will predominate. By contrast, in situations of relative economic security and affluence, attention may turn to fulfilling non- or post-material needs and wants. Post-material needs and wants might include forms of identity politics, such as equality and rights-seeking, as well as a turn in awareness to political issues such as the environment. The environment is a "new politics" issue[3] and concern about it has been found to be related to post-material values.[4] Regardless of the source, the very existence of green parties in political systems around the world indicates that the environment has become an important issue in many countries.

Empirical data provide a clearer picture of recent trends in Canada. Like most political issues, concern for the environment demonstrates an ebb and flow over time in the collective opinion of the Canadian public. Figure 1.1 presents the percentage of Canadians, on an annual basis, who have indicated, in Environics polls, that the environment is the "most important issue." The figure shows a sharp rise in concern for the environment in the late 1980s and early 1990s, followed by a deep trough through much of the 1990s. After the turn of the century there was a substantial upswing in concern about the environment. The proportion of Canadians who think the environment is the most important issue has increased several-fold since 2004.[5] This likely reflects the global focus on the Kyoto Accord and Canada's role in meeting (or not meeting) its international obligations and commitments. The high point in

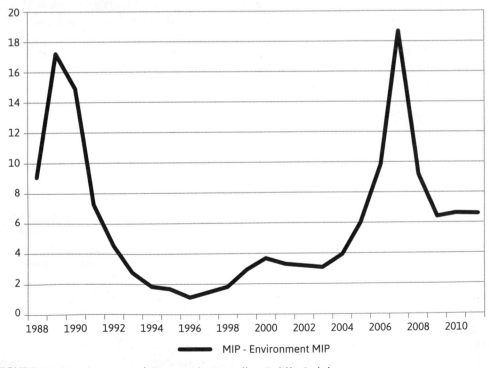

FIGURE 1.1 | Environmental Concern in Canadian Public Opinion

2008 coincides with the **"Green Shift"** electoral platform of Stéphane Dion and the Liberals. The decline after that also coincides with real-world events. In the fall of 2008, the American economy collapsed and many other countries, Canada included, suffered in its wake.

Before leaving this figure, it is important to note the vertical axis. The range of percentages of Canadians who named the environment as their most important issue tops off just under 20 per cent. Thus, while Canadians think the environment is an important problem, even in its most relevant year the concern does not extend to more than one-fifth of the population. However, there does appear to be a stable level of concern in recent years at around 6–7 per cent.

Another measure of environmental concern is opinion positions on whether the federal government should spend more or less on the environment. Data compiled from Environics polls by the Canadian Opinion Research Archive (CORA) demonstrate that while attitudes are dynamic, in recent years Canadians clearly support increased spending on environmental protection (Figure 1.2).[6] Indeed, for most of the period under consideration, a clear majority of respondents favoured more federal government spending on the environment. By contrast, the percentage of individuals who feel the federal government is spending too much on environmental protection has been under 10 per cent since the mid-1990s. Undoubtedly, Canadians believe in protecting the environment and think that the government should spend public money to do so.

Of course, attitudes can change when election campaigns make individuals consider other aspects of government activity. We can see whether environmental concern is evident during election periods by turning to the Canadian Election Study (CES). The surveys from the 2006, 2008, and 2011 federal elections contain a similar question: "Should the federal government spend more, less, or about the same as now on the environment?"

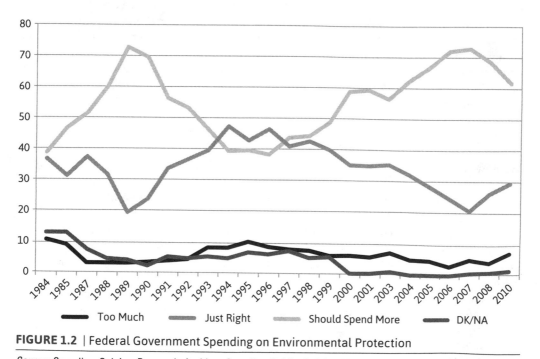

FIGURE 1.2 | Federal Government Spending on Environmental Protection

Source: Canadian Opinion Research Archive, Canadian Public Opinion Trends at http://www.queensu.ca/cora/3trends.html.

TABLE 1.1 Attitudes towards Government Spending on the Environment, Canadian Election Study 2006–11

Year	Less	Same	More
2006	4.3	35.2	60.5
2008	4.7	30.4	65.0
2011	4.8	36.7	58.5

Table 1.1 shows that around the time of the elections a clear majority of respondents indicated a preference for increased spending.[7] The peak of this demand was in 2008, when 65 per cent of respondents expressed a desire for more spending on the environment. This uptick in demand for more environmental spending reflects the pattern observed in Figure 1.1, where the environment was the most important issue for almost 20 per cent of respondents in 2008. The percentage indicating a preference for less spending has been remarkably small over this period of time. These election study data confirm the CORA data reflecting broad and sweeping support for the environment.

To conclude this section, we observe that up to 20 per cent of Canadians have indicated that the environment, among such other issues as health, education, and the economy, is the most important issue facing Canada over the past 25 years. Most recent estimates, as noted above, would put this number at about 6–7 per cent. While this may seem low, measuring salience by selecting the environment as the most important issue among all others is a strong requirement. A more realistic expectation might be that there is (or is not) broad public support for spending and policy attention to be given to the environment. On this account, we find resounding and consistent opinion support for the environmental issue among Canadians, in terms of strong recent support for increasing spending on the environment. We believe these data, collectively, support our initial assertion that Canadians are concerned about the environment. Furthermore, the data indicate that Canadians favour policy initiatives supporting the environment, meaning that they see the issue as one the government should address.

Political Implications of Environmental Concern

We now turn to consider the political implications of Canadians' support for the environment. Does it matter that Canadian opinion tends to support the environmental issue? Our guiding question here is: Does environmental concern differentiate public perceptions of and support for political parties in Canada?

Many studies have considered how environmentalism is related to political competition and other political issues.[8] Dalton demonstrates that the environment issue has been largely adapted into the traditional left–right spectrum of politics.[9] In the Canadian case, Anderson and Stephenson demonstrate that from 2000 to 2006 those who were more concerned about the environment were less likely to evaluate parties of the right (Canadian Alliance/Conservative Party of Canada) positively.[10] In light of this previous work, has environmental concern continued to differentiate opinion about political parties even after the economic downturn of 2008?

Table 1.2 provides an initial answer. We consider Canadians' ratings of the major political parties at the federal level and look to determine whether there are differences in the ratings

TABLE 1.2 Predicted Party Rating (Thermometer) Based on Environmental Spending Attitude

2006	Less	Same	More
Conservative	56.0	49.7	43.5
Liberal	37.3	42.0	46.8
NDP	35.9	42.1	48.2
BQ	38.5	45.1	51.7
Greens	20.2	26.3	32.3
2008	Less	Same	More
Conservative	67.2	57.5	47.9
Liberal	41.7	46.4	51.1
NDP	38.6	45.1	51.7
BQ	33.3	45.9	58.4
Greens	27.1	36.1	45.1
2011	Less	Same	More
Conservative	63.6	54.2	44.7
Liberal	33.5	40.6	47.7
NDP	33.2	42.7	52.2
BQ	30.0	40.8	51.7
Greens	17.8	29.4	41.1

of these parties based on respondents' positions on environmental spending. To do this, we predict ratings of political parties in Canada[11] on a 0–100 scale (where 0 means "really dislike" and 100 means "really like") at the different values of the environmental spending measure (spend "more," "less," or "about the same as now" on the environment).[12] This is the same procedure used by Anderson and Stephenson and thus updates that work with data from more recent electoral contests.

Based on the results presented in Table 1.2, there appear to be two main trends. The first is that rising environmental concern across these three election years consistently predicts lower ratings of the Conservative Party. In 2006, we predict a decline in party rating from "spend less" on the environment to "spend more" of 12.5 rating points. This decline increased to an almost 20 point difference in 2008 and then retreated slightly in 2011 (18.9 points). Despite the variation, it is clear that rising environmental concern is related to lower ratings for the Conservative Party of Canada.

The second trend is that the rating of every other party is predicted to increase as environmental concern rises across this time period. While there is variation in the extent to which party ratings are positively affected across the three elections and the various parties, the message is uniform. These trends are consistent with previous work on the topic[13] and suggest that the nature of party competition on the environmental issue has solidified within Canada.

However, a relevant point for our overarching research question is that the Conservative Party is predicted to have the highest rating of any political party for those who think environmental spending should be less or the same. This represents about 35–42 per cent of the electorate based on Table 1.1. Furthermore, although the party's popularity is predicted

TABLE 1.3 Predicted Conservative Vote Share, 2006, 2008, 2011

		2006	2008	2011
Baseline		38.1	37.4	38.9
Environmental	Less	67.3	73.8	75.9
Spending	Same	48.5	51.6	52.6
Preference	More	30.1	28.8	28.0

to decline when more environmental spending is preferred, it is also notable that the support for the Conservatives is not far behind other parties. In 2011, for example, fewer than 8 points separate the Conservatives and the party with the highest predicted rating, the NDP, under conditions of preferring more spending on the environment.

We can further substantiate the effect of environmental attitudes on support for the Conservative Party by looking at predicted vote share using Canadian Election Study data from 2006, 2008, and 2011 (see Table 1.3). Using a model of Conservative vote share, we can predict support for the party when environmental concern is at different levels.[14] Again, considering the 2006, 2008, and 2011 federal elections, each of which the Conservatives won, we see that environmental concern matters. In 2006, the predicted baseline share of Conservative vote is 38 per cent. If all respondents wanted more done for the environment, vote support is predicted to fall to about 30 per cent of the electorate. The 2008 and 2011 results are similar. In each case there is a difference of approximately 9 to 11 percentage points between the baseline predicted Conservative vote share and the share predicted when everyone wants more spending. When it comes to a hard-fought electoral battle, those 9 to 11 points can make a big difference.

The data we have presented so far are intended to make two points. First, the environment matters to Canadians in the twenty-first century. It is important for a non-trivial number of Canadians. Not only has its salience been substantial in recent years (especially 2008), but a majority of Canadians would prefer greater spending on the environment. Second, these attitudes have political consequences. Supporting environmental spending is related to a decline in support for the Conservatives and an increase in support for (all) other parties. Putting these pieces of information together results in a puzzle of sorts. How did the Conservatives win office in 2008 and 2011 if they were viewed poorly on the environmental issue? In the next section, we consider whether accounting for economic concern provides a way to understand the electoral success of the Conservative Party in light of these conflicting trends.

Environmental Support in Times of Economic Stress

There is no doubt that the economic climate in Canada since the fall of 2008 is vastly different from that of the early 2000s. The hardships, austerity, and government cutbacks of the 1990s were a bad memory when the 2008 recession began. Even though Canada was not the source of the decline, and indeed weathered the crisis better than many other countries,[15] nonetheless the Canadian economy was affected. Figure 1.3 plots the unemployment rate in Canada from 2008 to 2013.

This figure indicates a substantial increase in unemployment after the economic collapse in 2008. By the time of the 2011 election, the employment rate had improved but it was

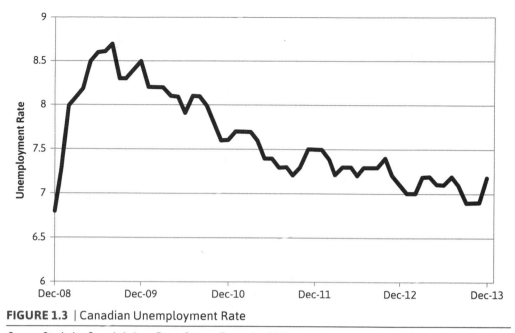

FIGURE 1.3 | Canadian Unemployment Rate

Source: Statistics Canada Labour Force Survey, December 2013.

still above its December 2008 level. Furthermore, living through an economic crisis that was not completely over would have affected the salience of the economy in the minds of many Canadians.

What might the economic downturn have meant for environmental attitudes? Figure 1.4 plots the relationship between actual national unemployment rates (on the horizontal axis) and net public opinion in favour of more federal government spending on the environment (on the vertical axis) between 1987 and 2009.[16] A line of best fit (or regression line) has been added to more clearly display the relationship. The trend is clear and informative. As unemployment increases, demand for more federal spending on the environment drops significantly. The coefficient for the regression line is −6.3 (a significant relationship at p < .001). This means that for each additional percentage point of national unemployment the average opinion support for more spending drops by 6.3 per cent. Thus, a strong negative relationship exists between national unemployment and support for environmental spending.

This suggests a trade-off in the minds of Canadians. They may support the environment when the economy is good, but there is a real and significant drop in public support for environmental spending when economic conditions deteriorate. Returning to Figure 1.1, the low percentage of individuals who named the environment as their most important issue during the 1990s can be understood as reflecting the economic distress of that period. The increase after the turn of the century, on the other hand, indicates that economic stability is related to a shift in concern towards the environment. When the economy is doing well the Canadian public is also more likely to support government initiatives for the environment. The difference in support for greater environmental spending between 2008 and 2011 indicated in Table 1.1 can also be understood as reflecting the economic downturn between the two election years.

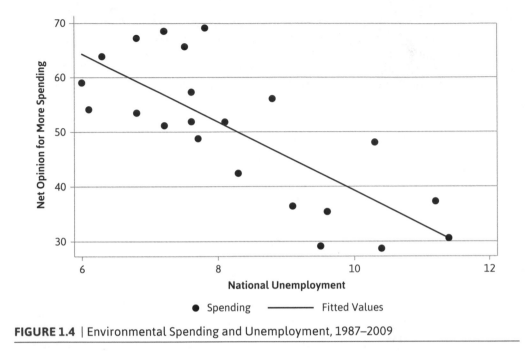

FIGURE 1.4 | Environmental Spending and Unemployment, 1987–2009

The final sections of this chapter bring all of these pieces of empirical evidence together to understand the 2008 and 2011 Canadian federal elections. We use Canadian Election Study data to demonstrate how opinions about the environment and the economy factored into support for the Conservative Party in those two contests.

We do not consider 2006, the first election won by the Conservative Party, for two reasons. First, 2006 marked the first change in the federal governing party since 1993. Throwing the Liberals out of office may have been a strong motivation for voters, and the Conservatives were the most obvious alternative. Second, the sponsorship scandal that emerged in 2004 no doubt factored into the minds of Canadians as they voted in 2006. The Conservatives campaigned as a "clean government" alternative, and the importance of this issue may have decreased the role that any other issue could have played in support for the political parties.

The 2008 Federal Election

The global economic recession began in September 2008 when Lehman Brothers Holding Inc. collapsed. Ripples were felt around the world and Canada was not exempt. The issue was obviously salient for the Canadian election held on 14 October of that year. Andrew et al., in their analysis of press coverage of the 2008 election campaign, note that the economy was prominent.[17] Nanos writes, "This campaign will likely be known as The 'Wall Street' election. It is very rare for a national election to be sideswiped by international financial turmoil, but that's exactly what happened in 2008."[18]

The parties were not prepared for the role that the economy would play in the election. Andrew et al. observe that while the 1988 election was also focused on the economy, "in 1988 the main parties and leaders all anticipated and primed the economy frame. It is not clear that the economy's presence as *the* critical ballot box question in 2008 was either anticipated or welcomed by any of the parties or leaders contesting this campaign."[19]

The timing of the financial crisis could not have been worse for the Liberal Party. The Liberals had staked their electoral fortune on the appeal of a plan to protect the environment. They were fighting under a new leader, Stéphane Dion, with a platform that promoted significant environmental action. Furthermore, the Liberal election plan tied economic action to addressing climate change. As the platform explained, "With the green shift plan and other measures included in this platform, we can help the economy and fight climate change at the same time."

The incumbent Conservative Party, on the other hand, put forward a different option for Canadians. Their platform characterized the election in this way:

> This election, Canadians face a clear choice. It's a choice between the Harper Conservatives' credible and affordable plan, and risky tax-and-spend experiments that will drive up the cost of everything from groceries to gas and throw Canada back into a deficit. It's a choice between strength and weakness. And it's a choice between moving forward and going back.

Although the Conservative plan did mention the environment, it was far less prominent and the policy ideas focused on enforcement, conservation, sustainability, renewable energy, and a cap-and-trade system, a much weaker stance than the "green shift" proposed by the Liberals.

Leading up to the election and prior to the economic collapse, it appeared that the environment would be a major issue in the campaign. In addition to the Liberal and Conservative platforms featuring environmental ideas, the NDP also put forward a plan. In his platform message, NDP leader Jack Layton explained, "We'll face the challenge of climate change—not with Mr. Harper's idle words or by taxing you and your family—but with tough laws that force polluters to clean up the mess they've made." However, the financial crisis and concern for the economy quickly overpowered the environment as the main election issue. The study by Andrew et al. of media coverage during the election shows that economic issues, broadly categorized, dominated about half of the press coverage, compared to less than 20 per cent for environmental issues.[20] Among all of the parties competing, the Conservatives were best placed to provide a plan for the economy. In the end, the election outcome was a minority Conservative government: the Conservatives won 143 seats, the Liberals 77, the Bloc Québécois 49, and the NDP 37.

With this election context in mind, we turn to empirical evidence detailing voter attitudes in the 2008 election. As shown in Table 1.1, over 65 per cent of respondents indicated a preference for more environmental spending in 2008. A different question from the 2008 survey asked about the importance to them personally of protecting the environment, and almost 67 per cent indicated that protecting the environment was very important.

However, these questions inquire about general attitudes regarding the environment. Voters may hold a wide variety of attitudes but their electoral decisions may give more weight to a single, specific concern. A long-standing survey question asks respondents to name the most important issue in the election.[21] In 2008, almost 10 per cent named the environment.[22] Among the vast list of issues raised by respondents, 10 per cent is not a trivial number. However, in comparison to concern related to the economy, it is not surprising that it is dwarfed. Just under 30 per cent of respondents indicated an economic issue was the most important in the election.

We demonstrated earlier that pro-environmental attitudes have negative consequences for Conservative Party support. But what about economic concern? CES respondents were asked to name the party they thought "would be best able to create jobs/deal with the economy." The most common response was the Conservatives (40 per cent) as compared to the next closest party, the Liberals, at 30 per cent. This is consistent with the different platform issues put forward by the parties, as well as with a general perception that parties on the right of the ideological spectrum are better for economic issues. Thus, although environmental concern might not have helped the Conservatives in 2008, economic concern did.

Of course, it is theoretically possible for individuals to be concerned about the economy *and* the environment. However, the opinion data suggest a trade-off exists in the minds of respondents. Figure 1.5 presents respondents' views from the CES on the importance of the economy among those with and without environmental concerns. In the 2008 election, among those who thought the environment was not important to them personally, 37.5 per cent believed the economy was the most important issue in the election. By contrast, among those who responded that the environment was personally important, 26 per cent—a drop of more than 10 points—believed the economy was the most important issue. This confirms an inverse relationship between these issues, as environmental concern was related to the somewhat weaker standing of the economy in the 2008 election.

The last piece of data to consider is the individual-level effect of different issue concerns on voting for the Conservative Party in the 2008 federal election. We ran a **logistic**

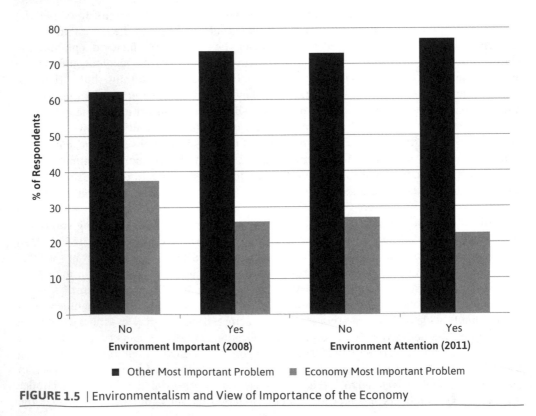

FIGURE 1.5 | Environmentalism and View of Importance of the Economy

regression with voting for the Conservatives as the **dependent variable**. The model included two **independent variables**—one dummy variable for naming the economy as the most important issue in the election and another dummy variable for naming the environment as the most important issue in the election. This basic setup allows for a consideration of how the salience of these two issues influenced Conservative support in the 2008 election. We expect that the economic variable will have a positive impact on Conservative support and the environmental one will have a negative impact. The results show that a respondent who thought the economy was the most important issue in the election was 34 points more likely to vote for the Conservative Party versus all other parties.[23] On the other hand, when the environment was seen as the most important issue in the election, respondents were over 80 points less likely to vote for the Conservative Party.[24]

Combining all of these data pieces together leads to a complete story. In 2008, the election was expected to have an environmental focus as voters were concerned about the environment and the parties were prepared to campaign on the issue. Voters thought the environment was important and supported greater public spending on it. Those who thought it was the most important election issue were also less likely to support the Conservatives. However, the environment was not the most salient issue in the election. Indeed, almost three times as many Canadians named the economy as most important as named the environment. In short, public concern for the environment was dwarfed by economic concerns, and on this issue trade-off the Conservative Party had an advantage. Thus, although the relationships demonstrated in our earlier study[25] continued through the 2008 election, environmental concern among voters at the time of the election was simply not enough to elect a more environment-friendly party.

The 2011 Federal Election

We can use empirical data to tell a similar story about the 2 May 2011 federal election. From Figure 1.3, we know that the economy was still in recovery in 2011. National unemployment was declining but it was still higher than before the recession. Compared to 2008, we might expect heightened salience of the economy in 2011 as the country continued to grapple with the after-effects of the 2008 economic collapse.

Certainly, the election platforms put forward by the parties reflected the economic crisis. Whereas the environment had been prominent in the platforms of the parties in 2008, it was not mentioned as one of the Conservatives' five priorities in 2011. Instead, the incumbent party focused on jobs, supporting families, eliminating the deficit, making the streets safe, and national security. Once again, the platform laid out how the party saw the election choice:

> In this election, Canadians will choose between principled leadership and opportunism; between a stable government and a reckless coalition; between a low-tax plan for jobs and growth and a high-tax agenda that will stall our recovery, kill jobs, and set you and your family back. It's a clear choice, a real choice—and it couldn't be more important.

The Liberals and NDP did mention the environment in their platforms. However, both also focused on economic concerns. For the Liberals, the first section in their platform was "The

Economy: Better Choices, New Directions." The NDP addressed economic issues through plans for benefits to families and by rewarding job creation.

The election outcome was dramatic but not because of the prominence of the economy or the environment as an election issue. The real story of the election was the "Orange Wave" of support for the NDP, particularly in Quebec. The NDP became the Official Opposition for the first time in Canadian history—winning 103 seats—and the Conservative Party won its first majority government under Stephen Harper (winning 166 seats). By contrast, the Liberals and Bloc Québécois were devastated, reduced to 34 and 4 seats, respectively. The Green Party also made history by winning its first seat in the House of Commons. While these dynamics cannot be traced to environmental issues in particular, we should note that the election of Green Party leader Elizabeth May to Parliament does suggest a general acceptance of the Green Party by Canadian voters.

Overall, the environment was less prevalent in the parties' 2011 election platforms. But does that mean the environment was unimportant to voters? Turning to the CES data in Table 1.1, we see that there was still majority support for increased spending on the environment. This is consistent with 2008 and the data from our earlier study. The 2011 CES also asked respondents how much attention they paid to the environment—almost 65 per cent indicated a lot of attention.[26] Clearly, general support for the environment continued in 2011. As noted above, however, the fact that a smaller percentage of individuals supported more spending on the environment could be a reflection of the tougher economic context underlying the 2011 election.

The response frequencies of the "most important problem" question asked in the CES are also revealing. Fully 24 per cent of respondents identified an economic issue as being the most important in the election. Slightly less than 3 per cent cited the environment. The proportions are even more dramatic than in 2008 and once again show that the environment was far less salient for voters than economic issues. Nonetheless, we cannot conclude that environmental attitudes were unimportant. The second panel of Figure 1.5 shows that economic concern was still negatively related to environmental attitudes in 2011. The number of individuals who indicated the economy was the most important issue was over four percentage points lower for those who paid attention to the environment compared to those who did not (27 per cent vs 22.6 per cent).

Beyond the relative salience and positioning on the environment and the economy, were the Conservatives still the preferred party to manage the economy? The short answer is "absolutely." Almost 43 per cent of respondents named the Conservative Party as best able to deal with the economy while about 24 per cent indicated the Liberals and 15 per cent named the NDP. Clearly, the Conservative Party has managed to earn and solidify a reputation as a good economic manager during its years in office. Soroka et al. note that the proportion of non-partisans who indicated the Conservatives were best able to manage the economy (56 per cent) provided a big advantage to that party.[27]

Relating these attitudes to individual-level vote choice once again, we repeated our analysis of Conservative voting with economic issue salience and environmental issue salience as independent variables. The results indicate that those who viewed economic issues as most important were twice as likely to vote for the Conservative Party as compared to all other parties (odds ratio = 2.08, p < 0.000). In 2011, the effect of thinking that the environment was the most important issue in the election on voting for the Conservative Party was a reduction in the likelihood of voting for the Conservative party of 71 points (odds ratio = 0.29, p < 0.001).

This reflects the same pattern of support as observed in 2008, although with even greater effect. Additionally, as in 2008, despite the strong influence of environmental concern at the individual level, the very fact that less than 3 per cent of the population thought the environment was the most important issue meant that the overall influence of the environmental issue on the outcome of the election was less. In our view, the Conservatives succeeded in swaying voters to support them due to the economic climate, their election platform, and their reputation as economic managers. The environment was not a salient enough concern to sway voters otherwise.

Is There Any Incentive for the Conservatives to Do Better on the Environment? No!

The data discussed above suggest that the Conservative Party won the 2008 and 2011 elections, despite their reputation as the least environment-friendly party, for two reasons: the environment was simply not the most salient issue for voters, and the Conservatives were seen as best on an issue that was salient—the economy. Although Canadians are, in general, supportive of the environment, other issues matter for electoral choices. In particular, when other issues become salient or take precedence, this can lead voters to make their decisions based on which party is better suited to deal with an issue other than the environment. Our position is that the economy took precedence over the environment in 2008 and 2011 and the Conservatives, seen as the party best able to deal with that issue, benefited.

In this last section, we offer some speculation about what this means for the Conservative Party in the future. Is there any reason for the party to pay more attention to environmental issues?

The short (and perhaps disheartening) answer is "no." In the first instance, referring back to Table 1.2 and party ratings, we know that pro-environmental attitudes are related to increasing support for parties of the centre and left. Yet, although ratings for the Conservative Party decline, they do not evaporate among those with pro-environmental attitudes. When we consider vote support among those who preferred more environmental spending in 2008 and 2011, it becomes evident that the Conservatives were not shut out by this group of voters. Among CES respondents in 2008 who thought there should be more spending on the environment, 28 per cent voted for the Conservatives, 28 per cent voted for the Liberals, and 19 per cent voted for the NDP. In 2011, among CES respondents holding the same pro-environmental opinions, 27 per cent voted for the Conservatives, 20 per cent voted for the Liberals, and almost 40 per cent voted for the NDP.

Collectively, these results reflect two important points. The first is that, even among those with pro-environmental attitudes, Conservative support is not eliminated. The party remains competitive for these votes with other, more pro-environmental parties. Second, there are at least three other parties in each local constituency electoral contest (Liberal, NDP, and Green outside of Quebec) that prioritize the environment to a greater extent than the Conservatives. If voters do not want to support the Conservatives due to their environmental concerns, they are still faced with multiple choices. This means that the competition facing the Conservatives is divided. Even if the environment was the most salient issue for half of the electorate, those votes would still be divided unless substantial co-ordination between those parties occurred. Should the Liberals and NDP merge, as has been speculated, this could pose a threat. Until such time, however, the prospect of defeat due to environmental attitudes is weak.

Simply put, strategically there is little reason for the Conservatives to become strong advocates for significant environmental policy change. There is little doubt that the party will continue to have a plan for environmental activity. However, that plan is likely to be mostly about the status quo and at risk of being set aside in the face of more pressing priorities. Unless and until more Canadians put the environment ahead of other concerns, especially the economy, the Conservatives will receive little electoral payoff from putting substantial resources into environmental protection. Further, until the party system adjusts to prevent vote-splitting on the left, the electoral return for such reallocation will remain minimal.

Key Terms

dependent variable

"Green Shift"

independent variable

logistic regression

post-materialist values

salience

Questions for Review

1. How has public opinion about the environment changed over the past two decades?
2. How does opinion about the environment affect voters' preferences over political parties?
3. What is the relationship between environmental support and concern for the economy? Why is this the case?
4. How is the relationship between environmental support and concern for the economy relevant to understanding the outcome of the 2008 and 2011 Canadian federal elections?
5. What was the effect of the economic collapse of 2008 on Canadian politics?

Internet Resources

Canadian public opinion on various political issues, politicians, and political parties.

www.queensu.ca/cora/3trends.html

www.lispop.ca/

Additional Reading

Abramson, Paul R. 1997. "Postmaterialism and Environmentalism: A Comment on an Analysis and a Reappraisal." *Social Science Quarterly* 78, 1: 21–3.

Anderson, Cameron D., and Laura B. Stephenson. 2011. "Environmentalism and Party Support in Canada: Recent Trends outside Quebec." *Canadian Journal of Political Science* 44, 2: 341–66.

Blake, Donald E. 2001. "Contextual Effects on Environmental Attitudes and Behavior." *Environment and Behavior* 33, 5: 708–25.

Blake, Donald E. 2002. "Personal Values and Environmental Attitudes." In Joanna Everitt and Brenda O'Neill, eds, *Citizen Politics*. Toronto: Oxford University Press.

Dalton, Russell J. 2009. "Economics, Environmentalism and Party Alignments: A Note on Partisan Change in Advanced Industrial Democracies." *European Journal of Political Research* 48, 2: 161–75.

Inglehart, Ronald. 1995. "Public Support for Environmental Protection: Objective Problems and Subjective Values in 43 Societies." *PS: Political Science and Politics* 28, 1: 57–72.

Kanji, Mebs, and Neil Nevitte. 1997. "Environmental Support, Concern and Action: An Exploratory Crossnational Analysis." *International Journal of Public Opinion Research* 9, 1: 66–76.

Notes

1. Cameron D. Anderson and Laura B. Stephenson, "Environmentalism and Party Support in Canada: Recent Trends outside Quebec," *Canadian Journal of Political Science* 44, 2 (2011): 349.
2. Donald E. Blake, "Personal Values and Environmental Attitudes," in Joanna Everitt and Brenda O'Neill, eds, *Citizen Politics* (Toronto: Oxford University Press, 2002); Ronald Inglehart, "Public Support for Environmental Protection: Objective Problems and Subjective Values in 43 Societies," *PS: Political Science and Politics* 28, 1 (1995).
3. Russell J. Dalton, *Citizen Politics*, 3rd edn (New York: Chatham House, 2002).
4. Blake, "Personal Values and Environmental Attitudes"; Inglehart, "Public Support for Environmental Protection"; Mebs Kanji and Neil Nevitte, "Environmental Support, Concern and Action: An Exploratory Crossnational Analysis," *International Journal of Public Opinion Research* 9, 1 (1997).
5. The exact question wording for this time series is: "In your opinion, what is the most important problem facing Canadians today?"
6. The question wording from 1984 to 2002 was "Do you think that Canada is spending too much, just the right amount or should be spending more on each of the following: environmental protection . . . ?" In 2003 the question changed to "Keeping in mind that increasing services could increase taxes, do you think the federal government should spend more, less or the same on each of the following?"
7. We present data from 2006 to provide a comparison with the previous period and a connection to the material covered in Anderson and Stephenson, "Environmentalism and Party Support."
8. Russell J. Dalton, "Economics, Environmentalism and Party Alignments: A Note on Partisan Change in Advanced Industrial Democracies," *European Journal of Political Research* 48, 2 (2009); Ian McAllister and Donley T. Studlar, "New Politics and Partisan Alignment: Values, Ideology and Elites in Australia," *Party Politics* 1, 2 (1995); Frank L. Davis and Albert H. Wurth Jr, "Voting Preferences and the Environment in the American Electorate: The Discussion Extended," *Society & Natural Resources* 16, 8 (2003); Neil Carter, "Party Politicization of the Environment in Britain," *Party Politics* 12, 6 (2006).
9. Dalton, "Economics, Environmentalism, and Party Alignments."
10. Anderson and Stephenson, "Environmentalism and Party Support."
11. The Bloc Québécois values are for Quebec respondents only.
12. Using a statistical program called "Stata," we run a bivariate regression of environmental spending on party ratings for each party in each of the elections under consideration. Using the "predict" command in Stata, we then predict a rating for each party if everyone in the sample held that view of environmental spending (i.e., in 2006, the rating of the Conservative Party is "56" when everyone in the sample thinks that the government should spend less on the environment).
13. Anderson and Stephenson, "Environmentalism and Party Support."
14. We estimated a simple bivariate model of Conservative electoral support based on environmental concern with no control variables. As above with the party ratings, we then predicted Conservative vote share under the scenarios of all respondents expressing a response of "less" spending on the environment, "more" spending, and spending at about the "same level as now."
15. See Tim Kiladze, Tara Perkins, Grant Robertson, Jaqueline Nelson, Boyd Erman, Joanna Slater, Jeffrey Jones, Paul Waldie, and Greg Kennan, "The 2008 Financial Crisis: Through the Eyes of Some Major Players," *Globe and Mail*, 14 Sept. 2013.
16. The unemployment data come from Cansim Table 282-0002 and the raw opinion data come from the CORA website at Queen's University. The polling firm collecting this data was Environics. Net spending preferences on the environment were calculated annually according to the following calculation: net spending = more spending − less spending. Missing opinion data for 2002 were interpolated through averaging the opinion of 2001 and 2003. The opinion data were lagged by one year.
17. Blake Andrew, Lori Young, and Stuart Soroka, "Back to the Future: Press Coverage of the 2008 Canadian Election Campaign Strikes Both Familiar and Unfamiliar Notes," *Policy Options* 29, 10 (2008).
18. Nik Nanos, "Closing the Deal: The Thanksgiving Election," *Policy Options* 29, 10 (2008).
19. Andrew et al., "Back to the Future," 82.
20. Ibid, 81.
21. This question is very similar in form to the earlier time series question presented in Figure 1.1.
22. This includes mentioning the environment in conjunction with other issues, for example, health care and the environment.
23. This is based on an odds ratio of 1.34 ($p < 0.001$).
24. Based on an odds ratio of 0.18 ($p < 0.000$)
25. Anderson and Stephenson, "Environmentalism and Party Support."
26. The question wording was: "In general, how much ATTENTION do you personally usually pay to the following issues? Do you pay a lot, a little, or no attention to the environment?"
27. Stuart Soroka, Fred Cutler, Dietlind Stolle, and Patrick Fournier, "Capturing Change (and Stability) in the 2011 Campaign," *Policy Options* 32, 6 (2011).

2 The Environmental Movement in Canada: Current Challenges

Clare Demerse and Nathan Lemphers

Chapter Summary

This chapter opens with a history of the Canadian environmental movement and then highlights four features of the environmental policy landscape since the Conservative Party took power in 2006. These are a lack of federal leadership on environmental policy; diminished federal capacity for environmental science; the marginalization of environmental voices; and the increasing influence of the oil and gas industry in Canada. The remainder of the chapter examines the changed approach that Canadian environmental non-governmental organizations, or ENGOs, have adopted in response to the election of a majority Harper government. That response features a shift in ENGO priorities away from work "inside" Ottawa to more fertile terrain outside the nation's capital—including a focus on provincial policy, public mobilization, and efforts to limit the expansion of the tar sands sector. The chapter concludes with an assessment of the effectiveness of ENGO campaigns against new pipeline proposals.

Chapter Outline

- History of environmental activism in Canada
- Current context of Canada's federal environmental policy landscape
  - Lack of federal leadership on environmental policy
  - Diminished role of environmental science
  - Marginalization of critics
  - Increasing influence of oil and gas industry
- Reconciling climate change and rapid tar sands expansion
- Environmental group (ENGO) responses to the Harper government: Turning away from Ottawa
  - Change in tactics after the election of a majority government
  - Greater emphasis on provincial policy
  - Greater emphasis on public mobilization
  - Greater emphasis on the tar sands sector's ability to reach markets
- Effectiveness of the ENGO response

A Brief History of the Environmental Movement

The popular notion of environmental activism—hanging Greenpeace banners from nuclear power plant silos, obstructing Japanese whaling ships in the Southern Ocean, and signing petitions against clear-cut logging or tar sands development—provides only a narrow glimpse into the history of environmental activism and its current manifestations. The environmental movement in Canada has its roots in a larger conservation movement that took place in North America near the turn of the last century.[1] In the 1880s and 1890s, the first national parks, such as Yellowstone and Yosemite in the United States and Banff in Canada, were being created alongside some of the first nature conservation organizations in the United States, such as the Sierra Club in 1892 and a growing number of field naturalist clubs and forestry associations in Canada.[2] The views of this conservation movement were largely based on the use of nature, or the management of components of the environment that have commercial value. Unlike the modern environmental movement, the early conservation movement was not founded on an integrated understanding of ecosystems where air, land, and water interact with plant and animal species and local communities.

The beginning of the modern environmental movement in North America is commonly dated to 1962 when Rachel Carson published *Silent Spring*, a book that decisively revealed the link between a commonly used pesticide (DDT) and the decline of songbirds in America.[3] Carson's book, which showed the impact that industrial agriculture can have on human and ecosystem health, coincided with the counterculture movement of 1960s North America, which strove to radically change the existing economic, social, and political order. As a result, modern environmentalism was birthed alongside the civil rights, women's rights, anti-war, and anti-nuclear movements. Canada's first outspoken environmental groups were founded a few years later, such as Pollution Probe in 1969. Pollution Probe successfully advocated for a federal ban on DDT and was an instrumental advocate in cleaning up Lake Erie. Greenpeace, among the most visible of environmental groups in the world, was founded in Vancouver in 1971 and helped bridge the peace and environmental movements through initial campaigns against nuclear arms testing in Alaska.[4] At the end of the 1970s, the environmental movement began to divide between those groups seeking direct action/radical environmental activism (e.g., Earth First and the Sea Shepherd Society) and those engaging governments and businesses (e.g., World Wildlife Fund [WWF] Canada, Sierra Club British Columbia). By the early 1980s, a major recession in Canada resulted in less public attention being paid to environmental issues. The recession also reduced funding for many environmental groups, muting their advocacy for several years. However, a series of high-profile environmental disasters in the mid- to late 1980s brought environmental concerns back to the forefront of the minds of Canadians. The Bhopal, India, toxic gas disaster (1984), the Chernobyl nuclear reactor meltdown in Ukraine (1986), and the *Exxon Valdez* oil tanker spill on the Alaskan coast (1989), along with other issues of global concern like acid rain, the ozone hole, and climate change, all served to heighten public concern over environmental issues. At this time, there was a focus in Canadian environmental activism on rainforest and biodiversity protection, which resulted in successful campaigns to save Vancouver Island's Clayoquot Sound and Carmanah Valley from clear-cut logging.[5] Environmental groups began to adopt new tactics, including turning to the courts as a venue to hold companies and governments accountable for environmental change. Ecojustice, which formed in Vancouver in 1990, worked alongside other longer-standing Canadian groups like West Coast Environmental Law and the Canadian Environmental Law Association, and leveraged the power of the courts to set legal precedents for stronger environmental protection. During the mid- to late 1980s, Canada's federal environmental leadership was gaining international recognition through the country's role in the Montreal Protocol, a global agreement that bans ozone-depleting substances; by playing a leadership role in organizing the Rio Earth Summit in 1992; and in addressing the acid rain problem in Ontario and Quebec. By the early to mid-1990s, another recession had hit Canada and both federal and provincial governments reprioritized away from environmental protection and towards balancing budgets.

Environmental activism in the twenty-first century continues to evolve. Many environmental groups in Canada are seeing increasing professionalization and are just as likely to employ engineers, lawyers, public policy analysts, fundraisers, and communications experts as they are to hire more "traditional" environmental advocates like biologists or community organizers. Improved communication through the Internet and social media has enabled Canada's environmental groups to form strong networks with other groups from around the world, and these networks are increasingly necessary to prevent global climate change. Climate change has become the most important environmental issue for twenty-first-century environmental activism in Canada. For example, sophisticated international campaigns against Alberta's tar sands development are using a host of tactics to raise awareness about the environmental implications of rapid tar sands development, from hanging banners and organizing local communities to participating in regulatory hearings and spearheading a fossil fuel divestment campaign with the investment community.

Environmental activists in Canada are also partnering and forming **coalitions** with a broader range of groups. In the 1990s, the "war in the woods" pitted environmental groups against forestry workers. More recently, some unions now partner with green groups to push for shared goals like a vibrant clean energy economy. For example, BlueGreen Canada brings together environmental groups like Environmental Defense with unions like Unifor and the United Steelworkers to advocate for environmental solutions that create jobs and positive economic benefits.[6] Increasing numbers of environmental groups are also collaborating with the forest industry to strengthen environmental protection. Sierra Club BC, ForestEthics, and Greenpeace Canada signed the Great Bear Rainforest Agreement alongside logging companies, First Nations, and the British Columbia government to protect the largest coastal temperate rainforest in the world.[7] Environmental groups such as the Pembina Institute, Équiterre, and WWF Canada are also working alongside many First Nations in campaigns against shale gas, pipeline, and tar sands development.

As Canada's environmental movement becomes more sophisticated, the need for ENGOs to have an equally sophisticated understanding of the policy landscape is critical if the movement is to see stronger environmental stewardship in Canada. We explore the major aspects of this landscape in the next section.

Current Context

This section highlights four main features of Canada's federal environmental policy landscape that have actively shaped the current context for the Canadian environmental movement since the Conservative Party took power in 2006. These are the lack of federal leadership on environmental policy; the diminished federal capacity for environmental science; the marginalization of environmental voices; and the increasing influence of the oil and gas industry in Canada.

Lack of Federal Leadership

In making the case for diminished federal leadership on environmental issues, we remind the reader of the division of authority on environmental responsibilities among the levels of government in Canada.[8] As discussed in detail by Valiante in Chapter 4 and Simmons in Chapter 8, jurisdiction with respect to protecting the environment differs across issues but generally favours the provincial role, and this is reinforced by the penchant of the federal government to delegate its authority to subnational governments. The result of decentralized and delegated authority has been a patchwork of environmental management in Canada.[9] This patchwork can make it challenging when facing environmental issues that impact various regions of Canada differently (e.g., transboundary pollution) or for major national issues that require immediate, concerted action (e.g., climate change).

Canada has had moments of strong federal leadership on environmental issues. The federal government of Liberal Prime Minister Pierre Trudeau ushered in the formation of a Department of the Environment as well as nine major environmental laws in his first term as Prime Minister (1968–72). Progressive Conservative Prime Minister Brian Mulroney, in power from 1984 to 1993, has been recognized as the greenest Prime Minister in Canadian history for his role in addressing acid rain, the ozone hole, and climate change.[10] Mulroney represented the "high-water mark" of environmental policy leadership, however; recent administrations have exhibited considerable ambivalence on this file. This ambivalence has reached its most stark expression to date under the Conservative government of Prime Minister Stephen Harper, and indeed we might reasonably speak of a leadership vacuum at the federal level in Canada—particularly in the crucial area of climate change policy.

This is unfortunate, as there are critical roles that only the federal government can occupy, including being the arbiter in environmental disputes between provinces, being the broker of nationally important policy discussion (such as with respect to Canadian climate policy), negotiating international agreements, and implementing new national environmental policies and regulations. For example, the Harper government has shown itself unwilling to step in on several recent environmental disputes between the provinces, including a disagreement between Alberta and the Northwest Territories (NWT) regarding the quantity and quality of water that upstream Alberta must ensure for the downstream NWT.[11] This is of particular concern given that water use in Alberta's tar sands has significant impacts on water quality and quantity in the Athabasca River, which eventually drains into the NWT.[12] Further, the federal government has traditionally brokered policy debates of national importance: on health care, constitutional reform, and Aboriginal concerns. These policy debates, although not constitutionally mandated, have then helped to inform federal action on potentially contentious issues. Yet despite requests by provinces, business and labour leaders, a coalition of some of Canada's leading think-tanks, and environmental groups, the federal government's active avoidance of brokering a national conversation about the development of Canada's energy resources, as discussed by Macdonald in Chapter 13, is frustrating a growing number of Canadians.[13]

While the federal government under Prime Minister Harper has moved forward on several environmental files in recent years (examples include banning the dangerous chemical BPA in children's toys, creating some new national parks, and improving vehicle fuel efficiency regulations), major policy areas remain where the federal government has shown its ambivalence. The most notable is climate change, which has been identified by Canada's environmental community as one of the most pressing challenges facing the country. In the absence of federal leadership, some provinces are moving ahead and engaging in ambitious carbon emissions reductions. While these initiatives are to be commended, the development of province-by-province climate policies means that a patchwork of approaches is beginning to emerge across Canada, with little to no co-ordination from the federal level. This lack of federal co-ordination makes harmonization difficult and results in higher implementation costs due to reduced economies of scale, inconsistent monitoring and enforcement of environmental legislation, and difficulty in assessing whether national pollution reduction targets will be reached.

Diminished Federal Capacity for Environmental Science

Through a series of federal budgets, the Conservative federal government has diminished its **capacity** to generate environmental science and communicate environmental science knowledge to the public, as discussed by Bocking in Chapter 6. Hundreds of federal scientific research programs, along with several internationally renowned research facilities, were eliminated between 2009 and 2013. Over 2,000 federal science positions have been lost, including 798 full-time equivalent (FTE) science positions at the National Research Council, 159 FTE science positions at Environment Canada, and 73 FTE science positions at Fisheries and Oceans Canada.[14] In the wake of these reductions, the number of scientific publications from Canada's National Research Council has declined sharply, from 1,800 in 2006 to 570 in 2012.[15] A 2013 survey revealed that nine out of 10 federal scientists at Fisheries and Ocean Canada believe the 2012 changes to the Fisheries Act will make it harder to protect fish and fish habitat in Canada.[16]

In addition, it is now more difficult for publicly funded federal environmental science to be shared with the public than it was before the Conservatives took power in 2006. Another 2013 survey of federal scientists, researchers, and engineers found that nearly one-quarter of the 4,069 respondents had been asked, for non-scientific reasons, to exclude or alter information from public communication about scientific findings.[17] New communications protocols mean that federal scientists can no longer speak freely to the news media regarding their research; instead, media requests are routed through their department's communications teams for approval.[18] All of these actions have prompted serious concerns from scientists across the country, not to mention the international scientific community;[19] in September 2013 there were demonstrations by scientists in 17 cities across Canada. Certainly, these budget cuts and the political scrutiny have had a clear impact on the federal government's ability to generate the scientific data that should support evidence-based environmental policy in Canada.

Marginalization of Environmental Voices in Canada

The Harper government also sought to marginalize environmental voices in Canada. In January 2012, then federal Natural Resources Minister, Joe Oliver, wrote an open letter to

Canadians critical of "radical" environmental groups that threaten to "hijack" the regulatory process for approving fossil fuel projects.[20] The letter clearly implied that environmental groups critical of fossil fuel projects are not part of a legitimate discussion on energy policy in Canada. Several months later, the federal government made the biggest changes to Canada's environmental laws since they were created (as outlined in Chapter 4 by Valiante), limiting the amount of public participation in regulatory hearings and fast-tracking resource development projects without any meaningful consultation with Canada's environmental community. Moreover, additional funding was given to the Canada Revenue Agency (CRA) to investigate any charities that may be engaging in political activities that could threaten their charitable status. The list of environmental charities under review by the CRA in 2014 is a "Who's Who" of Canada's environmental movement: the David Suzuki Foundation, Tides Canada, West Coast Environmental Law, the Pembina Foundation, Environmental Defense, Équiterre, and the Ecology Action Centre.[21] Further, in 2013 the federal government eliminated the National Round Table on the Environment and the Economy (NRTEE), an arm's-length environmental policy think-tank created by the Mulroney government to inform federal environmental policy-making. In the months preceding its elimination, the NRTEE had produced reports indicating that stronger government action was needed on climate change.

Increasing Influence of the Oil and Gas Industry

At the same time that the federal government has worked to diminish the role of environmental voices, the oil and gas industry has demonstrated increasing influence on government policies. This rising influence partially results from the industry's booming production in British Columbia, Alberta, Saskatchewan, and Newfoundland and Labrador, supported by oil-and-gas-friendly governments in all of those provinces and in Ottawa.[22] The fossil fuel industry's access to federal decision-makers is the highest of any interest group in Canada, according to **lobbying** records.[23] From 2008 to 2012, the Environment Minister and the Natural Resources Minister were consistently among the most lobbied ministers in the federal cabinet, with representatives from fossil fuel companies and their industry associations being by far the most frequent visitors.[24] The 2012 federal budget unveiled a **Responsible Resource Development** plan that, among other things, included tens of millions of dollars of public funding for advertisements promoting Canada's oil and gas industry.[25] The budget also included changes to Canada's environmental laws that had been requested by Canada's oil and gas industry to increase the predictability of the permitting process for new facilities and expansions.[26]

Environmental Groups and the Harper Majority

The remainder of this chapter examines the changed approach that ENGOs have adopted in Canada in response to the election of a majority Harper government in 2011 and the policy landscape as described above. It begins with a description of ENGO tactics during the Harper minority years, several of which effectively reached a dead end after the majority government adopted an emphatically pro-resource development agenda in the 2012 federal budget. The discussion below examines the tension between strong climate policy and the rapid tar sands development championed by the Harper majority government. It then looks at the shift in ENGO tactics away from Ottawa to more fertile terrain outside the nation's capital, including a focus on provincial policy, public mobilization, and limiting the tar sands sector's access to new markets by contesting proposals for tar sands pipeline expansion. The chapter concludes with an assessment of the effectiveness of ENGO campaigns against new pipeline proposals. Although environmental organizations in Canada work on virtually the full gamut of environmental issues, this chapter concentrates on climate change, which has become the single largest preoccupation of the Canadian environmental movement.

Manoeuvring under a Minority Government

Stephen Harper's first five years in power, during which he led a **minority government**, made it clear that environmental protection was not among the top priorities. As noted above, however, some environmental issues fared better than others under his watch, with climate change proving to be a particularly difficult file for the Harper government to address.

While previous Liberal governments promised far more than they delivered on climate change, the Conservative minority government elected in 2006 took office without even a rhetorical commitment to greenhouse gas (GHG) emission reductions. Instead, the Conservative government conveyed a clear suspicion of the Kyoto Protocol, and presented a climate agenda that could at best be called minimalist.[27] As a result, the Harper government sought ENGO advice and perspectives on climate change relatively infrequently. In contrast, the parties holding the majority of seats in Parliament—the Liberals, the New Democratic Party, and the Bloc Québécois—all called for a more ambitious agenda on climate change than the government did, and all gave the issue greater priority. Polling showed that a majority of Canadians worried about climate change and wanted to see stronger government action to combat it.[28] The Harper minority years also saw climate change gain unprecedented global attention, particularly in the run-up to the 2009 UN climate change talks in Copenhagen.

However, as the issue rose in political prominence—and, perhaps, as Conservative MPs learned more about it—federal officials led by the Environment Minister, John Baird, proposed a package of policies aimed at curbing GHG emissions from Canada's heavy industry sectors. This 2007–8 plan, called "Turning the Corner," would have required Canada's heavy industry sectors to reduce **GHG emissions intensity** (i.e., the emissions generated per unit of production, such as a tonne of steel or a barrel of crude oil), offering companies a number of different options to comply with their targets.[29] Environmentalists were critical of the system's design and doubted the government's claims that it was adequate to achieve Canada's national GHG target of a 17 per cent reduction below 2005 levels by 2020;[30] nonetheless, on paper at least, the target mattered to the federal government.

During the Harper minority government years (2006 to 2011), ENGOs worked successfully with federal opposition parties to put pressure on the government to strengthen its approach to tackling climate change. Tools like private members' bills, House of Commons committee meetings, and parliamentary motions allowed opposition parties to propose alternatives to the government's approach, thus generating debate, media coverage, and, in rare cases, action. By informing opposition party members that a given initiative mattered to the ENGO community, environmentalists were sometimes able to persuade opposition parties to work together, thus giving them the votes to push environmental actions forward even in cases where the Harper government actively opposed the initiative.

For example, a pair of climate change bills tabled by Liberal and NDP members of Parliament, and championed by the ENGO community, passed the House of Commons despite Conservative opposition during the Harper minority years.[31] One of those, the Kyoto Protocol Implementation Act, also became law, thus requiring the publication of annual (and invariably unflattering) assessments of the government's climate performance.

From Minority to Majority

The Conservative Party won a majority of the seats in Parliament in May 2011. Early in 2012, the Harper government provided a couple of pointed illustrations of its approach to climate and energy policy under a majority government—and in the process made it crystal clear to ENGOs that the game had changed profoundly.

In a perfect illustration of the new reality, the 2012 budget bill repealed the Kyoto Protocol Implementation Act.[32] ENGOs and opposition parties voiced strong concerns about the changes to environmental legislation and resource review processes in the 2012 budget, but in a **majority government**, Conservative MPs easily voted it into law. In other words, ENGO efforts to work with opposition parties could no longer trump the government's majority status. Second, Natural Resources Minister Oliver's letter labelling opponents of expanded fossil fuel infrastructure as foreign-funded "radicals" served notice that the government wanted the energy debate in Canada to be adversarial rather than collaborative.

Climate Change and Tar Sands Expansion

It is worth discussing why the federal government chose such an adversarial stance towards those who raised concerns about fossil fuel development and the infrastructure needed to support that development. Calling pipeline opponents foreign-funded "radicals" could simply be a reflection of the government's approach: the Harper government's ministers have sometimes been accused of attacking their critics rather than responding to them. But substance as well as style is at play here: the government's emphasis on rapid tar sands development is difficult to reconcile with reducing GHG emissions.

Because tar sands companies in Canada have been increasing production rapidly, the tar sands have become Canada's fastest-growing source of GHG emissions.[33] Federal projections to 2020[34] foresee continued increases in tar sands production, with the result that the sector would maintain its role as Canada's leading source of GHG emissions growth—although some projects could proceed far more slowly or be shelved altogether if the lower oil prices seen in early 2015 persist.

Over the life cycle of the fuel—extraction, processing, and then combustion—**unconventional oil** from the tar sands generates more GHG emissions than **conventional oil**.[35] Relative to other sources of crude, tar sands is also a very costly fuel to produce. As a particularly high-cost, high-carbon fuel, the tar sands sector's future production—in particular, planned projects that have not yet begun construction—is sensitive both to lower oil prices and to policies aimed at increasing demand for cleaner fuels. For example:

> With oil prices dropping significantly in late 2014 and into 2015, tar sands companies responded by cutting personnel and delaying capital spending on new projects,[36] thus slowing the pace of growth in the sector's production.

Under Prime Minister Harper, the Canadian government has lobbied vigorously against cleaner fuel standards like the European Union's Fuel Quality Directive[37] and California's Low Carbon Fuel Standard.[38] These policies aim to reduce the carbon footprint of fuels in their respective jurisdictions, which creates a disincentive to import high-carbon tar sands products.

Technologies can reduce the GHG impact of tar sands operations: for example, **carbon capture and storage** (CCS) could significantly improve tar sands emissions performance at many operations, but it is so expensive that only one tar sands project is currently adopting it.[39] Under current conditions, then, more tar sands development means more GHG emissions.[40] The converse is also true: according to the oil and gas industry, more stringent policies to reduce emissions in Alberta would slow the growth in tar sands production.[41]

Looking beyond the tar sands sector specifically, scientific assessments estimate that avoiding dangerous climate change will require leaving the majority of the world's fossil fuel reserves in the ground.[42] Many policy options aimed at reducing GHG emissions would have the effect of reducing oil use, including more stringent fuel efficiency standards, support for electric vehicles, and increased investment in public transit.

The bottom line? If you want to develop the tar sands as quickly as possible, action to tackle climate change—whether at home or abroad—can be seen as a threat to the future of a prized sector.

ENGOs, Climate Policy, and the Harper Majority

By the time the Harper majority took office in 2011, global concern about climate change had dropped from the unprecedented levels seen during Harper's minority tenure. The US had also failed to enact economy-wide carbon pricing policies. With the pressure from abroad diminished and a majority of votes in Parliament, the Harper government's political direction was now strongly in favour of rapid resource development to maximize short-term economic gain. As noted above, the 2012 federal budget's Responsible Resource Development initiative aimed to put companies on a smoother, faster track to developing oil, gas, and other natural resources. The government's approach to climate policy—never an area of strength or innovation for the Harper Conservatives—now included outright rejection of **carbon pricing**,[43] a principal and widely accepted tool for efficiently curbing GHG emissions.

As discussed in the Introduction to this volume, Canada's parliamentary system provides relatively few checks and balances on the power of the executive under a majority government. Indeed, for ENGOs, the Harper majority meant that work with environment-minded parliamentarians had shifted from the substantive to the rhetorical. Even the most optimistic ENGOs had to abandon any hope of strengthening the government's approach to climate change and environmental protection from the inside. As a result, certain types of policy engagement that ENGOs had pursued vigorously prior to 2011 became token at best. For example, ENGO efforts to inform legislators about the strengths and weaknesses of specific carbon pricing policies became obsolete in the face of a majority government that characterized carbon pricing as a "job-killing tax on everything."[44] In addition, ENGO efforts to work with "unusual allies" in the business community on carbon pricing also became virtually irrelevant. While ENGOs and the business community continue to share similar views on the need for economy-wide carbon pricing[45] (though not in regard to the required level of stringency), there is little benefit for companies in putting themselves offside with the Prime Minister's Office by communicating that position in a strong and public way. Thus, initiatives like an "ENGO–industry dialogue on no regrets climate policy"[46] lost momentum in the face of federal disinterest.

It is notable that the majority Harper government has shown no inclination to publish a plan, or design a package of policies, capable of achieving Canada's national 2020 climate target. Prior to 2011, ENGOs had made significant efforts to communicate the kinds of policy choices needed to hit our national goals,[47] but that kind of comprehensive approach is no longer of interest in Ottawa. The government has also made a concerted effort to mimic the American positions at international climate negotiations, arguing that Canada cannot afford to do anything more than its neighbour.[48] Partly as a result of Canada's lack of independent positioning, Canadian ENGO attention to and engagement in the UN climate negotiations has been reduced dramatically.

A few areas remained open to ENGOs with an interest in the federal scene. For example, there was still a niche for the "watchdog" role of monitoring Ottawa's environmental performance. Public communication of a lack of progress towards climate goals, or the federal government's failure to constrain the growing environmental footprint of tar sands development, could continue to be worthwhile terrain for ENGOs. However, the effectiveness of this approach was somewhat dulled by its repetitiveness. After the comprehensive sweep of the 2012 budget changes, added to the years of international critiques of Canada's climate performance, there was little "news" in the message that Canada was not taking climate change seriously. The idea that the Harper government prioritizes resource development over environmental protection is widely accepted by Ottawa-based reporters and pundits, and thus offered little novelty value to the news media. However, ENGOs that continued to track federal policy remained able to generate periodic media coverage reminding Canadians of their assessment of the federal government's performance as being inadequate.[49]

In addition, some non-political officials working in federal departments remain interested in the views of non-profit organizations. As a result, environmental think-tanks could pursue technical work with officials at Environment Canada, Natural Resources Canada, or other federal departments, hoping to influence specific, very detailed issues. For example, while the Prime Minister's Office and cabinet would decide Canada's climate target, officials at Environment Canada could decide issues related to reporting on those targets, and might welcome ENGO comments on how to do it better.

If Not Ottawa, Then What?

For national ENGOs, one response to the lack of opportunities in Ottawa was to turn more of their attention to the provinces. As noted above, provinces make many of the critical decisions about resource development, so they have always been key players in Canada's climate and energy landscape. While national ENGOs in Canada—including the David Suzuki Foundation, Greenpeace, and the WWF—paid attention to provincial policies before the Conservatives gained a majority government, their emphasis on provincial jurisdictions grew after 2011. Policies like British Columbia's carbon tax, Quebec's **cap-and-trade system**, and Ontario's coal phase-out and feed-in tariff to support renewable energy offered more interesting opportunities for emission reductions, and for ENGO policy influence, than anything happening in Ottawa. As a result, fewer ENGO staff were employed in Ottawa in 2014 than during the Harper government's minority years, and this is particularly the case with those ENGOs focused on climate change.

As noted above, the niche for ENGO work in Ottawa under a Harper majority is a narrow one. It was clear to ENGOs that playing a watchdog role and doing technical work in Ottawa, while useful, would not be sufficient to lead to meaningful policy change. So ENGOs have turned to two sources of pressure that matter to all democratic governments: votes and money.

Votes: Public Mobilization

It was clear after the 2012 budget (and arguably much earlier) that the federal government was willing to withstand critiques of its environmental policies from ENGOs, scientists, and other Canadian opinion leaders. But any democratic government pays close attention to *voters'* concerns. So if ENGOs could mobilize strong public support for environmental protection, they believed, governments in Canada would be more likely to move those issues up their priority lists.

Public mobilization by ENGOs on climate and energy issues was already taking place well before the Harper majority, but its importance grew after the May 2011 federal election. ENGO strategists concluded that lobbying in Ottawa could not succeed unless it was backed by adequate and tangible voter support, and put new emphasis on building that support. One consequence of this stronger focus on public mobilization is an emphasis on specific local issues, as these more tangible environmental concerns often carry the most weight with members of the public. For example, the British Columbia–based Dogwood Initiative is currently focused on stopping an increase in tanker traffic on the BC coast and stopping coal exports from BC ports.[50] While both issues have direct relevance to climate change, their local impacts may be the primary concern for many of Dogwood's supporters.

A perfect illustration of this shift is the career path of a prominent Ottawa-based environmentalist, Graham Saul. During the Harper government's minority years, Graham chaired the Climate Action Network (CAN)–Canada, an umbrella group of civil society organizations working on climate change. CAN–Canada focused on federal policy and paid close attention to the UN climate talks. After the Conservatives achieved a majority, Graham left CAN to work on public mobilization to solve local environmental problems at Ecology Ottawa, an ENGO he co-founded.[51]

Money: Getting Crude to Markets

Many ENGOs interpret the Harper government's stance on resource development as being one that sees strong climate policy as a threat to the tar sands sector's future. In the years since the Harper majority government took power, ENGOs have devoted an increasing amount of time and effort to illustrating the opposite proposition: that weak environmental policies are the real threat to the future of tar sands development.

For ENGOs, this approach is seen as perhaps the only way to pique the interest of the federal government in reducing the GHG footprint of the tar sands. While ENGOs see the Harper government as having virtually no interest in climate policy for its own sake, some believe that Ottawa's calculus would change if the tar sands' environmental footprint was impeding companies' ability to build new facilities or to ship their product to markets.

ENGO work linking weak environmental policies in the tar sands to the sector's economic future has several dimensions. These include:

Cleaner fuel standards. As mentioned above, several jurisdictions, including California[52] and the European Union,[53] have proposed policies aimed at reducing the GHG impact of their transportation fuels over time through a regulated target. These policies would create an economic disincentive to consuming tar sands oil in those jurisdictions because of its higher GHG footprint. ENGOs outside of Canada have mobilized to support these policies, and ENGOs in Canada have made the case that tar sands production won't be able to compete in a lower-carbon world unless companies and governments take steps to cut its GHG footprint.

Social licence. Tar sands companies need at least some public support for their operations and growth plans (as the cliché goes, governments grant permits but only the public can grant permission). Canadian ENGOs have argued that better environmental performance from oil and gas companies would help increase public support for the sector's operations.[54]

Divestment campaigns. Climate campaigners are also putting growing pressure on institutional investors, such as pension funds and university endowments—which often have a longer-term perspective than other investors—to divest their holdings of fossil fuel (or, more narrowly, tar sands) companies.[55]

However, easily the best-known facet of the ENGO effort to link weak environmental practices in the tar sands to the sector's future growth is the North-America-wide campaign against new oil pipeline proposals.

The tar sands sector has had ambitious growth plans, at a time when US domestic oil production is also growing rapidly. As a result, the current pipeline network out of Alberta is near capacity; in response, pipeline companies have brought forward a number of significant new proposals. These include the Northern Gateway proposal from Alberta to the BC coast; the Keystone XL proposal from Alberta to the US Gulf coast; and the Energy East proposal from Alberta to New Brunswick. Although some of these proposals were developed well before the 2011 federal election, the tenure of the Harper majority government has coincided with the regulatory assessment of a number of these projects. For ENGOs concerned about the pace and scale of tar sands development, pipelines represent an important chokepoint. The ENGOs campaigning against new pipeline proposals believe that constraints on new pipeline construction would lead to a slowdown in the pace and scale of tar sands development, and thus a slowdown in expanding the sector's environmental footprint.[56] Pipeline campaigns offer ENGOs a strategic blend of the local and the global, marrying the more local risk of oil spills with the long-term climate risk of locking in additional tar sands emissions.

The cross-border campaign against the Keystone XL pipeline proposal, the biggest ENGO anti-pipeline effort to date, is widely credited with reviving the US environmental movement after a period of despondency when Congress failed to adopt cap-and-trade legislation.[57] Many ENGO strategists interpreted that failure as being the result of too much focus "inside the Beltway" in Washington, and they resolved to build greater political power through public mobilization. Although the context was different in the US than in Canada, ENGOs on both sides of the border pivoted to a campaign focused on mobilizing the public against the Keystone XL pipeline after more comprehensive climate policy efforts had failed to win traction inside governments. Canadian ENGOs have worked closely with their US counterparts to oppose the Keystone XL proposal, and have already earned some significant victories. President Barack Obama rejected an earlier application of the Keystone XL proposal when congressional supporters of Keystone attempted to force a decision on a very short time-line.[58] The proponent, TransCanada, refiled its application for the cross-border pipeline with a different route that reduced its proximity to an important aquifer.[59]

In June 2013, President Obama announced that he would only approve the Keystone proposal if it would not significantly increase net GHG emissions.[60] Over the summer of 2013, he said in an interview about the Keystone XL proposal that Canada could "potentially be doing more to mitigate carbon release."[61] Throughout 2014 and into 2015, the President's position on Keystone XL moved closer to that of the pipeline proposal's ENGO opponents: Obama has linked the Keystone XL proposal to climate change and disputed its proponents' rosy projections of economic gains.[62] In February 2015, the US Environmental Protection Agency weighed in to the Keystone review process with a letter stating that tar sands development "represents a significant increase in greenhouse gas emissions relative to other crudes." The Agency's letter also indicates that in a time of lower oil prices—such as those seen in late 2014 and early 2015—approving or rejecting Keystone XL would make a significant difference in the economics of tar sands development "and the accompanying greenhouse gas emissions."[63] This appraisal, from an agency whose views carry weight in the decision-making process, provides President Obama with a rationale to reject the Keystone XL proposal on climate grounds, should he wish to do so.

President Obama's statements and actions are an excellent illustration of the "market access" approach working as ENGOs hoped it could, with the sector's most important "customer" calling on the tar sands industry to improve its environmental performance. One might argue that Obama's statements have put far more pressure on the Harper government to regulate GHG emissions from oil and gas than Canadian ENGOs on their own could ever deliver in Ottawa—an argument also put forward by VanNijnatten in Chapter 11.

Assessment

As of the time of writing, the fate of the Keystone XL proposal is still undetermined; of course, President Obama and Secretary of State John Kerry may ultimately decide to approve it. Meanwhile, Prime Minister Harper's government has yet to announce any federal GHG regulations on the oil and gas sector. Indeed, in late 2014, with oil prices dropping to a five-year low, Prime Minister Harper stated that imposing any GHG emission regulations on the industry would be "crazy economic policy."[64]

So with the pieces still in motion, it's too early to make a full assessment of the effectiveness of the ENGO strategy. However, ENGO campaigns against pipeline proposals have already generated unprecedented public debate about the specific risks of tar sands pipelines and tar sands development in general, including its climate change implications.

The Harper majority government opened its tenure by adopting an agenda in direct contradiction to the ENGO goals of greater environmental protection, more measured tar sands development, and significant reductions in GHG emissions. Arguably, ENGOs have responded relatively nimbly and effectively to the tough hand they were dealt. ENGOs got themselves back in the game with effective public mobilization campaigns, particularly the cross-border effort to slow or stop the approval of new tar sands pipelines. Given the rapid reorientation this required, it was an impressive feat. No matter what the outcome of the next federal election, building a broader base of mobilized public support for environmental protection will stand ENGOs in good stead. (However, it remains to be seen whether members of the public who are passionate about the impacts of specific projects will transfer that interest to other climate and energy issues.)

While ENGOs may have had little choice but to shift their efforts away from the federal scene, the turn away from Ottawa does carry some risk. For example, much of the ENGO effort to call into question tar sands access to markets depends on the actions of governments outside of Canada—jurisdictions where Canadian ENGOs have virtually zero influence. As long as California, the EU, and the US federal government are more ambitious in tackling climate change than Canada, these campaigns could prod the Harper government to greater climate action (or, at a minimum, open the Harper government up to critiques that its environmental inaction is hurting the tar sands sector's prospects). But if those governments choose to focus on other priorities, the strength of the market access argument risks crumbling away.

The hollowing out of ENGO capacity in Ottawa leaves these non-profits understaffed if comprehensive climate policy begins to matter again. This risk seems relatively small, however, as presumably the ENGOs would be only too happy to build federal teams back up if there were occasion and the funding to do so.

Finally, both the Harper majority government and the ENGO community have staked out stark and polarized positions on oil sands and climate issues. The oil and gas industry, particularly through its industry association, has done the same. As of today, none of those players are yet publicly looking for compromise or seeking out a middle ground. The binary nature of pipeline decisions—either they will proceed, albeit with conditions, or they won't—has likely contributed to a public debate that largely falls into one of two camps. While polarization is generally decried as unproductive, it does also serve to bring the arguments on either side into sharper focus. Perhaps the polarization we see today is a necessary stage in the evolution of Canada's approach to climate and energy policy.

Key Terms

capacity	GHG emissions intensity
cap-and-trade system	lobbying
carbon capture and storage	majority government
carbon pricing	minority government
coalitions	Responsible Resource Development
conventional oil	unconventional oil

Questions for Review

1. How has the environmental movement in Canada changed over the past 50 years?
2. How have the federal budget and program cuts to environmental science impacted environmental advocacy in Canada?
3. To what extent does the rise in influence of the oil and gas industry impact the effectiveness of environmental groups?
4. What were the main features of the Canadian environmental movement's response to the Harper majority government?
5. What are the major strategic benefits and risks of campaigning to limit the tar sands sector's ability to gain access to global markets?
6. What are the strengths and weaknesses of the ENGO response to the Harper majority? What could the movement have done differently?

Internet Resources

Climate Action Network
climateactionnetwork.ca/

Greenpeace Canada
www.greenpeace.org/canada/en/

Environmental Defence
environmentaldefence.ca/

WWF Canada
www.wwf.ca/

Pembina Institute
www.pembina.org/

Équiterre
www.equiterre.org/

David Suzuki Foundation
www.davidsuzuki.org/

Canadian Environmental Network
rcen.ca/home

Green Budget Coalition
www.greenbudget.ca/

Additional Reading

Adkin, Laurie E. *Environmental Conflict and Democracy in Canada*. Vancouver: University of British Columbia Press, 2009.

Forkey, Neil S. *Canadians and the Natural Environment to the Twenty-First Century*. Toronto: University of Toronto Press, 2012.

MacDowell, Laurel Sefton. *An Environmental History of Canada*. Vancouver: University of British Columbia Press, 2012.

McKenzie, Judith I. *Environmental Politics in Canada*. Toronto: Oxford University Press, 2002.

Weyler, Rex. *Greenpeace: The Inside Story*. Vancouver: Raincoast Books, 2004.

Notes

1. For more information about the conservation movement, see Robert Paehlke, "The Environmental Movement in Canada," in Debora VanNijnatten and Robert Boardman, eds, *Canadian Environmental Policy and Politics*, 3rd edn (Toronto: Oxford University Press, 2009).
2. Laurel Sefton MacDowell, *An Environmental History of Canada* (Vancouver: University of British Columbia Press, 2012).
3. Ibid.
4. Paehlke, "The Environmental Movement in Canada."
5. Judith I. McKenzie, *Environmental Politics in Canada* (Toronto: Oxford University Press, 2002).
6. Blue GreenCanada, at: www.bluegreencanada.ca.
7. "Take It Taller for the Great Bear Rainforest," www.savethegreatbear.org.
8. For a more detailed treatment of federalism in Canada and the impact on environmental policy-making, see Chapters 4 and 8 of this volume.
9. McKenzie, *Environmental Politics in Canada*.
10. *Ottawa Citizen*, "Mulroney to PM: Push U.S. to Go Green," 21 Apr. 2006, accessed 6 Apr. 2014, www.canada.com/story_print.html?id=ae348b17-23a8-4571-b699-5750990673c7&sponsor=.

11. Jennifer Grant, Simon Dyer, Nathan Lemphers, and Jennifer Dagg, *Northern Lifeblood: Empowering Northern Leaders to Protect the Mackenzie River Basin from Oilsands Risks.* Calgary: Pembina Institute. www.pembina.org/pub/2051.

12. Ibid.

13. Winnipeg Consensus.org,www.winnipegconsensus.org; Energy Policy Institute of Canada, www.canadasenergy.ca; The Council of the Federation—Canadian Energy Strategy Working Group, www.councilofthefederation.ca/en/initiatives/130-energy-working-group.

14. *The Fifth Estate*, "Silence of the Labs," www.cbc.ca/fifth/episodes/2013-2014/the-silence-of-the-labs; "Vanishing Science: The Disappearance of Canadian Public Interest Science," www.pipsc.ca/portal/page/portal/website/issues/science/vanishingscience.

15. Amanda Shendruck, "Are Scientists Being Muzzled? A Look at the Record," *Maclean's*, 4 Oct. 2013, www2.macleans.ca/2013/10/04/are-scientists-being-muzzled-a-look-at-the-record/.

16. "Vanishing Science."

17. "The Big Chill," www.pipsc.ca/portal/page/portal/website/issues/science/bigchill.

18. Ibid.

19. Editorial, "Death of Evidence: Changes to Canadian Science Raise Questions That the Government Must Answer," *Nature* 487 (2012): 271–2, accessed 4 Apr. 2014, doi:10.1038/487271b.

20. "An open letter from the Honourable Joe Oliver, Minister of Natural Resources, on Canada's commitment to diversify our energy markets and the need to further streamline the regulatory process in order to advance Canada's national economic interest," 9 Jan. 2012, www.nrcan.gc.ca/media-room/news-release/2012/1/1909.

21. Evan Solomon and Kirsten Everson, "7 Environmental Charities Face Canadian Revenue Agency Audits," CBC News, 6 Feb. 2014, accessed 4 Apr. 2014, www.cbc.ca/news/politics/7-environmental-charities-face-canada-revenue-agency-audits-1.2526330.

22. Roger Gibbins, "Like Her or Loathe Her, B.C. Premier Christy Clark Is Possibly Canada's Most Influential Energy Player," *Alberta Oil*, 3 Feb. 2014, accessed 4 Apr. 2014, www.albertaoilmagazine.com/2014/02/christy-clark-bc-premier/; Paul Chastko, *Developing Alberta's Oil Sands: From Karl Clark to Kyoto* (Calgary: University of Calgary Press, 2004); "Oil and Gas Industry—Government of Saskatchewan," accessed 6 Apr. 2014, http://www.gov.sk.ca/Default.aspx?DN=4a57f37e-88de-4da5-b6a8-411793a739d5; Paul Wells, Tamsin McMahon, and Alex Ballingall, "How Ottawa Runs on Oil: Suddenly Western Money and Influence Are Driving Everything That Happens in the Nation's Capital," *Maclean's*, 23 Mar. 2012, accessed 6 Apr. 2014, http://www2.macleans.ca/2012/03/23/oil-power/.

23. D. Cayley-Daoust and R. Girard, *Big Oil's Oily Grasp: The Making of Canada as a Petro-State and How Oil Money Is Corrupting Canadian Politics* (Ottawa: Polaris Institute, 2012), 23, http://polarisinstitute.org/files/BigOil'sOilyGrasp_0.pdf.

24. Ibid.; "The Top Lobby Groups in Ottawa," *Maclean's*, 5 Dec. 2013, accessed 6 Apr. 2014, http://www.macleans.ca/news/canada/the-top-lobby-groups-in-ottawa/.

25. Canadian Press, "Ottawa Ramps Up Ad Spending for U.S. Pipeline Fight," CBC News, 14 May 2013, accessed 6 Apr. 2014, http://www.cbc.ca/news/politics/ottawa-ramps-up-ad-spending-for-u-s-pipeline-fight-1.1307723.

26. Max Paris, "Energy Industry Letter Suggested Environmental Law Changes," CBC News, 9 Jan. 2013, accessed 6 Apr. 2014, http://www.cbc.ca/news/politics/energy-industry-letter-suggested-environmental-law-changes-1.1346258.

27. The Conservative Party of Canada's 2006 election platform committed to "Address the issue of greenhouse gas emissions, such as carbon dioxide (CO2), with a made-in-Canada plan, emphasizing new technologies, developed in concert with the provinces and in coordination with other major industrial countries." While the platform did not mention Canada's Kyoto commitment by name, it did critique the Liberal government for signing "ambitious international treaties" and sending "money to foreign governments for hot air credits." Conservative Party of Canada, "Stand Up for Canada: Conservative Party of Canada Federal Election Platform 2006," Jan. 2006, http://www.google.ca/url?sa=t&rct=j&q=&esrc=s&source=web&cd=1&cad=rja&uact=8&ved=0CC0QFjAA&url=http%3A%2F%2Fwww.cbc.ca%2Fcanadavotes2006%2Fleadersparties%2Fpdf%2Fconservative_platform20060113.pdf&ei=WIFRU6SuFoKh2QX9qIGICA&usg=AFQjCNGY_1gPJNrKRMCQkvCo=uxagDQv8Q&sig2=gOVPTFlkVnFpDB6d4XuqwQ&bvm=bv.65058239,d.b2I.

28. "Almost 4 out of 5 Canadians Believe in Global Warming: Poll," CBC News, 22 Mar 2007, accessed 18 Apr. 2014, http://www.cbc.ca/news/canada/almost-4-out-of-5-canadians-believe-in-global-warming-poll-1.653791.

29. A short description of the plan is available in Government of Canada, "Taking Action to Fight Climate Change: Turning the Corner," Mar. 2008, accessed 18 Apr. 2014, publications.gc.ca/collections/collection_2009/ec/En88-2-2008E.pdf.‌Ž

30. See, for example, Matthew Bramley and Clare Demerse, "The March 2008 Federal Regulatory Framework for Industrial Greenhouse Gas Emissions," Pembina Institute, 21 Mar. 2008, accessed 18 Apr. 2014, http://www.pembina.org/pub/1614.

31. Liberal MP Pablo Rodriguez introduced and championed the Kyoto Protocol Implementation Act in the House of Commons, and Liberal Senator Grant Mitchell sponsored the bill in the Senate. The bill became

law on 22 June 2007; the text of the Act is available at http://laws-lois.justice.gc.ca/eng/acts/K-9.5/20070622/ P1TT3xt3.html. NDP leader Jack Layton introduced the Climate Change Accountability Act, a bill requiring longer-term climate planning and deep reduction targets. A subsequent version of the same bill passed the House of Commons but was defeated in November 2010 by Conservative senators, who had by then gained a majority of seats in the Senate. See Gloria Galloway, "Tory Senators Kill Climate Bill Passed by House," *Globe and Mail*, 17 Nov. 2010, accessed 20 Apr. 2014, http://www.theglobeandmail.com/news/politics/ ottawa-notebook/tory-senators-kill-climate-bill-passed-by-house/article4348505/.

32. The legislation was repealed on 29 June 2012 (http:// laws-lois.justice.gc.ca/eng/acts/K-9.5/page-1.html) by Section 699 of the 2012 Jobs, Growth and Long-Term Prosperity Act (http://laws-lois.justice.gc.ca/eng/acts/ J-0.8/page-30.html#h-285).

33. Canada's National Inventory Report 1990–2012 (https://www.ec.gc.ca/ges-ghg/default.asp?lang= En&n=3808457C-1&offset=1&toc=show) provides historical and current context, while the Environment Canada publication Canada's Emissions Trends 2013 (http://www.ec.gc.ca/ges-ghg/default.asp?lang=En &n=985F05FB-1) contains projections that look forward to 2020.

34. Government of Canada, Canada's Emissions Trends 2014, accessed 16 Feb. 2015, http://ec.gc.ca/ges-ghg/ default.asp?lang=En&n=E0533893-1.

35. See "Oilsands 101" at the Pembina Institute (http:// www.pembina.org/oil-sands/os101/climate) for an overview and Appendix U of the US State Department's Final Supplemental Environmental Impact Statement for the Keystone XL pipeline proposal (available from http:// keystonepipeline-xl.state.gov/finalseis/) for a more detailed discussion.

36. See, e.g., Dan Healing, "Suncor Cuts $1B in Capital Spending, Plans to Chop 1,000 Positions," *Calgary Herald*, 14 Jan. 2015, http://calgaryherald.com/business/energy/ suncor-cuts-1b-in-capital-plans-to-chop-1000-positions.

37. See, e.g., Natural Resources Canada, "Minister Oliver Highlights Canada's Position on the Proposed European Union Fuel Quality Directive in Brussels," 2013, http://www.nrcan.gc.ca/media-room/news-release/ 2013/1709.

38. See, e.g., Alex Boutilier, "Federal Government Prepares $24-Million Oil Sands Advertising Blitz," Postmedia News, 10 Oct. 2013, http://o.canada.com/uncategor-ized/federal-government-prepares-24-million-oil-sands-advertising-blitz.

39. The project is Shell's Scotford upgrader: http://www. shell.ca/en/aboutshell/our-business-tpkg/upstream/ oil-sands/quest.html.

40. For more information, see P.J. Partington, "Oilsands Talking Point Collides with Reality," Pembina Institute, 16 Apr. 2014, accessed 20 Apr. 2014, http://www.pem-bina.org/blog/787.

41. Canadian Association of Petroleum Producers, "CAPP Concerns and Questions for AB and Consultants," 9 Apr. 2013, accessed 20 Apr. 2014, http://www.pembina.org/ pub/2492. (Document received under Alberta's Freedom of Information legislation.)

42. For example, UN Framework Convention on Climate Change Executive Secretary Christiana Figueres put it this way in an April 2014 speech: "If we are to stay within 2 degree maximum temperature rise . . . we have to stay within a finite, cumulative amount of GHG emissions in the atmosphere. We have already used more than half of that budget. This means that three quarters of the fossil fuel reserves need to stay in the ground, and the fossil fuels we do use must be utilized sparingly and responsibly." Christiana Figueres, "Statement to IPIECA 40th Anniversary Conference," 3 Apr. 2014, accessed 20 Apr. 2014, unfccc.int/files/press/statements/application/pdf/ 20140204_ipieca.pdf.

43. See, e.g., "Another Senior Liberal Calls for Job-Killing Carbon Tax," Conservative Party of Canada, 17 July 2012, accessed 20 Apr. 2014, http://www.conservative. ca/?p=1978.

44. Journalist David Akin provides a summary of the popularity of this phrase with Conservative MPs: "The Job-Killing Carbon Tax. Again and Again and Again," David Akin's On the Hill, 4 Feb. 2013, accessed 20 Apr. 2014, http://blogs.canoe.ca/davidakin/politics/the-job-killing-carbon-tax-again-and-again-and-again/.

45. For example, the Canadian Chamber of Commerce's 2013 "Climate Change Policy Resolution" recommends that the government "promotes an economy-wide carbon policy that allows for the participation of all emitters." Canadian Chamber of Commerce, "Climate Change Policy Resolution," 2013, accessed 20 Apr. 2014, http:// www.chamber.ca/download.aspx?t=0&pid=2efb0284-e094-e311-93a5-000c29c04ade.

46. The Pembina Institute and Shell convened a dialogue of ENGOs and companies to consider joint support for "no regrets" climate policies in 2011.

47. See, e.g., the David Suzuki Foundation and Pembina Institute report: Matthew Bramley et al., "Climate Leadership, Economic Prosperity," Pembina Institute, 29 Oct. 2009, accessed 20 Apr. 2014, http://www.pembina.org/ pub/1909.

48. Environment Canada's website describes Canada's relationship to the US this way: "Canada's economy is integrated with the United States' to the point where it makes absolutely no sense to proceed without aligning a range of principles, policies, regulations and standards. For this reason, Canada has fully aligned its 2020

emission reduction target to reduce emissions by 17 percent from 2005 levels with the United States. This target has been inscribed in the Copenhagen Accord and is subject to adjustment to remain consistent with the U.S. target." Environment Canada, "Canada's Action on Climate Change: Canada's Continental Action," accessed 20 Apr. 2014, http://climatechange.gc.ca/default.asp?lang=En&n=A4F03CA6-1.

49. For example, an annual international ranking of countries' climate change performance or Canada's "Fossil of the Day" prizes at the UN climate talks usually garner some media coverage. Examples of ENGO news releases on these topics can be seen at the Climate Action Network's website: Climate Action Network–Canada, "Canada Ranked as Worst Performer in the Developed World on Climate Change," 3 Dec. 2012, accessed 20 Apr. 2014, http://climateactionnetwork.ca/2012/12/03/canada-ranked-as-worst-performer-in-the-developed-world-on-climate-change/?rel=669; Climate Action Network–Canada, "Canada Wins 'Lifetime Unachievement' Fossil Award at Warsaw Climate Talks," 22 Nov. 2013, accessed 20 Apr. 2014, http://climateactionnetwork.ca/2013/11/22/canada-wins-lifetime-unachievement-fossil-award-at-warsaw-climate-talks/?rel=669.

50. Dogwood Initiative, "Focus—That's Our Promise to You," accessed 20 Apr. 2014, https://dogwoodinitiative.org/campaigns.

51. See the "More About" page on Ecology Ottawa's website: http://ecologyottawa.ca/about/more-about/ (accessed 20 Apr. 2014).

52. More information concerning California's Low Carbon Fuel Standard is available at California Environmental Protection Agency Air Resources Board, "Low Carbon Fuel Standard Program," accessed 20 Apr. 2014, http://www.arb.ca.gov/fuels/lcfs/lcfs.htm.

53. More information concerning the European Union's Fuel Quality Directive is available at European Commission, "Environment: Transport & Environment: Fuel Quality Monitoring," http://ec.europa.eu/environment/air/transport/fuel.htm (accessed 20 Apr. 2014).

54. For an example of this kind of reasoning, see Simon Dyer, "Protecting the Athabasca River Offers Industry a Chance to Earn Social License," *Oilsands Review*, 29 Aug. 2013, accessed 20 Apr. 2014, http://www.pembina.org/op-ed/2473.

55. US environmentalist Bill McKibben is arguably the best-known advocate of divestment. A Canadian example of divestment campaigning is the Canadian Youth Climate Coalition's "Fossil Free Canada" project. See http://gofossilfree.ca/about/ (accessed 20 Apr. 2014).

56. This case is made in general terms in Pembina Institute, "Oilsands Transportation Infrastructure Perspective,"

25 Nov. 2013, accessed 20 Apr. 2014, http://www.pembina.org/pub/2497.

57. *Grist* writer Dave Roberts provides an excellent summary of the appeal of the anti-Keystone campaign for US ENGOs in his blog "Climate Analysts Are from Mars, Climate Activists Are from Venus . . . But They Both Live on Earth," 16 Feb. 2012, accessed 20 Apr. 2014, http://grist.org/climate-change/climate-analysts-are-from-mars-climate-activists-are-from-venus-but-they-both-live-on-earth/.

58. White House, Office of the Press Secretary, "Statement by the President on the Keystone XL Pipeline," 18 Jan. 2012, accessed 21 Apr. 2014, http://www.whitehouse.gov/the-press-office/2012/01/18/statement-president-keystone-xl-pipeline.

59. Detailed information about the amended proposal is available from the US State Department's project website, http://www.keystonepipeline-xl.state.gov/ (accessed 21 Apr. 2014).

60. White House, Office of the Press Secretary, "Remarks by the President on Climate Change," 25 June 2013, accessed 21 Apr. 2014, http://www.whitehouse.gov/the-press-office/2013/06/25/remarks-president-climate-change. The President's Keystone "climate test" reads as follows: "Allowing the Keystone pipeline to be built requires a finding that doing so would be in our nation's interest. And our national interest will be served only if this project does not significantly exacerbate the problem of carbon pollution. (Applause.) The net effects of the pipeline's impact on our climate will be absolutely critical to determining whether this project is allowed to go forward. It's relevant."

61. Michael D. Shear and Jackie Calmes, "Obama Says He'll Evaluate Pipeline Project Depending on Pollution," *New York Times*, 27 July 2013, accessed 21 Apr. 2014, http://www.nytimes.com/2013/07/28/us/politics/obama-says-hell-evaluate-pipeline-project-depending-on-pollution.html?_r=0.

62. See, e.g., Paul Koring, "Keystone Pipeline Good for Canada, Not U.S., Obama Says," *Globe and Mail*, 14 Nov. 2014, http://www.theglobeandmail.com/news/world/obama-unmoved-as-us-house-set-to-back-keystone-today/article21585797/.

63. US Environmental Protection Agency, letter to Amos Hochstein and Judith Garber from Cynthia Giles, 2 Feb. 2015, http://www.epa.gov/compliance/nepa/20140032.pdf.

64. Les Whittington, "New Oil and Gas Regulations Would Be 'Crazy' Harper Says," *Toronto Star*, 9 Dec. 2014, accessed 13 Feb. 2015, http://www.thestar.com/news/canada/2014/12/09/new_oil_and_gas_regulations_would_be_crazy_harper_says.html.

3 The Current (Post-Staples?) State of Canada's Resource Industries

Michael Howlett and Nigel Kinney

Chapter Summary

Canada's resource history has long been the quintessential example of a staples economy based on the extraction and export of natural resources: fisheries, forestry, agriculture, mining, and energy. Each of these staples sectors evolved, albeit unevenly, from a frontier staples situation, to greater state involvement in an expanding staples sector, to a mature staples status and in some cases beyond this to the "post-staples" situation described below. Each sector has faced strong, though different, obstacles in its respective transition. In the most recent era following World War II, environmental considerations, including the push for conservation, sustainability, and "full-cost accounting," have forced policy-makers to integrate environmental policy with resource policy to a greater or lesser degree, although some governments have resisted these efforts in some areas and sectors in the name of economic development. Environmental considerations in general, however, continue to play a significant role in shaping Canadian resource policy as Canada engages in international climate change negotiations whose outcome will affect many staples sectors, especially energy.

Chapter Outline

- The four stages of evolution of the Canadian staples economy
  - Frontier Staples State > Classical Expanding State > Mature Staples State > Post-Staples State
- The major staples sectors in Canada (agriculture, forestry, fisheries, mining, and energy)
  - Moving to the mature staples state but with elements of a post-staples shift
- The major obstacles faced by each staples sector in transitioning to a post-staples status
- The role of environmental concerns in determining Canadian resource policies

Introduction

For generations, provinces such as British Columbia, New Brunswick, and Quebec were known for their forestry resources, whereas others, such as Prince Edward Island, Saskatchewan, and Manitoba, were known for agriculture. Ontario mining was legendary, as were the oil and gas wells of Alberta and the fisheries of Newfoundland and Nova Scotia.[1] It was common wisdom, for example, that 50 cents of every dollar in British Columbia came from the forestry industry and that sawmills, pulp and paper, shingle mills, and other related industries employed hundreds of thousands of people in cutting, hauling, and producing various wood products.

Those days are gone. The Douglas fir no longer reigns in British Columbia's economy; in its place tourism, film and television production, aquaculture, and other industries have taken a strong, if not leading, role in the province's economy.[2] Although still important to most provinces' economies, the original **staples resource industries** of farming, fishing, mining, and forestry have given way to service and other types of business. The wheat economy of the Prairies has diversified into the production of a wide range of high-technology agri-food and bio-agricultural products, including genetically modified crops, and wheat producers have been consolidated into large agribusinesses. On the east coast, the Atlantic cod fisheries have vanished due to overfishing and poor management, to be replaced by tourism, offshore oil and gas development, and government work; on the west coast as well, the Pacific salmon stocks have dwindled. In the energy sector, the staples of hydroelectricity, crude oil, and natural gas have been transformed by environmental regulation, the decreasing conventional reserves of liquid hydrocarbons, conflict over land use, new technology, and scarcity of supply outside of expensive tar sands and hydraulic fracturing ("fracking") operations. As well, a security premium on oil and gas reserves adds to the final production and consumption cost. Mining, too, now relies on sophisticated non-traditional products, such as diamonds, for much of its growth.

Nevertheless, the base of the Canadian economy still retains its roots in early staples industries but with many new activities grafted into, and onto, those traditional sectors in what has been termed a **post-staples pattern**.[3] No longer tied exclusively to the original staples industries, Canada is a sophisticated modern society but one whose economy remains different from the typical model of advanced manufacturing, high technology, and services found in Europe, the United States, and Japan. While this transformation of the old staples political economy has ushered in some elements of a desirable new political and social order, at the same time it has exacerbated or worsened many elements of the old.[4]

Most observers would agree that, historically, Canada can be characterized as having had a staples economy, and that this has had a significant impact on the evolution of Canada's resource regimes and practices.[5] Considerable disagreement remains over which aspects of this depiction continue to apply to Canada's primary industries, to what extent it continues to characterize the general Canadian economy, and whether or not it will continue to do so in future years.[6]

Earlier debates within the "Staples School"—the group of scholars centred at the University of Toronto who explored the impact of primary resource production on Canadian history—focused on whether Canada had emerged from its early reliance on staple products in the wake of the wheat boom and manufacturing activities associated with World War I. However, the failure of the manufacturing sector to grow outside of wartime led to a re-emergence of staples analysis in the 1960s and 1970s. This analysis sought to explain the weakness in manufacturing and move past it through, for example, reforms to foreign investment laws, regional development schemes, and the promotion of science and technology research and entrepreneurship.[7] Current debates focus less on the impact of this transition from primary to secondary activities than upon the undeniable growth in service sector employment and production in the post-World War II era,[8]—and the transition of many staples industries towards more capital- and technology-intensive forms of production, for example, with pulp and paper production supplanting the timber and lumber trade. Both developments were thought to undermine the association of large parts of the population directly with staples-extraction activities and exacerbate urban–rural divides in culture, wealth, and well-being.

Examining patterns in Canada and in other staples-oriented economies such as those of Chile, Argentina, Norway, Australia, and New Zealand, Clapp has argued most resource sectors typically follow a similar pattern of development caused by a fall in profits and dislocations over time, caused by the exhaustion of easily accessible resources and their "replacement" by dwindling or more difficult-to-access and therefore more costly supplies.[9] The changes in the staples economy that result are linked to the rise of new social movements such as environmentalism, which can protect wildlife stocks or geographic areas from exploitation, driving up the cost of staples; urbanization, which removes many people from any affinity with producers or awareness of their difficulties; and an increasingly disconnected regional politics as rural–urban divides sharpen. These changes are also affected by forces such as the globalization and regionalization of markets, which can result in increasing competition from lower-cost producers.[10]

Simply put, the traditional staples industries within Canada have been affected by a variety of factors, which together have transformed the Canadian political economy. In most provinces, this has involved a move from a "mature" staples economy characterized by the conditions described above towards a "new" or "post"-staples political economy in which the staples industries themselves shift in order to exploit higher-cost resources, demanding higher amounts of capital and technology, and a more skilled labour force, in their production.[11] This new economy is still very much linked to primary natural resource production, but in new forms and combinations. The idea that significant parts of the economy have entered this new post-staples mode has led to a variety of debates in Canada regarding the consequences for government policy-making, the environment, and the economy.

The Evolution of a Staples Political Economy

A staple refers to a raw or unfinished bulk **commodity** product that is sold in export markets. Timber, fish, and minerals are typical staples, usually extracted and sold in external markets without significant amounts of processing, but so are most agricultural products, oil and gas, hydroelectricity, and, increasingly, water.[12]

An economy based on a single or a multiple set of "primary" or resource industries or staples has been a common feature at various points of the history of many countries, ranging from the United States[13] to Argentina, Chile, New Zealand, Australia, Canada, Brazil, Norway, and many others.[14] Many countries still rely on a single resource industry, including oil-reliant states in the Middle East and Central Asia, as well as agriculture- and mineral-reliant countries in Africa.[15]

Individual staples sectors typically follow four phases as they grow and evolve. The first phase is a period of rapid expansion as the new staple is developed using easy-to-access, plentiful natural resource supplies. The second phase is a maturing phase, as the limits of easily accessible, low-cost resource supplies are reached and/or increased competition limits both market growth and the rate of the expansion of the sector. The third phase is one of

disequilibrium as the state and private sector respond to the slowing of growth by trying to force expansion through subsidies, weaker regulations, or the search for new resource supplies. These efforts at expansion can create some growth but it is usually short-lived, as subsidized supplies are again depleted and costs rise. The fourth phase is one of either decline or crisis as the subsidized expansion is shut down and the industry downsizes, moves to other countries still offering plentiful cheap supplies, or makes a transition to a new form of resource activity, as when aquaculture activities increase to offset declines in the wild fishery.[16]

Some countries have evolved from a staples base to a manufacturing or service base, such as, most notably, the United States and to a lesser extent Russia and Brazil, but others have not or have only partially done so.[17] An economy reliant on a single staple would be expected to follow the same four stages, overall, as its dominant industry. Countries based on multiple staples, of course, could have more complex patterns of development given the different time periods in which different industries would enter and exit different stages. Ultimately, however, these countries would also be expected to pass towards the final post-staples stage as each industry reaches its limits of growth.

In historical terms, an ideal-typical sequence of staples-based political-economic regimes in a "new" country is thus roughly as follows (see Figure 3.1).

First, there is the **frontier staples state**. In this initial period of staples development, easily available bulk commodities (for example, fisheries, furs, and timber) in the period of European exploration and colonial enterprise are exported to metropolitan countries. The extraction of these resources in raw or unprocessed form acts as a leading influence on social formation and settlement patterns, characterized by conflict both between contending colonial or staples-exploiting powers (for example, France, Britain, and the United States) and between trading companies over territory and resources. This is often marked by widespread displacement of existing populations, such as occurred with First Nations and other Aboriginal societies in Canada and with Aboriginal people in Australia.[18] The government often plays a minimal role in the frontier staples state as resources are abundant and small-scale extraction remains manageable. Governments can play a more significant role in associated activities such as transporting goods to market, however, by building links such as roads and highways, railways, and canals. This was the case in Canada where, according to staples scholar and historian Harold Innis, climate and topographic difficulties forced Canadian governments to play a heavier role in the provision of such infrastructure than was the case in many other countries, such as the US.[19] Innis argued this large-scale investment in turn stunted the development in Canada of a domestic industrial base by tying up investment capital in the resource sector and removing it from circulation and use for other industrial projects. In general, though, during this period state policies were focused mainly on free trade in resources globally and the promotion of the new staple industries across the country.

Second is the archetypal or **classical expanding staples state**. In Canada, this state developed with the expansion of agriculture, forestry, fisheries, and mining in the nineteenth and early twentieth centuries, based on a significant comparative advantage Canada held in natural resource endowments and its proximity and special status in first the UK and then the US markets. This classical staples state developed national and subnational core–periphery or "metropolis–hinterland" relationships between one or two major cities such as Montreal and Toronto and the rest of the country, as described in compelling terms by historians and economic geographers such as Innis[20] and Donald Creighton.[21] This state was dominated by the industrial metropolises of Montreal and Toronto and their satellites, such as Winnipeg and Halifax. Both federal and provincial governments were preoccupied with the financing and extraction of a succession of staples, each in turn constituting a lead development sector (that is, involved in investment, employment, and community formation) for the national and provincial (usually northern) periphery.[22] State involvement drastically expanded under the classical expanding staples state, a time marked by these staples sectors becoming a national priority.

Third is the **mature staples state**. Here, in Canada, the rapid expansion of staples extraction dating from World War I was facilitated by new industrial production technologies and Fordist organization of labour, involving the introduction of assembly lines and mass production replacing older skilled craftsmen and apprenticeship systems. Continued high levels of staples production and export earnings stimulated both domestic and export market demand, and were coincident with the growth of core cities linked to resource peripheries at the national and provincial scales.[23] This stage ushered in national strategies for each respective sector combined with large state investments to facilitate the needs of the mature industry. An example in Canada was former Prime Minister John Diefenbaker's late 1950s Road to Resources initiative, a platform to open up the Canadian North and its resources for development, especially mining.

Fourth, the new or **post-staples state** began to emerge in the late twentieth and early twenty-first centuries in previously staples-exporting countries in response to a set of new conditions shaping the trajectory of staples development. The emergence of this state has been influenced by increasing pressures on resources and allied staples sectors, as well as on communities experiencing resource depletion and global market pressures. As mentioned above, in countries like Canada this economy has seen the continued substitution of capital for labour and the growth of social factors—notably the emergence of environmentalism and its variants—within the context of increasing transnational urbanism. This has led some regions, and notably major metropolitan areas, to break away from a purely primary sector-based economy to one more reliant on services provision in a global marketplace, such as the creation of a leading film-making industry in Vancouver and software development in Toronto, Montreal, and on the west coast.[24] Other areas of the country, however, remain firmly within a mature staples mode of production.

As Clapp[25] and Hutton[26] suggest, however, if economic diffusion, diversification, and resource depletion continue, the result may be an economy that evolves even further overall in a post-staples direction. Under conditions whereby expensively procured unprocessed bulk commodities can no longer compete with low-cost suppliers in the traditional export markets, for example, a further reconfiguration of growth and development may occur. Such a transition typically requires a significant increase in the metropolitan shares of population and employment as rural employment declines, as well as the emergence of regional

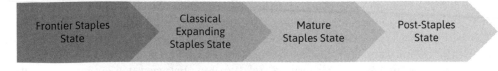

FIGURE 3.1 | The Evolution of a Staples Industry

economic centres in peripheral regions linked to government services and education and health care, for example. In addition, it features the decline of smaller resource-dependent communities, the increased prominence of the internal market for the remaining smaller-scale resource industries, and the transition of existing staples sectors towards high-tech, high-er-value-added activities and products.[27] To a certain extent, this type of political economy has emerged in many areas of the country like southern Ontario's Golden Horseshoe and the Lower Mainland–Victoria area of British Columbia as well as within the Montreal–Quebec City, Halifax–Dartmouth, Calgary–Edmonton, and Regina–Saskatoon corridors.

As Hutton has observed, however, other possible permutations can occur on this general staples evolutionary theme. Thus, rather than a post-staples state, a **degenerative mature, advanced staples political economy** can emerge, characterized by a substantial deple-tion of original resource endowments and consequent increasing pressure on industry to access more costly or protected stocks and supplies. In most countries, this intensification is resisted by environmental groups originating both in urban centres divorced from the resource economy and in hinterland communities desiring to replace "exploitation" with "sustainability" as the operating motif of their livelihood. Rather than diversifying away from primary sector activities, declining mature staples economies feature the increasing capital- and technology-intensiveness of resource extraction processes and consequent decreases in employment in the staples sector; large-scale emigration from affected regions; and the growth of public sector-led employment in areas such as local administration, education, health, and other social services.[28] This pattern has emerged in many areas of Canada, especially the provincial Norths, eastern Ontario, the Maritimes, and much of Nova Scotia and Newfoundland and Labrador.

For countries such as Canada that remain based on multiple staples resource extrac-tion,[29] knowing how these transitions are occurring is critical, as is knowing to what extent each component primary industry, and thus the entire country as a whole, has approached Clapp's final phase or is mired in Hutton's.

The Social and Environmental Significance of a Staples Political Economy

As has been set out above, the significance of having an economy based on exporting unfinished bulk goods is manifold. First, such an economy creates continuing issues with respect to resource technologies, supplies, profits, rents, location, and availability.[30] As Naylor and others have also shown,[31] the development of a staples-based economy can trig-ger government and private sector investments in specific large-scale infrastructure activ-ities, such as transportation and communications facilities required to co-ordinate the extraction and shipment of bulk commodities to markets in distant lands, as well as the pro-vision of export subsidies and credits designed to facilitate trade, at the expense of others. The distortion of the banking and financial system away from consumer and small business credit to a concentration on large industrial loans and profits can be one result.[32] Taken to the extreme, this kind of development can constitute, as Watkins[33] and Freudenburg[34] have noted, a **staples trap** or an "addictive economy," in which a cycle of large-scale resource exploitation is entrenched, with one staple succeeding another as supplies diminish or worldwide demand declines; this is sometimes referred to as the **resource curse**.

Second, the characteristics of natural resource exploitation or harvesting affect activities in related areas, such as education and training. As the Toronto School of staples theorists noted many years ago when undertaking their pioneering studies of Canada's primary sector,[35] frontier staples economies have only a limited need for education and technical skills, and this serves to entrench a system of metropolitan–hinterland links both in economy and also in culture.[36] The impact of natural resource exploitation on the structure and organization of public services as a whole is no less telling as government revenues and capabilities rise and fall with resource rents and taxes.[37]

Third, the relative success or failure of a natural resource or primary industry-based economy also indirectly affects many other areas of social life, such as the ability of governments to pay for or support welfare, health and social policies, or economic diversification and regional development.[38] Basing a country's wealth on foreign markets requires populations, governments, and industries to anticipate and react to their continued vulnerability to international market conditions. The fact that staples-reliant countries have tended to focus on markets in foreign lands is significant in itself. Because most staples-based countries have a monopoly or near-monopoly on the production of only a very few resources or agricultural goods, producers must sell at prices set by international conditions of supply and demand.

Although international demand for most resources—outside of wartime—has increased at a relatively steady but low rate, world supplies of particular primary products are highly variable. A good harvest, the discovery of significant new reserves of minerals or oil, or the addition of new production capacity in the fishery or forest products sectors can quickly add to world supplies and drive down world prices until demand slowly catches up and surpasses supplies, resulting in sudden price increases that trigger a new investment cycle and a subsequent downturn.[39] As Cameron[40] has noted, these fluctuations in international supplies account for the **boom-and-bust cycles** prevalent in most resource industries and, by implication, in most resource-based economies. This can lead affected populations to press governments to provide a range of social policies and to invest large-scale public expenditures in job creation and employment, although governments also are affected by these same boom-and-bust cycles in terms of the kinds of revenues they can collect.

Of course, one of the state's largest struggles as it transitions from a mature staples economy is establishing a new balance between (staples) economic policy and emerging environmental policy. In the 1960s and 1970s, as noted by Demerse and Lemphers in Chapter 2, environmental advocates were successful in lobbying the government in many areas of primary industry to incorporate the reduction of allowable resource yields, create new wilderness and park areas, and generally to adhere to higher standards of resource extraction.

The success of the environmental movement has varied among the major staples sectors of agriculture, fisheries, mining, and forestry, however, as discussed below. The growing environmental pressure at present is to conduct **full-cost accounting**, the practice of including social and environmental costs within standard economic metrics.[41] While environmental values have long been a part of Canada's history, the international discussions and negotiations associated with climate change have brought new pressures to bear on government staples policies. Indeed, before the Harper government backed out of the Kyoto Protocol, the regulation of emissions in some sectors—forestry, mining, and energy— brought about some minimal policy changes. Looking ahead, if Canada does seriously reengage with international climate change treaties, then environmental policy will play a much more significant role in future resource policy-making.

Variations by Staples Sector

Not surprisingly, in a large and geographically diversified country such as Canada, more than one staple sector has always been active. As suggested above, an analysis of the sectoral structure of Canada's primary industries supports the idea that Canada is currently involved in a very uneven transitional process from a mature staples state to a post-staples one. Each of the five major staple sectors of agriculture, fisheries, mining, forestry, and energy are examined below to identify and highlight their current stages of evolution and status, all of which have implications for environmental policy. While state investment has varied across sectors, it has remained significant, and overcoming this legacy of previous development efforts has been one of the largest factors that the Canadian environmental movement continues to try overcome. Despite this obstacle, as shown below, the environmental movement has had some impact, most notably in the (near) post-staples sectors.

Agriculture

Canada's agricultural sector is far removed from the days when the Prairies were synonymous with "King Wheat." Grains and oilseed still remain dominant commodities but they are now closely followed by other major commodities such as livestock, dairy, poultry and eggs, and horticulture. The evolution of the agricultural sector from a frontier staples state to a mature staples state occurred in four periods: the expansionist stage from the late 1800s to 1930; an interregnum from the 1930s to World War II; the structural and policy changes from World War II to the 1980s; and, finally, the state interventionism that has characterized the 1980s to the present.[42]

Agriculture's dominance as a staple resource began in the late nineteenth century with the production and export of wheat. Wheat represented the "keystone" of the National Policy established in the first decades after Confederation to create jobs, investment, and economic prosperity.[43] Its central role in the economy is best illustrated by the fact that wheat comprised more than 25 per cent of all exports during this period.[44] This economic power led to political power, with farm organizations developing into farmers' parties in the last decades of the nineteenth century. The Progressive Party, with its close ties to the Canadian Council of Agriculture, rode this new-found political power to become the second largest party in the House of Commons in the 1920s. The political success generated policy success with the farmer-friendly Crowsnest Pass freight rates becoming permanent in 1925.[45]

The second period, from the 1930s until the beginning of World War II, represented a mix of the frontier staples state and classical expanding staples state. Agriculture remained a dominant commodity while government enacted new policies to encourage further resource development in areas such as mining and forestry, a central tenet of the expanding staples state. The major policy initiatives in agriculture included the creation of the Canadian Wheat Board (CWB) and financial assistance to stabilize agricultural prices and protect farmers.[46]

The period ranging from World War II through the 1980s was marked by state intervention and restructuring. The government enacted a strategy to increase production and profitability. In the years from 1951 to 1967, capital investment more than doubled, largely due to government-subsidized credit.[47] The state also added direct assistance to farmers while restructuring its policies to promote larger "commercial" farms. This shift towards larger

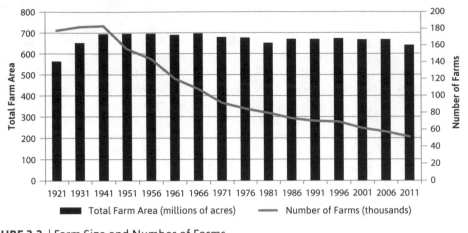

FIGURE 3.2 | Farm Size and Number of Farms

Source: Statistics Canada, "Census of Agriculture: 1921–2011."

farms can be seen in Figure 3.2. These actions were intended to reduce the farm poverty that became rampant through the 1960s.[48] Altogether, these policy changes represent a major evolution from a once-frontier staples state to a mature staples state.

The 1980s through the 2000s saw Canada's agricultural sector solidify its status as a mature staples industry and begin to move beyond it. Skogstad, for example, argues Canada's agriculture sector reached beyond that of a mature staples state during this period.[49] The introduction of genetically engineered (GE) food in Canada, for example, is evidence of such a step (see Figure 3.3). Indeed, the use of genetic engineering represents a long-standing

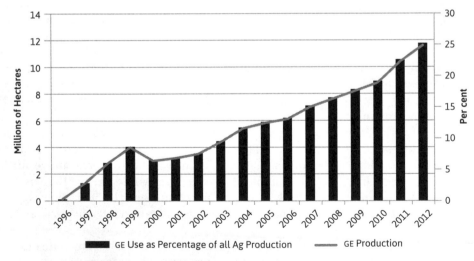

FIGURE 3.3 | Genetically Engineered Food Production in Canada

Sources: Statistics Canada, "Snapshot of Canadian Agriculture 2011"; International Service for the Acquisition of Agri-Biotech Applications (ISAAA), "Global Status of Commercialized Biotech/GM Crops: 1997–2012"; Environment Canada, "Land Use Practices and Changes: Agriculture."

mature staples practice of introducing technology with the hope of sustaining and increasing profitability through the development of new products.[50] The federal government took a central role in the promotion of GE adoption, first by funding their development, and later, through the creation of a regulatory framework designed to promote commercialization.[51] In 1983, the government formalized its role through the creation of the National Biotechnology Strategy (NBS). The NBS provided funding for research on GE crops. The funding grew through the 1990s with the focus remaining on crop breeding. The early 2000s brought a swift shift of funding towards genomics, with research focusing on the analysis of genetic information. It is still too early, however, to discern much about the results of this shift in research effort.

The growing diversification of agriculture towards crops such as wines and organic produce is another indicator of the progression of this sector in a post-staples direction. Further indicators of a movement in this direction are that "commodity and food production is capital-intensive; technologically advanced; and concentrated in fewer, larger, and more specialized enterprises."[52] The sector remains economically vulnerable, however, as nearly half of all production and an even greater percentage in grain and livestock are sent to export markets. Much of this vulnerability is attributed to the North American Free Trade Agreement (NAFTA), and the Canada–US Free Trade Agreement (FTA) that preceded it. These agreements led to greater integration in agricultural sectors (among others) previously excluded from trade deals, such as the General Agreement on Tariffs and Trade (GATT), and left Canada highly dependent on the American market.

Canada's agricultural sector has not shown many signs of nearing a crisis or significant decline that might lead towards a final paradigm shift to a post-staples state. Agricultural exports have remained strong post-NAFTA, with the exception of the 2008–9 period, which, of course, represented the start of the most significant recession in the US since the Great Depression. This short-lived decline does signal the sector's continued vulnerability to America's market strength. While Canada's agricultural exports have rebounded strongly through a greater diversification of trading partners, the risk of crisis remains in this sector in transition.

Fisheries

As a country with some of the world's largest reserves of freshwater and the longest coastline, it is natural that Canada's fisheries have deep historical roots.[53] Canadian fisheries have evolved significantly from their early days as a frontier staple to their present status. Unlike agriculture, the fisheries industry is currently facing a crisis that may lead to its evolution to fully post-staples status.

The first evolution of the fisheries from the frontier to the classical expanding staples state occurred alongside the 1850s debate about whether Canada should enter a free trade ("reciprocity") treaty with the United States. Fisheries stakeholders were among the main advocates for reciprocity as freer trade relations promised a much broader export market than the traditional markets for cod in the Caribbean and elsewhere, which had developed under the British mercantilist system. Only the collapse of these reciprocity agreements led to the enactment early in Confederation of Canada's National Policy of expanding its staple economy.[54] Coincidently, the United States' move towards a mature staples economy and increased population drove the need for greater fish imports, which led to the Fordist introduction of modern factories (canneries) in Canada needed to stabilize the supply of raw fish.[55]

In the 1950s, the fisheries sector evolved to the status of a mature staple state, as can be seen by its expansion to new technologies, featuring the growth of new markets such as exporting frozen fish, as opposed to canned or salted fish. The development of canneries and factory trawlers in this period led to the sustainability crisis that the industry still faces today.[56]

The conflict between sustainability and market forces is one that all staples sectors face to varying degrees, but the fisheries sector was especially hard hit. Overcapacity and over-harvesting began with the provision of government subsidies to fishing companies soon after World War II in an effort to alleviate rural poverty. The overfishing that resulted went unchecked until 1975, when new "buffering" strategies, such as limitations on fishing gear and net size and boat licensing, were enacted to conserve fish resources. These strategies can be effective, but were undermined when Canada (and the US) had to fight for their right to conservation against foreign fishing fleets and were only partially successful in doing so. On multiple occasions, GATT and, later, World Trade Organization (WTO) rulings went against Canada,[57] and fisheries stocks continued to decline and sometimes collapse, as occurred with the large cod fishery off the Atlantic coast in the 1980s and 1990s.

One innovative way to avoid the sustainability crisis facing the fisheries sector is through aquaculture, the farming of fish and other aquatic life. Initially, aquaculture seemed to have all the components of a post-staples resource industry—with its combination of high-capital investment and sophisticated new technologies that produced a new version of a classic staples resource.[58] However, aquaculture is currently suffering from an overly optimistic prediction of both its potential growth and its market share. The promise of this new post-staples resource soon met with the harsh reality that it faces many of the same obstacles as traditional fishery methods, as well as introducing new conflicts such as those between the traditional "wild" fishery and the new "caged" one.

Huge growth occurred in finfish aquaculture and, later, in shellfish aquacultural production in the 1990s thanks to high investments and favourable government policies, but this levelled off in the mid-2000s (see Figure 3.4). One of the major obstacles facing aquaculture's

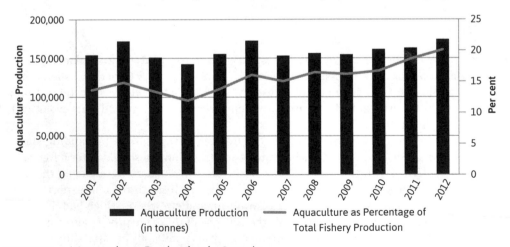

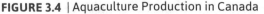

FIGURE 3.4 | Aquaculture Production in Canada

Sources: Statistics Canada, "Aquaculture Statistics: 2001–2012"; Fisheries and Oceans Canada, "Commercial Fisheries: Landings 1990–2012."

growth is conflict with environmental groups, traditional fisheries, and First Nations. Opponents have taken aim at the environmental impacts of aquaculture, citing "the use of wild fish stock to make feed pellets for farmed fish; the impact of wastes, parasites, and diseases on local wild stocks; and the human health implications of therapeutant residues, colourants, and contaminants contained in the final food products."[59] These environmental interests have been successful at undermining consumer confidence in farmed fish products and slowing down the growth of the sector.

While production has levelled off, value has incrementally increased until very recently. This increase in value, matched with steady production, does indicate an increase in efficiency, and the value of aquaculture fisheries is currently around half of the total landed value of all fish in the country. However, the weaker than expected growth, combined with a successful public campaign by opponents, has forced the state to move beyond the promotion of industry activity into legitimizing the entire process. Canada's access to freshwater and coastline, combined with a high demand for fish foods by its close trading partners, indicates fisheries will always remain an important economic sector. Nonetheless, it is one that Canadian policy must better serve if the sector is to be sustainable in its mature era.

Mining

Mining of minerals, like the other sectors, has a very long history in Canada, dating back to the first explorations of Martin Frobisher and others in the sixteenth century. After a lengthy frontier period, the mining sector was in an expanding staples stage until very recently. Today, the critical question facing mining, however, is whether it is becoming a "sunset industry" in its mature phase. Exploration for minerals peaked at more than $1 billion in 1987 before collapsing to less than half that by 1990,[60] and there is some debate as to whether Canada remains a top target for exploration or whether it has already reached its peak exploration potential.[61] While the mining industry remains large and profitable—Canada continues to be a world leader in mineral exports with a production value of $46.8 billion in 2012 (Figure 3.5)—it still faces considerable obstacles.[62]

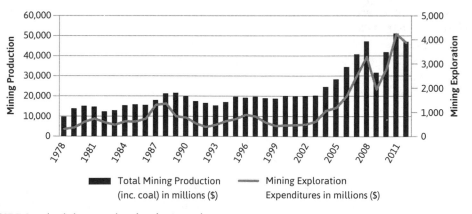

FIGURE 3.5 | Mining Production in Canada

Sources: Natural Resources Canada, "2012 Annual Mineral Production" and "Exploration and Deposit Appraisal Expenditures 1978–2012."

A sharp decline in exploration in the 1990s was impacted more by the strength and success of First Nations groups in pressing land claims in northern areas of the country, and to a lesser extent by labour and environmental organizations pressing for better practices, than by resource declines. The land claims and concerns about environmental impacts have produced more than just legal hurdles for the mining sector; they have also led to new social pressures to improve resource extraction processes. Whereas the crisis facing the fisheries is resource sustainability, the mining industry is instead an example of a crisis of political and social opposition (this is not to say that mineral sustainability is not the primary factor). Many Canadian firms moved offshore during this period and focused on mineral developments in other areas of the globe, including Kazakhstan and elsewhere in Central Asia, Indonesia, South America, and Africa. But the decline in mining activity in the 1990s in Canada proved to be only temporary, as an increase in exploration expenditures started soon after the government introduced a 15 per cent Mining Exploration Tax Credit (METC) in the 2000 federal budget.

Historically, the mining industry avoided facing much public opposition, beyond periodic conflicts with labour over wages and working conditions, given its generally remote rural location. In the current mature staples period, however, the mining industry has not been very successful in addressing social and political challenges. Mining has remained successful, to this point, in large projects like the Alberta oil sands and recent diamond mining projects in the North, but public perspectives of the industry as a dinosaur remain a huge obstacle to its future development. Examples of its poor reactions to new mature staples problems include inept negotiations with local communities (especially Indigenous peoples), the poor handling of industrial relations, a failure to meet national commitments, the poor handling of mining disasters, and bad relations with local property owners.[63] These failures are compounded and amplified by the ability of opponents to publicize their concerns on the Internet.

Forestry

Nearly half of Canada's land mass is comprised of forests, totalling over 400 million hectares, so it is not surprising that Canada is the world's largest exporter of forest products.[64] The forest industry followed a similar path as other staple sectors, beginning with the early settlers who initially viewed the forests as impediments to settlement but quickly realized their value as a resource.[65] These early days were marked by provincial licensing policies that created significant revenues from the forest industry in exchange for allowing the removal of trees on Crown lands.[66] This practice was heavily criticized for placing the state in the contradictory role of both regulating and profiting from increased harvesting.[67]

Until 1947, scientific innovation in the sector focused on greater extraction, not preservation. That changed in the 1950s and 1960s when new laws were passed that required **sustained yields**, meaning that the amount of tree fibre removed each year should equal the amount added through tree growth. Sustained yield was initiated with forest sustainability in mind, but critics claim these measures actually exacerbated the crisis by granting large companies guaranteed access to large swaths of public forests where they could balance harvesting and conservation activities over the long term.[68] The forest industry was able to manipulate the sustainable extraction rate through such practices as extracting older stands first, which is damaging to forest health, as well as through a variety of other means.

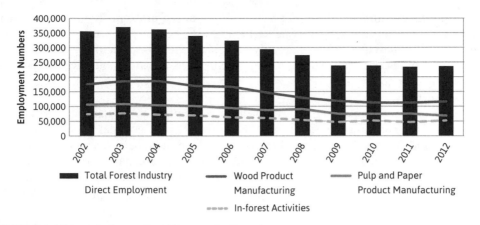

FIGURE 3.6 | Forest Industry Employment in Canada

Sources: Natural Resources Canada, "Forest Industry Employment 2012" and "Forest Industry Direct Employment 2002–2012."

Led by the work of environmental groups and First Nations, the forest industry evolved into a mature staples mode as new ecosystem management was implemented by Canadian governments in the 1980s and 1990s. However, insect plagues such as the mountain pine beetle and the effects of long-term overharvesting have reduced the amount of fibre available and led to many mill shutdowns and layoffs. Still, the industry continues to employ a significant portion of the Canadian workforce (Figure 3.6).

The crisis facing the forestry sector may be resolved through the appreciation of "other" non-forestry values rather than strict commodity production. Specifically, the forestry sector's evolution towards a post-staples future may come from its significance as a "carbon sink," that is, its ability to sequester greenhouse gases. This attribute could hold far more value than the production of forest products in a seriously degraded timber environment.

Energy

In recent years, the energy sector has been Canada's most visible lightning rod for criticism domestically and abroad. One need look no further than Alberta's (and to a much lesser

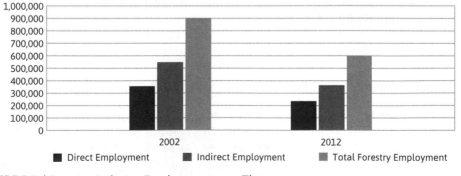

FIGURE 3.7 | Forestry Industry Employment over Time

Sources: Natural Resources Canada. "Forest Industry Employment 2012" and "Forest Industry Direct Employment 2002–2012."

extent, Saskatchewan's) oil sands to find the source of the problem. The use of expensive technology to exploit the vast oil reserves found in the oil sands represents a major shift from conventional to unconventional sources of energy, and the difficulty in extracting the oil from the sands has required massive investments in research and development. This has launched the sector, and some say the country, from a mature towards a **degenerative staples trajectory**.

Much like the other natural resource sectors, oil and gas production started with the discovery of the natural resource during the immediate post-colonial period (1867–1930). Initial demand was low and the world market had an abundance of more easily accessible oil, so development occurred at a slow rate. Under the Constitution Act of 1867, the provinces have control of natural resources, but it wasn't until 1930 that the federal government relinquished this control to Alberta, Saskatchewan, and Manitoba, three provinces created in the first 40 years following Confederation.

By the 1930s, demand for oil had increased exponentially thanks to automobiles and the conversion of many industries and heating from coal, leaving known reserves depleted. In this classical developing staples state, the provincial governments, especially Ontario, encouraged multinational companies to develop their reserves as quickly as possible.[69] Yet the post-war period saw little discovery or expansion of production, leading provincial governments to actively encourage and fund continued exploration by multinational companies. This resulted in the first major strikes in Alberta and Saskatchewan, and to a lesser extent British Columbia. After strong lobbying by the provinces looking for protection from cheaper foreign oil, the federal government erected a more efficient pipeline from Alberta to Ontario.[70] The success of the pipeline led to three additional trans-Canada pipelines and the flourishing of the industry.

The Organization of Petroleum Exporting Countries (OPEC) oil embargo of 1973 was the trigger that set the federal government scrambling to secure supplies of oil and gas, upsetting the status quo in the sector. In 1974, the federal government created Petro-Canada, a state-owned oil company that took the lead in exploration and development in the Arctic. Alberta resented the federal government for what it viewed as Ottawa overstepping its boundaries, and in 1985, under the sympathetic Mulroney government, the National Energy Program (NEP), which had been formally established by the federal Liberal government in 1980, was dismantled with the signing of the Western Accord. Other protectionist policies were dismantled by the Mulroney government. The signing of the Canada–US Free Trade Agreement (FTA), the precursor to NAFTA, eliminated many other regulations put into place to restrict oil and gas exports. This, combined with increasing oil prices, led to renewed exploration and the commercial exploitation of the oil sands, along with the development of a sizable offshore industry in Atlantic Canada, notably in Newfoundland and to a lesser extent Nova Scotia.

The signing of the Kyoto Protocol on greenhouse gas emissions in 1997, however, represented a direct challenge to the status of the sector as a mature or advanced mature staples sector actively expanding to support increases in demand in foreign markets. Restrictions placed on the greenhouse gas emissions emitted by the sector and involved in the burning of fossil fuels such as coal and oil and gas would have presented significant challenges for the status quo, and Alberta, joined by other provinces, was quick to push back against such proposals.[71] Real discussions of a policy shift were short-lived, however, as 2006 ushered in the Alberta-based Conservative government of Stephen Harper. The Harper government quickly shifted the power to regulate the industry back to the provinces, indicated it would not rat-ify the Kyoto Protocol, and, instead, focused on pipeline construction and fostering greater energy integration between the US and Canada.

The very high oil prices found in the run-up to the global financial collapse of 2007–8 benefited many governments and companies with windfall revenues and profits. However, oil prices dropped shortly thereafter and again starting in late 2014 as US shale gas and fracking activities increased supplies in that country dramatically. At the time of this book's printing, oil was trading at the threshold of profitability for much of the oil sands produc-tion, just at a time when production was increasing due to investments in the previous boom period. This new landscape has the potential to undermine the Conservative Party dream of Canada as an energy superpower just as it has for other presumptive petro-states such as Russia and Venezuela. The length of the slump in prices, as well as a possible turnover in gov-ernments in 2015, could lead to a re-evaluation of energy policy, while also eliminating the demand for the highly contentious proposed Enbridge pipelines—Keystone XL and Northern Gateway—to access foreign markets.

Conclusion

No longer on the periphery of empire, Canada became a mature staples state in the post-World War II period, and many of its regions—urban and rural—and resource sectors developed in ways characteristic of other staples or resource-based political economies. In all five sta-ples sectors—agriculture, fisheries, mining, forestry, and energy—these industries were in a mature staples status from World War II until at least the 1960s, when Aboriginal land claims, environmentalism, and declining resource stocks began to affect them, albeit in dif-ferent ways and to different degrees. Some sectors now have some post-staples elements, but none has fully evolved in this direction in the immediate future, and some, such as energy, may have moved into a degenerative state. These different trajectories highlight the strug-gles the Canadian state has faced in addressing the problems in these sectors, and more generally with respect to the environment. Faced with uneven development, policy-makers often continue to use a policy portfolio designed to solve mature staples problems, rather than promote a post-staples trajectory. This has manifested itself directly in environmental policy, where both the federal and the provincial governments have expressed a great deal of ambivalence in trying to balance environmental policies of conservation against deeply entrenched staples economic policies that underlie their large but fragile resource sectors.

Key Terms

boom-and-bust cycles

classical expanding staples state

commodity

degenerative mature, advanced staples political
    economy

degenerative staples trajectory

disequilibrium

frontier staples state

full-cost accounting

mature staples state

post-staples pattern

post-staples state

resource curse

staples resource industries

staples trap

sustained yields

Questions for Review

1. What are the key indicators that a particular resource sector is in one of the four staples states?
2. In which staples status is the current agriculture sector? Fisheries? Forestry? Mining? Energy?
3. What are the obstacles that face a resource sector as it transitions beyond a mature staples state?
4. What is a staples trap? Why does it matter?

5. What are some of the environmental considerations that the government takes into account when creating its economic policy?
6. What might be some of the benefits to environmental policy from Canada transitioning to a post-staples state?

Internet Resources

Statistics Canada, "Natural Resources, the Terms of Trade, and Real Income Growth in Canada: 1870 to 2010"
http://www.statcan.gc.ca/pub/11f0027m/2012079/part-partie1-eng.htm

The Progressive Economics Forum: "The Staple Theory @ 50"
http://www.progressive-economics.ca/2013/09/24/the-staple-theory-50-abe-rotstein/

Additional Reading

Clarke-Jones, M. *A Staple State: Canadian Industrial Resources in Cold War.* Toronto: University of Toronto Press, 1987.

Clement, W., ed. *Understanding Canada: Building on the New Canadian Political Economy.* Montreal and Kingston: McGill-Queen's University Press, 1997.

Hessing, M., M. Howlett, and T. Summerville. *Canadian Natural Resource and Environmental Policy: Political Economy and Public Policy.* Vancouver: University of British Columbia Press, 2005.

Howlett, M., and K. Brownsey, eds. *Canada's Resource Economy in Transition: The Past, Present, and Future of Canadian Staples Industries.* Toronto: Emond Montgomery, 2008.

Howlett, M., A. Netherton, and M. Ramesh. *The Political Economy of Canada: An Introduction.* Toronto: Oxford University Press, 1999.

Hutton, T.A. *Visions of a "Post-Staples" Economy: Structural Change and Adjustment Issues in British Columbia.* Working paper PI #3. Vancouver: University of British Columbia Centre for Human Settlements, 1994.

Lee, E., and A. Perl, eds. *The Integrity Gap: Canada's Environmental Policy and Institutions.* Vancouver: University of British Columbia Press, 2003.

Watkins, M.H. "A Staple Theory of Economic Growth." *Canadian Journal of Economics and Political Science* 29, 2 (1963): 141–58.

Watkins, M.H. "The Staple Theory Revisited." *Journal of Canadian Studies* 12, 5 (1977): 83–95.

Notes

1. M. Howlett and K. Brownsey, "From Timber to Tourism: The Political Economy of British Columbia," in R.K. Carty, ed., *Politics, Policy and Government in British Columbia* (Vancouver: University of British Columbia Press, 1996), 18–31.
2. Ibid.; T.W. Luke, "The Uneasy Transition from Extractive to Attractive Models of Development," in W. Magnusson and K. Shaw, eds, *A Political Space: Reading the Global through Clayoquot Sound* (Montreal and Kingston: McGill-Queen's University Press, 2002), 91–2.
3. M. Watkins, "Canadian Capitalism in Transition," in W. Clement, ed., *Understanding Canada: Building on the New Canadian Political Economy* (Montreal and Kingston: McGill-Queen's University Press, 1997), 19–42.

4. S. Clarkson, "The Multi-Level State: Canada in the Semi-Periphery of Both Continentalism and Globalization," *Review of International Political Economy* 8, 3 (2001): 501–27.
5. B. Wilkinson, "Canada's Resource Industries," in J. Whalley, ed., *Canada's Resource Industries and Water Export Policy* (Toronto: University of Toronto Press, 1985), 1–159.
6. M. Howlett, "Canadian Environmental Policy and the Natural Resource Sector: Paradoxical Aspects of the Transition to a Post-Staples Political Economy," in E. Lee and A. Perl, eds, *The Integrity Gap: Canada's Environmental Policy and Institutions* (Vancouver: University of British Columbia Press, 2003), 42–67.

7. D. Drache, "Re-discovering Canadian Political Economy," in W. Clement and D. Drache, eds, *A Practical Guide to Canadian Political Economy* (Toronto: Lorimer, 1978), 1–53; G. Williams, *Not for Export: Toward a Political Economy of Canada's Arrested Industrialization* (Toronto: McClelland and Stewart, 1983).

8. W. Clement, ed., *Understanding Canada: Building on the New Canadian Political Economy* (Montreal and Kingston: McGill-Queen's University Press, 1997); W. Clement and G. Williams, eds, *The New Canadian Political Economy* (Montreal and Kingston: McGill-Queen's University Press, 1989).

9. R.A. Clapp, "The Resource Cycle in Forestry and Fishing," *Canadian Geographer* 42, 2 (1998): 129–44.

10. Howlett, "Canadian Environmental Policy and the Natural Resource Sector"; M. Hessing, M. Howlett, and T. Summerville, *Canadian Natural Resource and Environmental Policy: Political Economy and Public Policy* (Vancouver: University of British Columbia Press, 2005).

11. T.A. Hutton, *Visions of a "Post-Staples" Economy: Structural Change and Adjustment Issues in British Columbia*. Working paper PI #3 (Vancouver: University of British Columbia Centre for Human Settlements, 1994).

12. H.A. Innis, *The Fur Trade in Canada* (Toronto: University of Toronto Press, 1930); H.A. Innis, *Problems of Staple Production in Canada* (Toronto: Ryerson Press, 1933).

13. D.C. North, *The Economic Growth of the United States* (Englewood Cliffs, NJ: Prentice-Hall, 1961).

14. A.O. Hirschman, *The Strategy of Economic Development* (New Haven: Yale University Press, 1958); Watkins, "Canadian Capitalism in Transition."

15. W.R. Freudenburg, "Addictive Economies: Extractive Industries and Vulnerable Localities in a Changing World Economy," *Rural Sociology* 57, 3 (1992): 305–32.

16. Ibid.

17. Ibid; M.H. Watkins, "A Staple Theory of Economic Growth," *Canadian Journal of Economics and Political Science* 29, 2 (1963): 141–58; M.H. Watkins, "The Staple Theory Revisited," *Journal of Canadian Studies* 12, 5 (1977): 83–95.

18. H.A. Innis, *Essays in Canadian Economic History* (Toronto: University of Toronto Press, 1956); A.R.M. Lower, *Great Britain's Woodyard* (Montreal and Kingston: McGill-Queen's University Press, 1972).

19. Innis, *Essays*.

20. Innis, *Problems of Staple Production*.

21. D.G. Creighton, *Empire of the St. Lawrence* (Toronto: Macmillan, 1937).

22. Watkins, "A Staple Theory"; G.W. Bertram, "Economic Growth and Canadian Industry, 1870–1915: The Staple Model and the Take-off Hypothesis," *Canadian Journal of Economics and Political Science* 29, 2 (1963): 162–84; K. Buckley, "The Role of Staple Industries in Canadian Economic Development," *Journal of Economic History* 18, 4 (1958): 439–52.

23. M. Clarke-Jones, *A Staple State: Canadian Industrial Resources in Cold War* (Toronto: University of Toronto Press, 1987).

24. Hutton, *Visions of a "Post-Staples" Economy*.

25. Clapp, "Resource Cycle in Forestry and Fishing."

26. Hutton, *Visions of a "Post-Staples" Economy*.

27. Ibid.

28. Ibid.

29. Hessing et al., *Canadian Natural Resource and Environmental Policy*.

30. Ibid.

31. R.T. Naylor, "The Rise and Fall of the Third Commercial Empire of the St. Lawrence," in G. Teeple, ed., *Capitalism and the National Question in Canada* (Toronto: University of Toronto Press, 1972), 1–42.

32. F. Stone, *Canada, the GATT and the International Trade System* (Montreal: Institute for Research on Public Policy, 1984); J. Whalley, *Canadian Trade Policies and the World Economy* (Toronto: University of Toronto Press, 1985); Naylor, "Rise and Fall."

33. Watkins, "A Staple Theory."

34. Freudenburg, "Addictive Economies."

35. C.R. Fay, "The Toronto School of Economic History," *Economic History* 3, 1 (1934): 168–71.

36. Ibid; Watkins, "A Staple Theory."

37. J.E. Hodgetts, *The Canadian Public Service* (Toronto: University of Toronto Press, 1973).

38. M. Howlett, A. Netherton, and M. Ramesh, *The Political Economy of Canada: An Introduction* (Toronto: Oxford University Press, 1999).

39. F.J. Anderson, *Natural Resources in Canada* (Toronto: Methuen, 1985); M.C. Webb and M.W. Zacher, *Canada and International Mineral Markets: Dependence, Instability and Foreign Policy* (Kingston, Ont.: Queen's University Centre for Resource Studies, 1988).

40. D.R. Cameron, "The Growth of Government Spending: The Canadian Experience in Comparative Perspective," in K. Banting, ed., *State and Society* (Toronto: University of Toronto Press, 1986), 21–52.

41. T.A. Hutton, "The Reconstruction of Political Economy and Social Identity in 21st-Century Canada," in M. Howlett and K. Brownsey, eds, *Canada's Resource Economy in Transition: The Past, Present, and Future of Canadian Staples Industries* (Toronto: Emond Montgomery, 2008), 46.

42. Ibid, 65.

43. W.T. Easterbrook and H.G.J. Aitken, *Canadian Economic History* (Toronto: University of Toronto Press, 1956), 46.

44. M. Hart, *A Trading Nation* (Vancouver: University of British Columbia Press, 2002), 96.

45. G. Skogstad, "The Two Faces of Canadian Agriculture in a Post-Staples Economy," in M. Howlett and K. Brownsey, eds, *Canada's Resource Economy in Transition: The Past, Present, and Future of Canadian Staples Industries* (Toronto: Emond Montgomery, 2008), 67.

46. W.M. Drummond, W.J. Anderson, and T.C. Kerr, *A Review of Agriculture in Canada* (Ottawa: Agricultural Economics Research Council of Canada, 1966).

47. Information Canada, *Canadian Agriculture in the Seventies: Reports of the Federal Task Force on Agriculture* (Ottawa, 1970), 334.

48. Skogstad, "Two Faces of Canadian Agriculture," 68.

49. Ibid.

50. E. Moore, "The New Agriculture: Genetically Engineered Food in Canada," in M. Howlett and K. Brownsey, eds, *Canada's Resource Economy in Transition: The Past, Present, and Future of Canadian Staples Industries* (Toronto: Emond Montgomery, 2008), 84.

51. Ibid, 87.

52. Ibid, 63.

53. Statistics Canada, "Aquaculture Statistics: 2001–2012."

54. N.C. Clement, G.D. Vera, J. Gerber, W.A. Kerr, A.J. McFadyen, A.J. Zepeda, and D. Alcon, *North American Economic Integration: Theory and Practice* (Northampton, Mass.: Edward Elgar, 1999); R. Hoogensen, "The Canadian Fisheries Industry: Retrospect and Prospect," in M. Howlett and K. Brownsey, eds, *Canada's Resource Economy in Transition: The Past, Present, and Future of Canadian Staples Industries* (Toronto: Emond Montgomery, 2008), 109.

55. Ibid, 109.

56. Ibid, 110.

57. A. Rugman and J. Kirton, *In a Perfect Ocean: The State of Fisheries and Ecosystems in the North Atlantic Ocean* (Washington: Island Press, 2003).

58. Hutton, *Visions of a "Post-Staples" Economy*; J. Rayner and M. Howlett, "Caught in a Staples Vise: The Political Economy of Canadian Aquaculture," in M. Howlett and K. Brownsey, eds, *Canada's Resource Economy in Transition: The Past, Present, and Future of Canadian Staples Industries* (Toronto: Emond Montgomery, 2008).

59. Rayner and Howlett, "Caught in a Staples Vise," 123–4.

60. M.L. McAllister, "Shifting Foundations in a Mature Staples Industry: A History of Canadian Mineral Policy," in M. Howlett and K. Brownsey, eds, *Canada's Resource Economy in Transition: The Past, Present, and Future of Canadian Staples Industries* (Toronto: Emond Montgomery, 2008), 153.

61. J. Gouveia, P. Rose, and J. Gingerich, "The Prospector Myth: Coming to Terms with Risk Management in Minerals Development," paper presented to the Prospectors and Developers Association of Canada international convention, 9–12 Mar. 2003, p. 9, http://www.pdac.ca/pdac/publications/papers/2003/Gingerich-Risk.pdf; D.A. Cranstone, A *History of Mining and Mineral Exploration in Canada and Outlook for the Future* (Ottawa: Natural Resources Canada, Public Works, and Government Services Canada, 2002), 3.

62. Howlett, "Canadian Environmental Policy and the Natural Resource Sector."

63. McAllister, "Shifting Foundations," 155; MiningWatch Canada, "The Need for MiningWatch Canada" (2005), http://www.miningwatch.ca/index.php?/About/Need_for_MWC; B. Russell, *More with Less: Work Reorganization in the Canadian Mineral Industry* (Toronto: University of Toronto Press, 1999).

64. J. Thorpe and L.A. Sandberg, "Knotty Tales: Forest Policy Narratives in an Era of Transition," in M. Howlett and K. Brownsey, eds, *Canada's Resource Economy in Transition: The Past, Present, and Future of Canadian Staples Industries* (Toronto: Emond Montgomery, 2008), 189.

65. K. Drushka, *Canada's Forests: A History*. Forest History Issues Series (Montreal and Kingston: McGill-Queen's University Press, 2003), 27.

66. M. Howlett and J. Rayner, "The Business and Government Nexus: Principal Elements and Dynamics of the Canadian Forest Policy Regime," in M. Howlett, ed., *Canadian Forest Policy: Adapting to Change* (Toronto: University of Toronto Press, 2001), 25–6.

67. Ibid, 43.

68. J. Lawson, M. Levy, and L.A. Sandberg, "Perpetual Revenues and the Delights of the Primitive: Change, Continuity, and Forest Policy Regimes in Ontario," in M. Howlett, ed., *Canadian Forest Policy: Adapting to Change* (Toronto: University of Toronto Press, 2001), 293.

69. K. Brownsey, "The New Oil Order: The Staples Paradigm and the Canadian Upstream Oil and Gas Industry," in M. Howlett and K. Brownsey, eds, *Canada's Resource Economy in Transition: The Past, Present, and Future of Canadian Staples Industries* (Toronto: Emond Montgomery, 2008), 238.

70. Ibid, 240.

71. Ibid, 248.

4 Environmental Law in the Time of Austerity

Marcia Valiante

Chapter Summary

This chapter considers the themes of ambivalence and austerity with respect to Canadian environmental law. It looks at a series of recent legislative changes that shift the federal role in the review of major resource development projects and delegate decision-making authority. It also considers recent court decisions involving the interplay of federal legislation protecting the creditors of insolvent companies and provincial legislation ensuring the cleanup of contaminated sites. In addition, the chapter considers the legal context in which these developments operate. The author concludes that the changes have the effect of reducing the federal role in environmental protection and reducing opportunities for public participation in decision-making. Some limited opportunities remain for turning to the courts to challenge these policy directions or to prompt reform.

Chapter Outline

- Context/background to understanding the recent changes
  - Constitutional authority
  - General patterns of Canadian environmental regulation
- Summary of recent legislative changes
  - Fisheries Act
  - Canadian Environmental Assessment Act (CEAA)
  - Navigable Waters Protection Act (NWPA)
  - Northwest Territories Devolution Act
- The role of the courts in a difficult economic context
- Implications of recent legal developments

Introduction

The recession that started in 2008 had profound effects across the global economy, which translated into serious impacts in many sectors of the Canadian economy. Governments in Canada responded to these forces much as other governments did, with "austerity" policies that, on the one hand, cut government spending and, on the other, provided stimulus to the economy.[1] While provinces such as Ontario and British Columbia pursued differing visions of a "green economy,"[2] the Canadian federal government adopted a more traditional approach: an economic strategy that would "capitalize on [Canada's] natural resource advantage" in the hopes of attracting billions of dollars of investment.[3] Investment in the exploitation and trade of Canadian resources was expected to "create jobs, growth and long-term prosperity for all Canadians." Pursuing this strategy led the government directly into changing some important environmental laws. Meanwhile, in the face of corporate failures brought about by the recession, the courts have struggled with the question of how to balance competing public interests in environmental protection and protection of creditors.

The themes of the book—ambivalence and austerity—are reflected in the development of Canadian environmental law and policy over the last several years. The purpose of this chapter is to highlight some aspects of this development, in particular the legislative agenda set by the federal government, how that agenda fits within the context of the legal and constitutional principles that govern, and the implications of that agenda for the development of environmental law. In addition, the chapter considers the role of the courts in the development of environmental policy and law during this "time of austerity."

Context/Background to Understanding the Recent Changes

Constitutional Authority

In Canada, legislative authority to address environmental concerns is shared between the federal and provincial governments. The courts have long accepted that the environment is not a single matter for constitutional purposes that could be or should be assigned to one order of government or the other. Instead, powers of all governments can be used to address environmental concerns, but different aspects will be recognized as appropriate to one order of government or the other, according to the formal division of powers in the Constitution Act, 1867.

Federal legislative powers over the environment flow from a number of different constitutional heads of power, including broad general powers respecting criminal law, national concerns within the residual **"peace, order, and good government"** power, all forms of taxation, interprovincial and international trade and commerce, federal public property, and spending. In addition, powers respecting specific subjects, including Aboriginal peoples and their rights and lands, fisheries, navigation and shipping, aeronautics, nuclear power, and federal works, can also be relied on to ground federal legislation touching on the environment.

Provinces, in turn, rely on powers to legislate with respect to non-renewable natural resources, forestry, management of provincial Crown lands, municipal institutions, direct taxation, local matters, and property and civil rights within their borders. **"Property and civil rights"** has been held to ground broad authority, including in particular the power to regulate business and industry operating within a province. Natural resources located within the provinces are generally owned by the provincial Crown and access to them is controlled by provincial governments.

Agriculture is expressly a shared power between the federal and provincial governments. International relations are also shared in practice. The federal executive has the prerogative to enter into international agreements and treaties, although it does not have corresponding authority to implement them. Legislation is required to bring the provisions of treaties into force in Canadian law. Other than for "British Empire" treaties—which applies only to those negotiated before 1930, such as the Boundary Waters Treaty—there is no legislative power for the federal government over international relations. Instead, implementation of international agreements must follow the usual division of powers. In other words, all treaties negotiated by the federal government must be implemented through an Act of Parliament or the provincial legislatures, and the power to do so will vary with the subject matter and substantive terms of the treaty.

As a result of the broad approach the Supreme Court of Canada takes to interpreting constitutional powers,[4] federal and provincial authority to address complex environmental matters through legislation and regulations is overlapping. The "environment" is not a single or independent matter for constitutional purposes; rather, each enactment is assessed separately. First, a statute's **pith and substance** or dominant purpose is determined, and then a link is made to a specific head of power. Overlapping authority allows flexibility for governments at all levels in how they respond to environmental problems, but it also creates a degree of uncertainty about whether new or innovative environmental regulations will be accepted as constitutionally valid.

One example of this is with climate change. As a matter of global concern, the federal government negotiated a multilateral convention as well as several protocols and agreements under which it made commitments, on behalf of the country as a whole, to meet targets for reducing greenhouse gas emissions and to adopt mitigation and adaptation measures.[5] Most of the measures to address climate change in Canada have been adopted at the provincial or municipal level. Although the federal government has not yet enacted comprehensive climate-related measures to fulfill its international commitments, a few regulations have been adopted[6] and several possible regulatory approaches have been suggested in various action plans. Some sources of greenhouse gas emissions, such as motor vehicles, were already regulated under federal law, so that more stringent targets, which Canada has committed to align with those adopted in the United States, are not constitutionally problematic. However, many of the sources of greenhouse gas emissions, including power plants, which in many provinces are owned by provincial Crown corporations, and industrial facilities, as well as many of the sinks for carbon dioxide, such as forests, are ordinarily regulated under provincial laws. The scope of federal authority to regulate those sources through emissions limits that mandate carbon capture and storage, or through adoption of an emissions trading scheme with offsets for provincial sinks, is a matter of some debate.[7]

Even if an enactment is within a constitutional power, the courts also apply doctrines that give priority to federal statutes when a conflict arises between a provincial enactment and a federal one; likewise, federal powers have priority when a provincial enactment deals with a matter within a core federal competency. Recent cases have held, for example, that provincial land-use planning laws—which are clearly constitutionally valid—cannot restrict the use of lands in a harbour such as Vancouver where the federal government has adopted its own land-use plan,[8] and cannot control the location of even unregulated private airstrips because of the exclusive nature of federal authority over aeronautics.[9]

Courts apply these interpretive rules when a government takes action and that action is challenged on constitutional grounds. The more difficult question is whether a government's failure to act, or its withdrawal from regulating in an area where it previously did so, can be challenged in the courts. In other words, can a government ignore a pressing environmental issue such as climate change and fail to act? Can it repeal legislation and walk away from an issue, such as the protection of aquatic ecosystems, that it formerly regulated under the Fisheries Act?

Most aspects of constitutional authority are expressed as *powers* to act, not as *duties* to act. In the Canadian system of government, the **doctrine of parliamentary sovereignty** has led to "the long-standing common law and constitutional prohibition on courts adjudicating the wisdom or desirability of government action."[10] The role of the courts is to ensure that the legislature and the executive act in accordance with their legal authority, but it is left to the electorate, and not the courts, to pass judgment on the wisdom of their policies. Thus, if Parliament and the executive choose not to act, that choice is a policy choice that cannot ordinarily be challenged in a court. The exception to this would be where there is a duty to act, for example, because of an international obligation, or where rights protected under the Canadian Charter of Rights and Freedoms are infringed by the inaction of the government. For example, section 35 of the Charter recognizes and affirms "existing aboriginal and treaty rights." This provision has been held to restrict government interference with the lands and resources traditionally used and controlled by First Nations, Inuit, and Métis communities.[11] The courts have also held that this provision imposes a duty, invoking the "honour of the Crown," on governments to consult with Aboriginal peoples and to accommodate their interests whenever governments contemplate action that may affect those interests.[12] The duty to consult is not limited to decisions or conduct having only an immediate impact on First Nations' lands and resources, but extends to "strategic, higher level decisions."[13] Breach of the duty can give rise to a range of remedies, depending on the circumstances.

In other Charter cases, the courts routinely scrutinize the rationale for and the content of government action or inaction to determine whether either can be "justified" under section 1 of the Charter, which "guarantees the rights and freedoms set out in it subject only to such reasonable limits prescribed by law as can be demonstrably justified in a free and democratic society."[14] There is a debate within the courts and legal academy over whether the Charter guarantees **positive rights**, such as the right to a minimum standard of living, that would compel the government to act. The Supreme Court of Canada has left that possibility open.[15] Relatedly, the first appointed Independent Expert on human rights for the United Nations has undertaken a mandate to "study the human rights obligations relating to the enjoyment of a safe, clean, healthy and sustainable environment."[16]

If the federal government fails to address an environmental problem, it would not necessarily mean that a province could step in to fill the void, despite broad provincial authority. The Canadian Constitution does not allow one order of government to delegate legislative powers to another, although administrative powers, such as the power to enforce a law, can be delegated. Therefore, even in the face of federal inaction, a province that wants to step in and regulate could only do so within the limits of its powers under the Constitution.

An example of how this might create a regulatory vacuum can be seen in the context of the regulation of aquaculture in British Columbia. At first, the federal government licensed aquaculture in BC, but it then withdrew from doing so pursuant to a 1988 agreement with the province. Under that agreement, BC adopted its own regulatory scheme and began issuing licences. When the provincial scheme was challenged on constitutional grounds, the British Columbia Supreme Court declared the scheme to be ultra vires—that is, beyond the powers of the province because regulation of aquaculture falls within the core of federal authority over fisheries.[17] To avoid a regulatory vacuum, the Court suspended its declaration of invalidity to give the federal government time to develop a regulatory regime for aquaculture. Although it eventually did adopt new regulations, the Court had no power to order the federal government to do so.

General Patterns of Canadian Environmental Regulation

At certain points in time, federal and provincial governments in Canada have competed in adopting progressive environmental laws, but the general pattern is more one of inter-provincial co-operation combined with harmonization of provincial laws with federal guidelines.[18] Despite strong potential authority to legislate with respect to environmental concerns, the federal government has most often played a modest role in practice. Most federal ambient environmental standards are in the form of non-binding guidelines, which operate as suggestions for adoption into provincial law. Exercising its criminal law authority, the federal government plays a lead role with respect to the management of industrial chemicals under the Canadian Environmental Protection Act, 1999[19] and, under the agriculture power, the registration of pesticides under the Pest Control Products Act.[20] The federal power in the Constitution over fisheries has provided the basis for adoption of a few targeted national regulations addressing the effluents from mining, pulp and paper mills, and municipal wastewater treatment plants,[21] and for the federal role in protecting aquatic species under the Species at Risk Act.[22] The federal power over trade and commerce and interprovincial undertakings has provided the basis for emission standards for motor vehicles and engines, fuel standards, and pollution standards applicable to railways, ships, and airplanes. Federal approvals are required for interprovincial and international pipelines and electric power lines. The residual peace, order, and good government power is the basis for federal regulation of nuclear facilities and ocean dumping. **Environmental impact assessment** (EA) is triggered for major projects having a federal component, as discussed in more detail below.

The pattern for environmental regulation in Canada has been for the provinces to take the lead in most of the routine regulation of air and water pollution and management of waste from private sector activities in Canada, under comprehensive provincial laws and regulations. Access to and management of natural resources are controlled exclusively by the provinces, except in offshore areas and in the North. The federal government has tended to defer to provinces, territories, First Nations, and Inuit communities, with such deference formalized in the adoption of co-operative agreements. A general forum for co-operative law-making is the Canadian Council of Ministers of the Environment (CCME), which administers the 1998 Canada-wide Accord on Environmental Harmonization.[23] The most important initiatives of the CCME under the Accord have been the development of "Canada-wide standards"[24] and the 2012 agreement to develop a national Air Quality Management System. Comprehensive land claims agreements have been signed with a number of Aboriginal governments that share the management of lands and natural resources, which is discussed by White in Chapter 10. The federal government has also taken steps to transfer decision-making authority over resources to territorial governments, as discussed below.

Overall, Canadian environmental law is no longer considered to be at the cutting edge compared with other industrialized countries; rather, it has been deemed a "damp squib."[25] Some of the reasons suggested for this assessment include the jurisdictional constraints of Canadian federalism, the resonance of neo-liberal policies on deregulation, the economic importance of primary industries in many provinces, and the structure of the electoral system.

Summary of Recent Legislative Changes

As noted above, even before the recession the Canadian federal government was ambivalent about taking a strong role in most areas of environmental protection. Since the election in 2006 of a Conservative government under Prime Minister Stephen Harper, the trend most in evidence has been the reduction of environmental scrutiny of resource development projects, as part of an agenda to reduce regulatory burden and smooth the way for energy and resource development.

Under its strategy of Responsible Resource Development, the federal government seeks to accelerate the exploitation and trade of energy and natural resources in order to attract investment and stimulate the economy. This can only happen in a timely way, according to the government, if changes to environmental regulations are made. The rationales for these changes are that processes required to attain approvals for projects with the potential to harm the environment are inefficient because they take too long and have uncertain outcomes, and that duplication of effort occurs between federal and provincial regulations.

This federal strategy led the government to make a number of significant changes to federal environmental legislation. These changes include, most importantly, revisions to the Fisheries Act, the Canadian Environmental Assessment Act, the National Energy Board Act, and the Navigable Waters Protection Act. All were adopted as part of two **omnibus budget bills**, rather than as stand-alone enactments. This approach meant that debate on the bills was limited. A further example of lumping controversial regulatory changes in with other legislative changes occurred with the Northwest Territories Devolution Act, discussed below.

Other trends link into broader ideological priorities for the Conservatives. One effort has been the expansion of enforcement tools and significant increases in statutory fines for environmental offences, as part of a larger "tough on crime" agenda.[26] However, despite these changes, a report by the Commissioner of the Environment and Sustainable Development concluded that Environment Canada's "enforcement program was not well managed to adequately enforce compliance with the Canadian Environmental Protection Act, 1999 and ensure that threats to Canadians and their environment from pollution were minimized."[27] More recently, environmental protection has been undercut further by significant reductions to the budgets of Environment Canada, the Department of Fisheries and Oceans (DFO), Parks Canada, and the Canadian Environmental Assessment Agency. These cuts have affected staffing, research, libraries and data collection, core programs, and enforcement.[28]

The Fisheries Act[29]

In 2012, the federal government adopted amendments to the Fisheries Act as part of its omnibus budget bills.[30] These changes have been phased in over two years. The Fisheries Act dates back to Confederation and for decades it contained two key environmental provisions: a prohibition on the discharge into water of substances that might harm fish and a prohibition on the **harmful alteration, disruption, or destruction**, known as HADD, of fish habitat. Potentially harmful substances could be discharged to water if allowed under regulations approved by the Governor-in-Council, i.e., the federal cabinet. Development that had the potential to harm fish habitat could be authorized by the Minister of Fisheries and Oceans.

The HADD authorization process triggered application of the Canadian Environmental Assessment Act, thus requiring at a minimum a screening assessment of the potential adverse effects of an authorization. Given the courts' broad view of the meaning of "fisheries" and the Act's operation across the country as a whole, these provisions had provided the federal government with broad authority to protect aquatic ecosystems and demand actions to restore or maintain habitats. While providing a common base of protection for aquatic ecosystems across Canada, these provisions were subject to criticism by the environmental community for lax enforcement and for leaving too much discretion in the hands of the Minister of Fisheries and Oceans.

The view of industry, apparently, was quite different. Companies found the process for authorizing HADD of fish habitat was an impediment to investment, was too unpredictable, and increased the costs and the time needed to get regulatory approvals.[31] The Minister of Fisheries and Oceans, in introducing changes to the Act, echoed this view, stating that the previous protections were "indiscriminate," applying to virtually all Canadian waters, and so it made "good, common sense that the government should be able to minimize or eliminate restrictions on commonplace activities that pose little or no threat, and at the same time, maintain appropriate, reasonable and responsible protection for Canada's fisheries."[32]

One of the goals of the new provisions is to reduce the regulatory burden on proponents of projects requiring HADD authorizations. In the amendments now in force, the HADD provisions have been rewritten and combined with a prohibition on the killing of fish to create a new prohibition against causing "serious harm to fish." Serious harm is defined as "death of a fish or any permanent alteration to, or destruction of, fish habitat." In addition, this prohibition applies only to fish "that are part of a commercial, recreational or Aboriginal fishery, or to fish that support such a fishery." In other words, altering or disturbing fish habitat that falls short of *permanent* habitat damage or destruction is no longer prohibited and the fish and habitat that are protected are limited to those that currently form part of a commercial, recreational, or Aboriginal fishery, rather than applying to aquatic life more broadly.

The power to issue an authorization to permanently alter or destroy habitat is retained in the Act, but the minister can exclude certain waters from its application by regulation. The amendments add factors that must be considered when determining whether to issue an authorization, which will reduce the minister's discretion. These factors are explained more fully in a new "Fisheries Protection Policy Statement" issued by DFO in October 2013. A new regulation specifies the information to be provided and sets a deadline for a decision on an application for an authorization.

Another goal of the Fisheries Act amendments is to reduce regulatory duplication and share the protection of fish habitat among a range of partners, including relying on user groups to foster habitat conservation. The amendments allow the minister to delegate the HADD authorization decision to a "designated person." In addition, the amendments give the minister the power to enter agreements with provinces that will divide the responsibilities under the Act between different orders of government. The federal cabinet can also recognize a provincial regulation as having equivalent effect to protection under the Fisheries Act and order that the Act will no longer apply in that province. Further, regulations can be adopted that will allow for the deposit of substances deleterious to fish in certain situations and under certain conditions. This authority forms the basis for regulations adopted in April 2014 that authorize the Minister of the Environment to issue regulations permitting deposits of harmful substances that are authorized under provincial laws or guidelines.[33] In other words, provincial regulations or guidelines will prevail, reducing uncertainty for industry and developers who have been faced with two levels of protection.

The Canadian Environmental Assessment Act

Also included in Bill C-38 in 2012 were provisions that repealed the Canadian Environmental Assessment Act (CEAA)[34] and replaced it with a new Act, known as CEAA 2012.[35] Changes to the EA process were a central plank in the federal government's Responsible Resource Development strategy, and are intended to "modernize the regulatory system and allow for natural resources to be developed in a responsible and timely way for the benefit of all Canadians." The thinking is similar to that behind the Fisheries Act changes, that is, that existing environmental regulations were impeding Canada's economic recovery. Joe Oliver, then Minister of Natural Resources, famously expressed the government's view that "environmental and other radical groups" were using EA hearings to deliberately block economically important projects:

> These groups threaten to hijack our regulatory system to achieve their radical ideological agenda. They seek to exploit any loophole they can find, stacking public hearings with bodies to ensure that delays kill good projects. They use funding from foreign special interest groups to undermine Canada's national economic interest. They attract jet-setting celebrities with some of the largest personal carbon footprints in the world to lecture Canadians not to develop our natural resources. Finally, if all other avenues have failed, they will take a quintessential American approach: sue everyone and anyone to delay the project even further. They do this because they know it can work. It works because it helps them to achieve their ultimate objective: delay a project to the point it becomes economically unviable.[36]

While the government has not gone so far as to abandon EA entirely, the changes do restrict the scope of that process and the opportunities for public participation.

The previous EA process was triggered whenever a federal authority—through federal agency participation, funding, or regulatory approval—had some involvement in a project that could have an impact on the environment. One of the changes under CEAA 2012 is to limit the number of projects that will require EA, generally to those with more significant potential for adverse environmental impacts. The only projects that will undergo EA are designated in a regulation.[37] The responsibility to carry out EA also shifts to one of three agencies, the Canadian Environmental Assessment Agency, the National Energy Board (NEB), or the Canadian Nuclear Safety Commission (CNSC). Designated projects regulated by the NEB or CNSC automatically require EA. For CEA Agency projects, which are most of the designated projects, the process requires an initial step, a new version of screening, which will determine if the designated project could have adverse effects on aspects of the environment that fall exclusively within federal jurisdiction, specifically First Nations peoples, lands, or resources; fish and fish habitat; aquatic species; migratory birds; federal lands; or interprovincial or international effects. The screening decision is based on information provided by the project proponent, in accordance with new regulations.[38] If it is determined that there could be such effects, an EA will be done by the CEA Agency. The Minister of the Environment may refer a project to a review panel, which could also include a joint panel with a province or other jurisdiction.

The members of a review panel are appointed, and the terms of reference for a review panel are established, by the Minister of the Environment. The role of the review panel is to conduct an EA of the project, make the information it uses available to the public, hold hearings, and prepare and submit a report to the minister on its conclusions and recommendations. The hearings are to be held "in a manner that offers any **interested party** an opportunity to participate" in the EA.[39] Unlike the previous CEAA, and unlike the open opportunity for any member of the public to provide comments on the screening decision, CEAA 2012 restricts public participation in panel hearings by defining "interested party" narrowly. Under s. 2(2) of CEAA 2012, an interested party is a person who is "directly affected by the carrying out of the designated project" or is a "person who has relevant information or expertise," as determined by the review panel. Nevertheless, there is some confusion in the drafting because the panel, in its report to the minister, must include a "summary of any comments received from the public, including interested parties" and the Agency must establish a "participant funding program to facilitate the participation of the public" in EAs referred to a review panel.[40] What an "opportunity to participate" will mean is unclear.

The restriction on public participation also applies to EAs carried out by the National Energy Board (NEB), where there is no screening decision. The NEB Act was amended to require the Board to "consider the representations of any person who, in the Board's opinion, is directly affected" or who has relevant information.[41] The NEB has identified the factors it will apply to determine status and has clarified the means of participation it will allow. To be considered "directly affected," a person must have a specific and detailed individual interest, such as a "commercial, property or financial interest," that will be affected, or must personally use or occupy affected land.[42] The NEB will consider the degree of connection, the frequency and duration of one's use of an area, and the likelihood and severity of potential harm. These factors are all measured against the list of relevant issues in the hearing. For example, in the hearing regarding the reversal of the Enbridge Line 9 pipeline running from Montreal to Sarnia to allow it to carry bitumen from the Alberta oil sands, the NEB notified potential participants that it would not consider the effects of upstream activities, development of the oil sands, or downstream use of the oil distributed through the pipeline. Those wishing to make submissions on the issue of the environmental impacts of oil sands expansion were denied the ability to do so.[43]

Once the NEB determines that a person is directly affected or has relevant information or expertise to be allowed to participate, it then determines how each person can participate. It recognizes two ways: one can either write a letter of comment or act as an **intervener** in the hearing. A letter from a recognized commentator will be considered and will form part of the public record; unsolicited letters from the public will not be considered at all. An intervener can expect to receive all the relevant documents, have an opportunity to present written evidence, question other parties and be questioned on their written evidence, cross-examine witnesses, and give final argument. However, this may not always be the case. For example, in the Hearing Order respecting the application for the Trans Mountain Expansion Project, the NEB accepted 1,468 out of 2,118 applications to participate. Four hundred of those were accepted as interveners, although the Hearing Order did not provide for the right of those interveners to cross-examine witnesses for the proponent.[44] The ultimate determination following an EA is whether the project will cause "significant adverse environmental effects" after taking into account the implementation of appropriate mitigation measures. If the decision-maker (which can be the NEB, the Minister of Environment, cabinet, or another "responsible authority" if designated by regulation, depending on the circumstances) determines that these are likely, then the project must be referred to cabinet to determine whether such effects "are justified in the circumstances." If it is determined that significant effects are not likely, or that they are justified, the decision-maker establishes conditions that the project proponent must meet in relation to mitigation and follow-up and a "decision statement" is issued making those conditions enforceable. If the decision-maker is the NEB, the final decision on the project is made by cabinet.

One of the accomplishments of CEAA 2012, intended to speed up regulatory approval, is the establishment of time limits on the process. The CEA Agency's screening decision as to whether EA is required must be made within 45 days from receipt of the project description from the proponent. This period includes a 20-day public comment period. The time to complete an EA is 365 days from commencement to the final decision or, if there is an assessment by a review panel, 24 months to reach a final decision. It has been suggested that one implication of the timelines is that there may not be sufficient time to allow for the preparation of scientific reports that are relevant and necessary to the decisions that must be made.[45]

Other measures that will save the federal government time and resources are opportunities to delegate the EA to other governments on a case-by-case basis. The new Act contains two levels of **delegation of responsibility** to a province. One level, known as "substitution," *requires* the Minister of the Environment to substitute a provincial EA process for the federal one when a province requests it and the minister is of the opinion that the provincial process constitutes "appropriate substitution."[46] This means that the conduct and findings of the EA are done under provincial law but the final decision is still made by federal authorities. The federal government signed a Memorandum of Understanding (MOU) regarding substitution with British Columbia in 2013,[47] and since then has authorized substitution for seven designated projects. The MOU allows for the province to carry out the "procedural aspects" of Aboriginal consultation.

The second level of delegation, known as "equivalent assessment," allows the federal cabinet to exempt a designated project that meets the conditions of substitution from application of the federal Act in its entirety. Before making an exemption order, cabinet must be satisfied that the provincial agency will ensure that mitigation measures and a follow-up program are implemented following the EA.[48]

Navigable Waters Protection Act (NWPA)[49]

Under its constitutional authority over navigation and shipping, the federal government has regulated navigable waterways since the 1880s under the NWPA. This Act, while protecting the public right of navigation, also incidentally protected the waters themselves. In addition, as the Supreme Court of Canada held in the *Friends of the Oldman River* decision,[50] since the 1980s the need for a NWPA permit triggered application of the federal EA process. In 2009, the Harper minority government allowed certain small projects in navigable waterways to go forward without NWPA or EA approval. Then, in 2012 with Bill C-45, the NWPA was significantly revamped and even renamed the Navigation Protection Act, emphasizing the decoupling of navigation from the waters themselves.[51] The major change was to limit federal oversight and approval to those projects on specific lakes and rivers, identified on a list in the Schedule to the amended Act, rather than to projects on all navigable waterways. This change was pushed by the pipeline industry,[52] and it means that projects that could affect navigation or waters on more than 99 per cent of the lakes and rivers in Canada no longer require a permit or EA approval.[53]

Northwest Territories Devolution Act

On 1 April 2014, legislation transferring resource management in the Northwest Territories (NWT) from the federal government to the territorial government came into force.[54] This is the culmination of many years of negotiations among the federal and territorial governments as well as five organizations representing First Nations governments in the NWT, and follows a similar process carried out in the Yukon Territory that came into effect in 2003. In both cases, comprehensive land claims were settled with the First Nations prior to negotiating **devolution**. The result of these devolution initiatives is that decisions on resource development will be made jointly.

While there had been widespread discussion and consultation on the terms of the devolution agreement, the implementing legislation, Bill C-15, when introduced in Parliament also included provisions that amended the Mackenzie Valley Resource Management Act (MVRMA).[55] Opposition members of Parliament objected that the two issues should be separated so that each could be debated on its own merits, but the government refused.

As discussed by White in Chapter 10, the effect of the amendments to the MVRMA is to dissolve four regional regulatory boards that had been agreed to under the First Nations governance agreements and to replace them with a single board, the Mackenzie Valley Land and Water Board, with jurisdiction for the entire NWT. This new Board is to be based in Yellowknife. Instead of each Aboriginal group being entitled to nominate half the members of a board, each will be entitled to one representative on the new Board. In addition, the amendments allow the federal minister to impose binding policy guidance on the new Board. The First Nations affected by this change claim that the federal government failed to consult them about the amendments, that the change is contrary to the terms of the governance agreements they signed with the federal government, and that there was no justification for the change, as the Auditor General and others found that the regional boards functioned efficiently.

The MVRMA amendments respond to industry complaints about the "delays, expense, and uncertainty of environmental regulatory processes and, of course, about some of the conditions imposed by the boards."[56] In 2008, the federal government had appointed a special representative to review the NWT land-use process and make recommendations for change. The MVRMA amendments respond to those recommendations, and were one of the conditions under which the federal government agreed to move the devolution legislation forward to 2014. In Parliament, the federal Minister of Aboriginal Affairs and Northern Development, Bernard Valcourt, commented only that the changes represent an effort to "modernize" the regulatory system by increasing the predictability and timeliness in the environmental assessment process, while also reducing the regulatory burden. The changes would make the system similar to that in Yukon and Nunavut. Minister Valcourt noted that the diamond industry was in favour of the change and stated, "this is how we can ensure that investors will look favourably at the Northwest Territories."[57] The Tlicho First Nation has brought a court action challenging the MVRMA amendments.[58]

The Role of the Courts in a Difficult Economic Context

Canadian courts have generally been very supportive of government action to protect the environment. In numerous cases, the Supreme Court of Canada has expressed the fundamental importance of environmental protection to Canadian society and the need to interpret legislation broadly to provide governments with the flexibility they need to respond to environmental problems.[59] The Court has endorsed the key values of the precautionary principle, the "polluter pays" principle, sustainability, intergenerational equity, and public trust.[60] In an economic downturn, however, when private firms struggle to stay in business and governments reduce expenditures, environmental values can be seen to come into conflict with competing public policies. In recent cases, the courts have been called on to interpret legislation addressing environmental protection in the context of corporate bankruptcy and insolvency.

For a company on the brink of insolvency or bankruptcy, environmental obligations and liabilities can require significant expenditures. The legal question is whether a failing company must continue to follow environmental regulations and orders. The answer is grounded in part in the Constitution because "bankruptcy and insolvency" is a federal head of power, while the environmental regulation of business and industry is primarily provincial.

When companies become insolvent, they can gain protection from their creditors and restructure by applying to the court under a federal statute, the Companies' Creditors Arrangement Act (CCAA).[61] Once a proceeding is commenced, the court typically orders a **stay**, that is, an order preventing the filing of new claims against the company and its directors while the company restructures. The process allows for negotiations with all of a company's creditors, with the goal of reaching a settlement of their claims against the debtor company. Claims are "compromised," meaning that creditors will often have to accept less in repayment than they are owed. Once a company comes out of this process, it can continue to operate and is free of its previous obligations. This process of using a single forum for negotiating restructuring is based on two ideas—fairness among creditors, and finality for the debtor so as to be able to make a fresh start. However, if restructuring fails, the company can declare or be forced into bankruptcy. The bankruptcy process is governed by the federal Bankruptcy and Insolvency Act.[62]

The environmental implications of these processes have been addressed in some high-profile court cases in the last few years. The Supreme Court of Canada confronted the issue in the 2012 case of *Newfoundland and Labrador v. Abitibi-Bowater*.[63] Abitibi, a pulp and paper manufacturer, had operated in the province for more than 100 years, but because of financial difficulties with its US and Canadian operations it announced the closing of its last mill in the province and sought CCAA protection in 2009. The court issued a stay, preventing further claims against the company. The province, concerned that it would be left to remediate sites that had been contaminated by Abitibi over the years, issued five cleanup orders under the provincial Environmental Protection Act and sought a ruling that they were legal obligations that would survive the CCAA restructuring. It also argued that the federal legislation could not interfere with orders validly enacted in the exercise of a constitutional power held by the province.

The Supreme Court ruled against the province, holding that the province was a creditor and the environmental orders were claims subject to compromise under CCAA but without any priority over other, private claims. This meant that Abitibi could emerge from restructuring free of any continuing obligation to clean up the sites that it had contaminated, the cost of which, estimated to be equivalent to the entire budget of the provincial Ministry of Environment and Conservation for the year, would then have to be borne by the public. The Court also noted that Parliament, in enacting the CCAA, had considered the balance between provincial regulations and the rights of corporate debtors and their creditors. The case turned on whether the provincial environmental orders could be viewed as monetary orders rather than regulatory ones. Because the Court considered that the province would have to clean up the sites if Abitibi did not, it held that the orders were in essence monetary orders. As such, the province could not issue the orders to defeat the scheme of the federal CCAA that provides for fairness among creditors.

Similar cases have arisen in Ontario courts. In *Re Nortel Networks*,[64] the company contaminated five sites of its former manufacturing operations, which it was voluntarily cleaning up, even though some had been sold, without the government having issued a remediation order. The company had spent more than $28.5 million on remediation, with another $18 million needed to complete the task, when it applied under the CCAA for protection. The Ontario Ministry of the Environment then issued remediation orders against Nortel and the current owners of the sites. The Ontario Court of Appeal distinguished this situation from the one in *Abitibi* on the basis that, because other parties were named in the orders, it was not sufficiently certain that the province itself would have to do the remediation and seek reimbursement of its costs. Thus, the Court held that these orders were regulatory in nature and not provable claims. As a result, the obligation for Nortel to comply with them continued.

In *Northstar Aerospace*,[65] by contrast, the company had been remediating its former manufacturing site in Cambridge and the surrounding neighbourhood when it ran into financial problems. The Ontario Ministry of the Environment issued orders against the company and its directors to continue the remediation, but the company then filed for creditor protection and later declared bankruptcy. At that point, the contaminated property was abandoned and the ministry took over remediation. In those circumstances, the Ontario Court of Appeal found that it was sufficiently certain that the province would carry out the cleanup and seek reimbursement, and therefore the orders were considered to be claims that could be compromised.

These cases illustrate the difficulties faced by regulators when corporations that have created significant environmental risks fall into financial hardship. The balance between the federal and provincial statutes does not give a priority to the cleanup of contaminated sites over other corporate financial obligations. When companies fail, they often abandon their contaminated sites, leaving the government as the owner and the public on the hook for cleanup costs. This approach could have serious consequences for resource-rich provinces, such as Alberta, and the liability in the coming years for the cleanup and remediation of contaminated sites, such as those associated with oil sands projects, likely will cost billions of dollars. Nevertheless, any reform of this "untidy intersection" between competing public policies will have to wait for action from Parliament.

Implications of Recent Legal Developments

In sum, the current federal government's view is that economic recovery through energy and resource exploitation and trade is a national priority, and that environmental review processes should be minimized to facilitate quick achievement of that priority, while continuing to ensure environmental protection. Part of achieving that goal has been through reducing the types of projects that are subject to EA review and reducing the time that reviews take. Reducing the time for reviews has been achieved, in part, by limiting the number of participants to those directly affected and, in part, by limiting the types of issues that can be raised and to which proponents must respond. It may be that this new approach reflects simple impatience with the time it takes to hear from the broader public, but it does mean that interested organizations and members of the public have no forum in which to raise concerns about larger policy choices. Truncated processes may also undermine science-based decision-making. This contributes to serious concerns about the effectiveness of these deliberative processes and about government accountability for environmental protection.

The federal government has also moved to reduce its regulatory role in ensuring the protection of navigable waterways and aquatic habitat. It has expanded de jure and de facto sharing of responsibility for the environment with the provinces and territories, decentralizing decision-making even further in an already decentralized system. In areas that remain in federal hands, the government has undertaken little new action to respond to emerging concerns, such as climate change. The addition of new enforcement measures and higher fines made headlines, but these have made little difference in practice due to budget cutbacks made in the name of austerity.

The legal and constitutional context in which this has occurred provides little opportunity to challenge the government's policy direction through the courts. The courts play an important role in ensuring government accountability and forcing adherence to legislative mandates and constitutional norms. When competing public priorities, such as environmental protection and creditor protection, come into conflict in a time of recession and austerity, the courts must find a way to rationalize these competing objectives that have been adopted by Parliament. Where the government or Parliament fails to act, guts legislation, or adopts policies that move away from strong environmental protection, the courts have limited power to interfere. Policy in our system is set by Parliament and by the executive, and the traditional role of the courts is to interpret and apply it. Courts cannot ordinarily rule on the wisdom of policy or disagree with the terms of legislation.

Nevertheless, there are opportunities to bring legal challenges to the government's actions. Lawsuits have been launched against the government by First Nations and by environmental groups in reaction to many of its recent actions. One example involves litigation over the report of the joint review panel that recommended approval of the Enbridge Northern Gateway pipeline project, the dual pipeline proposed to carry diluted bitumen from the Alberta oil sands to Kitimat on the BC coast for loading onto tankers. The cases argue a range of legal issues, including inadequate consultation with First Nations, violations of Aboriginal rights, and failure to follow principles of administrative law and the statutory requirements in both the CEAA and the Species at Risk Act. Lawsuits have also been started with respect to the NEB's hearing process for the Kinder Morgan Trans Mountain Expansion Project and the MVRMA amendments. The irony, of course, is that by seeking to speed up the approval process to fast-track resource exploitation, the federal government will likely face significant delays for many projects due to pending court proceedings.[66] Other kinds of court cases continue to be brought to force government adherence to legislation that has not been changed, including the Species at Risk Act and the Pest Control Products Act. In addition, although opportunities for public and NGO involvement in administrative processes have been diminished, participation and engagement are still essential to accountable decision-making and to the progressive development of environmental law and policy in Canada.

Key Terms

delegation of responsibility

devolution

doctrine of parliamentary sovereignty

environmental impact assessment

harmful alteration, disruption, or destruction (HADD)

interested party

intervener

omnibus budget bills

"peace, order, and good government"

pith and substance

positive rights

"property and civil rights"

stay

Questions for Review

1. What are the common themes in the recent legislative changes made to federal environmental legislation?
2. What impacts will these changes have?

3. How do the courts balance competing public policy objectives? Should Parliament take steps to give higher priority to environmental objectives?

Internet Resources

Canadian Council of Ministers of the Environment
http://www.ccme.ca/

Canadian Environmental Assessment Agency
http://www.ceaa-acee.gc.ca/

Commissioner of the Environment and Sustainable Development
http://www.oag-bvg.gc.ca/

Ecojustice
http://www.ecojustice.ca/

Environment Canada
http://www.ec.gc.ca/

Office of the High Commissioner for Human Rights, Independent Expert on human rights and the environment
http://www.ohchr.org/EN/Issues/Environment/IEEnvironment/Pages/IEenvironmentIndex.aspx

National Energy Board
http://www.neb-one.gc.ca/

West Coast Environmental Law
http://www.wcel.org/

Additional Reading

Benidickson, Jamie. *Essentials of Canadian Law: Environmental Law*, 4th edn. Toronto: Irwin Law, 2013.

Doelle, Meinhard. "CEAA 2012: The End of Federal EA As We Know It?" *Journal of Environmental Law and Practice* 24 (2012): 1–17.

Lucas, Alastair R., and Jenette Yearsley. "The Constitutionality of Federal Climate Change Legislation." *Journal of Environmental Law and Practice* 23 (2011): 205–36.

Valiante, Marcia. "The Courts and Environmental Policy Leadership." In Debora L. VanNijnatten and Robert Boardman, eds, *Canadian Environmental Policy and Politics: Prospects for Leadership and Innovation*, 3rd edn. Toronto: Oxford University Press, 2009.

Wood, Stepan, Georgia Tanner, and Benjamin J. Richardson. "What Ever Happened to Canadian Environmental Law?" *Ecology Law Quarterly* 37 (2010): 981–1040.

Notes

1. Government of Canada, Economic Action Plan, www.actionplan.gc.ca.

2. Ontario, Green Energy and Green Economy Act, 2009, S.O. 2009, c. 12; *BC's Green Economy: Growing Green Jobs*, http://bcge.ca/wp-content/uploads/2014/03/BCs_Green_Economy-20121.pdf, Update 2014: http://bcge.ca/wp-content/uploads/2014/03/GreenEconomy_2014.pdf.

3. Natural Resources Canada, *Report on Plans and Priorities*, 2013–14: "Minister's Message," accessed 19 July 2014, http://www.nrcan.gc.ca/plans-performance-reports/747.

4. Hoi Kong, "Beyond Functionalism, Formalism and Minimalism: Deliberative Democracy and Decision Rules in the Federalism Cases of the 2010–2011 Term," *Supreme Court Law Review* (2d) 55 (2011): 355.

5. The UN Framework Convention on Climate Change, the Kyoto Protocol, and the agreements of the parties are found at: unfccc.int.

6. *Reduction of Carbon Dioxide Emissions from Coal Fired Electricity Regulations*, SOR/2012-167.

7. See Alastair R. Lucas and Jenette Yearsley, "The Constitutionality of Federal Climate Change Legislation," *Journal of Environmental Law and Practice* 23 (2012): 205–36, which takes issue with Peter Hogg, "Constitutional Authority over Greenhouse Gas Emissions," *Alberta Law Review* 46 (2009): 207.

8. *British Columbia (Attorney General) v. Lafarge Canada Inc.*, [2007] 2 SCR 86.

9. *Québec (Attorney General) v. Canadian Owners and Pilots Association*, [2010] 2 SCR 536; *Québec (Attorney General) v. Lacombe*, [2010] 2 SCR 453.

10. Lorne Sossin, *Boundaries of Judicial Review: The Law of Justiciability in Canada*, 2nd edn (Toronto: Carswell, 2012), 204.

11. *Delgamuukw v. British Columbia*, [1997] 3 SCR 1010.

12. *Haida Nation v. British Columbia (Minister of Forests)*, [2004] 3 SCR 511.

13. *Rio Tinto Alcan Inc. v. Carrier Sekani Tribal Council*, [2010] 2 SCR 650, para. 44.

14. Canadian Charter of Rights and Freedoms, section 1.

15. *Gosselin v. Québec (Attorney General)*, [2002] 4 SCR 429.

16. Office of the High Commissioner for Human Rights, Independent Expert on human rights and the environment, accessed 19 July 2014, http://www.ohchr.org/EN/Issues/Environment/IEEnvironment/Pages/IEenvironmentIndex.aspx.

17. *Morton v. British Columbia*, [2009] BCSC 136, appeal dismissed [2009] BCCA 481.

18. Nancy Olewiler, "Environmental Policy in Canada: Harmonized at the Bottom?" in K. Harrison, ed., *Racing to the Bottom? Provincial Interdependence in the Canadian Federation* (Vancouver: University of British Columbia Press, 2005), 113–55.

19. S.C. 1999, c. 33.

20. S.C. 2002, c. 28.

21. *Metal Mining Effluent Regulations*, SOR/2002-222; *Pulp and Paper Mill Effluent Regulations*, SOR/92-269; *Wastewater Systems Effluent Regulations*, SOR/2012-139.

22. S.C. 2002, c. 29.

23. See www.ccme.ca.

24. Standards have been developed for benzene, dioxins and furans, mercury, particulate matter, ozone, and petroleum hydrocarbons in soil. See Chapter 8 by Simmons.

25. Stepan Wood, Georgia Tanner, and Benjamin J. Richardson, "What Ever Happened to Canadian Environmental Law?" *Ecology Law Quarterly* 37 (2010): 981–1040.

26. 40th Parliament, 2nd Session, Bill C-16, Environmental Enforcement Act, royal assent, 18 June 2009.

27. Commissioner of the Environment and Sustainable Development, December 2011 Report, Chapter 3: "Enforcing the *Canadian Environmental Protection Act, 1999*," 26.

28. See, e.g., Cindy Harnett, "Another Round of Cuts Planned for Fisheries and Oceans Canada," *Victoria Times Colonist*, 12 Mar. 2013; Paul Withers, "DFO at Risk from Budget Cuts, Change: Internal Report," CBC News, 8 Nov. 2013; Mike DeSouza, "Federal Budget Cuts Undermine Environment Canada's Mandate to Enforce Clean Air Regulations: Emails," *National Post*, 17 Mar. 2013; Alex Boutilier, "Environment Canada Braces for Cuts to Climate Programs," *Toronto Star*, 12 Mar. 2014. Annual reports on plans and priorities for Environment Canada are found at www.ec.gc.ca.

29. R.S.C. 1985, c. F-14.

30. Bill C-38, Jobs, Growth and Long-term Prosperity Act, enacted as S.C. 2012, c. 19; Bill C-45, Jobs and Growth Act, enacted as S.C. 2012, c. 31.

31. Gloria Galloway, "Fisheries Act Change Guided by Industry," *Globe and Mail*, 6 Aug. 2013.

32. Paddy Ashfield, Minister of Fisheries and Oceans, Speaking Notes, 24 Apr. 2012.

33. *Regulations Establishing Conditions for Making Regulations under subsection 36(5.2) of the Fisheries Act*, SOR/2014-91.

34. S.C. 1992, c. 37.

35. S.C. 2012, c. 19, s. 52.

36. "An open letter from the Honourable Joe Oliver, Minister of Natural Resources, on Canada's commitment to diversify our energy markets and the need to streamline the regulatory process in order to advance Canada's national economic interest," 9 Jan. 2012, www.nrcan.gc.ca/media-room/news-release/2012/1/1909.

37. *Regulation Designating Physical Activities*, SOR/2012-147.

38. *Prescribed Information for the Description of a Designated Project Regulations*, SOR/2012-148.

39. CEAA 2012, s. 43(1).

40. CEAA 2012, sections 43(1)(d)(ii) and 57, respectively.

41. NEB Act, s. 55.2.

42. NEB, *Hearing Process Handbook*, 2013, http://www.neb-one.gc.ca/clf-nsi/rthnb/pblcprtcptn/pblchrng/pblchrngpmphlt-eng.pdf.

43. As a result of this ruling, the Forest Ethics Advocacy Association has brought a constitutional challenge in the Federal Court, arguing a breach of freedom of expression: http://www.forestethics.org//sites/forest-ethics.huang.radicaldesigns.org/files/ForestEthics-Advocacy-NoticeofApplication-Federal-Court-Appeal.pdf. A similar ruling on the issues was made for the hearing on the Kinder Morgan Trans-Mountain Expansion Project. In that case, motions for a declaration that s. 55.2 violates the Charter guarantee of freedom of expression have been brought before the NEB: https://docs.neb-one.gc.ca/ll-eng/llisapi.dll/fetch/2000/90464/90552/548311/956726/2392873/2449981/2478040/A36%2D1_%2D_Letter_seeking_comments_%2D_Notices_of_Motion_from_Lynne_M._Quarmby_and_others%2C_dated_6_May_and_15_May_2014_-_Trans_Mountain_Expansion_Project_%2D_A3X3H3.pdf?nodeid=2477537&vernum=-2.

44. Motions challenging the NEB's Ruling on Participation, dated 2 Apr. 2014, were dismissed by the Board on 7 May 2014.

45. See Andrew Gage, "Why the NEB Downplayed the Impact of a Major Bitumen Spill," WCEL Environmental Law Alert, 29 Jan. 2014, http://wcel.org/resources/environmental-law-alert/why-neb-downplayed-impact-major-bitumen-spill; Gavin Smith, "Strict Timelines for Environmental Assessments, but Not for Government," *West Coast Environmental Law*, 14 Feb. 2014, http://wcel.org/resources/environmental-law-alert/strict-timelines-environmental-assessments-not-government.

46. CEAA 2012, s. 32.

47. *Memorandum of Understanding between the Canadian Environmental Assessment Agency (the Agency) and the British Columbia Environmental Assessment Office (EAO) on Substitution of Environmental Assessments (2013)*, http://www.ceaa-acee.gc.ca/default.asp?lang=En&n=CD2D2131-1.

48. CEAA 2012, s. 37.

49. R.S.C. 1985, c. N-22.

50. *Friends of the Oldman River Society v. Canada (Minister of Transport)*, [1992] 1 SCR 3.

51. Ecojustice, "Legal Backgrounder: Bill C-45 and the Navigable Waters Protection Act," Oct. 2012, 2.

52. Heather Scoffield, "Pipeline Industry Drove Changes to Navigable Waters Protection Act, Documents Show," 20 Feb. 2013, Canadian Press, www.thestar.com/news/canada/2013/02/20/pipeline_industry_drove_changes_to_navigable_waters_protection_act_documents_show.html.

53. Ecojustice, "Legal Backgrounder."

54. Northwest Territories Act, S.C. 2014, c. 2.

55. S.C. 1998, c. 25.

56. Graham White, "Aboriginal People and Environmental Regulation: The Role of Land Claims Co-management Boards in the Territorial North," in D.L. VanNijnatten and R. Boardman, eds, *Canadian Environmental Policy and Politics: Prospects for Leadership and Innovation*, 3rd edn (Toronto: Oxford University Press, 2009), 134.

57. Honourable Bernard Valcourt, Minister of Aboriginal Affairs and Northern Development, 41st Parliament, 2nd Session, Bill C-15, Third Reading, *Hansard*, 14 Feb. 2014, 1015.

58. Canadian Press, "Lawsuit Attacks Northwest Territories Resource Rules, Devolution Deal," *Ottawa Citizen*, 8 May 2014, http://www.ottawacitizen.com/news/Lawsuit1attacks1Northwest1Territories1resource1rules/9823515/story.html.

59. See, e.g., *Ontario v. Canadian Pacific Ltd.*, [1995] 2 SCR 1031; *Castonguay Blasting Ltd. v. Ontario (Ministry of the Environment)*, [2013] 3 SCR 323.

60. Jerry V. DeMarco, "The Supreme Court of Canada's Recognition of Fundamental Environmental Values: What Could Be Next in Canadian Environmental Law?" *Journal of Environmental Law and Practice* 17 (2007): 159–204; Jerry V. DeMarco, "Law for Future Generations: The Theory of Intergenerational Equity in Canadian Environmental Law," *Journal of Environmental Law and Practice* 15 (2005): 1.

61. R.S.C. 1985, c. C-36.

62. R.S.C. 1985, c. B-3.

63. [2012] 3 SCR 443.

64. *Re Nortel Networks Corporation*, 2013 ONCA 599 (CanLII).

65. *Re Northstar Aerospace Inc.*, 2013 ONCA 600 (CanLII).

66. Sandy Carpenter, "Fixing the Energy Project Approval Process in Canada: An Early Assessment of Bill C-38 and Other Thoughts," *Alberta Law Review* 50 (2012–13): 231.

5 Implementing Environmental Policy in Canada

Mark Winfield

Chapter Summary

This chapter examines the tools and strategies available to governments for the purpose of implementing environmental policy in Canada, including substantive, procedural, and institutional instruments. The factors influencing policy instrument choice by governments, such as considerations of effectiveness, efficiency, fairness, and political and policy acceptability, are explored as well. Political and policy factors generally outweigh substantive considerations in decision-making. The chapter highlights major shifts in direction with respect to procedural and institutional mechanisms particularly since 2008. These shifts have been away from strengthening consideration of the environment and public input in decision-making towards facilitating natural resources extraction and development. The tendency towards outright withdrawals from substantive requirements regarding environmental protection is noted, as is a longer-term shift towards "smart" regulation implementation models. The long-term implications of these shifts in approaches to policy implementation are discussed in terms of the legitimacy and public acceptance of public policy decisions and the potential risks to public safety, health, and the environment.

Chapter Outline

- Introduction to policy implementation
- Types of implementation tools
  - Three categories: substantive, procedural, and institutional
- Factors influencing policy instrument choice
  - Effectiveness, efficiency, fairness, and policy and political acceptability
- Recent shift away from procedural and institutional mechanisms
  - Increased emphasis on mechanisms to facilitate the development and export of natural resources
- Parallel withdrawal of substantive regulatory requirements
  - The shift towards "smart" regulatory implementation models, emphasizing "partnerships" with regulated entities
- Implications
  - Declining legitimacy and acceptance of the resulting policy decisions
  - Increased risks to the health, safety, and environment of Canadians

Introduction

Policy implementation is the stage in the policy cycle[1] where governments move from the identification of problems, the assessment of potential responses, and the establishment of desired outcomes, to actually trying to change the behaviour of individuals, companies, and institutions to achieve these results. It is the stage at which policy is, in theory, translated into reality. Policy instruments are the tools employed by governments to implement policy. This chapter examines the different types of policy instruments available to governments for environmental policy purposes and the considerations governments may take into account in choosing implementation tools. In addition, the chapter examines the recent changes in Canadian governments' approaches to environmental policy implementation, particularly since the 2008 economic downturn and the 2011 arrival of a majority Conservative federal government led by Prime Minister Stephen Harper. The discussion highlights the ways in which austerity has been used to weaken a policy regime whose commitment to environmental sustainability was already ambivalent.

Types of Implementation Tools

The types of tools or policy instruments used by governments to implement environmental policy decisions can be broadly organized into three categories: substantive, procedural, and institutional. Substantive policy instruments are intended to directly change behaviour on the part of individuals, households, communities, and corporations. Substantive instruments can include the use of law and regulation to prohibit or control certain activities; the application of taxes, charges, and incentives to activities that governments wish to discourage or encourage; the creation of markets for ecological services like the sequestration and storage of greenhouse gas (GHG) emissions; the dissemination of information about pollutant emissions and other environmental impacts of human activity; public information and education campaigns intended to motivate action at the individual, household, or classroom level; and encouraging voluntary action by companies, communities, and individuals to manage or reduce the environmental impact of their activities.

Procedural instruments are focused on modifying decision-making processes with respect to policies and projects that may affect the environment, rather than on directly changing the behaviour of individuals or firms.[2] Environmental assessment (EA) processes have been among the most prominent procedural environmental policy instruments used in Canada. Environmental assessment processes were intended to inject environmental considerations into the decision-making process where they would not normally have been present. Public participation requirements can work in a similar way, providing opportunities for members of the public to have input into decision-making in ways that would not otherwise be the case.

The third type of implementation tool is institutional instruments. These strategies focus on the creation or use of specific agencies inside or outside of government to act as focal points for policy development, implementation, and evaluation, or to provide specific services, such as the regulation of activities that pose risks to public safety and the environment, or to manage natural resources.

Substantive Policy Instruments

The principal types of substantive policy instruments and their key features are summarized in Table 5.1.

TABLE 5.1 Substantive Policy Instruments and Their Key Features

Instrument	Means of Influence on Behaviour	Decision-maker Regarding Behaviour	Effectiveness in Achieving Behaviour Change	Political and Policy Considerations
Regulatory	Coercion; penalties for non-compliance	Government	High when applied and enforced (e.g., acid rain control; pulp and paper discharges to water; vehicle fuel economy)	Strong ideological opposition among some governments; strong public support where important public goods at stake
Economic	Price/costs of different behaviours	Market; consumers; resource users	Uncertain: marginal costs needed to change behaviour must to be discovered	Potential acceptance if revenue neutral or supported by dedicated government revenue (e.g., BC, Quebec), but have been controversial (federal carbon pricing proposals, Ontario "eco-fees")
Informational	Information provision	Consumers	Uncertain:effective in some cases, especially in conjunction with other instruments (e.g.,NPRI; in-home displays for energy efficiency)	Moderate but weakening as governmental awareness of impacts of information increases; support for use except in specific applications (e.g., household energy efficiency)
Educational and outreach	Information; moral suasion	Consumers	Uncertain: some cases of significant impacts (e.g.,blue boxes)	Can provide appearance of action without coercion or cost
Voluntary	Moral suasion; pre-emption of more coercive measures	Industry/resource user	Low: poor outcomes from flagship initiatives (VCR, ARET)	Declining in light of weak performance; re-emerging in modified form through "smart" regulation models

Regulatory Instruments

Regulatory instruments have been the traditional tool of choice in Canadian environmental policy, particularly for the prevention and control of pollution, but also for the purposes of managing access to natural resources and land-use planning. Regulatory tools rely on the establishment of obligations, based in legislation, prohibiting certain types of behaviour or requiring the explicit permission of government to engage in specified activities. Where such permission is given it typically may be subject to whatever conditions, such as the installation of equipment to limit emissions of pollutants or limits on the height of buildings that can be built at a given location, that the government may choose to impose. In effect, the state acts as a trustee of environmental resources, controlling access to them and making decisions about who should be allowed to use the environment and for what purposes.

This regulatory model was strongly reflected in the initial round of environmental legislation adopted in the late 1960s and early 1970s, particularly at the provincial level. Provincial environmental protection statutes, for example, typically prohibited engaging in activities that would result in pollution,[3] unless approvals had been obtained from the provincial environment ministry and the activity was carried out in accordance with the terms and conditions of those approvals.[4] In addition, regulations could be adopted under environmental legislation that set specific rules in relation to particular activities. Regulations might be employed to prohibit the use or release into the environment of certain toxic substances or limit emissions of particular pollutants from specific industrial facilities or sectors.

Under environmental legislation, penalties are usually attached for engaging in prohibited activities without appropriate approvals or for carrying out activities that violate rules and conditions imposed by government. These penalties typically take the form of fines or imprisonment on conviction for an offence. Fines for environmental offences grew significantly in Canada from the mid-1980s onward. Maximum fines under the initial round of environmental legislation adopted in Canada in the early 1970s were in the range of $5,000–$10,000 per offence. In practice, the actual fines imposed for environmental offences were usually far below even these modest maximums, with the result that violators simply regarded the penalties they received as the "cost of doing business." Major offences under the federal Canadian Environmental Protection Act (enacted in its current form in 1999) can now be subject to penalties of up to $1 million and up to five years' imprisonment.[5] In actuality, the application of maximum fines remains rare. More broadly, the vigour with which Canadian governments have been willing to actually enforce environmental laws has been a long-standing problem in Canadian environmental policy.[6]

Economic Instruments

Regulatory approaches, when they have been applied vigorously, have been highly effective in Canada in reducing pollution from specific industrial sources. The implementation of regulations by the governments of Ontario and Quebec in the mid-1980s to control emissions of the pollutants that caused acid rain resulted in reductions in emissions of sulphur dioxide from the targeted sources, largely base metal smelting and coal-fired electricity generation facilities, by more than 50 per cent relative to a 1980 baseline by the mid-1990s (for more detail on the air quality case, see Chapter 19). The emission reduction goals of the federal–provincial Eastern Canada Acid Rain Control program were achieved as a result.[7] Similarly, regulations have been used to successfully phase out the manufacturing and import of highly toxic or otherwise problematic substances, like polychlorinated biphenyls (PCBs) or substances that deplete the ozone layer. New federal and provincial requirements resulted in major reductions in water pollution from the pulp and paper sector in the 1990s.[8]

Despite these successes, regulatory tools have been subject to criticism since the 1970s for being inefficient, inconsistently applied, and likely less effective in stimulating the kinds of deeper systemic changes in economic activities, such as dramatically reducing the use of fossil fuels, that seem to be necessary to ensure the sustainability of the global biosphere. As a result, economic policy instruments have been widely proposed as a complement or even alternative to regulatory strategies for achieving environmental policy goals. Rather than governments trying to prescribe the behaviour of individuals and companies through regulation, economic instruments rely on the responses of these actors to price signals in the marketplace to achieve policy goals.[9]

Economic instruments can take a number of different forms. Taxes or charges can be imposed on activities that governments wish to discourage or phase out. Such charges have the effect of raising the costs of these activities relative to alternative paths. **Carbon taxes**, based on the carbon content of fuels, and by implication the amounts of GHGs likely to be generated through their use, for example, have been widely proposed as a means of achieving economy-wide reductions in the use of fossil fuels, like coal and oil, to combat global climate change. Sweden was among the most prominent early users of environmental taxes, imposing substantial taxes on the carbon and sulphur content of fossil fuels in the early 1990s.[10]

Governments can also pursue strategies of providing economic incentives to encourage behaviour or the development and adaptation of technologies that are seen to be more environmentally sustainable. **Feed-in tariffs (FITs)**, which pay renewable energy (e.g., wind, solar photovoltaic, biogas, small-scale hydro) developers a fixed long-term price for the electricity they produce, have been widely and successfully employed in Europe over the past two decades to promote the large-scale deployment of renewable energy resources.[11] Ontario initiated a similar FIT program under its 2009 Green Energy and Green Economy Act.[12]

Federal and provincial subsidies were central in the near-universal installation of sewage treatment systems by Ontario municipalities in the Great Lakes Basin, a development that has been fundamental to the recovery of water quality in the lakes over the past four decades.[13] Subsidies can also be employed as complements to regulatory initiatives to assist affected business in dealing with the capital costs of installing new pollution prevention or control technologies. Federal regulations on water pollution from the pulp and paper sector, first introduced in the 1970s, were accompanied by substantial subsidies for the modernization of pulp and paper mills.[14]

Integrated strategies of environmental taxation and broader tax reform are sometimes referred to as **ecological fiscal reform** (EFR).[15] Under EFR strategies, the funds raised through environmental taxes and charges are recycled into subsidies for more environmentally sustainable behaviour or technologies, and even into broader reductions in employment and income taxes. The revenue from Sweden's carbon and sulphur taxes, for example, was used to reduce personal income taxes. Such strategies are generally seen to enhance the political acceptability of environmental taxes by ensuring no increase in the overall tax burden on households and businesses.

There has been extensive discussion in Canada of the potential roles of environmental taxes and charges in environmental policy from the time of the 1992 World Conference on Environment and Development onward, but until very recently almost no significant application of these tools has resulted. The introduction of a modest carbon tax in Quebec in the fall of 2007 and then a much more substantial and comprehensive carbon tax regime in British Columbia in July 2008[16] seemed to indicate a potential shift in the willingness of Canadian governments to employ environmental taxes and charges. However, the defeat of the federal Liberal Party, which had put forward a major ecological fiscal reform initiative, including a comprehensive carbon pricing regime in its October 2008 federal election campaign,[17] has caused other Canadian governments to hesitate to pursue such initiatives. Ontario, for example, explicitly ruled out a carbon tax as part of its GHG emission reduction strategy at the beginning of 2013.[18]

A second form of economic instrument involves the creation of markets for certain types of activities, such as the emission of pollutants or the harvesting of natural resources. The underlying theory is that by creating a limited number of permits to engage in a targeted activity, and then allowing market participants to decide whether to purchase the number of permits required to continue their existing activities (such as emitting greenhouse gases) or to change their behaviour to reduce the number of permits they need, will result in markets establishing economic values for the permitted activities. Companies will then make the most economically rational decisions, from their perspectives, about what strategy to pursue. Many economists argue that these types of trading systems are more economically efficient than traditional regulatory models.[19]

Numerous attempts have been made to establish trading systems, with mixed results. The trading system for sulphur dioxide emissions established under amendments to the US federal Clean Air Act in 1990 is generally regarded as an environmental and economic success.[20] The European Union's efforts to create a cap-and-trade system for industrial emitters of greenhouse gases, on the other hand, have produced much less positive results. In the EU system, the price of carbon emission permits has repeatedly collapsed as a result of the granting of permits to industrial GHG emitters well in excess of actual emission levels at the time of the establishment of the system.[21] Discussions of cap-and-trade systems for large final emitters of GHGs were central to the first 20 years of debates on climate change policy in Canada.[22] However, since 2009 the Harper government has stated that it intends to follow the lead of the Obama administration in the US, which, faced with an inability to pass GHG emission trading legislation through the US Congress, has adopted a sector-by-sector regulatory approach to dealing with industrial emissions of GHGs. The first such regulations, regarding emissions of GHGs from coal-fired electricity plants, were adopted in Canada in 2012.[23]

Informational Instruments

Although governments have collected environmental data and information from the beginnings of the establishment of government agencies concerned with the management of natural resources and the environment, the gathering and dissemination of environmental information really only came into its own as an instrument for achieving specific policy outcomes in the 1990s. The first **pollutant release and transfer registry**, the United States' Toxic Release Inventory (TRI),[24] was established in 1987 in the aftermath of the Bhopal chemical plant disaster in India. Under these systems, facilities are required to report annually on their releases and off-site disposal of specified lists of pollutants. The information is then made available to the public. The emerging World Wide Web and developments in web server technologies offered enormously enhanced public access to the information collected through pollutant release inventory systems, and opened major new possibilities for the use of this information. Customized user-designed data searches and the combination of pollutant release data with geographic, demographic, and economic information became possible.[25] Canada was the second country in the world to establish a pollutant release inventory, the National Pollutant Release Inventory (NPRI), in 1992.[26] However, after an initial period of expansion, including the addition of criteria air pollutants and the lowering of reporting thresholds for priority toxic substances in the early part of the last decade, development of the NPRI stalled. Part of the explanation for this outcome may have been the growing recognition on the part of industry and governments of the potential public impact of assessments of their environmental performance based on the information made available through the inventory.

Public Outreach and Education

Environmental education and awareness initiatives have generally been regarded as the "softest," or least coercive, of the substantive environmental policy instruments available to governments. Education and awareness programs encourage rather than require action, and do not provide direct economic incentives for changes in behaviour. In practice, these initiatives can provide a number of important functions as parts of overall strategies for environmental sustainability. Formal (i.e., school classroom) and informal educational initiatives are central to building constituencies for policy action both in the present and in the future.

Education and awareness strategies have also been effective in motivating and sustaining behavioural changes at the individual and household level. In Canada, such strategies have been used to achieve widespread participation of households in increasingly ambitious waste diversion activities. In some communities this has involved major transitions in household behaviour. Household waste management in Toronto, for example, has been transformed from a simple process of taking bags of mixed waste to the curb twice a week, to sorting household wastes into six or seven streams, which are then collected according to complex weekly schedules.[27] The result, in the case of single-family dwellings, has been waste diversion rates exceeding 65 per cent.[28] The achievement of such outcomes with little or no direct economic incentive or regulatory enforcement highlights the potential impacts of education and awareness initiatives.

Voluntary Instruments

Voluntary initiatives became a highly prevalent approach to environmental policy implementation in Canada in the 1990s. For public policy purposes, these instruments were typically characterized by public challenges to industry by governments to reduce their emissions of pollutants in exchange for public recognition of their performance or, alternatively, avoidance of future regulatory requirements. Two such programs, the Accelerated Reduction and Elimination of Toxics (ARET) launched in 1994 and the Voluntary Climate Registry (VCR) initiated in 1995, constituted the federal government's principal initiatives on industrial sources of toxic substances and GHG emissions, respectively. By the early years of the new millennium, however, evidence of the failures of these high-profile voluntary initiatives,[29] reinforced by the roles of "voluntary" compliance regimes in the 2000 Walkerton, Ontario, and 2001 North Battleford, Saskatchewan, drinking water contamination disasters,[30] became increasingly obvious. In the context of the re-emergence of high levels of concern over environmental issues in the middle of the last decade, proposals by governments for voluntary action by industry in response to major environmental problems came to be seen as an indication, on the part of government, of a lack of seriousness about taking action.

Other forms of "voluntary" action by industry that emerged in the 1980s and 1990s were more complex and have resulted in more complicated relationships to regulatory regimes. Industrial sectors began to formulate and formalize safety and quality management systems independently of government. These developments were epitomized by the chemical industry's "Responsible Care" initiative, where membership in chemical industry associations became subject to meeting industry-formulated standards for safe practices. Independently verified quality and environmental management systems (ISO 9000 and ISO 14000, respectively) also were widely adopted within industry. Although outside of government-established regulatory requirements, and in some cases formulated to pre-empt the imposition of formal and potentially more stringent regulatory requirements by governments,[31] these systems were regarded by governments as complements and even potential substitutes for such requirements. The consequences of this development are discussed later in the chapter.

Integrated Use of Policy Instruments and Regimes

Traditional academic discussions of policy instruments tended to make sharp distinctions among regulatory, economic, voluntary, and other types of instruments. In practice, it is rare for any type of instrument to be used in isolation. In fact, the most effective environmental policy strategies have used combinations of instruments to achieve their goals. The successful strategies pursued by Canadian governments with respect to acid rain control in the 1980s and water pollution from the pulp and paper sector in the early 1990s, for example, employed a combination of regulatory requirements and substantial subsidies to the affected industries to assist them with the installation of new equipment to meet the new emission and discharge requirements.[32]

Strategies that rely on single instruments or simple combinations of instruments, such as regulation and subsidy, can be adequate where the policy goals being sought are relatively limited, such as the reduction of emissions of a specific pollutant from a specific industrial sector. Deeper structural, economy-wide changes in behaviour are more likely to require an integrated regime that uses a combination of different instruments. Examples of such strategies have been seen among US states; California's approach to energy efficiency, employing a combination of regulatory, economic, and informational tools is particularly noteworthy in this regard (see Box 5.1).[33] Similar strategies have been seen within the European Union with respect to waste management and climate change. However, consistent with the much more limited environmental policy goals pursued by Canadian governments, these types of integrated strategies or regimes rarely have been employed in Canada.[34]

BOX 5.1 | California's Approach to Energy Efficiency

California has achieved major progress on energy efficiency over the past 35 years through the use of a combination of policy instruments. Aggressive use of standards and codes (i.e., regulatory instruments) has pushed low-energy-efficiency products like older models of air conditioners and refrigerators out of the marketplace. In addition, energy is priced to ensure that it reflects the real costs of production, financial incentives are provided for the adoption of energy-efficient technologies and practices, and investments are made in research on energy-efficient technology design and program evaluation. At the same time, aggressive outreach and education programs on energy efficiency are carefully targeted at specific audiences and markets, and sophisticated monitoring and information systems, including in-home displays that allow consumers to monitor their own energy use, are used to provide feedback on program effectiveness.

Procedural Instruments

Procedural instruments reflect a less direct but more structural and systemic approach to dealing with environmental issues. These instruments focus on modifying decision-making processes with respect to all policies and projects that may affect the environment, rather than directly changing the behaviour of individuals or firms. Two prominent examples of procedural environmental policy instruments that have emerged in Canada are environmental impact assessment processes and mechanisms for public participation in decision-making.

Environmental Assessment

Environmental impact assessment, which first emerged in the late 1960s and early 1970s, is the most prominent and widely adopted procedural policy instrument with respect to environmental issues. Assessment processes have been established through legislation at the federal level and across all of the provinces and territories.[35] Environmental assessment was designed to ensure the proper evaluation of potential environmental effects of major development projects and industrial plans. In some cases, their rationale and the availability of alternative ways of meeting identified needs were subject to assessment as well. The process was designed to introduce consideration of environmental effects into decision-making processes, particularly with respect to large infrastructure and resource development projects, where typically there had been little or no thought of such consequences. Assessment also became important for managing social conflicts over major development projects and for fulfilling governments' **duty to consult** with Aboriginal peoples prior to making decisions that may affect their rights or interests.[36]

Public Participation

Public participation mechanisms, such as opportunities for members of the public to receive notice of pending decisions, file comments with decision-makers, and participate in public hearings on major projects and plans, are a second example of the use of procedural instruments in environmental policy-making. As with the consideration of the environmental effects of major decisions, prior to the mid-1970s it was rare for members of the public to have any input into decisions affecting the environment or their communities, particularly at the federal and provincial levels. However, public participation provisions were widely incorporated into environmental assessment and land-use and resource planning and management legislation between the early 1970s and early 1990s.

Ontario's Environmental Bill of Rights, adopted in 1994, represents the most systemic effort to date to establish opportunities for members of the public to contribute to decision-making. The bill established rights to notice-and-comment on pending decisions via an electronic registry, rights of appeal of decisions for third parties where such rights existed for proponents, and rights to petition for the enforcement of environmental laws or for the establishment of new laws, regulations, and policies. The government is required to respond to such petitions within set timeframes, and must provide a rationale for rejecting requests.[37] Similar requirements for public participation have been established at the international level through the 1998 United Nations Economic Commission for Europe (UNECE) Convention on Access to Information, Public Participation in Decision-Making and Access to Justice in Environmental Matters, although Canada has declined to sign the convention.

Institutions as Policy Implementation Tools

The creation of specific agencies and institutions inside and outside of government has been an essential element of environmental policy implementation in Canada. At the most basic level, the creation of ministries and departments of the environment at the federal and provincial levels since the early 1970s, usually through the consolidation of pre-existing agencies and functions scattered among multiple agencies,[38] was a watershed event in the emergence of the environment as a public policy issue. The creation of such agencies provided the means to advance and defend environmental interests in governmental decision-making processes at the political and bureaucratic levels. Environment ministers had seats at the cabinet table, the centre of the political decision-making process, and became institutional focal points for environmental concerns on the part of the public, media, interest groups, and legislative opposition parties. The integration of public service functions related to the environment provided the institutional capacity to support ministers at the political level with information and analysis, administer the then newly adopted environmental legislation, and engage in discussion and negotiation with other government departments, whose conventional views on economic development had hitherto gone unchallenged.

The second modern wave of public concern for the environment, which ran from the mid-1980s to the early 1990s, brought with it a round of significant institutional innovation with respect to the environment in Canada. Environmental commissioners' offices were created in the mid-1990s at the federal level and in Ontario. The federal Commissioner of the Environment and Sustainable Development (CESD)[39] and the Environmental Commissioner of Ontario[40] were mandated to report publicly to Parliament and the Ontario legislature, respectively, on the effectiveness of environmental policies and the overall environmental performance of governments. The commissioners' offices were intended to strengthen the effort put into addressing environmental issues by establishing permanent independent public evaluation and reporting mechanisms. These mechanisms would be relatively immune to shifts in levels of public concern for environmental issues—effectively providing a form of institutional "automatic stabilizer" through their regular evaluation and reporting functions. In addition, round tables on the environment and economy were created at the federal level and in each of the provinces, mandated to consider the implications of the sustainable development concept of the World Commission on Environment and Development (the Brundtland Commission) for their economies and societies.[41] The creation of the round tables, which included representation from government, industry, non-governmental organizations, and academics, reflected a conscious decision to move these discussions outside of traditional governmental structures, which tended to be dominated by institutions committed to conventional models of resource development and economic growth. An International Institute for Sustainable Development[42] was created by the federal government to investigate similar questions at the international level.

Choosing Implementation Strategies

Given the range of potential options for addressing a given problem or goal, the question arises as to how governments make decisions about what approaches to employ. Typically, either implicitly or explicitly, a number of criteria are considered.

Effectiveness

Perhaps the most basic criterion is the question of whether a particular instrument will be effective in achieving the desired policy outcome. Certainty of the results is particularly important where human health and safety are directly at risk. The timeliness of the result can also be an important consideration. Economic instruments, such as environmental taxes and charges, may result in the required changes in behaviour, but the timeframes within which consumers respond to the higher prices may be uncertain. Regulatory instruments, when backed with a credible expectation of enforcement, are generally seen to offer relatively high certainty of outcomes,[43] and generally set the timelines within which these results need to be achieved. The importance of effectiveness as a criterion in selecting policy implementation tools is also a function of how seriously the government is committed to achieving a specific outcome.

Efficiency

A second factor likely to be considered by policy-makers is the potential efficiency of different options. In the context of competing demands on the resources of government and society, governments will generally seek to achieve their policy goals at the lowest possible cost, with the intent of maximizing the resources available to address other problems. Efficiency can be defined in terms of a number of different dimensions. These aspects include the achievement of the desired result at minimum cost to society as a whole, to the government agencies that will have to implement and administer the chosen instruments, and to the individuals and organizations whose behaviour will be affected. Governments facing significant resource or financial constraints, for example, have tended towards the use of what they perceive as lower-cost instruments like voluntary initiatives, despite the fact that they may be less effective than options like regulation, as the latter are seen to be associated with higher administrative costs.[44]

Distributional Fairness

A third consideration is the likely distribution of the costs and benefits of a given strategy. In general, it is seen to be difficult to use relatively more coercive (and potentially effective) tools, such as regulatory and economic instruments, where the resulting costs will be concentrated among a small number of firms or sectors and the benefits will be widespread. Those who would suffer the costs of such strategies have strong incentives to resist them, while the benefits may be so widely distributed that no specific constituency emerges to argue for action.[45]

The fairness of the distribution of the costs and benefits of a given choice of instruments within society must also be considered. Is the strategy consistent, for example, with the widely accepted **polluter pays principle**[46] that those who generate the pollution should internalize the resulting environmental costs? Does the strategy impose disproportionate costs on vulnerable sectors of society or, conversely, offer disproportionate benefits for other members of society? The problem of free riders was central to critiques of the use of voluntary instruments in Canadian environmental policy.[47] The option of **free riding** is typically much more difficult where economic or regulatory instruments are employed.

Political and Policy Factors

Besides these considerations inherent to a particular instrument and in relation to a specific environmental problem, a number of other factors are likely to enter into the decision-making process. Implementation strategies must be seen to be politically acceptable by decision-makers as well as being effective, efficient, and fair. These considerations can have a major impact on policy instrument choice.

Since the mid-1980s, neo-liberal ideas about the role of governments have dominated at the federal and provincial levels. These models emphasize the reduction of governmental interference in private sector economic activity. Instead, the role of markets as the most efficient mechanisms for allocating access to resources, including environmental resources, has been highlighted, with the state's role being focused on the facilitation of the efficient functioning of markets.[48]

One of the practical manifestations of the prevalence of these ideas has been the establishment at the federal level and in many provinces of increasingly elaborate **regulatory management systems**. In most cases these systems incorporate explicit biases against the use of regulatory instruments, and typically establish extensive analytical and procedural tests, such as requirements of cost–benefit analyses, to ascertain if there would be "net" economic benefits from regulatory environmental, health, or safety initiatives. The effect of these requirements, reflected in the succession of policies and cabinet directives on regulatory management adopted under the Mulroney, Chrétien, and Harper governments[49] and some provinces,[50] was to make the use of regulatory instruments in environmental policy extremely difficult under normal circumstances.

In a democratic society, the public acceptability of different options is also a key consideration. Strong evidence, for example, suggests that a carbon tax could be a highly effective policy instrument for combating climate change.[51] However, even in the context of the adoption of a substantive carbon tax in British Columbia in 2008 and the subsequent electoral successes of the BC Liberal government that brought in the tax, the threat of the adoption of such a tax by a federal Liberal or New Democratic government has been employed aggressively as a political weapon at the national level by the Conservative government.[52]

Other factors may also enter the equation. International trade regimes, such as the North American Free Trade Agreement (NAFTA) and the World Trade Organization (WTO), impose important restrictions on strategies that may be employed to address environmental problems that might also affect international trade. The investor–state provisions contained in Chapter 11 of NAFTA may further increase the reluctance of government agencies to pursue the use of regulatory instruments.[53] Similar provisions are included in the proposed Canada–European Union Trade Agreement.[54]

Federal–provincial relations may be an additional consideration in implementation choices, particularly at the federal level. Traditionally, provincial governments have strongly opposed substantive interventions by the federal government in the environmental field. Rather, provinces have preferred to be the primary regulators of industrial sources of pollution and the principal assessors of proposed resource development projects. They have preferred that the federal government restrict itself to a supporting role, such as through the provision of subsidies to assist firms in installing additional pollution prevention and control technologies and research and information services.[55]

Environmental Policy Implementation in the Harper Era

Prime Minister Stephen Harper's personal hostility to major interventions around environmental issues, particularly climate change, was already well known at the time of his government's arrival in 2006.[56] The new government's preferred focus, reflecting both its overtly neo-liberal ideological orientation and its western Canadian base, was on natural resources development and export. In the context of the high levels of public concern over the climate change issue it encountered upon arrival in office, the Harper Conservatives briefly flirted with the possibility of significant federal regulatory interventions on air pollution and GHG emissions.[57] However, these directions were abandoned as levels of public concern fell in the context of the 2008 economic crisis and the Harper government's defeat of the federal Liberals, who campaigned on their "Green Shift" ecological fiscal reform platform. The government's one significant regulatory intervention was to require, for the first time in Canada, vehicle fuel economy standards. That move was compelled by the need to match the standards adopted by the Obama administration in the United States in order to maintain access to the North American automobile market for Canadian manufacturers.[58] In the past, Canadian vehicle fuel economy standards had been established through voluntary agreements with automobile manufacturers.

Procedural and Institutional Strategies

The Harper government took an explicit and dramatic approach, shifting the institutional and procedural dimensions of environmental policy away from an emphasis on embedding environmental considerations and public input into decision-making and towards facilitating natural resources development and export. The long period of Conservative minority government from 2006 to 2011 witnessed a steady incremental erosion of the federal environmental assessment process through a succession of amendments to the Canadian Environmental Assessment Act and related legislation.[59] These moves were accompanied by a gradual wearing down of institutional capacity, particularly at Environment Canada, through budgetary reductions.

Two events in 2011 would produce an even more fundamental shift in the federal government's approach. First, the Conservatives' achievement of a majority government in the May 2011 federal election removed the constraints imposed by minority government status. Second, the Obama administration's fall 2011 decision to delay approval of the proposed Keystone XL pipeline from Alberta to the US Gulf coast prompted major concerns on the part of the Harper government about market access for the products of expanded production from Alberta's oil sands. Oil sands expansion by then had emerged as the centrepiece of the government's overall economic strategy. The government placed a dramatic new emphasis on the need to access non-US markets and sought the removal of any obstacles to the construction of the transportation infrastructure, principally pipelines from Alberta to the British Columbia coast, in order to move bitumen to Asian markets. Under the banner of "Responsible Resource Development," described in Chapter 4, environmental assessment and approval processes were specifically targeted as such obstacles. These were seen by the government as being used by opponents of oil sands expansion to block and delay important projects.[60]

Accordingly, the government's 2012 budget implementation legislation, Bill C-38, repealed the existing Canadian Environmental Assessment Act (CEAA) and replaced it with new legislation. As laid out by Valiante in Chapter 4, the new CEAA dramatically reduced the types of projects for which environmental assessments would be required and made the application of the process to those projects to which it might apply discretionary. Even where assessments are required they will only examine a very narrow range of issues, typically where federal regulatory approvals will be required. Considerations of the need and rationale for projects; their overall environmental impacts, cumulative effects, social and economic consequences (except narrowly in relation to Aboriginal peoples), and contributions to sustainability; and the availability of alternatives were eliminated from the process. Other provisions of the revised statute were specifically designed to limit public participation in the process to those determined to have a direct "interest" in designated projects.[61] Bill C-38 made similar amendments with respect to public participation to the National Energy Board Act. These amendments resulted in the introduction of requirements that members of the public fill in a 10-page form establishing their interest in a project before even being able to file a letter of comment with the Board.[62]

Institutionally, a Major Projects Management Office, housed within Natural Resources Canada, was established in 2007 to co-ordinate and expedite federal regulatory approvals for "major resource projects." The 2012 budget incorporated major reductions (of more than 20 per cent) in the budgets and staff of Environment Canada, the Department of Fisheries and Oceans, Health Canada, and Parks Canada Agency, representing major losses in institutional capacity, particularly in relation to climate change and air quality, toxic substances, and ecosystem management. These cuts included the closure of the Experimental Lakes Area in northwestern Ontario, a unique and internationally important freshwater research facility. To date the facility has been kept open under the direction of the Winnipeg-based International Institute for Sustainable Development and through the support of the Ontario and Manitoba governments.[63] Bill C-38 also dissolved the National Round Table on the Environment and the Economy (NRTEE),[64] one of the major institutional legacies of the second modern wave of public concern for the environment. Over the 25 years of its existence, the NRTEE had undertaken research and consultations and published reports and recommendations on a wide range of major federal and national environmental policy issues, and it had come to be highly regarded for the quality of its work.[65]

A less dramatic but significant movement in the same direction has been occurring at the provincial level. Ontario's environmental assessment process, for example, has gradually been "streamlined" to focus very narrowly on the mitigation of the direct impacts of proposed projects, and to reduce opportunities for public input.[66]

Substantive Policy Instruments

While the approaches of the federal government and the provinces to the procedural and institutional dimensions of environmental policy implementation have been readily apparent, their approach to the question of the application of substantive policy instruments to the protection of public goods, like the environment, has been more complicated and subtle. The approaches at both levels have reflected governmental sensitivity to public concerns about the role of government in the protection of public safety and health, particularly in the aftermath of the contamination of water supplies in Walkerton and North Battleford and more recent events affecting public safety, such as the July 2013 Lac-Mégantic rail disaster in which 47 people were killed.

In some cases, governments have engaged in outright withdrawals of regulatory requirements related to the environment. Among the most significant examples has been the major weakening of the fish habitat protection provisions of the federal Fisheries Act through Bill C-38.[67] In a similar vein, the second 2012 budget implementation bill (C-45) repealed the Navigable Waters Protection Act. The legislation had required the approval of the federal Minister of Transport for any activity that might interfere with navigation, such as the construction of dams and bridges, and was regarded as an important mechanism for protecting the integrity of waterways.[68]

Such behaviour has not been limited to the federal level. In the spring of 2013 Ontario granted a series of outright exemptions to the province's major resource industries, including mining and forestry, from the requirements of its 2007 Endangered Species Act.[69] British Columbia has been reported to be considering major revisions to the rules regarding its Agricultural Land Reserve (ALR) to permit oil and gas and other forms of development on ALR lands. The ALR was established in 1973 to protect prime agricultural land from development.[70]

New Implementation Models

More generally, over the past two decades Canadian governments have approached the question of their substantive regulatory functions with respect to the protection of public goods like public health, safety, and the environment in a manner that has emphasized the theme of building "partnerships" with regulated entities. These approaches have reflected international trends related to the concepts of "New Public Management."[71] These principles, generally advanced under the concept of **smart regulation**,[72] are grounded in arguments that it has become impossible for governments alone to carry out the required levels of standards development, inspection, and oversight, particularly in periods of fiscal restraint, and that non-state actors, including regulated firms, need to be enlisted as "partners" in the implementation of regulatory systems. In practice in Canada, these models have taken three major forms: delegated administrative authorities; permit-by-rule systems; and self-inspection and safety management systems. Each is discussed in detail below.

Delegated Administrative Authorities

Delegated administrative authorities (DAAs) are not-for-profit corporations, usually created by statute, for the purpose of assuming the technical, safety, or economic regulatory responsibilities of a previously existing government agency in relation to a specific set of activities or sector. The boards of directors of DAAs are typically made up of representatives of the sectors whose activities they are to oversee, with some (a minority of) members appointed by government. DAAs first emerged in the early 1990s during the Ralph Klein era in Alberta, but the model was subsequently adopted in Ontario (e.g., Technical Safety and Standards Authority [TSSA] and Electrical Safety Authority) and British Columbia (e.g., BC Safety Authority). DAAs have been assigned responsibility for regulating a wide range of activities with significant health, safety, and environmental implications, including boilers and pressure vessels, and petroleum and natural gas handling and storage facilities.[73] Variations on the model have also been employed for the implementation of municipal waste diversion strategies in Ontario[74] and Alberta.[75] In Ontario, the model has been proposed repeatedly as a potential mechanism for carrying out the approval functions of the Ministry of the Environment, and most recently to carry out regulatory inspection and enforcement functions with respect to municipal waste diversion and stewardship.[76]

The DAA model has been controversial. Proponents of the model argue that it offers a more efficient mechanism for the regulatory oversight of "mature" industries.[77] Critics of the model point out that it embeds fundamental conflicts of interest in terms of the roles of the regulator and regulated sector, and that as private corporations DAAs initially escaped most of the oversight mechanisms, such as audits by auditor generals and the application of freedom of information that would normally apply to government agencies, and blurred lines of oversight, control, accountability, and responsibility.[78] The performance of DAAs as regulators has been the subject of considerable criticism as well, particularly after a major propane explosion and fire at a TSSA-regulated facility in Toronto in 2008.[79] In the aftermath of that event, the Ontario government adopted legislation significantly strengthening its oversight and control of DAAs.[80] At the same time, the province has remained an enthusiastic supporter of the model for any significant new provincial regulatory functions.[81]

Permit by Rule

A second model for the implementation of environmental regulatory systems that has been widely adopted in Canada over the past two decades is "registration" or "permit by rule." This model, too, was first adopted in Alberta during the Klein period, following approaches adopted in some US states. Under the registration model the relevant government departments and agencies no longer actively review most applications for approvals to release pollutants into the environment, nor do they handle and dispose of waste materials under the legislation they administer. Rather, proponents simply affirm their compliance with a set of required practices and procedures by "registering" with the regulating agency before proceeding with their proposed activities. Under the model, the responsibility (and cost) of assessing compliance with the relevant regulatory requirements is transferred from government officials to proponents. The model has been at the core of modernizations of the environmental and natural resource management approvals processes in Alberta,[82] Saskatchewan,[83] and Ontario.[84]

The permit-by-rule model has been subject to considerable criticism from environmental non-governmental organizations (ENGOs). The loss of proactive assessment of potentially harmful activities, the inability of the process to address the cumulative effects of these activities, and the loss of opportunities for the public to comment on proposals before they are approved and to appeal the resulting decisions have been important points of concern.[85]

Self-Inspection/Management Systems

While DAAs and registration systems have dominated provincial efforts in the "reform" of their environmental regulatory systems over the past two decades, the federal government has taken a different approach. In situations where the federal government is the front-line safety regulator, as is the case with foods, drugs, and rail, air, and marine transportation, it has adopted a model of "safety management systems."[86] Under this model, regulated entities are required to develop their own strategies for protecting public safety and health in their operations and products. These strategies are then subject to approval by the relevant federal regulator. Once the plans are approved, the federal government largely relies on the regulated firms to conduct internal inspections of their own operations for compliance with their approved plans. Federal regulatory oversight and inspection are then focused on reports generated by these internal processes rather than on the actual observation of the regulated firms' activities in the field.[87] Many provincial natural resources agencies have adopted similar models related to forestry and other resources.[88]

The model has been the subject of extensive criticism from public safety advocates,[89] organized labour[90] in the affected sectors, and the Auditor General of Canada. These criticisms have emphasized numerous shortcomings in this approach:

- the loss of first-hand knowledge of operational practices on the part of federal regulators;
- reliance on the regulated firms to establish appropriate levels of safety and risk;[91]
- reliance on firms to conduct inspections and report on their own compliance to regulators;
- the lack of transparency with respect to the safety management plans that are developed;[92]
- the lack of adequate oversight capacity on the part of federal regulators;[93]
- poor monitoring of outcomes;[94]
- failures on the part of the regulatory agencies to adequately train their own staff on implementation of the new systems or to identify companies and facilities where risks of problems are high.[95]

These criticisms have been heightened by a number of significant incidents where such systems have been in place, including the Maple Leaf Foods listeria contamination incident in 2008 that resulted in 23 deaths,[96] the XL Foods meat contamination episode that led to a massive meat recall in 2012,[97] and the Lac-Mégantic rail disaster in July 2013 (see Box 5.2).

BOX 5.2 | The Lac-Mégantic Rail Disaster

In the early hours of 6 July 2013 an unattended train of 73 carloads of crude oil from the Bakken shale formation in North Dakota ran away and then derailed, exploded, and burned in the heart of the small Quebec town of Lac-Mégantic, killing 47 people. The disaster stands as the deadliest rail accident in Canada in the past century. The tragedy has focused attention on consequences of the development of "unconventional" fossil fuel sources, such as the Bakken shale deposits and Canada's oil sands, at a pace that has far outstripped the capacity of regulatory agencies on both sides of the Canada–US border to protect public safety, health, and the environment. The disaster also raised serious questions about Transport Canada's "safety management system" approach to overseeing the movement of dangerous goods on Canada's railway systems and about the federal government's reliance on these types of industry self-regulatory models. Several years earlier, as Mike McBane of the Canadian Health Coalition said, in referring to **self-regulatory models**: "We've replaced a culture of safety with a culture of risk. We've replaced proactive regulation with industrial self-regulation. We've replaced active inspections with paper inspections."[98]

Conclusions

Implementation models in Canadian environmental policy have shifted significantly over the past 40 years, with major periods of innovation coinciding with high levels of public concern for the environment. The period following the 2008 economic downturn and federal election has been one of profound retrenchment, particularly at the federal level. In the context of an overriding emphasis on resource extraction and export, the focus of institutional innovation shifted to mechanisms to facilitate those directions, such as the establishment of the Major Projects Management Office, and on the elimination of those institutions, such as the NRTEE, which were potential sources of criticism of such a course. The policy and operational capacity of federal environmental agencies has been significantly eroded through substantial budgetary reductions. Procedural mechanisms are now being employed to establish barriers to public participation in decision-making rather than to facilitate it, and the application and scope of environmental assessment processes have been radically narrowed.

The long-term impact of these procedural and institutional strategies is unknown. However, they may carry with them the possibility of creating at least as many problems for project proponents as they solve. The changes to environmental assessment and the curtailment of opportunities for public participation have a strong potential to undermine the legitimacy of decision-making processes and, therefore, public acceptance of their outcomes. Such results can lead to additional political conflict, which can produce further delays or even block project approvals. The saga of the Northern Gateway pipeline project to transport bitumen from Alberta to Kitimat, BC,[99] recent events regarding the Line 9 pipeline proposal in Ontario[100] and shale gas development in New Brunswick,[101] and the Idle No More movement all speak to these possibilities. The loss of institutional capacity increases the risk for governments of being blindsided by emerging issues and of being unable to formulate effective or credible responses. More importantly, the loss of capacity weakens governments' ability to identify and address emerging problems before they become crises or disasters. Such an outcome implies significantly increased risks for the health, safety, and environment of Canadians.

Although law and regulation have remained the tools of choice where governments have felt compelled to demonstrate a willingness to act on environmental matters, outright withdrawals from substantive regulation, particularly where it is seen to be a barrier to resource development, have become common at the federal and provincial levels. More broadly, so-called "smart" regulatory models, such as delegated administrative authorities, permit-by-rule systems, and safety management systems, which emphasize "partnerships" with regulated firms, have become increasingly prevalent over the past two decades. Again, the long-term consequences of these directions are uncertain. Recent high-profile failures and disasters, such as the Lac-Mégantic tragedy, that involve facilities and activities regulated under these models have raised serious questions about their effectiveness. The result may lead to demands for a more active re-engagement by Canadian governments in implementing regulatory regimes to protect public goods, including the environment. So far, however, the responses have reflected the minimum level of intervention needed to deflect criticism, as opposed to any fundamental change in direction with respect to the protection of the environment and public safety.

Key Terms

carbon taxes

duty to consult

ecological fiscal reform

feed-in tariffs (FITs)

free riding

pollutant release and transfer registry

polluter pays principle

regulatory management systems

self-regulatory models

smart regulation

Questions for Review

1. Define substantive, procedural, and institutional policy instruments and give examples of each.
2. Why have Canadian governments been reluctant to employ combinations of policy instruments in the way seen in some US states and in the European Union?
3. Are other provinces likely to follow BC's model of adopting a carbon tax?
4. What will be the impact of the Bill C-38 changes to the Canadian Environmental Assessment Act and National Energy Board Act on public acceptance of resource development decisions?
5. Why have governments moved towards "smart" regulatory implementation models? Will these models improve protection of public health, safety, and the environment or put these things at greater risk?

Internet Resources

Canadian Environmental Law Association
http://www.cela.ca

EcoJustice
http://www.ecojustice.ca

Environmental Commissioner of Ontario
http://www.eco.on.ca

Commissioner for the Environment and
Sustainable Development
http://www.oag-bvg.gc.ca/internet/English/
cesd_fs_e_921.html

Environment Canada
http://www.ec.gc.ca

Ontario Ministry of the Environment and
Climate Change
http://www.ontario.ca/ministry-environment-
and-climate-change

Pembina Institute
http://www.pembina.org

Additional Reading

Benidickson, J. *Environmental Law*. Toronto: Irwin Law, 2009.

Commissioner for Environment and Sustainable Development. *Annual Report*. Various years.

Environmental Commissioner of Ontario. *Annual Report*. Various years.

Hessing, M., M. Howlett, and T. Summerville. *Canadian Natural Resource and Environmental Policy: Political Economy and Public Policy*. Vancouver: University of British Columbia Press, 2005.

Howlett, M., M. Ramesh, and A. Perl. *Studying Public Policy: Policy Cycles and Public Subsystems*, 3rd edn. Toronto: Oxford University Press, 2010.

Macdonald, D. *Business and Environmental Politics in Canada*. Peterborough, Ont.: Broadview Press, 2007.

Muldoon, P., A. Lucas, R. B. Gibson, and P. Pickfield. *An Introduction to Environmental Law and Policy in Canada*. Toronto: Emond Montgomery, 2009.

Pal, L. *Beyond Policy Analysis*, 5th edn. Toronto: Nelson, 2014.

Winfield, M. *Blue-Green Province: The Environment and Political Economy of Ontario*. Vancouver: University of British Columbia Press, 2012.

Notes

1. On the "policy cycle" concept, see M. Hessing, M. Howlett, and T. Summerville, *Canadian Natural Resource and Environmental Policy: Political Economy and Public Policy*, 2nd edn (Vancouver: University of British Columbia Press, 2005), 102–34.

2. On the concepts of substantive and procedural instruments, see M. Howlett, "Policy Instruments and Implementation Styles: The Evolution of Instrument Choice in Canadian Environmental Policy," in D.L. VanNijnatten and R. Boardman, eds, *Canadian Environmental Policy: Context and Cases*, 2nd edn (Toronto: Oxford University Press, 2002), 26–7.

3. See, e.g., the Ontario Environmental Protection Act, R.S.O. 1990, Chapter E-19, s. 14.

4. Ibid, s. 9.

5. Canadian Environmental Protection Act, 1999, (1999 c-33) ss. 272–4.

6. See, e.g., K. Webb, "Between Rocks and Hard Places: Bureaucrats, the Law and Pollution Control," in R. Paehlke and D. Torgeson, eds, *Managing Leviathan* (Peterborough, Ont.: Broadview Press, 1990), 201–28. More recently, see Commissioner for Environment and Sustainable Development *2011 December Report* (Ottawa: Minister of Supply and Services, 2011), ch. 3, "Enforcing the Canadian Environmental Protection Act, 1999," accessed 22 Nov. 2013, http://www.oag-bvg.gc.ca/internet/English/parl_cesd_201112_03_e_36031.html.

7. Environment Canada, "Acid Rain: What's Being Done, What Has Canada Done?" accessed 12 Oct. 2006, http://www.ec.gc.ca/acidrain/done-canada.html. Although the program's emission reduction goals were achieved, it subsequently became apparent that further emission reductions would be necessary to halt the environmental and health impacts of acid rain.

8. National Water Research Institute, *National Assessment of Pulp and Paper Environmental Effects Monitoring Data* (Ottawa: Environment Canada, 2003).

9. See, e.g., Organisation for Economic Co-operation and Development, *Economic Instruments for Environmental Protection* (Paris: OECD, 1989).

10. On the Swedish initiative, see Runar Brännlund, "Green Tax Reforms: Some Experiences from Sweden," in Kai Schlegelmilch, ed., *Green Budget Reform in Europe: Countries at the Forefront* (New York: Springer, 1999), 67–91.

11. See D. Jacob, *Renewable Energy Policy Convergence in the EU* (Burlington, Vermont: Ashgate, 2012).

12. On the Ontario program, see L.C. Stokes, "The Politics of Renewable Energy Policies: The Case of Feed-in Tariffs in Ontario, Canada," *Energy Policy* 56 (2013): 490–500.

13. *The Great Lakes Water Quality Agreement: Promises to Keep; Challenges to Meet* (Toronto: Alliance for the Great Lakes, Biodiversity Project, Canadian Environmental Law Association, and Great Lakes United, Dec. 2006), accessed 27 Nov. 2013, http://cela.ca/uploads/f8e04c51a8e04041f6f7faa046b03a7c/553GLWQA_promises.pdf.

14. K. Harrison, *Passing the Buck: Federalism and Canadian Environmental Policy* (Vancouver: University of British Columbia Press, 1996), 103.

15. For an overview of the EFR concept, see Frédéric Beauregard-Tellier, *Ecological Fiscal Reform* (Ottawa: Library of Parliament, 2006).

16. See BC Ministry of Finance, "Carbon Tax Review, and Carbon Tax Overview," accessed 27 Nov. 2013, http://www.fin.gov.bc.ca/tbs/tp/climate/carbon_tax.htm.

17. *The Green Shift* (Ottawa: Liberal Party of Canada, June 2008).

18. Ontario Ministry of the Environment, *Greenhouse Gas Emission Reductions in Ontario: A Discussion Paper* (Toronto: Queen's Printer for Ontario, 2013).

19. See, e.g., "The Regulation of Sulphur Dioxide," in G. Bruce Doern, ed., *Getting It Green: Case Studies in Canadian Environmental Regulation* (Toronto: C.D. Howe Institute, 1990), 129–54.

20. See, e.g., C. Carlson, D. Burtaw, M. Cropper, and K. Palmer, *Sulphur Dioxide Control by Electric Utilities: What Are the Gains from Trade?* (Washington: Resources for the Future, 2000), accessed 28 Nov. 2013, http://www.rff.org/Documents/RFF-DP-98-44-REV.pdf.

21. "Carbon trading: ETS, RIP?" *The Economist*, 20 Apr. 2013.

22. On the evolution of federal policy regarding large final emitters of GHGs up to 2009, see D. Macdonald, "The Failure of Canadian Climate Change Policy," in D. VanNijnatten and R. Boardman, eds, *Canadian Environmental Policy: Prospects for Leadership and Innovation* (Toronto: Oxford University Press, 2009), 152–66.

23. *Reduction of Carbon Dioxide Emissions from Coal-fired Generation of Electricity Regulations*, SOR/2012-167, 30 Aug. 2012.

24. US Environmental Protection Agency, "Toxics Release Inventory (TRI) Program," http://www.epa.gov/tri/.

25. See M.Winfield, "North American Pollutant Release and Transfer Registries," in D.L. Markell and J.H. Knox, eds, *Greening NAFTA: The North American Commission for Environmental Cooperation* (Stanford, Calif.: Stanford University Press, 2003), 38–56.

26. Environment Canada, "National Pollutant Release Inventory," accessed 27 Nov. 2013, http://www.ec.gc.ca/pdb/npri/npri_home_e.cfm

27. Recyclable metals and plastics (blue box), paper and paper products (grey box), household organics (green bin), leaf and yard wastes, household hazardous wastes, residual wastes, and in some households, disposable diapers.

28. City of Toronto, "Residential Diversion Rate," accessed 11 Nov. 2013, http://www.toronto.ca/garbage/residential-diversion.htm.

29. M. Bramley, *The Case for Kyoto: The Failure of Voluntary Corporate Action* (Edmonton: Pembina Institute and the David Suzuki Foundation, 2002); Review Branch, Environment Canada, *Evaluation of the ARET Initiative* (Ottawa: Environment Canada, 2000); Ontario Medical Association, *The Health Effects of Ground Level Ozone* (Toronto: Ontario Medical Association, 1998).

30. See the conclusions of the resulting public inquiries: D. O'Connor, *Report of the Walkerton Inquiry: Part 1* (Toronto: Queen's Printer for Ontario, 2002); R. Laing, *Report of the Commission of Inquiry into Matters Relating to the Safety of Drinking Water in North Battleford, Saskatchewan* (Regina: Queen's Printer for Saskatchewan, 2002).

31. See, generally, D. Macdonald, *Business and Environmental Politics in Canada* (Peterborough, Ont.: Broadview Press, 2007).

32. Harrison, *Passing the Buck*, 103.

33. A.H. Rosenfeld, Commissioner, California Energy Commission, "Energy Efficiency for California, the US, the World: No. 1 in the California 'Loading Order'," presentation to the Manatt Forum, 28 Sept. 2007, accessed 24 Oct. 2007, http://www.energy.ca.gov/papers/index.html.

34. See M. Winfield, "An Unimaginative People? Instrument Choice in Canadian Environmental Law and Policy," 2007 Saskatchewan Law Review Lecture, *Saskatchewan Law Review* 71, 1 (2008).

35. See A.J. Sinclair and M. Doelle, "Environmental Assessment in Canada: Encouraging Decisions for Sustainability," in B. Mitchell, ed., *Resource and Environmental Management in Canada*, 4th edn (Toronto: Oxford University Press, 2010), 462–94; J. Benidickson, *Environmental Law* (Toronto: Irwin Law, 2009), 249–71.

36. K.M. Lambrecht, *Aboriginal Consultation, Environmental Assessment, and Regulatory Review in Canada* (Regina: University of Regina Press, 2013).

37. Environmental Commissioner of Ontario, *Ontario's Environmental Bill of Rights and You* (Toronto: ECO, n.d.).

38. On the early development of environmental agencies in Canada, see M. Winfield, *Blue-Green Province: The Environment and Political Economy of Ontario* (Vancouver: University of British Columbia Press, 2012), ch. 2; G. Bruce Doern and T. Conway, *The Greening of Canada: Federal Institutions and Decisions* (Toronto: University of Toronto Press, 1995); D. Macdonald, *The Politics of Pollution: Why Canadians Are Failing Their Environment* (Toronto: McClelland & Stewart, 1991).

39. Commissioner of the Environment and Sustainable Development, http://www.oag-bvg.gc.ca/internet/English/cesd_fs_e_921.html.

40. Environmental Commissioner of Ontario, http://www.eco.on.ca/.

41. See S. Boutros, "A Child of Brundtland: The Institutional Evolution of the National Round Table on Environment and Economy," in G. Toner and J. Meadowcroft, eds, *Innovation, Science and Environment: Charting Sustainable Development in Canada 1987–2007* (Montreal and Kingston: McGill-Queen's University Press, 2009).

42. International Institute for Sustainable Development, www.iisd.org.

43. See D. Macdonald, "Coerciveness and the Selection of Environmental Policy Instruments," *Canadian Public Administration* 44, 2: 161–87.

44. Howlett, "Policy Instruments and Implementation Styles," 28–9.

45. See, generally, James Q. Wilson, *The Politics of Regulation* (New York: Basic Books, 1980).

46. Organisation for Economic Co-operation and Development, *The Polluter Pays Principle* (Paris: OCED, 1975).

47. See K. Harrison, "Voluntarism and Environmental Governance," in E.A. Parson, ed., *Governing the Environment* (Toronto: University of Toronto Press, 2001), 207–46.

48. See, e.g., A. Kranjc, "Wither Ontario's Environment: Neo-Conservatism and the Decline of the Ministry of the Environment," *Canadian Public Policy* (Jan. 2000). See also D. Eberts, "Globalization and Neo-Conservatism: Implications for Resource and Environmental Management," in B. Mitchell, ed., *Resource and Environmental Management in Canada* (Toronto: Oxford University Press, 2004), 54–79.

49. Most recently, Government of Canada, *Cabinet Directive of Regulatory Streamlining* (Ottawa: Treasury Board Secretariat, 2012).

50. See, e.g., *Government of Ontario Regulatory Policy* (Toronto: Ministry of Economic Development and Trade, 2010)

51. See, e.g., National Round Table on the Environment and Economy, *Getting to 2050: Canada's Transition to a Low Carbon Economy* (Ottawa: NRTEE, 2007).

52. P. Wells, *The Longer I'm Prime Minister: Stephen Harper and Canada 2006–* (Toronto: Random House, 2013), 395.

53. Eberts, "Globalization and Neo-Conservatism."

54. N. Bernasconi-Osterwalder, "The Draft Investment Chapter of the Canada–EU Comprehensive Economic and Trade Agreement: A Step Backwards for the EU and Canada?" (Winnipeg: IISD, 2013), accessed 19 Nov. 2013, http://www.iisd.org/itn/2013/06/26/the-draft-investment-chapter-of-canada-eu-comprehensive-economic-and-trade-agreement-a-step-backwards-for-the-eu-and-canada/.

55. See, generally, Harrison, *Passing the Buck*. See also M. Winfield and D. Macdonald, "Federalism and Canadian Climate Change Policy," in G. Skogstad and H. Bakvis, eds, *Canadian Federalism: Performance, Effectiveness and Legitimacy*, 3rd edn (Toronto: Oxford University Press, 2012), 241–60.

56. In a 2002 Canadian Alliance Party fundraising letter, Harper described the Kyoto Protocol as "essentially a socialist scheme to suck money out of wealth-producing nations." Quote from CBC News, "Harper's

Letter Dismisses Kyoto as 'Socialist Scheme'," 30 June 2007, accessed 19 Nov. 2013, http://www.cbc.ca/news/canada/harper-s-letter-dismisses-kyoto-as-socialist-scheme-1.69316.

57. See L. Martin, *Harperland: The Politics of Control* (Toronto: Viking, 2010), 72–90.

58. Winfield and Macdonald, "Federalism and Canadian Climate Change Policy."

59. On the revisions to federal environmental assessment during the Harper period, see M. Winfield, "The Environment, 'Responsible Resource Development' and Evidence-Based Policy-Making in Canada," in Shaun Young, ed., *Evidence Based Policy-Making in Canada* (Toronto: Oxford University Press, 2013).

60. "An open letter from the Honourable Joe Oliver, Minister of Natural Resources, on Canada's commitment to diversify our energy markets and the need to further streamline the regulatory process in order to advance Canada's national economic interest," 9 Jan. 2012, www.nrcan.gc.ca/media-room/news-release/2012/1/1909.

61. For a summary of CEAA 2012, see M. Doelle, "CEAA 2012: The End of the Road for Federal EA in Canada?" *Journal of Environmental Law and Practice* 25 (2012).

62. G. Galloway, "Energy Board Changes Pipeline Complaint Rules," 5 Apr. 2013.

63. For an overview of these reductions and their impact, see Winfield, "The Environment, 'Responsible Resource Development' and Evidence Based Policy-Making."

64. The provincial round tables were dissolved in the early 1990s.

65. J. Simpson, "Ottawa Kills the Emissions Messenger," *Globe and Mail*, 20 June 2012.

66. See Environmental Commissioner of Ontario, *2007/08 Annual Report: Getting to K(no)w* (Toronto: ECO, 2008).

67. See EcoJustice, "Legal Backgrounder: Fisheries Act," Feb. 2013, accessed 19 Nov. 2013, https://www.ecojustice.ca/files/fisheries-act.

68. EcoJustice, "Legal Backgrounder: Bill C-45 and the *Navigable Waters Protection Act* (RSC 1985, C N-22)," accessed 19 Nov. 2013, http://www.ecojustice.ca/files/nwpa_legal_backgrounder_october-2012/.

69. See Environmental Commissioner of Ontario, *Laying Siege to the Last Line of Defence: A Review of Ontario's Weakened Protection for Species at Risk* (Toronto: ECO, 2013).

70. M. Hume, "B.C. Government Documents Summarize Proposal to Dismantle Agricultural Land Commission," *Globe and Mail*, 7 Nov. 2013.

71. See L. Pal, "The New Public Management in Canada," in Pal, *Beyond Policy Analysis* (Toronto: Nelson, 2006), 202–36. See also L. Pal, *Beyond Policy Analysis*, 5th edn (Toronto: Nelson, 2014), 195–204.

72. See N. Gunningham and D. Sinclair, *Designing Smart Regulation* (Paris: OECD, 1998), http://www.oecd.org/env/outreach/33947759.pdf.

73. On the development of DAAs in Canada, see M. Winfield, D. Whorley, and S. Kaufman, "Public Safety in Private Hands: A Study of Ontario's Technical Standards and Safety Authority," *Canadian Public Administration* 45, 1 (2002): 24–51.

74. See Stewardship Ontario, www.stewardshipontario.ca.

75. The Alberta Beverage Container Management Board and the Alberta Recycling Management Authority.

76. See Bill 91, Waste Reduction Act, 2013, First Reading, 6 June 2013.

77. See, e.g., Commission on Reform of Ontario Public Services, *Report* (Toronto: Ministry of Finance, 2012), ch. 16, "Operating and Back-Office Operations," http://www.fin.gov.on.ca/en/reformcommission/.

78. See Canadian Environmental Law Association, "Re: Proposal to Transfer Inspection and Enforcement Powers to the Waste Reduction Authority under Bill 91," 25 Sept. 2013, http://www.cela.ca/sites/cela.ca/files/953Bill91.pdf. See also Ombudsman Ontario, *Submission to the Standing Committee on Finance and Economic Affairs Relating to Bill 55, the Strong Action for Ontario Act (Budget Measures), June 11, 2012* (Toronto: Ombudsman Ontario, 2012).

79. See Auditor General of Ontario, *2009 Annual Report*, ch. 3, Section 3.03, "Consumer Protection," accessed 19 Nov. 2013, http://www.auditor.on.ca/en/reports_en/en09/303en09.pdf. See also *2003 Annual Report, Ministry of Consumer and Commercial Relations*, Section 3.04, "Policy and Consumer Protection Services Division," and *2011 Annual Report. Ministry of Consumer Services*, Section 4.03, "Consumer Protection."

80. Delegated Administrative Authorities Act, 2012 S.O. 2012, ch. 8.

81. Ontario Ministry of Finance, *2012 Ontario Budget*, ch. 1, "Delegated Administrative Authorities," accessed 22 Nov. 2013, http://www.fin.gov.on.ca/en/budget/ontariobudgets/2012/ch1.html#c1_delegatedAA.

82. Alberta Environment and Sustainable Resource Development, "EPEA Registration Process," accessed 19 Nov. 2013, http://environment.alberta.ca/02244.html.

83. Saskatchewan Ministry of the Environment, "Saskatchewan Environmental Code," accessed 19 Nov. 2013, http://www.environment.gov.sk.ca/Code.

84. Ontario Ministry of the Environment, *Modernization of Approvals*. Toronto, Feb. 2010.

85. R. Nadarajah, M. Carter-Witney, and E. Macdonald, *Modernizing Environmental Approvals: EBR Registry No 010-9143* (Toronto: Canadian Environmental Law Association, Canadian Institute for Environmental Law and Policy and Ecojustice.ca, Apr. 2010).

86. Hazard Analysis and Critical Control Point (HACCP) systems employed in the food industry are similar in concept.

87. Auditor General of Canada, *Report of the Auditor General of Canada to the House of Commons: Spring*

2012 (Ottawa: Ministry of Supply and Services, 2012), ch. 5, "Oversight of Civil Aviation," Transport Canada exhibit 5.3.

88. M. Winfield, "Alternative Service Delivery in the Natural Resources Sector: An Examination of Ontario's Forestry Compliance Self-Inspection System," *Canadian Public Administration* 48, 4 (2005): 552–74.

89. CTV.ca, "Deregulation a Disaster for Rail Safety: Report," 29 May 2007, regarding Canada Safety Council report on rail safety.

90. M. McBane, *Ill-Health Canada Putting Food and Drug Company Profits Ahead of Safety* (Ottawa: Canadian Health Coalition, 2004).

91. B. Campbell, *The Lac-Megantic Disaster: Where Does the Buck Stop?* (Ottawa: Canadian Centre for Policy Alternatives, 2013).

92. W. Gillis, "Railway Safety Plans Kept Secret," *Toronto Star*, 5 Nov. 2012.

93. M. DeSousa, "Watchdogs Contradict Transport Canada Safety Oversight Claims Following Lac-Megantic Disaster," *PostMedia*, 12 July 2013, http://www.canada.com/news/Auditor+General+denies+giving+Transport+Canada+extensions+safety+oversight+commitments/8645940/story.html.

94. R.A. Holley, "Smarter Inspection Will Improve Food Safety in Canada," *Canadian Medical Association Journal* 182, 5 (2010): 471–3

95. Auditor General of Canada, *Spring 2012 Report*, "Oversight of Civil Aviation." See also Auditor General of Canada, *Fall 2013 Report*, ch. 13, "Oversight of Rail Safety—Transport Canada," accessed 27 Nov. 2013, http://www.oag-bvg.gc.ca/internet/English/parl_oag_201311_07_e_38801.html.

96. B. Curry and B. Fenlon, "Conservatives' Pro-Industry Approach Compromises Food Safety, Dion Says," *Globe and Mail*, 22 Aug. 2008.

97. B. Curry, "XL Foods Recall Was Product of Preventable Errors, Review Finds," *Globe and Mail*, 5 June 2013.

98. M. McBane, quoted in *Globe and Mail*, 25 Jan. 2010.

99. N. Vanderclippe, "How Enbridge's Northern Gateway Pipeline Lost Its Way," *Globe and Mail*, 10 Aug. 2013.

100. J. McDiarmid, "Enbridge Pipeline: Protesters Converge on Line 9B Hearings," *Toronto Star*, 18 Oct. 2013.

101. K. Bissett, "N.B. Shale-Gas Fight Will Go On, Elsipogtog Chief Vows Despite Ruling," *Globe and Mail*, 18 Nov. 2013.

6 Science and Canadian Environmental Policy

Stephen Bocking

Chapter Summary

Science plays essential roles in environmental governance, anticipating, managing, and solving environmental issues and conflicts. However, the application of science in environmental policy-making involves numerous challenges, especially in the context of recent restrictions imposed by the federal government on its practice and communication. The diversity of environmental science today, as practised in universities, governments, industry, and civil society, can be understood in terms of four models of science: basic research, regulatory science, advocacy science, and innovation science. Each model has distinctive purposes, institutions, and governance arrangements. Together they demonstrate the need for a diversity of approaches to policy-relevant science. However, in recent years federal policy changes have resulted in an imbalance in national scientific activity, including inadequate support for regulatory science. Effective science requires better communication and ensuring scientific credibility, relevance, and legitimacy. It also requires support for all four models of research, as well as attention to research needs that span these models. A new model of modest science, with appropriate institutions, can meet these requirements.

Chapter Outline

- The role of science in environmental policy
  - Surveying environmental science
- Four models of science
  - Basic research, regulatory science, activist science, and innovation science
  - The unmet challenge of science in environmental governance
- Science and environmental leadership
  - The requirements: credibility, relevance, and legitimacy
  - A new model: modest science

The Role of Science in Environmental Policy

While transforming their environment over the last century, Canadians also created a complex and contested terrain for science and governance. Consider a few examples. On the Pacific coast, salmon are raised in pens for market. Some see this industry as environmentally sustainable and economically essential; others consider it a threat to wild salmon, commercial and sport fisheries, and coastal cultural identity. Both sides invoke scientific arguments to support their claims. On the Prairies, computer models forecast drought as climate change takes hold and oil sands plants and irrigated agriculture demand more water—exemplifying how scientific knowledge adds larger meaning to everyday observations, like those of shrinking glaciers in the Rocky Mountains. And in laboratories and industrial facilities across the country, products are being developed that incorporate nanotechnologies: coatings, powders, and structures that promise novel benefits, as well as health and environmental risks both unknown and largely unexamined by scientists.

As these instances illustrate, science plays essential roles in environmental governance, shaping how we understand, argue over, and protect or exploit our environment. Regulatory agencies frame their objectives in terms defined by science, with contaminants measured in the parts per billion and the status of endangered species evaluated in terms of population size and habitat condition. Industries hire scientists to assess impacts, defend their interests, and develop "green" technologies. Activist groups assemble scientific information to strengthen their arguments. All of these activities build on research accomplished by scientists in universities, government laboratories, and other institutions, in Canada and elsewhere.

But these examples also exemplify the challenges encountered in applying science to environmental leadership. Debates about the science of salmon farming have often hindered formation of a shared vision for the future of coastal communities and ecosystems. The implications of water scarcity in Alberta have been obscured by scraps over energy and provincial autonomy. Research into **nanotechnology** products attracts heavy investment, but study of their consequences is almost ignored.

The status and roles of science have long been fiercely contested, contradicting the notion of scientific knowledge as merely the objective, rational foundation of wise policy. In recent years, the federal government's actions relating to science and the environment have also generated controversy. These have included cutbacks to research funding; closing of or withdrawal of funding for laboratories (including some with distinguished records in policy-relevant science, such as the Experimental Lakes Area); muzzling of government scientists; abolition of the post of National Science Advisor and the National Round Table for the Environment and Economy; weakening of environmental laws, including the Fisheries Act (for over a century the foundation for aquatic environmental protection); and a continuing failure to respond to the scientific consensus on climate change.[1] These actions have generated heavy criticism within Canada and internationally.

Effective environmental policy relies on science for several essential functions. Science anticipates emerging environmental problems such as climate change. It contributes to new environmental policy (for example, the designation of **ecological integrity** as the basis for national parks management). It guides the management of environmental resources, such as forests and fish, by evaluating the impacts of harvesting and the state of the resource. And finally, it provides a basis for adjudicating conflicting uses or values regarding the environment.

Fulfilling these functions requires, at least, steady funding, an openness to new information, and avoidance of undue interference in research and its communication. But leadership must go beyond these minimal requirements. Scholars have identified a variety of other obstacles to effective science in policy contexts, including competing interpretations of scientific information, failures to weigh scientific evidence in relation to economic or political imperatives, and an absence of necessary research on environmental hazards. Their analyses have also generated insights into the challenge of connecting knowledge to visions of natural and social well-being. As a result, various practical efforts aimed at ensuring science can play effective roles in governance are underway. These approaches are grounded in awareness that environmental leadership demands knowledge that is scientifically sound, practically relevant, credible to all parties, and politically legitimate. Producing such knowledge, in turn, depends on a new model of scientific practice and application, as well as a commitment to diverse strategies for generating knowledge.

Surveying Environmental Science

Environmental knowledge today comes from many sources: federal and provincial agencies, universities, industry, environmental organizations, and citizens. This knowledge is produced for a similarly wide range of purposes, such as managing resources, improving scientific theory, meeting regulatory requirements, and understanding local environmental concerns. The consequences of this pluralistic research landscape include the use of a broad range of forms of knowledge in policy-making, debates over contrasting scientific interpretations, and a questioning of the assumptions that underpin the practices, objectives, and application of science. Science thus plays roles in governance that are nothing like the ideal often invoked of a rational process in which scientists are kept separate from politics, simply determining the neutral facts regarding an environmental problem, which are then matched with an optimal solution by policy-makers. Instead, science is deeply implicated in politics. This political character must be considered in determining how science can play effective roles in policy. Ethical and political possibilities and preferences are implicated in the practice of science itself—in scientists' choices of research methods, scales of inquiry, standards of proof, and strategies for managing uncertainties. Far from being neutral arbitrators, scientific knowledge and the practice of science itself embody particular ideas about nature and human conduct, with consequences that may or may not be benign for local communities or ecosystems.[2]

This entanglement of science and politics is evident not just in science, but in the relation between science and broader political priorities.[3] For example, while a chief goal of Canadian federal and provincial science policy is to encourage the development and commercialization of innovative environmental technologies, achieving these goals depends as much, if not more, on effective environmental regulation—which creates a demand for these technologies—as on specific policies for guiding scientific activities.[4] Similarly, shifts in the focus of scientific research often depend on changes in policy. Thus, while Natural Resources Canada laboratories in recent years have begun to examine the environmental dimensions of resource extraction, their continuing focus on oil sands and other developments of questionable environmental rationality reflects the larger departmental mandate of service to the resource industry.[5] Political and economic preferences also have wider implications for science. How the goals of environmental policy are defined in terms of human health, intact ecosystems, or sustainable resource use determines what forms of expertise are considered most relevant. Aspects of governance—the relative roles of government and the market, and the importance of public versus private goods—also help determine how science will be structured and applied.

These implications become especially evident in debates over the definition of an issue as a matter of science or of politics. It is often argued that environmental decisions should be based on **sound science**, as an objective, rational alternative to political considerations. Yet this argument has political implications: it suggests that action must wait until scientific standards of proof have been satisfied. This is why those urging deregulation have often invoked the need to base decisions on science. It also accords an advantage in environmental debates to those with the most scientific (and often, economic) resources, disadvantaging communities and individuals, particularly Indigenous peoples. And finally, defining a contested issue as a matter of science tends to distract attention from the political preferences or economic structures that may be at the root of environmental problems. Such has been the case in natural resource management, where a commitment to science-based decisions has long reinforced a preference for the industrial transformation of nature. In practice, therefore, insistence on the need for "sound science" may be less about rational policy than about favouring more powerful interests.

Over the last several decades, the complex relations between science and politics have been especially evident in international affairs. Canada's contribution and vulnerability to climate change and long-range transport of contaminants, Canadian scientists' leadership in understanding these phenomena, and the application of knowledge from elsewhere to domestic environmental issues all exemplify the porous nature of national borders, at least where environmental science is concerned. This international dimension is also evident in continental and global trade agreements, where standards of evidence based on "sound science" frame disputes over barriers to trade.[6]

Four Models of Science

But how can we move beyond the notion of "sound science" and construct a more useful perspective on the place of science in environmental governance?[7] One such perspective might be framed in terms of various "models" of science, that is, sets of ideas that guide the relation between science and governance. Through these models, it is possible to understand the diversity of ways in which science relates to environmental governance, their shortcomings, and the assumptions about society and nature embedded in the ideas and practice of science.[8]

Basic Research

For several decades basic research has been closely associated with universities and (until recent cutbacks and closures) federal laboratories. In this model, scientific disciplines define scientists' agendas, with research problems framed in terms of those considered most interesting within the discipline, as well as in terms of strategic areas set by the Natural Sciences and Engineering Research Council (NSERC) or by policy-oriented programs such as the Canadian Foundation for Climate and Atmospheric Sciences (closed by the federal government in 2012). Underlying this model is the view that useful knowledge can be best obtained through research directed by scientists themselves. Such research has often generated highly useful knowledge, regarding, for example, the mechanisms of long-range transport of contaminants and the role of CFCs (chlorofluorocarbons) in damaging the stratospheric ozone layer. These and other episodes illustrate how the contribution of research to governance can often be unexpected, with the scientific community building intellectual capital to be drawn on when attention becomes focused on an emerging crisis.

Yet basic research alone cannot fulfill all the roles of science in environmental governance. It tends to neglect environmental challenges that lack theoretical significance or require long-term monitoring or other practices of less interest to scientists. The disciplinary structure of science can also impose a limited vision. For example, Canadian atmospheric scientists, most trained in physical meteorology, were slow to identify the changes in atmospheric chemistry that were eventually recognized as acid rain. Such episodes also illustrate how interdisciplinary research is essential; however, the departmental structure of many universities presents obstacles to such work (although interdisciplinary programs in environmental science are now growing rapidly).

Regulatory Science

Environmental administration has an insatiable appetite for knowledge, generating research activities known as regulatory science. This research encompasses everything from estimating tree growth as part of a forest harvesting regime to studying the toxicity of contaminants in order to set water quality standards. Regulatory science is one of the largest components of environmental research in Canada. For example, historically Environment Canada's science budget has emphasized "related scientific activities"—a category that encompasses regulatory science. These activities, while essential, often attract little attention. Environmental monitoring by the Water Survey of Canada is a case in point. Long-term knowledge of water quality and quantity is an essential public good, yet it is collected almost entirely outside the public eye, and with modest funding.[9] Regulatory research is conducted within federal and provincial agencies, and by university faculties of applied science. Industry, including consulting firms, is also a major player, in part in response to regulatory requirements, but also because federal policy encourages the private sector to contribute to funding research. Collectively, these activities fulfill their role by transforming knowledge into distinct arenas of professional practice, imparting the authority of expertise to decisions made by administrative agencies and regulated industries.

Recent cutbacks in federal environmental research have diminished national capabilities in regulatory science. These cuts have been substantial: as of 2013, nearly $600 million had been cut from the budgets of federal science-based departments and agencies, with the loss of 2,141 full-time positions. The cuts include, for example, $125 million from Environment Canada's science budget (a loss of 17.5 per cent) and $28 million from the Department of Fisheries and Oceans (DFO) (more than 10 per cent). Programs eliminated included, among others, Environment Canada's team of scientists that measured air pollution from smoke stacks and DFO's Ocean Contaminants and Marine Toxicology Program. The government is also planning to make much larger cuts in science budgets by 2016.[10]

While essential, regulatory science also has shortcomings. Because industry often pays the bills, the results may be proprietary and closed to public scrutiny. Beyond the challenge of assuring the quality of private information, this can hinder regulators' efforts to protect the public interest, reinforce obstacles to public participation in decision-making, and facilitate close ties between regulators and private interests. Information generated may also only be relevant to immediate government or industry priorities. For example, forestry studies often focus strictly on tree growth and fail to assess the health of the entire ecosystem. This research has also been criticized for failing to accommodate local conditions, whether in nature or in human communities. The tacit prescriptive commitments embedded in scientific knowledge may be inconsistent with local attitudes towards nature, and consequently this knowledge is often perceived as irrelevant to, or even a deliberate misunderstanding of, the places in which people live.[11]

Most fundamentally, defining issues as related strictly to technical, regulatory science, like the assumptions of **administrative rationalism** that underpin it, focuses debate not on ends (about which it is assumed all agree) but on efficiency of the means. In doing so it discourages public attention to the political dimensions of environmental issues, implicitly justifying the existing order. The consequences include a failure to challenge the assumptions of conventional **risk assessment** and natural resource management, including those regarding how "nature" itself should be used. For example, regulatory science leaves unexamined the role of the oil sands in Canada's energy economy, or of salmon aquaculture in coastal resource use. Regulatory science can also reinforce the tendency of bureaucratic organizations to resist learning, favouring standardized programs over efforts to understand the unexpected or to experiment with alternative approaches.

Advocacy Science

In the last two decades, advocacy science has emerged as a significant phenomenon in environmental governance, often challenging the assumptions and practice of regulatory science. Citizens and environmental organizations have become significant consumers and, to some extent, producers of scientific knowledge. Experience shows that if an issue is perceived to have a direct impact on a community, people will actively acquire technically sophisticated information, often sufficient to challenge professional expertise. Community groups may seek volunteer expertise at local universities, while larger groups hire scientists to review issues and prepare position papers. Non-governmental organizations have also emerged as knowledge brokers, relating information to policy options and acting as conduits between scientists, the media, and the public. Until its elimination in 2012, the National Round Table for the Environment and Economy fulfilled this role. The Pembina Institute has also contributed by relating climate change science to energy efficiency, development of the oil sands, and other policy issues.

Other organizations seek to influence the research agenda itself by providing funding or facilities for researchers or by conducting research in areas of special interest. Smaller groups may do community-based monitoring of environmental resources, while larger groups have their own scientists or commission research. For example, the World Wildlife Fund supports studies of endangered species; the Raincoast Research Society provides facilities for research on the implications of salmon farms for marine ecosystems; and conservation groups urging protection of transboundary natural areas have co-ordinated wildlife research, demonstrating capacities in these areas beyond those of provincial, state, or federal governments.[12]

These activities share with regulatory research the view of science as essential to the policy process. But they also challenge policy agendas, the structures of environmental governance (including the close relations between government and industry), the status of these actors as the dominant providers of knowledge, and even conventional definitions of issues. Such challenges are essential because they broaden both the policy agenda and participation in the policy process. But advocacy science has its own shortcomings, some of which stem from the political context of this research. Communicating science in the context of controversy often polarizes debates, as advocates accept whatever evidence is consistent with their own views and discount contrary information. Advocacy science can also exacerbate controversy by focusing attention on conflicting interpretations of knowledge.

nally, as in regulatory science, advocates in a controversy can evade responsibility for value choices by hiding behind the protective veil of science, with the consequence that debate shifts from whatever political, economic, or moral values or interests may be at stake to focus instead on scientific issues.

Innovation Science

During the last two decades a fourth model of science has gained prominence. In the environmental field, as in other policy realms, innovation science—usually defined in terms of the pursuit of marketable technologies—has become a chief focus of federal and provincial science policies. The motivation is economic: new technology is seen as contributing to prosperity. Innovation policies are founded on the view that economic benefits are not the inevitable outcome of research, but instead depend on careful attention to the ecology of research, particularly active collaboration among scientists, industry, and policy-makers.[13] Among other initiatives, this view is evident in the increasing emphasis of federal granting agencies (including NSERC and Genome Canada) on partnerships between scientists and industry, so as to ensure that research is focused on the most relevant, commercially viable opportunities. These partnerships are usually encouraged by requirements for matching funding from industrial or other sources. In the environmental field, the innovation agenda is evident in efforts to facilitate commercialization of **green technologies**, both to improve the environmental performance of conventional industry and to build an environmental industry. These objectives are pursued, for example, by the three Canadian Environmental Technology Advancement Centres (in western Canada, Ontario, and Quebec); by Sustainable Development Technology Canada (a federal foundation that works in partnership with the private sector to support development of innovative technologies); and, at the provincial level, by the Ontario Research Fund and the British Columbia Innovation Council. Internationally, this approach has been most evident in the substantial investments by many governments in research on renewable energy technologies.

Innovation research has been adopted by federal and provincial governments alike as a strategy for combining environmental and economic priorities. For example, a collaboration between university scientists and an aquaculture company found a way of farming "organic" salmon that does not require antibiotics—an innovation that promises to be both profitable and sustainable.[14] Innovation research contributes to reducing the impacts of economic activities, particularly by reaching into decision-making processes within firms that would otherwise be inaccessible to regulatory action or advocacy pressures. Its shortcomings, however, reflect its reliance on commercialization potential and market forces as the basis for determining research priorities. Innovation research tends to neglect research on topics that lack economic potential, including emerging and long-term concerns, or species and habitats that lack economic significance. It also tends to shortchange contributions to the scientific basis for public policy, and, more generally, the building of environmental knowledge that is accessible to all.

For example, the Canadian Biotechnology Strategy has emphasized promotion of this technology, neglecting balanced assessment of its environmental risks and benefits. A similar pattern has emerged with nanotechnology: research on its environmental implications remains patchy and unco-ordinated. There is also reason for concern regarding the potential for universities—recipients of considerable innovation funding over the last decade—to be distracted from their public service roles.[15] And as is the case with regulatory s[...] links between science and economic interests raise concerns regarding access to pr[...] etary knowledge, as well as the problematic nature of research that serves economic in[...] ests and yet is presented as acting in the service of a single, undifferentiated public. Such a view effectively disallows questions regarding who does and who does not gain from these investments. Finally, there is the problematic view of technology itself as the solution to environmental problems. This bias often motivates political leaders to neglect other dimensions of environmental challenges.

As this review of models of science and environmental governance illustrates, the landscape of Canadian environmental science reflects responses to a multiplicity of motivations and circumstances. While certain sectors are most closely associated with certain models—universities for basic research, environmental organizations for advocacy science—the diversity of relations between institutions and models of science makes such generalizations risky. In particular, the federal government has historically pursued research that conforms to several models, including basic, regulatory, and innovation science. Ironically, this diversity often remains unrepresented in public presentations of research, particularly those of the federal government. These instead tend to emphasize innovation science because it fits more readily within the storyline of science in the service of prosperity. In contrast, much less attention is directed to **public-good science**, including that devoted to providing a basis for regulation.[16] That research tends instead to become visible only at times of crisis, such as when cod stocks are forced to near-extinction or a potentially hazardous contaminant is identified. It has also become more prominent recently because of concerns regarding shifts in funding between these models of science. Public-good regulatory science has sustained large cutbacks in recent years, while innovation science has received greater support. Some areas of basic research relevant to environmental issues (such as climate science) are receiving less financial support, while other areas are receiving more, through new programs for university research such as the Canada First Research Excellence Fund announced in the February 2014 federal budget. (No information is currently available regarding trends in funding for advocacy science.)

Controversies regarding the "muzzling" of scientists have also focused attention on public-good science and its contribution to public discussion about environmental and other issues. Rules imposed after 2006 require federal government scientists to obtain permission before responding to requests for information from the media, particularly if the query relates to controversial subjects such as the environment. As a result, according to a 2013 survey, 90 per cent of government scientists now feel they cannot speak freely to the media about their work. One prominent case involved Kristi Miller, a Department of Fisheries and Oceans scientist who in 2011 published a paper in *Science* journal on possible links between a viral infection and declining sockeye salmon stocks in British Columbia. Officials in the Privy Council Office (which serves the Prime Minister) apparently refused to allow Miller to talk to the media about her research.[17] Because obtaining permission from senior administrators generally takes a great deal of time, journalists (who must usually meet same-day deadlines) are now much less likely to ask government scientists for comment.

These shifts in support for various models of science, and efforts to obstruct communication of scientific knowledge, are of concern because all models are essential to good environmental policy. Only by applying a variety of models can science respond effectively to diverse requirements for environmental knowledge. This becomes especially evident if we consider how environmental challenges can become evident through a variety of means, including basic research, evolving public concerns, or routine monitoring. Responses to these challenges—through regulation, incentives, education, or other approaches—can similarly depend on a variety of strategies, including discipline-oriented basic research, targeted regulatory science, studies and communications by environmental organizations, and better technologies.

These models can also give us a sharper understanding of the challenges involved in applying science to environmental governance. Environmental knowledge is often uncertain or contested, tied to powerful interests or committed advocates, inaccessible to the public, neglectful of essential political requirements, or heedless of demands for participation in decisions involving its production. As a result, there is often widespread skepticism regarding the reliability of scientific information. Other challenges are also evident. Environmentalists find that science cannot provide the support they expect. Regulatory agencies find that science provides only fragmentary grounds on which to base their decisions. Parties to controversies find that scientific evidence does not resolve divisions but instead exacerbates them. Those who oppose environmental initiatives invoke—and sometimes exaggerate—scientific uncertainties, a practice most evident today in climate change debates, but one that dates back to at least the 1920s, when evidence of the health effects of leaded gasoline began to emerge. (It took another 60 years before it was phased out.) And beyond the shortcomings of each model of science lies the uncertainty and ignorance prevalent in all but the simplest issues, stemming from incomplete theoretical understanding, insufficient research, or the complexity of natural and human systems. In such contexts, a single answer is rarely possible. Often there may be no answer at all, particularly in complex policy areas that push scientific inquiry to the outer edge of accepted facts.

These characteristics of knowledge—uncertain or incomplete, embodying objective authority but incorporating subjective values and attitudes, providing not one single "truth" but multiple partial perspectives—define the essential challenge of science in environmental governance. How, then, can it be possible to ensure that science provides the knowledge we need to achieve environmental policy leadership?

Science and Environmental Leadership

At least two key issues must be considered. One relates to the agenda of science and the need for scientific priorities to consider the overall public interest. The second concerns how science relates to the changing landscape of environmental governance, particularly to the need to resolve debates over contentious environmental challenges. Both issues relate to shortcomings in the four models that frame contemporary Canadian environmental science.

As we have seen, each of these models emphasizes a particular agenda: the disciplinary priorities of basic research, the information requirements of regulatory agencies, the demand for knowledge for advocacy, or the potential for innovative commercial technologies. All are important, and yet these agendas neglect some urgent knowledge needs. Consider, for example, the study of agriculture and its environmental implications. The overwhelming emphasis in Canadian agricultural science is on higher yields through intensive laboratory-based practices, including genetic engineering. The ultimate objective is to create marketable innovations, such as seed varieties and chemical products. But this neglects research on alternative strategies, including organic agriculture, as well as other approaches that emphasize resilience over maximum production, and that produce public, rather than private, intellectual property.[18]

An even more significant gap between research and emerging challenges is evident in energy technologies. In recent years a number of observers have argued that, even with appropriate pricing of energy through a carbon tax or other measures, market forces alone will not call into existence the technologies required for a drastic reduction in carbon emissions.[19] A massive expansion of research is also required, and yet public investment in solar, wind, and other forms of renewable energy has not kept pace. This gap between research needs and funding parallels the gap between research as a public good (such as basic research on climate change) and research on innovative technologies; while basic research can predict (at least roughly) future climate challenges, innovation science is failing to produce the technologies that can help us deal with these challenges. What environmental leadership therefore requires is research that combines the anticipatory capacity of environmental science with the practical goals of innovation research, generating technologies that address not just possibilities for commercialization, but the public interest, now and in the future.

Other requirements for leadership relate to the landscape of environmental governance. Science is only rarely able to provide a single best option for action. Unavoidable uncertainties and areas of ignorance are one factor, but another consists of our diverse preferences regarding action: while informed by science, these also incorporate myriad political differences. Resolution of these differences depends not only on science but on working through the many different ways we relate to and value our relationship with the environment.[20] An additional consideration is the evolution of environmental governance, from conventional "end-of-pipe" regulation towards extensive collaboration among various stakeholders. Governance thus requires attention to not just the substance of policy, but the processes required for networks of actors to be guided towards sustainability, including dissemination of information, reflexive regulation (also known as "smart" regulation), and partnerships.[21] These processes, in turn, require careful design if they are to be considered legitimate, including ample consultation and other forms of participation. These changes imply new requirements for scientific practice, beyond mastery of the theoretical literature and rigorous technical procedures. Foremost is a capacity for effective communication and collaboration.

Communication and collaboration are essential in science itself. For most scientists research involves collaboration with colleagues in numerous institutions and sectors. Thus, the boundaries between scientific institutions are blurred, with scientists in governments, universities, industry, and advocacy organizations working (if not always smoothly) together. These collaborative relationships are inevitably affected when scientists are not able to communicate freely (as is now the case with federal scientists), or when centres of collaboration, such as the Experimental Lakes Area, lose funding or are closed.

The need for effective communication of science beyond the scientific community is widely acknowledged. But this involves multiple challenges, beyond the muzzling of scientists by government discussed above. The specialized journal article—the traditional medium for conveying scientific information, especially that which is generated by basic research—often fails to communicate knowledge to those who might apply it. Neither are the news media always able to communicate science effectively, because of how they frame and simplify issues, their tendency to present issues as more contentious than may be justified by the actual scientific consensus (a problem most evident with respect to climate change), and restrictions on scientists' communication with the media.[22] At least in part in response to these shortcomings, various interests—both industrial and environmental—now use the Internet to communicate directly to selected audiences.

More generally, the obstacles to communicating science to decision-makers are both structural (relating to where scientists are situated within government departments and other institutions) and substantive (reflecting the divergent objectives, communication strategies, and relations of trust between scientists and those who use scientific information). Communication practices for science are evolving rapidly in response to these challenges. This evolution has become particularly evident in diverse issue-specific forums for discussion and consensus-building across institutions and sectors (for example, with respect to aquaculture, the Speaking for the Salmon process conducted by Simon Fraser University), as well as in formal expert committees, such as the Committee on the Status of Endangered Wildlife in Canada (COSEWIC).[23] These forums, and effective communication generally, depend on trust between scientists and those who use scientific information. Communication is affected not just by its format but by evaluations of the individual or institution that is communicating. Such communication, furthermore, must be in both directions, that is, a true dialogue, so that research will be not only relevant but communicated in ways consistent with public and institutional concerns and priorities.

But effective roles for science, and therefore environmental leadership, depend on more than communication.[24] Given the networked character of science, it is not always clear who will apply the results and whether the knowledge will be considered public or private. This is particularly the case in the context of controversy, when the conduct of science must be considered acceptable to all parties if it is to contribute to resolving differences. As a result, just as policy is being evaluated in terms of both content and process, so is scientific knowledge now being evaluated not just in terms of what it adds to our understanding but in terms of how it was obtained and applied. In other words, policy and science are converging in how they are received and evaluated by environmental actors.

This convergence can be understood in terms of three aspects of scientific practice. The first relates to evaluations of **scientific credibility**. Peer review—familiar in basic research, and also now often used in regulatory and advocacy contexts—plays an important role in these evaluations. Peer review is not infallible, especially in practical contexts, but its value can be enhanced by understanding that it serves best not simply by assuring the truth of scientific results, but by "witnessing" research, helping to ensure its quality and rigour. This function, in turn, implies reconsidering the structure of the review process, relying less on individual reviewers than on groups of independent experts, and widening participation beyond the scientific community to include, for example, holders of local knowledge. Scientific credibility also depends on aspects of the process of science less accessible to peer review, such as the relations between scientists and economic or other interests and the perceived openness of scientists to considering other perspectives and forms of knowledge.

A second aspect relates to **scientific relevance**. To solve problems and advance the policy agenda, science must fulfill a diversity of roles, from anticipating emerging issues to understanding the basis of persistent conflicts. This, in turn, requires a broad definition of relevance, implemented through a pluralistic research strategy that draws on a diversity of participants in setting the research agenda.[25]

The third aspect is **scientific legitimacy**. It depends, in part, on transparency regarding the objectives of research and its consequences for all interests. This can be assured through open arrangements for funding science and determining research objectives—being clear, for example, about whether the research results affect the interests of those funding the research. It also requires open, inclusive negotiation of the relation between knowledge and action—whether, say, action on a problem can be taken on the basis of a weight-of-evidence approach (in which a conclusion is drawn on the basis of what the evidence tends to indicate), or must wait until there is absolute proof of the need for action. Explicit articulation of how decisions using uncertain or incomplete evidence will be made is also required: will it be by, say, balancing benefits and risks, or by invoking the precautionary principle? Such requirements acknowledge that legitimacy is achieved not through universal norms of scientific conduct but through a context-dependent process that takes into account local interests and concerns.[26] The significance of legitimacy is illustrated by how criticisms of federal research cutbacks and efforts to "control" science often invoke transparency and democracy. Legitimacy also poses challenges for science and its relation to other ways of thinking about nature; it requires defining which questions may be addressed by science and which require other approaches, while acknowledging that science is only one of several ways of knowing the world.

These requirements relating to credibility, relevance, and legitimacy imply a new model of science as the basis for environmental leadership. This model might be described as **modest science**—that is, science that contributes distinctive knowledge but is cognizant of the value of other forms of knowledge, and is also mindful of democratic imperatives and the boundaries between science and other perspectives. Essential to this model are transparent, consensual approaches to distinguishing between those questions that can be answered by science and those that, while perhaps illuminated by scientific knowledge, depend for resolution on political, economic, or moral considerations.

A chief implication of this new model of science is that institutions framed in terms of conventional models of science are not sufficient for science to be fully effective. Neither science that is insulated from the policy world, as in basic research, nor science fully integrated within this world, as in regulatory or advocacy science, can provide the information required. Science that fails to relate to pressing environmental problems risks irrelevancy. Science too closely enmeshed in politics risks becoming itself the focus of dispute, distracting attention from genuine political, economic, and moral differences. Such an outcome has been too commonly encountered, as is evident in issues ranging from climate change to the assessment of big energy projects, such as the proposed Northern Gateway pipeline in British Columbia.

Instead, new kinds of institutions for science, those able to integrate scientific and non-scientific considerations, are required. **Boundary organizations** are among the more promising innovations. These organizations, rather than insisting on a clean demarcation of science and policy, straddle the boundary between them and thus provide the basis for stabilizing this boundary. Experience has shown that such organizations (the Intergovernmental Panel on Climate Change is a well-known example; the National Round Table on Environment and Economy was another) are able to synthesize knowledge and contribute to setting the research agenda, while achieving agreement on consensual knowledge, even across diverse interests and scientific disciplines.[27] Other innovations in institutional design, such as learning organizations that embody the capacity to adapt to changing conditions and to new knowledge, suggest further possibilities.

These new kinds of institutions and the networked character of science and governance have implications for various sectors, particularly for government. It is becoming increasingly evident that agencies with both policy and scientific responsibilities need to evolve from serving as the primary source of scientific information to facilitating the use of science from a diversity of sources. Acting as reliable, trusted knowledge brokers, these agencies could fulfill such tasks as disseminating information and facilitating dialogue among diverse actors. While some agencies are beginning to acknowledge the importance of these tasks, distrust founded on histories of lack of transparency and perceptions of conflict of interest (as when an agency both regulates and promotes an industry) accentuates the challenges involved. As noted throughout this chapter, recent federal actions restricting environmental science and its communication have only heightened these challenges, diminishing the likelihood of federal agencies facilitating the modest and effective use of science.

Canadians have learned a great deal about their natural environment through scientific research (although many uncertainties and areas of ignorance remain). This knowledge should be able to provide the basis for environmental leadership. But for it to do so, research must go beyond those models that have traditionally guided its pursuit, instead embracing modest approaches to scientific practice and institutional structures that produce knowledge that all parties will consider credible, relevant, and legitimate.

Key Terms

administrative rationalism

boundary organizations

ecological integrity

green technologies

modest science

nanotechnology

public-good science

risk assessment

scientific credibility

scientific legitimacy

scientific relevance

sound science

Questions for Review

1. What have been the roles of science and of scientists in the making of Canadian environmental policy? Should they have greater influence in policy processes?

2. How should scientific, economic, social, and other concerns and interests be combined in forming Canadian environmental policy?

3. To what extent is science culturally relative? Are there blind spots towards local communities, traditional knowledge, and the perspectives of non-scientists, and if so what are the consequences?

4. What are the differences among basic science, regulatory science, advocacy science, and innovation science? In what ways does each of these contribute to or act as a constraint on environmental policy?

5. How have recent federal actions relating to environmental research and communication affected the national capacity to apply science to environmental policy?

6. How can the practice of science be revised to provide an effective basis for environmental leadershi'

Internet Resources

Canadian Association of University Teachers, "Get Science Right"
http://getscienceright.ca/

Canadian Broadcasting Corporation, "Silence of the Labs"
http://www.cbc.ca/fifth/episodes/2013-2014/the-silence-of-the-labs

National Round Table for the Environment and Economy
http://collectionscanada.gc.ca/webarchives2/20130322140948/http://nrtee-trnee.ca/

Additional Reading

Bocking, Stephen. *Nature's Experts: Science, Politics and the Environment*. New Brunswick, NJ: Rutgers University Press, 2004.

Doern, G. Bruce, ed. *Innovation, Science, Environment: Canadian Policies and Performance, 2007–2008*. Montreal and Kingston: McGill-Queen's University Press, 2007.

Doern, G. Bruce, and Jeffrey S. Kinder. *Strategic Science in the Public Interest: Canada's Government Laboratories and Science-Based Agencies*. Toronto: University of Toronto Press, 2007.

Hackett, Edward J., et al., eds. *The Handbook of Science and Technology Studies*, 3rd edn. Cambridge, Mass.: MIT Press, 2008.

Jasanoff, Sheila. *Science and Public Reason*. New York: Routledge, 2012.

Nature. "Frozen Out: Canada's Government Should Free Its Scientists to Speak to the Press, as Its US Counterpart Has." 443, 1 (2012): 6.

Pielke, Roger A., Jr. *The Honest Broker: Making Sense of Science in Policy and Politics*. Cambridge: Cambridge University Press, 2007.

Professional Institute of the Public Service of Canada. *Vanishing Science: The Disappearance of Canadian Public Interest Science*. Ottawa, 2014.

Notes

1. Peter Calamai, "The Struggle over Canada's Role in the Post-Kyoto World," in G. Bruce Doern, ed., *Innovation, Science, Environment: Canadian Policies and Performance, 2007–2008* (Montreal and Kingston: McGill-Queen's University Press, 2007), 32–54; Andrew Nikiforuk, "Librarians Say Cullings Signify Harper's New Info Policy," *The Tyee*, 18 Jan. 2014.

2. S. Bocking, *Nature's Experts: Science, Politics, and the Environment* (New Brunswick, NJ: Rutgers University Press, 2004), 25–44.

3. S. Jasanoff, *Designs on Nature: Science and Democracy in Europe and the United States* (Princeton, NJ: Princeton University Press, 2005).

4. Bert Backman-Beharry and Robert Slater, "Commercializing Technologies through Collaborative Networks: The Environmental Industry and the Role of CETACS," in G. Bruce Doern, ed., *Innovation, Science, Environment: Canadian Policies and Performance, 2006–2007* (Montreal and Kingston: McGill-Queen's University Press, 2006), 169–93.

5. G. Bruce Doern and Jeffrey S. Kinder, *Strategic Science in the Public Interest: Canada's Government Laboratories and Science-Based Agencies* (Toronto: University of Toronto Press, 2007), 94–116.

6. G. Bruce Doern, "The Martin Liberals: Changing ISE Policies and Institutions," in Doern, ed., *Innovation, Science, Environment: Canadian Policies and Performance, 2006–2007* (Montreal and Kingston: McGill-Queen's University Press, 2006), 3–34.

7. See, e.g., G. Bruce Doern and Ted Reed, eds, *Risky Business: Canada's Changing Science-Based Policy and Regulatory Regime* (Toronto: University of Toronto Press, 2000); W. Leiss, *In the Chamber of Risks: Understanding Risk Controversies* (Montreal and Kingston: McGill-Queen's University Press, 2001); Doern and Kinder, *Strategic Science*.

8. Bocking, *Nature's Experts*.

9. Doern and Kinder, *Strategic Science*.

10. Professional Institute of the Public Service of Canada, *Vanishing Science: The Disappearance of Canadian Public Interest Science* (Ottawa, 2014).

11. B. Wynne, "Public Understanding of Science," in Sheila Jasanoff et al., eds, *Handbook of Science and Technology Studies* (Thousand Oaks, Calif.: Sage, 1995), 361–88.

12. J.N. Sanders and P. Stoett, "Extinction and Invasion: Transborder Conservation Efforts," in P. LePrestre and P. Stoett, eds, *Bilateral Ecopolitics: Continuity and Change in Canadian–American Environmental Relations* (London: Ashgate, 2006), 157–77.

13. G. Bruce Doern, "The Reshaping of an Agenda for Innov-
    ation, Science, and Environment (ISE)," in Doern, ed.,
    *Innovation, Science, Environment: Canadian Policies
    and Performance, 2007–2008* (Montreal and Kingston:
    McGill-Queen's University Press, 2007), 3–31.
14. Natural Sciences and Engineering Research Council,
    "Bolstering the Business Case for Organic Salmon,"
    http://www.nserc-crsng.gc.ca/Media-Media/Impact-
    Story-ArticlesPercutant_eng.asp?ID51102.
15. M.G. Bird, "Harmful Distraction: The Commercializa-
    tion of Knowledge at Canada's Public Universities," in
    G. Bruce Doern, ed., *Innovation, Science, Environment:
    Canadian Policies and Performance, 2007–2008* (Mont-
    real and Kingston: McGill-Queen's University Press,
    2007), 281–98.
16. Doern and Kinder, *Strategic Science*, 117–65, 201–2.
17. CBC, "DFO Scientist Says Privy Council Silenced Her,"
    25 Aug. 2011, http://www.cbc.ca/news/canada/british-
    columbia/dfo-scientist-says-privy-council-silenced-
    her-1.987107.
18. See, e.g., E. Ann Clark, "Has Ag Biotech Lived Up to Its
    Promise? (and what should the scientific community
    do about it?)," 2004 Helen Battle Lecture, University
    of Western Ontario, 25 Nov. 2004, http://www.plant.
    uoguelph.ca/research/homepages/eclark/pdf/uwo.pdf.
19. See, e.g., J. Sachs, *Common Wealth: Economics for a
    Crowded Planet* (New York: Penguin, 2008).
20. S. Jasanoff, "Technologies of Humility," *Nature* 450, 1
    (Nov. 2007): 33.
21. Michael Howlett and Jeremy Rayner, "(Not So) 'Smart
    Regulation'? Canadian Shellfish Aquaculture Policy

and the Evolution of Instrument Choice for Industrial
Development," *Marine Policy* 28 (2004): 171–84.
22. Bocking, *Nature's Experts*.
23. R. Routledge, Patricia Gallaugher, and Craig Orr, "Con-
    vener's Report—Summit of Scientists on Aquaculture
    and the Protection of Wild Salmon," Simon Fraser Uni-
    versity, 2007; D.L. Vanderzwaag and J.A. Hutchings,
    "Canada's Marine Species at Risk: Science and Law at
    the Helm, but a Sea of Uncertainties," *Ocean Develop-
    ment and International Law* 36, 3 (2005): 219–59.
24. Dan M. Kahan et al., "Biased Assimilation, Polarization,
    and Cultural Credibility: An Experimental Study of
    Nanotechnology Risk Perceptions," *Project on Emerging
    Nanotechnologies*, Brief No. 3. 2008.
25. Bocking, *Nature's Experts*.
26. See, e.g., C.A. Miller, "Challenges in the Application
    of Science to Global Affairs: Contingency, Trust, and
    Moral Order," in Clark A. Miller and Paul N. Edwards,
    eds, *Changing the Atmosphere: Expert Knowledge and
    Environmental Governance* (Cambridge, Mass.: MIT
    Press, 2001), 247–85.
27. David H. Guston, ed., "Special Issue: Boundary Organ-
    izations in Environmental Policy and Science," *Science,
    Technology, and Human Values* 26, 4 (2001): 399–500. On
    the significance of boundary organizations and analo-
    gous mechanisms in an interjurisdictional context, see
    D.L. VanNijnatten and W. Henry Lambright, "North
    American Smog: Science–Policy Linkages across Mul-
    tiple Boundaries," *Canadian–American Public Policy* 45
    (2001).

PART II
Environmental Governance Across Scales

As Mary Louise McAllister notes in Chapter 9, "[s]cale is important." The chapters in this section explore how governments in Canada work as political units at different jurisdictional scales, contributing to (or drawing down) the environmental protection framework. Together, they also provide a sense of the richness of the environmental policy toolkit, which spans the formal and the informal, from legislation and regulation, to administrative agreements and policy statements, to operating rules and norms. Critically, these chapters show the myriad ways in which these political units are linked through constitutional, statutory, and administrative means, as well as by practical politics. The result is a multi-level, interlinked, and variegated latticework.

The critical message in this section is that federal leadership is necessary for driving, co-ordinating, and facilitating environmental policy progress in Canada—and that such leadership is completely lacking. While all of the chapters in Part II are at some pains to explain both the complex nature of environmental policy jurisdiction and the important roles that sub-national governments (provinces, territories, local and Aboriginal governments) as well as the international system play, the gap left by a retreating (and some would argue antagonistic) federal government yawns widely. Certainly, environmental policy analysts agree that the Canadian federal government, in terms of its constitutional and statutory authorities as well as its policy capacity, does not begin to approximate the US federal government in terms of its environmental policy power. Yet, it is also clear from the chapters here that there are roles only the federal government can play in Canadian environmental policy-making, but it chooses not to.

We begin with an assessment of the federal "struggle" to institutionalize sustainable development in the policies, practices, and institutions of the national government. Glen Toner, James Meadowcroft, and David Cherniak, in Chapter 7, argue that while "a substantial effort [was made] to instill sustainable development values and insights" under the earlier Mulroney, Chrétien, and Martin administrations, the longer-term integrative perspective required by sustainable development "did not penetrate deeply into the core of government activity." In some ways, the early innovations—which included a new parliamentary standing committee, a Commissioner of Environment and Sustainable Development, the establishment of the National Round Table on Environment and Economy (NTREE), and State of the Environment reporting—seem rather bold by comparison with the lack of positive action under the Harper Conservative government. The extensive revisions to the environmental legislative framework, the closing off of various channels of parliamentary engagement, the termination of the NRTEE, and the loss of considerable policy capacity that would support sustainable development programming have set back the "process of change" initiated by previous governments. While some provinces and local governments are making serious attempts to fashion programs and policies that further sustainable development, these offer only a partial solution to what is a national challenge.

These findings are echoed by Julie Simmons in Chapter 8. Despite a context that is characterized by constitutional and jurisdictional uncertainties, and that demands "constructive entanglement" by the federal and provincial/territorial governments, Simmons argues that the intergovernmental machinery is weakly institutionalized and lacks capacity. The Harper government is certainly not the first to emphasize respect for the provincial role and a view of the federal role as "enabling" rather than "directing"; indeed, this defines the approach of successive federal governments spanning the 1980s to the present, and explains the lack of robust intergovernmental institutions and agreements. However, the current government has retreated almost completely, with the result that intergovernmental environmental relations are at a standstill. At the very least, the critical tasks associated with co-ordinating the environmental policy activities of a large and diverse set of lower-order governments are simply not being performed.

One line of argumentation that winds across the contributions to this volume is that subnational governments offer potential as environmental policy experimenters and innovators. In Chapter 9, Mary Louise McAllister surveys the local government landscape, highlighting cases where watershed- and place-based approaches, as well as green and digital infrastructure, have been put in place. Such innovations indicate a willingness at the local level to pursue policies that recognize the interdependence of biophysical and socio-economic properties. However, local governments face serious constraints on such experimentation, including limits on their jurisdictional authority, policy capacity, financial resources, and political will. To some considerable extent, local governments rely on higher orders of government to put in place the appropriate conditions to stimulate progressive environmental policy.

In a similar vein, in Chapter 10 Graham White portrays co-management boards in the Northwest Territories as "unique institutions" engaged in the delicate task of striking a balance between much-needed resource development and protection of the northern environment. White attributes the accomplishments of co-management boards, created under the terms of modern comprehensive land claims agreements, to Aboriginal involvement and influence, as well as to the increased use of traditional knowledge (TK). Here, too, however, actions taken by the Conservatives, in particular through the Northwest Territories Devolution Act, threaten to change the composition and structure of co-management boards, lessening the role of local Aboriginal representatives in the environmental regulatory process.

If Chapters 7 through 10 explore the federal willingness to engage seriously with the challenges posed by environmental degradation and to undergird the environmental policy efforts of governments at other scales, Chapter 11, by Debora VanNijnatten, wrangles with the important question of whether and how the "North American influence" operates on Canadian environmental policy. Using the language of "push-pull" dynamics, the chapter tracks the shifts in the intensity of transboundary activity across the bilateral, subnational, and trilateral scales, the locus of leadership, and the types of mechanisms in use (collegial "pushing" vs formal mandates that "pull"). It is argued that we seem to be entering a new phase in transboundary interactions where co-operative energies have waned at all levels. The austerity context is partly to blame here, as is the sorry state of Canada–US relations.[1] However, the infrastructure associated with cross-border regional co-operation, along with the more formal bilateral (and trilateral) environmental architecture, offers a platform for encouraging environmental policy leadership in Canada.

In the final chapter of this section, Neil Craik and Tahnee Prior look farther afield, to Canada's engagement at the international level. Craik and Prior argue that, if we understand the system of international environmental law as consisting of multilateral treaties but also general principles and customary norms, then Canada's environmental policy actions can impact the system as whole. In particular, they examine the degree to which the Harper government has supported the four foundational principles arising out of the Rio Declaration: the no-harm principle; the principle of common but differentiated responsibilities; the public participation principle; and the precautionary principle. Craik and Prior argue that the Canadian government has to some extent retreated from the Rio consensus by shifting the basis of its engagement towards a narrower, (economic) interest-based interpretation and application of these principles.

Note

1. Paul Wells, "Obama, Harper and the End of the Affair," *Maclean's*, 9 June 2014, accessed 5 July 2014, www. macleans.ca/politics/ottawa/obama-harper-and-the-end-of-the-affair/.

7 The Struggle of the Canadian Federal Government to Institutionalize Sustainable Development

Glen Toner, James Meadowcroft, and David Cherniak

Chapter Summary

Sustainable development (SD) is a normative framework for merging the social, economic, and environmental spheres of our society. The implementation of SD by governments has had a rocky history in Canada. Successive federal governments have been willing to construct institutions focused on enshrining sustainable development (with successful results in many cases), but these institutions are often far removed from the halls of power and limited in both their scope and their ability to influence policy decisions. Under the current Conservative government, the attention paid to sustainable development has been drastically reduced, replaced with the phrase "Responsible Resource Development," with resource development and economic growth placed far above environmental concerns. In the absence of federal leadership, provincial and municipal governments have to some extent begun to shoulder the responsibility for implementing sustainability principles. Provincial policies directed towards renewable electricity, the transport sector, and experimentation with carbon taxes all promote sustainable development. Similarly, municipalities across Canada are focusing their policies on urban design, mass transit, and local agriculture.

Chapter Outline

- The scale of the sustainable development change agenda
- Federalism, politics, and voters
- Ideas, instruments, and institutions: an overview of the Mulroney, Chrétien, and Harper governments
- Provinces and cities: hotbeds of experimentation, challenges, and a new wave of SD
  - Provincial initiatives
  - Municipal initiatives

Introduction

Environmental policy is usually reactive. It involves creating recovery plans for species once they are threatened, adopting regulations to govern the use of toxic substances endangering human and animal life, cleaning up sites contaminated by industrial activity, and studying, monitoring, and documenting the decline in natural capital and ecological systems impacted negatively by human activity. Development is the activity that humans engage in every day when they get out of bed and contribute to economic and social life in a multitude of ways. For the past two centuries or so, this development process has become increasingly unsustainable as nature can no longer sustain the natural capital upon which life depends. Recognition in the 1980s that this human development process had to shift from unsustainable to sustainable had a profound impact on public policy discourse in national, subnational, and local governments and in international organizations. Two things happened: environmental policies were strengthened to contain and fix increasingly serious problems imposed by industrial activity; and **sustainable development** (SD) policies were created to address the causes of these problems, by altering the corporate and governmental decision-making processes that had triggered the unsustainable practices of human systems in the first place.

Our Common Future, the 1987 report of the World Commission on Environment and Development (WCED), made the following prescient observation: "in the end, sustainable development is not a fixed state of harmony, but rather a process of change in which the exploitation of resources, the direction of investments, the orientation of technological development, *and institutional change* are made consistent with future as well as present needs."[1] William Ruckelshaus, former head of the United States Environmental Protection Agency, clarified the transformative nature of the shift required in human thinking and practice when he said:

> Can we move nations in the direction of sustainability? Such a move would be a modification of society comparable in scale to only two other changes: the Agricultural Revolution of the late Neolithic, and the Industrial Revolution of the past two centuries. Those revolutions were gradual, spontaneous, and largely unconscious. This one will have to be a fully conscious operation, guided by the best foresight science can provide. If we actually do it, the undertaking will be absolutely unique in humanity's stay on earth.[2]

Given the transformative agenda of SD, it is not surprising that the post-1987 period has been characterized by both breakthroughs and setbacks. In reference to this change process, the WCED (commonly known as the Brundtland Commission after its chair, former Norwegian Prime Minister Gro Harlem Brundtland) added the profound insight that "[w]e do not pretend that the process is easy or straightforward."[3] Indeed, it has not been.

Since 1987, various Canadian federal and provincial governments have formally committed to this transformation by introducing SD policies, institutions, and practices. Indeed, in the 1990s Canada was considered an innovator and leader in this "change process"—but that is most certainly not the case today. Certain critical factors have both driven and constrained the nature and pace of engagement of Canada's federal governments under Prime Ministers Brian Mulroney, Jean Chrétien, and Stephen Harper. While scientific evidence and international pressure have been major drivers, the impact of economic conditions, Canadian federalism, and partisan politics have been more mixed. However, the depth and severity of the 2008–9 economic crisis and the election of a majority Harper Conservative government in 2011 significantly changed the governance game in this area. Indeed, the Harper government introduced a new governing philosophy called "Responsible Resource Development" (RRD), discussed in the Introduction, which rejected the core principle of SD by reasserting the pre-eminence of economic growth and diminishing environmental protection to a secondary level.

In a rushed attempt to institutionalize the RRD approach, the Conservatives rolled back much of the legislative base of SD in 2012 and 2013,[4] and actively sought to undermine the influence of science and scientists in the decision-making process.[5] The goal was to reduce the influence of environmental considerations in constraining the pace of oil, gas, mining, and pipeline projects at the heart of RRD, and to minimize constraints on cabinet in making the decisions needed to expedite these developments. To some extent countering the thrust of the Harper government, several provinces have introduced policies and institutions that tend to strengthen sustainable development. This chapter will assess the scope and dynamics of this institutional change process over the past 25 years.[6] But before addressing the Canadian experience, it is necessary to say something more generally about the challenge SD presents to contemporary governments.

The Scale of the Sustainable Development Change Agenda

Over the past two decades, SD has come to represent an emergent **international norm** that emphasizes the protection of global life support systems, equity within and between generations, the importance of meeting basic human needs, and public participation in environment and development decision-making.[7] The idea was formulated as a "bridging concept" to draw together the concerns of rich and poor countries, and to denote a new form of development that would be more equitable and more sensitive to environmental limits.

Institutionalizing SD certainly represents a real challenge. Its constructive ambiguity is typical of normative terms (think of other examples such as "freedom," "equality," and "democracy") that have clear core meanings and play a central role in political life, but about which we argue continuously. But this ambiguity does mean that SD cannot be invoked as a mechanical formula that cranks out a specific policy recommendation in any given context. Rather, it must be applied to a particular circumstance, and it inevitably involves value choices about the sort of development we want to encourage and the kind of society in which we want to live.[8]

Conventional governance structures have evolved over centuries of political experimentation and struggle, as societies tried to find acceptable ways to manage their affairs. Elements such as a written constitution; responsible government; periodic elections; the party system; individual civil, political, and social rights; and civil service neutrality are all the result of generations of innovation, trial and error, reform and counter-reform, and adjustment. Yet the history of the second half of the twentieth century has revealed an emerging set of societal problems that our inherited governance institutions have been ill-equipped to manage.

Compared to conventional approaches, governance for SD implies a longer-term perspective that does not fit neatly into the political cycle of elections. This sort of governance must be intergenerational, considering consequences two, three, or more generations in the future. It deals with issues that cut across established jurisdictions and have implications at multiple scales, from the local community to the global commons. It requires integration of economic, social, and environmental considerations and the breaking down of traditional partitions among government departments responsible for different dimensions of policy. And, it requires that public officials interact with many societal actors, because the solutions are not just in the hands of government but depend on innovation at all levels in society. Moreover, although it is usual to emphasize collaboration and consensus, the transition towards more sustainable ways of living is likely also to involve acute struggles, as those who gain from existing (unsustainable) activities resist the transition to more ecologically sound ways of doing things. The current intergenerational struggle between those social interests invested in the ongoing dominance of fossil fuels and those driven to expedite a low-carbon energy future is a prominent example.

SD is often described in terms of three "pillars"—the economic, social, and environmental. Yet, in a rich country like Canada the environmental pillar has been systematically neglected, and the integration of the environmental dimension into development decision-making is both critical and often contested. Environmental integration requires a reconceptualization of what "growth," "development," and "the public good" imply. And it points towards a dramatic transformation of key economic sectors (energy, transport, agriculture, construction, and so on) to reduce the environmental impacts of production and consumption.[9]

Federalism, Politics, and Voters

Over the past 20 years, federal–provincial entanglements and partisan politics have hindered consistent and sustained federal government engagement with SD. International experience suggests that geographically extensive federal states face particular challenges articulating a coherent response to SD, but in Canada the situation seems especially acute. Here, the constitutional division of powers, federal–provincial tensions over energy resources, long-standing regional sensitivities, the influence of local resource industries over provincial governments, and nationalist feelings in Quebec have combined into a particularly potent brew.[10] This has been manifest in climate change policy, where different regional resource endowments, economic structures, energy systems, and levels of affluence have underpinned very different perspectives. Vacillating between a deferral to provincial sensibilities and unilateral action that ignored previous commitments, the federal government has failed to provide consistent leadership and to establish fruitful interactions with provincial and municipal governments required to advance this file. These tendencies are highlighted by Macdonald in Chapter 13, for example, in his analysis of climate policy.

Partisan disputes have also taken their toll: the Liberals abandoned the Green Plan, which had been initiated by their Conservative rivals; and the Conservatives shut down Liberal climate programs as soon as they returned to power. The polarized political style associated with the **Westminster model** and **first-past-the-post electoral system** presents something of a challenge. Most democratic states now incorporate some form of **proportional representation**, which generates more balanced assemblies, encourages cross-party collaboration, and favours coalition governments.

Yet, it is possible to exaggerate the operation of these features. Constitutional complexities and jurisdictional tensions are simply facts of doing politics in Canada. When there is enough pressure for action, solutions are usually found. Indeed, in some circumstances, the federal distribution of power can favour innovation, as governments are able to move ahead with reforms in their areas of authority even when others are unwilling to act. Consider, for example, the carbon tax initiative in British Columbia. Moreover, substantial regional autonomy should in principle allow SD policies to be better adjusted to local conditions. And it is also true that features of the electoral and party systems that may have hampered substantive engagement with SD at the federal level may, in other circumstances, have the opposite effect. Arguably, this was the case in the late 1980s and early 1990s, when pioneering SD efforts were introduced by the Mulroney Conservatives and then the Chrétien Liberals.

Hence, the priorities of politicians and electorates, rather than characteristics of the political system, deserve a more important place in the story. One can argue, for example, that over the last few decades Canadians and their political leaders have been confronted with tough issues—relating to free trade, deficit reduction, periodic recessions, and Quebec's unique status and occasional thrusts towards independence—that have made it a challenge for concerns about SD to hold their ground. Yet governments everywhere face difficult issues, and evidence from some countries indicates that SD has found a more important place on the political agenda.[11] For example, in the 1990s, Sweden faced serious economic difficulties that threatened its established welfare state model, but the government placed SD at the core of its political program, calling for efforts to build a **green welfare state**.

The general assumption of politicians, journalists, and other analysts, it appears, is that Canadian voters want to protect the environment, but do not appreciate the economic consequences of their desires and are unwilling to pay for the measures required to deal with the major problems. Polls suggest that Canadians remain committed to environmental protection, although the relative ranking of environmental issues varies considerably over time, an argument developed by Anderson and Stephenson in Chapter 1. Certainly, political leaders do not feel a significant and sustained demand from the electorate to take vigorous action over long-term environmental risks such as climate change. Environmental issues can seem remote in a large and sparsely populated country like Canada, which has abundant water, land, forest, and energy resources. The relative weakness of Canadian environmental organizations, the strong ideological influence from the US (for example, climate change deniers), and the unrelenting campaign by fossil energy producers (through lobby organizations such as the Canadian Association of Petroleum Producers) to slow down and weaken GHG regulation should not be forgotten.

Ideas, Instruments, and Institutions: An Overview of the Mulroney, Chrétien, and Harper Governments

As noted above, the SD paradigm integrates environmental, social, and economic goals and insights from the natural and social sciences to encourage an approach to development that accounts for natural capital. The idea was to "anticipate and prevent" environmental damage from industrial development. The two previous Canadian economic development paradigms have been characterized as "frontier economics" (from the eighteenth century through to the 1960s) and "resource management" (from the 1960s to the 1980s). In the frontier staples economy era, resource extraction was conducted without any concern for the environment and pollution, and resource scarcity simply drove extraction further into the hinterland.[12] Resource management introduced the "react and cure" era in response to the first wave of environmental consciousness by attempting to repair environmental damage from resource extraction, processing, and transportation projects, while continuing to subjugate the environment to the economy.[13]

The SD era began with the Mulroney Conservative government around 1990. Brian Mulroney had committed on the dais of the United Nations General Assembly to implement the principles of *Our Common Future*, and the effort culminated in the 1990 Green Plan: "Sustainable Development is *what* we want to achieve. The Green Plan sets out *how* we are going to achieve it."[14] Mulroney played a prominent role at the Rio Earth Summit in 1992, and is credited with convincing American President George H.W. Bush to sign the UN Biodiversity Convention. Significant institutional gains were made during this period when the National Round Table on the Environment and Economy and the International Institute for Sustainable Development were created. SD principles also informed the legislative beachhead that the Mulroney Conservatives built with the Canadian Environmental Protection Act (1988), the Canadian Environmental Assessment Act (1992) and its accompanying agency (established in 1995), and the first Strategic Environmental Assessment (SEA) directive, a decision-making tool to integrate environmental considerations into all government policies and programs. Canada also gained a reputation as a world leader in State of the Environment reporting.

The Liberals' 1993 election manifesto highlighted a number of SD innovations that the government went on to implement after its victory. These included strengthening institutional capacity by creating a Parliamentary Standing Committee on Environment and Sustainable Development, a Commissioner of the Environment and Sustainable Development (CESD), and Sustainable Development Technology Canada (SDTC).[15] The legislation creating the CESD also produced the first requirement that federal departments create sustainable development strategies every three years, which were to be assessed by the CESD. The Liberals also established the Office of Greening Government Operations and ratified the Kyoto Protocol of the United Nations Framework Convention on Climate Change. The Chrétien Liberal government further strengthened the SD legislative base with the Species at Risk Act in 2002.

Interestingly, the most creative institutional innovations were made outside of the executive branch. This shows that governments are capable of institutional innovation, but are inclined to do it in a way that minimally impacts the autonomy of ministers and cabinet. The International Institute for Sustainable Development, for example, is headquartered in Winnipeg and is now largely autonomous of the government, as it has developed a financial base that is no longer primarily reliant on federal funds. It is a highly respected research-based organization that works on both Canadian and international issues. Sustainable Development Technology Canada is an arm's-length agency that invests federal funds in innovative clean technology developments to leverage private sector investment. While these two organizations have carved out interesting and valuable domains in the suite of SD institutions in Canada, neither is directly involved in the day-to-day decision-making process of government that influences the development trajectory of the country.

The Commissioner of the Environment and Sustainable Development has proven to be the most controversial of the innovative non-executive SD agencies, not surprising perhaps since it is also the closest to the day-to-day operations of government. The CESD was created by the Chrétien government in 1995, in fulfillment of a commitment made in the 1993 election campaign to create an environmental auditor general. Interestingly, the idea of such a position was introduced by the environmental community during the development stage of the Green Plan but was rejected by the Conservatives. The House of Commons Standing Committee on Environment and Sustainable Development, in its 1994 deliberations on the structure and functions of such an office, recommended the creation of a fully independent commissioner who would report directly to Parliament. The combination of stiff resistance to the creation of an independent official by bureaucrats in the key line departments and the offer from the Auditor General to house the new office within his existing apparatus resulted in the location of the CESD at a second-tier level within the Office of the Auditor General (OAG).

This was a mistake in organizational design. The OAG is a long-standing and highly regarded audit office that reports directly to Parliament and has a legitimate proscription against commenting on policy. Yet, the transformative SD change agenda is inherently forward looking and policy oriented. Placing a commissioner-type function within an audit office that is only allowed to audit existing programs—i.e., to ask if departmental activity met its stated objectives—was bound to come up against its inherent contradictions. The CESD established a strong reputation for audit work but was never really able to exercise the commissioner functions expected of independent commissioners like the Commissioner of Official Languages. The Harper Conservatives later argued that an independent CESD would become an advocate for SD within the parliamentary system, and that advocacy should only be exercised by political parties and interest groups. This, significantly, has never been a charge levelled at the Commissioner of Official Languages, who is an expected and respected advocate for the growth and development of both official languages in the practices of the federal government across Canada.

Hence, one must acknowledge that, at one level, the period 1990–2006 was characterized by a substantial effort to instill sustainable development values and insights into the practices of the government of Canada, and into the policies and programs influencing Canadian society and economy. But such major societal transformations as that represented by SD take time and will be subject to push back. Despite the rhetorical endorsement of SD by political leaders, such new thinking did not penetrate deeply into the core of government activity. Both politics and the public service remained largely rooted in a traditional mindset—with established production-oriented and distributional issues at centre stage. For politicians, time horizons are typically short, with an emphasis on regional trade-offs, the concerns of key economic sectors, the management of day-to-day crises and embarrassments, and partisan point-scoring.

The arrival of the Harper minority Conservative government in 2006 began a significant rollback of the SD implementation efforts of the previous Liberal and Conservative governments. However, the majority Harper victory in 2011 had an even greater chilling effect on SD and the scientific knowledge at its base;[16] in fact, it might be argued that Harper has set out to fundamentally undermine the core values of SD. Indeed, Harper has chosen to make environment and resource development a "wedge issue" in an attempt to separate his core supporters from other Canadians.[17] He made his position abundantly clear in a revealing back-to-the-future moment when speaking about the development of a gold mine in Nunavut, stating that "[e]nvironment issues . . . can't stop development" while defending the dumping of toxic tailings into fish habitat in a lake near the mine site. His rationale was a combination of frontier economics ("we can't stop development [in the North] any more than we would let that stop development in Toronto, Montreal or Vancouver") and resource management ("are there effects of development on the environment? Absolutely . . . we seek to minimize . . . and remediate those effects").[18] This approach plays well to the Conservative base (representing roughly 30 per cent of voters), and may be an effective technique for soliciting donations. It also turns the clock back to pre-1987.

As discussed in detail by Valiante in Chapter 4, in a pair of sweeping budget bills the Conservatives reversed federal SD commitments and began to implement Responsible Resource Development, which emphasizes the rapid extraction of resources from the Earth's crust and the construction of transportation infrastructure to ship these largely unprocessed commodities to world markets. Transforming Canada into a global quarry required "correcting" the SD legislation and practices created by the Mulroney and Chrétien governments. The Conservatives slipped fundamental reforms into "omnibus" budget bills C-38 (2012) and C-45 (2012), rather than introducing, debating, and passing amendments through routine parliamentary processes. This unconventional approach to wholesale environmental regulatory reform was largely recognized as an abuse of Parliament. The omnibus bills provided cover to roll back environmental regulations and eliminate key agencies that were part of the Brundtland Commission's legacy in Canada. The National Round Table on the Environment and Economy (NRTEE) was terminated, arguably for publishing independent research-based positions critical of the government. Further, arm's-length regulatory agencies such as the Canadian Environmental Assessment Agency and the National Energy Board saw their mandates reduced in the interests of "efficiency and timeliness" as part of the government's approach to project development. Changes to the environmental assessment process were explicitly designed to restrict public participation.

While still a minority government, the Conservatives had supported a Liberal private member's bill to create a Federal Sustainable Development Act. The core purpose of this Act, which came into effect in 2008, is to provide a legal framework for developing and implementing a federal sustainable development strategy to provide context and direction to departmental SD strategies. The first strategy covered the period 2010–13. It may strike the reader as odd that the Harper Conservatives, once they reached majority government status, would continue with this requirement, when clearly their articulation of the RRD framework and their rollback of environmental protection legislation in Bill C-38 and Bill C-45 showed they did not support the SD paradigm. Just two examples from the 2010–13 strategy will show how it is possible to engage in empty rhetoric.

One technique was to appropriate the language of SD and deploy it to legitimize RRD. SD concepts like "natural capital" and "strategic environmental assessment" were redefined to legitimize "sustainable economic growth and responsible resource development" at the same time that environmental considerations were diminished in development decisions.[19] Another technique has been to mislead Canadians about the government's efforts in this area. In the 2013 CESD *Review* of the Conservative's 2012 *Progress Report* of the FSDS, the CESD chastised the government for being misleading by failing to "present a representative, clear, and complete picture. . . . Furthermore, balanced reporting ensures there are no distortions of information through presentation or tone, or through the omission of information and context."[20] The CESD was referring to a broader practice but also to specific text that was deceptive. A narrative box in the *Progress Report* painted a picture of Canada being well on its way to meeting the greenhouse gas reduction targets agreed to by Harper for the Copenhagen Accord in 2009; in other forums, however, the government was simultaneously reporting that, due to rapid expansion of absolute oil sands emissions, Canada would not only not meet the Copenhagen targets but would likely remain 20 per cent above them.[21] Simply put, the growth of oil sands production is swamping all the progress made in all other sectors. At the time of writing, the Conservatives were no closer to announcing emission reduction regulations for the oil and gas sector than they were when they announced their plans to do so three years earlier. The CESD pointed out that the Conservatives were not being honest with Canadians, and lacked the political will to impose the kinds of regulations on the oil and gas sector that they had applied to the coal-fired electricity and vehicle transportation sectors.[22]

Provinces and Cities: Experimentation, Challenges, and a New Wave of SD?

Despite the recent moves away from sustainability by the Harper government, it would be incorrect to describe Canada as a whole as being negligent on SD. Within the Canadian constitutional framework, two subnational levels of government (provincial and municipal) have substantial powers and unique responsibilities that allow them to implement SD principles. Moreover, given their geographic and institutional proximity to citizens, provincial and municipal governments are able to design and implement policies that reflect diverse circumstances across the country. These two factors, along with an acknowledgement by many officials at these governance levels of the need to advance SD, have led to a number of initiatives over the last 5–10 years. These initiatives have often begun as a response to climate change, but the central tenets of SD—including the core consideration of the economic, social, and environmental spheres—are present throughout.

Provincial Initiatives

Canada's three largest provinces, representing nearly three-quarters of the Canadian population, have been the most active. Other provinces have certainly introduced various initiatives, but we focus here on the big provinces.

Quebec has established a Commissioner of Sustainable Development, introduced a carbon charge, and advanced plans to accelerate **low-carbon electrification** in many sectors, including transportation. Interestingly, Quebec has established a new Institute of Electrical Transportation that will advance transportation electrification by acting as a bridge between companies and technological developments in the field. In particular, the Institute will support the development of industrial and commercial collaborations focused on the needs of both the heavy vehicle industry (e.g., vehicles used in public transit, for example) and the light vehicle industry. This initiative is intended to build on the province's obvious strengths in hydroelectric power generation and electrical systems by bringing knowledge and expertise together in the design and manufacture of electrical vehicles. Planned projects will target a variety of transportation electrification fields, including batteries, electric motors, smart grids, information networks, design, lightweight materials, and electronics. The Institute will manufacture short runs of pre-production prototypes as well as provide access to a test track adapted for this type of vehicle.[23]

Ontario, for its part, has institutionalized programs to increase the share of low-carbon renewable energies in the electricity supply mix and to strengthen energy conservation practices in the industrial, commercial, and residential sectors. Garnering perhaps the most press, in 2003 Ontario committed to phasing out coal power facilities within 10 years because of the detrimental effects on human health and contribution to greenhouse gas emissions of coal combustion. The province has met this commitment. Yet, the idea of retiring coal power was part of a larger plan centred on renewable electricity development in the 2009 Green Energy and Green Economy Act (GEA). The Act is a multi-part strategy to encourage new renewable energy generation, promote energy conservation, and stimulate the creation of "clean energy jobs" in Ontario.[24] A centrepiece of the strategy is the feed-in tariff (FIT) program for renewable electricity, designed to encourage the development of new renewable energy projects in the province. With its emphasis on renewable electricity, energy conservation, and the creation of jobs around these industries, the Act has combined the economic, social, and environmental spheres within one piece of legislation.

Since its inception, the FIT program has led to the rapid development of new renewable energy projects and has helped generate a vibrant discussion about Ontario's future. The government's pursuit of upstream and downstream economic spinoff benefits of the program has been more difficult to achieve, however, and this has led to criticisms of the GEA as an industrial strategy. Additionally, there has been a backlash against the GEA due to increases in electricity prices in recent years. This criticism is misdirected, in that price increases since the mid-2000s have had a number of drivers, including the continued high costs associated with the nuclear power system.[25] Despite these recent setbacks, the government of Ontario has not significantly backed away from the strategy as a whole, showing once again that changing political landscapes pose challenges, which major SD initiatives must navigate. Moreover, the majority Liberal government of Ontario, re-elected in May 2014, has committed to placing a price on carbon, likely in 2015.

British Columbia also implemented a broad SD agenda in the late 2000s. In 2008, the BC Liberal government introduced the Climate Action Plan as a multi-pronged approach to addressing climate change. The centrepiece of the Plan is a revenue-neutral carbon tax, which was designed to intensify over time, increasing from an original rate of $10 per tonne of carbon emissions in 2008 to $30 per tonne in 2013. In addition to the tax, the plan would also work towards longer-term economic and behavioural adjustments by committing to energy conservation measures, creating a carbon-neutral government, and establishing numerous investment funds dedicated to clean energy research.[26] As is the case in Ontario, BC's Climate Action Plan is forward thinking, inclusive of economic, social, and environmental factors, and underscores the need for a fundamental shift in our business and private behaviour.

Much like Ontario's Green Energy and Green Economy Act, however, BC's Climate Action Plan has faced challenges. Early in its history (2009), the Plan was the subject of a fundamental challenge during the provincial election with the major opposition party running on a promise to "axe the tax." BC voters rejected this option and the Plan has proved resilient; in fact, public support increased even as the carbon tax reached its highest level. Some of this success might be attributed to the cultural attitudes of British Columbians and the notions of environmental stewardship that have long run through the province, although specific aspects of the tax's implementation are also at play.[27] As the tax was intended to strengthen over time, British Columbians have had time to adjust their expectations, behaviours, and views. This does not imply that the BC Plan is complete, however, as there are ongoing questions about whether some resource industry processes should be brought under the tax, as well as whether the tax should be raised in coming years. Overall, however, public acceptance of the Plan is strong, and recent studies have shown that the tax appears to be decoupling economic growth from fossil fuel usage, while also stimulating investment in clean technologies and research, a stated goal of the Climate Action Plan and a hallmark of SD policy overall.

Municipal Initiatives

Decisions at the municipal level affect people on a day-to-day basis, in an immediate and intimate way. Decisions about where to build new houses, where to repair roads and build public transit, and how to plan the community have profound impacts on the citizens. Similarly, SD initiatives at the municipal level, due to their proximity to citizens, have a greater chance of influencing specific aspects of individual behaviour.

Two of the most wide-ranging SD plans currently adopted at the municipal level can be found in Vancouver and Edmonton. The Vancouver approach was adopted by city council in 2011 and is titled the *Greenest City 2020 Action Plan*. As the title implies, the primary goal is to make Vancouver the greenest city in the world by 2020. In developing the *Plan*, the city consulted over 35,000 people who helped shape 15 specific targets, the intermediate goals, and the overall plan to reach the targets by 2020.[28] Many of these specific goals go to the very heart of daily life and include such things as developing alternative methods of transportation, mandating waste reduction measures, and developing district (as opposed to individual) heating and cooling systems for offices and residential areas.

While Vancouver's *Action Plan* should be commended for its near-term goals and aspirations, Edmonton's plan is notable for its scale and ambition. Since 2008, Edmonton has been developing a comprehensive strategy to rebuild and rebrand the city around SD principles. A focal point of this plan involves comprehensive redevelopment for the downtown core as a way to slow urban sprawl. Edmonton has moved forward on this in a number of ways, including construction of a new multi-purpose arena downtown, intended to coax residential and commercial development in the area. The cornerstone project, however, is the redevelopment plan for a vast piece of property that had been a downtown airport until it was closed several years ago. Once completed around 2035, the former airport lands will become a 30,000-person community that is completely carbon neutral.[29] Such transformative urban sustainability plans will no doubt face challenges along the way, but the fact that the strategies were developed with broad public input, were adopted by city councils, and are already underway bodes well for the future. These are examples from just two cities, and similar sorts of SD-inspired projects are being undertaken in cities across the country. When combined with provincial-level initiatives, such recent municipal actions show that SD experimentation and implementation are continuing to unfold at the subnational levels across Canada.

Conclusion

As noted by both *Our Common Future* and William Ruckelshaus, the transformation of a society in the direction of sustainability is an ongoing intergenerational challenge and opportunity. Given the transformative agenda of SD, it is not surprising the post-1987 period has been characterized by setbacks as well as breakthroughs. In reference to this change process, *Our Common Future* noted that there will be strides forward, sideways, and backward. Changes in the executive offices of governments do matter at all levels. But so do changes in large and small business, in civil society and educational organizations, and at the household level. Canadian engagement with sustainable development is a mixed story to date—and an evolving one, at that.

Key Terms

first-past-the-post electoral system
green welfare state
international norm
low-carbon electrification

proportional representation
sustainable development
Westminster model

Questions for Review

1. In small groups, discuss the term "sustainable development." What does it mean to you and how can governments foster sustainability in a society?
2. Are Canadian citizens just as guilty as governments in failing to implement sustainable development?

3. Which is more capable at implementing sustainable development, the federal government or subnational governments?
4. Which of the post-1990 sustainable development institutions, processes, and policies would you keep? What would you add?

Internet Resources

The Delphi Group
http://wwww.delphi.ca

International Institute for Sustainable Development (IISD)
http://www.iisd.org

International Renewable Energy Agency (IRENA)
http://www.irena.org

Pembina Institute
http://www.pembina.org

Sustainable Development and Technology Canada (SDTC)
http://www.sdtc.ca

Sustainable Prosperity
http://www.sustainableprosperity.ca

World Business Council on Sustainable Development
http://www.wbcsd.org/

Additional Reading

Boutros, Serena, Lillian Hayward, Anique Montambault, Laura Smallwood, and Glen Toner. "Growing the Children of Brundtland: The Creation and Evolution of the NRTEE, IISD, CESD, and SDTC." In Glen Toner, Leslie A. Pal, and Michael J. Prince, eds, *Policy: From Ideas to Implementation—Essays in Honour of Professor G. Bruce Doern*, 257–85. Montreal and Kingston: McGill-Queen's University Press, 2010.
Braungart, Michael, and William McDonough. *The Upcycle*. New York: North Point Press, 2013.

Lafferty, William. *Governance for Sustainable Development: The Challenge of Adapting Form to Function*. Cheltenham: Edward Elgar, 2004.
Lafferty, William, and James Meadowcroft, eds. *Implementing Sustainable Development: Strategies and Initiatives in High Consumption Societies*. Oxford: Oxford University Press, 2000.
Lundqvist, L. *Sweden and Ecological Governance*. Manchester: Manchester University Press, 2004.

Meadowcroft, James. "National Sustainable Development Strategies: A Contribution to Reflexive Governance?" *European Environment* 17 (2007): 152–63.

Toner, Glen, and Francois Bregha. "Institutionalizing Sustainable Development: The Role of Governmental Institutions." In Glen Toner and James Meadowcroft, eds,

Innovation, Science, Environment: Charting Sustainable Development in Canada, 1987–2027, 30–53. Montreal and Kingston: McGill-Queen's University Press, 2009.

World Commission on Environment and Development (WCED). *Our Common Future*. Oxford: Oxford University Press, 1987.

Notes

1. World Commission on Environment and Development (WCED), *Our Common Future* (Oxford: Oxford University Press, 1987), 9 (our emphasis).
2. As quoted in David Suzuki Foundation, *Sustainability within a Generation* (Vancouver: David Suzuki Foundation, 2004).
3. WCED, *Our Common Future*, 9.
4. For a detailed analysis of the nature and impact of these legislative changes, see Chapter 4 by Valiante.
5. For a detailed analysis of the orientation of the Harper administration towards science and scientists, see Chapter 6 by Bocking.
6. For detailed assessments of earlier parts of this period, see Glen Toner, "Canada: From Early Frontrunner to Plodding Anchorman," in William Lafferty and James Meadowcroft, eds, *Implementing Sustainable Development: Strategies and Initiatives in High Consumption Societies* (Oxford: Oxford University Press, 2000), 53–84; Glen Toner and James Meadowcroft, eds, *Innovation, Science, Environment: Charting Sustainable Development in Canada, 1987–2007* (Montreal and Kingston: McGill-Queen's University Press, 2009).
7. William Lafferty, "The Politics of Sustainable Development: Global Norms for National Implementation," *Environmental Politics* 5 (1996): 185–208; James Meadowcroft, "Sustainable Development: A New(ish) Idea for a New Century?" *Political Studies* 48 (2000): 370–87.
8. See, e.g., James Meadowcroft, "Who Is in Charge Here? Governance for Sustainable Development in a Complex World," *Journal of Environmental Policy and Planning* 9 (2007): 299–314.
9. Bob Masterson, "From Eco-efficiency to Eco-effectiveness: Private Sector Practices for Sustainable Production," in Glen Toner, ed., *Sustainable Production: Building Canadian Capacity* (Vancouver: University of British Columbia Press, 2006), 27–41.
10. See Glen Toner and Francois Bregha, "Institutionalizing Sustainable Development: The Role of Governmental Institutions," in Glen Toner and James Meadowcroft, eds, *Innovation, Science, Environment: Charting Sustainable Development in Canada 1987–2027* (Montreal and Kingston: McGill-Queen's University Press, 2009), 30–53.
11. Consider P. Dreisen and P. Glasbergen, *Greening Society: The Paradigm Shift in Dutch Environmental Politics* (Dordrecht: Kluwer Academic, 2002); L. Lundqvist, *Sweden and Ecological Governance* (Manchester: Manchester University Press, 2004); William Lafferty, *Governance for Sustainable Development: The Challenge of Adapting Form to Function* (Cheltenham: Edward Elgar, 2004); James Meadowcroft, "National Sustainable Development Strategies: A Contribution to Reflexive Governance?" *European Environment* 17 (2007): 152–63.
12. For a detailed discussion of Canada's experience as a staples economy, and the impact on environmental policy, see Chapter 3 by Howlett and Kinney.
13. Glen Toner, "The Green Plan: From Great Expectations, to Eco-Backtracking . . . to Revitalization?" in Susan Phillips, ed., *How Ottawa Spends 1994–95: Making Change* (Ottawa: Carleton University Press, 1994), 229–60.
14. Canada, *Canada's Green Plan—For a Healthy Environment* (1990), 4–6.
15. Serena Boutros, Lillian Hayward, Anique Montambault, Laura Smallwood, and Glen Toner, "Growing the Children of Brundtland: The Creation and Evolution of the NRTEE, IISD, CESD, and SDTC," in Glen Toner, Leslie A. Pal, and Michael J. Prince, eds, *Policy: From Ideas to Implementation—Essays in Honour of Professor G. Bruce Doern* (Montreal and Kingston: McGill-Queen's University Press, 2010), 257–85.
16. Kathryn O'Hara and Paul Dufour, "How Accurate Is the Harper Government Misinformation? Scientific Evidence and Scientists in Federal Policy Making," in G. Bruce Doern and Christopher Stoney, eds, *How Ottawa Spends 2014–2015: The Harper Government—Good to Go?* (Montreal and Kingston: McGill-Queen's University Press, 2014): 178–191.
17. Glen Toner and Jennifer Mckee, "Harper's Partisan Wedge Politics: Bad Environmental Policy AND Bad Energy Policy," in G. Bruce Doern and Christopher Stoney, eds, *How Ottawa Spends 2014–2015: The Harper Government—Good to Go?* (Montreal and Kingston: McGill-Queen's University Press, 2014), 108–21.
18. Mike de Souza, "Harper Defends Dumping Waste from Gold Mine into Fish Habitat," *Ottawa Citizen*, 25 Aug. 2011, A4.
19. Canada, *Planning for a Sustainable Future: A Federal Sustainable Development Strategy for Canada 2010–2013* (Ottawa: Sustainable Development Office, Environment Canada, 2013), 8.

20. Commissioner of the Environment and Sustainable Development, *Federal and Departmental Sustainable Development Strategies Part 2—Review of the 2012 Progress Report of the Federal Sustainable Development Strategy* (Ottawa: Office of the Auditor General of Canada, 2013), ch. 8, p. 31.

21. For the latest information on Canada's GHG emissions status, see Environment Canada, *Canada's Emissions Trends*, Oct. 2013, accessed 4 July 2014, http://www.ec.gc.ca/ges-ghg/985F05FB-4744-4269-8C1A-D443F8A86814/1001-Canada's%20Emissions%20Trends%202013_e.pdf.

22. Shawn McCarthy, "Emissions Will Soar after 2020 without Oil Sector Regulation, Federal Report Says," *Globe and Mail*, 8 Jan. 2014.

23. Government of Quebec, *Transportation Electrification Strategy 2013–2017* (2013), 51–2.

24. Government of Ontario, An Act to enact the Green Energy Act, 2009 and to build a green economy, to repeal the Energy Conservation Leadership Act, 2006 and the Energy Efficiency Act and to amend other statutes, 14 May 2009. See Preamble.

25. Environmental Commissioner of Ontario, *2014 Annual Energy Conservation Program Report: Planning to Conserve* (Toronto, 2014), 79–83.

26. Government of British Columbia, *British Columbia's Climate Action Plan* (June 2008), 2–5.

27. Kathryn Harrison, *The Political Economy of British Columbia's Carbon Tax*, OECD Environment Working Papers, No. 63 (Paris: OECD, 2013), 12–13.

28. City of Vancouver, *Greenest City 2020 Action Plan*, 6.

29. Perkins + Will Canada, *Civitas Group Two: Draft Plan Presented to Edmonton City Council July 17, 2012*, 39.

8 Federalism, Intergovernmental Relations, and the Environment

Julie M. Simmons

Chapter Summary

This chapter considers how the operation of federalism and federal–provincial relations affects environmental policy in Canada. It argues that the complex nature of environmental challenges, on the one hand, and jurisdiction over environmental policy, on the other, demand that federal and provincial governments work together. However, to date, Canada's forums for intergovernmental decision-making have not tended to produce robust environmental agreements, owing to a variety of factors including their weak institutionalization and limited policy capacity. The history of intergovernmental relations in this policy field shows that federal governments have put a premium on co-operative relations with provinces, often at the expense of stronger environmental policies. During Stephen Harper's tenure as Prime Minister, we have seen a slightly different approach, one potentially more harmful to the environment. This approach is characterized by very limited intergovernmental interaction and the simultaneous weakening of federal environmental policies.

Chapter Outline

- Jurisdiction over environmental policy in the Canadian federation
  - Attributes of federations
  - Federal and provincial roles in environmental policy
- Institutions of intergovernmental decision-making
  - Why executive federalism exists and the forms it takes
  - The degree of institutionalization and policy capacity of intergovernmental forums for the discussion of policies related to the environment
- Environmental policy and intergovernmental decision-making, 1970–2006
  - Federal legislative activism (early 1970s and late 1980s–early 1990s)
  - The equilibrium of federal–provincial co-operation through enabling rather than mandatory action

- Stephen Harper's "open federalism" and its impacts on the environmental policy sector
  - ○ Respect for provincial jurisdiction
  - ○ Smaller state (fewer regulations that impede the free flow of the market)
  - ○ Limited executive federalism and federal retreat from environmental policy
- Future of intergovernmental relations regarding environmental policy

Introduction

Given the complex nature of environmental challenges, and given that federal and provincial governments both have constitutional jurisdiction over the environment, interaction between the two orders of government is a necessity for the development of effective environmental policy. This chapter explores the nature of intergovernmental forums that exist to co-ordinate federal and provincial environmental policies, and argues that they are weakly institutionalized or, in other words, largely informal. Their reliance on consensus-based decision-making has produced a largely enabling, rather than mandatory, environmental policy legacy. Also inhibiting the development of robust environmental policy in Canada is a historical lack of federal interest in testing the scope of its own jurisdiction in the field and, instead, a focus on maintaining federal–provincial harmony. Steven Harper's approach to environmental policy and relations has been guided by his general preference for a small state (an economy free from state intervention) and for an untangling of federal and provincial areas of responsibility. This preference is sometimes referred to as "open federalism" or "the Harper doctrine." As a result, the most recent era of intergovernmental relations is characterized by federal–provincial harmony, achieved through an absence of interaction and a federal retreat from the environmental policy sphere.

This chapter develops these arguments, first, by outlining federal and provincial jurisdiction over the environment and, then, by exploring the nature of the intergovernmental institutions that co-ordinate federal and provincial and/or interprovincial environmental policy. It discusses whether it is possible in theory to have robust, collaborative environmental policies, and uses a variety of contemporary examples to illustrate the weakness of intergovernmental policy outputs. The chapter then traces, over time, the pattern of intergovernmental decision-making pertaining to the environment. Against the backdrop of open federalism, we consider the federal government's measures to limit federal–provincial co-ordination, as well as to weaken those environmental laws that potentially impede the growth of the economy through greater natural resource extraction. The chapter concludes with a discussion of the factors that might have to be present in order to pursue collaborative intergovernmental decision-making on environmental policy matters in the future.

Jurisdiction over Environmental Policy in the Canadian Federation

In a federation, territorially defined political communities agree to share in the making and administering of laws in some areas and to pursue other laws independently. **Federalism** is a legal construct, offering one way to sustain the diversity of geographically based communities while uniting those communities. The **constituent units** of every federation (called provinces in Canada) always have some form of representation in the political institutions of the central government (referred to as the federal government in Canada), and laws made by the central government apply to all individuals in the country as a whole. The laws of the constituent unit governments only apply to those individuals who live in those subnational political communities. All federations have constitutions that outline the policy areas over which the central and constituent unit governments have power to make laws, as well as court systems to arbitrate disputes arising between the central and constituent unit governments. In Canada, as in all federations, neither the federal nor provincial governments are subordinate to one another, because this division of policy jurisdiction cannot be changed unilaterally by either of them. In other words, in Canada the two orders of government (federal and provincial) are equal, inasmuch as neither can change the division of powers in the Constitution Act, 1867 without the consent of the other, and in accordance with a specified amending formula.

Federated states may be contrasted with **unitary states**, such as New Zealand or France. In unitary states, different levels of government (central and local) still exist, but the central government has the authority to determine what kinds of powers the local governments will have. Another alternative is a **confederated state**, where local governments have the authority to determine the powers and jurisdiction of the central government. It is important to appreciate that, unlike federations, both unitary states and confederal states have one level of government that is subordinate to the other.

There are a variety of reasons why communities choose federalism over unitarism, in which the tyranny of the majority can trump the will of a geographically concentrated minority. Principally, the diversity of the constituent units can be preserved, while the benefits of union can be accrued. Federalism works when communities desire unity but not necessarily uniformity.[1] But even if scholars and citizens disagree on whether federalism is sufficiently democratic, inclusive, respectful of diversity, or responsive to citizens' needs, it defines how the Canadian governmental system functions, and solutions to complex problems like global warming and endangered species must be found within our federal arrangements.

Federations differ on how they distribute powers among the central and constituent unit governments. As discussed in detail by Valiante in Chapter 4, the Canadian Constitution identifies areas of exclusive jurisdiction of the federal government (section 91 of the Constitution Act, 1867) and of provincial governments (section 92). There is also a third small set of concurrent powers, or policy areas in which both orders of government might legislate. Anything not mentioned in these lists of powers was intended to be captured by the residual clause, which gives the federal government the general power to legislate for the "peace, order, and good government" of Canada. In practice, however, Canada's final court of appeal has historically interpreted this clause narrowly, while interpreting provincial jurisdiction broadly.[2] An alternative approach to the federal division of powers can be found in the German constitution, which outlines those areas where the central government has exclusive jurisdiction, concurrent powers (which it shares with the constituent unit governments, or Länder), and framework powers. All policy areas not enumerated in the constitution are the purview of the Länder. The central government is limited to providing general policy guidelines in the areas listed as framework powers, such as nature conservation. In turn, the Länder determine how they will translate these guidelines into detailed legislation. Canada's Constitution does not have an equivalent to Germany's framework powers.

Like many other modern policy challenges, "environmental protection" was not foreseen in 1867 as a subject of legislation, and is not identified as such in Canada's Constitution. However, provinces are said to have jurisdiction over environmental policy because of their exclusive jurisdiction over provincially owned public lands and natural resources; municipal institutions and services; property and civil rights; local works and undertakings; forestry; mining; and "matters of a local and private nature" within a province. At the same time, the federal government is said to have jurisdiction over environmental policy because of its jurisdiction over seacoasts and fisheries; navigation and shipping; interprovincial trade and commerce; international relations; and its authority to negotiate international treaties such as the Kyoto Accord. In addition, Supreme Court decisions in cases such as *Crown Zellerbach* in 1988 strengthened federal authority over environmental policy, relying on an expanded interpretation of Parliament's power to legislate for the "peace, order, and good government of Canada." In this case, the Court upheld the federal government's Coastal Dumping Act, arguing that coastal water pollution constitutes a "national concern" (a bar established through criteria that have evolved through Supreme Court rulings). In the landmark 1997 *Attorney General of Canada v. Hydro-Québec* case, the Supreme Court found that Parliament may use its power over criminal law when exercising its environmental authority. The Court upheld the federal government's authority to regulate toxic substances under the Canadian Environmental Protection Act, on the basis that "the stewardship of the environment is a fundamental value of our society, and that Parliament may use its criminal law power to underline that value."[3]

Given that both orders of government have different sources of authority to act to protect the environment, there are compelling reasons why the two orders of government should co-ordinate their efforts, rather than develop strategies independent of each other. For example, as discussed in greater detail by Macdonald in Chapter 13, climate change cannot be addressed simply by the federal government making commitments in international treaties to reduce greenhouse gas emissions. The extraction of natural resources like oil and gas are emissions-intensive processes, but the provinces have jurisdiction over those natural resources, and the strength of many provincial economies rests on the extraction of those resources. "Buy-in" is thus required by provinces, such as Alberta, whose natural resource extraction is disproportionately responsible for our national emission levels. The problem, of course, is that there is little economic incentive for these provinces to commit to aggressive emission reductions.[4] It comes as no surprise that, absent federal leadership in co-ordinating intergovernmental efforts, the 2012 *Report* of the Commissioner of the Environment and Sustainable Development conveyed that "GHG emissions are expected to be 805 million tonnes above Canada's Kyoto Protocol target of 2792 million tonnes during the 2008–2012 period."[5] And the oil and gas sector provinces are not the only ones to confront the challenge of balancing the protection of their natural resource industries against protection of the environment. The same could be said for other sectors such as forestry, important to the British Columbia government in particular, and the mining of potash in Saskatchewan.

The key point is that the federal government often cannot act alone; but neither should it rely on provincial governments to act, given the uneven distribution of the negative economic consequences among provinces of doing so. The interdependencies of modern policy-making require some kind of flexible approach in order to overcome the rigidities of the Constitution.

Institutions of Intergovernmental Decision-Making

Through what channels can the federal and provincial governments co-ordinate policies? In Canada there is a tradition of executive federalism, defined as "the relations between the elected and appointed executives of the two orders of government."[6] Executive federalism arises from the marriage of Westminster-style decision-making, federalism, and the ineffective representation of the provinces in the central institutions of government.[7] Provincial interests are not well represented in the central institutions of government (for example, the unelected Canadian Senate), and this lack of effective representation means that provincial governments can claim to be best able to represent the interests of Canadians living within their provinces. At the same time, the Westminster parliamentary system concentrates political authority in the hands of the executive. The elected executive is comprised of the cabinet (ministers of various policy areas) and is almost always drawn from members of the legislature (Parliament in Ottawa, the provincial legislature in the case of each province) who are part of the governing party. In instances where the governing party has a majority of seats, through the exercise of party discipline, the cabinet essentially controls every outcome of the legislature. Accordingly, the executives of the federal and provincial governments have the ability to speak authoritatively on behalf of their governments in intergovernmental meetings with their counterparts from other jurisdictions, even though these meetings take place outside of legislative settings.

Sometimes these meetings result in formalized intergovernmental agreements that have real impacts on federal and provincial policy developments. The highest level of these kinds of negotiations takes place at meetings of provincial premiers and the Prime Minister. Such summits, known as First Ministers' meetings, have become rare and ad hoc.[8] However, meetings of federal ministers in specific policy areas—e.g., health or natural resources—with their respective provincial counterparts are more routine. At such meetings, discussion takes place and commitments might be made to direct bureaucrats to further examine specific issues with an eye towards developing a consensus on how governments will collectively proceed. There are also a variety of interactions between the unelected bureaucrats who support ministers. These interactions take the form of face-to-face meetings, telephone calls, and written correspondence. All of this communication constitutes executive federalism.

On the one hand, these intergovernmental forums offer the potential for swift federal–provincial decision-making; a limited number of individuals are involved (ministers from each participating jurisdiction) and they can circumvent the process of debate associated with the obligations of first, second, and third readings of a bill in a legislature. These forums can also build trust among governments. As they operate on the principle of consensus, to a considerable extent the federal and provincial governments are participating as equals—a key principle in federations. On the other hand, the lack of transparency of these forums also can be interpreted as a democratic deficiency. Further, these forums can get bogged down in balancing the disparate interests of the participating governments, resulting in a consensus that reflects the "lowest common denominator," or the lowest standard among them. Worse yet, intergovernmental paralysis can lead to a policy void, and provinces potentially engage in a race to the bottom, competing among themselves to maximize their economic benefit.[9] Both the lowest common denominator and race-to-the-bottom dynamics are strongly criticized by environmentalists, who advocate for more assertive national legislation that challenges the boundaries of the scope of federal jurisdiction, even if it is at the expense of intergovernmental co-operation.[10]

Environmental issues are potentially discussed in a variety of venues for executive federalism, including intergovernmental meetings of ministers of environment, mining, wildlife, parks, forestry, energy, and fisheries and aquaculture, not to mention First Ministers' meetings. The Council of the Federation, comprised of the premiers of the provinces and territories, meets twice yearly, and has also been the setting of interprovincial discussion pertaining to climate change in the last decade. Table 8.1 identifies the pattern of meetings of these sectoral ministers and deputy ministers (the highest-ranking bureaucrats in their relevant departments) over the last decade.

The most obvious intergovernmental forum for discussion of environmental policy is the Canadian Council of Ministers of the Environment (CCME), which coincidentally is the most fully institutionalized forum with respect to sectoral federal–provincial interactions. The CCME has a full-time secretariat in Winnipeg (currently with a staff of eight) that provides bureaucratic support to ministers; a formal "constitution" that embeds consensus as the decision-making rule of the Council; a series of subcommittees on specific aspects of environmental policy comprised of bureaucrats drawn from all jurisdictions; and an annual work plan (Figure 8.1 depicts the organization of the CCME). While a handful of other ministerial forums also have websites, such as the Canadian Council of Forest Ministers (CCFM), the CCME website stands apart because of its information on CCME priorities, access to its publications, calendar of public consultation, and the transparency it provides in terms of how the Council functions.[11] The CCME also has a formalized commitment to joint federal–provincial action on environmental issues, the harmonization of environmental legislation, policies, procedures, and programs, and the development of "nationally consistent environmental objectives (and) standards."[12] Put another way, the CCME is committed to unity—though without uniformity.

Other sectoral intergovernmental forums pertaining to the environment are less institutionalized. Generally speaking, they constitute annual meetings of ministers who, at the end of their deliberations, may or may not issue a communiqué explaining to the public what took place in the meeting. Moreover, these meetings rarely result in new deals or agreements struck among ministers.[13] For example, fisheries and aquaculture ministers have been working on developing new regulations to manage the threat of aquatic invasive species. However, the communiqué from their 2013 meeting reads: "Ministers re-affirmed their commitment to continue to work together in a manner consistent with their respective jurisdictions of the two levels of government to bring this most important project to fruition."[14] A skeptic might be inclined to conclude from this statement that ministers could *not* agree on how to work together!

Another reason why Canada's forums for executive federalism are considered less institutionalized, especially when compared to those in other federations,[15] is that much of the output of intergovernmental relations assumes actors (whether governments or industries) will voluntarily comply. For example, perhaps the only major output of the Canadian Council of Forest Ministers since 2008 has been the work of its Climate Change Taskforce. While its 2012 report is rather voluminous, the voluntary nature of this output is evident in the authors' introduction, which notes that "it is our sincere hope that these documents . . . will benefit forest practitioners from coast to coast to coast as they seek innovative ways to adapt sustainable forest management policies and practices for a changing climate."[16] As

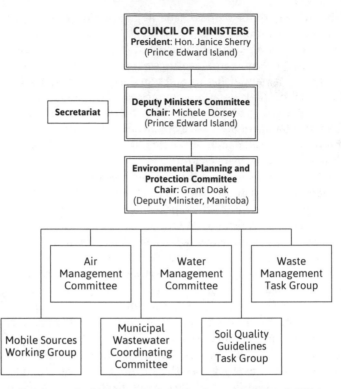

FIGURE 8.1 | Canadian Council of Ministers of the Environment, March 2014

Winfield demonstrates in Chapter 5, however, *hoping* for voluntary compliance is a rather weak policy instrument.

Finally, we might say that Canada's forums for executive federalism lack intergovernmental policy capacity because there is limited cross-sectoral discussion.[17] It is noteworthy that ministers of the environment, energy, forestry, wildlife, fisheries and aquaculture, and so on rarely meet together. In fact, in the last 10 years, only three meetings that might be described as intersectoral took place at the ministerial level. Yet, it would seem that such meetings, particularly given the rarity of First Ministers' meetings (another forum for intersectoral co-ordination), are especially important—indeed, necessary—given the complexities associated with developing effective environmental protection frameworks.

Upon its inception in 2003, the Council of the Federation held potential as a way to increase intergovernmental policy-making capacity in Canada. This Council effectively formalizes the long-standing Annual Premiers' Conferences, and is the only intergovernmental forum with a formal commitment to meet at least twice a year.[18] The Council's founding agreement establishes a steering committee composed of provincial deputy ministers, a secretariat, and a mechanism to create subcommittees to examine specific policy areas. Unfortunately, it does not codify a decision rule other than consensus and, as a result, its output with respect to climate change, for example, has been particularly weak, exposing the fissures between those provinces with carbon emission-intensive economies and those without. In 2012, the Council of the Federation established an Energy Strategy Working group co-chaired by Alberta, Newfoundland and Labrador, and Manitoba. The goal of the working group is to establish an agreement among provinces on energy conservation, development, and use so that "provinces and territories are better positioned to build the energy infrastructure they require; improve sustainable energy use, development, and protection for the environment; and expand production to help meet global demand."[19] However, British Columbia and Quebec, the two provinces with arguably the strongest records in combating climate change,[20] only joined the working group in 2013 and 2014, respectively.

Thus far, I have argued that a need exists for intergovernmental co-ordination, given divided jurisdiction over the environment and the complexity of environmental protection. While there is a strong tradition of executive federalism in Canada, our intergovernmental decision-making forums are weakly institutionalized, lack policy capacity, and are vulnerable to deadlock or lowest-common-denominator outcomes because they operate on the basis of consensus. The next section traces how the federal government, in this intergovernmental context, has developed environmental policy since the 1970s.

Environmental Policy and Intergovernmental Decision-Making, 1970–2006

Since the creation of federal and provincial environment departments in the 1970s, the federal government has not been particularly aggressive in testing the limits of its jurisdiction with respect to environmental policy. In the early 1970s, the federal government passed seven major pieces of legislation related to pollution control: the Inland Waters Act, the Arctic Waters Pollution Prevention Act, the Canada Water Act, the Clean Air Act, and the amendments to the Fisheries Act, the Ocean Dumping Control Act, and the Environmental Contaminants Act. However, generally speaking, the Canadian federal government has sought to support provincial efforts, avoiding the use of inducements or threats to bring provinces in line. This federal hesitancy to flex its muscle was apparent even during the initial period of federal legislative activism, and contrasts the experience in federations such as the United States. There, the federal government adopted a more domineering approach towards states in the initial development of environmental policies, and then solidified its jurisdiction over the subsequent decade. By contrast, from the mid-1970s to the mid-1980s in Canada, the federal government played less of a role in environmental protection, declining to enforce many of the national regulations established under the statutes mentioned above, and instead trusting provincial governments to enforce federal environmental standards as well as their own.[21]

The other period of federal environmental "activism" is marked by the passage of the 1988 Canadian Environmental Protection Act and the 1992 Canadian Environmental Assessment Act (CEAA). The former regulated toxic substances and had the potential to establish consistent standards across Canada. Unlike its predecessor, the Environmental Contaminants Act, it did not allow provincial governments to veto federal action. Provinces could only bypass federal regulations if they could prove, according to strict criteria, that their regulations were equivalent.[22] For its part, the CEAA was a source of considerable federal and provincial conflict since it impacted provincial efforts to develop their own natural resources. While the federal government had been involved in environmental impact assessments for decades, they acted under the terms of discretionary "guidelines." However, in a key 1987 court case, environmentalists were successful in compelling the federal government to conduct an environmental assessment on a dam project in Saskatchewan. This finding of the court prompted the federal government to adopt the CEAA. Afterwards, in many cases, both a provincial and a federal environmental assessment of a project would be required.

In the 1990s, public attention to issues like global warming waned, and provincial and federal governments became fixated on reducing their deficits. Environmental departments found their budgets cut. In this context, reducing the overlap and duplication of federal and provincial environmental policies became the focus of federal and provincial intergovernmental activities. After a series of negotiations in the CCME, environment ministers (with the exception of Quebec) signed the 1998 Canada-Wide Accord on Environmental Harmonization, with sub-agreements on Canada-Wide Standards, Inspections, and Environmental Assessment. At the macro level, these agreements reflect a renewed emphasis on federal–provincial co-operation and federal politeness towards provinces. But they also informed the federal government's 1999 amendments to the Canadian Environmental Protection Act and the drafting of the 2002 Species at Risk Act. As Winfield laments, "(t)he CEPA amendments require(d) the federal government to 'make offers to consult' with the provinces before taking virtually any substantive action under the Act."[23] More specifically, the Canada-Wide Accord on Environmental Harmonization put in place a framework for the negotiation and implementation of future sub-agreements (bilateral between the federal government and one province; or multilateral among all governments) to "harmonize" environmental management. In practice, this has translated into what a critical observer might call an obsession with ensuring that only one order of government acts in any specific area of environmental policy (either federal or provincial). A good example here is environmental assessment.

The Canada-Wide Environmental Standards sub-agreement outlines a "federal, provincial and territorial approach" for identifying toxic substances requiring standards, and developing the standards,[24] offering the possibility of co-ordinated action in lieu of federal unilateralism. Yet, the process of developing standards in this manner highlights some of the obstacles embedded in executive federalism, discussed above. First, developing consensus on specific standards has been a slow process. To date, there have been approximately 15 substances for which ministers have developed a Canada-Wide Standard (CWS). Examples include dioxins and furans; mercury emissions from specific sectors like coal-fired electric power generation plants; and most recently, fine particulate matter and ozone (the two main components of smog).[25] In general, the standards have been characterized as "unambitious," [26] owing in part to the consensus decision rule of the CCME.

The very careful approach to delineating federal and provincial responsibilities is also apparent in the Species at Risk Act (SARA). A key goal of this Act is to provide recovery plans for plants and animals that are extirpated, endangered, or threatened due to human activity. The Act itself only applies to federal lands: Parks Canada is responsible for species at risk in national parks; Fisheries and Oceans Canada is responsible for protecting aquatic species at risk; and Environment Canada is responsible for all other species at risk, including co-ordinating with provinces and territories to ensure that land-based species on non-federal lands are protected. The latter objective is to be achieved through the Canadian Endangered Species Conservation Council (CESCC), comprised of federal, provincial, and territorial ministers responsible for wildlife. The National Accord for the Protection of Species at Risk, which resulted from CESCC negotiations, commits governments to establishing "complementary legislation and programs that provide for effective protection of species at risk throughout Canada."[27] Like the Species at Risk Act, the Accord recognizes the Committee on the Status of Endangered Wildlife in Canada (COSEWIC) as the source of independent advice on the status of species at risk throughout Canada, and commits provincial governments to establishing recovery strategies within one year for species that become listed as endangered.[28] Ultimately, a federal minister (the minister responsible for Parks Canada Agency, the Ministry of Fisheries and Oceans, or the Minister of the Environment, depending on the location of the species) is responsible for ensuring that the provincial strategies meet the requirements of SARA and that provincial action plans are implemented in a timely manner. However, the discrepancy between lists of endangered species of various provinces and that of the federal government, the federal government's own record on the development of action plans, and the limited activity of the CESCC (discussed below) suggest that federal ministers have not provided the necessary leadership and co-ordination of provincial activity.

To sum up, the federal government has never been particularly ambitious about testing the scope of its jurisdiction in the field of environmental policy, with two eras of legislative activism punctuating an equilibrium that can be described not so much by the co-ordination of federal and provincial policy, but rather by the federal government declining to occupy policy space. Forays into joint development of policy through the CCME or other intergovernmental forums have placed a premium on federal–provincial co-operation, resulting in policy that is largely enabling rather than mandatory, in contrast to the United States. The next section assesses how Prime Minister Stephen Harper's approach to intergovernmental relations and the environment fits with this pattern.

Stephen Harper's Open Federalism

Prime Minister Stephen Harper's approach to federalism has been one of limited engagement in intergovernmental relations. Known to some as "the Harper doctrine,"[29] this approach was initially referred to as **open federalism** by Harper.[30] While it has several facets—and Harper has not been wholly consistent in applying it—the component most relevant to this chapter is Harper's retreat from areas of provincial jurisdiction (such as social policy) and concentration on major federal responsibilities (like national defence). In a sense, this approach has been an attempt to return to a classical "watertight" interpretation of the Constitution Act, 1867, rather than navigating a constructive entanglement with provinces that recognizes the interconnected complexity of modern policy problems. Disentanglement of the two orders of government out of so-called respect for provincial jurisdiction is the objective.[31] Some have argued that such an approach to intergovernmental relations is a means to the end of a smaller federal state that promotes **free markets** and "constrain(s) market-inhibiting forms of government intervention."[32]

Clearly, Harper's retreat from intergovernmental relations applies in the field of environmental policy. As Table 8.1 reveals, the total number of deputy ministers' and ministers' meetings has declined considerably since 2007. When one considers the frequency of ministerial meetings, the pattern is even more unambiguous, with meetings of those ministers in sectors pertaining to the environment declining from at least one per *month* during the Chrétien/Martin years (and up until 2008), to three meetings per *year* from 2011 to 2013. Another intriguing observation is the cessation of any form of intersectoral meetings that might properly reflect the complexity of tackling environmental issues such as biodiversity. Also evident from the table is the Conservative government's disinterest in any intergovernmental discussion of endangered species. The CESCC has met just three times in the last *decade*, with no meetings taking place during the Harper era at all. Indeed, wildlife ministers have not met during this period either. The Canadian Council of Forest Ministers—the most institutionalized forum apart from the CCME—did not meet for three years between

TABLE 8.1 Intergovernmental Meetings of Ministers and Deputy Ministers, 2003–2013

Name of Intergovernmental Forum	Year										
	2003	2004	2005	2006	2007	2008	2009	2010	2011	2012	2013
Canadian Council of Fisheries and Aquaculture Ministers	1	1	1	1	2		1	1	1	1	1
Canadian Council of Forestry Ministers	1	1	1	1	1	1	1	1			
Canadian Council of Ministers of the Environment	1	2	1	1	2	1	2	1	1	1	1
Canadian Council of Resource Ministers/Canadian Council of Ministers of the Environment				1	1						
Federal/Provincial/Territorial Meeting of Mines Ministers	1	1	1	1	1						
Federal/Provincial/Territorial Council of Energy Ministers	1	1	1	1	3						
Ministers Responsible for Energy and Mines							1	1	1	1	1
Northern Mines Ministers' Conference	1	1									
Ministers Responsible for Renewable Fuels				1	1						
Ministers Responsible for Forests, Wildlife, Endangered Species, Fisheries and Aquaculture	1	1	1								
Canadian Endangered Species Conservation Council		1	1								
Canadian Endangered Species Conservation Council and National Aboriginal Committee on Species at Risk				1							
Total Ministers' Meetings	7	9	7	8	11	3	5	4	3	3	3
Deputy Ministers' Meetings	4	7	3	7	6	4	5	5	2	4	5
Total Deputy Ministers' and Ministers' Meetings	11	16	10	15	17	7	10	9	5	7	8

Source: Canadian Intergovernmental Conference Secretariat 2003–2013.

2011 and 2014. And, while the CCME has continued to meet, it has not issued a press release since its 2012 meeting. Interestingly, the meetings of energy and mines ministers have continued, perhaps not surprising given the Harper government's emphasis on strengthening a national economy that is so reliant on the oil and gas sector.

One might argue that the lack of intergovernmentalism in the Harper era is not wholly negative, given that intergovernmental processes—like that associated with setting Canada-Wide Standards through the CCME—have yielded weak environmental policies. However, unlike other eras during which the federal government did not put a premium on intergovernmental co-operation (the early 1970s and the mid-1980s to early 1990s), the Harper era also has been one of deepening austerity—serious attempts to reduce budget deficits by targeting government programs—at the same time that the government seeks to generate economic growth by freeing the natural resource economy from any constraints, including from environmental requirements. The 2012 omnibus budget bill contained thoroughgoing changes to a wide variety of Acts pertaining to the environment, including the Canadian Environmental Assessment Act, the Fisheries Act, the Species at Risk Act, and the Canadian Environmental Protection Act.[33] The resulting changes to the Canadian Environmental Assessment Act allowed Ottawa to formally shift responsibility for environmental assessments to provinces, and federal ministers now have greater discretion to decide what projects need an environmental assessment, and what the scope of those assessments should be, as discussed in detail by Valiante in Chapter 4.[34] According to the Leader of the Opposition in Ottawa, these changes have reduced the number of annual federal environmental impact assessments from 3,000–6,000 to just 30, and amount to "a regulatory blank cheque for [the Conservatives'] friends in the resource extraction industry."[35] As of 2013, the Fisheries Act now only protects fish that are part of a commercial, recreational, or Aboriginal fishery. As a result of this change, described as "eras(ing) forty years of enlightened and responsible legislation," the habitats of most freshwater fish species in Canada and roughly 80 per cent of threatened or endangered fishes are no longer protected under the Act.[36]

The Conservative government's orientation towards environmental policy has also been evident in its lack of enforcement of the 1999 Canadian Environmental Protection Act, something highlighted in the 2011 report of the Commissioner of the Environment and Sustainable Development (CESD).[37] The Commissioner at the time, Scott Vaughan, left this position before the end of his term, according to some musings, out of exasperation with the Conservatives' "passive aggressive approach" to the environment.[38] Also revealing has been the Conservative approach to the implementation of SARA. The 2013 report of the CESD notes that 146 recovery strategies were outstanding for the 518 species listed at risk under the Act. Just seven of the required 97 action plans were in place, and the Commissioner estimated it would be 10 years before the outstanding plans were completed.[39] Another indicator has been the government's chronic delay in listing species at risk following a recommendation of COSEWIC. In every case, the government has up to nine months to determine whether it will accept the recommendation of the Committee of scientists to list a species, a prerequisite for the commencement of deliberation as to how to best protect a species. If it does not make a decision, then the species is automatically listed. One academic study found that over a four-year period, from 2009 to 2013, 92 of 141 COSEWIC assessments were in limbo, neither accepted nor rejected. Because successive Conservative environment ministers had not been officially transmitting these assessments to cabinet, the nine-month stopwatch could not begin.[40]

Future of Intergovernmental Relations Regarding Environmental Policy

Why does it seem like robust environmental policy in Canada is a remote possibility? Federalism as a principle for organizing decision-making among geographically communities is not the problem. Certainly, other federations, such as Germany and the United States, have been able to establish a stronger national framework for environmental protection. Some might be inclined to argue that a different division of powers would make for more effective policies, particularly if natural resources were in the hands of the federal government. But it is highly unlikely that governments would ever agree to such a change, and so solutions need to be found within the existing institutional context.

Looking forward, one option might be to increase the policy capacity of Canada's forums for intergovernmental decision-making by making them more institutionalized, with permanent bureaucratic support in the form of secretariats, formalized regular meeting schedules, and decision-making rules that do not rely on consensus. Such changes would bring them in line with other federations like Germany. However, this chapter has also revealed that federal leadership is a necessity. Such leadership is in conflict with Stephen Harper's so-called "open federalism," whether we think of this approach as a return to a watertight interpretation of federal and provincial jurisdiction, or the reduction of government interventions in the form of environmental policies that are seen to impede the free flow of the market.

Key Terms

confederated state

constituent units

executive federalism

federalism

federated states

free markets

open federalism

race to the bottom

unitary states

Questions for Review

1. What is executive federalism and why does it exist in Canada's federation?
2. What are the strengths and weaknesses of current intergovernmental institutions of decision-making?
3. What are some instances of unilateral federal environmental policy-making (achieved without provincial co-operation)?
4. What are some instances of environmental policy-making that have resulted from federal–provincial co-operation through intergovernmental forums?
5. Imagine you are the next Prime Minister of Canada. How would you go about exercising environmental leadership, given the nature of constitutional jurisdiction and the weaknesses of current intergovernmental institutions of decision-making?

Internet Resources

Canadian Council of Ministers of the Environment
www.ccme.ca

Canadian Council of Forest Minsters
www.ccfm.org

Council of the Federation
www.councilofthefederation.ca

Reports of the Commissioner of the Environment and Sustainable Development
http://www.oag-bvg.gc.ca/internet/English/parl_lp_e_901.html

Additional Reading

Council of the Federation, Canadian Energy Strategy Working Group. *Canadian Energy Strategy: Progress Report of the Council of the Federation.* 2013.

Courchene, Thomas J., and John R. Allan, eds. *Canada: The State of the Federation 2009: Carbon Pricing and Environmental Federalism.* Montreal and Kingston: McGill-Queen's University Press, 2010.

Harmes, Adam. "The Political Economy of Open Federalism." *Canadian Journal of Political Science* 40, 2 (2007): 417–37.

Harrison, Kathryn. "Federalism and Climate Policy Innovation: A Critical Reassessment." *Canadian Public Policy* 39, 2 (2013): S95–S108.

Holmes, Miranda. *All Over the Map 2012: A Comparison of Provincial Climate Change Plans.* Vancouver: David Suzuki Foundation, 2012.

Inwood, Gregory J., Carolyn Johns, and Patricia L. O'Reilly. *Intergovernmental Policy Capacity in Canada: Inside the Worlds of Finance, Environment, Trade and Health.* Montreal and Kingston: McGill-Queen's University Press, 2011.

Olewiler, Nancy. "Environmental Policy in Canada: Harmonized at the Bottom?" In Kathryn Harrison, ed., *Racing to the Bottom? Provincial Interdependence in the Canadian Federation.* Vancouver: University of British Columbia Press, 2006.

Simeon, Richard, and Amy Nugent. "Parliamentary Canada and Intergovernmental Canada: Exploring the Tensions." In Herman Bakvis and Grace Skogstad, eds, *Canadian Federalism: Performance, Effectiveness and Legitimacy,* 3rd edn. Toronto: Oxford University Press, 2012.

Weibust, Inger. "The Great Green North? Canada's Bad Environmental Record and How the Feds Can Fix It." In Gordon DiGiacomo and Maryantonnett Flumian, eds, *The Case for Centralized Federalism.* Ottawa: University of Ottawa Press, 2010.

Winfield, Mark, and Douglas Macdonald. 2012. "Federalism and Canadian Climate Change Policy." In Herman Bakvis and Grace Skogstad, eds, *Canadian Federalism: Performance, Effectiveness and Legitimacy,* 3rd edn. Toronto: Oxford University Press, 2012.

Notes

1. On this observation of Dicey and the democratic benefits of federalism, see Jennifer Smith, *Federalism* (Vancouver: University of British Columbia Press, 2004).
2. See Gerald Baier, "The Courts, The Constitution and Dispute Resolution," in Herman Bakvis and Grace Skogstad, eds, *Canadian Federalism: Performance, Effectiveness and Legitimacy,* 3rd edn (Toronto: Oxford University Press, 2012).
3. Supreme Court of Canada, *Attorney-General of Canada v. Hydro-Québec* (Supreme Court of Canada, 1997 No. 24652).
4. This argument is developed in more detail in Chapter 13 by Macdonald. See also Kathryn Harrison, "Multi-level Governance and Carbon Pricing in Canada, the United States and the European Union," in Thomas J. Courchene and John R. Allan, eds, *Canada: The State of the Federation 2009: Carbon Pricing and Environmental Federalism* (Montreal and Kingston: McGill-Queen's University

Press, 2010); Douglas Macdonald, "Harper Energy and Climate Change Policy: Failing to Address the Key Challenges," in Christopher Stoney and G. Bruce Doern, eds, *How Ottawa Spends 2011–2012: Trimming Fat or Slicing Pork?* (Montreal and Kingston: McGill-Queen's University Press, 2011).

5. Office of the Auditor General of Canada, *Report of the Commissioner of the Environment and Sustainable Development* (Ottawa: Minister of Public Works and Government Services, Spring 2012).
6. Donald V. Smiley, *Canada in Question: Federalism in the 1980s,* 3rd edn (Toronto: McGraw-Hill Ryerson, 1980), 91.
7. For a more detailed explanation of this interaction, see Richard Simeon and Amy Nugent, "Parliamentary Canada and Intergovernmental Canada: Exploring the Tensions," in Herman Bakvis and Grace Skogstad, eds, *Canadian Federalism: Performance, Effectiveness and Legitimacy,* 3rd edn (Toronto: Oxford University Press, 2012).

8. For example, during their tenures as Prime Minister, Brian Mulroney held 14 of these meetings over seven years; Jean Chrétien held seven over 10 years, and Paul Martin held two over one year. Peter Graefe and Julie M. Simmons, "Assessing the Collaboration That Was 'Collaborative Federalism' 1996–2006," *Canadian Political Science Review* 7 (2013): 25–36. Stephen Harper held one First Ministers' meeting in 2009, prompting Paul Wells to observe in January of 2015 that this gap between First Ministers' meetings was the longest in 97 years. "Why the PM Won't Meet with the Premiers," *Maclean's*, 28 Jan. 2015, Accessed 6 Mar. 2015, http://www.macleans.ca/politics/ottawa/why-pm-wont-meet-premiers/.

9. For a review of the race-to-the-bottom literature, see Kathryn Harrison, "Provincial Interdependence: Concepts and Theories," in Kathryn Harrison, ed., *Racing to the Bottom? Provincial Interdependence in the Canadian Federation* (Vancouver: University of British Columbia Press, 2006). The alternative to a race to the bottom is when individual provinces become "laboratories for innovation" with successful environmental policies in one province transferring to another, or diffusing among many. Kathryn Harrison carefully explains these dynamics and why they are unlikely the case in regard to climate change, in particular in "Federalism and Climate Policy Innovation: A Critical Reassessment," *Canadian Public Policy* 39, 2 (1997): S95–S108. Nancy Olewiler's investigation of provincial pollution control absent federal leadership finds neither a race to the bottom nor a race to the top. Olewiler, "Environmental Policy in Canada: Harmonized at the Bottom?" in Harrison, ed., *Racing to the Bottom?*

10. See, e.g., Inger Weibust, "The Great Green North? Canada's Bad Environmental Record and How the Feds Can Fix It," in Gordon DiGiacomo and Maryantonnett Flumian, eds, *The Case for Centralized Federalism* (Ottawa: University of Ottawa Press, 2010).

11. For a comparison, see Julie M. Simmons, "Securing the Threads of Co-operation in the Tapestry of Intergovernmental Relations: Does the Institutionalization of Ministerial Conferences Matter?" in Harvey Lazar, Peter Meekison, and Hamish Telford, eds, *Canada the State of the Federation 2001–2002: The Institutions of Intergovernmental Relations in Canada Today* (Montreal and Kingston: McGill Queen's University Press, 2004).

12. Canadian Council of Ministers of the Environment Secretariat, "CCME History," unpublished document, n.d.

13. Herman Bakvis, Gerald Baier, and Douglas Brown, *Contested Federalism: Certainty and Ambiguity in the Canadian Federation* (Toronto: Oxford University Press, 2009).

14. Ministers Responsible for Fisheries and Aquaculture, "Fisheries Ministers Commit to Working Together to Protect Fisheries and Develop Canadian Fishing and Aquaculture Industry," news release, 5 Sept. 2013.

15. Nicole Bolleyer and Lori Thorlakson, "Beyond Decentralization—The Comparative Study of Interdependence in Federal Systems," *Publius: The Journal of Federalism* 42, 4 (2012): 566–91.

16. J.E. Edwards and K.G. Hirsch, *Adapting Sustainable Forest Management to Climate Change: Preparing for the Future* (Ottawa: Canadian Council of Forest Ministers Climate Change Taskforce, 2012).

17. A comparison of limited intergovernmental policy capacity across sectors, including the environment, is Gregory J. Inwood, Carolyn Johns, and Patricia L. O'Reilly, *Intergovernmental Policy Capacity in Canada: Inside the Worlds of Finance, Environment, Trade and Health* (Montreal and Kingston: McGill Queen's University Press, 2011).

18. See Graefe and Simmons, "Assessing the Collaboration."

19. Council of the Federation, Canadian Energy Strategy Working Group, *Canadian Energy Strategy: Progress Report of the Council of the Federation* (July 2013).

20. For a comparison of provincial climate change strategies, see Miranda Holmes, *All Over the Map 2012: A Comparison of Provincial Climate Change Plans* (Vancouver: David Suzuki Foundation, 2012).

21. For a comparative history of federal–provincial interaction, see Kathryn Harrison, "The Origins of National Standards: Comparing Federal Government Involvement in Environmental Policy in Canada and the United States," in Patrick Fafard and Kathryn Harrison, eds, *Managing the Environmental Union: Intergovernmental Relations and Environmental Policy in Canada* (Kingston, Ont.: Queen's School of Public Policy, 2000); Kathryn Harrison, *Passing the Buck* (Toronto: University of Toronto Press, 1997). With respect to non-enforcement of the Fisheries Act, see Kernaghan Webb, "Gorillas in Closets? Federal–Provincial *Fisheries Act* Pollution Control Enforcement," in Patrick Fafard and Kathryn Harrison, eds, *Managing the Environmental Union: Intergovernmental Relations and Environmental Policy in Canada* (Kingston, Ont.: Queen's School of Public Policy, 2000).

22. Harrison, "Origins of National Standards," 59.

23. Mark Winfield, "Environmental Policy and Federalism," in Herman Bakvis and Grace Skogstad, eds, *Canadian Federalism: Performance, Effectiveness and Legitimacy* (Toronto: Oxford University Press, 2002), 131.

24. Canadian Council of Ministers of the Environment, *Canada-Wide Environmental Standards Sub-Agreement* (1998).

25. Canadian Council of Ministers of the Environment, "Environment Ministers Take Steps to Improve Air Quality in Canada," press release, 11 Oct. 2012.

26. Douglas Macdonald and Mark Winfield, "The Harmonization Accord and Climate Change Policy: Two Case Studies in Federal–Provincial Environmental Policy," in Herman Bakvis and Grace Skogstad, eds, *Canadian*

Federalism: Performance, Effectiveness and Legitimacy, 2nd edn (Toronto: Oxford University Press, 2006), 272.

27. Ministers Responsible for the Protection of Species at Risk, *National Accord for the Protection of Species at Risk*, n.d.

28. Ibid.

29. Geoff Norquay, "The Death of Executive Federalism and the Rise of the 'Harper Doctrine': Prospects for the Next Health Care Accord," *Policy Options* (Dec. 2011–Jan. 2012).

30. Office of the Prime Minister of Canada, "Prime Minister Promotes Open Federalism," news release, 21 Apr. 2006.

31. Ibid.

32. Adam Harmes, "The Political Economy of Open Federalism," *Canadian Journal of Political Science* 40, 2 (2007): 423.

33. A summary of the scope of these changes is Elizabeth May, "Bill C-38: The Environmental Destruction Act," *The Tyee*, 10 May 2012.

34. Shawn McCarthy, "Budget Bill Gives Harper Cabinet Free Hand on Environmental Assessments," *Globe and Mail*, 9 May 2012.

35. Tom Mulcair, "Building a Balanced, Sustainable Energy Future," *Policy Options* (May 2013).

36. Jeffrey A. Hutchings and John R. Post, "Gutting Canada's Fisheries Act: No Fishery, No Fish Habitat Protection," *Fisheries* 38 (Nov. 2013): 497.

37. Office of the Auditor General of Canada, *Report of the Commissioner of the Environment and Sustainable Development* (Ottawa: Minister of Public Works and Government Services, Dec. 2011).

38. Karl Nerenberg, "Species at Risk Are Victims of Harper's Love Affair with Big Oil," *Rabble.ca*, 7 Nov. 2013.

39. Office of the Auditor General of Canada, *Report of the Commissioner of the Environment and Sustainable Development* (Ottawa: Minister of Public Works and Government Services, Fall 2013). For an earlier NGO account of implementation, see David Suzuki Foundation, *Canada's Species at Risk Act: Implementation at a Snail's Pace* (Apr. 2009).

40. Sarah Otto, Sue McKee, and Jeannette Whitton, "Saving Species at Risk Starts at the Top: Where Is Our Environment Minister?" *Globe and Mail*, 14 Aug. 2013.

9 Sustaining Twenty-First-Century Canadian Communities in an Era of Complexity

Mary Louise McAllister

Chapter Summary

Healthy cities depend on decision-makers who know how to foster desirable, resilient socio-ecological systems. Yet local governments encounter barriers related to jurisdictional authority, financial resources, and limits on capacity when attempting to address complex environmental challenges. In order to foster sustainability, local governments need to adopt (and be allowed to adopt) flexible tools that will allow them to respond to and cope with complexity and uncertainty, particularly in this era of climate change. Watershed-based approaches and place-based governance are two approaches that attempt to transcend the limitations set by municipal jurisdictional boundaries, and have been the subject of some local experimentation. Further, some Canadian local governments are facilitating community initiatives and approaches such as local food security, green infrastructure, and partnership approaches with private and non-profit groups. Information and communications technologies are also increasingly being used to address some sustainability challenges, yet they should be employed carefully such that they do not also undermine desired socio-environmental outcomes.

Chapter Outline

- Understanding the determinants of local environmental politics
    - Local governments as "creatures of the provinces"
    - Mechanization, efficiency, and the "city beautiful"
    - Healthy communities
- Socio-ecological systems perspectives
    - Ecosystems approaches
    - Watershed approaches
- Resilient cities: local innovations
    - Intergovernmental co-operation, place-based governance, eco-infrastructure, re-localization, and digital technologies
- The governing challenges of complex systems and administrative silos

Introduction

Healthy cities depend on a governing system equipped to foster desirable, resilient **socio-ecological systems**. Canadian local governments, which are constitutional "creatures of the provinces," that is, they are created by and exist in a particular governmental and jurisdictional form at the mercy of the provinces, are ideologically, institutionally, and financially constrained from promoting biophysical or socio-economic sustainability now, or for future generations. Nevertheless, in partnership with, and influenced by, community-based local groups, municipalities are adopting a number of policies and establishing programs aimed at sustaining healthier communities.

It is not easy sailing. Promoters of healthy, resilient cities invariably find their agendas submerged by a tidal wave of property development plans—projects supported by the unceasing municipal quest for revenues required to support burgeoning societal demands. The property tax, originally designed to fund infrastructure and "hard" services such as roads, sewerage, and utilities, is now being stretched to finance social, public health, and other "soft" services. Local governments are seeking other sources of revenue by fostering private sector partnerships, licensing, and charging fees for services. In addition to cities having only limited fiscal resources, path-dependent behaviours based on historical practices serve to limit institutional innovations. Throughout the twentieth century, Canadian cities were planned to separate "incompatible" land uses, and local governments were structured according to organizing principles assumed to be rational and efficient. These approaches, based on a "silo" mentality, may have worked reasonably well throughout much of the last century, but they are not well designed to protect and support vital interconnected biophysical and socio-economic ecosystems essential to sustaining twenty-first-century communities.

Despite the constraints, pressure from various quarters has led to a diversity of governing initiatives to protect the environment. Local policies are increasingly designed to recognize the value of ecological goods and services as well as their interrelationship with community health. Moreover, the growing public acceptance and legitimacy of watershed-based approaches are contributing to the emergence of a system of governance that includes a diversity of players: governments, businesses, non-governmental organizations, and individual volunteers. A number of these efforts transcend administrative and political jurisdictional boundaries to achieve more sustainable approaches to governance. Outcomes include innovations ranging from greenbelt preservation, to alternative energy and food projects, to ecosystem approaches to health.

Underpinning these developments is a growing theoretical body of literature that reconceptualizes what is meant by "good" environmental policy. Historically, urban environmental concerns were viewed in terms of the city's biophysical properties. To the extent that they were considered at all, they were managed through departments of public health and safety and, in time, through the use of zoning to separate uses. Today, decision-makers are beginning to recognize that environmental health will not be achieved through reductionist approaches, and that biophysical and socio-economic factors are mutually dependent, requiring nuanced and adaptive policy approaches. To some extent, institutional learning is taking place with respect to the long-term sustainability of Canadian urban areas. A review of selected initiatives indicates that local decision-makers are beginning to test the turbulent waters of complex systems and integrated policy approaches, in hopes of nudging Canadian cities in a more sustainable direction.[1]

Mechanization and Efficiency:
Early Local Environmental Politics

Health for Efficiency
Efficiency for Production
Production for Well-being

– *Slogan at 1924 Town Planning Institute of Canada meeting*[2]

Constitutionally, local governments do not possess the authority to pass important pieces of legislation, as is the case with the federal and provincial governments. As the country urbanized at the turn of the twentieth century, the job of local governments as "creatures of the provinces" was largely confined to promoting economic development and maintaining social order and public safety through the provision of services such as sewers, fire protection, waste removal, and policing. With rapid urbanization and industrialization, adverse social and physical impacts were becoming evident in cities. City dwellers became further removed from the responsibility of producing, maintaining, and conserving the natural resources that sustained them with the growing separation of the rural from the urban.

Local environmental policy was not on the political agendas of the early 1900s, although its precursors might be identifiable in two ways: a concern with urban public health, and a collective desire to foster attractive and appealing cities. An early urban reform movement generated by a growing middle class to clean up cities led to some social assistance, housing, and improved health conditions for the poor. At the heart of the urban development initiatives was a dynamic business community that envisioned how public and social well-being could be advanced through the economic prosperity of the cities. Environmental concerns were relatively low on the agenda. Residents of early Canadian cities suffered from a toxic combination of noxious emissions from smokestacks, poisonous wastewaters, and untreated garbage when industrial enterprises intermingled with residential housing. The urban planning profession emerged to deal with these "incompatible" land uses through subdivision and zoning. The groomed "city beautiful" approach was based on notions of efficient, scientific planning and zoning. The policy goal stressed fostering the aesthetic beauty of a city so that new residents and investors would be drawn to the community. Land developers, businesses, and homeowners whose views dominated municipal councils reinforced the value placed on private property. As one individual claimed, "the real business of city government is property."[3] A few early radical thinkers, such as Thomas Adams, believed that planning should more holistically incorporate the goals of a healthy social, living, and natural environment.[4]

Throughout the following decades, however, land development for the purposes of raising revenues became a pressing priority, with little thought given to the impact on environmental goods and services. The unceasing quest for property-based revenues set the stage for a conflict between two communities of interest, a conflict that continues today. It consisted of opposing views held between those whose vision for sustaining cities was predicated on values of economic growth and land development, and those belonging to an emerging social and environmental movement.

Emerging Local Environmental Policy: Healthy Communities

They paved paradise and put up a parking lot
With a pink hotel, a boutique, and a swinging hot spot . . .

—Joni Mitchell, "Big Yellow Taxi" (1970)

During the intense 1960s–1970s era of social and environmental activism, critics questioned municipal decision-making processes that promoted large real estate development projects while neglecting the housing and health problems of the urban, inner-city working class. Rapidly growing suburbs fuelled the demand for expensive, high-maintenance infrastructure and services. Shopping centres, big box stores, and, ultimately, power centres gobbled up land, resources, and retail dollars. In the early 1980s, the opening of the mammoth West Edmonton Mall offered one of the most prominent examples of the times. Christopher Leo claimed it to be the "prime cause" of inner-city Edmonton's stress.[5]

By the 1980s, recognition of the interconnections between social, economic, and biophysical health increasingly brought environmental concerns into the mainstream of local governmental policy and planning. One notable movement, Healthy Cities, based on concepts of "community conviviality, environmental viability, and economic adequacy," rapidly gained public recognition first in Canada, and then around the world.[6]

Socio-Ecological Systems Perspectives

As the twentieth century drew to a close, **ecosystem perspectives** and approaches garnered policy attention. Socio-ecological systems perspectives have generated many new prescriptions in local decision-making. One such approach is **watershed-based planning** that crosses local jurisdictional boundaries. Poverty, food insecurity, air pollution, groundwater contamination, overpopulation, and habitat fragmentation do not respect political jurisdiction and operate in multiple spatial and temporal scales. One way of determining natural boundaries is to assess them on the basis of physical characteristics such as drainage patterns, landforms, vegetation, and climate.[7] As Hodge and Robinson point out, ecosystem approaches have been influencing how theorists, planners, and practitioners are carrying out their work throughout the country.[8] One analyst has suggested that it is necessary to "build influence for political and institutional change in the political sphere at the local level supported by strong, horizontal efforts to define new cultural watershed identities, develop norms of cooperation and civic solidarity and build networks of restoration activists."[9]

An influential application of such an approach in the 1990s was that of the Royal Commission on the Future of the Toronto Waterfront. The Crombie Commission (established in 1988) was asked to formulate recommendations about how to deal with the contaminated waterfront and related lands in the face of "jurisdictional gridlock."[10] The Commission's mandate covered the Greater Toronto bioregion, extending from the Niagara Escarpment on the west, the Oak Ridges Moraine on the north and east sides, and Lake Ontario's shoreline. The Commission initiated an extensive consultation process, which involved teams composed of developers, environmentalists, traffic engineers, landscape architects, scientists, community activists, federal and provincial public servants, and city officials.[11] Gibson et al. observed that the Crombie Commission introduced Canadian decision-makers to the idea of ecosystem planning as an alternative to conventional planning. Ecosystem planning "rejects business as usual."[12] It recognizes that not all economic growth is good; in fact, growth can undermine the biophysical, social, and economic resilience of a community. Among many other principles, Gibson et al. suggested that ecosystem planning needed to be linked with other aspects of democratic change, social learning, community building, and environmental enlightenment.[13]

In the 1990s, land-use round tables and public consultative initiatives across the country gained steam; at the same time, many provinces were engaged in slashing budgets and offloading responsibilities for environmental and social programs to the municipalities. During this same period, however, American governments were actively occupied with strengthening the "livability" of their cities. To that end, they were working on harnessing urban sprawl with investment in transit, green spaces, mixed-use developments, and downtown revitalization initiatives while also engaging in collaborative community participation. These **smart growth** approaches were adopted throughout the United States and eventually in Canada, where in 1999 a non-profit group introduced Smart Growth BC.[14] As John Sewell notes, however, smart growth proponents face some fairly intractable challenges:[15] rapid growth continues to gobble up land in and around cities; the Canadian public relies heavily on cars to get around; and suburbs are inexorably munching their way through valued wetlands and other green spaces.

In Ontario, a series of provincial legislative planning and policy efforts have been introduced since 2005 to address the problems caused by urban sprawl. Initiatives have included the 2006 Places to Grow Act, the 2005 Greenbelt Act, and a revised Ontario Planning Act (2007). Such initiatives have encouraged cities—including Toronto, one of North America's largest cities—to plan for a denser urban form. As Mark Winfield has noted, however, these pieces of legislation still left plenty of room for urban development as it "leapfrogs" the more protected greenbelt. He also noted that insufficient consideration was given to the ability of municipalities to absorb the projected growth.[16] The ongoing legal dispute between the Region of Waterloo and the Ontario Municipal Board illustrates the powerful influence of private developers on decision-making processes (see Box 9.1).[17]

BOX 9.1 | Who Has the Power: Developers or Government?

In January 2013, the Ontario Municipal Board (OMB), an arm's-length planning tribunal, ruled in favour of developers who wanted hundreds of additional hectares set aside for development that the Region of Waterloo's Official Plan would not allow. The Official Plan set limits on urban sprawl to guide growth that met and exceeded the recommendations in the provincial Places to Grow Act. The provincial government joined the region in appealing the OMB's decision, and the Region of Waterloo now is seeking a full judicial review of the case.

Sources: CBC News, "Waterloo Region Takes OMB to Court over Alleged Bias," 14 Aug. 2013, http://www.cbc.ca/news/canada/kitchener-waterloo/waterloo-region-takes-omb-to-court-over-alleged-bias-1.1315015; Paige Desmond, "Region of Waterloo Seeks Judicial Review on OMB Decision," *Waterloo Region Record*, 13 Oct. 2014, http://www.therecord.com/news-story/4912135-region-of-waterloo-seeks-judicial-review-on-omb-decision/.

By the end of the first decade of the twenty-first century, political debates over how much growth cities could sustain were far from over, with some constituencies placing faith in technological solutions while others emphasized the need for material constraint and conservation.

Resilient Cities: Local Innovations in the Twenty-First Century

> In seeking sustainability, we must look to the human potential for selective adaptability. We cannot afford to maintain outmoded nineteenth-century views of the dominance and invincibility of technological "man". . . . Success will be found and must be measured in terms of our ability to foster both urban and global systems of feedback that simultaneously detect and communicate threats to our ecological, social and economic systems.[18]

By 2014, global climate change was making its presence known most publicly and visibly in the form of more frequent extreme weather events, from droughts to devastating floods to ice storms. The year 2013 was on record as the "costliest" ever in economic terms.[19] Along with the direct economic costs, however, unpredictable climate change events pose longer-term ecological costs to valued ecosystem goods and services (e.g., local food, urban forests, and water systems), while creating social disruption, particularly for already vulnerable and marginalized members of society. Such "wicked" challenges, characterized by complexity and uncertainty, require ecosystem-based approaches to governance.

Currently, one of the most salient approaches in the literature is based on **resilience thinking**. This concept is not new; it was the premise of all traditional societies immediately dependent on the land for survival.[20] According to Walker and Salt, resilience thinking recognizes that "socio-ecological systems are complex adaptive systems. . . . Its focus is on how the system changes and copes with disturbance. Resilience, a systems capacity to absorb disturbance without a regime shift, is the key to sustainability."[21] If this type of thinking were adopted, new approaches to governing would be required. The following examples discuss some promising initiatives taking place in Canada and elsewhere that might succeed, given the right mix of incentives and contextual factors.

Intergovernmental Co-operation: A Nested Approach

Sustaining valued socio-ecological systems requires a level of co-operation between municipalities that would have been inconceivable 100 years ago when they actively competed with each other to attract businesses and industry to locate in their own cities. Yet, co-operation is now taking place at all levels. The national Federation of Canadian Municipalities (FCM) plays an important co-ordinating role between governments. For example, the FCM and the ICLEI—Local Governments for Sustainability (founded as the International Council for Local Environmental Initiatives)—have worked together to foster partnerships to combat the effects of climate change and reduce contributions to greenhouse gases. The Canadian organization Partners for Climate Protection (a subgroup of ICLEI's international entity, Cities for Climate Protection) is comprised of 240 municipalities throughout the country.[22]

Nationally, after years of decreasing grant transfers to municipalities and intensive municipal lobbying, senior governments have funded some new programs for local governments. Of particular note was the $33 billion federal infrastructure program being rolled out over 2007–14. Half of that amount—funded through the municipal GST rebate and the gas tax fund—was directed towards the municipalities to invest in transit, local infrastructure, water, and waste and energy management systems, while encouraging conservation.[23] One of the more notable municipal "federal-to-local" government programs was the "green municipal funds" designed to encourage investment in innovative environmental projects. These funds included a $550 million endowment that operates through the Federation of Canadian Municipalities. The organization announced that there was to be a new funding offer beginning 1 April 2015.[24]

Despite these and other encouraging funding signs from senior levels of government, they fall far short of what is required to surmount disparate urban environmental policy challenges. Moreover, increased funding and resources only go so far; different approaches are needed when governing sustainable communities. Political scientist Christopher Leo has called for a more flexible approach to intergovernmental relations; he has coined the term **deep federalism**, whereby federal government programs are adapted to the unique needs of specific communities while drawing on local knowledge and resources.[25]

Place-based Governance and Municipalities

Geographer Becky Pollock, among others, has developed the notion of **place-based governance** predicated on more fluid boundaries than those dictated by political jurisdiction. The concept combines ecological and political interpretations of "space" with social and cultural interpretations of "place." To achieve this, a different view of what constitutes good local governance is required, one that contains a comprehensive understanding of the diverse individuals, communities, and interests residing within a particular place, as well as knowledge about how these actors are affected by (and contributors to) local socio-ecological conditions.[26] In this context, good governance includes an informed and engaged public, along with trustworthy, supportive, and inclusive institutions capable of developing and promoting collaborative networks.[27]

With place-based governance, co-ordination takes place among municipalities and other local bodies in order to protect valued socio-ecological systems such as could be offered through the mechanism of a biosphere reserve. These were first created over 30 years ago under the United Nations Educational, Scientific, and Cultural Organization (UNESCO) Man and the Biosphere program to help protect biodiversity on a global scale through local-level initiatives. They have evolved beyond a primary preoccupation with conservation, research, and education to include concerns such as sustainable livelihoods and development practices. As of 2012, there were 564 reserves throughout the world, 16 of them in Canada—one of which is the Long Point Biosphere Reserve (see Box 9.2).[28]

The biosphere reserve model is an example of collaborative governance[29] across nested scales, although in practice these reserves face a number of challenges, including a heavy reliance on volunteers and limited resources. While the biosphere reserves offer an attractive approach for fostering participatory, watershed-based co-operation, a number of other place-based approaches are gaining salience in public agendas across the country, including community forests, conservation areas, protected greenbelt areas, and watershed-based initiatives.

BOX 9.2 | Long Point Biosphere Reserve

In 1986, UNESCO designated Long Point, a 32-kilometre sand spit located on the north shore of Lake Erie, in Norfolk County, Ontario, as a biosphere reserve. Long Point has some of the largest remaining forest tracts in Carolinian Canada. The core area of the biosphere reserve consists in part of the 3,250-hectare Long Point National Wildlife Area. The biosphere reserve is located in what was once a thriving tobacco-producing area that is populated by farmers and other rural property owners. Long Point Provincial Park and nature-related tourism revenues are important to the area. Communities are encouraged to promote sustainable resource management and socio-economic practices compatible with biosphere reserve ideals.

Sources: Long Point World Biosphere Reserve Foundation, accessed 14 Mar. 2014, http://www.longpointbiosphere. ca/about/; George Francis and Graham Whitelaw, "Long Point Biosphere Reserve Periodic Review Report," Canadian Biosphere Reserves Association, 2001.

From Grey to Green Infrastructure (Eco-infrastructure)

Along with federal–provincial and inter-municipal co-operation are initiatives that can be undertaken within the city itself. One of the primary responsibilities of local government has always been the provision of infrastructure to service property. Infrastructure has been defined as "the substructure or underlying foundation, especially the basic installations and facilities on which the continuance and growth of a community or state depends."[30] Canada's crumbling "grey" infrastructure of roads, public transport, water and sewerage systems, and the like, and the costs of repairing it, frequently makes the news. But another kind of infrastructure is gaining local policy attention. "Green" or "eco-infrastructure" offers a counter-approach to traditional, centralized infrastructural approaches to energy, transportation, water, and waste systems.

Green infrastructure is "an integrated infrastructure *system* with a reduced ecological footprint over its life cycle, and with significant benefits for the community economy and quality of life."[31] It can also be viewed as a biophysical natural life support system. These closed-loop or soft-path approaches look to regenerate natural systems and focus on "augmenting the self-design of natural flows, or perhaps, mimicking these flows with engineered designs that nevertheless allow natural flows much scope for taking their own course."[32] The goals are to foster resilience; reliance on renewable, smaller, dispersed, flexible systems with lower life-cycle costs; and responsiveness to local social and physical conditions. Some funding for such green initiatives has been provided by governments at all levels—local, provincial, and federal, including Infrastructure Canada. Green infrastructure covers a wide range of initiatives including the installation of green roofs on municipal buildings, water[33] and energy conservation programs, community gardens, and green spaces, as well as projects that encourage a community sense of place and stewardship. Some cities have taken a leadership role (see Box 9.3).

BOX 9.3 | The Greenest City in the World

Vancouver, British Columbia, has undertaken an aggressive and comprehensive green action plan; green infrastructure is an important component of the initiative. In 2009 the Vancouver mayor, Gregor Robertson, launched a team-based initiative to become the greenest city in the world. Building on that initiative, the city quickly developed an action plan to reach this objective by 2020. Its 10 target areas for "greening" the city are green economy, climate leadership, green buildings, green transportation, zero waste, access to nature, lighter footprint, clean water, clean air, and local food. By 2014, it had made notable headway in reaching many of these areas by revising by-laws, introducing financial and other incentives, conducting public information campaigns, and leading by example with its own green procurement, green building, and local food initiatives.

Source: City of Vancouver, "Greenest City 2020 Goals and Targets," https://vancouver.ca/green-vancouver/targets-and-priority-actions.aspx.

City bylaws and zoning can be huge obstacles to the development of green infrastructure approaches. Recent years, however, have seen a number of changes to bylaws and zoning as environmental initiatives gain legitimacy on public agendas and are incorporated into local policy. Examples include bans on the cosmetic use of pesticides, local food charters, no-smoking bylaws, tree protection bylaws, water conservation initiatives, and active transit initiatives. Bylaws also quite often make their way into provincial policies and legislation once they have been passed by a number of municipalities.

(Re)Localization and De-Growth

A movement advocating localization (sometimes referred to as de-growth) has been developing in response to public concerns that the era of cheaply available fossil fuels, as well as inexpensive, readily available food, is rapidly coming to a close. Localized communities come in a diversity of forms and functions.[34] The concept of **Transition Towns**, for example, spread rapidly throughout the world, including Canada, after it was introduced in 2006 in the United Kingdom. Transition Towns might be defined as a grassroots network of communities whose primary goal is to find ways of "transitioning" away from their heavy reliance on fossil fuels and global food systems. The movement emerged in response to an awareness that the global fossil fuel supply has its limits, and our reliance on it has contributed to climatic and economic instability. The ultimate goal is to foster adaptable, resilient cities through sustainable (re)localization of the economic activities on which communities depend. Transition Peterborough in Ontario defines this phenomenon as localization focusing on "securing our food, water, energy, wellness and culture."[35] As of 2012, Canada had a reported 66 Transition Towns.[36] Although these initiatives are non-profit and run by volunteers, they often receive various types of support and encouragement from local governments.

These critiques of modernity and globalization, and the accompanying growth of alternative localization movements, do have their appeal; they conjure up somewhat idyllic vistas of community-sharing, people-friendly "urban pastoralism."[37] There are, however, serious questions related to power, gender, inclusiveness, and, for that matter, practicality. As Mikulak argues, if such projects are to contribute to sustainability, they will have to be conducted not with a blueprint based on a romanticized, and regressive, Arcadian past but in an "ethical engagement with the current historical-ecological context."[38] Related to (re)localization is the concept of local **food security**. Xuereb and Desjardins suggest food security in a community is present when "all residents have access to, and can afford to buy safe, nutritious, and culturally-acceptable food that has been produced in an environmentally-sustainable way and that sustains our rural communities."[39] Examples of food security initiatives throughout Canada include the widespread adoption of municipal food charters, as well as municipal food policies that address all steps of the food production and distribution process in order to achieve a number of goals. The emphasis is on reducing the reliance on "fossil foods" (reducing food miles) as well as encouraging a local food economy, community economic development, social justice, and ecological health.[40] Although there are diverse models, the municipal government frequently plays a role in partnering with volunteer organizations and helping to facilitate these initiatives.

Complexity and Governing Cities in a Digital Era

> An urban "network mind" can be continually dialed and consulted, revealing not just the circulations of urban messages and information but also informing the pathways of people who are reliant on these systems of navigation.[41]

Operating simultaneously at global and local scales, ever reconfiguring social notions of time and space, "[l]ocative technologies, wireless sensors, geotaging, and Web 2.0 or Environmental 2.0 technologies are now all-pervasive in urban-settings."[42] So observes Jennifer Gabrys, who conjures up juxtaposing visions. In the one scenario, local government is depicted as "Big Brother" tracking citizens through surveillance systems and webcams. In an alternative scenario, data bits blanket a city with "smart dust" operating as an autonomous ungovernable "network mind," collectively shaping how people unconsciously navigate and, in turn, reconfigure their urban environment. The automated gathering of data bits about public transit use and traffic patterns, or to regulate energy or water use or public safety, may all individually be part of a deliberative local government strategy. As yet unaccounted for, however, are the complex and unintended consequences of "all-encompassing sense technologies than can continually scan general data from, and even regulate and modify, our natural-cultural environments."[43]

For better or worse, cities and various forms of human interaction are being fundamentally altered by the rapid adoption of information technology (IT) in all aspects of life. With good reason, the application of technology in environmental circles has often been discussed in a critical way when observing the perils of introducing innovations in the absence of a broad understanding of their socio-ecological implications. IT innovations are being applied by governments in efforts to reduce the consumption of natural resources or to stimulate local economic development. The implication of such innovation is an area of inquiry that needs closer policy attention from those interested in sustainable cities. As an example of its positive potential, telecommuting can reduce the amount of time commuters spend on the road and the demand for more highways, and possibly improve quality of life for those working at home. IT is also being used in smart-metering, which is intended to encourage water and electricity conservation by measuring the amount and time of usage. The information is then used to encourage conservation through education about individual consumption practices, as well as the application of various pricing mechanisms, although it should be noted that such programs can be contentious if they are not well-designed or implemented. The Internet could also be used to encourage local information exchanges for the purpose of bartering services or used goods; to promote small business and local food; to encourage public adoption of green ideas; and to stimulate public engagement through **citizen science**, thereby generating information exchanges and publicly mapped information about the social and ecological aspects of a community. Throughout the country, many local governments are making "open data" freely available on city websites; this provides anonymous data that can be used to enhance the quality and governance of life in the city. In Vancouver, for example, the public can find open data about its "greenest city" project, community food assets, city initiatives, and road construction.[44] These kinds of initiatives can both foster civics and help to ensure more open and transparent government.

This being said, the application of information technology is far from a panacea for solving environmental problems; it can also serve to undermine sustainability. As Neil Bradford notes, "the premium placed on creativity and innovation in the knowledge-based economy offers tremendous rewards to those who develop and apply the best ideas. On the other hand, these same dynamics leave many more people and places struggling to find their way without resources or opportunity."[45] Moreover, in this era of highly complex and rapidly evolving technological interactions at various scales, it is difficult for governments to anticipate the possible environmental implications of technological applications that have yet to be invented.

The Governing Challenges of Complex Systems and Administrative Silos

Local government can take many initiatives to enhance valued social, built, and natural aspects of cities; a great number of environmental issues, however, exceed temporal, spatial, and political boundaries. Adequate responses frequently require resources and authority that local governments do not possess. This is particularly the case in Canada, where the central and provincial governments wrangle for resources while cities have been largely left out of the debate, lacking as they do any constitutional legitimacy. Transformative institutional learning and political will are needed to overcome global political, economic, and societal expectations and practices. Ecosystem perspectives are now beginning to inform the way in which some government decision-makers, such as planners, view their cities.

Sometimes, these ideas are introduced into public consultative processes, particularly when local decision-makers are engaged in community "visioning" exercises. Such perspectives may even be nibbling at the edges of established assumptions about the kinds of values that should drive a city's future. As yet, however, these perspectives do not appear to have resulted in the restructuring of government administrations and policy processes in a manner that might reverse the burgeoning pressures on socio-ecological life support systems. The concept of sustainable or **healthy communities** seems to be well entrenched among activists and a few other communities of interest. The means, mechanisms, and political desire needed to effectively implement those concepts, however, are far from being realized in daily local government decision-making.

This situation is partly attributable to the building blocks of governing structures. Government institutions are established in a way that allows them to maintain social control. Institutional structures offer a means to impose order and organize civil society in a complicated environment. The more intricate the problems, the more risk-averse organizations become. As environmental concerns become more imperative, governments react in crisis mode and are less able and less willing to explore innovative models for governance. Ann Dale observes that "[w]hen one is stuck in a spiralling pattern of exploitation and conservation, systemic learning cannot take place, and reactive rather than proactive policy choices become the norm."[46]

There are few built-in incentives for changing existing practices and venturing into a much less certain decision-making environment. Holistic approaches to decision-making require adaptive management techniques, long-range decision-making, the relinquishment of control, the sharing of information, consensus-building exercises, and the abandonment of long-held world views revolving around notions of rationality, efficiency, and effectiveness. In government in general, and at the local level in particular, one of the primary historic objectives has been to provide services in the most economically efficient manner assessed in today's dollars—not tomorrow's ecological costs. Nevertheless, new ecosystem, biodiversity, and social well-being assessment tools are now emerging in Canada and globally that would assist decision-makers in assessing trade-offs and developing models that would allow them to consider different scenarios.[47] Theory is making its way into practice in various city initiatives, though pre-existing economic and political demands serve as powerful counterweights. Quite apart from needing the political will and initiative, it is a challenge to craft policies that can accommodate numerous variables, including various spatial and time scales, and span the boundaries of sub-systems and larger systems.

The degree to which desired local ecosystems (including human systems) are healthy constitutes the single most crucial factor in determining the long-term future of cities. The ability to plan on an ecosystem basis is a prerequisite of sustainability as well as of preventing environmental crises from happening. A striking example of governance failure is the environmental tragedy that occurred in 2000 in Walkerton, Ontario, where seven people died and 2,300 were sickened as a result of *E. coli* contamination in the water supply, and the speed with which political actors were forced to respond after the fact.[48] As Ann Dale notes in her thoughtful analysis:

> It would . . . be prudent for human activity systems to reconcile methods of production with the rehabilitation and maintenance of ecosystems that provide the essential services for all life. We need a common language and an adequate conceptual framework within which to work, institutional reform based on a convergence of human and natural system cycles.[49]

Urban planners, such as Patsy Healey, observing these institutional constraints, suggest that new collaborative processes are required "where territorial political communities can collectively address their conflicts and maximize their chances to shape their places and their future."[50] Collaborative planning, Healey argues, serves a valuable "countervailing force to functional service delivery logics for organizing government."[51]

Conclusion

Effective local policy that can counter the cumulative environmental effects of unsustainable urban living calls for transformative institutional and social learning and adaptation, at all scales, from international organizations to local neighbourhoods. It is, without doubt, a daunting task. Political will is required. Local governments and their citizens need to have the means and authority to make changes happen. They require a much more meaningful degree of self-governance than is currently the case in Canada. Scale is important. Just as bureaucracies require tasks to be broken down into manageable pieces, problems that are most readily dealt with are smaller and closer to home, what systems thinkers refer to as "tight feedback loops." Natural processes need to once again be visible, tangible, and meaningful to the public.

To be sure, steps are being taken. Soft paths to energy and water consumption are now being seriously investigated, as is green infrastructure. Naturalized gardens are springing up in place of "bowling green" lawns. Neighbourhood markets and community gardens are blossoming in abandoned lots. Solar panels are no longer seen as a curiosity. And, in some places, the chickens, banned for 100 years, are returning to peck their way around coops in urban backyards. Yet, for such initiatives to be more than entertaining human interest stories for the local media, they need to take place within the context of wide-sweeping structural and policy change that represents socio-ecological imperatives.

The journey towards healthy, sustainable communities follows a winding, frequently diverging, and always elusive path. Nevertheless, despite numerous constraints at work in public institutions, the functions and practices of local governments are dynamic; as institutions, they do learn and evolve. Possibilities do exist, opportunities arise, and the collective environmental costs of retaining the status quo are becoming painfully apparent. The urgent need for institutional change that can produce effective local environmental policies is an imperative that is increasingly difficult for decision-makers to ignore.

Key Terms

citizen science

deep federalism

ecosystem perspectives

food security

healthy communities

place-based governance

resilience thinking

smart growth

socio-ecological systems

Transition Towns

watershed-based planning

Questions for Review

1. In what ways are Canada's local governments important environmental policy actors?

2. What factors might constrain environmental policy activism on the part of local governments and what factors might serve to encourage such activism?

3. What is green infrastructure? Can you think of current examples in your community?

4. What are the possible implications of the application of information technologies for accountable and democratic local government?

5. Is (re)localization or de-growth feasible?
6. What should local governments be doing to respond to complex challenges posed by such issues as climate change?

7. Should chickens and goats be permitted in urban backyards even if residents in affected neighbourhoods don't like the idea?

Internet Resources

Canadian Biosphere Reserve Association
http://biospherecanada.ca/en/

Christopher Leo: Research Based Analysis and Commentary: Category, City Politics
http://christopherleo.com/category/city-politics/

ICLEI Canada: Local Governments for Sustainability
http://www.icleicanada.org/

Federation of Canadian Municipalities
http://www.fcm.ca/home.htm

Resilience Alliance
http://www.resalliance.org/

Transition Network
http://www.transitionnetwork.org

Additional Reading

Alternatives Journal: Canada's Environmental Voice. http://www.alternativesjournal.ca/policy-and-politics.

Bradford, Neil. "Territory and Local Development: A Place-Based Perspective." *Universitas Forum* 3, 2 (2012). http://www.universitasforum.org/index.php/ojs/article/view/106/427.

Harcourt, Michael. *From Restless Places to Resilient Communities: Building a Stronger Future for All Canadians, Final Report.* Ottawa: Infrastructure Canada, 2006. http://www.ontariomcp.ca/library/reference-materials/restless-communities-resilient-places.

Lightbody, J. 2006. *City Politics, Canada.* Peterborough, Ont.: Broadview Press.

Mikulak, Michael. *The Politics of the Pantry: Stories, Food, and Social Change.* Montreal and Kingston: McGill-Queen's University Press, 2013.

Thompson, David, and Shannon A. Joseph. *Building Canada's Green Economy: The Municipal Role.* Ottawa: Federation of Canadian Municipalities, 2011. http://www.fcm.ca/Documents/reports/Building_Canadas_green_economy_the_municipal_role_EN.pdf.

Walker, B.H., and David Salt. *Resilience Thinking: Sustaining Ecosystems and People in a Changing World.* Washington: Island Press, 2006.

Winfield, M. "From Walkerton to McGuinty." In Winfield, *Blue-Green Province: The Environment and the Political Economy of Ontario,* 121–51. Vancouver: University of British Columbia Press, 2012.

Notes

1. Portions of this chapter are based on Mary Louise McAllister, *Governing Ourselves? The Politics of Canadian Communities* (Vancouver: University of British Columbia Press, 2004).
2. Thomas I. Gunton, "The Ideas and Policies of the Canadian Planning Profession, 1909–1931," in Alan J. Artibise and Gilbert A. Stelter, eds, *The Usable Urban Past: Planning and Policies in the Modern Canadian City* (Toronto: Macmillan, 1979), 182.
3. James Lorimer, *A Citizen's Guide to City Politics* (Toronto: James, Lewis and Samuel, 1970), 4.
4. Gerald Hodge, *Planning Canadian Communities: An Introduction to the Principles, Practices and Participants* (Toronto: ITP Nelson, 1998), 108.
5. Christopher Leo, *The Subordination of the Local State: Development Politics in Edmonton* (Winnipeg:

University of Winnipeg, Institute of Urban Studies, 1995).
6. Trevor Hancock, ed., *Healthy Sustainable Communities: Concept, Fledgling Practice, and Implications for Governance* (Gabriola Island, BC: New Society, 1997).
7. David Crombie, Royal Commission on the Toronto Harbourfront, *Regeneration: Toronto's Waterfront and the Sustainable City: Final Report* (Toronto: Minister of Supply and Services Canada, 1992).
8. Gerald Hodge and Ira M. Robinson, *Planning Canadian Regions* (Vancouver: University of British Columbia Press, 2001).
9. Mike Carr, *Bioregionalism and Civil Society: Democratic Challenges to Corporate Globalism* (Vancouver: University of British Columbia Press, 2004), 287.
10. Crombie, *Regeneration*, 1–2.

11. Hodge and Robinson, *Planning Canadian Regions*, 330.
12. Robert B. Gibson, Donald H.M. Alexander, and Ray Tomalty, "Putting Cities in Their Place: Ecosystem-based Planning for Canadian Urban Regions," in Mark Roseland, ed., *Eco-City Dimensions: Healthy Communities, Healthy Planet* (Gabriola Island, BC: New Society, 1997), 25–40.
13. Ibid.
14. Deborah Curran and Ray Tomalty, "Living It Up," *Alternatives* 29, 3 (2003): 10–18; Ann Dale, *At the Edge: Sustainable Development in the 21st Century* (Vancouver: University of British Columbia Press, 2001), 11.
15. John Sewell, "Breaking the Suburban Habit," *Alternatives* 29 (2003): 22–9; Alisa Smith and J.B. MacKinnon, *The 100-Mile Diet: A Year of Local Eating* (Toronto: Random House Canada, 2007).
16. Mark Winfield, *Blue-Green Province: The Environment and the Political Economy of Ontario* (Vancouver: University of British Columbia Press, 2012), 163.
17. CBC News, "Waterloo Region Takes OMB to Court over Alleged Bias," 14 Aug. 2013, http://www.cbc.ca/news/canada/kitchener-waterloo/waterloo-region-takes-omb-to-court-over-alleged-bias-1.1315015.
18. Robert Woollard and William Rees, "Social Evolution and Urban Systems: Directions for Sustainability," in J.T. Pierce and Ann Dale, eds, *Communities, Development, and Sustainability across Canada* (Vancouver: University of British Columbia Press, 1999), 27–45.
19. CBC News, "Extreme Weather Cost Canada Record $3.2 Billion Insurers Say," 20 Jan. 2014, http://www.cbc.ca/news/business/extreme-weather-cost-canada-record-3-2b-insurers-say-1.2503659.
20. B.H. Walker and David Salt, *Resilience Thinking: Sustaining Ecosystems and People in a Changing World* (Washington: Island Press, 2006).
21. Ibid, 38.
22. Federation of Canadian Municipalities, "Partners for Climate Protection," updated 29 Nov. 2013, http://www.fcm.ca/home/programs/partners-for-climate-protection.htm.
23. Infrastructure Canada, "Building Canada," 2008, http://www.buildingcanada-chantierscanada.gc.ca/index-eng.html?wt.ad5infc-eng.
24. Federation of Canadian Municipalities, Green Municipal Fund, "GMF Update: New Funding Offer," 2015, updated 26 Jan. 2015, http://www.fcm.ca/home/programs/green-municipal-fund/about-gmf/gmf-update.htm.
25. Christopher Leo, "Minimalist Government in Winnipeg," in Martin Horak and Robert Young, eds, *Sites of Governance: Multilevel Governance and Policy Making in Canada's Big Cities* (Montreal and Kingston: McGill-Queen's University Press, 2012), 323–4.
26. Rebecca Pollock, "Place-based Governance for Biosphere Reserves," *Environments* 32, 3 (2004): 27–42.
27. Sara Edge and Mary Louise McAllister, "Place-based Local Governance and Sustainable Communities: Lessons from Canadian Biosphere Reserves," *Journal of Environmental Planning and Management* 52, 3 (2009): 279–95.
28. Biosphere Canada, accessed 29 Jan. 2014, http://biospherecanada.ca/en/about-2/frequently-asked-questions/.
29. Patsy Healey, "Collaborative Planning in Perspective," *Planning Theory* 2, 2 (2003): 101–23; Gerald Hodge, *Planning Canadian Communities: An Introduction to the Principles, Practice, and Participants* (Toronto: ITP Nelson, 1998); M. Raco and J. Flint, "Communities, Places, and Institutional Relations: Assessing the Role of Area-based Community Representation in Local Governance," *Political Geography* 20 (2001): 585–612.
30. Elisa Campbell and The Sheltair Group, Inc., "The Five W's of Green Infrastructure," in *FCM Sustainable Communities Conference* (Ottawa: Federation of Canadian Municipalities, 2002).
31. Ibid.
32. Brian Milani, *Designing the Green Economy: The Postindustrial Alternative to Corporate Globalization* (Lanham, Md: Rowman & Littlefield, 2000), 103.
33. Econics, *Blue City: The Water Sustainable City of the Near Future*, Blue City Initiative, Jan. 2014, http://www.blue-economy.ca/sites/default/files/BEI%20Blue%20City%20report_econics_final.pdf.
34. P. Newman, T. Beatley, and H. Boyer, *Resilient Cities: Responding to Peak Oil and Climate Change* (Washington: Island Press. 2009).
35. Transition Town Peterborough, accessed 29 Jan. 2014, http://transitiontownpeterborough.ca/.
36. Trevor Hancock, "Healthy and Sustainable : Two Sides of the Same Coin," FCM, Jan. 2012, http://www.fcm.ca/Documents/presentations/2012/webinars/Healthy_and_Sustainable_Two_Sides_of_the_Same_Coin_EN.pdf.
37. M. Mikulak, *The Politics of the Pantry: Stories, Food, and Social Change* (Montreal and Kingston: McGill-Queen's University Press, 2013), 105.
38. Ibid, 118.
39. Marc Xuereb and Ellen Desjardins, *Towards a Healthy Community Food System for Waterloo Region* (Waterloo, Ont.: Public Health, 2005), 24.
40. Vancouver Food Policy Council, "Vancouver Food Charter: Context and Background," City of Vancouver, Jan. 2007, accessed 29 Jan. 2013, http://vancouver.ca/your-government/vancouver-food-policy-council.aspx.
41. Jennifer Babrys, "Telepathically Urban," in A. Boutros and W. Straw, eds, *Circulation and the City: Essays on Urban Culture* (Montreal and Kingston: McGill-Queen's University Press, 2010), 59.
42. Ibid.
43. Ibid.

44. City of Vancouver, "VanMap," last modified 2 Dec. 2013, accessed 30 Jan. 2014, http://vancouver.ca/your-government/vanmap.aspx.

45. Neil Bradford, "Territory and Local Development: A Place-based Perspective," *Universitas Forum* 3, 2 (2012), http://www.universitasforum.org/index.php/ojs/article/view/106/427.

46. Ann Dale, *At the Edge: Sustainable Development in the 21st Century* (Vancouver: University of British Columbia Press, 2001).

47. Heidi Wittmer and Haripriya Gundimeda, eds, *Economics of Ecosystems and Biodiversity in Local and Regional Policy and Management* (Washington: Earthscan, 2012).

48. Dennis R. O'Connor, *Part 1: A Summary: Report of the Walkerton Inquiry: The Events of May 2000 and Related Issues* (Toronto: Ontario Ministry of the Attorney General, Queen's Printer, 2002).

49. Dale, *At the Edge*, 58.

50. P. Healey, "Building Institutional Capacity through Collaborative Approaches to Urban Planning," *Environment and Planning A* 30 (1998): 1531.

51. Healey, "Collaborative Planning," 116.

10 Aboriginal People and Environmental Regulation: Land Claims Co-Management Boards in the Territorial North

Graham White

Chapter Summary

This chapter examines the contribution of co-management boards to territorial environmental governance, and provides an analysis of the degree to which they have been able to include Aboriginal people and their perspectives in public policy decisions relating to wildlife management and environmental regulation. As unique institutions that exist at the intersection of the federal government, the territorial governments, and Aboriginal self-government, these boards have brought about real change in the environmental regulatory process. Focusing specifically on boards in the Mackenzie Valley of the Northwest Territories the analysis highlights how Aboriginal members are directly involved in striking a balance between environmental protection and resource development, and how the boards emphasize the importance of respecting Aboriginal culture and lifestyle. The devolution legislation passed by Parliament in April 2014 threatens to change these processes through a reduction in the number of co-management structures, as well as by altering the roles and responsibilities of different levels of governance. In addition, austerity measures are posing difficulties for board operations.

Chapter Outline

- Comprehensive claims, territorial government, and co-management boards
  - Understanding the role of territorial government
  - The 2014 Northwest Territories Devolution Act
- Claims boards in the Mackenzie Valley
  - The Mackenzie Valley Land and Water Board (MVLWB)
  - The Mackenzie Valley Environmental Impact Review Board (MVEIRB)
- The environmental regulatory process
- Aboriginal involvement and influence on the claims boards
  - Use of traditional knowledge (TK)

- Board accomplishments
  - ○ Screening and environmental protection
- Board shortcomings
  - ○ Lack of intervener funding, incorporation of TK into decision-making, enforcement of board decisions, board independence

Introduction

As recent attention to issues of global warming has brought home, the fragile environment of Canada's Far North is especially vulnerable to damage wrought by human activity. The North is rich in natural resources, particularly non-renewable natural resources such as oil, gas, diamonds, gold, uranium, and iron ore, but exploiting them often comes at significant environmental cost. The Aboriginal peoples, for whom the North is home and who constitute an overwhelming proportion of the population in most northern communities, have a special relationship—both spiritual and economic—with the land that renders them acutely sensitive to the potential environmental consequences of resource development.

This mixture creates a difficult setting for establishing environmental policy that would allow for exploitation of the North's non-renewable resources—the principal hope for much-needed economic development—in an environmentally sensitive manner that takes fully into account the perspectives and preferences of the local Aboriginal people.

For most of the twentieth century, protection of the environment was of negligible concern in northern resource development projects and other activities. This is evidenced in two prominent features of the present-day landscape. Rivers in the central Yukon remain massively disfigured by seemingly endless miles of dredge tailings—enormous mounds of gravel dug up from riverbeds from the early 1900s to the 1960s by huge placer mining barges in search of gold. To the east, throughout Nunavut, the tundra is littered with rusting oil drums, abandoned machinery, and PCB-laden ground left from the construction of the DEW Line in the 1950s and from other defence and mining projects. These and other environmental depredations occurred in no small measure because of the complete exclusion of local Aboriginal people from governmental institutions and decision-making processes, which in turn meant that their experience, insights, and wishes were all but completely ignored.

More recently, as elsewhere in Canada, strong concern for the environment has come to the fore in the North. The last few decades have also witnessed remarkable changes in the political-governmental complexion of the North, not least in the prominent role that Aboriginal leaders and political organizations have come to play. Among the most far-reaching of these changes has been the settlement of **comprehensive land claim agreements** across most of the territorial North. The myriad governance provisions of these constitutionally protected modern-day treaties include the establishment of a host of **co-management boards** designed to include Aboriginal people and their perspectives in public policy decisions relating to wildlife management and environmental regulation.

The chapters in this book demonstrate that, overall, Canadian governments have been decidedly ambivalent in their approaches to environmental policy. The creation of these claims boards may be something of an exception. The boards are new, unique institutions within the Canadian federation. They are not extensions of the federal government or of the provincial/territorial governments; nor are they species of Aboriginal self-government.

Rather, they exist at the intersection of the three orders of government. That they are new and distinctive, however, is not to say that they are effective; assessing their effectiveness is a central objective of this chapter.

The chapter looks at the environmental regulatory boards created under the land claims agreements in the territorial North. It examines their operations and processes, paying special attention to the extent to which Aboriginal peoples participate in and influence their activities. Though comprehensive claims have been finalized in three provinces—Quebec, British Columbia, and Newfoundland and Labrador—the chapter will examine only the claims boards in the three territories of Yukon, the Northwest Territories (NWT), and Nunavut, with the lion's share of the analysis focused on boards in the NWT. Following a brief overview to set the comprehensive land claims and the territorial governments in context, the chapter describes the principal environmental regulatory boards in the Mackenzie Valley of the NWT and examines their role in the regulatory process. It then looks at various aspects of Aboriginal participation in environmental regulation through the claims boards, highlighting a few especially notable decisions arising from board reviews; it outlines some of the far-reaching changes to the regulatory regime stemming from recent federal legislation; and it surveys some of the shortcomings of the boards.

Background: Comprehensive Claims and Territorial Governments

In much of southern Canada between the eighteenth century and the 1920s, the Aboriginal peoples who occupied the land before the coming of the Europeans signed treaties with the British government, and later the Canadian government. While fundamental disagreements exist as to the nature and intent of these treaties, and about the Canadian government's record in fulfilling its obligations under them, the historic treaties provide a legal basis for the control exercised by the Canadian state over the lands they cover.[1] Across great swaths of the country, however, the Aboriginal people were never conquered militarily and did not sign treaties with British or Canadian authorities, and thus they never agreed to accept the sovereignty of the Canadian state. Nonetheless, their lands were subsumed into Canada and their long-standing status as self-governing nations had been dismissed by Canadian governments. By the early 1970s, however, spurred on by the landmark *Calder* decision of the Supreme Court of Canada in 1973 acknowledging that **unextinguished Aboriginal title** might still exist in areas without treaties, the federal government had accepted the need to settle the outstanding claims of the Aboriginal peoples who had never signed treaties.[2]

Since the mid-1970s, claims have been finalized covering all of Nunavut, northern Quebec, most of Yukon, and the Northwest Territories,[3] as well as parts of Labrador and British Columbia. Negotiations are still underway on other comprehensive claims across the North and in some provinces. Finalized land claim agreements are complex, highly detailed legalistic documents that, once ratified by vote of the affected Aboriginal people, by Parliament, and by the relevant provincial or territorial legislature, achieve constitutional protection under section 35 of the Constitution Act, 1982. As a result, they are far, far more than simple contracts or policy statements, not least in that their provisions supersede those of ordinary laws.[4]

Each comprehensive claim is unique, but all share common features. In return for giving up title to their traditional lands (but not other Aboriginal rights), the claimant Aboriginal group receives a substantial cash payment, fee simple ownership of selected parcels of land (including some with subsurface rights), and other economic benefits. As well, each claim involves a range of far-reaching governance provisions, including co-management boards to manage wildlife, regulate the environment, and carry out related functions such as land-use planning.[5]

Because this chapter is exclusively devoted to claims boards in the northern territories, a word about the territories and their governments is in order. Constitutionally, territories lack the status of provinces. For example, the federal government has the technical power to abolish or reconstitute the territories at will, though it is inconceivable that it would do so. More significantly, the jurisdictional scope of the territories, though substantial, is not as broad as that of the provinces. The territorial governments exercise many of the key powers that provinces wield, including jurisdiction over health, education, social welfare, local government, civil law, local and regional transportation, and so on. Ottawa, rather than the territorial governments, has jurisdiction over a few fields that "south of 60" fall under provincial control; most are of minor consequence but one is central, both in overall terms and for this analysis.

Elsewhere in Canada, **Crown land**—or public land—is owned and controlled by the provinces; in the territories, the federal government still retains ownership and, thus, in important ways, control of Crown land (as it did in the three Prairie provinces until 1930). Since most land in the three territories is Crown land, this has huge economic implications. The many millions of dollars in royalties generated by the diamond mines of the NWT and Nunavut, for example, have until recently accrued entirely to Ottawa rather than to the territorial treasuries. In April 2014, a **devolution** agreement between the government of the Northwest Territories and Ottawa transferred administrative responsibility for (though not actual ownership of) lands and non-renewable resources to the NWT. Accordingly, some royalties are now shared with the territorial government and with Aboriginal governments and organizations, though most royalties still go to the federal government. Federal ownership of Crown land has also effectively meant that most issues of environmental policy and regulation fell within the federal, rather than the territorial, government's ambit. Yukon is an important exception since under its devolution agreement, signed in 2003, the territorial government takes the lead in setting and implementing environmental policy, including matters coming before the claims boards. Significantly, the NWT agreement differs substantially from the Yukon arrangement, leaving many essential regulatory powers with Ottawa rather than transferring them to the NWT government. (Although Nunavut has vigorously sought a devolution agreement from its earliest days, Ottawa has been unwilling to enter serious negotiations, and consequently virtually no progress has occurred.)

Much could be said of the geographic, economic, demographic, and political characteristics of the territories. For present purposes, let us simply highlight two characteristics relating to the place of Aboriginal peoples in territorial society and governance. First, the territories are distinctive in the demographic predominance of Aboriginal people: Aboriginal people constitute roughly 23 per cent of the population in Yukon, 50 per cent in the NWT, and 85 per cent in Nunavut. These overall figures, however, can be misleading; the non-Aboriginal population is heavily concentrated in a few larger centres, so that most communities have large Aboriginal majorities. Second, in all three territories, the Aboriginal political organizations—governments in a very real sense—are integral to the system of governance to an extent scarcely imaginable in most of southern Canada.

BOX 10.1 | "Devolution" in the Northwest Territories

Passage in early 2014 of the federal Northwest Territories Devolution Act marked a significant milestone in the political and constitutional development of the NWT. Many years in the making, the complex devolution agreement assigned significant authority over lands and waters to the NWT government; as well, some 200 staff from Aboriginal Affairs and Northern Development Canada (AANDC) engaged in land and water administration were transferred to the NWT government. Important as these changes were, they did not include transferring ownership of Crown land to the territorial government. A key component of the devolution agreement gives the NWT, for the first time, a substantial share—up to 50 per cent—of royalties from non-renewable resource development. In turn, the NWT government passes on 25 per cent of these new revenues, termed the "net fiscal benefit," to Aboriginal governments and organizations. The devolution agreement was highly controversial. Some Aboriginal governments at first rejected it but later signed on; others never consented to it on the grounds that it abrogated their **Aboriginal and treaty rights**. Still others in the NWT objected that the deal itself was inadequate. The Act not only authorized the devolution agreement, it also made major changes to the environmental regulatory system created in 1998 by the Mackenzie Valley Resource Management Act, most notably doing away with the regional land and water boards. These provisions had little to do with devolution but were central to the Conservative government's agenda of streamlining environmental regulatory processes. The NWT government, desperate to finalize the devolution deal, had little choice but to accede to this aspect of the bill, despite extensive local opposition.

Claims Boards in the Mackenzie Valley

A great many variations are evident in environmental regulatory boards established by and under the settled claims (one in Nunavut, four in the NWT, and one in the Yukon[6]) across the territorial North, in terms of structure, mandate, budget, process, effectiveness, and the like. No point would be served in enumerating these variations; instead, the balance of this discussion will focus on two of the largest, most active boards: the Mackenzie Valley Land and Water Board (MVLWB) and the Mackenzie Valley Environmental Impact Review Board (MVEIRB), with occasional reference to boards in Yukon and Nunavut.

Under the provisions of the 1992 Gwich'in and 1993 Sahtu land claims in the northern NWT and the 2005 Tlicho agreement in the central NWT, the federal government was required to establish a series of co-management boards to deal with land-use planning and environmental protection in the Mackenzie Valley (essentially the entire NWT south of the delta of the Mackenzie River[7]). After some delay, which led to Ottawa finding itself in court over unfulfilled treaty obligations, the MVLWB, the MVEIRB, and two (later three) regional land and water boards in the Gwich'in, Sahtu, and Tlicho areas were created under the federal Mackenzie Valley Resource Management Act (MVRMA), passed by Parliament in 1998. This might suggest that a simple Act of Parliament could substantially alter or indeed abolish these boards, with the implication that their existence and influence rest precariously on the favour of the federal government. However, this is only partially true. On the one hand, were Ottawa to do away with the boards, it would immediately be faced with a constitutional obligation to create replacement boards with similar mandates and composition. On the other hand, the federal government does have extensive scope to change the boards and their operations. This is illustrated in the passage early in 2014 of Bill C-15, the Northwest Territories Devolution Act, which, in addition to implementing the devolution agreement mentioned earlier, did away with the three regional land and water boards, folding them into the territory-wide MVLWB.

The organization of the MVEIRB is relatively straightforward. The Board, whose mandate covers the entire Mackenzie Valley, is composed of eight members, who serve on a part-time basis, and a chair, who effectively works full-time on Board business. Its core funding from Ottawa is roughly $2.6 million a year, and until recently it usually received supplementary funds to cover unpredictable expenses, such as the need for public hearings on proposals that had not come forward when the budget was prepared. In 2013, however, Ottawa significantly reduced its financial support for the Board, requiring it to lay off nearly half its staff.[8] The Board now has eight full-time professional staff and hires consultants to provide technical expertise that Board staff may lack. Its office is in the territorial capital, Yellowknife.

As initially created, the MVLWB was far more complex. The three regional boards were responsible for projects that affected only their regions, with the MVLWB responsible for applications coming from the "unsettled areas"—the parts of the southern NWT where claims have yet to be finalized—plus projects that might affect the environment in more than one region or that might be transboundary in nature, that is, with implications for an adjacent province or territory. All members of the regional land and water boards belonged to "the big Board" (the MVLWB) and, with additional members from the unsettled areas, at full strength it had 19 members (including the chair). The MVLWB's staff complement of about a dozen works out of its Yellowknife office with an annual budget of roughly $3 million. The regional land and water boards, headquartered in their own regions, together have roughly 20 staff. The consolidation of boards mandated by the Northwest Territories Devolution Act only occurred in April 2015, so that many aspects of the organization and operation of the new MVLWB will not be clear for some time. The Act specifies that one member of the Board, which has 11 members under the new regime, must come from each of the regions that previously had its own board. Aboriginal groups in the NWT objected, to no avail, that this is a poor substitute for having regional boards. The balance of this chapter is presented as the process existed at the time of writing—i.e., when the regional land and water boards still existed.

A fundamentally important feature of these boards is their co-management nature. "Co-management" is widely used in resource management to denote various forms of power-sharing between government and other organizations or individuals.[9] In this instance, it refers primarily to the all-important composition of board membership. Typically, decisions about who will be appointed to public boards are made exclusively by government, though they sometimes consult with important stakeholders about possible members. Under the MVRMA (as stipulated in the claims agreements), although the federal government formally makes most appointments to the Mackenzie Valley boards, half the members are nominees of government (the federal government and the government of the Northwest Territories) and half are nominees of Aboriginal organizations and governments. Since the Aboriginal organizations and governments almost always nominate Aboriginal members, and many territorial government nominees as well as some federal appointees are also Aboriginal, the result is that a majority of board members, often a strong majority, are Aboriginal. This is enormously important.

The boards and their members are required to be independent. Like judges, they are to make decisions based on their best judgment without direction or influence from outside entities, whether government or Aboriginal organizations. In that sense, board members do not "represent" government, Aboriginal organizations, or regions. At the same time, the parties are careful to nominate only persons whose views they find compatible. Moreover, the elemental fact of a strong Aboriginal presence on the boards is of huge importance in determining how the boards operate and the decisions they reach.

The Environmental Regulation Process

All but the tiniest construction, infrastructure, or resource extraction projects require land-use permits and/or water licences, which specify in great detail what project proponents may or may not do to the geophysical environment, as well as what measures they must take to ensure against potential (as opposed to actual or predictable) environmental damage, plus remedial actions to restore the environment once the project is completed. Thus, anyone—governments included—proposing anything from a major pipeline, road, or diamond mine to a culvert carrying a small creek under a road must secure formal government approval based on environmental acceptability. The land and water boards and the MVEIRB mainly determine whether proposed projects meet environmental standards, and they impose conditions on the projects to ensure that the environment is protected. In this respect, except in very unusual circumstances, the Canadian Environmental Assessment Act, the principal federal legislation covering most of Canada, does not apply to the NWT; the MVRMA is the operative statute.

The MVRMA is long, highly complex, and replete with barely comprehensible legal language. So, too, board processes are convoluted and confusing (a simplified schematic diagram setting out basic processes fills an entire page). Very much simplified, the process unfolds as follows.[10]

Applications from project proponents are screened by various governmental bodies, usually a land and water board, though other government entities, including the federal AANDC, also screen projects. If the screener believes the potential environmental impact to be minimal, either because the project is very small or because the applicant has identified and committed to specific detailed measures to mitigate possible environmental damage, the land and water board will issue the requisite licences or permits or, in the case of certain larger projects, recommend to the NWT Minister of Environment and Natural Resources that the project be approved.[11] If the screener concludes, in the words of the Act, that the proposed development "might have a significant adverse impact on the environment or might be a cause of public concern,"[12] it refers the application to the MVEIRB for an environmental assessment (EA). Only a small proportion of projects are sent for EA. The MVEIRB can also decide to conduct an EA on a project even if none of the screening bodies has sent it forward, but only rarely does this happen.

An EA is a prolonged, formal process that typically involves public hearings; detailed reviews of technical data; and extensive exchange of information and opinion among the MVEIRB, government agencies, the project proponent, and the people and communities in the potentially affected area. It can easily take a year or more. All documents generated in this process become part of the public record, readily accessible via the public registry on the Board's website.

Once the information has been assembled and analyzed, and all those potentially affected by the project—including the local Aboriginal communities—have been heard from, the Board issues a report to the federal minister recommending that the project be approved as is, that it be rejected entirely, or that it be approved subject to specific measures to mitigate possible environmental damage. Recommended measures are often extensive and detailed. Approval of the federal minister (who responds on behalf of other federal departments, as well as territorial departments that may be involved) is required to confirm the Board's recommendation. Once ministerial approval is received, the application is sent to the appropriate land and water board for issuance of the detailed licences or permits. Putting it this way makes it seem that it is purely a pro forma exercise. It is not. Although the land and water boards have no discretion to deny a licence or permit at this stage, they can and do impose rigorous conditions that may not be to the proponent's liking.

This summary might suggest that the boards are purely advisory and that in the final analysis decisions rest with Ottawa, which would in turn raise questions about Aboriginal influence and about "co-management." In a strictly legal sense, the final decision on most large or controversial applications is indeed made by federal or territorial ministers, though many routine decisions on smaller projects are made by the land and water boards without federal or territorial approval. Since Ottawa in general and the AANDC minister in particular are eager to facilitate large economic development projects such as pipelines and mines, it might be supposed that the apparent federal control of the decision would produce less stringent environmental conditions on proposed projects than the boards would recommend. In terms of real-world politics and policy, however, such a reading greatly underestimates the boards' power and influence.

In the first place, the boards' reports are thorough and professional, based on extensive review of relevant technical data and expert opinion, and thus carry significant credibility and political weight. In addition, virtually the entire process is carried out in public[13] and all documents—including the formal response from the minister to the EA report and its recommendations—are public. This transparency adds to the credibility of the board and its reports, and requires Ottawa to justify any objections it may have to board recommendations.

More significantly, the MVRMA itself makes it difficult for the federal minister to simply reject recommendations from an MVEIRB environmental assessment report, and all but impossible to substitute his or her conditions for those proposed by the Board. The only route open to a minister who wishes to reject an EA report is to refer the matter to an Environmental Impact Review (EIR), but this is an unpalatable option since EIRs are more formal, extensive, costly, and time-consuming than EAs (and thus disagreeable and frustrating to proponents). Not surprisingly, no federal minister has chosen this route. Ottawa may negotiate with the Board about revising its recommended conditions through an informal "consult to modify" process. Many disputes between the federal minister and the Board are resolved this way, though the process can take considerable time. If this fails to resolve differences, stalemate ensues. Without Board agreement to modify its recommendations, the minister cannot impose his preferred conditions; but without ministerial approval, no licences or permits may be issued and the project cannot proceed. Such standoffs are not common, but neither are they unknown. Until they are resolved, which can take months or occasionally years, the project cannot go forward.

The expansive mandates of the MVRMA boards significantly enhance their clout and the influence of Aboriginal people in the environmental assessment process. This was not accidental: "in many instances the language of the legislation was kept deliberately broad to ensure maximum involvement for Indigenous people, and to ensure that all uses of land that could have an impact would be subject to proper environmental assessment."[14] A crucial illustration relates to the definition of the "environment," which the boards are to protect: the definition includes not only the geophysical environment—the land, water, air, and the flora and fauna—but also "the social and cultural environment . . . [and] heritage resources."[15] This broad remit gives the Mackenzie Valley boards (and the Yukon Environmental and Socio-Economic Assessment Board, whose Act contains a similar provision) significantly wider leeway to examine issues relating to the human environment than other agencies conducting EAs elsewhere in Canada.

Moreover, as noted above, the land and water boards are to send applications to EA if they perceive that the proposed project "might have a significant adverse impact on the environment or might be a cause of public concern." Since nowhere in the Act, or in the regulations supplementing it, are such key terms as "significant adverse impact" or "public concern" defined, the boards are left with wide discretion in interpreting them. This ambiguity serves to enhance the boards' ability to establish the ground rules in their efforts at protecting the environment.

A final important point about the boards' legal mandates: in keeping with one of the MVRMA's guiding principles—that is, enhancing the well-being and preserving the way of life of the Aboriginal peoples of the Mackenzie Valley—the Act explicitly sets the **traditional knowledge** (TK) of the Aboriginal people on an equal footing with Western "scientific knowledge."[16] This noteworthy provision is examined more extensively below.

Aboriginal Involvement and Influence on Claims Boards

Beyond TK, two important characteristics of claims boards make for significant Aboriginal influence in environmental regulation (as, indeed, on other claims boards such as wildlife management boards and planning commissions). One is the substantial number of Aboriginal board members and the other is the requirement for extensive, genuine consultation with local communities—most overwhelmingly Aboriginal—potentially affected by proposed developments.

As noted above, the boards were explicitly designed on a co-management basis, in the sense of guaranteed representation by the nominees of Aboriginal governments and organizations on the boards, and not in token numbers. One analysis found that across the three territories between 40 and 90 per cent of claims board members were Aboriginal.[17] Since its creation, 67 per cent of MVLWB members have been Aboriginal; for the MVEIRB, the figure is 57 per cent.[18] That board members—Aboriginal and non-Aboriginal—act independently and do not take instructions from the parties that nominated or appointed them does not mean that Aboriginal sensibilities are left behind. Consider the following episode involving Gabrielle Mackenzie-Scott, a Dene member (and later chair) of the MVEIRB, during a public hearing on a proposed diamond drilling project:

> . . . a Dene woman stepped forward, pleading with the board to protect the area because her baby teeth were buried there.

"A lot of people would have found that to be strange, but I could relate to the woman," says Mackenzie-Scott. "She was about my age and I too had the experience of having my baby teeth buried in a ceremony. This was an important moment in life for both me and my mother. I know where my baby teeth are buried. Many people have sacred places like this."[19]

As the specific board decisions mentioned below illustrate, Aboriginal board members bring their distinctive world views to bear when evaluating the environmental consequences of projects they review.

Not only are Aboriginal people involved as decision-makers, they participate in the process via consultations and public hearings. The Mackenzie Valley boards are required by the MVRMA to ensure that the people who stand to be affected by proposed projects are taken into account in environmental reviews. These are not merely pro forma consultations. Guidelines set out by the MVLWB make it clear that project proponents are required to engage in extensive and genuine interaction with local communities about their projects, and to do so before submitting an application. Tellingly, the guidelines refer to "engagement" rather than consultation, with would-be applicants warned that permit or licence applications must include an "engagement record," which "must be comprehensive and provide the Board with evidence of which engagement activities took place prior to an application, a summary of key issues, resulting changes to the proposed project, and which issues remain unresolved."[20]

Once an application is received, the Board informs local communities, Aboriginal organizations, governments, and other potentially affected groups, and actively solicits their views. Should a project be sent for EA—often on the basis of "public concern"—the MVEIRB process is likely to entail public hearings in which community representatives, officials of Aboriginal organizations, and local people are invited to appear and to address the Board. Not only do they have the right to speak, but they also have the right to question representatives of the companies or governments, and to ask them to explain or justify their plans and assertions—all in public.

In all phases of their activity, boards strive to include Aboriginal TK in environmental decision-making. A widely cited definition of TK describes it as "a cumulative body of knowledge, practice and belief, evolving by adaptive processes and handed down through generations by cultural transmission about the relationship of living beings (including humans) with one another and with their environment."[21] In practice, giving voice to TK entails such things as giving as much credence to information and opinion provided by Aboriginal elders with decades of experience on the land as is accorded to that offered by professional consultants and biologists with university credentials. Aboriginal people with daily experience of the location, numbers, and behaviour of wildlife, of long- and short-term changes in the health and spatial distribution of plants and trees, of patterns of water movement in rivers, lakes, and the like may have a better understanding of the complex interrelationships of the myriad elements of the natural environment than those trained in Western science, whose focus is typically more narrow and lacks long-term perspective. Aboriginal hunters and elders, with generations of observation and experience to draw on, may be better placed to predict the consequences of putting a road across a caribou migration route than Western scientists. This is not to say that TK is necessarily at odds with the findings of Western science—indeed, they often complement one another—but to emphasize the involvement of

Aboriginal people and their experiences and perspectives in the process. Prior to the advent of the Mackenzie Valley boards, TK played a far less significant role in environmental regulation in the NWT and certainly had no legal status, as it does under the MVRMA.

Notable Board Accomplishments

Given the number, range, and complexity of the proposed projects that the boards have screened and reviewed since the MVRMA came into effect, it is possible only to highlight a small number of specific illustrations of the boards' contribution to environmental protection in the Mackenzie Valley.[22]

Early in 2005, the MVEIRB issued its EA report on a proposal for a small exploratory diamond drilling project at Drybones Bay, roughly 45 kilometres southeast of Yellowknife on Great Slave Lake. The actual biophysical environmental effects of the proposed drilling were relatively minor but the Board unanimously recommended that the project be rejected in its entirety because of a "cultural impact so severe it could not be mitigated . . . the cultural groups that have long utilized Drybones Bay consider it to be of utmost importance—as a spiritual place, as a gathering place, as a burial grounds, as a place of rest and respite, as a learning place, and as a harvesting place."[23] After an initial hesitation, the federal government accepted the Board's recommendations, killing the project. This was an unusual occurrence not only because it was the first time the Board had recommended complete rejection of a project, but also because the Board subsequently recommended approval, with appropriate mitigation measures, for similar projects in the vicinity of Drybones Bay. Nonetheless, it serves to underline both the Board's clout and the influence on decision-making, via the boards, of Aboriginal peoples' holistic appreciation of "the environment."

A more far-reaching episode was the disposition of an application by a mining company to explore for uranium at Screech Lake in the watershed of the upper Thelon River, some 80 kilometres south of the Thelon Game Sanctuary, which spans the NWT–Nunavut border. The MVLWB had referred the project to EA on the basis of concerns expressed by the people of the small Dene community of Łutsël K'e, the closest community to the proposed development (though more than 200 kilometres distant). At the MVEIRB's public hearing in Łutsël K'e, community members expressed profound disquiet at the prospect of uranium mining in this pristine and ecologically sensitive area central to their traditions and lifestyle. In its EA report, the Board noted that "at the heart of this issue is the belief that the Upper Thelon is a spiritual place that must be protected from any type of desecration . . . the Review Board agrees that the potential for industrial development of the area is incompatible with the aboriginal values of this spiritually significant cultural landscape."[24] With the Board's recommendation that the project be rejected, in short order the federal minister accepted the recommendation.

A more recent example of board influence is that of the Nunavut Impact Review Board (NIRB) decision on a major coal mine proposed for Ellesmere Island. Early in 2010, the NIRB—effectively the Nunavut equivalent of the MVEIRB—recommended to the federal government that the project be rejected entirely or very substantially modified on the grounds that it "may have significant adverse effects on the ecosystem, wildlife habitat or Inuit harvesting activities . . . [and that it] may have significant adverse socio-economic effects on northerners."[25] Before Ottawa could respond, the developer withdrew the proposal.

Very few projects have been rejected outright by the Mackenzie Valley boards or by their counterparts in Yukon and Nunavut, though certainly others have been abandoned before the process was completed, as it became evident that proposed developments would not pass muster. But the measure of the boards' success is not the number of projects they have halted. Far more numerous and important have been recommendations leading to mitigation measures designed to protect and preserve the geophysical and cultural environment for projects given the go-ahead. By way of illustration, the boards routinely recommend—and the federal and territorial governments typically accept—such measures as reduction in the number and size of "seismic lines" (clearings in the bush to accommodate seismic exploration); limitations on times and seasons when drilling and other activities may take place, so as not disturb wildlife; more stringent water quality standards and monitoring than project developers proposed; extensive baseline studies to document the size, nature, and health of fish and wildlife stocks in potentially affected areas; strict conditions, and sometimes outright prohibitions, on location of access roads and campsites; involvement of local Aboriginal elders in determining the location of archaeologically or spiritually important sites to be avoided in exploration and exploitation activities.

These and other measures are designed to strike a balance between environmental protection and resource development, with substantial emphasis on the importance of maintaining and respecting Aboriginal culture and lifestyle. To be sure, such measures may fall short of what some—both Aboriginal and non-Aboriginal—think necessary to protect and preserve the environment, but by the same token they are often significantly more extensive than development proponents would otherwise put in place. It is also worth bearing in mind that, as board approaches and policies become better known across the Mackenzie Valley, would-be developers include tougher environmental protection measures in their initial proposals in anticipation of board recommendations.

Shortcomings

Although the MVEIRB environmental assessment process has been described as "exemplary," especially as a contrast to the typical failings of such processes to give adequate voice and influence to Aboriginal people,[26] the regulatory regime of the Mackenzie Valley claims boards has significant shortcomings. Some, such as the lack of **intervener funding** and the often limited incorporation of TK into board processes, relate directly to Aboriginal participation and influence. Other failings affect Aboriginal influence less directly but are no less important. These include the complexity of the process, problems of enforcement, and concerns about board independence, mostly but not entirely arising from statements and activities of the federal government.

While Aboriginal organizations and communities fully appreciate the importance of being involved in the process through participation in public hearings and submission of written documents, they often lack the capacity—the human and financial resources—to take on the myriad issues confronting them, only some of which involve environmental assessments of projects proposed for their lands. The Mackenzie Valley boards have long argued that, without intervener funding, Aboriginal organizations and communities are often unable to make their views and concerns known. Intervener funding refers to money made available to organizations and groups to enable them to participate effectively in regulatory processes. It could be used, for example, to have staff prepare submissions, to hire experts to provide evidence to support their case, or to defray travel costs for representatives to attend hearings and meetings.

The boards do take TK seriously in gathering and evaluating information, and in reaching recommendations. Genuine as these efforts are, criticisms are sometimes heard that TK is not always given the same respect as Western science or that board staff (who tend to be non-Aboriginal and typically have university backgrounds) and proponents will always ensure that information acquired and analyzed according to the Western science paradigm will be presented to the boards, whereas TK may not be as readily available.[27] Additionally, while boards make sincere and extensive efforts to utilize TK in their deliberations, certain spiritual-cosmological aspects of TK, involving, for example, ethical understandings of how humans should relate to one another, are incompatible with the world views of the Western bureaucratic state in which the boards are embedded.[28]

A particularly weak link in the Mackenzie Valley environmental regulatory regime is enforcement. The claims boards have no enforcement authority or capacity. They must depend entirely on the staff of the federal and territorial governments to inspect projects once they are licensed and to enforce the conditions of licences and permits. The often substantial gap between conditions imposed by the boards and compliance, as enforced by government inspectors and other officials, has long been a sore point. An appeal for action from the chairs of the MVEIRB and of all the land and water boards to the senior department official in the NWT estimated that "only about 46% of the [MVEIRB's] measures accepted by the Minister of INAC [AANDC's previous acronym] are being implemented by regulatory authorities and that, of those, less that [*sic*] 50% are actually inspected for purposes of compliance or enforcement. At best, only 25% of the Review Board's measures are having any affect [*sic*] on the impacts they were designed to mitigate."[29] It does not necessarily follow that conditions set out in permits and licences were being ignored, but without systematic inspection and follow-up to ensure compliance, the effectiveness of the regime is cast into some doubt. In response, INAC contended that many of the conditions that the boards argue it is not enforcing either are beyond the boards' mandates or are too imprecise to make enforcement possible. Under the devolution arrangements, the NWT government rather than the federal government is now responsible for most inspection and enforcement. Northerners will be watching closely to see whether this increase in territorial authority will make for different approaches to enforcement. In the short term, at least, this seems unlikely since all of the former AANDC inspection staff were transferred to the territorial government when devolution occurred.

The effectiveness of the boards is heavily contingent on their independence from government, especially the federal government. And, while the boards, especially the MVEIRB, have not been reluctant to criticize AANDC or to issue reports or take other actions unwelcome in Ottawa, the question of board independence is never far below the surface. Every penny of the boards' funding comes from Ottawa. Although their core funding is secure, the number, scope, and thus the cost of the EAs, public hearings, and other activities the boards will be required to conduct in any given year are unpredictable and largely funded through special transfers that have to be negotiated every year. Ottawa has thus far generally provided the boards with adequate funding, though this is rarely as much as the boards argue they need to fulfill their mandates properly. For example, representatives of the Nunavut Impact Review Board and the Nunavut Planning Commission recently warned a House of Commons committee that they simply could not meet their obligations under a new piece of federal legislation with their current level of funding.[30] Ottawa does not appear to have used its financial upper hand over the boards to attempt to influence their decisions and recommendations. Nevertheless, the boards, as well as those who interact with them, remain acutely aware of "the golden rule of politics": he who has the gold, rules.

Board independence also stands to be affected by the appointment process. Aboriginal organizations and governments (and the territorial governments) nominate people to serve on boards, but in most cases Ottawa makes the appointment.[31] Thus, the federal government can reject a nominee not to its liking, though it cannot make a substitute appointment. Since the appointment process is highly secretive, it is unclear how often Ottawa rejects nominees put forward by Aboriginal governments, though it unquestionably happens. Robert Alexie Jr, former president of the Gwich'in Tribal Council, recently complained that "we have nominated about five people over five years [to the MVEIRB], and all five have been rejected by Canada for whatever reason. They don't give us a reason."[32] Certainly, Ottawa on occasion has been willing to use its appointment and dismissal powers to promote its interests. The most noteworthy example of the federal government using its political muscle to affect board membership involved its abrupt and questionable removal of a veteran member of the MVEIRB who had vigorously opposed the Board's chair on the grounds that his actions were motivated by subservience to the federal government and its priorities.[33]

Overall, in terms of the appointment process, delays on Ottawa's part—often long, disruptive delays, occasionally leaving boards short of quorum and thus unable to act—in making appointments to board vacancies have been more of a concern than federal attempts at influencing boards through its appointment prerogative. The potential for high-handed intervention by Ottawa in this fashion, however, remains a concern. Along these lines, in the 2014 revisions to the MVRMA, Ottawa enhanced its power to choose the chair of the MVLWB, eliminating the Board's role in the process.[34]

It is also clear that the federal government, especially but not exclusively under the Conservative administration of Stephen Harper, has wanted to rein in some of the boards and render environmental protection processes in the NWT less time-consuming and less complex. Industry long complained about the delays, expense, and uncertainty of environmental regulatory processes, and of course about some of the conditions imposed by the boards. Former Conservative INAC Minister Jim Prentice complained vigorously about what he termed the "spider's web" of regulatory processes in the NWT and vowed improvements.[35]

An Ottawa-commissioned 2008 report agreed with some of industry's criticisms about the complexity and unpredictability of the regulatory system in the Mackenzie Valley, proposing sweeping changes to the boards and their operations. In putting forward his recommendations, the report's author was at some pains to emphasize that "this is not an attempt to diminish or reduce the influence that Aboriginal people have on resource development in the North."[36] Following a protracted, conflict-ridden process, the federal government, as mentioned earlier, brought in a host of major changes to the MVRMA, the most notable of which was elimination of the regional land and water boards. Aboriginal opposition to this move was widespread and vehement. "Canada has returned to the old colonial ways of thinking they know what is best for us. They are silencing our voice," said Tlicho Grand Chief Eddie Erasmus. According to Herb Norwegian, Dehcho Grand Chief, "people right down the valley, people in the communities are just up in arms, wondering what is going on? Why is this being shoved down our throats?"[37]

It should not be thought that challenges to board independence come solely from Ottawa (or, under devolved regimes, the territorial capitals). A disturbing episode from Nunavut illustrates that Aboriginal organizations and governments may also threaten board independence. An application for a water licence for a gold mine had been languishing for some time at the Nunavut Water Board, which exercises similar functions to the Mackenzie Valley land and water boards. Pressing for quick approval, in order to create jobs and economic opportunities, were the Kitikmeot Inuit Association and other, largely Inuit-dominated political and business organizations. When Board staff issued a long, detailed critique of the proponent's most recent revision of its application, the Board summarily fired its long-serving and highly respected executive director, whereupon the Board's entire technical staff resigned in support, citing blatant political interference.[38]

Conclusion

In northern Canada, economic development projects such as mines, roads, and oil and gas wells and pipelines are both substantial in number and far-reaching in their potential environmental consequences. Especially given the economic, cultural, and spiritual significance of the land to the Aboriginal peoples, its protection looms as a critically important issue. Accordingly, having in place stringent processes for environmental regulation of resource extraction and infrastructure projects, processes that afford the Aboriginal peoples of the North meaningful involvement and influence, is crucially important.

The regulatory boards created to fulfill the northern comprehensive land claims, such as the MVLWB and the MVEIRB, were designed to provide just such processes. To be sure, the boards have their shortcomings, but overall their record—both in maintaining a high-quality regime of environmental impact assessment and of imposition of mitigation measures, and in assuring that the concerns and the approaches of the local Aboriginal people are taken into account in decision-making—is one of solid accomplishment. This is not to say that Aboriginal peoples or their governments are always satisfied with the outcome of the regulatory process in the North; at times, they can be as vocally critical of the boards and the board process as the mining industry.

Nor should it be thought that Aboriginal opposition to government decisions respecting the recommendations of claims boards is always directed against Ottawa. As this chapter is written, environmentalists and Aboriginal leaders are fighting an attempt by the Yukon government to override the recommendations of a claims-mandated land-use planning board regarding the Peel watershed, a pristine region of northeast Yukon.

After years of study and consultation, in 2011 the Peel Watershed Planning Commission, a body established under the Yukon Umbrella Final Agreement (the territory-wide framework for land claims and self-government) recommended that 81 per cent of the Peel watershed be designated a special management area where, among other things, mining development would be prohibited. Early in 2014, the Yukon government, claiming the power to override such recommendations, announced a plan that would protect only 29 per cent of the area, leaving 71 per cent open to exploration and mining. Yukon First Nations and environmental organizations challenged the government's decision in court. In a stunning rebuke, late in 2014 Justice R.S. Veale of the Supreme Court of Yukon struck down the government's plan. To some extent, he based his decision on the technically flawed process the government followed in its dealings with the Planning Commission, but more critical was what he held to be the fundamental principle underpinning modern-day treaties, and by extension the institutions created to implement them:

> Treaties are as much about building relationships as they are about the settlement of past grievances. They are to be interpreted in a manner that upholds the honour of the Crown . . . the process adopted by the Government of Yukon . . . [did not] enhance the goal of reconciliation. It was an ungenerous interpretation not consistent with the honour and integrity of the Crown.[39]

The Yukon government almost immediately announced that it would appeal the decision.

A theme of this book has been the pronounced effects of federal government austerity in weakening environmental policy by reducing funds for development, monitoring, and enforcement of environmental standards. Cutbacks have clearly affected the environmental co-management boards in the territories, but so too have changes in federal legislation and policy, which continue to shape environmental regulation in the North in fundamental ways. The story of claims-based co-management boards continues to be a positive one, but not as positive as it was when the previous edition of *Canadian Environmental Policy and Politics* was published.

At the time of writing it is unclear what the effects of the enforced consolidation of the land and water boards in the Northwest Territories will be. As the Conservative government pushed the legislation through Parliament, it insisted that the smaller MVLWB would be more efficient than the system of regional boards, and that environmental standards would not be compromised. Opponents vociferously rejected this claim, arguing that regional perspectives crucial in environmental regulatory processes will be lost; this is a very real and disheartening possibility. The opponents also pointed out that even if overall staff complement is not reduced in the revamped MVLWB—an uncertain proposition at best—closing the regional offices will mean a serious loss to the small communities where the offices were located. These communities, which need as many opportunities as possible to develop their governance capacity, will see their capacity decline as the professional staff of the regional boards are all moved to the centralized operation in Yellowknife.

Overall, just as the whole notion of comprehensive land claim agreements represents an innovative restructuring of the relationship between the Canadian state and Aboriginal peoples, the northern claims board process qualifies as innovative and ambitious. It remains, to be sure, a work in progress, requiring commitment to environmental protection on the part of government, industry, and the Aboriginal peoples of the North.

Key Terms

Aboriginal and treaty rights

co-management boards

comprehensive land claim agreements

Crown land

devolution

intervener funding

traditional knowledge

unextinguished Aboriginal title

Questions for Review

1. What balance should be struck in the North between the right to develop natural resources and the need to protect the environment?
2. Do the co-management boards involved in environmental regulation in the North offer Aboriginal people an adequate opportunity to influence important environmental policy decisions?

3. What should be the role of traditional Aboriginal knowledge in environmental policy?
4. Why do the roles, powers, and composition of co-management boards matter for environmental policy?

Internet Resources

AANDC, "Comprehensive Claims"
http://www.aadnc-aandc.gc.ca/eng/1100100030577/1100100030578

Mackenzie Valley Environmental Impact Review Board
http://www.reviewboard.ca

Mackenzie Valley Land and Water Board
http://www.mvlwb.com

Nunavut Impact Review Board
http://www.nirb.ca

NWT Board Forum
http://www.nwtboardforum.com

Protect the Peel
http://www.protectpeel.ca

Yukon Environmental and Socio-economic Assessment Board
http://www.yesab.ca

Additional Reading

Alcantara, Christopher. *Negotiating the Deal: Comprehensive Land Claims Agreements in Canada.* Toronto: University of Toronto Press, 2013.

Anderson, Robert B., and Robert M. Bone, eds. *Natural Resources and Aboriginal Peoples in Canada*, 2nd edn. Concord, Ont.: Captus Press, 2009.

Armitage, Derek. "Collaborative Environmental Assessment in the Northwest Territories, Canada." *Environmental Impact Assessment Review* 25 (Apr. 2005): 239–58.

Bielawski, Ellen. *Rogue Diamonds: The Rush for Riches on Dene Land.* Vancouver: Douglas & McIntyre, 2003.

Bone, Robert M. *The Canadian North: Issues and Challenges*, 4th edn. Toronto: Oxford University Press, 2012.

Christensen, Julia, and Miriam Grant. "How Political Change Paved the Way for Indigenous Knowledge: The Mackenzie Valley Resource Management Act." *Arctic* 60 (June 2007): 115–23.

Kassam, Karim-Aly. *Biocultural Diversity and Indigenous Ways of Knowing: Human Ecology in the Arctic.* Calgary: University of Calgary Press, 2009.

Myers, Heather. "Changing Environment, Changing Times: Environmental Issues and Political Action in the Canadian North." *Environment: Science and Policy for Sustainable Development* 43 (July–Aug. 2001): 32–44.

Nadasdy, Paul. *Hunters and Bureaucrats: Power, Knowledge, and Aboriginal–State Relations in the Southwest Yukon.* Vancouver: University of British Columbia Press, 2004.

Spak, Stella. "The Position of Indigenous Knowledge in Canadian Co-management Organizations." *Anthropologica* 47 (2005): 233–46.

White, Graham. "Cultures in Collision: Traditional Knowledge and Euro-Canadian Governance Processes in Northern Land-Claim Boards." *Arctic* 59 (Dec. 2006): 401–14.

Notes

1. On the nature and importance of the historic treaties and the controversies surrounding the adequacy of the government's fulfillment of its treaty obligations, see J.R. Miller, *Compact, Contract, Covenant: Aboriginal Treaty-making in Canada* (Toronto: University of Toronto Press, 2009).

2. Christa Scholtz, *Negotiating Claims: The Emergence of Indigenous Land Claim Negotiations in Australia, Canada, New Zealand, and the United States* (New York: Routledge, 2006), ch. 4.

3. Much of the current NWT was covered by Treaty 8 (1899) and Treaty 11 (1921) but the government's policy tacitly

accepts that in areas, such as the NWT, where existing treaties were fundamentally flawed, comprehensive land claims could be negotiated.

4. Bernard Funston, "Canada's North: Barren Lands or Blind Spot," in Ian Peach, ed., *Constructing Tomorrow's Federalism: New Perspectives on Canadian Governance* (Winnipeg: University of Manitoba Press, 2007), 87.

5. Comprehensive claims are very different from "specific" claims, in which First Nations seek redress or compensation for the federal government's failure to live up to the terms of historic treaties.

6. In Yukon, an Umbrella Final Agreement sets out an overall framework covering the entire territory. Individual First Nations negotiate their claims and self-government agreements within this framework. As of 2015, 11 of 14 Yukon First Nations had settled claims.

7. An earlier claim, the 1984 Inuvialuit Final Agreement, created a series of boards with responsibility for the northern part of the Mackenzie Delta and the portions of the Arctic coast and the Arctic islands within the NWT.

8. Thandiwe Vela, "Major Layoffs at Review Board," *News/North NWT*, 11 Feb., 2–13.

9. Fikret Berkes, P.J. George, and R.J. Preston, "Co-management: The Evolution of Theory and Practice of the Joint Administration of Living Things," *Alternatives* 18, 2 (1991): 12.

10. Any number of nuances, exceptions, and complications are ignored in this overview.

11. Until the April 2014 changes to the water licence process, the role now played by the territorial Minister of Environment and Natural Resources was the responsibility of the federal Minister of AANDC. Because of the territories' constitutional status, AANDC takes the federal lead in policy areas that elsewhere in Canada would be the responsibility of other departments, such as the Department of the Environment.

12. Mackenzie Valley Resource Management Act (MVRMA), s. 125.1(b).

13. The principal exception is that, as required by the Act, the various boards meet behind closed doors to formulate their reports and decide on recommendations.

14. Graham White, Vern Christensen, and Alan Ehrlich, "Involving Canada's Indigenous Peoples in Environmental Impact Assessment: Co-management through the Mackenzie Valley Environmental Impact Review Board," paper presented at the annual conference of the International Association for Impact Assessment, Seoul, Korea, June 2007, 5.

15. MVRMA, s. 115.

16. MVRMA, s. 60.1(b), s. 115.1.

17. Graham White, "'Not the Almighty': Evaluating Aboriginal Influence on Northern Claims Boards," *Arctic* 61, Suppl. 1 (2008): 75, Table 1.

18. Author's calculations. Note that this is only one way of measuring Aboriginal participation. Some members serve a decade or more and others for just three years, so that one could also calculate the proportion of "board years" held by Aboriginal and non-Aboriginal members.

19. Ed Struzik, "Guardian of Sacred Place," *Edmonton Journal*, 24 Feb. 2008.

20. MVLWB, "Engagement and Consultation Policy," 1 June 2013, 20.

21. Fikret Berkes, *Sacred Ecology: Traditional Ecological Knowledge and Resource Management* (Philadelphia: Taylor and Francis, 1999), 8.

22. Despite its potential importance, no reference is made here to the mammoth, multi-billion dollar proposed Mackenzie Gas Project, the centrepiece of which is a plan to construct a pipeline from the Arctic Ocean, through the Mackenzie Valley, to northern Alberta. In part this is because the regulatory process was staggeringly complex and thus not easily summarized (involving as it did a host of regulatory agencies, such as the National Energy Board, beyond those of the MVRMA) and in part because at the time of writing the project appeared to be close to defunct.

23. Mackenzie Valley Environmental Impact Review Board (MVEIRB), "Further Considerations of the Ministers' Questions," attachment to a letter from Gabrielle Mackenzie-Scott, chairperson of the MVEIRB, to Hon. Andy Scott, Minister of Indian Affairs and Northern Development, 23 June 2005, 4.

24. MVEIRB, Report of Environmental Assessment, Ur Energy Exploration Project, 7 May 2007, 4.

25. Letter from Lucassie Arragutainaq, NIRB Chair, to INAC Minister Chuck Strahl, 22 Feb. 2010.

26. Lindsay Galbraith, Ben Bradshaw, and Murray B. Rutherford, "Towards a New Supraregulatory Approach to Environmental Assessment in Northern Canada," *Impact Assessment and Project Appraisal* 25 (Mar. 2007): 33, 36.

27. Stephen C. Ellis, "Meaningful Consideration? A Review of Traditional Knowledge in Environmental Decision-making," *Arctic* 58 (Mar. 2005), 66–77.

28. Graham White, "Cultures in Collision: Traditional Knowledge and Euro-Canadian Governance Processes in Northern Land-Claim Boards," *Arctic* 59 (Dec. 2006): 401–14.

29. Letter from Mackenzie Valley board chairs to Trish Merrithew-Mercredi, Regional Director General, INAC, Yellowknife, 11 Dec. 2007.

30. "Nunavut Boards Say They Can't Pay for Bill C-47 Obligations," *Nunatsiaq News*, 15 Feb. 2013.

31. Under the Yukon devolution agreement, Ottawa no longer makes the appointments to claims boards, the territorial government does. Significantly, despite the 2014 devolution settlement in the NWT, board members are still appointed by the federal government.

32. Quoted in Paul Bickford, "Don't Fix What's Not Broken," *News/North*, 2 Dec. 2013.

33. Bob Weber, "Nault Muzzling Regulatory Agency, Critics Say," *Globe and Mail*, 11 Oct. 2003, A14.

34. Previously, Ottawa appointed the chair from a list of persons nominated by the Board, though it could substitute its own choice if none of the Board's nominees were acceptable. Now, Ottawa simply makes the appointment.

35. Hon. Jim Prentice, "Notes for an Address to the Canadian Energy Pipeline Association Annual Dinner," Calgary, 23 May 2006.

36. Neil McCrank, *Road to Improvement: Report to the Honourable Chuck Strahl, "The Review of the Regulatory Systems across the North"* (Ottawa: Indian and Northern Affairs Canada, May 2008), 13.

37. Canada, House of Commons, Standing Committee on Aboriginal Affairs and Northern Development, *Evidence*, 27 Jan. 2014 (transcript of public hearing in Yellowknife), 12, 28.

38. John Thompson, "Technical Staff Quits in Protest," *Nunatsiaq News*, 13 Apr. 2007.

39. Supreme Court of Yukon, *The First Nation of Nacho Nyak Dun v. Yukon (Government of)*, 2014 YKSC 69, 63 and 74.

11 The Push and Pull of North America on Canadian Environmental Policy

Debora L. VanNijnatten

Chapter Summary

This chapter considers the North American influence on Canadian environmental policy-making and policy. The first section introduces the reader to the mechanisms by which North American ideas and actors can feed into Canadian environmental policy-making across governance scales (bilateral, subnational/cross-border regional, and trilateral) and across issues, using the language of "push-pull" dynamics. The second section sets out the argument that, looking at the North American environmental policy landscape, we seem to be entering a new phase in transboundary interactions; whereas bilateral relations between the Canadian and American national governments dominated until the early 1990s, followed by a significant increase in cross-border interactions between subnational governments (states and provinces) in the late 1990s and early 2000s, it is now the case that co-operative energies seem to have waned in both arenas. Further, trilateral environmental policy activities, which had begun to serve as a supportive backdrop for actors across scales who wished to exercise environmental policy leadership, have lost traction. Certainly, the austerity context has impacted both domestic capacity and transboundary willingness at all levels. The third section discusses how the decline of collaborative efforts across borders serves to reinforce both the current federal government's unwillingness to act in the environmental policy arena as well as policy fragmentation across the country as provinces go their own way.

Chapter Outline

- How might we understand the "North American" influence on Canadian environmental policy?
  - ○ Governance across scales
  - ○ Push-pull dynamics and the potential of transboundary environmental co-operation
- Phase One: Building the bilateral environmental architecture
  - ○ Politics and pragmatism—pushing and pulling
  - ○ The parallel politics of austerity

- Phase Two: The emergence of subnational and cross-border regional environmental governance
  - State-led innovation and the push for collaboration
  - Trilateralism: early hopes, subtle pushing
- Phase Three: The waning of transboundary effort
  - The federal turn inward
  - Discovering the limits to bottom-up efforts: pushing alone
  - Whither trilateralism?
- North American transboundary co-operation: Can Canada stay away?

Introduction

In the third edition of *Canadian Environmental Policy and Politics*, this chapter focused on the ways in which Canada's environmental policy landscape had changed, particularly its North American "backyard." It argued that our backyard had become simultaneously deeper and longer. The chapter highlighted the disaggregation of policy voices in the United States, such that the country could not be viewed as a monolithic, unitary actor exerting pressure on its northern neighbour but more as a loose collection of voices at different scales conveying diverse messages with regard to environmental matters. States had become among the loudest of these, and on various issues they were forcing environmental action by moving ahead with ambitious policies in their own jurisdictions. Canadian jurisdictions were often encouraged to co-operate in these ventures, and sometimes they did. At the same time, our backyard was longer, reaching down into Mexico; the NAFTA partner was becoming something of a policy partner, though the US continued to overshadow continental relationships. Further, Mexico's participation in trilateral institutions and processes was encouraging a broader conception of sustainability and more thoroughgoing reflection on how co-operation might best occur, given profound asymmetries in policy capacity across the continent.[1]

A key concern of this revised chapter, in keeping with the theme of the volume, is whether North American environmental policy dynamics are likely to reinforce or challenge the increasing environmental policy ambivalence in Canada. It makes the argument that, while our backyard remains deeper and longer, Canada appears to have turned away, focused on its own front yard instead. One might argue that we have entered a new phase of interactive dynamics, whereby Canadian jurisdictions are engaged less in co-operative activities at the bilateral, subnational, and trilateral levels than they were when the last edition was being written, and that "push factors" for environmental policy leadership, emanating from transboundary governance sites, are weakening. Canadian federal policies are more likely to reflect domestic priorities (austerity and natural resource development), and less likely than just a few years ago to reflect innovation in policy instrument choice. Further, this may reinforce the differences in environmental policy approach that already exist among provinces, between the provinces and the federal government, and between jurisdictions on either side of the border.

Understanding the North American Influence

"North America" in many ways has become a more concrete entity for Canadian environmental policy-makers and policy analysts. After years of debate about the impacts of NAFTA on the environment, we have arrived at a nuanced and broader view of environmental policy dynamics in a liberalized, continental trade context. Careful convergence studies have found little compelling evidence of a generalized race to the bottom in environmental standards; in fact, there are some examples of upward harmonization. We have come to realize that Canadian environmental performance is (increasingly) not what we would wish to race "up" to anyway, given our rather mediocre standards in many areas. At the same time, we have also acquired a greater awareness of the yawning development gap on the continent, and indeed globally, the challenge this poses for future sustainability, and the need for governance frameworks that will allow us jointly to address these challenges, using a wider range of policy tactics.

The reader will note that the term **governance** has been used, rather than "government." While we associate "government" with the exercise of authoritative decision-making within a particular political unit (e.g., Canada or Ontario), "governance" might best be understood as the ability to wield and co-ordinate resources from public and private actors, generally in a more informal manner than government and with the participation of a wider range of actors.[2] Governance often entails a shift from formal, top-down modes of interaction (i.e., through conventional political institutions, such as cabinet and the legislature) to more informal, **networked arrangements** in which public and private sectors as well as civil society can participate.[3] It implies a form of political steering that does not necessarily depend on regulation or other interventions by the nation-state; instead, it can involve the use of "soft" mechanisms such as fostering mutual understanding and learning, creating new norms and expectations for policy performance, and exerting peer pressure to achieve these norms.[4]

What might explain the shift from "government" to "governance"? Certainly, one key factor is the recognition that, if we are to solve the increasingly complex public policy problems we now face (e.g., climate change), we need to involve all actors that are able to contribute to the problem-solving exercise, such that more extensive and varied resources can be brought to bear.[5] This is complicated enough in North America, given the reality that all three countries have federal systems that divide environmental policy-making and implementation across levels of government. Yet, as Anne-Marie Slaughter observes, it is also the case that many problems—environmental degradation among them—pay no attention to jurisdictional boundaries.[6] It is just a short step from there to envisioning governance sites that are primarily transboundary, involving actors from different governments and from outside these governments. None of this is to say that governments matter less; in the North American context (as elsewhere), governments continue to dominate and officials, often at a particular level, take the lead in defining and implementing policy activities in transboundary governance sites.[7] Given this reality, North American influences can be understood here as being generated in a context that includes governance sites at three levels—bilateral, subnational, and trilateral—corresponding to where policy jurisdiction originates.[8]

One way of thinking about how North American transboundary governance works is to use the language of **push-pull factors**. This terminology has been employed in a variety of policy contexts: to understand why people emigrate (i.e., "push" factors, such as a lack of economic opportunity, drive migrants out of their countries of origin, while "pull" factors, such as high standards of living, influence where they end up);[9] to explain the drivers of industry innovation (i.e., a technology "push" implies that a new invention is pushed forward to market from research discoveries, while a market need "pulls" innovation out of targeted research);[10] and to understand the impact of policies and legislation on the behaviour of private actors (i.e., "push" factors such as energy conservation practices in the building industry encourage "greener" designs while government regulations "pull" them up to higher standards of efficiency).[11] We might think of the "pull" motivation as a stronger force (an external goal pulls actors towards it), while the "push" motivation puts in place a set of self-incentives (the actors themselves push towards a goal).

In thinking about how this might apply to transboundary governance, we can observe instances where transboundary activities serve to "push" actors towards certain policy choices and behaviours by fostering dialogue on new approaches, creating consensus on how to move forward and exhorting actors to meet the new goals. Transboundary governance architecture that includes more binding mechanisms, like treaties or formal agreements, exerts a stronger "pull," committing actors (likely governments) to specified actions and regular reporting. Admittedly, this portrait highlights the potential positive impact of transboundary deliberations, which is inherent in studies of "push-pull" factors, but also reflects how they have played out in the North American context.

The Shifting North American Transboundary Dynamic

The above discussion highlights how transboundary institutions and processes might exert influence on environmental policy-making in Canada; they provide arenas through which jurisdictions in North America can "push" us to adopt policy goals or instruments, or put in place binding instruments that "pull" us in specific directions. Over the past decades, environmental policy activity has occurred at all three governance levels—bilateral, subnational/cross-border regional, and trilateral. One might delineate three phases of interaction, in which the intensity of activity across scales, the locus of leadership, and the types of mechanisms in use (collegial "pushing" vs formal mandates that "pull") have shifted.

Phase One: Building the Bilateral Environmental Architecture

In the 1980s and into the early 1990s, Canada–US federal interactions dominated and this period saw the Canadian government push its neighbour on many issues, including air quality and climate change. Those studying the Canada–US environmental relationship in these earlier decades emphasized the key roles of bilateralism and diplomacy in creating the infrastructure for the environmental relationship. As Maxwell Cohen noted in 1983: "Canada and the United States occupy and inevitably have to jointly manage a vast continental region. . . some five thousand miles of boundary [that] are the major fact of sovereign life for both countries."[12] This "major fact" underlay what Cohen saw as the burgeoning scope of interactions between federal actors in the two countries across the length of the border, and across the full range of issues. In the early 1990s, Don Munton and Geoffrey Castle focused on the structures of "the emerging bilateral regime," which posed complications for the "legal sovereignty and substantial political autonomy" of the two countries,[13] yet resulted in the development of relatively complex Great Lakes pollution and acid rain regimes.

This emerging bilateral regime rested on both formal agreements and institutions and a broadening range of inter-agency ties. The International Joint Commission (IJC), established under the 1909 Boundary Waters Treaty, has been perhaps the most prominent bilateral institution operating in Canada–US environmental relations.[14] Engagement under the treaty and through the IJC resulted in the Great Lakes Water Quality Agreement (signed in 1972, updated in 1978, 1987 and 2012), a binational accord that highlighted areas within the

Great Lakes experiencing severe environmental degradation and provided a framework for addressing these. On the west coast, the Pacific Salmon Commission was established under the Pacific Salmon Treaty in 1985 to set and implement long-term goals for the joint management of the salmon fishery. The treaty established a framework to prevent overfishing and to allocate the resource between various interests in the two countries. When this framework broke down in the 1990s, the treaty was renegotiated and the Commission now plays a more active role in resource conservation. In addition, when the highly politicized conflict between the two countries over acid rain in the 1980s came to a conclusion with the 1991 passage of the Canada–United States Air Quality Agreement, this led to the creation of another bilateral institution, the Canada–US Air Quality Committee. Effective co-operation and diplomacy by the Air Quality Committee (and its subcommittees) resulted in binational "annexes" to reduce the flow of acid rain precursors and ground-level ozone.[15]

These binational institutions have had a fair degree of success in "pulling" the two countries in directions mandated by formal agreements, though this success has been more marked with regard to narrowly defined environmental disputes or issues. The IJC, for example, has often been an effective mechanism for mediating disputes regarding the management and use of shared water resources. The Pacific Salmon Commission finds itself treading carefully among various and conflicting proprietary interests in a resource that is allocated according to nationality. Efforts to protect chinook stocks, which involve the "sale" of fishing rights between the two countries, is a case in point.[16] For its part, the Canada–US Air Quality Committee has had some high-profile successes, but precisely because it has restricted its engagement to reducing specific pollutants, one at a time, and in such a way that actions taken remain firmly within the restricted mandates of domestic agencies.[17]

Bilateralism during this first phase was certainly not without its bumps. Some of these relate to the **politics of sovereignty**; the Canadian and American national governments, as well as domestic agencies in the two countries, have been reluctant to cede any policy territory to international organizations and processes. For example, while many stakeholders had hoped that the IJC would be a forceful advocate for transboundary environmental quality, the two national governments have stymied attempts—whether originating inside or outside the Commission—to assign to the IJC a more independent role in studying and adjudicating border issues. Munton, for example, has observed that, "by the very nature of its unique and rather anomalous position vis-à -vis the governments, the IJC remains a vulnerable institution with limited capabilities and authority . . . less than an equal match for the sovereign will of the two governments which created it."[18] Other bumps relate to the politics of personality, e.g., Jean Chrétien and Bill Clinton looked at the world through similar ideological and policy lenses, but Chrétien and George W. Bush did not. While it is conventionally understood that, through the ups and downs of personality politics, a significant part of the Canada–US relationship unfolds quietly behind the scenes through myriad interactions among departmental officials established in response to existing mandates,[19] there can be no doubt that the personalities at the political apex have an impact on the nature and scope of shared activities.[20]

And, certainly, the scope of these shared activities increased in 1993, with the signing of the North American Agreement on Environmental Cooperation (NAAEC) and the creation of its institutional offshoot, the Commission for Environmental Cooperation (CEC). The NAAEC and CEC "promised to transform a hitherto almost exclusively bilateral relationship into a new trilateral community, by making many issues, processes, and institutions into a new trilateral structure."[21] While its origins were highly political (Clinton pushed the NAAEC and CEC on Canada and Mexico as a counterbalance to NAFTA, after considerable lobbying by US environmental groups), great hopes accompanied these additions to the North American environmental policy architecture.

Yet, the early 1990s appeared to mark the high point of federal environmental engagement by Canada and the US, with commitments made domestically, bilaterally, and at the continental level, after which engagement waned. By the mid-1990s, the bilateral "building" phase had come to an end, as environmental institutions and initiatives along the border were impacted by the changing policy and financial priorities of national governments. Environmental agencies, which provide much of the support for bilateral programming, did not fare well. In Canada, deficit reduction through "program review" exercises became the primary concern and Environment Canada lost almost one-third of its budget and one-quarter of its staff. In the US, the Republican-dominated Congress blocked Clinton's environmental initiatives with its deregulatory Contract with America. After the election of George W. Bush in 2000, the political agenda became even more explicitly anti-environmental, this time directed from the White House. US EPA programs also underwent cuts beginning in 2002–3 as a result of the Bush administration's attempts to address a sizable budget deficit. In both countries, cuts encouraged a retreat to the fulfillment of core regulatory responsibilities, and funding for transboundary projects became less imperative. Moreover, with the increased focus on domestic and border security post-9/11, the two countries (but especially the US) shifted their focus to security and federal monies were diverted to associated programs and technology.

Phase Two: The Emergence of Subnational and Cross-Border Regional Environmental Governance

By the later 1990s, it appeared that the environmental policy torch had been passed down to subnational governments, often working within cross-border regional co-operative institutions initiated and fostered in most instances by activist American states. This second period also featured an increase in trilateral initiatives, a "settling in" whereby the Commission for Environmental Cooperation and other trilateral organizations found their modest place in the continental order. These organizations provided a framework for dialogue among environmental policy-makers and non-government organizations in the three countries, broadened their perspectives to take continental pollutant pathways into account, and encouraged the three countries to set and pursue joint goals in particular areas.

A sizable literature, based on considerable case study work over the 2000s, indicated that subnational governments, particularly US states and to some extent Canadian provinces, often acting through cross-border co-operative mechanisms, had become the primary locus of environmental policy initiative and innovation to address transboundary problems.[22] Earlier empirical work by VanNijnatten provided evidence that distinct **environmental cross-border regions**, possessing observable boundaries and capable of autonomous action, were developing on the Canada–US border.[23] The concept of "cross-border region" (CBR) was approached through multiple lenses: a focus on how major ecological regions provided impetus for joint action; results from an elite survey targeting government, private sector, academic, and civil society representatives who work in a cross-border capacity;[24] and efforts to trace the formal imprint of cross-border environmental governance.[25] Three environmental cross-border regions were identified: the Pacific Northwest (encompassing British Columbia, Alberta, Washington, Idaho, Oregon, and Montana); the Great Lakes–Heartland (including Ontario, Minnesota, Michigan, New York, Illinois, Indiana, Ohio, Wisconsin, and Pennsylvania); and New England (including Quebec and the four Maritime provinces as well as Vermont, Maine, New Hampshire, Massachusetts, Rhode Island, and Connecticut). These three core clusters, it was argued, could radiate influence outward to draw in other states and provinces in the sub-regions or on the periphery for particular purposes.

In the early years of the new century, the three environmental CBRs showed considerable evidence of autonomous action. Climate change was the foremost example. While national governments did little on the climate file, either domestically or bilaterally, subnational governments, often working within cross-border regions, undertook a variety of initiatives, including a number of continental "firsts": a 2001 Climate Change Action Plan by the Conference of New England Governors–Eastern Canadian Premiers (NEG/ECP), which included greenhouse gas reduction targets as well as sector-specific initiatives to achieve these reductions; inventory and modelling work to support the launching of cap-and-trade programs (the Regional Greenhouse Gas Initiative, RGGI, in the US Northeast; the Western Climate Initiative, WCI, in the US/Canadian West; and the Midwest Greenhouse Gas Regional Initiative, MGGRA); and carbon taxes in Quebec and British Columbia. In addition, states and provinces undertook far-reaching and broad-based initiatives with respect to watershed management, via a new Great Lakes Charter.

An important aspect of the shift from bilateral to cross-border regional environmental governance was the accompanying shift in the locus of leadership. Under the previous bilateral regime the Canadian government was often the initiator of co-operation (propelled by its "environmental dependence" on the US), but at the subnational level it was American states that were "pushing" for more ambitious transborder environmental action. From air quality and climate change, to non-point-source water pollution and toxics reduction, many states committed to ambitious policy goals and experimented with new policy instruments to achieve these goals. The reasons for this activism were complex; states, particularly those in the Northeast and along the west coast, were driven forward by a peculiar mix of electoral politics, interest group pressures, legacies associated with earlier legislative commitments and (ironically) federal support for capacity-building in the 1990s, as well as supportive state professional associations such as the Environmental Council of the States (ECOS). Some American states were reacting to the gearing down of the federal environmental regulatory machine in the US under the Bush administration and chose to move ahead on their own.

This innovation was in some cases transferred northward; states, rather than Canadian provinces, were the driving force behind some of the most ambitious cross-border regional initiatives. For example, the Western Climate Initiative emerged out of the energies of certain west coast US states; only when the Initiative was up and running did British Columbia and then other Canadian provinces become interested. RGGI was driven by northeastern states; while waiting for Canadian provinces to join in, they created a regional electricity emissions reduction program. The original impetus for the Great Lakes Charter was concern on the US side that there would be major demands on the water resources of the Great Lakes Basin in the future.[26] Such dynamics created "peer pressure" on provinces, which were meeting regularly with their state colleagues in cross-border forums, to follow their lead.

Also during this second phase, some noteworthy initiatives at the trilateral level served as a supportive backdrop for subnational and federal activities. By the end of the 1990s, it was argued that the NAAEC had "brought trilateralism in an intense and permanent way to North America and to Canada–US environmental governance."[27] Into the 2000s, the CEC—with its mandate "to promote trinational cooperation for sustainable development, conservation, and environmental protection" through the provision of "tangible services, in the form of activities and outputs"[28]—was promoting technical training; developing methodologies, tools, and databases to support policy formulation; and funding community-based projects in the three countries. More controversially, the CEC, through its citizen submission process and its powers to undertake research on specific environmental policy problems provided for under the NAAEC, made initial forays into an "environmental watchdog" role.

These activities were not particularly popular with the three national governments. Attempts by the CEC Secretariat to be ambitious in its undertakings or, some would argue, even to fulfill the basic requirements of its mandate were met with resistance—not unlike national governments' treatment of the IJC. Indeed, the autonomy of the Secretariat was constrained at numerous points over this period by the involvement of national executives in the Secretariat's program operations and attempts to restrict the scope of the citizen submission process.[29] The CEC also struggled to operate within the meagre budget provided by the three national governments—$3 million US from each government. Given that the budget had not changed since 1994, its real value declined every year.[30]

Despite these difficulties, however, the CEC was able to carve out a modest place for itself in the continental environmental policy architecture. It has been argued that the institution's most notable accomplishment "may be the creation of a trilateral North American community joining the governments and the public,"[31] and certainly the CEC has been able to increase the number and range of contacts among government officials at different levels and their various stakeholder groups. As early as 1997, Kirton noted that, "although the [CEC's] autonomous political impact is limited by its lack of formal policy advisory responsibilities, it has nevertheless exerted influence through the scientific credibility it has commanded and the broader support base and **epistemic community** it is fostering through the many expert groups, study teams, and consultations it has created."[32]

In its own quiet way, the CEC was able to push action forward in several areas, including toxic release reporting (now done according to a comparable methodology in all three countries), the establishment of North American Regional Action Plans (NARAPs) for reducing persistent and toxic chemicals such as PCBs, dioxins and furans, and mercury, and targeted projects for biodiversity protection. All of these initiatives served to broaden the perspective of governments and foster dialogue on shared environmental objectives, while providing some (albeit minimal) support for implementation—especially for those jurisdictions willing to engage in environmental policy innovation.

Phase Three: The Waning of Transboundary Effort

In this most recent phase, transboundary activity has declined at all levels, as federal and subnational governments turn inward, responding both to domestic political polarization and to a difficult fiscal context. Moving into the mid-2010s, one might observe that, across the continental environmental policy landscape, "the voices" remain disaggregated but are fading to background noise, more easily ignored in the din of daily policy-making.

At the federal level, the turn inward has been pronounced. The 2009 collapse of the American effort to put in place comprehensive national climate legislation, in the face of lasting fallout from the 2008 recession, was disappointing for many who had hoped for a more activist, comprehensive, and uniform policy. However, it did not signal an end to the US federal role in climate change. Instead, President Obama indicated that he would move ahead with a regulatory approach to reducing GHG emissions. A December 2009 ruling by the US Environmental Protection Agency (EPA) that GHGs endanger human health provided Obama with the means to regulate emission sources under the existing 1990 Clean Air Act, even without new legislative action by Congress.[33] The agency thus proceeded to regulate mobile and stationary sources, and in April of 2010 new fuel economy standards as well as the first-ever tailpipe GHG standards were introduced for cars and light trucks, with a further tightening of standards mandated for the 2017–20 period.[34] The regulatory effort continued to move forward in 2012–13, as the EPA began creating a GHG permitting program, requiring the use of **best available control technology** (BACT) for large industrial emission sources.[35] Then, in June 2014, the EPA proposed state-specific targets for lowering carbon pollution from power plants by 2030, but indicated it would allow states to use their own mix of instruments to achieve these goals.[36] This strategy holds considerable promise for reducing GHGs by maximizing energy efficiency but it is a purely "made-in-the-USA" policy solution.

The Canadian federal government also announced that it would develop a new regulatory program to reduce GHG emissions on a sector-by-sector basis.[37] Initial signs were promising; just days after the American announcement on vehicle standards, the Canadian government indicated that it would follow suit with fuel economy and GHG tailpipe standards, announcing equivalent regulations under the Canadian Environmental Protection Act 1999 (CEPA).[38] Yet, this appears to have been the high point of government action. Regulations put in place (after long delays) to reduce emissions from Canadian coal plants only apply to plants built after 2015; existing plants built in the last 50 years are grandfathered and will continue to emit GHGs and other pollutants.[39] A comparison of the Canadian and American coal-fired power plant regulations by the International Institute for Sustainable Development indicates that "the U.S. regulations have a much deeper cut in providing real meaningful, substantial reductions in greenhouse gases compared to Canada."[40] Meanwhile, regulations for the oil and gas sector, long promised by the Conservative government, have not materialized. As Prime Minister Harper stated in December 2014 when gas prices seemed to be in freefall: "Under the current circumstances of the oil and gas sector, it would be . . . crazy economic policy to do unilateral penalties on that sector. We are clearly not going to do it."[41]

Differences between Canada and the US in terms of regulatory style are not new, as the US Clean Air Act and the Canadian Environmental Protection Act embody quite different regulatory aims and methods. Neither is the reality of Canadian standards lagging behind those of the US.[42] As well, the strong role of the provinces in setting emission standards (and the delicate position of the federal government in regulating stationary sources) is not replicated in the American context, where states are brought much more firmly under a national legislative framework. What is notable here, though, is the rather obvious desire on the part of the Harper government to choose its own approach to environmental policy, one that is apparently less open to American influences. When introducing the new federal measures limiting emissions from coal-burning power plants in 2010, Canada's Environment Minister, Jim Prentice, noted that, "while our firm intent is to co-ordinate key environmental decisions and actions with the United States, where Canadian circumstances and American circumstances are not the same, we will not hesitate to pursue a policy direction that reflects our differing circumstances."[43]

While the two federal governments are tending their own regulatory gardens, they are also interacting less across borders. Personal antipathy may be a factor here. Bilateral relations, pronounced *Maclean's* magazine in mid-2014, are in a "sorry state," such that "[t]he collapse of the Harper–Obama relationship is so complete that at least one of them will have to go before co-operative leadership at the top returns."[44] A January 2015 *Huffington Post* article derided the Canadian Prime Minister's singular ability to alienate the one person that might have handed him what he most wanted—approval for the Keystone pipeline to carry Canadian tar sands oil to American refineries: "Harper's unbending ambition [to be an energy superpower] set him on a collision course with a president intent to act on climate change. For anyone watching closely, all the signals were there that Obama would turn to the environment as a major pillar of his legacy."[45] The storyline accompanying the apparently "broken" relationship between the Canadian and American leaders makes for interesting reading, winding as it does across alleged attempts by the Harper Conservatives to support Republicans in the 2008 presidential election, to very public swipes by each at the climate policy of the other (Obama in his June 2013 address at Georgetown University; Harper during the visit of the Australian Prime Minister to Canada in 2014), to the ongoing war of words over the proposed Keystone pipeline.

Though one should not overstate the role of personality in cross-border relations, given the complex bilateral infrastructure already in place, as discussed above, it is difficult to overlook the relative absence of interaction. The Canada–US Clean Energy Dialogue, the Canada–US Regulatory Cooperation Council, and negotiations on a new annex to the Canada–US Air Quality Agreement are all initiatives that seem effectively to be stalled.[46] The (admittedly significant) exception here is the successful 2012 revision to the Canada–US Great Lakes Water Quality Agreement; here, though, the "pull" dynamics of existing mandates and reporting requirements have to some extent continued to provide forward impetus.

At the subnational level, where hope for environmental policy leadership so recently resided, it appears that the limits to bottom-up environmental efforts are being discovered. According to Barry Rabe, ambitious climate efforts at the subnational level "were clearly designed to give [states] added influence over the design of such a [national] system and to also position themselves for advantages if any were created," including early emission reduction credits or influence in the operational design of a larger system.[47] A national system (and/or transborder systems) also appeared to offer a more cost-effective way to launch a cap-and-trade program. With the collapse of national climate legislation in the US, however, the incentives underlying state and regional climate programs have changed significantly.

Critical also in terms of gauging policy directions at the subnational level has been the fiscal situation of American states and, Canadian provinces. It is difficult to underestimate the impact of the recession on the states which caused the largest collapse in state revenues on record.[48] The primary focus of state officials, not surprisingly, has been the struggle to fulfill their commitment to entitlement programs (health, education, and social security). The precarious position of California, which is a key driver of environmental policy innovation continentally, has been of particular concern.[49] On the northern side of the border, the largest province, Ontario, has posted record deficits and is seeking broad-scale changes to how the health and educational sectors are funded; its financial commitment to clean energy and climate programming is unclear. Other provinces are also experiencing fiscal difficulties; a range of public sector cuts, tax increases, and other measures are being employed from the west coast to the east.

The budgetary situation across subnational jurisdictions, along with changes in governorships and premierships, has to some extent undercut the kind of climate policy innovation, capacity-building, and cross-border co-operation seen over the 2000s. For example, most states have pulled out of the WCI, leaving California and some Canadian provinces (British Columbia, Ontario, and Quebec)—jurisdictions that have taken no actions to implement its provisions. The RGGI has experienced some troubles, including the defection of several states, but it continues to operate stateside and has reached an agreement on a substantial reduction in its greenhouse gas emissions cap. The MGGRA is long dead.

One might argue that cross-border regional co-operation is inherently unstable, based as it is on "push" rather than "pull" forces. Most cross-border regional programming rests on regional memorandums of understanding (MOUs) by state and provincial authorities; MOUs are non-binding and rely to a considerable extent on the high-level political support of all jurisdictions. Yet this support is difficult to maintain given varying patterns of governing party ideology, shifting political priorities, and leadership transitions. Cross-border regional initiatives also rely on the personal interaction of officials within agencies in participating jurisdictions and their willingness to continue to commit time and resources; both are vulnerable in light of staff changes and tight budgets. Rabe argues that building a sustainable network among states and provinces—one that promotes trust and encourages bonds of reciprocity—is critical to regional co-operative efforts, yet such bonds are difficult to create and maintain.[50]

The bonds of trilateralism are even more tenuous, particularly given the increasing tendency towards "dual bilateralism." The Canadian–Mexican relationship has not exactly flourished in recent years; in a recent statement, Mexico's ambassador to Canada characterized his country's relations with Canada as "stagnant," and indicated that Canada held an anglocentric view of the world in which Mexico does not exist.[51] The US–Mexico relationship remains intense, but has been overshadowed by transitional issues associated with the new administration in Mexico.[52] In the background, the CEC continues to labour on various fronts, including capacity-building, monitoring environmental enforcement, and facilitating continental approaches to common pollution problems. Its activities draw strength from the formal trilateral agreement that lends it legitimacy and purpose. Interestingly, however, the three governments have tasked the CEC with examining its "governance" in order to "enhance accountability; improve transparency of the Secretariat's activities; ensure alignment with the Council priorities; and, set clear performance goals."[53] In conjunction with this, the Council has committed to "making operational changes" over the course of the CEC's 2010–15 Strategic Plan. One might wonder, here, if this is another attempt by the governments to keep a tight rein on the CEC's activities.

North American Transboundary Co-operation: Can Canada Stay Away?

What does this apparent waning of transboundary effort mean for environmental policy-making in Canada? In the last edition of this volume, it was argued that North American forces, particularly co-operation at the subnational level within cross-border regions, had created opportunities in Canada for environmental policy action and leadership—and perhaps even some innovation in terms of policy instrument choice— that might not otherwise exist. In this sense, transboundary co-operation had an agenda- and goal-setting function, whereby Canadian jurisdictions were encouraged to consider more seriously both the adoption of targets and a range of alternative (especially market-based) policy instruments.

Climate change has been a good example of the "push" dynamic. The consideration and implementation of a wide range of "harder" initiatives, including legislated reductions, mandated targets, and technical frameworks for cap-and-trade programming at the state level was beginning to figure into cross-regional initiatives (RGGI, WCI, and MGGRA), and also into discussions in the two countries on the appropriate tools to use with respect to national climate change plans. Congress's consideration of various new elements of climate legislation included discussion of state-level initiatives,[54] and the Harper government announced the day after the 2008 US election (reiterated in the 18 November 2008 Speech from the Throne) that Canada would be interested in joining a North America-wide cap-and-trade system.[55] In this scenario, the American influence has seemed to be a relatively positive one, encouraging more ambitious action and consideration of a wider range of policy tools. Many of the US states bordering Canada have been instrumental in terms of acting as climate policy entrepreneurs, both for their own national government and for neighbouring provinces.

Cross-border regional interaction, undergirded by the trilateral framework, thus presented potential opportunities for environmental policy action. These opportunities are undoubtedly fewer in number and less readily available at the present time. However, cross-border regionalism has created something of a policy legacy in the form of public political commitments, action plans, technical and policy documents, reporting briefs, and programming infrastructure buttressed by (often) years of effort and preciously expended political will. Policy legacies leave an imprint; some can have considerable staying power. In this respect, it is worth noting that the province of Ontario is, at the time of writing, more seriously exploring the prospects of a cap-and-trade system, one that is linked to systems in Quebec and California.

The "pull" effect of bilateral treaties, agreements, and institutions is stronger; while governments can ignore their obligations for a time, they cannot completely avoid them. In those issue areas where the formal architecture is denser, as with water or air quality, governments—no matter what political stripe—are carried forward by mandates, reporting requirements, and the constant flow of information generated by implementation. Although little new has been added to this architecture of late, and political leadership is lacking, it remains in place, exerting its own force. To a lesser extent, this is true of the CEC, which can continue to prod us to adopt a broader political and environmental perspective, based on trilateral commitments made under the NAAEC.

It is hard to avoid concluding that Canada's environmental policy context has become less "transnationalized" over the past five years. At the same time, however, the infrastructure associated with cross-border regional co-operation and the more formal bilateral (and trilateral) environmental architecture together offer a "push-pull" platform for encouraging environmental policy leadership in Canada. Canada might turn its back for a time (and on certain issues), but it will not be able to stay away.

Key Terms

best available control technology

environmental cross-border regions

epistemic community

governance

networked arrangements

politics of sovereignty

push-pull factors

Questions for Review

1. How does the "push-pull" dynamic operate in trans-boundary environmental relations?
2. How effective have the more formal Canada–US bilateral frameworks been, relative to subnational and cross-border environmental co-operation?
3. What has contributed to the recent decline of American states and Canadian provinces as important North American environmental policy actors?
4. What is the current significance for Canadian environmental policy of the North American Agreement on Environmental Cooperation and the North American Commission for Environmental Cooperation?
5. What impact has the austerity context had on trans-boundary environmental co-operation?

Internet Resources

Government of Canada—Canada–US Relations
http://can-am.gc.ca/relations/environment-environnement.aspx?lang5eng

Great Lakes Commission
http://glc.org/about/

International Joint Commission
http://www.ijc.org/en_/

North American Commission for Environmental Cooperation
http://www.cec.org/

Regional Greenhouse Gas Initiative
http://www.rggi.org/

Additional Reading

Bow, Brian, and Greg Anderson. 2015. *Regional Governance in Post-NAFTA North America: Building without Architecture*. New York: Routledge.

Healy, Robert G., Debora L. VanNijnatten, and Marcela López-Vallejo. 2014. *Environmental Policy in North America: Approaches, Capacity, and the Management of Transboundary Issues*. Toronto: University of Toronto Press.

López-Vallejo, Marcela. 2014. *Reconfiguring Global Climate Governance in North America: A Transregional Approach*. The New Regionalism Series. Burlington, Vt: Ashgate.

Petraeus, David H., and Robert B. Zoellick. 2014. *North America: Time for a New Focus*. New York: Council on Foreign Relations Task Force Report.

Vogel, David. 1997. "Trading Up and Governing Across: Transnational Governance and Environmental Protection." *Journal of European Public Policy* 4: 556–71.

Notes

1. Robert G. Healy, Debora L. VanNijnatten, and Marcela López-Vallejo, *Environmental Policy in North America: Approaches, Capacity, and the Management of Transboundary Issues* (Toronto: University of Toronto Press, 2014).
2. Lamont C. Hempel, *Environmental Governance: The Global Challenge* (Washington: Island Press, 1996), 10.
3. Healy, VanNijnatten, and López-Vallejo, *Environmental Policy in North America*, 48.

4. Debora VanNijnatten, Carolyn Johns, Kathryn Friedman, and Gail Krantzberg, "Assessing Adaptive Transboundary Governance Capacity in the Great Lakes Basin: The Role of Institutions and Networks," *International Journal of Water Governance* (forthcoming).

5. R.D. Jessop, "Governance and Metagovernance: On Reflexivity, Requisite Variety, and Requisite Irony," in H. Heinelt, P. Getimis, G. Kafkalas, R. Smith, and E. Swyngedouw, eds, *Participatory Governance in Multi-Level Context: Concepts and Experience* (Opladen, Germany: Leske and Budrich, 2002), 33–58.

6. A.M. Slaughter, *A New World Order* (Princeton, NJ: Princeton University Press, 2004).

7. Debora L. VanNijnatten, "Cross-Border Environmental Governance in North America: Building from the Bottom-Up?" paper prepared for "National Solutions to Trans-border Problems? The Challenges for Building Cross-Border Governance Practices in Post-NAFTA North America conference, First Meeting of Tri-national Academic Group for the Study of Emerging Governance Institutions in North America (TAGGINA), Mar. 2008, Monterrey, Mexico.

8. Healy, VanNijnatten, and López-Vallejo, *Environmental Policy in North America*, 48.

9. Everett S. Lee, "A Theory of Migration," *Demography* 3, 1 (1966): 47–57, JSTOR2060063.

10. Michael J.C. Martin, *Managing Innovation and Entrepreneurship in Technology-based Firms* (New York: Wiley-IEEE, 1994), 44.

11. Kemi Adeyeye, Mohamed Osmani, and Claire Brown, "Energy Conservation and Building Design: The Environmental Legislation Push and Pull Factors," *Structural Survey* 25, 5 (2007): 375–90.

12. Maxwell Cohen, Preface to John E. Carroll, *Environmental Diplomacy: An Examination and a Prospective of Canadian–U.S. Transboundary Environmental Relations* (Ann Arbor: University of Michigan Press, 1983), ix.

13. Don Munton and Geoffrey Castle, "Air, Water and Political Fire: Building a North American Environmental Regime," in A. Claire Cutler and Mark W. Zacher, eds, *Canadian Foreign Policy and International Economic Regimes* (Vancouver: University of British Columbia Press, 1992), 333.

14. The treaty, which dealt primarily with the "levels and flows" of boundary waters, also included a strongly worded prohibition on the pollution of boundary waters: "the waters herein defined as boundary waters and waters flowing across the boundary shall not be polluted on either side to the injury of health or property on the other."

15. Debora L. VanNijnatten, "Analyzing the Canada–United States Environmental Relationship: A Multi-Faceted Approach," *American Review of Canadian Studies* 33, 1 (2003): 93–120.

16. Justine Hunter, "Salmon Deal Sells Out Fishermen, B.C. Trollers Say," *Globe and Mail*, 24 May 2008, accessed 24 May 2008, http://www.theglobeandmail.com/servlet/story/LAC.20080524.BCTREATY24/TPStory/?query=pacific+salmon.

17. Debora L. VanNijnatten, "Negotiating the Canada–U.S. Ozone Annex: A Case Study in Transboundary Environmental Relations," Global Affairs Institute Transboundary Case Program, Maxwell School for Citizenship and Public Affairs, Syracuse University, 2001.

18. Don Munton, "Paradoxes and Prospects," in Robert Spencer, John Kirton, and Kim Richard Nossal, eds, *The International Joint Commission Seventy Years On* (Toronto: University of Toronto, Centre for International Studies, 1981), 81.

19. Greg J. Anderson and Christopher Sands, eds, *Forgotten Partnership Redux: Canada–U.S. Relations Today* (New York: Cambria Press, 2011).

20. Debora L. VanNijnatten, "Environmental Policy in Canada and the United States: Climate Change and Increasing Distinctiveness," in David M. Thomas and David N. Biette, eds, *Canada and the Unites States: Differences That Count*, 4th edn (Toronto: University of Toronto Press, 2014), 342–5.

21. J. Kirton, "The Commission for Environmental Cooperation and Canada–U.S. Environmental Governance," *American Review of Canadian Studies* 27, 3 (1997): 459.

22. See, e.g., Barry G. Rabe, *Statehouse and Greenhouse: The Emerging Politics of American Climate Change Policy* (Washington: Brookings Institution Press, 2004); Debora L. VanNijnatten, "The Constituent Regions of the Canada–United States Environmental Relationship," in George A. MacLean, ed., *Canada and the U.S.: A Relationship at a Crossroads?* (Winnipeg: Centre for Defence and Security Studies, Proceedings of the University of Manitoba Political Science Students Conference, 2006); Debora L. VanNijnatten, "Environmental Constituent Regions and the Canada–U.S. Relationship," paper prepared for Linnea Terrarum: International Borders Conference, Mar. 2006, El Paso, Texas; Debora L. VanNijnatten, "Mercury Reduction in the United States and Canada: Policy Diffusion across Internal and International Borders," paper prepared for the annual meeting of the American Political Science Association, Sept. 2005, Washington, DC.

23. Debora L. VanNijnatten, "Towards Cross-Border Environmental Policy Spaces in North America: Province–State Linkages on the Canada–U.S. Border," *AmeriQuests: The Journal of the Center for the Americas* 3, 1 (2006); Debora L. VanNijnatten, "Environmental Cross-Border Regions and the Canada–U.S. Relationship: Building from the Bottom-Up in the Second Century?" paper prepared for the authors' workshop on *Transboundary Environmental Governance: The Second Century*, Barry Rabe and Stephen Brooks, eds (Washington: Woodrow Wilson Institute, 8–9 May 2008).

24. As part of its "North American Linkages" research project, Policy Research Initiative (Government of Canada)

researchers and three university academics (including this author) constructed a detailed 12-page Elite Survey, the purpose of which was to examine the nature of relationships and interactions at the cross-border level. Respondents were surveyed from the four cross-border regions outlined by the PRI and from a range of organizations—provincial–state governments, cities, nongovernmental organizations, think-tanks, chambers of commerce, regional economic development agency, and associations. A total of 547 people were contacted and received the survey. One hundred individuals completed the survey for a response rate of 19 per cent. Surveys were completed between 20 July and 7 October 2005. This author acted as academic adviser in the formulation and implementation of the survey.

25. As a first step in building the database, existing studies were consulted, such as R.E. Stein and G..Grenville-Wood's *Between Neighbours: How U.S. States and Canadian Provinces Settle their Shared Environmental Problems* (Ottawa and Washington: Environmental Mediation International, 1984) as well as the CEC Transboundary Agreements Database. Research was then conducted to determine whether additional linkages could be discovered. Preliminary lists of linkages—including the name, date of establishment, and membership—were then sent to each state and province for verification. Input from state and provincial officials resulted in deletions from the database, as additional linkages were declared inactive. A few additions also resulted from the verification process. Particular conditions were imposed for the inclusion of state–province linkages in the database. First, there must be some form of documentation on the linkage which provides evidence of its existence and nature, and, second, states and provinces must be the primary agents of the linkage. The database is current to the end of 2005.

26. International Joint Commission, *Protection of the Waters of the Great Lakes: Final Report to the Governments of Canada and the United States*, Feb. 2000.

27. Kirton, "The Commission for Environmental Cooperation," 481.

28. Stephen P. Mumme and Pamela Duncan, "The Commission on Environmental Cooperation and the U.S.–Mexico Border Environment," *Journal of Environment and Development* 5, 2 (1996): 203.

29. Kirton, "The Commission for Environmental Cooperation," 474; Laura Carlsen and Hilda Salazar, "Limits to Cooperation: A Mexican Perspective on the NAFTA's Environmental Side Agreement and Institutions," in C.L. Deere and D.C. Esty, eds, *Greening the Americas: NAFTA's Lessons for Free Trade* (Cambridge, Mass.: MIT Press, 2002), 224.

30. Ten-year Review and Assessment Committee, *Ten Years of North American Environmental Cooperation*, 19.

31. Ibid, 4.

32. Kirton, "The Commission for Environmental Cooperation," 473.

33. US Environmental Protection Agency, "EPA Finds Greenhouse Gases Pose Threat to Public Health, Welfare: Proposed Finding Comes in Response to 2007 Supreme Court Ruling" (2009), http://yosemite.epa.gov/opa/admpress.nsf/0/0ef7df675805295d8525759b00566924.

34. US Environmental Protection Agency and US Department of Transportation, *Light-Duty Vehicle Greenhouse Gas Emission Standards and Corporate Average Fuel Economy: Final Rule*. Federal Register (2010), http://www.gpo.gov/fdsys/pkg/FR-2010-05-07/pdf/2010-8159.pdf.

35. US Environmental Protection Agency, "Clean Air Act Permitting for Greenhouse Gases" (2011), http://www.epa.gov/nsr/ghgpermitting.html.

36. US Environmental Protection Agency, "Clean Power Plants Proposed Rule," http://www2.epa.gov/carbon-pollution-standards/clean-power-plan-proposed-rule.

37. Government of Canada, "Canada's Action on Climate Change," http://www.climatechange.gc.ca/default.asp?lang=En&n=72F16A84-1.

38. Department of the Environment, Canadian Environmental Protection Act, 1999, "Notice of Intent to Develop Regulations Limiting Carbon Dioxide Emission from New Cars and Light-Duty Trucks," *Canada Gazette* 143, 14 (4 Apr. 2009), http://www.gazette.gc.ca/rp-pr/p1/2009/2009-04-04/html/notice-avis-eng.html#d110.

39. *Proposed Regulations: Reduction of Carbon Dioxide Emissions from Coal-Fired Generation of Electricity Regulations, Canada Gazette* 145, 35 (27 Aug. 2011), http://gazette.gc.ca/rp-pr/p1/2011/2011-08-27/pdf/g1-14535.pdf.

40. Margo McDiarmid, "New Coal Plant Regulations Have 'Negligible Effect,' Report Says," CBC News, 19 Sept. 2014, http://www.cbc.ca/news/politics/new-coal-plant-regulations-have-negligible-effect-report-says-1.2770385.

41. Shawn McCarthy, "Harper Calls Climate Regulations on Oil and Gas Sector 'Crazy Economic Policy'," *Globe and Mail*, 9 Dec. 2014, http://www.theglobeandmail.com/news/politics/harper-it-would-be-crazy-to-impose-climate-regulations-on-oil-industry/article22014508/.

42. Debora L. VanNijnatten, "Environmental Policy in Canada and the United States: Climate Change and Continuing Distinctiveness," in David Thomas and Barbara Boyle Torrey, eds, *Canada and the United States: Differences that Count*, 2nd edn (Peterborough, Ont.: Broadview Press, 2007).

43. Speaking points for the Honourable Jim Prentice, Minister of the Environment, to the University of Calgary School of Public Policy and the School of Business, Calgary, Alberta, 1 Feb. 2010.

44. Paul Wells, "Obama, Harper and the End of the Affair," *Maclean's*, 9 June 2014, http://www.macleans.ca/politics/ottawa/obama-harper-and-the-end-of-the-affair/.

45. Sandy Garossino, "Keystone News Unsurprising after Harper Wrecked Canada's Relationship with the U.S.,"

Huffington Post, 7 Jan. 2015, http://www.huffingtonpost.ca/sandy-garossino/keystone-pipeline-harper-obama_b_6427762.html.

46. Embassy of the United States, Ottawa, "U.S.–Canada Cooperation on Environment: Air Quality Issues," accessed 25 May 2008, http://ottawa.usembassy.gov/content/textonly.asp?section=can_usa&subsection1=environment&document=environment_airquality.

47. Barry G. Rabe, "Building on Sub-Federal Climate Strategies: The Challenge of Regionalism," in Neil Craik, Isabel Studer, and Debora VanNijnatten, eds, *North American Climate Change Policy: Designing Integration in a Regional System* (Toronto: University of Toronto Press, 2013), 103–4.

48. Phil Oliff, Chris Mai, and Vincent Palacios, "States Continue to Feel Recession's Impact," Center on Budget Policy and Priorities, updated 27 June 2012, http://www.cbpp.org/cms/?fa=view&id=711.

49. Debora L. VanNijnatten, "Standards Diffusion: The Quieter Side of North American Climate Policy Cooperation?" in Neil Craik, Isabel Studer, and Debora VanNijnatten, eds, *North American Climate Change Policy: Designing Integration in a Regional System* (Toronto: University of Toronto Press, 2013).

50. Rabe, "Building on Sub-Federal Climate Strategies."

51. "Canadian–Mexican Relations: Rivals More Than Friends," *The Economist*, 17 Feb. 2014, http://www.economist.com/blogs/americasview/2014/02/canadian-mexican-relations.

52. Clare Ribando Seelke, "Mexico: Background and U.S. Relations," Congressional Research Service, 16 Dec. 2014, https://fas.org/sgp/crs/row/R42917.pdf.

53. Commission for Environmental Cooperation, "Proposal to Examine the Governance of the CEC and the Implementation of the NAAEC," 24 June 2009, http://www.cec.org/Storage/101/10004_Governance_Proposal_May_2010_final2e.pdf.

54. Jeffrey Simpson, "What America's Clean-Air Booster Means for Canada," *Globe and Mail*, 22 Nov. 2008, http://www.theglobeandmail.com/servlet/story/RTGAM.20081121.wcosimp22/CommentStory/special-Comment/.

55. Jonathan Fowlie, "Three Premiers Say They'll Bypass Harper, Go with B.C. on Climate Change," *Vancouver Sun*, 30 Jan. 2008, accessed 23 May 2008, http://www.canada.com/vancouversun/news/story.html?k=22306&id=382d49c8-04a1-4775-b652-dfc02aaddc67.

12 Retreat from Principle: Canada and the System of International Environmental Law

Neil Craik and Tahnee Prior

Chapter Summary

In this chapter, we examine Canada's participation in the institutions of international environmental law (IEL), with a view to assessing the extent to which Canada has supported or detracted from the system of international environmental law that emerged after the Rio Declaration in 1992. In addition to looking at the overall pattern of engagement by Canada in multilateral environmental agreements, we look at the extent to which Canada has supported four foundational principles arising out of Rio: the harm prevention principle (Principle 2), the principle of common but differentiated responsibilities (Principle 7), the public participation principle (Principle 10), and the precautionary principle (Principle 15). We argue that, contrary to the commonly held view that Canada has gone from leader to laggard, this is not a simple story of disengagement or one of complete repudiation of the normative consensus that came out of Rio. Instead, Canada has taken a more nuanced approach in seeking to shift the basis of global environmental co-operation towards a more narrow footing that favours a less interventionist approach to IEL. This shift is crucial for understanding Canada's present and future role in the formation and maintenance of the system of IEL.

Chapter Outline

- Understanding the system of international environmental law (IEL)
  - The Rio principles
- Canada's participation in IEL
  - A nuanced assessment: the role of individual Canadians, multilateral engagement, funding commitments, compliance, and conforming to norms

- Canada's support for Rio Principles—from adherence to the normative framework to economic interests
  - No harm/common concern
  - Common but differentiated responsibilities
  - Precautionary principle
  - Participation principle

Introduction

A dominant narrative in both popular and academic writing respecting Canada's contribution to the development of international environmental law (IEL) is Canada's transition from global "leader" on environmental issues to "laggard."[1] According to this account, Canada has evolved from a country that was once regarded as a strong voice in developing new international rules to protect the environment to one that actively obstructs international progress on environmental issues. These criticisms stand in apparent contrast to Canada's prior support for the institutions of IEL. Canada played a catalytic role in the formation of the climate change regime, organizing and hosting a global conference on CO_2 emissions in Toronto in 1988 that called for sharp reductions in emissions and set the stage for the United Nations Framework Convention on Climate Change (UNFCCC) process that was to follow.[2] Alongside the United States, Canada pushed the international community towards the acceptance of a phase-out of chlorofluorocarbons (CFCs) under the Montreal Protocol. It was the first developed country to ratify the United Nations Convention on Biological Diversity (UNCBD), shortly after it was opened for signature in 1992.[3] Canada also pushed for the successful conclusion in 1991 of the treaty with the US on acid rain and was instrumental in the formation of the United Nations Straddling Fish Stocks Agreement in 1995.

Canada's leadership position on IEL was strongly associated with the emerging global consensus surrounding the 1992 United Nations Conference on Environment and Development (the "Rio Conference"). Emboldened by the success of the United Nations Convention on the Law of Sea (1982) and then the Vienna Convention for the Protection of the Ozone Layer (1985), international opinion coalesced around the concept of sustainable development, in particular, around the statement of principles, known as the Rio Declaration, that arose out of the United Nations Conference on Environment and Development (UNCED).[4] This emerging global consensus was intended to provide the basis of "a new and equitable global partnership."[5] The Rio Conference was a watershed moment because it appeared to successfully bridge the divide between the twin imperatives of continued economic development and environmental preservation.[6] For IEL, the Rio consensus signalled the emergence of a set of principles, captured by the Rio Declaration, that provided structure and coherence to the development and implementation of a *system* of IEL. This point was echoed by David Freestone, who concluded:

> [T]he Rio Process . . . has accelerated the emergence of a discrete discipline of international environmental law with its own distinctive principles, its own mechanisms and instruments designed to address issues which are different in kind from other issues of international law. In other words, a system of international environmental law has emerged, rather than simply more international law rules about the environment.[7]

Understood in this light, Canada's failure to support a number of key international environmental initiatives that succeeded the Rio Declaration can be potentially understood as not merely a rejection of the individual initiatives themselves, but also as detracting from the consensus underpinning the emerging system of IEL. Indeed, Canada's engagement in IEL institutions is often characterized as a broader retreat from **global environmental multilateralism**. In relation to Canada's withdrawal from the UN Convention to Combat Desertification (UNCCD), Robert Fowler, a former Canadian ambassador to the UN, stated that this amounted to a "departure from global citizenship."[8] An op-ed piece in the journal *Biodiversity*, also reacting to the same withdrawal, expressed a similar sentiment:

> Withdrawal from the UNCCD—together with the unprecedented decision to remove Canada's support for the Kyoto Protocol and Canada's checkered domestic environmental record—raises fundamental questions about Canadian commitment to the community of nations, respect for multilateral institutions, and dedication to achieving the global outcomes agreed at the 1992 Rio Earth Summit.[9]

David Boyd notes Canada's "dramatic shift" from the Rio period, citing the country's diplomatic position in climate negotiations. In relation to negotiations on the trade of genetically modified organisms (GMOs), Boyd maintains that "Canada, along with the United States and Australia, has become one of the leading opponents of meaningful international agreements to address environmental issues."[10]

The intent of this chapter is to examine Canada's participation in the institutions of international law with a view to assessing whether Canada's engagement can indeed be characterized as a "dramatic shift" away from the Rio consensus. We are also interested in the extent to which, and in what ways, Canada has moved away from the normative foundations of IEL. Animating this analysis is the assumption that if multilateral environmental treaties, along with the system of general principles and customary norms, are understood as being interdependent and underlain by a common normative framework, then Canada's actions in relation to a particular issue area can be understood as impacting the system as a whole. This, we argue, is important because the strength of the system of IEL influences the ability of states to co-operate with one another. Dan Bodansky frames the role of a **shared normative framework** as playing "a significant role by setting the terms of the debate, providing evaluative standards, serving as a basis to criticize other states' actions, and establishing a framework of principles within which negotiations may take place to develop more specific norms."[11] Where states view the actions of other states as being shaped by adherence to shared principles and common goals, the possibility for co-operation is deepened. On the other hand, actions defined by self-interest may erode those same possibilities.[12]

Our approach is twofold. First, we look at the pattern of Canadian participation in international environmental legal institutions, focusing on Canada's acceptance of international obligations as well as its ongoing support of, and participation in, treaty structures. However, while looking at Canadian participation in IEL institutions may give us some broad sense of the degree of engagement, it tells us less about those aspects of the system of IEL that Canada supports and those where Canada has moved away from the Rio consensus. With this in mind, we also look more closely at Canada's position with respect to the set of principles that are foundational to the system of international environmental co-operation arising out of Rio, namely, the no-harm principle, the principle of common but differentiated responsibility, the precautionary principle, and the participation principle. In relation to the leader-to-laggard thesis, the argument we present is that the story is not simply one of disengagement or of complete repudiation of the normative consensus that came out of Rio. Instead, we argue that Canada's approach has sought to shift the basis of global environmental co-operation towards a more narrow footing that favours a less interventionist approach to IEL. While we present this shift as being more nuanced than a simple turn away from global environmental co-operation, we maintain the shift has importance for understanding Canada's present and future role in the formation and maintenance of the system of IEL.

The subject of this chapter is Canada's broader contribution to IEL, not its domestic environmental performance or reputation relative to other states.[13] Support or lack of support for international law is only indirectly tied to domestic environmental performance. In some cases, international law only provides minimum standards, and adherence to those standards may not be sufficient. In many cases, international law simply does not address matters of an entirely domestic nature that will impact domestic environmental performance. That said, there is a growing recognition that many of the most pressing environmental problems, such as climate change, biodiversity, and marine pollution, transcend national boundaries and require international co-operation.

Principles and the System of IEL

The premise from which this paper proceeds is that there does exist a *system* of IEL. Understanding IEL as a system stands in contrast to the dominant institutionalist approach in international relations theory that focuses on individual **regimes**, which can be understood as comprising an interconnected set of principles, norms, rules, and decision-making procedures associated with a particular issue area, such as biological diversity, climate change, ozone depletion, or the marine environment.[14] As a consequence, there is a tendency to view IEL merely as a collection of multilateral environmental agreements, each of which addresses a discrete issue and operates independently from the others.

What regime theory downplays, however, is that individual regimes are themselves nested in a set of common rules and shared understandings regarding how we should be addressing a given problem. At the systems level, environmental treaties are formed, interpreted, and implemented in accordance with the rules of public international law,[15] but they are also subject to principles surrounding the basis of agreement that are unique to environmental issues. Principles play a critical role because they express common purposes and justifications of those outcomes that structure the system. For example, the Rio principle of "common but differentiated responsibilities" alters the basic formula of **reciprocity** in international environmental agreement-making, by acknowledging that developed countries owe a historic responsibility for global environmental harm and have acquired greater capacity through their development activities. This, in turn, places a greater onus on developed states to address global environmental harms, resulting in differentiated legal responsibilities. The precautionary principle, as a second example, alters the burden of evidence justifying international action on an environmental threat.

Unlike legal rules, which operate directly on legal subjects and dictate a fixed outcome, principles tend to operate at a higher level and provide more flexibility for those doing the negotiating. In international law, principles also guide future law-making processes.

This function is particularly evident in the framework treaty/protocol structure of many international treaty structures, whereby states negotiate a framework treaty, such as the UNFCCC, which sets the normative parameters that guide the future negotiation of more precise agreements, such as the Kyoto Protocol. The underlying logic of this staged negotiation structure is that precise legal commitments are more likely to arise under conditions where parties first agree to the overarching goals of co-operation in a particular issue area. Again, by way of example, the inclusion of the principles of common but differentiated responsibilities and precaution in the UNFCCC provided the starting point for negotiations under the Kyoto Protocol—namely, that developed states should take the lead, and that scientific certainty was not a prerequisite for action.

The 1992 Rio Declaration, we argue, captures important aspects of these systemic elements. The argument is not that the Rio Declaration is itself an authoritative source of international law. It is not a formally binding document, but rather a political declaration. That said, the Rio Declaration was framed in overtly normative language—it is a set of principles intended to guide state behaviour, not merely a set of aspirational policy goals. The Rio Declaration and the surrounding processes of IEL-making, in particular the parallel negotiation of the UNCBD and the UNFCCC, best represent the global consensus on the normative foundations of the system of IEL that existed in 1992. At the heart of this consensus is the fundamental compromise made between developed states and developing states, which sought to reconcile development aspirations with the need to protect the global environment from continuing degradation.[16] It was, in the words of Boyle and Freestone, a "package deal."[17] Rio signalled a shared commitment to multilateral environmental co-operation and sought to identify the basis upon which those multilateral efforts would proceed.

Canada's Participation in IEL

Consistent with the leader-to-laggard thesis, Canada was very active in its participation in IEL instruments through the 1980s and 1990s, as discussed in the introduction to this chapter. Part of Canada's leadership reputation was generated by individual Canadians who played an instrumental role in the development of the key ideas informing the Rio process. Notable personalities were Jim McNeill and Maurice Strong, who acted as the Secretary General of the World Commission on Environment and Development (the Brundtland Commission) and the Secretary General of the Rio Conference, respectively. As Steven Bernstein argues, the foundational ideas respecting the mutually supportive interaction between economic growth and environmental protection outlined in the 1987 Brundtland Report were taken up within the UN system and the OECD, as a basis for future international environmental governance approaches.[18] As part of the Brundtland Report process, a group of legal experts, also chaired by a Canadian, developed a Summary of Proposed Legal Principles for Environmental Protection and Sustainable Development.[19] This document informed the approach taken in the lead-up to the Rio Conference, which saw the promotion of an "Earth Charter," a rights-based approach to identifying global principles for integrating environmental and development goals. While this approach was rejected in the preparatory meetings, Canada unsuccessfully sought support for a further statement of legal rights and obligations as a part of the Rio process.[20] Prime Minister Brian Mulroney, in his official statement at the Rio Conference, again promoted the idea of a revived Earth Charter to be adopted by 1995.[21] Canada's leadership legacy continued into 1993 when Elizabeth Dowdeswell became the first female executive director of the United Nations Environment Programme (UNEP), where she led the agency's implementation of sustainable development throughout the UN system.[22]

During this time, Canada also played an important role in the development of the UNCBD and UNFCCC, again hosting key meetings, providing leadership through the early adoption of domestic legislation, and supporting the underlying scientific processes that justified international intervention. The international community recognized this role when it chose to locate the UNCBD secretariat in Montreal. In the aftermath of Rio, Canada continued its position of leadership in the Straddling Fish Stocks Agreement negotiations, becoming party to a number of other important international agreements, such as the Antarctic Environmental Protection Agreement and the Espoo Convention on Transboundary Environmental Impact Assessment (EIA).

Following this intensive period of multilateral instrument creation around the Rio process, Canada became more selective about the treaties in which it chose to engage. In particular, Canada has opted not to engage in treaty-making in four particular areas. Despite being actively engaged in the IEL processes initiated under the auspices of the United Nations Economic Commission for Europe (a regional body consisting of European states, the US, and Canada) through the Long-range Transboundary Air Pollution (LRTAP) Convention and the Espoo Convention on Transboundary EIA, Canada has not become a party to more recent initiatives on procedural obligations, including the Aarhus Convention on Access to Information, Public Participation in Decision-making and Access to Justice in Environmental Matters, and the Kiev Protocol on Strategic Environmental Assessment. Canada has also declined to participate in treaties respecting freshwater resources, preferring instead to rely on long-standing bilateral agreements with the US, the only state with which Canada shares freshwater resources.[23] Nor has Canada chosen to join the Cartagena Protocol on Biosafety or the Nagoya Protocol on Access and Benefit-sharing, both of which fall under the Convention on Biological Diversity. Perhaps most notably in terms of its international participation was Canada's decision to withdraw from the Kyoto Protocol and the UNCCD, where its non-participation places Canada as a definite outlier.

It would be mistaken, however, to describe Canada's participation in environmental multilateralism as one of disengagement. Indeed, on many key environmental issues Canada has continued to remain involved in constructive, even leadership, roles, as was the case in Canada's guidance in the development of the Stockholm Convention on Persistent Organic Pollutants. It signed the Minamata Convention on mercury pollution in 2013, and is a party to two other multilateral treaties on hazardous substances—the Basel Convention and the Rotterdam Convention—as well as being party to six of the eight protocols under the LRTAP Convention. In fact, Canada's record of signing and ratifying multilateral environmental agreements (MEAs) is considerably stronger than that of the United States, which has yet to become a party to the UNCBD, the London Protocol, the Basel Convention, the Rotterdam Convention, and the Stockholm Convention.[24]

Looking beyond signing international agreements, it is also useful to consider Canada's activities under the agreements to which it has become a party. Here Canada's record is mixed, with some actions appearing quite supportive of these institutions, while other actions appear calculated to undermine the development of a system of IEL. For example, Canada's record on financing activities under various multilateral environmental agreements is strong. Canada has provided approximately $110 million in financing to the Multilateral Fund under the Ozone Convention, approximately $785 million to the Global Environment

Facility, a multilateral fund that supports activities under a variety of IEL treaties, as well as $1.2 billion in climate finance funding under the UNFCCC.[25] Many of the financing commitments, including those agreed to under the climate change regime, have been made within the last 10 years, showing willingness on Canada's part to continue supporting multilateral environmental institutions well beyond the Rio era. This support stands in contrast to Canada's withdrawal from the UNCCD, which was based on concerns over the Convention's spending—the ratio of funds spent on programming versus bureaucratic measures.

The use of Conferences of the Parties (COPs) as decision-making bodies is an innovation that has become pervasive in IEL. COPs are regular meetings of the parties, but as an institutional feature of a treaty they are endowed with certain decision-making powers to manage the treaty commitments. This process of expected, continual interaction within the treaty framework can serve to maintain and strengthen the legal character of the system by creating an expectation that states frame their positions in relation to the accepted rules and principles of the treaty.[26] The ongoing interactive structure stands in contrast to traditional forms of international law-making, characterized by a treaty standing as a static agreement in time. In many cases, COPs provide for a simplified form of international rule-making that avoids states making recourse to the more cumbersome processes of treaty amendment and ratification.[27] Often these mechanisms provide for a measure of individual state control, by either requiring consensus, or in the case of majoritarian voting, allowing for states in disagreement to opt out, although both the Montreal Protocol and the Cartagena Protocol allow for binding majoritarian voting in limited circumstances. Canada has accepted, and continues to participate in, a large number of treaty structures that provide for this form of delegated decision-making.

Participation in international legal institutions provides only a partial understanding of Canada's contribution to the system of IEL. A central contributor to Canada's reputation in relation to IEL is compliance with agreed-upon rules, as well as assessments of Canada's willingness to adhere to the underlying goals and principles of the agreements. It is beyond the scope of this chapter to explore Canada's record of compliance with IEL, but there are few formal instances of states claiming that Canada has not met its international obligations. The glaring exception is Canada's actions under the climate regime.

In 2002, Canada ratified the Kyoto Protocol, and in doing so accepted legally binding greenhouse gas emission (GHG) limits for the 2008–12 compliance period. It subsequently became clear that Canada was not only going to fail to reach its commitments, it was not even going to try, a position that Canada justified on economic and competitive grounds. To defend this position, Canada offered a tortuous interpretation of the Kyoto Protocol that effectively denied its legal character. In essence, Canada argued that the non-compliance procedure adopted by the parties (by consensus) was non-binding because it was not adopted as an amendment to the Protocol itself. In the absence of a binding non-compliance procedure, the argument continued, Canada's commitments under the Kyoto Protocol were political, not legal.[28] Notwithstanding this argument, Canada withdrew from the Kyoto Protocol one year before the expiry of the commitment period. By disregarding its obligations under the Kyoto Protocol, and then by denying its legal character, the Canadian government can be understood as destabilizing the broader system of IEL, which depends in part on each state's acknowledgement of its intent to have its conduct constrained by these arrangements. Certainly, non-compliance is not the only salient practice that impacts legality, but it remains one important factor.[29]

Even in international agreements without binding rules, treaty structures can impose normative expectations on states to take steps to meet the principles that underlie the regime. Under the UNFCCC processes that sought a new arrangement to replace the Kyoto Protocol, Canada agreed to a set of non-binding emission reduction commitments as part of that negotiation process. However, Canada's latest report to the UNFCCC, which shows its failure to make any substantial progress on emission reductions to which it had agreed, may further erode global trust in multilateral processes.[30]

Canada has faced similar pressures to conform to treaty norms in the context of negotiations under the Rotterdam Convention to list certain substances (e.g., chrysotile asbestos) for control under the treaty and in relation to the regulation of GMOs under the Cartagena Protocol (to the UNCBD). The expectation that Canada ought to agree to certain restrictions arises from the perception of a disjuncture between the treaty objectives and the Canadian position on accepting new rules. For example, under the Rotterdam Convention, which provides for a system of prior informed consent for the importation of hazardous chemicals and pesticides by the importing country, the controlled substances are listed within an annex to the treaty, to which substances can be added by consensus vote of the COP. For a substance to be considered for listing, a scientific risk assessment is carried out by a review committee, which recommends listing in accordance with established criteria.[31] Despite such a finding in relation to chrysotile asbestos, Canada resisted its listing on three separate occasions. On the one hand, Canada was acting within its rights under the treaty when it blocked the listing. However, in the face of a scientific finding of the substance's harmful nature and near unanimous support for its listing, the decision to invoke a veto signalled an intention to regulate the movement of hazardous substances on the basis of economic expediency, and not in accordance with the environmental and human health objectives of the treaty. Nor was the decision consistent with Canada's domestic treatment of chrysotile asbestos.[32] The strong condemnation that Canada received for its decision is interesting in that it indicates that compliance with the formal requirements of a treaty may not overcome the underlying normative expectations of the community. Canada was the subject of similar condemnation from states and non-governmental organizations (NGOs) in relation to its opposition (along with other exporter nations) to trade restriction on GMOs. The impact of these kinds of decisions on the system of IEL, we argue, depends in part on the degree to which these actions are understood as derogating from established principles of IEL.

Canada's Support for the Rio Principles

The Rio Declaration contains 27 principles, including some—such as the duty to conduct EIAs and duties to notify and consult in the face of possible transboundary harm—that operate as primary rules of IEL.[33] Others are much more aspirational in character, expressing desirable goals but providing minimal direction to guide state behaviour. Our interest is in a set of principles that provide direction to states on how they ought to engage one another in the generation and interpretation of IEL, and in this regard these principles have a structural character. The discussion that follows considers four such principles. The harm prevention principle (Principle 2), coupled with the concept of "common concern," defines the scope of international legal jurisdiction over the environment. The principle of common but differentiated responsibilities (Principle 7) identifies the structure of reciprocity between developed and developing states. The public participation principle (Principle 10) expands the range of actors to which international law may address itself, and internationalizes the obligations of states to engage citizens in environmental decision-making. And, finally, the precautionary principle (Principle 15) defines the onus of justification for international and state intervention on environmental issues. The role of these principles is evident in the development of global treaties on ozone depletion, climate change, and biological diversity immediately prior to or in conjunction with the Rio process, and in two treaties, on straddling fish stocks and desertification, that were contemplated during the Rio process. All of these expressly incorporate these principles. The degree to which Canada has embraced or moved away from these four principles provides a measure of those elements of the system of IEL that Canada supports and those from which it has retreated.

No Harm/Common Concern

The **no-harm principle** has a long pedigree in IEL that far precedes the Rio process. As a basic rule of IEL, it affirms the right of states to non-interference in the exploitation of their natural resources within their territory, but requires states to avoid causing significant harm to the environment of other states or to areas beyond national jurisdiction, such as the high seas. The no-harm principle effectively defines the scope of international legal jurisdiction (that is, when the international community may be justified in intervening) as protecting the territory of other states or areas where states have collective interests. The Rio process can be understood as further extending international jurisdiction to issues of common concern, such as ozone depletion, biological diversity, and climate change.

Unlike the global commons, which refers to a physical area such as the high seas, outer space, or the Antarctic that is not part of the territory of any one state, issues of common concern identify a class of issues over which international jurisdiction is asserted on the basis that there is a shared interest in addressing the issue, and that the issue is a collective action problem. For example, the conservation requirements under Articles 8 and 9 of the UNCBD relate to activities whose direct physical impacts are solely within the state; however, the UNCBD acknowledges a collective interest in the conservation of biological resources, regardless of their location. To this end, the Convention speaks to a more expansive understanding of the jurisdictional reach of IEL.[34] The climate change and ozone depletion regimes also rely on the concept of common concern in relation to changes to the atmosphere that occur on a global scale and, therefore, require broad participation. Common concern as a legal concept suggests state responsibility for contribution to a shared environmental problem. The Rio instruments, by embracing the notion of common concern, in Alan Boyle's words "broaden the idea of what is international about the environment."[35] By extending the reach of IEL to include issues of common concern, the Rio outputs can be understood as embracing a de-territorialized version of state interest and state responsibility, which extends those interests to the protection of resources based on their value to humankind as a whole.

Canada has been strongly supportive of a robust application of the no-harm principle based on international control over environmental externalities. This is evident in Canada's support for the protocols under the LRTAP regime, as well as its support for treaties that address toxins, marine pollution, and marine resources. This support is not surprising, as Canada is a net recipient of airborne pollution due to the continental movement of air pollutants and the accumulation of toxins in the Arctic. Canada also has an interest in an expansive marine pollution regime, given its extensive coastline and historic reliance on fisheries. These treaties, however, are very much rooted in the traditional understanding of the no-harm principle. Canada's embrace of the more expansive approach to international jurisdiction over the environment rooted in common concern is more hesitant.

Canada has not backed away from the concept of justifying international regulation over climate or biodiversity based on the notion of common concern. Rather, it has continued to participate in the conventions that are structured as issues of common concern. But Canada has resisted internationally imposed limitations on its GHG emissions, and has not attempted to regulate its own activity on the basis of a generalized obligation to support the provision of global public goods. For example, it has firmly maintained in relation to the oil sands that expansion of those resources is an internal matter and beyond the competence or even legitimate interest of groups outside of Canada.[36]

The UNCCD can also be understood as reflecting a broader approach to the no-harm principle insofar as the Convention imposes obligations on developed states in recognition of the broader interest in protecting biological resources wherever they are located, and also in recognition of the link between climate change and desertification.[37] The Canadian withdrawal signals an unwillingness to accept this more expansive form of international responsibility. As noted above, Canada's position here is inconsistent with its previous acceptance of this approach in the UNCBD and with its ongoing support of international projects in support of the UNCBD through the Global Environment Facility. Canada's stated reason for withdrawal related to its concerns over the effectiveness of the treaty, as opposed to an express disavowal of commitment to this problem. However, the relatively small amounts of funding ($350,000) and the absence of any overt attempts to address its concerns within the treaty structure suggest a lack of international solidarity that belies the community aspirations of the treaty.

Common but Differentiated Responsibilities

The identification of issues of common concern also finds expression in Principle 7 of the Rio Declaration, which states that, "[s]tates shall cooperate in a spirit of global partnership to conserve, protect and restore the health and integrity of the Earth's ecosystem." The need for global co-operation is fundamental to addressing issues of common concern, but different states have contributed to those issues in disproportionate ways, have diverse capacities to address environmental issues, and may be impacted disproportionately to other states. The **principle of common but differentiated responsibilities** (CBDR) acknowledges these differences and affirms the greater burden that developed states must bear in addressing solutions. The CBDR principle moves away from structuring IEL on the basis of the formal equality of states and reciprocity of obligations, towards a theory of equity based on historic responsibility, current capacity, and need.[38]

The legal recognition that international environmental obligations must account for the capabilities of the state in question predates the Rio process, but was institutionalized first in the Montreal Protocol, which, while not explicitly referring to the principle of common but differentiated responsibilities, expressly adopts a form that acknowledges the "special situation" of developing countries.[39] Subsequently, the principle was reflected in the UNFCCC and, to a lesser degree, the UNCBD. The principle is implemented in the Montreal Protocol through differential timeframes for compliance (that is, developing countries had more time to phase out CFCs),[40] and in amendments in 1990 that put in place a robust system of technology transfer and financial support for developing countries.[41] In the UNCBD, the principle is implemented through provisions for **technology transfer** (particularly around biotechnology) and financial support, but also through provisions respecting the "fair and equitable" sharing of the scientific and commercial benefits that flow from access to genetic resources.[42] The UNFCCC is expressly premised on the principle of common but differentiated responsibilities, and is notable for its acknowledgement within the preamble that developed countries have contributed the largest historic share of emissions,[43] while developing countries' emissions will need to grow to meet development demands.[44] Like the UNCBD and the Ozone Convention, part of the differentiation relates to the provision by developed states of financial resources to developing states, but the UNFCCC and, subsequently, the Kyoto Protocol institutionalized differentiation to a greater degree by a clear intention to impose greater emission reduction obligations on developed states.

The CBDR principle stands at the centre of the Rio consensus in that it is at the heart of the compromise between developed and developing states. The willingness of the developing states to accept restrictions on their development activities hinges on developed states' willingness to provide financial support, to make technology available, and to take the lead in imposing constraints on their own development activities. Climate change looms large in the implementation of the CBDR principle because it is within this context that the stakes are highest.

Canada's acceptance of the principle of CBDR is reflected in the many treaties during and after the Rio process that are premised on differential responsibilities. Again, Canada has implemented some of those commitments through its financial support of the multilateral fund and the Global Environment Facility. This support includes funding that flows under the UNFCCC and through subsequent agreements around climate finance that were negotiated through the COP process before and after Canada's withdrawal from Kyoto. Canada has directly engaged in international co-operation on the basis of differentiation, notably in the Ozone Convention and in the UNCBD.

Where Canada has clearly retreated from the principle of CBDR is in its non-compliance and withdrawal from the Kyoto Protocol, and in its insistence that it will only accept binding emission reductions if other large emitter nations, such as China, India, and Brazil, do the same. Canada's stance undercuts the theory of equity that animates the CBDR principle in three ways. First, it is a rejection of the idea that historic contributions to a global environmental problem impose international responsibility. Second, by refusing to cut its emissions, Canada is imposing harm on countries that are more vulnerable to climate change impacts, and thus disregards the obligations that flow from the greater need and urgency of those countries most vulnerable to climate change. Third, Canada's insistence on emission cuts from developing countries ignores the very different per capita emissions of developed countries and developing countries.

Canada's approach to date has been to support **capacity-building**, but it has moved away from accepting costly obligations on the basis of its historical responsibility. This position is consistent with the US position, as articulated in the Byrd-Hagel Senate resolution,[45] which directs that any future climate agreement must include emission reduction commitments from developing states. While developing state commitments are consistent with a framework that respects the principle of common but differentiated responsibilities (for example, large emitter nations could accept less onerous reduction commitments than developed states, instead of no commitments at all), the inability of developed states, including Canada, to take the lead, erodes the trust-building function of the principle.

Precautionary Principle

The **precautionary principle** first arose in the mid-1980s in response to a growing number of scientifically complex environmental issues where causal links between existing or predicted environmental harm and human activity were difficult to establish.[46] What Principle 15 requires is that, "where there are threats of serious or irreversible damage, lack of full scientific certainty shall not be used as a reason for postponing cost-effective measures to prevent environmental degradation."[47] The invocation of the principle in the Ozone Convention, the UNCBD, and the UNFCCC served as a justification for the development of the regime in the face of scientific skepticism. For example, under Article 3.3 of the UNFCCC, "[p]arties should take precautionary measures to anticipate, prevent or minimize the causes of climate change and mitigate its adverse effects." The most extensive elaboration of the principle is found in Article 6 of the Straddling Stocks Agreement, which requires states to "be more cautious when information is uncertain, unreliable or inadequate," to implement a suite of science-based activities, to obtain and share scientific evidence, and to properly account for uncertainty in their decision-making.

Insofar as the precautionary principle directs that state regulators not require scientific certainty as a precursor to regulation, it is uncontroversial. Canada has accepted numerous instruments that include reference to the precautionary principle in the post-Rio period, including the 2013 Minamata Convention. Canadian legislation, including the Canadian Environmental Protection Act and the Canadian Environmental Assessment Act, has adopted the wording of Principle 15, and Canada has developed a detailed decision-making framework for applying the precautionary principle. The Canadian approach to applying precaution has focused on the need to provide "a sound and credible basis that a risk of serious or irreversible harm exists."[48] This approach recognizes that risk preferences will differ among members of society, and requires that regulators account for levels of acceptable risk within affected groups. This approach is more conservative than the approach favoured by many environmentalists and embraced by some states, whereby the principle would operate to lower the threshold of proof necessary to require regulatory action or even reverse the burden of proof, requiring that those who seek to introduce a new substance into the environment must show that it is safe.[49] Canada's circumspection in relation to the international principle is indicated in its insistence that the precautionary principle is not a principle of **customary international law**; that is, it is not a general obligation that binds Canada beyond specific treaty commitments.[50]

Canada's ambivalence towards the precautionary principle can be seen in its position during the negotiation of the Cartagena Protocol where, as part of a negotiating block that included other states that produce GMO crops, Canada sought to ensure that the agreement would not limit the trade of goods containing GMOs on the basis of the precautionary principle. In particular, the concern was that other states would take the position that they would be justified in refusing to import GMOs if they believed those items posed an environmental risk.[51] During this same period, Canada was involved in a number of trade disputes over the same issue. Canada's position under World Trade Organization rules was that countries could only impose restrictions where scientific assessments demonstrated that there were real risks, as opposed to merely uncertain risks.[52] This is a position reflected in international trade law, and Canada has resisted any weakening of it in favour of environmental considerations. A similar line of argumentation was raised in relation to whether the listing of chrysotile asbestos under the Rotterdam Convention was justified.

Further, there is an argument that Canada's unwillingness to accept GHG emission reductions is contrary to the precautionary approach because it fails to respond to the risks associated with climate change. Clearly, Canada's approach is not precautionary in the ordinary sense of the word, but Canada has not sought to justify its inaction on the basis of a lack of certainty, and it has accepted formulations in numerous climate meetings that acknowledge the real and urgent danger climate change poses.[53] Canada's refusal to accept binding emission limits can explained by economic self-interest, but it would be a mistake to confuse this reasoning with a rejection of the precautionary principle. However, at the 2013 Conference of the Parties meeting under the UNFCCC, Canada was one of five states to stand in the way of establishing an international mechanism on climate change loss and damage whereby the precautionary principle would require states to support and implement proactive measures for managing slow-onset climate hazards (i.e., allocating long-term financing).[54]

The effect of the Canadian position has been to make it harder for states to adopt unilateral measures based on low risk tolerances associated with uncertainty for particular substances. Effectively, Canada is concerned about allowing other states to exercise too much discretion in imposing trade restrictions based on risks associated with uncertainty. These differences, which were evident in the negotiations of the Cartagena Protocol, were certainly present in the Rio process. Concerns over the use of environmental considerations, in conjunction with the precautionary principle, resulted in the inclusion of wording within the Rio Declaration clarifying that environmental trade measures should not be used as a way to arbitrarily restrict trade.[55] In this regard, Canada has not so much turned away from the precautionary principle as it has cemented its adoption of a narrow interpretation of the principle that requires that uncertainty and risk preferences be accounted for, while still requiring a clear scientific justification to support international regulation.

Participation Principle

The principle of public participation responds to a growing concern about the legitimacy, transparency, and accountability in environmental decision-making at both domestic and international levels. Within the Rio Declaration, Principle 10 requires that states provide access to environmental information, public participation in decision-making processes, and effective access to judicial and administrative proceedings at both domestic and international levels. The environmental specificity of this principle, in particular, distinguishes it from other participatory rights included in human rights instruments. Furthermore, its significance lies in its recognition of procedural or participatory rights as a means for upholding both human rights and environmental law. The principle also gets recognition in Principles 20 and 22, which recognize the important role of women and Indigenous people, respectively, in environmental management and development.

The Rio Conference itself, which was open to diverse groups of non-state actors, was a reflection of the principle. A similar opening-up was also seen within treaty structures, with provisions allowing for the admission of non-state parties to the meetings of the treaty parties found in such agreements as the Montreal Protocol, UNCBD, and UNFCCC. The UNCBD also contains specific obligations, like Article 8(j), respecting the important role of Indigenous people in biological diversity.[56] The structural significance of the principle of public participation relates to the conditions of how IEL is made and implemented, resulting in a strong normative expectation that policy processes will be transparent and consultative, and that environmental information will be made widely available. The result is a reorientation towards a less state-centric system of IEL, which provides an enhanced role for non-governmental organizations in treaty negotiations and in COPs, as well as a move towards minimum standards for participation and access to environmental information in domestic decision-making processes.

Canada gained much of its past international reputation for its leadership and respect for the promotion of participation and access to information. Canada advocated in favour of the inclusion of participatory principles within the Rio Declaration. It was a leader, along with the United States, in the development of processes of EIA, including the adoption of international rules respecting EIA under the Espoo Convention, as well as the development of domestic pollution disclosure mechanisms, such as the National Pollutant Release Inventory. In the lead-up to the 1992 Rio meeting, Canada also used consultative processes—dubbed the "Rio Way"[57]—to open decision-making to public input and scrutiny. This was regarded as a "profound transformation" in the way Canadian governments made decisions and as "the most significant innovation in the Canadian policy process in the past decade."[58] Through the North American Agreement on Environmental Cooperation, Canada provided an innovative mechanism for public participation with a **citizen submission process** that allowed members of the public to initiate investigations into state non-compliance with its domestic environmental laws. This process, which was negotiated as part of the North American Free Trade Agreement, was intended to ensure that the parties maintained a level playing field in terms of environmental regulation; it went beyond transparency and participation by giving non-governmental groups a right of standing to promote enforcement of environmental laws. Another innovative participatory institution that Canada had a hand in creating was the Arctic Council, which provided for three Indigenous organizations to be permanent participants in the Arctic Council.[59]

In the post-Rio era, Canada has not abandoned its commitment to participation, but its commitments have not kept pace with key international developments. Most prominently, Canada decided not to become a party to the Aarhus Convention on Access to Information, Public Participation in Decision-making and Access to Justice in Environmental Matters. The Convention provides a comprehensive set of process standards governing environmental decision-making in both domestic and international contexts, and it is the only treaty that explicitly implements Principle 10. The Aarhus Convention falls under the auspices of the UN Economic Commission for Europe, so Canada is entitled to become a party, but it has not ratified the Convention on the basis that:

> Canada maintains a well-established and advanced system of engaging the public. There already exist a number of mechanisms in Canada that permit public access to environmental information and the appropriate recourse to address concerns in environmental matters. For example, there are provisions to facilitate public participation generally in the Federal Access to Information Act, which gives Canadian citizens and permanent residents of Canada access to records held by federal government institutions.[60]

This reasoning does not appear convincing, however. Canada has often promoted treaties to ensure that other states are adhering to the same standards for which it has already taken domestic actions. The Aarhus Convention would have constrained the ability of the Canadian government to exercise greater discretion with respect to a wide range of procedural matters that would impact domestic policy-making. Canada has also decided not to join the Protocol on Strategic Environmental Assessment (under the Espoo Convention) and the Protocol on Pollutant Release and Transfer Registers (under the Aarhus Convention, but which is open for accession by non-parties to the Aarhus Convention).

In relation to the citizen submission process under the North American Agreement on Environmental Cooperation, the Canadian government has come under fire from environmental groups and academics alleging that the three member governments have sought to undermine the Commission for Environmental Cooperation (CEC) by obstructing and limiting the scope of its investigations.[61] In a letter to top environmental officials, 20 groups and individuals called on the United States, Mexico, and Canada to stop interfering with the CEC's core citizen complaint procedure.[62] Among the complaints, several pertaining to delays and political interference relate to factual records that found the Canadian government had failed to enforce its environmental laws. The actions of the three governments are in direct contradiction of the democratic purposes of the citizen submission process.

Canada's Commitment to the Rio Consensus

The first part of the leader-to-laggard thesis is strongly borne out by Canada's activities in relation to IEL in and around the time of the Rio Declaration. Canada played an important leadership role in the establishment of key treaties, but also in its support for the underlying architecture of IEL. The second part of the thesis is more nuanced. Canada remains an active and engaged participant across most multilateral environmental initiatives. Canada continues to sign on to environmental treaties and to support IEL institutions through financial contributions. But increasingly, it also has taken decisions in relation to treaty commitments that depart from the prevailing position of the international community. From an interest-based perspective, Canada's interpretation or non-acceptance of particular IEL rules is simply an exercise of **sovereignty**, in which Canada can be understood as weighing the costs and benefits of a particular commitment, accepting those rules that favour Canada's self-interest and rejecting those that do not. However, the Rio consensus ought to be understood as signifying a commitment to a normative framework intended to move the international community away from a simple calculus of individual state interests and towards a more global perspective. This commitment was most clearly signalled by the principle of common concern, but was reinforced by the principles of common but differentiated responsibilities, precaution, and participation. In this regard, Canada's pattern of activities indicates a move away from the global partnership established at Rio.

The clearest example of Canada's retreat is in relation to the principle of common but differentiated responsibilities, where Canada has refused to accept commitments premised on its historic contribution to global environmental problems. This is not necessarily a complete repudiation of the principle, since Canada does appear to engage in activities, such as financial and technical support, that recognize its greater capacity. It does, however, point to the government's non-acceptance of the equitable arguments attached to CBDR. Canada's position on this principle largely plays out in climate change, because in this context the threats to international economic competitiveness are most apparent. The primacy of economic interests also appears to have influenced Canada's position in relation to the precautionary principle, which has favoured a narrow interpretation of the principle that limits the ability of states to interfere with trade activities based on lower-risk preferences. Canada's position also indicates a less expansive role for IEL than the Rio consensus suggested. This is evident in relation to Canada's tepid embrace of the principle of common concern, which would provide a stronger basis for international legal intervention based on the shared global interest in an environmental resource. Canada's disinterest in implementing Principle 10 by adopting international standards for participation and access to environmental information similarly indicates a preference on the part of the federal government to restrict the penetration of IEL into internal decision-making processes, where international rules could constrain domestic development activities.

Because states are both subject to and the authors of international law, their interactions with other states with respect to the creation and interpretation of international law play a crucial role in the maintenance of normative systems. The principles of IEL require constant reinforcement, with the legal character of norms being affirmed by adherence to those norms and being diminished where states fail or undermine these practices. Thus, taken together, Canada's post-Rio stance ought to be understood as advancing a systemic shift back towards a more interest-dominated structure of IEL, while the Rio consensus sought to reframe environmental issues from a less state-centric perspective by refocusing IEL on a more open, equitable, precautionary, and global normative framework. The difficulty, which is vividly illustrated in the climate change negotiations, is that the environmental problems facing the international community are not easily resolved when viewed solely through the lens of individual state interests.

Key Terms

capacity-building

citizen submission process

customary international law

global environmental multilateralism

no-harm principle

precautionary principle

principle of common but differentiated responsibilities

reciprocity

regimes

shared normative framework

sovereignty

technology transfer

Questions for Review

1. Should Canada only accept international legal obligations that are in its national interest? What role should equity and fairness play in the creation of international rules on the environment?

2. In Canada, the federal government (through the Department of Foreign Affairs, Trade and Development) is primarily responsible for negotiating international agreements, but the provinces are primarily responsible for implementing environmental law. In what ways will the division of powers under Canada's federal structure impact the creation of international environmental law?

3. As non-state actors (both NGOs and private, commercial entities) become more prominent in international affairs, concerns have been raised about the legitimacy of non-state actors influencing international law-making processes. What are some of the potential problems with non-state actor involvement in international environmental law? What are the benefits?

4. The Canadian government has maintained that major resource developments, such as the oil sands, are a matter of domestic, not international, policy. Do you agree? What principles would support the claim that such activities ought to be subject to greater international oversight?

Internet Resources

Rio Declaration on Environment and Development
http://www.un.org/documents/ga/conf151/aconf15126-1annex1.htm

American Society of International Law Electronic Resources Guide
http://www.asil.org/resources/electronic-resource-guide-erg

Environment Canada—International Affairs
http://ec.gc.ca/international/default.asp?lang5En&n54E60822B-1

Center for International Environmental Law
http://www.ciel.org/

Foundation for International Environmental Law and Development
http://www.iied.org/foundation-for-international-environmental-law-development

Centre for International Sustainable Development Law
http://www.cisdl.org/

Additional Reading

Brunnée, Jutta. "Beyond Rio? The Evolution of International Environmental Law." *Alternatives Journal* 20, 1 (1993): 16–23.

Benidickson, Jamie. *Environmental Law*, 4th edn, ch. 4. Toronto: Irwin Law, 2013.

Freestone, David. "The Road from Rio: International Environmental Law after the Summit." *Journal of Environmental Law* 6 (1994): 193–218.

Najam, A. "Developing Countries and Global Environmental Governance: From Contestation to Participation to Engagement." *International Environmental Agreements* 5 (2005): 303–21.

Palmer, Geoffrey. "New Ways to Make International Environmental Law." *American Journal of International Law* 82 (1992): 259–83.

Wood, Stepan, Georgia Tanner, and Benjamin Richardson. "What Ever Happened to Canadian Environmental Law?" *Ecology Law Quarterly* 37 (2010): 981–1038.

Notes

1. Jennifer Ditchburn, "Canada a Laggard, Not a Leader, Sierra Club Says," *Edmonton Journal*, 28 Apr. 2007, accessed online 27 Apr. 2014; David Suzuki, "Canada's Growing Reputation as an Environmental Laggard," 26 June 2012, accessed 27 Apr. 2014, straight.com; Greenpeace International, "Who to Blame Ten Years after Rio? The Role of the USA, Canada, and Australia in Undermining the Johannesburg Summit," Aug. 2002, accessed online 27 Apr. 2014; David R. Boyd, *Unnatural Law: Rethinking Canadian Environmental Law and Policy* (Vancouver: University of British Columbia Press, 2003), 256–7.

2. Daniel Bodansky, "The History of the Global Climate Change Regime," in Urs Luterbacher and Detlef F. Sprinz, eds, *International Relations and Global Climate Change* (Cambridge, Mass.: MIT Press, 2001).

3. The UNCBD was signed 11 June 1992 and ratified 4 December 1992.

4. Declaration of the United Nations Conference on Environment and Development, 14 June 1992, UN Doc A/CONF.151/26 (Volume 1), 31 ILM 874 ("Rio Declaration").

5. Ibid, Preamble.

6. See A. Najam, "Developing Countries and Global Environmental Governance: From Contestation to Participation to Engagement," *International Environmental Agreements* 5 (2005): 303–21.

7. David Freestone, "The Road from Rio: International Environmental Law after the Summit," *Journal of Environmental Law* 6 (1994): 193–218.

8. "Why Canada Chose to Leave a Global Fight against Desertification," *Globe and Mail*, 28 Mar. 2013, accessed online 27 Apr. 2014.

9. Ole Hendrickson and Stephen Aitken, "Statement of Concern Regarding the Government of Canada's Withdrawal from the United Nations Convention to Combat Desertification (UNCCD)," *Biodiversity* 14, 3 (2013): 131.

10. Boyd, *Unnatural Law*, 257.

11. Daniel M. Bodansky, "Customary (and Not So Customary) International Environmental Law," *Indiana Journal of Global Legal Studies* 3, 1 (1995): 117.

12. Jutta Brunnée and Stephen Toope, *Legitimacy and Legality in International Law: An Interactional Account* (Cambridge: Cambridge University Press, 2010); but see Jack Goldsmith and Eric Posner, *The Limits of International Law* (Oxford: Oxford University Press, 2005).

13. But see Boyd, *Unnatural Law*, and Stepan Wood, Georgia Tanner, and Benjamin Richardson, "What Ever Happened to Canadian Environmental Law," *Ecology Law Quarterly* 37 (2010): 981–1038, both of which argue convincingly that Canada's relative environmental performance and its domestic policy leadership have dropped significantly since 1992.

14. The classic definition of a regime comes from Stephen Krasner: "Regimes can be defined as sets of implicit or explicit principles, norms, rules and decision-making procedures around which actors' expectations converge in a given area of international relations." Stephen Krasner, "Structural Causes and Regime Consequences: Regimes as Intervening Variables," *International Organization* 36 (1982): 185.

15. For example, the expectation of compliance is rooted in the international legal norm *pacta sunt servanda* (agreements must be kept).

16. See also Najam, "Developing Countries and Global Environmental Governance."

17. Alan Boyle and David Freestone, eds, *International Law and Sustainable Development: Past Achievements and Future Challenges* (Oxford: Oxford University Press, 1999), 3.

18. Steven Bernstein, "International Institutions and the Framing of Domestic Policies: The Kyoto Protocol and Canada's Response to Climate Change," *Policy Sciences* 35 (2002): 212.

19. See "Our Common Future, Annex 2: The Commission and Its Work", accessed 27 Apr. 2014, http://www.un-documents.net/ocf-a2.htm.

20. Steven Bernstein, *The Compromise of Liberal Environmentalism* (New York: Columbia University Press, 2001), 98.

21. Statement by Brian Mulroney, Prime Minister of Canada, in *Report of the United Nations Conference on Environment and Development*, v.III, A?CONF.151/26/Rev.1 (Vol. III), 72.

22. "Statement by Elizabeth Dowdeswell, Executive Director of UNEP, to the International Media Conference (World Environment Day)," 5 June 1997.

23. Boundary Waters Agreement.

24. See Jutta Brunnée, "The United States and International Environmental Law: Living with an Elephant," *European Journal of International Law* 15, 4 (2004): 617–49.

25. Global Environment Facility, *Instrument for the Establishment of the Restructured Global Environment Facility*, 11 Oct., CRS report; Executive Committee of the Multilateral Fund, *Status of Contribution and Disbursements*, 31 Oct. 2013, UNEP/Ozl.Pro/ExCom/71/3, Table 3—1991–2013 Summary Status of Contributions; Government of Canada, *Canada's Fast-Start Financing: Delivering on Our Copenhagen Commitment*, May 2013.

26. Jutta Brunnée, "COPing with Consent: Lawmaking under Multilateral Environmental Agreements," *Leiden Journal of International Law* 15 (2002): 16.

27. For example, Article 2(9) of the Montreal Protocol provides for binding decisions respecting adjustments to control measures for ozone-depleting substances to be made on the basis of double-weighted two-thirds majoritarian voting.

28. This interpretation was based on Article 18 of the Kyoto Protocol, which provides for the parties to negotiate a non-compliance procedure, but notes that any procedure that entails binding consequences shall be adopted by means of an amendment to the Protocol.

29. Brunnée and Toope, *Legitimacy and Legality*, 40.

30. Stephen Leahy, "Canada's Carbon Emissions Projected to Soar by 2030," *The Guardian*, 14 Jan. 2014, accessed 27 Apr. 2014.

31. 2244 UNTS 337; 38 ILM 1 (1999), Art. 7.

32. See Amir Attaran, David Boyd, and Matthew Stanbrook, "Asbestos Mortality: A Canadian Export," *Canadian Medical Association Journal* 179, 9 (2008): 871–2.

33. *Pulp Mills on the River Uruguay (Argentina v. Uruguay)*, International Court of Justice, 20 Apr. 2010.

34. 1760 UNTS 79; 31 ILM 818 (1992), Art. 4.

35. Alan Boyle, "The Gabčíkovo-Nagymaros Case: New Law in Old Bottles," *Yearbook of International Environmental Law* 8, 1 (1997): 19.

36. Joe Oliver, "An open letter from Natural Resources Minister Joe Oliver," *Globe and Mail*, 9 Jan. 2012, accessed online 27 Apr. 2014.

37. Principle 2 cited in Preamble of 1954 UNTS 3; 33 ILM 1328 (1994).

38. Dinah Shelton, "Equity," in Daniel Bodansky, Jutta Brunnée, and Ellen Hey, eds, *The Oxford Handbook of International Environmental Law* (Oxford: Oxford University Press, 2007), 639.

39. 1522 UNTS 3; 26 ILM 1550 (1987), Art. 5.

40. Ibid.

41. Ibid, Art. 10.

42. 421760 UNTS 79; 31 ILM 818 (1992), Art. 15.

43. 431771 UNTS 107; S. Treaty Doc No. 102-38; UN Doc.A/AC.237/18 (Part II)/Add.1; 31 ILM 849 (1992), Art. 3(1).

44. Ibid, Preamble.

45. Senate Resolution 98, *Congressional Record*, Report No. 105-5412, June 1997.

46. Philippe Sands, *Principles of International Environmental Law*, 2nd edn (Cambridge: Cambridge University Press, 2003), 267.

47. UN Doc. A/CONF.151/26 (vol. I) / 31 ILM 874 (1992), Principle 15.

48. Government of Canada, "A Framework for the Application of Precaution in Science-Based Decision-Making about Risk," 4.

49. Jonathan Weiner, "Precaution," in Bodansky, Brunnée, and Hey, eds, *Oxford Handbook of International Environmental Law*, 597.

50. Government of Canada, "A Framework for the Application of Precaution in Science-Based Decision-Making about Risk," 6.

51. See Steven Bernstein and Benjamin Cashore, "Globalization, Internationalization and Liberal Environmentalism: Exploring Non-domestic Sources of Influence on Canadian Environmental Policy," in Debora VanNijnatten and Robert Boardman, eds, *Canadian Environmental Policy: Context and Cases* (Toronto: Oxford University Press, 2001).

52. See, e.g., "European Communities—Asbestos," World Trade Organization, accessed 27 Apr. 2014, http://www.wto.org/english/tratop_e/envir_e/edis09_e.htm; "European Communities—Measures Concerning Meat and Meat Products (Hormones)," World Trade Organization, 25 Sept. 2009, accessed 27 Apr. 2014, http://www.wto.org/english/tratop_e/dispu_e/cases_e/ds26_e.htm; "European Communities—Measures Affecting the Approval and Marketing of Biotech Products," World Trade Organization, access 27 Apr. 2014, http://www.wto.org/english/tratop_e/dispu_e/cases_e/ds291_e.htm.

53. UNFCCC, "Bali Action Plan," Decision 1/CP.13, FCCC/CP/2007/6/Add.1; UNFCCC, "Copenhagen Accord," Decision 2/CP.15, FCCC/CP/2009/11/Add.1.

54. See "Don't Hold Up an International Mechanism on Loss and Damage at COP 19," WWF, 20 Nov. 2013, accessed online 27 Apr. 2014; Ronald Bailey, "Loss and Damage: The Third Era of Climate Change?" teason.com, 20 Nov. 2013, accessed online 27 Apr. 2014.

55. UN Doc. A/CONF.151/26 (vol. I) / 31 ILM 874 (1992), Principle 12.

56. 1760 UNTS 79; 31 ILM 818 (1992), Art. 8(j). See also "Akwé: Kon Guidelines," Convention on Biodiversity, 2004, accessed 27 Apr. 2014, http://www.cbd.int/doc/publications/akwe-brochure-en.pdf.

57. The Rio Way was defined by three characteristics: transparency, accountability, and inclusion. See Rod Dobell and Justin Longo, "From Commitment to Compliance: Dealing with Atmospheric Risks in Canada and the United States," prepared for Conference on Environment Policy Implementation: A Comparison of Canada and the United States, convened by the Indiana University School of Public and Environmental Affairs, San Diego, 9 July 1999.

58. See Michel Dorais, "Environmental Assessment: Consequences of the Emergence of Procedural Democracy," *Optimum* (Winter 1994–5): 36–9; Glen Toner, quoted in Ronald L. Doering, "Evaluating Round Table Processes," *National Round Table Review* (Winter 1995): 1–3.

59. *Joint Communiqué and Declaration on the Establishment of the Arctic Council* (1996), 35 I.L.M. 138, art. 2.

60. "Right to Clean Air, Clean Water, and a Healthy Environment," Response to Question 4, Office of the Auditor General of Canada, 6 Feb. 2006, accessed 27 Apr. 2014, http://www.oag-bvg.gc.ca/internet/English/pet_163A_e_28897.html.

61. "Canada, US and Mexico Interfering with NAFTA Watchdog," Ecojustice, 12 Jan. 2010, accessed 27 Apr. 2014.

62. "Letter to Baird, Johnson, and Elvira," Ecojustice, 23 Apr. 2008, accessed 27 Apr. 2014, http://www.ecojustice.ca/media-centre/media-release-files/CEC.LTR.INTERFERFENCE.FINAL.2008.04.23.pdf/at_download/file.

PART III
Cases

The environmental policy cases examined in Part III provide concrete examples of the kinds of dynamics and constraints identified in Parts I and II of this volume. The cases explored here highlight a profound ambivalence in policy regimes, which have tended to graft environmental protection or sustainability goals onto policy and program structures put in place primarily to encourage extractive activities and resource use. This phenomenon, where we see environmental policy primarily as a surface-layer "add-on" rather than entailing (as it should) programmatic renovation, has clear implications for future planning and prospects. The first is that the present era of austerity has made things worse by weakening (or washing away) many of the programs and provisions in place, particularly since most are not deeply rooted enough in the bedrock of policy and legal frameworks. Second, environmental policy advocates have faced considerable hurdles to getting effective protections in place, maintaining them, and countering rollbacks; consumptive and extractive actors have quite successfully operated in a policy game where the rules have not fundamentally changed.

In this section, too, our cases uniformly highlight the lack of federal willingness to take a leadership role in environmental policy. From climate change and energy policy, to water and air quality, to wildlife and protected areas management, the federal disinclination to bring the relevant actors together, to co-ordinate the actions of the provinces and territories, to provide scientific, policy, and capacity support, and to take actions designed to effectively change behaviours is all too clear. Worse, there is some evidence in the following chapters that the federal government is actively undermining those constraints that are (or were) in place to support environmental management efforts. Budget cuts and austerity measures have had very real, and likely lasting, impacts on environmental policy capacity, such that future attempts to fortify environmental safeguards will involve considerable "backfilling," while some earlier investments and practices will never be regained.

Chapter 13 by Douglas Macdonald sets the stage by providing a broad analysis of the major factors underlying Canada's "consistent failure" to gain purchase on our biggest, most encompassing environmental challenge: climate change policy. Why has Canada consistently failed to reach successive greenhouse gas reduction targets, with current policies expected to achieve only half of the national 2020 greenhouse gas emission reduction target? While sketching the broad outlines of climate policy dynamics in Canada, Macdonald drills down to a key obstruction: effective climate policy will inevitably impose much higher costs on the oil-producing provinces than it does on others. Yet, the weak rules of decentralized Canadian federalism and total absence of leadership from the federal government mean that there is no means to reach agreement on ways to equitably share the total reduction cost. In fact, as Simmons has argued in Chapter 8, there is at present *no* co-ordination of policy among federal and provincial governments. Since the provinces own the resources, they inevitably will be the major players in effective policy, and they are taking their own approaches (or doing little). What this means is that any steps taken towards effective climate policy—such as in

British Columbia (with its carbon tax) and Ontario (which has phased out use of coal to generate electricity)—are being undercut by emission increases in the oil-producing provinces.

Policy variation across provinces, alongside locally distinctive debates about the costs and benefits of supporting various forms of energy, is also reflected in the generation and use of renewable electricity. As Ian Rowlands notes in Chapter 14, the present means of generating electricity are, for the most part, unsustainable, and policy changes—particularly increased use of renewable resources like wind, solar, and water through price-based or quota-based measures—are required. Clearly, any progress we make on climate change will require the increased use of renewables across the country, a task complicated by the fact that provinces have primary jurisdiction over electricity systems and have developed markedly different systems, utilizing available resources to varying extents. While some jurisdictions in Canada have adopted and deployed a broad portfolio of measures, others have largely restricted their actions to the articulation of ambitions. What is lacking, according to Rowlands, is a holistic (and national) consideration of the full impacts of different energy sources that stretches across both space and time. Indeed, such a conversation is difficult to initiate in the current austerity context.

The next two chapters examine the politics of water in Canada and highlight the acute difficulties associated with placing water regimes and use on a more sustainable basis. Carolyn Johns and Mark Sproule-Jones provide insights into the complexities and challenges of water policy and governance in the Great Lakes in Chapter 15. The authors trace decades' worth of policy activity in conjunction with efforts to balance the multiple uses of water; they show how the waxing and waning of political and policy attention, not to mention policy capacity, has impeded efforts to address water quantity and quality problems. To a considerable degree, this policy history can be linked to a "myth of abundance," which underpins a popular and political ambivalence in water and environmental policy in the Great Lakes. Also critical has been the webbing of historically rooted uses, legal rights, and policy regimes that generate conflicts and do not fit comfortably with new use restrictions, as well as the complex nature of transboundary, multi-level governance structures in the Great Lakes Basin. The new 2012 Great Lakes Water Quality Agreement recommits the Canadian government to action on water quality but it is not clear that the sustained leadership required by the new mandates will be forthcoming.

In Chapter 16, Timothy Heinmiller demonstrates the ambivalence in the water policy regimes of western Canada. While the preceding chapter highlights the challenges associated with water management in a context of (relative) abundance, Heinmiller gives us a glimpse of how water scarcity in some parts of western Canada—specifically southern Alberta, southern Saskatchewan, and the BC interior—influences policy dynamics. He shows how new environmental demands have been planted onto a strongly pro-irrigation regime, resulting in considerable uncertainty for users, policy-makers, and environmental advocates. In these regions, water has long been allocated and managed using a system known as prior allocation. This system has been resistant to attempts to modernize in response to concerns about sustainability. The storyline developed by Heinmiller highlights how more pro-environment policy instruments, both substantive and procedural (as introduced by Winfield in Chapter 5), have been grafted onto the existing allocation system. However, the provincial reforms have continued to prioritize irrigators, and there is considerable uncertainty about the future application of environmental instruments in the face of increased scarcity and further pressure from newer stakeholders.

Underpinning so much of what is happening with environmental policy in Canada, as the Introduction to this volume highlights, is the politics of oil. Angela Carter leads us onto this terrain in Chapter 17, with a discussion of how the federal government, with some examples drawn from provincial cases, has supported oil development. After underlining the environmental impacts of oil, focusing on emissions causing climate change, Carter emphasizes the degree and extent of the Canadian economic dependence on oil, going so far as to reference the "oil curse." She then details how the federal government has actively facilitated the growth of Canada's oil economy through support for, and defence of, oil development; the obstruction of environmental research; environmental policy retrenchment; and the suppression of public debate. This case, perhaps unlike others in Part III, sheds stark light on the entrenchment and protection of political and policy choices that have direct environmental impacts. It remains unclear whether the burgeoning of civil society dissent and pressures associated with discussion of alternatives to the current oil-centred economy will have any impact on current dynamics.

Moving into the policy territory of biodiversity, Chapter 18 by Christopher J. Lemieux contrasts the layering of international and national commitments to protect and sustainably use biodiversity over time with continuing ecosystem degradation and lengthening endangered species lists in Canada. Although public support for biodiversity is high and Canada has participated in international efforts (most recently, the 2011–20 Aichi Biodiversity Targets and the Biodiversity Convention's new *Strategic Plan*), as a country we have been unable to achieve the targets set in such international agreements. Lemieux reviews a number of events that have shaped biodiversity conservation policy and management in Canada, and assesses Canada's ability to meet formal conservation commitments, given the federal Conservative government's science policy agenda and related austerity challenges. He concludes that immediate investments are required in biodiversity programming and governance, in the protected areas network, and in biodiversity policy capacity.

The final case presented here provides us with a different lens for observing federal government environmental policy activity, though its conclusions mirror those of other cases. In air pollution policy, explored by Owen Temby, Don Munton, and Inger Weibust in Chapter 19, we see that the Harper government has shown a greater openness to regulation and control, to fostering a more energetic environmental image. In recent decades, the authors argue, attention to the problem of air pollution in Canada and to action on pollution abatement has tended to be highly episodic, implemented through technological controls, and symbolic, often promising more than it delivers. The result is an air quality regime based on laws that do not constrain, regulations that make little or no difference, bilateral treaties that appear to promise more than they accomplish, and a redundancy of standards across multiple scales of government. The question posed by the authors, then, is whether the most recent initiative represents leadership by the Harper government, or if these policies are "smoke and mirrors" aimed at creating the appearance of progress while actually achieving little. Temby, Munton, and Weibust conclude that the ambivalence noted elsewhere in this book continues to be reflected in federal clean air regulations that, while unprecedented, are nevertheless so lax that they will likely have little positive influence on polluting industrial practices. Further, the new federal–provincial Air Quality Management System and the Harper government's coal-fired power plant program actually represent a continuation of long-standing tendencies.

13 Climate Change Policy

Douglas Macdonald

Chapter Summary

Why has Canadian climate change policy been such a consistent failure, with current policies expected to achieve only half the 2020 greenhouse gas emission reduction target? A major reason is that effective policy imposes much higher costs on the oil-producing provinces than it does on others. Steps towards effective policy, such as the BC carbon tax and Ontario's phasing out coal-generated electricity, are being undercut by emission increases in the oil-producing provinces. Today there is *no* co-ordination of policy among federal and provincial governments. The weak rules of decentralized Canadian federalism and the absence of leadership from the federal government mean that we cannot reach agreement on ways to equitably share the total reduction cost. Since the provinces own the resources, they inevitably will be the major players in effective policy, but the federal government must use the carrots and sticks of diplomacy to co-ordinate their actions.

Chapter Outline

- Canada has failed to meet all of its greenhouse gas emission reduction targets and current policies will fail again to meet the 2020 target.
- Effective climate change policy will impose higher costs on the oil-producing provinces than on others.
- The federal government led by Prime Minister Harper has no interest in acting on the issue itself or in co-ordinating actions of the provinces.
- Some provinces such as BC, Ontario, Quebec, and Nova Scotia are acting, but any reductions in greenhouse gas emissions they achieve are overwhelmed by emission increases in Alberta and Saskatchewan.
- Another problem is that Canadian business and government leaders traditionally have been convinced our policy must be harmonized with that of the United States.
- The provinces will inevitably be the major actors in development of effective policy, but the federal government must co-ordinate processes for reaching agreement on the sharing of the total Canadian reduction cost.

Introduction

Canadian federal and provincial governments have been attempting to reduce greenhouse gas (GHG) emissions in this country since 1990, when Prime Minister Brian Mulroney announced Canada would stabilize its greenhouse gas (GHG) emissions by the year 2000.

That commitment was reaffirmed when Canada signed and ratified the United Nations Framework Convention on Climate Change (UNFCCC) in 1992. While **emissions intensity** (the ratio of emissions to economic activity) has decreased, total Canadian emissions have actually increased, climbing 18.7 per cent between 1990 and 2011.[1] Canadian federal and provincial governments have set many targets since that initial 1990 commitment. The most recent federal government target is a commitment to reduce total Canadian GHG emissions to 17 per cent below the 2005 level, by 2020. If achieved, total Canadian emissions in 2020 would be 607 megatonnes (Mt) (i.e., million tonnes). Analysis by the former National Round Table on the Environment and the Economy (NRTEE) confirmed by that of Environment Canada, shows that, in total, all current and planned federal and provincial programs will have the effect merely of bringing emissions in 2020 down to 724 Mts.[2] Not only are we very likely to miss the 2020 target, but the government of Canada predicts that total emissions will continue to rise after that, to 815 Mts by 2030.[3] For these reasons, the research institute Germanwatch ranks Canada as the "worst performer of all industrialized countries."[4]

Why has Canada been unable to achieve its climate change goals since the first target was set in 1990? To answer that question, we need to understand the nature of climate change as a policy issue and then map that against the particulars of the Canadian case—a country giving priority to wealth created by fossil fuel exports, which are generated in certain provinces, primarily Alberta and Saskatchewan, but not in others. Having an economy closely integrated with that of the US, Canada has traditionally been under enormous pressure from Canadian business interests to harmonize its policies with those of the US. Furthermore, Canada is governed by a system of federalism that, next to that of Belgium, is one of the most decentralized and dysfunctional in the world. In summary, I argue that Canadian policy failure is explained by three factors. The first is the perception, shared by business and governments alike, that Canadian policy must be harmonized with that of the US and in particular that of the US federal government. (That perception may have changed with the November 2014 announcement of an agreement between the US and China that includes a significant commitment by the US President to future reductions—the Canadian government has not announced anything similar, despite its stated policy of harmonization with US federal government policy.) While some US states are taking effective action (and others are not), the Obama administration has not fulfilled its 2008 election promise of effective action on the issue, even with the 2014 US–China agreement, which means Canada has yoked itself to a slow-moving horse. The second is the fact that meaningful reduction of emissions will impose much higher costs on the oil-producing provinces, in particular Alberta, whose economic well-being, government revenues, and job prospects are so closely tied to the oil and gas industry, than it will upon other provinces. Not surprisingly, the oil-producing provinces have resisted the development of a national, co-ordinated policy in favour of maintaining the status quo, which has prevailed since 2003. Since that date each Canadian government has unilaterally developed its own climate change policy without regard to what others are doing. That approach dooms Canadian policy to failure, since reductions achieved in one part of the country will be overwhelmed by emission increases in other parts. The third explanatory factor is the failure of Canadian governments—and particularly of the federal government, which has a greater responsibility than the provinces to show leadership on national problems—to explicitly and publicly recognize this problem. By hiding their heads in the sand and avoiding any discussion of the need to equitably share the costs of emission reductions, Canadian governments, and in particular the

Prime Minister, prevent the possibility of effective national action as Canada's contribution to solving a global problem. The weakness of Canadian federalism contributes to this third problem but is not by itself the causal factor, which is the failure of Canada's elected leaders to even *attempt* to use the weak instruments available to them to put in place national, co-ordinated climate change policy.

The Nature of the Policy Issue

Climate change is the issue that broke the back of the environmental movement in Canada, the US, and other industrialized countries. From the 1960s to the 1990s, environmentalists made progress, albeit slow and uneven, in convincing governments, business firms, and citizens to act on issues such as toxic pollution, wilderness protection, and recycling. They have had nothing like that level of success on the climate change file since it became the dominant issue in the late 1990s. Perhaps their biggest defeat came in the US. In 2008, President Obama was elected on a campaign platform of action on climate change, and Democrats held a majority in both houses of Congress. The issue was by then highly visible and, as a consequence, environmentalists were very well funded. Yet, environmentalists have failed to achieve their goal of getting new federal climate change legislation in place, and there is no prospect of any such legislation before the end of Obama's term in January 2017. American environmentalists have switched their focus to stopping the Keystone XL pipeline, a relatively minor battle (although with symbolic resonance) in a much larger war. In Canada, the federal government in 2011 withdrew from the Kyoto Protocol with virtually no outcry from Canadians. As in the US, the focus of public debate has moved away from reducing emissions through improved energy efficiency and switching from fossil fuels to renewable sources. Instead, we now discuss whether construction on the Northern Gateway pipeline (which received regulatory approval in September 2014) has "social licence" to begin; what the prospects may be for a new west–east pipeline; and, since the August 2013 train wreck and oil spill disaster in Lac-Mégantic, how to address the safety issues associated with moving oil by rail.

Why has the climate change issue proven so intractable? In part, it is because those most threatened by climate change are not the humans (and other species) living today, but their offspring who will be born 30, 40, or 50 years from now—the grandchildren and great-grandchildren of those who are now undergraduate students in Canadian universities. Polar bears facing extinction and humans who will not be born until 2050 have no voice in today's climate change decision-making.

The fact that those most affected cannot participate in policy-making is important, but more so is the fact that climate change is an energy issue. The NRTEE states: "In Canada, roughly 82 per cent of emissions come from energy."[5] As such, the issue is fundamentally different from an issue such as toxic pollution that causes damage in the form of smog or acid rain. Toxic contamination can be addressed relatively easily because effects are apparent, immediate, and the costs to firms and other sources of reducing it are relatively low. Pollution is a *by-product* of resource extraction, manufacturing, and transportation that nobody (including those who produce it) wants, not only because of its effects on ecological health but also because it results from inefficiency and wasted resources. Fossil fuel energy—such as oil, coal, and natural gas—on the other hand, is a *product*, something firms sell to make money (as discussed in Chapters 3 and 17 in this volume). Energy firms have a powerful

TABLE 13.1 Sources of Canadian GHG Emissions by Economic Sector, 2011

Economic Sector	% of Total Emissions
Transportation	24
Oil and gas	23
Electricity	13
Buildings	12
Emissions-intensive industries	11
Agriculture	10
Waste and other	7

Source: Government of Canada, *Canada's Sixth National Report on Climate Change 2014* (Ottawa: Her Majesty the Queen in Right of Canada, 2013).

financial motivation to see *more* fossil fuels combusted, not less. To the extent that fossil fuel industries provide employment, tax revenues, and economic growth, governments tend to share that motivation. As can be seen in Table 13.1, the fossil fuel energy needed to extract oil and natural gas, which is then sold domestically and exported, accounts for a significant portion of total emissions. The fossil fuel then used, such as gasoline for motor vehicles or natural gas for generating electricity, accounts for a large part of remaining emissions.

Within Canada, the production of fossil fuel has been concentrated in some parts of the country—primarily Alberta and Saskatchewan—although that pattern is changing with the production of offshore oil on the Atlantic coast and the prospect of further production on both the east and the west coasts and in the Arctic, as well as the possibility of fracking of natural gas in Quebec, and a new focus on liquefied natural gas in BC. The NRTEE provides this summary: "On an absolute basis, the majority of emissions (58 per cent) originate from just two provinces—Alberta and Ontario. Alberta has the highest number of GHG emissions because it is the largest energy producer in the country."[6] Table 13.2 shows the contribution of each province to total Canadian emissions.

TABLE 13.2 Provincial Portions of Total Canadian GHG Emissions, 2009

Province	% of Total Emissions
Alberta	34
Ontario	24
Quebec	12
Saskatchewan	11
British Columbia	9
Nova Scotia	3
Manitoba	3
New Brunswick	3
Newfoundland and Labrador	1

Source: National Round Table on the Environment and the Economy, *Reality Check: The State of Climate Progress in Canada* (Ottawa, 2012).

The State of Climate Progress in Canada

These basic facts of Canadian geography and economy cause enormous problems for effective policy-making because of the third aspect of the climate change issue—it poses a **collective action problem**. No one country or government can solve its climate change problem by itself—Canada contributes a tiny portion of global emissions, which means if this country stopped all emissions tomorrow it would still suffer the same problems created by global emissions, such as rising sea levels, extreme weather, and the extinction of polar bears. To address the problem, countries must act collectively, which means there must be a sufficiently strong system of rules in place to ensure that if one incurs the cost of action others will as well. The tragedy of the commons metaphor holds that, as rational actors, countries will see this need for co-operation and work together to put in place a sufficiently robust system of rules. The difficulty is that in the "tragedy of the commons" all the actors—herders putting cows to feed in a commonly owned pasture—have identical interests to avoid depletion of the pasture and so are equally motivated to act. With respect to climate change, the actors have very different interests—some countries, such as low-lying island states, are more vulnerable to climate impact than others. At the same time, some countries, such as Russia, Saudi Arabia, and Canada, gain financially from selling fossil fuels, while others, such as France and Germany, do not. These differences in motivation make co-operation to address the collective action problem very difficult. France and Germany are not oil producers and so it is much easier for them to press for collective action, but they immediately bump into resistance from the producing nations.

We find exactly the same problem of differing motivation within Canada. These differences among Canadian provinces are illustrated by the differences in per capita emissions, shown in Table 13.3.

The two major oil-producing provinces have much higher **per capita emissions** than any others, which is an indication of the importance of fossil fuel production to their provincial economies. As a result, they will pay a higher cost for achieving Canadian reduction goals than will other provinces since, if it is effective, that policy will bring about a reduction in

TABLE 13.3 Provincial Per Capita GHG Emissions (tonnes/person), 2008

Province	Per Capita Emissions (tonnes/person)
Saskatchewan	72.5
Alberta	68.1
New Brunswick	25.7
Nova Scotia	23.1
Newfoundland and Labrador	19.4
Manitoba	17.9
British Columbia	15.0
Ontario	14.7
Prince Edward Island	14.3
Quebec	10.6

Source: Environment Canada, *Canada National Inventory Report*, 2011.

the fossil fuel production so important for their economies. Economic modelling has shown that the costs associated with climate change policy will not be evenly distributed. Jaccard states: "These policies are expected to trigger significant impacts on GDP with significant regional differences, especially for Alberta and Saskatchewan."[7] This means that if other provinces act unilaterally to reduce their own emissions, their contribution to achieving the overall Canadian reduction target is overwhelmed by increasing emissions in the oil-producing provinces, which, very understandably, seek to gain economic benefit from the fact that geography has blessed them with fossil fuel reserves.

There is another significant similarity between the Canadian and global contexts. At the global level, there is no government, so sovereign states can work together only by means of voluntary agreement. Since any country can opt out at any time, the efficacy of such agreements is driven down to the lowest common denominator—a standard of action that all, even the oil-producing states, are willing to accept. Within Canada, because of both the nature of Canadian federalism and the refusal of the Harper government to make any effort to develop a co-ordinated national program, exactly the same dynamic is found.

Canadian Federalism and Climate Change

As discussed in Chapters 4 and 8, Canada is a federated state, which means that the Canadian Constitution grants the federal government and each provincial government the right to govern—and this certainly is the case in the climate policy field. The federal government has authority over nuclear energy (because of its origins as a World War II national security issue) and over energy, such as oil in pipelines or trains, that crosses the international or provincial borders. Everything else having to do with the generation, transport, use, and conservation of energy—the bundle of issues that constitute climate change policy—falls squarely in the jurisdictional domain of the provinces. Although it has not been tested in the courts, the federal government does have constitutional jurisdiction to directly regulate greenhouse gas emissions. As discussed below, it has done so in the case of motor vehicles and coal-fired electricity plants. The point is that the provinces *also* have that constitutional authority and are implementing climate policy. Canadian climate change policy consists of policy action by both levels of government, and for that reason requires co-ordination.

Unfortunately, Canada does not have a strong and effective system for achieving that co-ordination, with clear rules and decisive means of making decisions. Within a federation such as Germany, the subnational governments (equivalent of Canadian provinces) are directly represented *within* the federal government by sending representatives to the upper house, the Bundesrat. The German federal government develops policy that applies to the whole country by deliberation and majority voting in the Bundesrat and the Bundestag (the lower house, equivalent to the House of Commons) and the subnational governments accept the outcome because they have participated in the decision. In Canada, the provinces are similarly represented in the upper house, but because the Senate is not elected it lacks democratic legitimacy and so effectively has no power to influence federal government decisions. As a result, policy applied to the whole country in an area of both federal and provincial jurisdiction, such as climate change, can only be developed through negotiating agreements among all of the federal government, provinces, and territories. Decisions are made by consensus, since any province has the right to not participate, with the result that, as at the international level, the effectiveness of policy is diluted down to the level that all will accept. Implementation is also weak, since there are few checks on a government that does not fully do what it had agreed to do. The inherent weakness of this system of inter-governmental relations, together with the great differences in motivation described above, make it very difficult for Canadian governments to work together to address the collective action problem of climate change.

Nevertheless, to be successful, they *have* to work together. Global policy can only be effective if countries agree on what portion of the overall reduction effort each will provide. As it has in the past and is about to do again for the post-2020 period, Canada makes a commitment to other countries to provide a certain portion of the total global effort. However, setting one overall target for reduction by the whole country, such as Prime Minister Mulroney's 1990 stabilization target, the Kyoto target of reduction to 6 per cent below 1990 levels, or the Copenhagen target of 17 per cent below 2005 levels, inherently carries with it the question of how that overall reduction effort will be allocated among the Canadian provinces. To date, that question has not been publicly addressed by Canadian governments.

Between 1990 and 2002, the federal and provincial governments attempted to work together using an institutional structure known as the National Climate Change Process, which consisted of a hierarchical network of committees staffed jointly by federal and provincial civil servants, reporting regularly to joint meetings of ministers (federal and provincial environment and energy ministers). Because a number of provinces, in particular Alberta, objected strongly to the federal government decision in 2002 to ratify the Kyoto Protocol (discussed below), that process came to an end. Alberta formally withdrew and established its own climate change policy target, which differed from the Canadian Kyoto target. For its part, the federal government announced it would regulate emission sources, regardless of what the provinces did. Those two actions effectively ended the attempt to develop co-ordinated policy, and since then each of the 11 federal and provincial governments has developed policy unilaterally without regard to what other Canadian governments are doing.[8] Prompted by Alberta's need for agreement from other provinces to new pipelines to ship Alberta oil to markets, a discussion of a possible "national energy strategy" has arisen; to date, however, nothing has materialized, in part because the federal government has shown no interest in leading any such effort.[9]

For those reasons, it is impossible for Canada to meet its current goal of a reduction to 17 per cent below the 2005 level. As noted, current analysis shows the total of current unco-ordinated federal and provincial policies will achieve only half that goal. However, no one Canadian government, federal or provincial, will pay the costs—its own administrative cost and the cost measured in terms of political repercussions from the fact of imposing controls and costs on its industries and firms—of making up the missing half of emission reductions on behalf of the rest of the country. Furthermore, reductions generated by some provincial policies, such as the BC carbon tax, will be undercut by future increases in emissions from the oil-producing provinces. Jeffrey Simpson, using federal government data, has noted that emissions will increase by "nearly 100 million tonnes in that province [Alberta] from 2005 to 2030. That's more than the increase for the entire country, where emissions are expected to hold steady or shrink elsewhere."[10] The decentralized nature of Canadian federalism, which has led to unilateral, completely unco-ordinated policy-making by all governments, coupled with a refusal to face the fact that setting one target for the whole country implicitly requires setting targets for each province, is a central factor explaining the failure of Canadian climate change policy.

Canada's External Relations and Climate Change

Since 1990, Canadian climate policy has been developed within two primary external contexts: (1) the international regime; and (2) the fact of living beside, and having an economy closely integrated with that of, the United States. The latter has had far more influence on Canadian policy. Each of these contexts is briefly discussed below.

As noted, having already adopted the goal of stabilizing GHG emissions, it was relatively easy for the federal government to accept that same goal when it was embedded in the UNFCCC reached at the 1992 Rio Conference on Environment and Sustainable Development. Canada then became one of the first signatory countries to ratify the Convention that same year. (Diplomats representing countries sign multilateral environmental agreements at the relevant international meeting, but the country does not finally commit itself until it ratifies the agreement by action of its government, at home.) Implementation of that commitment, due to opposition from the oil industry and oil-producing provinces, was much harder. Membership in the UNFCCC meant Canada had to develop a national plan, which led to the 1995 federal–provincial National Action Program on Climate Change. Alberta objected strongly to the fact that the federal government signed the 1997 Kyoto Protocol, but was mollified by the Prime Minister's commitment to not ratify the Protocol until there had been extensive consultation with industry, the provinces, and Canadian citizens. In 2001, President George W. Bush announced the US would not participate in the Kyoto Protocol. Surprisingly, because Canada has almost always followed the US lead throughout the UNFCCC/Kyoto process, the Chrétien government did not follow suit. Instead, it took advantage of the regime's desperate need for Canadian participation in the wake of the US pullout to negotiate a lower Canadian target, through recognition of the carbon stored in Canadian soil and wood, known as **carbon sinks**. Canada then proceeded to ratify the Protocol at the end of 2002, despite the largest lobbying campaign mounted by business before or since and the vigorous opposition of many provinces.

While it was in power from 2003 until the end of 2005, the Liberal Party government led by Prime Minister Paul Martin was an enthusiastic participant in the UNFCCC/Kyoto regime, due both to Martin's international perspective and commitment to strong global governance, as well as to Environment Minister Stéphane Dion's personal commitment to the issue. All that changed in January 2006, when the Conservative Party led by Stephen Harper took power. Harper has a mistrust of the United Nations, has shown little interest in international affairs apart from supporting Israel and Ukraine and following the US lead in fighting "terrorism," does not seem to believe climate change poses any threat, and leads a party that depends on electoral support from the western, oil-producing provinces. Once he achieved majority government status in 2011, Prime Minister Harper was able to act on these ideological and political interests seemingly without constraint, and announced in December of that year that Canada would withdraw from the Kyoto agreement. At the international meetings, his government actively worked to prevent global progress on achieving the Kyoto goal, a fact regularly pointed out by environmentalists. At the 2012 Kyoto Conference of the Parties meeting in Durban, South Africa, the Climate Action Network gave Canada, for the fifth year in a row, its "Fossil of the Year" award. Canada was selected for this satirical "honour" because, as the Network noted: "The Canadian government has made headlines and earned criticism from the international community in Durban for refusing to sign on to a second Kyoto commitment period, calling critical climate financing 'guilt payments,' and bullying least developed countries into leaving the Kyoto Protocol."[11] Nevertheless, Canada is still formally part of the international process intended to develop a new global target for the period after 2020 and as such must announce a new Canadian post-2020 target by the end of 2015.

As can be seen, Canada's enthusiasm for the international regime has weakened over the years and, in return, the regime has had almost no influence on Canadian policy. That cannot be said for Canada–US relations, which have very much influenced Canadian actions on the issue. Because most Canadian exports go to the US, Canadian business has always argued strongly that this country's climate policy must match that of the US, to ensure Canadian firms are not paying higher costs for energy than are their US competitors. Governments have accepted that argument, and Canadian climate policy—with the exceptions of the failure to leave Kyoto when the US did in 2001 and the November 2014 failure to announce a post-2020 reduction target similar to that announced by President Obama—has mirrored that of the US.[12] Since 2008, the Harper government, while showing no interest in co-ordinating its policy with that of Canadian provinces, has said explicitly it will *only* put in place policy measures previously implemented in Washington—of which there have been very few.

At one time it was thought that, despite this failure at the federal level, regional agreements between American states and Canadian provinces might result in effective policy. In particular, the Western Climate Initiative, led by California, one of the US states most active on the issue, seemed to offer promise. However, the other US states have abandoned the effort and Canadian provinces, with the exception of Quebec, have not yet implemented the proposed cap-and-trade system. Recent analysis has concluded that: "In the end, these multilateral subnational networks have been incapable of sustaining the linkages among participants."[13] In summary, Canada's external relations are another factor explaining Canadian policy failure—in particular, the inability of the UNFCCC regime to influence Canadian policy; the failure of the US, which certainly *can* exert such influence, to propel Canadian policy; and the failure of the promise of subnational cross-border linkages.

Federal Government Policy

Given the jurisdictional responsibilities outlined earlier, the federal government has responsibility for two roles respecting climate change policy: (1) developing and implementing its own policy measures to bring about emission reductions, and (2) facilitating with the provinces the co-ordination of overall Canadian policy. In terms of the first, as noted, during the period 1992–2002 the Ottawa government developed its own policy as part of a co-ordinated federal–provincial effort. It provided funding for technology research and development, implemented new efficiency-enhancing regulatory standards for refrigerators and other appliances, and encouraged voluntary action. When it left the federal–provincial process in late 2002, the federal government announced plans that it would directly regulate the fossil fuel, manufacturing, and electricity sectors, which account for half of total emissions. After taking power in 2006, the Harper government indicated it would essentially continue this approach of using law to put limits on emissions from different industrial sectors, rather than using broader and perhaps more efficient instruments such as a cap-and-trade system or carbon tax.

Yet, as of the time of writing, aside from a legal control on coal-fired electricity generation emissions that will come into effect in 2015 (but does not require action until existing machinery reaches the end of its natural life sometime in the 2020s), no such regulations have been put in place. The Harper government has repeatedly promised, and then deferred, regulatory controls on the oil and gas industry. It has taken two actions to regulate products, including mandating increases in the energy-efficiency of motor vehicles, following the lead of the Obama administration, and it has required that gasoline be made up of at least 5 per cent of a renewable source such as ethanol. With respect to spending, the Harper government has transferred funding from technological development of renewable energies to carbon capture and storage (CCS), the primary method Alberta plans to use to reduce its emissions.

In terms of the second role, successive federal governments have failed to take effective action to bring about co-ordinated, effective national policy. As discussed, the Chrétien government did play a lead role in developing national federal–provincial plans in 1995 and 2000 that might have provided the basis for more effective co-ordinated action, even though they did not use effective legal or tax instruments. That government refused, however, to face the central problem of much higher reduction costs in the provinces, such as Alberta, with high emissions per capita. Instead, it created anger and mistrust among the provinces when it ignored the negotiating position decided at a formal federal–provincial meeting immediately before the December 1997 international meeting at Kyoto and instead agreed there to a different target. The federal government then later ignored a united call by all provinces, in October 2002, for a prior meeting of the Prime Minister and provincial premiers to discuss the issue before it ratified the Kyoto Protocol in December of that year. The Martin government did attempt to develop a series of bilateral federal–provincial agreements, but since then the Harper government has made absolutely no effort to develop co-ordinated policy. As discussed above, it has shown no interest in leading the proposed national energy strategy (just as the Harper government has avoided federal–provincial policy development in any other field, and as the Prime Minister has always refused to convene a meeting of First Ministers). The weakness of Canadian federalism (not to mention the perceived constraints of electoral politics) certainly makes that leadership difficult, but not impossible, as discussed in the conclusion.

Provincial Climate Policy

In a 2012 study, the NRTEE found that provincial government climate policies and programs will account for approximately three-quarters of the total emission reduction expected to take place by 2020, "with only about one-quarter being derived from existing federal measures."[14] Some provinces are striking out on bold new paths for emission reduction. As an example, British Columbia has put in place a carbon tax that took effect on 1 July 2008, at the rate of $10 per tonne of carbon dioxide equivalents, payable at the point of sale. This tax then increased by $5 a year to its present level of $30 a tonne. The tax was one of a suite of measures introduced that year by the Liberal government of Premier Gordon Campbell, intended to meet the goal of reducing that province's GHG emissions by 33 per cent relative to 2005 levels by 2020. This policy effort came about because of a commitment by Premier Campbell, who a year or two before had become personally convinced that the problem was real and policy action was required. He may also have been aided in that conviction by the fact that action on climate change represented good politics prior to the 2009 BC election.[15] As it turned out, he was right: Campbell won the 2009 election, despite having introduced the carbon tax; the state of the provincial economy, rather than the tax, ended up being the central issue in the election campaign.[16]

The tax is revenue-neutral, meaning that any revenues it generates are offset by tax reductions elsewhere (an important point in its public support). Since 2008, the carbon tax has generated $3.7 billion in revenues, which have been funnelled into reductions to income tax and other taxes.[17] A 2013 study of the effects of the tax has suggested that it has brought about a 19 per cent reduction in consumption of the fossil fuels subject to the tax, compared to the rest of Canada, without having negative effects on the BC economy.[18] Noting that in 2012 the tax was supported by 64 per cent of BC residents, the study's authors argue it has been an environmental, economic, and political success, showing that pricing carbon at that level is both feasible and effective.[19]

The target set out in the Ontario government's 2007 Action Plan is to reduce emissions in that province to 15 per cent below 1990 levels by 2020. The primary means of achieving this is to eliminate the use of coal to generate electricity, a campaign promise made by the Liberal Party, led at the time by Dalton McGuinty, when it won the 2003 election. Indeed, emissions from coal-fired electricity were completely eliminated by the end of 2014. The Ontario plan is to replace those coal-fired emissions with increased generation of electricity from renewable sources and high-efficiency gas plants. The Ontario Green Energy and Green Economy Act came into force in 2009, providing guaranteed prices for renewable energy from different sources through the mechanism of a feed-in tariff, a tool that has been used in countries such as Germany. The goal was to both achieve environmental ends and boost the Ontario economy through expansion of its renewable energy industry. The policy has resulted in considerable controversy, as local residents resist the nearby siting of wind turbines and as concern has increased over rising electricity prices. In consequence, the scale of the program has been reduced, but so far the Ontario government remains committed to taking effective action. The coal phase-out has been referred to by one environmentalist as "by far the country's most effective climate policy."[20] In 2015, the Ontario government began consultations on a new mechanism to put a price on carbon.

Quebec policy is most notable for being the one successful example of state–province, cross-border collaboration. The Quebec 2013–2020 Climate Change Action Plan, adopted in June 2012, sets the goal of reducing emissions to 25 per cent below 1990 levels by 2020. One way of achieving that is participation in the California-led Western Climate Initiative (WCI) cap-and-trade program. In January 2012, the Quebec legislature enacted a cap-and-trade law, which came into effect in 2013. As of January 2014, that program has been integrated with the California trading system, and Quebec electricity generators and manufacturing industries are buying and selling emission allowances in one Quebec–California market.[21]

In Nova Scotia, the government has set an absolute cap on emissions from Nova Scotia Power, requiring by law that they decline from 10.2 Mts in 2009 to 4.5 Mts by 2030. The law also requires that 25 per cent of electricity be generated from renewable sources by 2015 and 40 per cent by 2020. As a result, the portion of electricity generated by coal has declined from 80 per cent in 2006 to 59 per cent in 2012, with a corresponding increase in renewable sources, supported by a community-based feed-in tariff system.[22] The province is also working actively to promote energy conservation.

Alberta in 2002 was the first province to enact climate change legislation (motivated by a desire to ward off any threat of the federal government itself regulating Alberta sources).[23] As of 1 July 2007, sources emitting more than 100,000 tonnes per year were required to reduce their GHG intensity (ratio of emissions to production) by 12 per cent. They can do that by increased efficiency, buying offsets, or contributing $15 per tonne to a special fund. This has resulted in a reduction of 20 Mts, with another 20 Mts avoided through purchase of offsets. By 2013, $398 million had been paid to the Climate Change and Emissions Management Fund, with $182 million of that used to fund clean energy projects.[24] Alberta is relying heavily on **carbon capture and storage** (CCS) to reduce provincial emissions and has committed funding to date of $1.3 billion, supplemented by federal government spending. The difficulty with this approach is that the cost of CCS is higher than the $15 cost of paying into the clean energy fund—one estimate puts the cost at between $23 and $90 (US).[25] As a result, without significant public subsidy there is no incentive for private sector operations to invest in CCS. Not surprisingly, Alberta emissions are expected to increase significantly over the coming years, cancelling out gains from provincial initiatives such as those discussed above.

Conclusion

At the outset, we asked why Canada has been unable to meet its emission reduction goals. As we have seen, some provinces have begun to take effective action, but unfortunately, those positive contributions to achieving the overall Canadian target are undercut by the failure of the high-emission provinces, in particular Alberta and Saskatchewan, to take comparable action. This problem is compounded by the fact of living next door to the US, with closely intertwined economies. Whether their fears are real or it is a convenient excuse for inaction, Canadian business and governments consistently say that, for competitiveness reasons, Canadian policy must remain harmonized with that of the United States (although apparently not when a US President announces a bold initiative like the 2014 China–US agreement). Efforts by Canadian provinces to harmonize with leading US states such as California have produced few effects. To these two factors we must add a third: the failure of successive federal governments to provide leadership in policy development. That failure has been particularly marked since the Harper government took power in 2006, but previous Liberal governments did little better. That failure takes two forms: first, a failure to develop effective policy using the federal government's own policy instruments such as law or spending; and, more importantly, a failure to address the uneven nature of provincial efforts and the basic factor producing that result, the major disparities in costs of emissions reduction.

Given provincial ownership of resources, the high degree of provincial motivation to resist federal intrusion, and the inevitable electoral consequences of severely alienating any of the large-population provinces, there is little that any federal government, no matter how motivated, can realistically be expected to do by itself. Although it receives most of the blame, the pro-oil industry, pro-economic growth ideological stance of the Harper government, combined with the Prime Minister's notorious personal aversion to acting on the issue, is not the essential problem. It is unrealistic to think that *any* federal government, even one led by Elizabeth May of the Green Party, can solve the problem alone. The provinces simply will not allow it.

What a committed federal government *could* do is to publicly recognize and begin to discuss the problem of differing reduction costs, and the consequent need to find a way of equitably sharing the total cost associated with reaching the overall Canadian emission reduction goal. This wilful refusal to even admit that the problem exists has been the greatest failing of the Chrétien, Martin, and Harper governments. That failing, along with the other factors discussed, explains Canadian policy failure to date. A first step in this recognition would be to acknowledge that any overall Canadian effort, be it to reduce emissions to 17 per cent below the 2005 level or a subsequent post-2020 target, will come primarily from provincial policy rather than from federal policy. Then, the central issue of the distribution of the associated provincial costs must be brought out from the closet, put squarely on the table, and examined under the bright light of open, public dialogue. As discussed, analysis exists of the different costs achieving the current 2020 Canadian target will impose on different provinces, and similar analysis was done throughout the effort from 1990 to 2002 to develop co-ordinated federal–provincial policy. Interviews with policy-makers reveal that throughout the 1990–2002 period they were all very aware of the basic issue associated with each policy option being considered, i.e., "What will it cost my province?"[26] The issue of cost distribution and the closely related question of how fair that distribution is seen to be are always top of mind for policy-makers if they attempt to develop co-ordinated policy, which means there is no harm but, instead, considerable benefit in explicitly addressing it.

Facing a similar problem, the European Union has twice negotiated a **burden-sharing agreement**—once in 1998 and again in 2008—to decide how the overall EU reduction effort will be allocated among member states.[27] Similarly, countries negotiated an agreement on what portion each would provide of the overall reduction effort represented by the 1997 Kyoto Protocol. In both cases, it seemed obvious that such an agreement was needed because the participants were sovereign states. In the absence of any authority above them to tell them what share each would provide, they had to reach common agreement. That was done by using the mechanism of differing reduction targets—those facing higher reduction costs are not required to reduce as much as those with lower costs, making the distribution of overall cost more equitable. Nor yet in Canada today, given the nature of Canadian federalism, is there any higher authority to dictate to provinces how much each will contribute to the overall national effort. However, agreement could be reached by means of federal–provincial intergovernmental relations, using the same mechanism of differing provincial targets (which already exists, in any case).

While it cannot dictate, the federal government could use diplomacy, combined with the carrot of federal spending to assist regions or industrial sectors particularly hard-hit by the reduction effort and the stick of threatened direct federal regulation, to broker a burden-sharing agreement. In 2012, the NRTEE called for this approach: "An equal reduction across all provinces would be neither fair nor effective. Yet, burden-sharing in Canada is a hallmark of our unique brand of federalism and suits this policy challenge well."[28] One example of that "hallmark" was seen with the 1992 collapse of the cod fishery in Newfoundland. One province for environmental reasons was forced to pay a significant cost, but by using the mechanism of federal government spending, that cost was to some extent spread across the entire country. Here, also for environmental reasons, Alberta and Saskatchewan are being asked to pay a higher cost than other provinces. Given their economic prosperity, particularly that of Alberta, giving those provinces federal money does not seem equitable (although there may well be a role for federal spending directly on those affected, such as dislocated workers), but negotiating an agreement based on differing reduction targets does.

Canada does not have to stay in its present quagmire of failed climate change policy. Some provinces have shown that effective action is possible without immediately running up against economic disaster or defeat at the next election. Now we must take the next step and work together as one nation to reach our national emission reduction goals.

Key Terms

burden-sharing agreement

carbon capture and storage

carbon sinks

collective action problem

emissions intensity

per capita emissions

tragedy of the commons

Questions for Review

1. What are the major factors explaining the failure of Canada to achieve its stated GHG emission reduction goals?
2. Why are some provinces doing more than others?
3. Could the federal government simply take responsibility for all Canadian climate change policy, with the provinces taking no action of their own?

4. If not, is it feasible for the federal government to negotiate with the provinces an effective Canadian policy? Is this likely to occur, and, if not, what other course of action do you propose?

Additional Reading

Bakvis, Herman, and Grace Skogstad. "Canadian Federalism: Performance, Effectiveness and Legitimacy." In Bakvis and Skogstad, eds, *Canadian Federalism: Performance, Effectiveness and Legitimacy*. Toronto: Oxford University Press, 2012.

Berman, Tzeporah, with Mark Leiren-Young. *This Crazy Time: Living Our Environmental Challenge*. Toronto: Alfred A. Knopf Canada, 2011.

David Suzuki Foundation. *All Over the Map: A Comparison of Provincial Climate Change Plans*. Vancouver, 2012.

Harrison, Kathryn. "The Path Not Taken: Climate Change Policy in Canada and the United States." *Global Environmental Politics* 7 (2007): 92–117.

Jordan, A., and T. Rayner. "The Evolution of Climate Policy in the European Union: An Historical Overview." In A. Jordan,

D. Huitema, H. van Asselt, T. Rayner, and F. Berkhout, eds, *Climate Change Policy in the European Union: Confronting the Dilemmas of Adaptation and Mitigation?* Cambridge: Cambridge University Press, 2010.

Newell, Peter. *Climate for Change: Non-State Actors and the Global Politics of the Greenhouse*. Cambridge: Cambridge University Press, 2000.

Simpson, Jeffrey, Mark Jaccard, and Nic Rivers. *Hot Air: Meeting Canada's Climate Change Challenge*. Toronto: McClelland & Stewart, 2007.

Weibust, Inger. *Green Leviathan: The Case for a Federal Role in Environmental Policy*. Farnham, UK: Ashgate, 2009.

Winfield, Mark. *Blue-Green Province: The Environment and the Political Economy of Ontario*. Vancouver: University of British Columbia Press, 2012.

Internet Resources

Environment Canada, *National Inventory Report: Greenhouse Gas Sources and Sinks in Canada*, Submission to the UN Framework Convention on Climate Change (2013)
http://www.ec.gc.ca/ges-ghg/default.asp?lang=En&n=83A34A7A-1

Government of Alberta, Environment and Sustainable Development, Alberta and Climate Change
http://esrd.alberta.ca/climate-change/default.aspx

Macdonald, Douglas, et al., *Allocating Canadian Greenhouse Gas Reductions amongst Sources and Provinces: Learning from the European Union, Australia and Germany*, report of an SSHRC-funded research project (2013)
http://www.environment.utoronto.ca/Allocating

GHGReductions2013/docs/AllocatingGHGReductions2013.pdf

National Round Table on the Environment and the Economy, *Reality Check: The State of Climate Progress in Canada* (2012)
http://www.collectionscanada.gc.ca/webarchives2/20130322165455/http:/nrtee-trnee.ca/reality-check-the-state-of-climate-progress-in-canada

Pembina Institute for Climate Change
http://www.pembina.org

United Nations Framework Convention on Climate Change
http://unfccc.int/2860.php

Notes

1. Environment Canada, *National Inventory Report: Greenhouse Gas Sources and Sinks in Canada*, Submission to the UN Framework Convention on Climate Change (Ottawa: Her Majesty the Queen in Right of Canada, 2013), 7.

2. National Round Table on the Environment and the Economy (NRTEE), *Reality Check: The State of Climate Progress in Canada* (Ottawa: NRTEE, 2012); Environment Canada, *National Inventory Report*.

3. Government of Canada, *Canada's Sixth National Report on Climate Change 2014* (Ottawa: Her Majesty the Queen in Right of Canada, 2013), 8.

4. Germanwatch, *The Climate Change Performance Index: Results 2014* (Bonn, Germany: Germanwatch, Nov. 2013), 6.

5. NRTEE, *Reality Check*, 38.

6. Ibid, 36.

7. M.K. Jaccard and Associates Inc., *Exploration of Two Canadian Greenhouse Gas Emissions Targets: 25% below 1990 and 20% below 2006 Levels by 2020*. Final report prepared for the David Suzuki Foundation and the Pembina Institute (Vancouver, 18 Oct. 2009), http://www.pembina.org/pub/1910, p. 12.

8. Douglas Macdonald et al., *Allocating Canadian Greenhouse Gas Reductions amongst Sources and Provinces: Learning from the European Union, Australia and Germany*, report of a SSHRC-funded research project (2013), http://www.environment.utoronto.ca/AllocatingGHGReductions2013/docs/AllocatingGHGReductions2013.pdf.

9. "National Energy Strategy Is All Talk," *Financial Post*, 16 Apr. 2013.

10. Jeffrey Simpson, "Don't Buy the Spin on Our Emissions Cutting," *Globe and Mail*, 7 Feb. 2014.

11. Climate Action Network, "Canada Wins Fossil of the Year Award in Durban," http://climateactionnetwork.ca/?p=26720.

12. Douglas Macdonald and Debora L. VanNijnatten, "Canadian Climate Policy and the North American Influence," in Monica Gattinger and Geoffrey Hale, eds, *Borders and Bridges: Canada's Policy Relations in North America* (Toronto: Oxford University Press, 2010).

13. Robert G. Healey, Debora L. VanNijnatten, and Marcela López-Vallejo, *Environmental Policy in North America: Approaches, Capacity and the Management of Transboundary Issues* (Toronto: University of Toronto Press, 2014), 151.

14. NRTEE, *Reality Check*, 112.

15. Kathryn Harrison, "A Tale of Two Taxes: The Fate of Environmental Tax Reform in Canada and the Province of British Columbia," presentation at the annual meeting of the American Political Science Association, Toronto, Sept. 2009.

16. Ibid.

17. Government of Canada, *Canada's Sixth National*, 72.

18. Stewart Elgie and Jessica McClay, "BC's Carbon Tax Shift after Five Years: Results" (Ottawa: Sustainable Prosperity, 2013), http://www.sustainableprosperity.ca/dl1026&display.

19. Ibid.

20. P.J. Partington blog, Pembina Institute, "More Trouble with 2030," 15 Jan. 2014, http://www.pembina.org/blog/776.

21. Mark Purdon, David Houle, and Erick Lachapelle, "The Political Economy of California and Québec's Cap-and-Trade Systems," *Sustainable Prosperity Research Report* (2014), http://www.sustainableprosperity.ca/dl1174&display.

22. Anders Hayden, "Ecological Modernization in a 'Have-Not,' Coal-Powered, Energy-Insecure Province: Nova Scotia's Promotion of Green Energy and Carbon Reduction," unpublished paper, Nova Scotia, 2012; "Greenhouse Gas Emissions from the Electricity Sector: Canada and Nova Scotia Draft Equivalency Agreement," Backgrounder (Halifax: Government of Nova Scotia), accessed 28 May 2013, http://www.gov.ns.ca/nse/climate-change/docs/Equivalency-Agreement-Backgrounder.pdf.

23. Douglas Macdonald, "The Influence of Federalism upon Quebec and Alberta Climate-Change Policy," paper delivered at the annual meeting of the Société québécoise de science politique, Université Laval, 20–1 May 2010.

24. Government of Canada, *Canada's Sixth National Report*.

25. Global CCS Institute, "The Costs of CCS and Other Low-Carbon Technologies," 2 Nov. 2011, http://www.globalccsinstitute.com/publications/costs-ccs-and-other-low-carbon-technologies.

26. Macdonald et al., *Allocating Canadian Greenhouse Gas Reductions*.

27. Andrew Jordan and Tim Rayner, "The Evolution of Climate Policy in the European Union: An Historical Overview," in Andrew Jordan, Dave Huitema, Harro van Asselt, Tim Rayner, and Frans Berkhout, eds, *Climate Change Policy in the European Union: Confronting the Dilemmas of Adaptation and Mitigation?* (Cambridge: Cambridge University Press, 2010).

28. NRTEE, *Reality Check*, 117.

14 Renewable Electricity: Provincial Perspectives and National Prospects

Ian H. Rowlands

Chapter Summary

The present means of generating electricity are, for the most part, unsustainable. Consequently, changes—including increased use of renewable resources like wind, solar, and water—are required. To encourage this, a variety of policies can be put in place. Price-based measures offer subsidies for capacity expansion or payments for energy generation. Quantity-based measures reserve parts of the market for renewable resources. While indirect measures focus on other issues—for instance, climate change mitigation—they nevertheless have positive impacts on renewable resource use. Policies vary across Canada: some jurisdictions have adopted a broad portfolio of measures; others have largely restricted their actions to the articulation of ambitions. In many parts of the country, debates continue about the scale and distribution of costs and benefits of supporting renewable electricity. A holistic consideration of the full impacts that stretches across both space and time could well serve to encourage the further development and deployment of renewable resources in electricity systems in years to come.

Chapter Outline

- Increased use of renewable resources in electricity systems can serve to advance sustainability.
- Constitutionally in Canada, provinces have primary jurisdiction over electricity systems, and they have developed markedly different systems, using different resources to different extents.
- Governments can encourage the uptake of renewable resources in electricity supply, often by means of so-called price-based measures (using financial incentives) or quantity-based measures (reserving parts of the broader market for renewables).
- Canadian provinces have adopted different kinds of policies to encourage increased use of renewable resources in electricity systems, and they have deployed them to different extents.

- The associated benefits and costs of more renewable resources in electricity systems have been discussed and debated.
- Ambivalence and austerity have been influential in the policy and politics of this issue to date; that will probably continue into the future.

Introduction

While access to electricity services in Canada has been critical to improving the national standard of living, it is nevertheless also accepted that the traditional arrangement of electricity systems—large, centralized power plants fuelled by fossil fuels, uranium, or large-scale dams—is not sustainable. It has led to a variety of environmental and social problems; air pollution at various scales (smog, acid precipitation, and global climate change), waste management challenges, and community disruption are but some examples.[1] In response, the increased use of renewable resources (for example, solar and wind) is often presented as an integral component of a sustainable energy strategy.[2] Indeed, ongoing work by the Intergovernmental Panel on Climate Change highlights that this issue is critical: the identified "transformation pathways"—that is, the means to decarbonize our energy supply systems—make great use of renewable electricity.[3]

The purpose of this chapter is to examine Canadian policies to promote the increased use of **renewable resources** in electricity systems. After briefly setting the scene by describing electricity systems, reviewing the structure of electricity systems in Canada, and highlighting the role of renewable resources therein, the range of conceivable policy options is presented. Strategies to promote the increased use of renewable resources have, to varying degrees, relied on price-based measures, quantity-based measures, or indirect measures. Attention then turns to experiences, achievements, and issues across Canada, examined on a jurisdiction-by-jurisdiction basis. After this sequential review, issues that arise from a cross-provincial/territorial analysis are examined. The differences and similarities lead to an investigation of the ways in which ambivalence and austerity have impacted policy and politics across Canada. This, in turn, launches a final discussion investigating the prospects for renewable electricity policies across the country. The ambivalence surrounding renewable electricity is noted; not only do different constituencies within a single community hold different views about renewable electricity (some supporting, others opposing), there are even instances in which individuals finds themselves acting alternatively as "concerned citizens" (voicing support) and as "cost-conscious consumers" (articulating opposition). The impact of austerity is also highlighted: the costs of transformational energy options (like renewable electricity) often attract scrutiny and disdain; those options that do "more of the same," regardless of their cost, seem to have an easier time. Ways in which a broader understanding of the issue could allow both ambivalence and austerity to promote renewable electricity as part of a sustainable energy future are investigated.

Setting the Scene

Electricity services are central to human life in Canada today, and have been for well over a century. In our homes, many appliances, entertainment devices, and heating/cooling systems are powered by electricity. In our offices, lighting and HVAC (heating, ventilation, and air conditioning) systems are major consumers of electricity. In our factories, motors, in particular, are central to the sector's electricity demand profile. Collectively, these and other services are critical to our social and economic well-being.[4]

To meet these various electricity service demands, Canada's electricity supply structures have arisen (largely) along provincial/territorial lines. Encouraged by a Constitution that assigns individual provinces the responsibility for the "development, conservation and management of sites and facilities in the province for the generation and production of electrical energy" (Constitution Act, 1867, s. 92A[1c]), these subnational governments have traditionally worked to develop secure, reliable, and economical means of supplying electricity to homes and workplaces and, as appropriate, to export markets as well. This should not be taken to mean that there is no role—past, present, or future—for the Canadian federal government. A national energy strategy, something that has been viewed as taboo by many for more than three decades, could help encourage a more sustainable future, and this point is pursued towards the end of this chapter.[5] For now, only a few largely isolated actions—like the regulations aiming to reduce greenhouse gas emissions from coal-fired electricity—have any kind of impact (and that impact is, as described below, "indirect").[6]

At the national level, 2011 figures from the International Energy Agency reveal that almost 59 per cent of the electricity produced in Canada was from hydropower facilities (the vast majority of them of the "large-scale" variety); nuclear energy provided almost 15 per cent, coal almost 12 per cent, and natural gas just under 10 per cent. Other resources—including a variety of other renewable resources—played a relatively modest role: biofuels at 1.7 per cent, wind at 1.6 per cent, and oil at just over 1 per cent. No other resource contributed more than one-quarter of 1 per cent of Canada's electricity.[7] There are, however, significant differences across provinces and territories. Hydropower dominates some jurisdictions, while others have a more balanced supply portfolio. Table 14.1 provides additional details.

TABLE 14.1 Total Electricity Generation in Canada by Province/Territory and Type (TWh), 2012

Province or Territory	Hydro	Nuclear	Conventional Steam	Internal Combustion	Combustion Turbine	Tidal	Wind	Solar
British Columbia	63.9		4.4	0.1	1.1			
Alberta	2.6		45.8	0.1	14.7		3	
Saskatchewan	4.2		16.4	~0	0.5		0.8	
Manitoba	32.1	0.1	0.1	~0	~0		0.4	
Ontario	33.8	86.8	8.5	0.1	9.0		2.6	0.3
Quebec	193.7	3.9	1.0	0.3	0.1		0.7	
New Brunswick	2.83	0.3	4.21	~0	1.7		0.6	
Nova Scotia	0.83		8.18		5.84	~0.03	0.44	
Prince Edward Island			~0.01	~0	~0		0.15	
Newfoundland and Labrador	41.7		0.86	0.05	0.25		0.1	
Yukon	0.4			~0			~0	
Northwest Territories	0.3			0.4	~0		~0	
Nunavut				0.2				

Source: Canadian Electricity Association, "Key Electricity Statistics (release May 21, 2013)," at: http://www.electricity.ca/media/IndustryData/KeyCanadianElectricityStatistics21May2013.pdf.

TABLE 14.2 Provinces'/Territories' Installed Capacity (MW), Wind Power, January 2013

Province or Territory	Installed Capacity (MW)
Ontario	2,470.5
Quebec	2,398.3
Alberta	1,120.3
British Columbia	488.7
Nova Scotia	335.8
New Brunswick	294.0
Manitoba	258.4
Saskatchewan	198.4
Prince Edward Island	173.6
Newfoundland and Labrador	54.7
Northwest Territories	9.2
Yukon	0.8

Source: Canadian Wind Energy Association, "Powering Canada's Future, January 2013," at: http://www.canwea.ca/pdf/Canada%20Current%20Installed%20Capacity_e.pdf.

Depending on how "renewable" is defined (and this definition is often contested),[8] Canada can be considered to already have significant renewable resources in its supply portfolio. However, if the category is restricted to the so-called "new renewables"—often defined in terms of low-impact renewable resources, such as solar, wind, small hydro, and biomass[9]— then the contribution to the supply portfolio across Canada is much more modest. In addition to the hydropower noted above (though recognizing that only a small portion of that would be included in this "new" category), a similar observation could be made about the aforementioned biomass category; only some of it is generated in a sustainable manner. Further to these observations, and continuing to use the same data as referenced above, solar photovoltaics supplied approximately 0.04 per cent of Canadian electricity production in 2011, waste approximately 0.03 per cent, and tidal-generated power approximately 0.004 per cent.[10] With wind being the most significant of these new renewables, it is worth noting here (as shown in Table 14.2) the distribution of installed capacity across the country. Further information about different provinces' respective wind power portfolios is presented later in this chapter.

Government Policies to Promote Increased Use of Renewable Electricity

To attempt to increase the use of renewable resources in electricity systems, governments around the world have deployed a variety of strategies. Most can be categorized into one of two types: price-based measures or quantity-based measures.[11]

Price-based measures provide financial support to renewable electricity generators, which may involve a subsidy payment for every kW of capacity installed or a performance payment for every kWh of electricity generated. A feed-in tariff (FIT) is the most widely known of the price-based measures. In its most basic form, a FIT involves a payment (usually at a premium to the market price for conventional electricity) to renewable electricity facilities for every unit of electricity generated, guaranteed for a number of years by a contract between the generator and some public and/or utility authority. Payment levels may be differentiated by technology, or even by facility location. Feed-in tariffs have been widely credited with spurring the original development of Denmark's wind industry and Germany's development of its world-class renewable electricity industries.[12]

Quantity-based measures consist of a government-declared goal for a desired level of renewable electricity in the electricity system, perhaps in the form of a share of the overall system total or an absolute amount (either of which, in turn, may be technology specific). A **renewable portfolio standard** (RPS) is the most widely known of the quantity-based measures. An RPS reserves a portion of the broader electricity market for renewable resources by obliging market participants to ensure that a predetermined share of their total electricity supply is provided by qualifying facilities. This predetermined share may gradually "ramp up" over time. Fulfillment of this obligation on the part of all electricity generators within the market may be facilitated by the use of some kind of **tradable renewable energy certificates**. Renewable portfolio standards have been popular in promoting renewable electricity development in a number of states in the United States;[13] Texas, for example, is an oft-cited success story.[14]

Put most succinctly, price-based measures fix the subsidy or payment, and then the level of interest on the part of potential participants determines how much renewable electricity is deployed. Alternatively, quantity-based measures identify the amount of renewable electrical capacity built and/or electricity generated, and it is left to the market players to determine the cost of the same.

Other measures also exist. Sometimes called "indirect support instruments," these may include environmental taxes or voluntary agreements (taken on board by non-governmental actors).[15] Many climate change strategies, for instance, have consequences for renewable electricity levels, and they are included in what will be called "indirect measures" in this chapter.[16] Collectively, then, these represent the primary means of encouraging the increased use of renewable resources in any jurisdiction's electricity system. Attention now turns to Canada, to explore recent history on this topic.

Provincial Policies in Canada
British Columbia

British Columbia—a province already using vast amounts of renewable resources to power its electricity system (see Table 14.1)—has the continued, and even increased, use of hydropower and other "clean or renewable resources" as a central goal of its energy objectives. As outlined in its 2010 Clean Energy Act, at least 93 per cent of its electricity is to be generated in this way[17]—an increase from the 90 per cent share that had been part of the 2007 BC Energy Plan.[18] Noteworthy, as well, in the 2010 Act are the links between energy goals and other societal goals, particularly the importance of ensuring that renewable electricity also serves to encourage economic development and that, through its net export, it contributes to reducing greenhouse gas emissions in neighbouring jurisdictions.

To push its renewable electricity goals, British Columbia has largely relied on a quantity-based measure—more specifically, a renewable portfolio standard (RPS). In

British Columbia parlance, it is usually referred to as a "clean power call," and a process of soliciting, evaluating, and selecting renewable electricity projects has been carried out twice: once between 2005 and 2006, and again between 2006 and 2010. In all, more than 60 projects were selected across the two calls, the vast majority of which (49) were hydropower (mainly run-of-river); other projects included nine wind, three waste heat, two biomass, and two coal/biomass. Together, they represented more than 10,000 GWh of electricity annually.[19] To put this into perspective, this represents more than 10 per cent of the province's 2012 electricity generation.

British Columbia has also used the RPS strategy to develop biomass-based renewable electricity projects. A similar sequence of events—solicitation, evaluation, and selection—was carried out twice: the first phase (2008–9) resulted in four projects being selected, which will generate 579 GWh of electricity a year;[20] the second phase (2010–11) also chose four projects, with a cumulative commitment to generate 754 GWh annually.[21] Smaller community-based calls (also biomass-based) yielded contracts for just under 85 GWh annually (from five projects).[22]

Interestingly, the province has also pursued, to a more modest extent, a price-based measure (more specifically, a feed-in tariff). The Standing Offer Program (again, the particular local terminology used to refer to the measure) was first introduced in 2008 to encourage small, clean electricity projects; it was reviewed in 2009–10 and relaunched in 2011. By offering set payments for electricity generation, it is designed to encourage projects rated between 50 kW and 15 MW.[23] By April 2014, uptake had been modest, with 61 MW of projects offered electricity purchase agreements and another 77 MW under review.[24]

Finally, the 2013 Integrated Resource Plan—prepared by BC Hydro and approved by the provincial government—points to at least a couple of renewable electricity issues that will likely become important during the coming years.[25] First, with significant development of **shale gas** fields in the northeastern part of the province, the extent to which this energy-intensive project will be powered by renewable electricity—something that proponents are demanding—remains unclear.[26] And, second, the sheer scale of the proposal to build "Site C"—a hydropower dam on the Peace River in northeast BC—will inevitably attract attention. Potentially operable in 2024, this facility could generate 5,100 GWh of electricity annually from an installed capacity of 1,100 MW.[27]

Alberta, Saskatchewan, and Manitoba

While Canada's Prairie provinces may share a common geography, they have significantly different energy-related resource endowments (see Table 14.1). These differences, among other factors, have led to varying levels of interest in and strategies for renewable electricity development in Alberta, Saskatchewan, and Manitoba.

Alberta established a voluntary renewable electricity target soon after its power market opened to competition on 1 January 2001. In its 2002 climate change plan, the government expected the "renewable and alternative energy portion of the province's total electricity capacity to grow by 3.5 per cent by 2008."[28] That target—interpreted as a movement to a 5.5 per cent share (from its then 2 per cent share)—was achieved. The publication of both a Provincial Energy Strategy[29] and a Climate Change Strategy[30] in 2008 contributed to keeping discussions about increased use of renewable resources in the electricity system active, though neither trumpeted any particular target or financial support; instead, it was left to other forces to spur the sector to change.

For one, Alberta's Greenhouse Gas Reduction Program, which requires facilities that emit more than 100,000 tonnes of greenhouse gases a year to reduce emissions intensity by 12 per cent, as of 1 July 2007, encourages the adoption of renewable resources in electricity systems.[31] Following the categories laid out earlier in this chapter, this is largely an example of an indirect measure. Facilities unable to comply with this requirement can either purchase offsets or pay $15/tonne of carbon dioxide emissions into a technology fund administered by the Climate Change and Emissions Management Corporation (CCEMC). The CCEMC grants funds to research and projects that reduce emissions, and several renewable electricity projects have made successful bids for this funding.[32]

The province also has a price-based measure in place: through its Bioenergy Producer Credit Program, per-kWh payments are made.[33] In addition, the provincial government has purchased 100 per cent green electricity for all government-owned buildings connected to the provincial grid.[34] Also, municipal levels of government have taken action. For instance, the city of Calgary has declared that, by 2036, 30 per cent of the city's energy will be derived from low-impact renewable sources.[35]

As of the beginning of 2014, however, Alberta appeared to be at something of a crossroads regarding renewable electricity issues. A new associate minister, with explicit responsibilities for "electricity and renewable energy," had been appointed in late 2013, and a process to develop an "Alternative and Renewable Energy Policy Framework" was expected to get underway soon.[36]

Saskatchewan has pursued renewable electricity along two paths.[37] Aiming to utilize its extensive wind potential—and to meet its stated goal of ensuring that, by 2017, 9 per cent of its total generating capacity is wind[38]—the provincial utility, SaskPower, has adopted quantity-based measures, issuing a variety of RfPs ("requests for proposals"). In April 2013, it was reported that: "Some 198 MW of wind capacity is currently operational and a further 177 MW is to be procured and commissioned by 2017."[39]

Saskatchewan also took an initiative with a price-based measure, but subsequently appeared to back away from the program. With its "Green Options Partners Program" introduced in 2010, which was somewhat akin to a feed-in tariff, smaller producers were invited to participate in an annual lottery. If selected, they were subsequently screened to ensure that they met a variety of economic and technical obligations. If so, they would then be paid a fixed price by SaskPower for the electricity they produced; moreover, the contract would last 20 years (or up to 40 years for some low-impact hydropower projects). The program generated relatively little interest, however, and was suspended in 2012.[40]

Completing our journey across the Prairies, Manitoba is one of the least-engaged places in the country with respect to non-hydro renewable electricity. While a commitment to develop 1,000 MW of wind power capacity is "on the books"—as articulated in 2004[41]—there has been relatively little activity to pursue it (as Table 14.2 reveals, the province is approximately one-quarter of the way towards that goal). Instead, the province's vast hydropower resources are the focus of electricity discussions. A new joint project between Manitoba Hydro and four Manitoba First Nations has begun at Keeyask on the Nelson River; study and planning for another and larger project, at Conawapa on the lower Nelson, was suspended by Manitoba Hydro in August 2014.[42]

Ontario

Canada's most populous province has also been the most active in terms of renewable electricity promotion. Ontario has run the entire gamut of major approaches to policy.[43]

The publication of a report by an Advisory Committee on Competition in Ontario's Electricity System in 1996 marked the beginning of a period of specialized discussion on the issue. At the beginning of the 2000s, as parts of the electricity market were opened to increased competition, alternative providers could offer products to customers. Accordingly, the prevailing sentiment was that if people want renewable electricity, they can demand it, and providers will step up and offer it. Notwithstanding some apparent interest, as evidenced by survey responses, uptake was relatively modest (not least because these offerings were at a premium price).[44]

A confluence of events, however, served to change the government's position in 2003. Towards what turned out to be near the end of Premier Ernie Eves's brief term in office, the Progressive Conservatives came to support a quantity-based measure—their particular terminology for this was a "Green Power Standard." Announced in June 2003, the Standard never had the chance to be introduced, however, as the Liberal Party was victorious at the polls in the October 2003 provincial election.[45]

The newly elected Liberal government soon introduced its own quantity-based measure. Following a "Request for Proposals" approach, a series of calls served to generate significant responses and activity, particularly in terms of wind power, and contracts for 1,370 MW of capacity were signed during 2004 and 2005. Soon into the Liberals' first term of office, however, a confluence of events caused the government to rethink its strategy for promoting renewable electricity and thus opened the door for an alternative policy in Ontario.[46]

Between 2005 and 2010, much of the discussion around the promotion of renewable electricity turned to price-based measures: a so-called "Renewable Energy Standard Offer Program" was followed by a "Feed-in Tariff Program," which was part of the larger 2008 Green Energy and Green Economy Act. With generous 20-year contracts guaranteeing payment for every kWh of renewable electricity generated, the programs attracted significant attention. By the time the first program was paused for a scheduled review, more than 27,000 contracts had been offered (from more than 50,000 applications), collectively representing approximately 5,000 MW of renewable electricity capacity.[47] On a larger scale, the Niagara Tunnel Project, begun in 2006 and completed in 2013, created a 10.2-kilometre tunnel with a diameter of 12.7 metres through the bedrock beneath the city of Niagara Falls to divert additional waters from the Niagara River to the Sir Adam Beck Generating Stations.

Public debate about the programs and the renewable electricity facilities they brought about were prominent in Ontario during the lead-up to the 2011 election (in which the Liberal Party retained its position as governing party, but lost its majority) and beyond.[48] Critics noted, in particular, the high costs to the ratepayer and the minimal input into decision-making of those community members who would live and work near the renewable energy projects.[49] Numerous concerns, for example, were expressed regarding the negative health impacts for those living in proximity to wind farms. To attempt to address such challenges the revised version of the Feed-in Tariff Program that emerged in 2012 called for additional incentives to engage communities and First Nations, program participation caps, and a commitment to review, annually, the prices paid for the renewable electricity generated.[50]

Finally, in an intriguing turn, quantity-based measures—in the form of RfPs for large-scale renewable electricity—have returned to Ontario. The Ontario Power Authority had, at the beginning of 2014, responded to a directive from the Minister of Energy and started a process of consultation designed to result in the selection and deployment of projects generally over 500 kW.[51]

Quebec

In Quebec, activity regarding renewable electricity (apart from the dominance of hydropower, as shown in Table 14.1 and discussed below) largely concerns wind.[52] Between 2003 and 2008 the province's dominant utility—Hydro-Québec—initiated and executed two quantity-based measures ("calls for tenders"). Together, they resulted in the signing of contracts totalling approximately 3,000 MW of wind power capacity. Of note in these contracts was the requirement to have a particular share of the project contain "local and/or Quebec content." Another call was initiated in 2009: totalling 500 MW, it aimed specifically to increase community-based and/or First Nations involvement. Success at securing the engagement of such involvement was modest, with only one 25 MW project being awarded to a First Nations proponent from the potential pool of 250 MW. In 2013, Hydro-Québec issued another call, seeking 800 MW of wind energy capacity. Again, local and/or Quebec content was a key requirement, as was community involvement: local communities (which potentially may include a regional county municipality, a local municipality, a First Nation, an inter-municipal board, or a co-operative) will be required to hold an interest representing at least 50 per cent of the control in each of the projects.[53]

Notwithstanding this wind activity, hydropower remains the predominant source of renewable electricity in the province and it continues to grow. The Romaine complex, in the Côte-Nord region of the province, will be commissioned between 2014 and 2020. During that time, more than 1,500 MW of hydropower capacity will be added to Quebec's system, contributing 8,000 GWh annually. (For sake of comparison, that is equivalent to more than 4 per cent of the province's annual generation.) Other such projects across the province are in various stages of development.[54] Finally, the process to produce a new energy strategy for the province, to cover the years 2016–25, is expected to begin during 2014.[55]

Atlantic Provinces

Among Canada's four Atlantic provinces, Nova Scotia and New Brunswick stand out as having paid the greatest policy attention to renewable electricity.

Nova Scotia's interest in policy measures, especially in quantity-based measures, is relatively long-standing, dating back to at least 2001.[56] This interest took more tangible form in 2004, when the government's new Electricity Act embodied, in law, what was being called a "renewable energy standard"; this Act also set the stage for the details to be laid out in subsequent regulations.[57] Those regulations were forthcoming in early 2007, at which time it was mandated that, by 2010, renewable electricity levels be 5 per cent above what was present in 2001 (the identified base year), and 10 per cent above by 2013.[58] Ambitions increased with the ability to use at least some of the hydropower from Newfoundland and Labrador's Lower Churchill Falls (to be transmitted by means of a new subsea Maritime Link between the two provinces), which is planned to be on stream in 2017. More specifically, the province's 2010 Renewable Electricity Plan established targets of 18.5 per cent by 2013, 25 per cent by 2015, and 40 per cent by 2020.[59] While larger projects would have many of the characteristics found in quantity-based measures, smaller projects could be stimulated by price-based measures.

Nova Scotia has a community-based feed-in tariff (COMFIT). This applies to relatively small projects (usually under 6 MW) that are community-owned. Conceived in the 2010 Renewable Electricity Plan, the first projects were launched in 2013 with the commissioning of six 50 kW turbines.[60] Tidal power has also received attention, with its own developmental feed-in tariff being launched.[61]

New Brunswick also has a quantity-based measure to promote renewable electricity. And discussions around its version also date back many years, at least back to a 1998 discussion paper.[62] Eight years later, the Electricity from Renewable Resources Regulation—Electricity Act obliged "standard service suppliers" to ensure that, in 2007, at least 1 per cent of their electricity was sourced from "new" (post-2001) renewable electricity generators. This obligation would ramp up by 1 per cent a year until it reached 10 per cent in 2016 (and beyond).[63] Beyond that, the government is committed to a policy to increase the RPS to 40 per cent by 2020.[64] To do this, NB Power is procuring 300 MW of new wind power resources.

In 2004, Prince Edward Island developed and implemented its Renewable Energy Act. In this, the province committed to a quantity-based measure to generate 15 per cent of its electricity from renewable resources by 2010. With development of the island's wind resources by the PEI Energy Corporation, that target was met early. Consequently, in 2008, a new target—30 per cent by 2013—was introduced.[65] Debates continue about what happens next, including discussion about the potential for price-based measures.[66]

Newfoundland and Labrador's approach follows, in many ways, that of Manitoba, a similarly hydropower-dominated jurisdiction in Canada. Indeed, Newfoundland and Labrador's level of activity may be considered even lower than that of Manitoba. There are no stated targets, but instead a public desire to continue to develop renewable resources, particularly given the contributions that can be made in isolated areas for lessening the dependence on diesel.[67]

Territories

Moving from west to east across Canada's North, the three territories have adopted strategies to promote renewable electricity. In Yukon's 2009 Energy Strategy, there is a commitment to increase the supply and use of renewable resources in the energy system as a whole—to 20 per cent by 2020. An intention also has been expressed to develop a policy framework that will encourage more renewable electricity.[68]

In 2013 the Northwest Territories released its Energy Action Plan in conjunction with the Northwest Territories Energy Corporation's NWT Power System Plan. In it, the desire for more renewable resources, including hydropower, solar, and wind, to contribute to its electricity portfolio is identified. The ways in which an extended and strengthened power grid could support this, and other, goals are also noted.[69]

Finally, Nunavut is implementing Ikummatiit, which is an energy strategy focused on alternative energy sources and efficient use of energy. With respect to the former, increased use of hydropower is the stated priority.[70]

Reflection and Prospects

As discussions about the increased use of renewable resources in electricity supply have continued to unfold across Canada during the past few years, consideration of the associated benefits has often been central. Environmental improvement and increased resilience are two sets of positives that have been identified, and will undoubtedly continue to be identified in the future.

When renewable electricity displaces dirty forms of power generation, there are improvements in local air quality and reductions in greenhouse gas emissions. Accordingly, a number of provinces have seen this as a key part of their broader environmental strategy or as part of their specific climate change strategy. Alberta's climate change strategy, for instance, consists of three areas of focus, with one being "greening energy production."[71] Of course, efforts to "firm up" the delivery of renewable electricity—that is, have it readily available on demand (e.g., hydropower or storage)—would ensure that these green benefits cannot be eroded by the need for natural gas-powered backup generation.[72]

An electricity supply system using more renewable resources (which are, by definition, locally available) decreases reliance on others for the supply of commodities (i.e., particular fuels) and has the potential to generate more economic activity locally (e.g., the installation and maintenance of renewable electricity facilities). In Quebec, for instance, one analyst observes that "Quebec's interest in renewable power development appears to be largely driven by an interest in sustaining manufacturing and local economic development."[73] Beyond the case of Quebec, when such activities are also accompanied by movement towards a more distributed electricity system, communities' resilience, more broadly, may well increase.[74]

Notwithstanding these oft-identified benefits, a number of drawbacks have arisen alongside efforts to increase the use of renewable resources in electricity systems. These have attracted considerable attention in Canada during the past few years across local, provincial, and international levels.

Locally, a number of communities have opposed the development of renewable electricity projects within their jurisdictions—particularly with respect to wind farms. Ontario, as noted earlier, has seen the most vocal and the most organized opposition in this manner. While anti-wind forces in that province were active before the introduction of the Green Energy and Green Economy Act in 2009, passage of that legislation served to foster further opposition.

Anticipating **NIMBY**-type reactions, with local communities declaring that while they supported renewable electricity in principle they did not want it "in their back yard," the Ontario government created a new "Renewable Energy Approvals" process that, among other things, removed the power of municipalities over wind turbine siting.[75] This allowed for the flurry of wind power development in Ontario described above. Many municipalities felt helpless, and citizen groups continued to protest wind turbine planning and operation.[76] In response, Ontario has required more local engagement and support before new renewable electricity developments can proceed.[77]

Within provinces, debates about the cost of renewable electricity projects have grown in scope and intensity. While many may remind us that once the "true costs" of conventional forms of electricity generation are calculated (for example, once the full costs of additional health care required as a result of pollution caused by coal-fired power plants have been calculated), the cost of renewable electricity does not seem particularly high. For the most part, however, our current economic system does not account for such costs; instead, politicians, who sooner or later have to face voters, focus on the immediate impact on the wallet. We see this in many provinces. In Nova Scotia, for instance, solar-photovoltaics (PV) was not part of the province's community feed-in tariff because it was deemed to be too costly to support (and would divert solar energy from the task of heating water and/or air, which was deemed to be preferable).[78]

Finally, there has been push-back from the international system, that is, actors located outside of Canada. Thus, after Ontario included domestic content requirements in its feed-in tariff—that is, at least a certain percentage of the components in a renewable energy facility had to have been made in Ontario—Japan challenged this obligation through the World Trade Organization (WTO). The countries' differences could not be resolved through informal mechanisms or by means of other good offices offered by the WTO; consequently, it became a formal case within the WTO's dispute settlement mechanism procedure. A panel was struck, and it found that WTO rules had been breached; in response, the Ontario government agreed to amend its program of support for renewable electricity.[79]

Recent experience regarding renewable electricity across Canada's provinces would seem, on balance, to reinforce the themes of ambivalence and austerity that are central to this volume.

With respect to ambivalence, a love-hate relationship with renewable electricity continues in many parts of Canada; the various positives and negatives identified earlier in this section attest to this. Moreover, following this volume's focus on politics and policy, it is important to note that we can often see such conflicting positions towards renewables reflected within individual governments and within individual communities. Government bureaucracies can see this file in many ways. Finance departments may see it as a potential drain on public funds, while environment departments may see it as a means to achieve stated goals. Given the reach of energy issues, moreover, virtually every portfolio will have a stance, some pro and some con. Community members, for their part, see different realities when they are confronted with a wind turbine or a solar-PV array: cottagers may see industrial structures spoiling their views, while community organizers may see employment opportunities for disadvantaged youth. What is clear is that the issue has served to divide communities. Ambivalence can be poisonous.

With respect to austerity, meanwhile, attention to how policies to promote renewable electricity affect governments' spending clearly has increased during the past few years. This trend has already been noted in the discussion above: debate about the cost impact of feed-in tariffs, for instance, is one example; concern about the fiscal consequences of any move forward with renewable resources (irrespective of policy choice) is another. And this echoes broader global trends; the world's leading report on renewable energy noted in 2013 that "[t]he rate of adoption of new policies and targets has remained slow relative to the early to mid-2000s. As the sector has matured, revisions to existing policies have become increasingly common."[80] Interestingly, "big-ticket items" that replicate the currently dominant system of energy supply in the country—for instance, fossil fuel production and transportation—seem to be subject to less economic scrutiny.

Ambivalence and austerity probably will continue to be influential in the future. Proponents of renewable resources—and those who value the goals that would be served (e.g., climate change mitigation and local resilience) by increased support for renewables—would prefer to see the ambivalence reflected not in whether to pursue renewable resources as part of an electricity system strategy going forward, but instead in "how" to do so. They would hope that increasingly vibrant debates about the effectiveness of various strategies, either singly or in combination, would mean that any choices are about which path to follow rather than whether or not to depart for the destination.

Such proponents would also maintain that there is the potential for a continued focus on austerity to similarly promote increased use of renewable resources. More sophisticated consideration of how energy systems sit within societies' broader socio-ecological systems would soon reveal that greater deployment of, for instance, solar-PV panels and wind turbines could well lead to lower net government expenditures (as noted above). In addition, greater interprovincial co-operation on this file—what renewed attention to national energy strategies during the past few years may be foreshadowing—would similarly lead to policies that exploit resource and demand differences across provinces. The potential set of benefits associated with increased Quebec–Ontario co-operation is one example; the development of a western Canada grid is another.[81] Taking this to the continental level, there are opportunities to exploit climatic differences between Canada and the US in the creation of cross-border energy regimes, which could serve to augment positive outcomes even further.[82] Technological advances in energy storage and societal decisions to electrify additional loads, particularly space heating (where not already done) and transportation, could further push interest in this issue. While both ambivalence and austerity present significant challenges to proponents of renewable resources in Canada, they also have the potential to drive a more sustainable future in Canada.

Summary

The purpose of this chapter has been to review the means whereby provinces have attempted to promote the use of renewable resources in their respective electricity systems. This review has revealed that a number of different strategies are in operation across Canada, with many of them using either price-based measures, quantity-based measures, or indirect measures. The perceived benefits and drawbacks that have occupied the politics and policy of renewable electricity in Canada were then investigated. Ambivalence accurately characterizes how these various traits have been viewed. Similarly, austerity has been a critical influence on politics and policy. Looking forward, however, a broader perspective on the issue could lead to greater support for renewable electricity in Canada. This perspective must recognize the long timelines that should be used for assessment, consider diverse potential partners across interprovincial and international borders, identify multiple contributors to calculations of benefits, and anticipate additional electricity services in the future.

Acknowledgements

The author would like to thank George Hoberg, Maya Jegen, and Tim Weis for comments on an earlier draft of this chapter. The author, however, is fully responsible for the contents.

Key Terms

NIMBY

renewable portfolio standard

renewable resources

shale gas

tradable renewable energy certificates

Questions for Review

1. Which electricity services are important in your life?
2. What kinds of environmental/sustainability problems are associated with different parts of different electricity systems?
3. From various perspectives, what are the advantages and disadvantages of, respectively, price-based measures and quantity-based measures?
4. Why have the provinces and territories varied in their commitments to renewable electricity, as well as in their strategies for encouraging renewable electricity?
5. How could a new Canadian energy strategy serve to support—or, alternatively, to inhibit—renewable electricity?
6. To what extent, and in what ways, will ambivalence and austerity continue to influence the development of renewable electricity in Canada?

Internet Resources

Canadian Electricity Association, "We Are the Electricity Industry in Canada"
http://www.electricity.ca/

Canadian Wind Energy Association
http://www.canwea.ca/index_e.php

International Energy Agency and International Renewable Energy Agency, "IEA/IRENA Joint Policies and Measures Database"
http://www.iea.org/policiesandmeasures/renewableenergy/

National Energy Board, "Energy Report"
http://www.neb-one.gc.ca/clf-nsi/rnrgynfmtn/nrgyrprt/nrgyrprt-eng.html

Natural Resources Canada, "Comprehensive Energy Use Database, 1990 to 2011"
http://oee.nrcan.gc.ca/corporate/statistics/neud/dpa/menus/trends/comprehensive_tables/list.cfm

US Energy Information Administration
http://www.eia.gov/

Additional Reading

Boyle, Godfrey, ed. *Renewable Energy: Power for a Sustainable Future*, 3rd edn. Toronto: Oxford University Press, 2012.

Edenhofer, Ottmar, et al., eds. *IPCC Special Report on Renewable Energy Sources and Climate Change Mitigation*. New York: Cambridge University Press, 2011.

Gattinger, Monica. "A National Energy Strategy for Canada: Golden Age or Golden Cage of Energy Federalism?" In Loleen Berdahl, André Juneau, and Carolyn Hughes Tuohy, eds, *Canada: The State of the Federation 2012: Regions, Resources, and Resiliency*. Kingston, Ont.: Institute of Intergovernmental Relations, Queen's University, 2015.

GEA. *Global Energy Assessment: Toward a Sustainable Future*. New York: Cambridge University Press, 2012.

MacKay, David J.C. *Sustainable Energy: Without the Hot Air*. Cambridge, UK: UIT Cambridge Ltd, 2008.

Natural Resources Canada. *Energy Efficiency Trends in Canada, 1990–2010*. Ottawa: Office of Energy Efficiency, Mar. 2013.

Pineau, Pierre-Olivier. "Fragmented Markets: Canadian Electricity Sectors' Underperformance." In Fereidoon P. Sioshansi, ed., *Evolution of Global Electricity Markets: New Paradigms, New Challenges, New Approaches*, 363–92. Waltham, Mass.: Academic Press, 2013.

Standing Senate Committee on Energy, the Environment and Natural Resources. *Now or Never: Canada Must Act Urgently to Seize Its Place in the New Energy World Order*. Ottawa: Senate of Canada, July 2012. http://www.parl.gc.ca/Content/SEN/Committee/411/enev/rep/rep04jul12-e.pdf.

Notes

1. See, e.g., José Goldemberg and Thomas B. Johansson, eds, *World Energy Assessment: Overview, 2004 Update* (New York: United Nations, 2004); Lisa Emberson, He Kebin, and Johan Rockström, "Energy and Environment," in GEA, *Global Energy Assessment—Toward a Sustainable Future* (Cambridge: Cambridge University Press, 2012), 191–254.

2. See, e.g., Keywan Riahi, "Energy Pathways for Sustainable Development," in GEA, *Global Energy Assessment—Toward a Sustainable Future* (Cambridge: Cambridge University Press, 2012), 1203–1306.

3. Chapter 6: "Assessing Transformation Pathways," in *Climate Change 2014: Mitigation of Climate Change* (Cambridge: Cambridge University Press, 2014).

4. More information about electricity end-use may be found in Natural Resources Canada, "Comprehensive Energy Use Database, 1990 to 2011," http://oee.nrcan.gc.ca/corporate/statistics/neud/dpa/comprehensive_tables/list.cfm?attr=0.

5. Monica Gattinger, "A National Energy Strategy for Canada: Golden Age or Golden Cage of Energy Federalism?" in Loleen Berdahl, André Juneau, and Carolyn Hughes Tuohy, eds, *Canada: The State of the Federation 2012: Regions, Resources, and Resiliency* (Kingston, Ont.: Institute of Intergovernmental Affairs, Queen's University, 2015).

6. Government of Canada, "Reducing Greenhouse Gas Emissions from Electricity Generation," http://www.ec.gc.ca/cc/default.asp?lang=En&n=C418B47C-1.

7. International Energy Agency, "Canada: Electricity and Heat for 2011," http://www.iea.org/statistics/statisticssearch/report/?country=CANADA&product=electricityandheat&year=2011.

8. Mary Jane Patterson and Ian H. Rowlands, "Beauty in the Eye of the Beholder: A Comparison of 'Green Power' Certification Programs in Australia, Canada, the United Kingdom and the United States," *Energy & Environment* 13, 1 (2002): 1–25.

9. EcoLogo, "CCD-003: Electricity—Renewable Low-impact," http://www.ecologo.org/en/seeourcriteria/details.asp?ccd_id=228.

10. International Energy Agency, "Canada: Electricity and Heat for 2011."

11. See, e.g., Reinhard Haas et al., "Efficiency and Effectiveness of Promotion Systems for Electricity Generation from Renewable Energy Sources: Lessons from EU Countries," *Energy* 36 (2011): 2186–93; Aviel Verbruggen and Volkmar Lauber, "Assessing the Performance of Renewable Electricity Support Instruments," *Energy Policy* 45 (2012): 635–44.

12. See, e.g., Reinhard Haas et al., "A Historical Review of Promotion Strategies for Electricity from Renewable Energy Sources in EU Countries," *Renewable and Sustainable Energy Reviews* 15, 2 (2011): 1003–34.

13. Thomas P. Lyon and Haitao Yin, "Why Do States Adopt Renewable Portfolio Standards? An Empirical Investigation," *Energy Journal* 31, 3 (2010): 133–57.

14. David Hurlbut, "A Look Behind the Texas Renewable Portfolio Standard: A Case Study," *Natural Resources Journal* 48 (2008): 129–62.

15. Mario Ragwitz and Sione Steinhilber, "Effectiveness and Efficiency of Support Schemes for Electricity from Renewable Energy Sources," *WIREs Energy and Environment* 3, 2 (2014): 213–29.

16. Chapter 15: "National and Subnational Policies and Institutions," in *Climate Change 2014: Mitigation of Climate Change* (Cambridge: Cambridge University Press, 2014).

17. Government of British Columbia, "Bill 17—2010: Clean Energy Act," http://www.leg.bc.ca/39th2nd/1st_read/gov17-1.htm.

18. Government of British Columbia, *The BC Energy Plan: A Vision for Clean Energy Leadership*, http://www.energyplan.gov.bc.ca/PDF/BC_Energy_Plan.pdf.

19. BC Hydro, "CFT Results," http://www.bchydro.com/energy-in-bc/acquiring_power/closed_offerings/open_call_for_power.html; BC Hydro, "Clean Power Call," http://www.bchydro.com/energy-in-bc/acquiring_power/closed_offerings/clean_power_call.html.

20. BC Hydro, "Bioenergy Phase I Call RFP," http://www.bchydro.com/energy-in-bc/acquiring_power/closed_offerings/phase_1_rfp.html.

21. BC Hydro, "Bioenergy Phase 2 Call RFP," http://www.bchydro.com/energy-in-bc/acquiring_power/closed_offerings/bioenergy_phase2_rfp.html.

22. BC Hydro, "Community-Based Biomass Power Call RFQ," http://www.bchydro.com/energy-in-bc/acquiring_power/closed_offerings/cbb_rfq.html.

23. BC Hydro, "Standing Offer Program," http://www.bchydro.com/energy-in-bc/acquiring_power/current_offerings/standing_offer_program.html.

24. BC Hydro, "Current Applications & Offered EPAs," http://www.bchydro.com/energy-in-bc/acquiring_power/current_offerings/standing_offer_program/current_applications.html.

25. BC Hydro, "Integrated Resource Plan (IRP)," http://www.bchydro.com/energy-in-bc/meeting_demand_growth/irp.html.

26. See, e.g., James Glave and Jeremy Moorhouse, *The Cleanest LNG in the World? How to Slash Carbon Pollution from Wellhead to Waterline in British Columbia's Proposed Liquefied Natural Gas Industry* (Vancouver: Clean Energy Canada at Tides Canada, Sept. 2013),http://cleanenergycanada.org/wp-content/uploads/2013/09/CEC_Cleanest_LNG_World.pdf. It is interesting to note, as well, that in 2012 the BC government amended the 2010 Clean Energy Act so that the "electricity to serve demand from facilities that liquefy natural gas for

export by ship" was to be outside of the aforementioned "93 per cent" target. See http://www.bclaws.ca/EPLibraries/bclaws_new/document/ID/freeside/234_2012.

27. For studies on British Columbia's electricity policy landscape, see, e.g., Amy Sopinka and Lawrence Pitt, "British Columbia Electricity Supply Gap Strategy: A Redefinition of Self-Sufficiency," *Electricity Journal* 26 (2013): 81–8; Mark Jaccard, Noel Melton, and John Nyboer, "Institutions and Processes for Scaling Up Renewables: Run-of-river Hydropower in British Columbia," *Energy Policy* 39 (2011): 4042–50.

28. *Albertans & Climate Change: Taking Action* (Edmonton: Alberta Environment, 2002), 3.

29. *Launching Alberta's Energy Future—Provincial Energy Strategy* (Edmonton: Ministry of Energy, 2008).

30. *Alberta's 2008 Climate Change Strategy: Responsibility/ Leadership/Action* (Edmonton: Alberta Environment, 2008).

31. Government of Alberta, "Greenhouse Gas Reduction Program," http://environment.alberta.ca/01838.html.

32. Climate Change and Emissions Management Corporation, "About," http://ccemc.ca/about/.

33. Alberta Energy, "Bioenergy Producer Credit Program Frequently Asked Questions," http://www.energy. alberta.ca/BioEnergy/1826.asp.

34. Alberta Environment, "Greening Government Strategy," http://environment.gov.ab.ca/info/library/8351.pdf.

35. City of Calgary, "Pathways 2 Sustainability Calgary 2013," http://www.imaginecalgary.ca/project-status/ completed.

36. Susan Carlisle, "Alternative and Renewable Energy Policy in Alberta" (Edmonton: Alberta Department of Energy, 4 Oct. 2013), http://cansia.ca/sites/default/files/2013_ solar_west_plenary_are_policy_in_alberta.pdf.

37. For an additional perspective, see Garrett Richards, Bram Noble, and Ken Belcher, "Barriers to Renewable Energy Development: A Case Study of Large-scale Wind Energy in Saskatchewan, Canada," *Energy Policy* 42 (2012): 691–8.

38. Tweet from Premier Brad Wall, 12 Mar, 2013, https://twitter.com/PremierBradWall/status/311595710703345665.

39. *2013: A New Era for Clean Energy in Canada, Issue 1* (Toronto: KPMG, Apr. 2013), 11.

40. SaskPower, "Green Options Partners Program," http:// www.saskpower.com/efficiency-programs-and-tips/ generate-your-own-power/green-options-partners-program/. For a historical perspective on power system planning in Saskatchewan, see Margot Hurlbert, Kathleen McNutt, and Jeremy Rayner, "Policy Pathways: Transitioning to Sustainable Power Generation in Saskatchewan," *Renewable Energy Law and Policy Review* 1 (2010): 87–100.

41. Miranda Holmes, *All Over the Map 2012: A Comparison of Provincial Climate Change Plans* (Vancouver: David Suzuki Foundation, Mar. 2012), 42.

42. For investigations into the Manitoba situation, see, e.g., Christopher J. Ferguson-Martin and Stephen D. Hill, "Accounting for Variation in Wind Deployment between Canadian Provinces," *Energy Policy* 39 (2011): 1652–3; Jacob Snell, David Prowse, and Ken Adams, "The Changing Role of Hydropower: From Cheap Local Energy Supply to Strategic Regional Resource," *International Journal of Water Resources Development* 30, 1 (2014): 121–34.

43. For broader overviews, see, e.g., Daniel Rosenbloom and James Meadowcroft, "The Journey Towards Decarbonization: Exploring Socio-Technical Transitions in the Electricity Sector in the Province of Ontario (1885–2013) and Potential Low-Carbon Pathways," *Energy Policy* 65 (2014): 670–9; Mark S. Winfield, *Blue-Green Province: The Environment and the Political Economy of Ontario* (Vancouver: University of British Columbia Press, 2012), 134–41, 163–9.

44. Ian H. Rowlands, "The Development of Renewable Electricity Policy in the Province of Ontario: The Influence of Ideas and Timing," *Review of Policy Research* 24, 3 (2007): 185–207.

45. Ibid.

46. Ibid.

47. Ontario Power Authority, "Bi-Weekly FIT and MicroFIT Report, data as of August 7, 2012," http://fit.power authority.on.ca/sites/default/files/page/Bi_Weekly ReportAugust7-2012.pdf, pp. 2, 7.

48. Leah C. Stokes, "The Politics of Renewable Energy Policies: The Case of Feed-in Tariffs in Ontario, Canada," *Energy Policy* 56 (2013): 490–500.

49. See, e.g., Parker Gallant and Glenn Fox, "Omitted Costs, Inflated Benefits: Renewable Energy Policy in Ontario," *Bulletin of Science, Technology & Society* 31, 5 (2011): 369–76.

50. *Ontario's Feed-in Tariff Program: Two-Year Review Report* (Toronto: Ministry of Energy, 19 Mar. 2012).

51. Ontario Power Authority, "Development of the Large Renewable Procurement," http://www.powerauthority. on.ca/large-renewable-procurement.

52. For an additional perspective, see Maya Jegen and Gabriel Audet, "Advocacy Coalitions and Wind Power Development: Insights from Québec," *Energy Policy* 39 (2011): 7439–47.

53. See, e.g., Hydro-Québec, "Electric Power Purchases: Québec Market," http://www.hydroquebec.com/ distribution/en/marchequebecois/index.html.

54. Hydro-Québec, "Developing Québec's Hydropower Potential," http://www.hydroforthefuture.com/projets/ 9/developing-quebec-s-hydropower-potential.

55. Matthew Sherrard, Thomas J. Timmins, and Ali Amadee, "Québec Announces Procurement of 800 MW of Wind Energy" (Montreal: Gowlings, May 2013), http://www. gowlings.com/KnowledgeCentre/article.asp?pub

ID=2907); for further context, see Commission sur les enjeux énergétiques du Québec, *Maîtriser Notre Avenir Énergétiques du Québec*, http://consultationenergie. gouv.qc.ca/pdf/Rapport-consultation-energie.pdf.

56. For a perspective highlighting the importance of stake-holder engagement, see Michelle Adams, David Wheeler, and Genna Woolston, "A Participatory Approach to Sustainable Energy Strategy Development in a Carbon-intensive Jurisdiction: The Case of Nova Scotia," *Energy Policy* 39 (2011): 2550–9.

57. Government of Nova Scotia, "Electricity Act," http:// nslegislature.ca/legc/statutes/elctrcty.htm.

58. Government of Nova Scotia, "Renewable Electricity Regulations,"http://www.novascotia.ca/just/regulations/ regs/elecrenew.htm.

59. Government of Nova Scotia, "2010 Renewable Electricity Plan," http://www.novascotia.ca/energy/renewables/ renewable-electricity-plan/.

60. Government of Nova Scotia, "Community Feed-in Tariff Program," http://nsrenewables.ca/feed-tariffs.

61. Government of Nova Scotia, "Tidal Array Feed-in Tariff," https://nsrenewables.ca/tidal-array-feed-tariff.

62. *Electricity in New Brunswick Beyond 2000, Discussion Paper* (Fredericton: Government of New Brunswick, Feb. 1998), 12.

63. Government of New Brunswick, "New Brunswick Regu-lation 2006-58 under the Electricity Act (O.C. 2006-274)," http://www.gnb.ca/0062/PDF-regs/2006-58.pdf.

64. Government of New Brunswick, "Renewable Port-folio Standard," http://www2.gnb.ca/content/gnb/en/ departments/energy/energy_blueprint/content/ renewable_portfolio.html.

65. Government of Prince Edward Island, *Prince Edward Island Energy Strategy, Securing Our Future: Energy Effi-ciency and Conservation* (Charlottetown, PEI: Depart-ment of Environment, Energy and Forestry, 2008), 22–3.

66. See, e.g., *Final Report: Charting Our Electricity Future* (Charlottetown, PEI: PEI Energy Commission, Sept. 2012); Tracey Allen, "The Future of Renewable Energy on Prince Edward Island," http://halifax.mediacoop. ca/story/future-renewable-energy-prince-edward-island/19331.

67. Government of Newfoundland and Labrador, "Energy Plan," http://www.nr.gov.nl.ca/nr/energy/plan/index. html.

68. Yukon Government, "Energy Strategy," http://www. energy.gov.yk.ca/energy_strategy.html.

69. Government of the Northwest Territories, "NWT Energy Action Plan Focuses on Efficiency; Alternative Energy," http://www.iti.gov.nt.ca/news/nwt-energy-action-plan-focuses-efficiency-alternative-energy.

70. *Ikummatiit: The Government of Nunavut Energy Strat-egy* (Iqaluit: Government of Nunavut, Sept. 2007).

71. Government of Alberta, "Climate Change Strategy," http://environment.alberta.ca/0909.html.

72. See, e.g., D. Lew et al., *The Western Wind and Solar Inte-gration Study Phase 2* (Golden, Colo.: National Renew-able Energy Laboratory, NREL/TP-5500-55588, Sept. 2013).

73. Marlo Raynolds, "Year in Review 2013: Canada's Renew-able Energy Markets," http://www.bluearthrenewables. com/blog/december-23-2013/. See also OECD, *Linking Renewable Energy to Rural Development* (Paris: OECD, 2012).

74. For a broader discussion, see Andreas Koch, Sébastien Girard, and Kevin McKoen, "Towards a Neighbourhood Scale for Low- or Zero-carbon Building Projects," *Build-ing Research & Information* 40 (2012): 527–37.

75. Ian Watson, Stephen Betts, and Eric Rapaport, "Deter-mining Appropriate Wind Turbine Setback Distances: Perspectives from Municipal Planners in the Canadian Provinces of Nova Scotia, Ontario, and Quebec," *Energy Policy* 41 (2012):782–9.

76. See, e.g., Chad Walker, Jamie Baxter, and Danielle Ouel-lette, "Beyond Rhetoric to Understanding Determinants of Wind Turbine Support and Conflicts in Two Ontario, Canada Communities," *Environment and Planning A* 46, 3 (2014): 730–45.

77. Ontario Power Authority, "FIT Program Version 2," http://fit.powerauthority.on.ca/faqs/fit-version-2.0.

78. Government of Nova Scotia, "Community Feed-in Tariff Program," http://nsrenewables.ca/feed-tariffs.

79. See, generally, Scott Sinclair, *Saving the Green Econ-omy: Ontario's Green Energy Act and the WTO* (Ottawa: Canadian Centre for Policy Alternatives, 2013).

80. REN21, *Renewables 2013: Global Status Report* (Paris: REN21 Secretariat, 2013), 14.

81. Pierre-Olivier Pineau, *Integrating Electricity Sectors in Canada: Good for the Environment and for the Economy* (Montreal: The Federal Idea, 2012).

82. Jatin Nathwani, "Beyond Keystone: Canada's Clean Elec-tricity," *Policy Options* (2013): 27–8.

15 Water Policy in Canada: The Great Lakes Case

Carolyn Johns and Mark Sproule-Jones

Chapter Summary

This chapter focuses on the Great Lakes to highlight the complexities and challenges of environmental policy and water policy in Canada. Like other water systems in the world, the Great Lakes support multiple human uses. Water is not only essential for human life, but many species and living systems are dependent on freshwater ecosystems. This chapter argues that, despite political efforts to balance the multiple uses of water, many challenges related to water quantity and quality remain. The myth of abundance is alive and well, and this myth underpins a general ambivalence in water and environmental policy in the Great Lakes, despite periods of heightened awareness and action. This chapter focuses on two cases in the Great Lakes— water quality in Lake Erie and the politics of water withdrawals and water levels—to illustrate the implications of this ambivalence and the important governance challenges that remain.

Chapter Outline

- Water politics and governance in the Great Lakes
  - Understanding governance arrangements relating to water
  - The waxing and waning of political action and engagement
- Ambivalence sets in
  - Program review, austerity, and the decline of policy capacity
- Enduring problems and outstanding challenges
  - Water quality and pollution in Lake Erie
  - Water uses and water levels
- Prospects for change or continuing ambivalence?

Introduction

For thousands of years water has been at the heart of human settlement, supporting critical human uses such as drinking water, agriculture, fishing, transportation, energy, mining, industry, recreation, and everyday domestic uses. Ancient civilizations and Indigenous peoples have long understood the critical value of water in terms of sustaining life and communities, and some of the most important uses of water to civilizations are cultural and spiritual. It is not surprising, then, that water, particularly universal access to fresh drinking

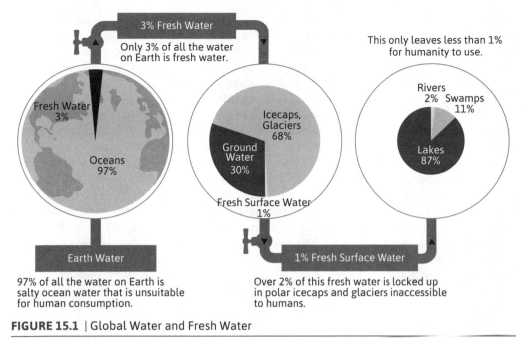

FIGURE 15.1 | Global Water and Fresh Water

Source: aquainnovations.com

water, is an important global issue. Although our planet is known as "the blue planet," the 7 billion people on Earth are dependent on roughly 3 per cent of the world's total freshwater supply and only a small percentage of that is accessible in the form of surface water and groundwater (see Figure 15.1). Although technology exists to make the Earth's vast ocean waters more usable for human populations, and some jurisdictions are pursuing this supply option for drinking water, to date, desalination is not a viable alternative to fresh water for many human uses and particularly for other species.

Given the fact that water is critical to human existence, food production, and numerous industrial activities, it is not surprising that multiple and competing uses of water have created conflicts over water quantity and quality. Indeed, water conflict and security have long been a source of discord at local, national, and international scales.[1] However, these multiple uses largely coexist in water bodies across the globe, and humans generally co-operate and share waters. International principles do exist relating to the governance of water, such as the United Nations' Dublin Principles (see Table 15.1), and declarations of water as a human

TABLE 15.1 The Dublin Statement on Water and Sustainable Development, 1992

Principle No. 1	Fresh water is a finite and vulnerable resource, essential to sustain life, development and the environment
Principle No. 2	Water development and management should be based on a participatory approach, involving users, planners and policy-makers at all levels
Principle No. 3	Women play a central part in the provision, management and safeguarding of water
Principle No. 4	Water has an economic value in all its competing uses and should be recognized as an economic good

right are embodied in other international laws and agreements. For the most part, however, water governance—particularly laws and policies related to water use, access, and quality—are left up to different countries and, in some cases, transboundary agreements between countries. Water use and rights are thus connected to territorial rights and property rights.

Despite the value of water to life, the global significance of water, and international principles recognizing the importance of water, water politics and policies in Canada have evolved under what some call the myth of abundance based on our wealth of fresh water. Attitudinal surveys conducted annually since 2008 consistently indicate that Canadians take water for granted and are not very concerned about water quantity or quality, as compared to other policy issues. In a 2014 national survey on water attitudes, only 2 per cent of respondents identify water pollution or supply as the most important issue facing Canada, well below the 20 per cent that identified the economy and the 18 per cent who identified health care. Water also ranks below climate change (at 4 per cent) and overall quality of the environment (identified by 3 per cent of those surveyed) in terms of the most significant issues facing the country.[2]

While water does not seem to rank highly as compared to other policy issues, other recent public opinion research reveals that residents of the Great Lakes in particular are strongly connected to the lakes; 96 per cent believe that the lakes significantly impact their local economy and 71 per cent indicate the lakes significantly impact their everyday lives. Pollution or contamination is by far the most widely cited environmental concern, mentioned by 74 per cent of residents as one of their top three concerns, with Asian carp (21 per cent), water levels (16 per cent), and invasive species generally (11 per cent) registering as other important concerns. The majority (86 per cent) of residents believe the Great Lakes are in at least fair condition, but not necessarily improving; some 50 per cent believe that the lakes are *not* in better health than they were 20 years ago.[3]

These variations in opinion are not surprising. Water as a global or national issue can seem abstract or remote to many citizens. But when probed at a more regional, local, or personal scale, water can mobilize people and political action. Like other environmental issues, salience and public engagement ebb and flow. This is clearly evident in the Great Lakes region.

Water Politics and Governance in the Great Lakes

The Great Lakes Basin is the largest freshwater basin on Earth, containing roughly 20 per cent of the world's freshwater supply and 84 per cent of North America's supply. The Great Lakes contain about 23,000 km^3 of water, covering a total area of 244,000 km^2 (94,000 square miles); only the polar ice caps contain more fresh water.[4] The Basin is home to nearly 40 million people, including more than 10 per cent of the population of the United States and 30 per cent of the population of Canada.[5] Collectively, the five lakes and their draining river systems span more than 1,200 kilometres, two provinces, and eight US states, more than 3,000 municipalities, and hundreds of Indigenous communities (see Figure 15.2). The Basin has played a major role in the economic development of the United States and Canada, and it continues to provide water for domestic consumption, industry, transportation, power, recreation, and a host of other uses. Some of the world's largest concentrations of industrial activity are located in the Great Lakes region, which accounts for 28 per cent of combined economic activity in Canada and the US. In comparative terms, the region's output ranks ahead of Germany, France, Brazil, and the United Kingdom, and it would rank as the fourth largest economy in the world if it were a country.[6]

Like other large water systems, the Great Lakes are sensitive to the effects of a wide range of pollutants from all of the various users, as well as human and economic activities in the region.

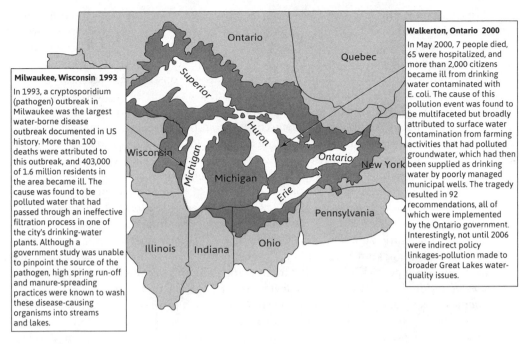

Milwaukee, Wisconsin 1993

In 1993, a cryptosporidium (pathogen) outbreak in Milwaukee was the largest water-borne disease outbreak documented in US history. More than 100 deaths were attributed to this outbreak, and 403,000 of 1.6 million residents in the area became ill. The cause was found to be polluted water that had passed through an ineffective filtration process in one of the city's drinking-water plants. Although a government study was unable to pinpoint the source of the pathogen, high spring run-off and manure-spreading practices were known to wash these disease-causing organisms into streams and lakes.

Walkerton, Ontario 2000

In May 2000, 7 people died, 65 were hospitalized, and more than 2,000 citizens became ill from drinking water contaminated with E. coli. The cause of this pollution event was found to be multifaceted but broadly attributed to surface water contamination from farming activities that had polluted groundwater, which had then been supplied as drinking water by poorly managed municipal wells. The tragedy resulted in 92 recommendations, all of which were implemented by the Ontario government. Interestingly, not until 2006 were indirect policy linkages-pollution made to broader Great Lakes water-quality issues.

FIGURE 15.2 | Jurisdiction Map and Major Pollution Events

Source: Adapted from the Great Lakes Information Network at http://gis.glin.net/.

Water pollution in the Great Lakes, and in other basins in Canada, can be divided into two broad types: (1) **point-source water pollution**, which is contamination caused by easily identifiable sources, such as industrial waste and outfall from municipal sewage treatment facilities; and (2) **non-point-source pollution**, which is contamination caused by dispersed, multi-source inputs, such as urban and agricultural runoff (which may carry sediment, fertilizers, oil, gasoline, pesticides, chemicals, heavy metals, and other toxic substances into water bodies), overflow sewage inputs, and groundwater contamination. Both types of pollution are evident in water bodies. A variety of measures are used to assess water and ecosystem health, including baseline measures to gauge whether waters are fishable, swimmable, and drinkable, as well as more complex scientific measures of water quality, fish and wildlife diversity, and toxic contamination.

Political Action and Engagement

Water governance in the Great Lakes region has existed for thousands of years. Indigenous peoples in particular have had long-standing governance arrangements related to water. In Canada, the politics of water plays out in the context of Indigenous rights to water, our colonial foundations, and the regime of laws that evolved along with property and land rights, many that predate Confederation. Most of the Great Lakes region falls under common law that grants landowners adjacent to rivers **reasonable use** of the water flows, provided they do not interfere with downstream or other users. Common law also grants landowners the **rights of capture** over the groundwaters under their property, but these groundwaters must be shared with any other landowners with surface lands above the aquifer. These common-law rights are called **riparian rights**. In Ontario, for example, they are essentially enjoyed only by landowners who have rights to take less than 50,000 litres per day without requiring a government permit. Common law underpins many existing laws in Ontario and the eight Great Lakes states, and similar pre-Confederation rights stem from the civil code in Quebec. Over time, common laws have been modified or replaced by laws passed under various constitutional authorities.

Since Confederation in Canada, and independence in the US, policies to govern water quantity and quality have evolved significantly to support a wide range of water uses. Many of the early politics and policy related to water focused on allocation of water rights and benefits, not environmental concerns. In the Canadian Constitution, neither the environment nor water is specifically mentioned. Thus, jurisdiction over water resources has evolved into a shared responsibility between the federal and provincial governments under sections 91 and 92.

Under section 91 of the British North America Act of 1867 (since renamed the Constitution Act, 1867), and later the Constitution Act, 1982, the federal government has legislative authority in a number of areas indirectly related to water resource management, including section 91(10), "navigation and shipping," and section 91(12), "sea coast and inland fisheries." Residual powers are acknowledged under "peace, order, and good government," plus the so-called "spending powers" provision that gives the federal government legislative leeway on issues of national and international concern, including the Great Lakes.

Under section 92 of the Constitution Act, 1867, the provinces have jurisdiction over natural resources within their geographic boundaries. These powers were reinforced in a 1982 constitutional amendment, section 92A, that clarified provincial rights over the development, conservation, and management of non-renewable resources, forests, and the generation and production of electrical generation from water. Under these constitutional provisions, provincial governments have historically been much less concerned about the quality of their water resources and more concerned about ensuring that the water necessary for economic expansion is available to various users.[7]

Because of this constitutional framework, legislative responsibility for water quality management and the corresponding bureaucratic machinery for implementation have developed at both the federal and the provincial levels. Provinces clearly have significant jurisdiction over water resources. In addition, municipal and local governments, as well as specialized agencies such as conservation authorities and watershed boards, possess some responsibilities delegated by provincial authorities. The well-documented water policy regime at the federal level[8] has its roots in a combination of legislation, court decisions, policy directives, and funding initiatives under various constitutional authorities. In Ontario, most early legislative activity was aimed at enabling the use of water for increasing economic development within provincial borders. Although pollution controls did exist under the federal Fisheries Act and other federal statutes, Ontario and other jurisdictions in Canada first began water quality regulations as part of public health protection legislation in the nineteenth century.[9] For the purposes of this chapter, the emphasis is on the key legislation and policies that relate to the Great Lakes.

Transboundary management of the vast watersheds shared by Canada and the United States began over 100 years ago with the signing of the Boundary Waters Treaty in 1909. The treaty established the International Joint Commission (IJC) as a unique transboundary institution for the resolution of binational water disputes. Headed by six commissioners (three appointed by the US President and three appointed by the Canadian Prime Minister), the IJC acts on **references** from both governments to co-operatively address disputes over the use of water resources. Initially, the emphasis was placed on water quantity impacts of industrial uses, hydro uses, shipping, and diversions in the Great Lakes–St Lawrence Seaway.

This began to change when visible environmental degradation and major pollution events resulted in political awareness and demands for government action.

Industrial waste, human sewage, and the use of man-made chemicals—including PCBs (polychlorinated biphenyls) introduced in the 1920s and DDT (dichloro-diphenyl-trichloroethane) introduced in the 1940s—began to have serious ecosystem effects. Chemicals, fertilizers, and untreated human waste from cities caused an acceleration of biological production (eutrophication) in the lakes. By the 1950s, Lake Erie, the shallowest of the lakes, showed serious signs of stress in the form of massive, lake-wide **algal blooms** (mats of algae) that severely depleted oxygen levels and resulted in the decline of several fish species.[10] Indications of obvious pollution began to be documented in scientific studies by the IJC in the 1940s and 1950s. However, not until the 1960s and 1970s, in the face of overwhelming scientific evidence that pollution was becoming a severe problem in the lakes, did governments act.

By the early 1970s, growing public concern about the deterioration of water quality stimulated citizens to push for basin-wide action by Canadian and US governments. Shocking events, including fish kills in Lake Erie, the Cuyahoga River in Cleveland, Ohio, catching fire in 1969 due to extremely high levels of pollutants in the water, the contamination of the walleye fishery by mercury, and the toxic contamination of land in the Love Canal area near Niagara Falls, New York, all brought environmental issues to the forefront of government agendas. The initial policy push was focused on point-source controls in the form of effluent limits for industries and municipal sewage treatment systems, followed shortly thereafter by a focus on toxic contaminants. Ultimately, several laws were passed in each country and the federal governments in Canada and the United States signed the Great Lakes Water Quality Agreement (GLWQA) in 1972. This "non-binding, good-faith agreement" between the two governments[11] resulted in action by federal and subnational governments in the form of new laws, policies, and programs. By the 1970s, several US environmental organizations had established Great Lakes programs and Canadian environmental groups were developing Great Lakes agendas.[12]

The 1970s was a key decade in terms of national, state, and provincial legislation related to water, including the federal Department of Environment Act (1971), the Canada Water Act (1970), the Ontario Water Resources Act (1970), and the Quebec Environment Quality Act (1972). As a result of legislation, government regulations, and other actions, major reductions were made to some pollutant discharges from industrial point sources and municipal sewage treatment plants. The initiatives of the 1970s showed that improvements could be made through collective action.

A renewed commitment to address Great Lakes pollution in 1978 was reflected in updates to the GLWQA, which recognized the need for an ecosystem-based approach and placed greater emphasis on toxic substances. Yet, in the 1980s, an estimated 57 million tonnes of liquid waste were still being poured into the Great Lakes annually by its inhabitants, their industries, and their municipalities, and toxic substances had emerged as a key water quality issue.[13] Clearly, despite the progress, serious challenges remained.

In 1984, in response to growing concerns about water quality in the Great Lakes and other watersheds across Canada, the federal government established the Inquiry on Federal Water Policy to examine the federal government's role in water resource management and protection. The Inquiry's report made several recommendations, including the need for new federal water legislation. In response to the report, instead of amending the Canada Water Act or developing new legislation, the federal government opted to develop the Federal Water Policy (FWP) in 1987, a directive outlining the ways in which the federal government would contribute to existing water quality objectives through its own programs, co-operation with provinces and stakeholders, the development of information and expertise, and promotion of public awareness. The goals of the

FWP are to protect and enhance the quality of water resources and to promote the wise and efficient use of water—two broad policy goals that highlight the conflicting values we hold vis-à-vis water in Canada.[14] Ultimately, the FWP simply reconfirmed the federal government's commitment to water quality research and a water infrastructure support role. To this day, there has not been any new federal water legislation. However, the FWP did support the need for action and was released during the same year that the third revision to the GLWQA was signed.

The 1987 GLWQA identified 43 Areas of Concern (AOCs) (see Figure 15.3) and called for Remedial Action Plans (RAPs) to address 14 **beneficial use impairments** such as to the health and reproduction of various species (including fish populations), wildlife habitat, and human health, and to restore other human uses and ecosystem functions in the AOCs. Of the AOCs, 26 are in the US, 17 in Canada; five of the total of 43 are shared by both countries.

RAPs required the multi-stakeholder involvement of citizens, non-governmental organizations, industries, and both the federal and the state/provincial levels of government in a two-stage process: first, water pollution problems in each AOC were assessed, and second, an implementation plan was formulated to address the identified impaired uses. In addition, Lake-wide Management Plans were to be formulated for each of the five lakes in order to supplement efforts in AOCs, as well as other programs and initiatives involving federal, provincial, state,

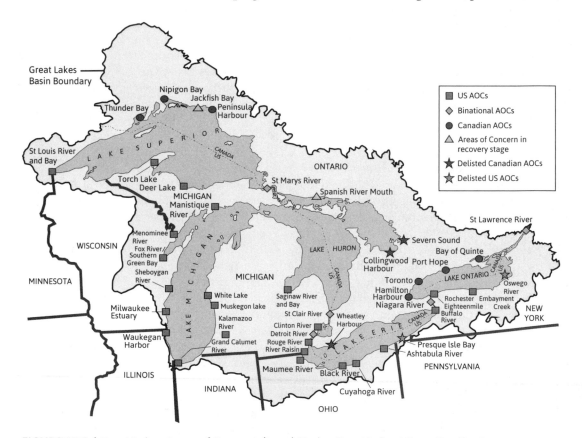

FIGURE 15.3 | Great Lakes Areas of Concern (AOCs) Under Great Lakes Water Quality Agreement

Source: US EPA, 2013. http://epa.gov/greatlakes/aoc/images/aoc-glbasin-map-20130215.pdf.

local, and Indigenous governments and a variety of non-governmental stakeholders on both sides of the border. Although the IJC's authority was not expanded beyond its investigative role, in effect it was given a "standing reference" and "permanent watchdog role" in the Great Lakes.[15]

In addition to the federal government's leadership flowing from the FWP and the GLWQA, the Canadian Environmental Protection Act (CEPA) was passed in 1988, emphasizing pollution prevention, an ecosystem approach, and toxic substance regulation. This legislation reinforced the federal government's focus on toxic substance regulation as central to its water quality mandate, and maintained the emphasis on point-source pollution problems and solutions.

The AOC approach gradually resulted in a shift in focus from IJC-level efforts to a more decentralized approach related to RAPs. Transboundary initiatives, such as the State of the Lakes Ecosystem Conferences (SOLECs), brought researchers and policy-makers together in the transboundary context to ensure ongoing research, monitoring, and regular reporting.[16] Despite this multi-stakeholder, watershed-based approach, local governments had almost no direct participation in the early years of the GLWQA, and a general lack of industry engagement reflected the sector's limited participation in the Great Lakes community.[17] Although local governments became increasingly involved over time and industry associations increased their environmental activities related to toxic chemicals, industries were not active participants in implementation of the GLWQA.[18]

Ambivalence Sets In

Although the focus on AOCs and RAPs resulted in some progress in the late 1980s and early 1990s,[19] progress began to slow by the mid- to late 1990s. After a period of heightened public awareness in the 1970s and 1980s, and a proliferation of policies and government institutions with related mandates, by the 1990s a period of government indifference to the environment and water issues took hold.

Progress as a result of point-source regulations slowed, and the RAP process began to document the extent of remediation and cleanup required. A consensus began to emerge that spending on municipal wastewater treatment facilities and point-source industrial pollution control was only part of the challenge of improving water quality.[20] Although conditions were much improved from the 1960s and 1970s, basic environmental policy goals of fishable, swimmable, drinkable waters remained elusive in many watersheds. Also at this time, environmental policy shifted away from regulatory approaches towards voluntary, market-based approaches.[21] This shift was reinforced by mounting scientific evidence indicating that non-point sources were a significant cause of water pollution in many Great Lakes watersheds and were more difficult to address.[22]

The early 1990s recession and the consequent focus on debts and deficits resulted in the Chrétien government's budget-cutting "program review," which significantly reduced funding for Environment Canada[23] as the lead agency for Great Lakes and water-related programs. Although two progress reports on the FWP were issued in 1990 and 1994, water-related policies and programs in the Great Lakes witnessed a marked decline alongside the environmental budget cuts in the mid- to late 1990s.[24] The fragmentation within Environment Canada became so severe in the 1990s[25] that a "Where's water?" team was assembled to determine whether the government's water duties were still being performed.[26]

Not surprisingly given this context, federal and also provincial environmental bureaucratic capacities related to water were much diminished. The long-standing Canada–Ontario

Agreements (COAs)—put in place to implement environmental policies related to the Great Lakes since 1971—were weakened significantly by funding reductions. A report by the federal Commissioner of the Environment and Sustainable Development in 2001 noted that the Minister of the Environment had committed $150 million for the Great Lakes program for the 1995–2000 period, yet only $14.9 million had been disbursed to participating departments.

By the late 1990s, the general sense of community between researchers and stakeholder groups in the Great Lakes began to decline.[27] There had also been a shift in focus in intergovernmental relations, with provinces spending much of their intergovernmental policy effort "posturing" on climate change and the Kyoto Protocol,[28] and focusing on water quantity concerns after the bulk water export controversy in Ontario in 1998 (see Box 15.1).

Under the Conservative government of Premier Mike Harris from 1995 to 2002, environmental policy and water policy in Ontario also experienced a marked decline, "in effect diluting the Great Lakes focus and losing much of its capacity to take an active role in Great Lakes matters."[29] Water policy during this period was significantly affected by cuts to the Ministry of the Environment (MOE), conservation authorities, and other agencies with water-related mandates. According to one report, MOE business plans during this period barely mentioned Great Lakes efforts, and in 1997 the Ontario MOE laid off the co-ordinators for most of the provincially led RAPs.[30]

During this period, significant water pollution events occurred in Milwaukee, Wisconsin, in 1993 and in Walkerton, Ontario, in 2000 (see Figure 15.2). People died from water pollution. This, however, did not generate a public response in connection with broader water quality issues in the Great Lakes. Although the Walkerton tragedy did result in a public inquiry and all of the recommendations of the Walkerton Inquiry were implemented by the

BOX 15.1 | Great Lakes Water Bound for Asia?

In 1998 the Ontario Ministry of the Environment issued a five-year "water-taking" permit to a private company, the Nova Group of Sault Ste Marie, Ontario, allowing withdrawal by tanker of 158 million litres a year of Lake Superior water. The issue erupted into a Canada–US Great Lakes controversy and Ontario cancelled the permit and kicked a state–provincial process into gear. This resulted in the signing of the 2001 Annex to the 1985 Great Lakes Charter and ultimately to a ban on water exports from the Great Lakes under the Great Lakes–St Lawrence Sustainable Water Resources Compact and Agreement, which was agreed to by Ontario and Quebec and the eight American Great Lakes states.

In contrast to the non-binding character of the GLWQA, this binding subnational transboundary agreement focuses on water quantity issues, does not involve the federal governments in Canada or the United States, and illustrates transboundary policy efforts outside the auspices of the IJC, despite the fact that the IJC did issue a relevant study following the incident. The Sustainable Water Resources Compact and Agreement also highlights the separate water quantity and quality policy regimes in the Basin and the need for more integration in the future (as the water levels issue discussed below and forecasted implications of climate change clearly indicate).

Source: Adapted from K. Cooper and S. Miller, "Selling Our Water: Water Taking in Lake Superior," Canadian Environmental Law Association, 1998, at: http://www.cela.ca/article/selling-our-water-water-taking-lake-superior.

Ontario government through passage of the Nutrient Management Act and the Safe Drinking Water Act in 2002, explicit connections between provincial drinking water policy efforts and water quality in the Great Lakes were only made when the provincial Clean Water Act was passed in 2006 and commitments to the COA were reconfirmed.[31] As a result of the Walkerton tragedy and Inquiry, Ontario was re-engaged in water policy by this time, though the federal government remained ambivalent.

On the other side of the border, progress had also slowed. However, congressional reporting and statutory funding requirements under the US Clean Water Act and Safe Drinking Water Act, as well as economic concern for the region, resulted in President George W. Bush and Congress passing the Great Lakes Legacy Act in 2002. This legislation allocated $270 million over five years for remediation projects, particularly the cleanup of contaminated sediments; over 2004–8, approximately $50 million per year were provided to support cleanup efforts. Comparative policy research clearly indicated that Canada was lagging behind the United States in terms of water policy efforts.[32] Indeed, in 2002, the federal Commissioner of the Environment and Sustainable Development (CESD) noted that "the limited use of federal powers, weakness in basic management and accountability and the politics of federal–provincial relations have all played a part" in diminishing the federal water policy role generally and in the Great Lakes specifically.[33] The federal government's weak support of the IJC was criticized in the report:

> What is the value of making domestic and international commitments when in some cases there is no capacity to deliver? When the federal government signed the *Great Lakes Water Quality Agreement*, for example, it assumed an obligation to ensure that action would be taken. The government decided to rely on others, and when others failed to deliver, it did not assume the lead. The time has come for it to either take responsibility for its commitments or change them.[34]

Although funding was committed for Great Lakes mandates for the 2000–5 period, Environment Canada and eight other federal departments reportedly received only $40 million of the $160 million requested.[35] A Senate committee characterized the federal role in the area of water management and research as "in retreat" and urged the federal government, "once a well-respected leader in advancing the scientific study of water," to reinvest and "take up that leadership role once again."[36] Clearly, the federal government was not fulfilling its role in relation to the GLWQA. However, given the non-binding status of this international agreement, little recourse was available.

In contrast, Great Lakes efforts were gearing up in the mid-2000s in the US. The Great Lakes Legacy Act had re-engaged the US federal government and states. In 2003, the efforts of the Association of Great Lakes and St Lawrence Mayors, as well as the Great Lakes and St Lawrence Cities Initiative, indicated growing involvement by local governments.[37] In 2004, President Bush issued an executive order that recognized the Great Lakes as a national treasure and that created a federal Great Lakes Interagency Task Force to improve federal agency co-ordination and efforts. The order also directed the US EPA Administrator to convene a "regional collaboration of national significance for the Great Lakes."[38] Together with the Council of Great Lakes Governors and the Great Lakes and St Lawrence Cities Initiative, a Great Lakes Regional Collaboration Strategy and implementation plans were developed in 2005 and 2006. In 2007, a study by the Brookings Institution clearly laid out the economic benefits of ecosystem restoration,[39] and government as well as non-governmental groups became more active in Great Lakes issues. Around the same time, the IJC initiated a multi-stakeholder consultation process to review the 1987 GLWQA because scientific knowledge and ecological conditions had changed dramatically in the 20 years since the previous agreement had been signed. In its thirteenth biennial report in 2006, the IJC set out the need to develop an effective accountability framework, and the body urged the two federal governments to replace the current GLWQA with a new agreement with achievable goals and timelines, measures for evaluating performance, and provisions for monitoring and reporting to allow for greater accountability related to cleanup of the Great Lakes.

The IJC review, ongoing initiatives in the US, and pollution events in the region also resulted in a coalition of environmental groups, known as the "Blue Group," releasing a blueprint and eight key priorities for the Basin.[40] Despite these developments, and evidence of increased attention to the federal role in water policy in 2006,[41] the election of Stephen Harper and a Conservative minority government in the same year—with virtually no environmental agenda—clearly indicated that water and environmental policy would not be a political priority. Despite almost a decade of budget surpluses and economic prosperity, ambivalence in water policy was to continue. Interestingly, this state of affairs only began to change due to significant momentum south of the border.

Shortly after the election of President Barack Obama in the United States, and as part of the celebrations associated with the IJC's 100th anniversary, it was announced in 2009 by US Secretary of State Hillary Clinton and Canadian Minister of Foreign Affairs Lawrence Cannon that the US and Canada would renegotiate the Great Lakes Water Quality Agreement last signed in 1987. The following year, President Obama announced in his 2010 budget that $475 million would be provided that year and each year through to 2014 under the Great Lakes Restoration Initiative (GLRI) to address the most significant problems in the region, including invasive aquatic species, non-point-source pollution, and contaminated sediment.[42] Although a collaboration of 11 US federal agencies developed an action plan to implement the initiative, the US EPA is the lead agency overseeing cost-shared projects on the US side of the Basin, with AOCs being specific targets of GLRI funding.

Three years after the announcement that the GLWQA would be renegotiated, the new protocol amending the GLWQA was signed in 2012.[43] It contained 10 issue annexes, including new annexes on climate change, groundwater, and aquatic invasive species. The new agreement reflected a consensus that there was no need for new laws, policies, or transboundary institutions, but rather a need to focus on action and implementation. The primary governance challenge is to make the complex governance arrangements produce better outcomes than they have over the past 40 years and rise to the challenge of new problems in the region.

Results to Date and Outstanding Water Policy Challenges: Two Cases

Some 40 years after the first GLWQA and 25 years after designating AOCs, only seven of the 43 AOCs have been delisted (three in Canada and four in the US), and two are now designated as "areas in recovery" (see Figure 15.3). The progress in the remaining AOCs and in many other watersheds in the Great Lakes remains slow—and pollution continues. An increasing number of water uses continue to have negative impacts on water quality, as does an imbalance in water uses. More than two-thirds of the original wetlands in the Great Lakes Basin have been lost, thousands of miles of rivers have been impaired, and shorelines have been degraded.[44] Many new and re-emerging issues have surfaced in the Great Lakes, including new evidence of pharmaceutical chemicals, the enduring problem of the importation of invasive species, new energy developments such as offshore wind and shale gas "fracking," and new toxic blue-green algae pollution. All of these issues highlight the significant and enduring governance challenges that exist in the Great Lakes and many water systems across the country. In the next section, we focus on two of these challenges—water quality in Lake Erie and water levels/water quantity.

Enduring Problems and Challenges in Lake Erie

Like other water systems across Canada and the Great Lakes, Lake Erie is part of a complex ecosystem. Lake Erie is the smallest of the Great Lakes by volume and surface area. It is also the shallowest. Water quality is related to a variety of factors, including climate, species (both native and invasive), changing land-use patterns and human activities, and the engineering of waterways. In contrast to the other Great Lakes, where surrounding land use is primarily forest and agriculture, land use in Lake Erie has for some time been significantly affected by agriculture and urban land uses. Because of the fertile soils surrounding the lake, the area is intensively farmed. The lake receives runoff from the agricultural area of southwestern Ontario and parts of Ohio, Indiana, and Michigan. In terms of water quality and pollution, the negative effects of agriculture clearly manifest themselves in Lake Erie (see Figure 15.4). But urban land uses are also significant sources of pollution. Approximately one-third of the total population in the Basin is within the Lake Erie watershed, which has 17 metropolitan areas with populations over 50,000 and receives the greatest amount of effluent from wastewater treatment plans. The lake is thus exposed to significant stress from urbanization and industrialization.[45]

Throughout the twentieth century, the lake has demonstrated signs of stress in the form of declining fish populations and contamination of fish and wildlife, and there has been ongoing concern related to the overloading of nutrients from fertilizers as well as human and animal

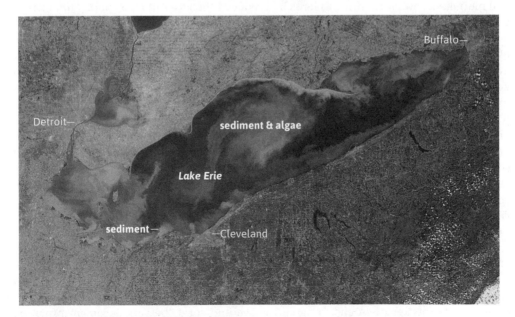

FIGURE 15.4 | Image of Lake Erie Water Pollution

Source: NASA 2012. Visible Earth Gallery, www.visibleearth.nasa.gov.

waste. Too much phosphorous and nitrogen cause **eutrophication**, a process that depletes the lake of oxygen and negatively affects fish, wildlife, and their food supplies, and also impacts water quality for human uses such as drinking water, fishing, and recreation. While eutrophication can be caused by both natural and human causes, urban and agricultural runoff, particularly of fertilizers, as well as sewage effluent are the major problems in Lake Erie.

Serious signs of environmental degradation in the form of fish and waterfowl deaths became evident in the late 1940s and 1950s.[46] Combined with major episodes of drought and water shortages, public and societal groups including fishers, hunters, and women's groups demanded government action.[47] *Time* magazine in 1965 declared that "Lake Erie is dead." Phosphorus inputs to Lake Erie accelerated through the 1970s from domestic sewage, increased use of detergents, agricultural operations, and industrial wastes. In areas like Detroit, the consequences of pollution surfaced in the form of substantial wildlife and fish deaths, hepatitis outbreaks, and debris-covered shorelines. Degraded water quality conditions were also evident in taste and odour problems in water supplies. Public demands for government action were becoming louder by the 1960s.

In response, phosphate detergent bans were put in place by 1972 and lake-wide phosphorus loading limits were set under the 1978 GLWQA. Significant investments were made in new wastewater treatment facilities, and fisheries management strategies were formulated by states and provinces. The results were dramatic. In 1973, 47 per cent of municipal sewage was being discharged into the lake with no treatment, but by 1985 over 97 per cent of wastewater was receiving treatment.[48] "By the mid-1980s the recovery of Lake Erie was a globally-known success story,"[49] and water quality conditions improved.[50] There was significant ecological recovery, with the return of bald eagles and fish species like walleye and whitefish.[51] Oxygen levels increased and food sources for various fish species also increased.[52] Contaminants in sediments also improved significantly over this period.[53] Point-source controls of industry and municipal sewage treatment plants had reduced the levels of phosphorus and nitrogen entering the lakes. However, some of these successes were short-lived.

Ironically, the successes contributed in part to a growing ambivalence about the state of the Great Lakes. Efforts waned. Declining funding in the mid-1990s, followed by almost a decade of minimal action on point-source regulation, meant that progress slowed in addressing the "dead zone" in Lake Erie.[54] Although a variety of voluntary policy instruments and programs aimed at addressing non-point sources of pollution were being supported by governments across the Basin,[55] Lake Erie again began to show signs of stress. This was compounded by invasive species and mounting evidence that climate change was having an impact on water quality in the lake. By 2002, the water quality in the lake was in serious condition again[56] and multiple stressors were responsible for Lake Erie's decline.[57]

In 2011, Lake Erie experienced the largest algal bloom in its history.[58] Again in 2012, widespread drought was associated with the largest dead zone since the mid-1980s.[59] The same year, the IJC initiated the Lake Erie Ecosystem Priority (LEEP) study in response to the enduring problems of phosphorus enrichment from both rural and urban sources, now recognized as being compounded by the influence of climate change and aquatic invasive species. The LEEP report clearly documented the declining state of water quality and the impacts on ecosystem health, drinking water supplies, fisheries, recreation and tourism, and property values.[60] The human and ecosystem costs were deemed significant, and the report called for governments to strengthen and "scale up" urban and rural "best management programs" (BMPs) and partnership efforts. It also called for jurisdictions to put supports in place to move from grey to green infrastructure, such that water running off the land travels through natural green filtration features rather than hard, impervious urban surfaces.

Under the revised 2012 GLWQA, there is a new annex related to nutrient management and a renewed commitment to nearshore and lakewide management approaches. Although the 2012 Agreement and annexes have mobilized policy efforts, there are serious concerns about the prospects for governments actually implementing the Agreement and whether the necessary funding support is available. Environment Canada is playing a leadership role, and a new COA has recently been negotiated with Ontario (2014–19). Ontario also has a proposed Great Lakes Protection Act moving through the legislature, but only time will tell if these commitments will put Lake Erie back on the path to ecosystem health.

In 2014, a half-million US citizens in Toledo, Ohio, were without water for a weekend in August due to algae toxins in Lake Erie, indicating the transboundary dimensions of the pollution problems in the lake.[61] Addressing the problems in Lake Erie will require partnerships and behavioural change by citizens, industry, and the agriculture sector in Canada and the US. Yet, the current context of austerity at the federal and provincial levels in Canada makes government-led implementation partnerships challenging. Further, the challenges of addressing non-point-source water pollution are daunting, as no current governments want to regulate agriculture, citizens, or the fertilizer and chemical industries. As highlighted in the IJC's LEEP report, the preferred solutions lie in BMPs, partnerships, and mobilizing collective action through voluntary approaches to curb the cumulative effects of pollution—despite some environmental activists calling for the development of lake-wide standards and regulatory instruments such as bans on phosphorus lawn fertilizers and restrictions on agricultural fertilizers. This challenging governance context is exacerbated by uncertainties such as climate change impacts. As we show in the next case example, some of these same uncertainties and challenges underpin the politics of water levels and water quantity.

Great Lakes Water Levels[62]

Water levels in the Great Lakes represent a continuous struggle between natural forces that replenish the lakes and human (anthropogenic) forces that struggle to control and withdraw waters for many different human uses. The lakes were formed around the conclusion of the last ice age, some 10,000 years ago. Lakes Superior, Michigan, Huron, Erie, and Ontario (and their connecting channels) were shaped such that their combined gravitational flows end in the Gulf of St Lawrence and the Atlantic Ocean. This formation still remains, with the lakes tilting slowly to the southeast. The lakes are replenished (largely) by rain and snow in the Basin, by groundwater, and by rivers and streams. Evaporation is a major natural withdrawal and is exacerbated by global warming.

Human interventions have kept lake levels largely constant for 150 years, partly through the building of dams and in the face of diversions and withdrawals. Figure 15.5 shows how, historically, average lake levels have remained relatively constant despite periodic fluctuations. However, beginning in 1997–8, much of the Basin has experienced an extended period of lower water levels than previously recorded since co-ordinated measurement began in 1918.[63] Water levels rebounded to some degree throughout the region in 2013–14 due to cooler temperatures in the Basin and extensive ice coverage and snowfall. However, it is unclear if the rebound marks an end to a low water trends or if it represents an exception to this general dynamic. A recent study concludes there could be significant economic fallout

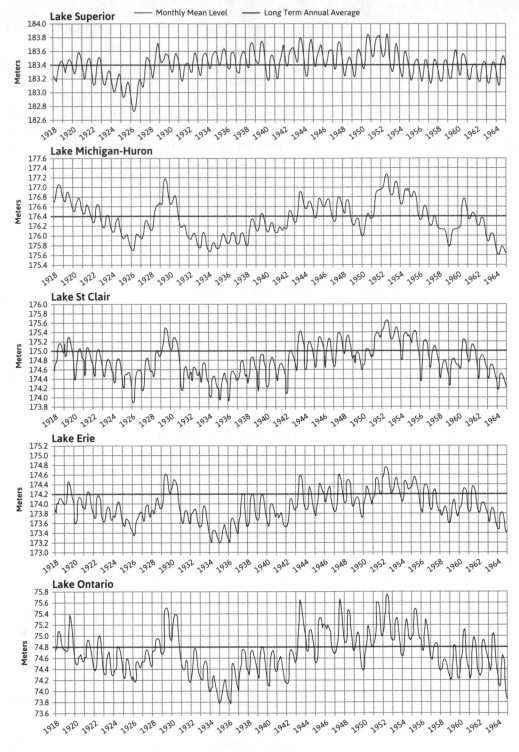

FIGURE 15.5 | Great Lakes Water Levels (1918–2012)

Source: United States Army Corp of Engineers, 2013. At http://www.lre.usace.army.mil/Portals/69/docs/GreatLakesInfo/docs/WaterLevels/LTA-GLWL-Graph.pdf.

FIGURE 15.5 | (Continued)

from a continuation of these lower water levels in the future, estimated at over $9 billion from the present through 2030.[64] But there is much uncertainty related to climate change and our ability to manage this issue.

Water levels clearly generate questions related to natural vs human causes. Like the Lake Erie case and many environmental issues in this book, uncertainty is an important part of the politics and policy challenge. Historically, water levels have been the source of a number of conflicts between different interests, and attempts to manage various uses by intervening in the natural processes of this massive lake and river system have accelerated. Currently, for example, the Lake Michigan–Lake Huron system is the site of major disagreements between shoreline users like marinas, boaters, and cottagers and the primary body mandated to regulate water flows, namely the International Joint Commission. Unusually low water levels in Huron, in particular, have created a number of negative impacts (see Figure 15.6).

The politics related to ensuring relatively constant levels in the Great Lakes can be illustrated by briefly focusing on dams, withdrawals (water takings), and diversions. These human interventions illustrate the complex governance arrangements that relate to water quantity, quality, and environmental politics in the Great Lakes. Dams were one of the earliest means for intervening in natural processes to change water levels for human benefit.

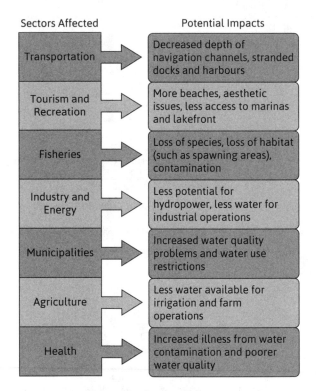

FIGURE 15.6 | Potential Impacts of Low Water Levels

Source: Adapted by Great Lakes Environmental Research Laboratory from Field, "North America." In *Climate Change 2007: Impacts Adaptation and Vulnerabilty*, edited by M. L. Parry, O. F. Canziani, J. P. Palutikof, P. J. van der Linden and C. E. Hanson, 617-652. Contribution of Working Group II to the Fourth Assessment Report of the Intergovernmental Panel on Climate Change. Cambridge, UK and New York, NY: Cambridge University Press, 2007.

There are two major sets of dams in the Great Lakes Basin: one on the St Mary's River, which is the connecting channel from Lake Superior to Lakes Michigan and Huron; and the other on the St Lawrence, which regulates the flow from Lake Ontario downstream past Montreal and Quebec City and away to the Atlantic Ocean. Both sets of dams are under the direct administrative control of the IJC.

The St Mary's River received its first dam in 1797, and the dams constructed later came under the regulation of the IJC in 1921. The St Lawrence River was also subject to continuous dredging and channelization over time. Much of its reaches were important for shipping interests both upstream and downstream of Montreal, and state and provincial authorities were heavily involved in the development of the seaway.[65] The Great Lakes–St Lawrence Seaway was built as a binational partnership between the US and Canada, and continues to operate as such. Administration of the system is shared by two entities, the Saint Lawrence Seaway Development Corp. in the US, a federal agency within the US Department of Transportation, and the St Lawrence Seaway Management Corporation in Canada, a not-for-profit corporation (ownership of the Canadian portion of the Seaway remains with the Canadian federal government).[66] The regulated flows are managed by the IJC. The IJC tries to balance the interests of upstream users like fishers and cottagers with the downstream interests in deep navigational channels for the Port of Montreal. In recent low-flow years, neither set of interests seems to be fully satisfied. In addition to these large dams, there are many small-scale dams on rivers and streams within the Basin itself, constructed largely for hydroelectric purposes. They have minimal impacts on the water levels in the Great Lakes.

In addition to dams, some larger human impacts on levels are a result of water takings. As outlined in Figure 15.7, all jurisdictions in the Basin use its water. Ontario is a significant user for hydroelectric power and a wide range of other domestic, industrial, and agricultural uses.

Waters taken from the Great Lakes can take two forms—withdrawals and consumptive uses. A water withdrawal is when water is taken from surface or groundwater sources and then returned to the lakes. The largest withdrawals are for power generation and for municipal, industrial, and agricultural uses. Consumptive water uses, on the other hand, are uses that permanently withdraw water from its source. The biggest consumptive uses are for agriculture and irrigation. Only about 5 per cent of withdrawn waters are consumed.[67]

The estimates of water withdrawals from surface waters and groundwater are acknowledged to be varied and debatable. The amounts of many small withdrawals from wells and streams are "guesstimates" and often do not occur according to the terms of government permits. Not all permitted withdrawals are metered, and volumes can vary due to local factors like micro-climates. Jurisdictions are making some efforts to calculate groundwater volumes, but sub-lake aquifers contain uncertain amounts of water that have percolated from land-based sources. In terms of cumulative impact, by the time the flows reach the St Lawrence dams the net impact of diversions and withdrawals is estimated as roughly 1 per cent of the stock of all lakes in an average year. There is one exception to this generalization.

A vigorous dispute involving cottagers and environmentalists against the IJC has dominated much of the last decade. The residents around Georgian Bay argue that mining of sand and gravel in the connecting channel between Lakes Michigan and Huron has increased the flow down the St Clair River. Suggestions to install water weirs and dams, which might lessen the flow, are opposed by some fishing and shipping interests. The IJC

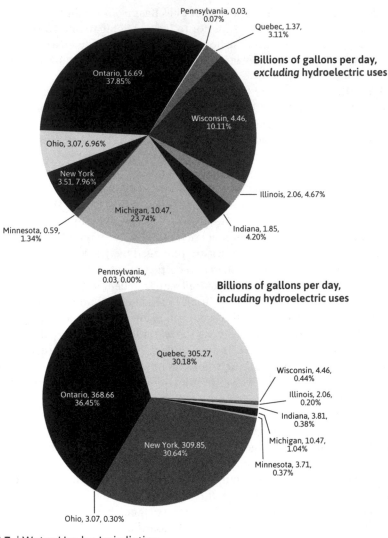

FIGURE 15.7 | Water Use by Jurisdiction

Source: Great Lakes Commission 2013, Annual Report of the Great Lakes Regional Water Use Database Representing 2011 Water Use Data http://projects.glc.org/waterusedata//pdf/wateruserpt2011.pdf.

seems largely content with its own research that the water levels in lakes are not exceptionally low by historical standards (see Figure 15.5). However, projections that water levels may increase or decrease due to climate change and other human uses make water levels an issue of concern, particularly as they relate to decision-making on withdrawals and dams.

The other contested issue related to water levels is diversions. The oldest major diversion on the Great Lakes is the so-called "Chicago Diversion" (completed in 1900) of waste waters (sewage) from outfalls discharging into the near-coastal waters of Lake Michigan and then diverted instead into the Chicago River and thence to the Mississippi Basin. The second major undertaking, constructed in 1940, is the Long Lac/Ogoki Diversion that redirects water from the James Bay watershed into Lake Superior. It adds significant volumes of water into the lake system, while the Chicago Diversion subtracts from water levels. Neither diversion involved the IJC.

The history of the Chicago Diversion can actually be traced back to the early days of North American exploration, when the feasibility of connecting the Great Lakes with the Mississippi River—to facilitate vessel traffic—was contemplated. Over the nineteenth century, the population of Chicago more than doubled, and large volumes of untreated sewage were regularly discharged into Lake Michigan. Under a federal permit from the War Department, a new outlet canal redirected the sewage into the Chicago River in 1848 and 1900. Some 60 years of legal cases between the Chicago Diversion District and Illinois (on one side) and downstream states like Missouri (on the other side) followed this engineering solution. It was left to the US Supreme Court in 1967 to finally referee the dispute, setting dilution limits and dischargeable volumes for Illinois to implement. It was a drawn-out effort to balance waste disposal interests and navigational interests against environmental concerns downstream of the diversion.

The Long Lac/Ogoki Diversion was not undertaken to sustain lake levels. It was built primarily to facilitate hydroelectric generation on the Albany River system as well as downstream on the Niagara River (which had the largest hydro capacity in the Basin). The Canadian and American governments were concerned about energy sufficiency during World War II. The Long Lac Diversion was completed in 1939 and the Ogoki in 1943. Together, they have an average annual flow of 158 cubic metres per second—roughly double the outflow of the Chicago Diversion at 91 cubic metres per second. The two national governments were so concerned about energy sufficiency that they made a direct agreement without the involvement of the IJC.

Finally, several proposals have been made for other water diversions. During the 1960s three proposals sought to divert Great Lakes waters out of the Basin, which potentially would have lowered water levels. One involved the dyking of James Bay, channelization to Lake Superior, and then pipeline diversion to the southwest US. A second was for a pipeline diversion for ultimate export to Asia. A third proposal was to export water from Lake Ontario through the Erie Canal. None of these proposals came to fruition. However, many citizen groups and governments in the Basin became increasingly mobilized against these potential threats to "their" waters. Ultimately, the governance system for the Great Lakes was changed to make out-of-basin diversions legally difficult if not impossible under the 2005 Great Lakes Sustainable Water Resources Compact and Agreement. Diversions or bulk water exports by pipeline or vessel like the Nova proposal (see Box 15.1) are now essentially banned by an agreement among the eight US states and the two Canadian provinces. The Compact and Agreement requires all major withdrawals to be approved by all 10 parties. Further, since 2008, the US government joined the group by approving the Compact, which is now legally binding under US law.

Communities and their governments on both sides of the American–Canadian border have struggled, largely with success, to stabilize water levels in the Great Lakes. Some historical withdrawal rights, dams, and diversions continue to have implications for water levels, but such threats as greater evaporation due to climate change have been of more recent concern. History suggests we should expect these struggles to continue.

Governance Challenges from the Cases

The governance of the Great Lakes is as complex and varied as the multiple uses and eco-systems in the Basin. Most important for understanding the basic rules, and hence the governance frameworks, is that the challenges in both of these cases stem from historical uses, rights, and legal regimes that for the most part govern water quality and quantity separately. Since 1909, the IJC has had primary responsibility and direct administrative powers over transboundary water level issues but the two national governments, and in particular state and provincial governments, have played a significant role in managing water uses. As noted, the IJC was not included as a participant in the two major historical diversions, the Chicago Diversion and the Long Lac/Ogoki Diversion. The diversion cases illustrate how Chicago and, ultimately, the US Supreme Court and the state of Illinois, were the final authorities. The two national governments handled the Long Lac/Ogoki Diversion by themselves. There are some parallel international agreements affecting the Great Lakes water environment, including the Convention on Great Lakes Fisheries that led to the establishment of the Great Lakes Fisheries Commission in 1965. The Commission works with all of the jurisdictions in the Basin to improve fish yields, control invasive species, and advance wetland ecologies, yet the states and provinces have the leading role.

Broadly speaking, under the Boundary Waters Treaty both water quantity and quality are governed binationally, but complex arrangements and constitutional authorities have given states and provinces a central role in Great Lakes governance, particularly when it comes to implementation of this treaty and the GLWQA. Finally, local governments, Indigenous governments, and public agencies operate in this mix of institutions, laws, and policies related to water levels and water pollution management.

Action to control pollution in the case of Lake Erie also illustrates the role of various levels of government, in terms of both action and inaction. This case clearly indicates that government efforts and collective action can make a difference, but that ambivalence can have consequences. In both cases, governments at all levels remain the authorities for action, but the engagement of citizens and stakeholders is critical.

In conclusion, more than 100 years after the Boundary Waters Treaty was signed and some 40 years after the first GLWQA, there has indeed been progress. The progress is evident to those who have lived their lives in the Basin. Although a more centralized IJC approach once generated significant research and policy responses related to water quality and quantity governance and the more decentralized effort related to Remedial Action Plans in Areas of Concern has made some progress, significant governance challenges remain.

The new GLWQA recommits the federal government to action on water quality, and the 2005 Great Lakes Sustainable Water Resources Compact and Agreement has demonstrated a commitment by states and provinces to take water levels and uses seriously. However, sustained commitment and action is required at all levels of government, and both the quality and quantity fronts require the engagement of governments, industry, stakeholders, and citizens at a variety of scales. In addition, engagement at the watershed level must involve local authorities and a wide range of diverse users in order to ensure sustainability of the Basin in light of many different user interests. The cases in this chapter clearly indicate that water quantity and quality are important issues in the Great Lakes region that need to be governed in a more integrated way. The effects of climate change may bring this into focus in the future.[68] All of these complexities and uncertainties require leadership and sustainable commitments that are very challenging in the current context of austerity at the federal and provincial levels of government. The cases presented here indicate that not much may change even with different parties in power. As indicated in this chapter and the next, Canadians cannot afford to be ambivalent about their water.

Key Terms

algal blooms

beneficial use impairments

eutrophication

myth of abundance

non-point-source pollution

point-source water pollution

reasonable use

references

rights of capture

riparian rights

Questions for Review

1. What does this chapter illustrate about water policy in Canada?
2. What can be done about water pollution in Lake Erie?
3. What kinds of governance challenges do water levels and withdrawals in the Great Lakes pose for policy-makers?
4. Imagine you are a policy adviser to the federal deputy minister responsible for the Great Lakes Water Quality Agreement. What barriers exist to implementing the Agreement and improving environmental outcomes in the next decade?
5. How do the water governance challenges in the Great Lakes compare to other water governance challenges in Canada and other jurisdictions?

Internet Resources

Alliance for the Great Lakes
www.greatlakes.org

Canada–Ontario Agreement Respecting the Great Lakes Basin Ecosystem
http://publications.gc.ca/collections/collection_2014/ec/En161-5-2007-eng.pdf

Environment Canada, Freshwater
www.ec.gc.ca/water

Environment Canada, Shared Responsibility
https://www.ec.gc.ca/eau-water/default.asp?lang=En&n=035F6173-1

Glossary of Great Lakes
www.seagrant.umn.edu

Great Lakes Biological Diversity
www.epa.gov/glnpo/ecopage

Great Lakes Environmental Atlas and Resource Book
www.epa.gov/glnpo

Great Lakes Information Network
www.great-lakes.net

Great Lakes Policy Research Network
www.greatlakespolicyresearch.org

Great Lakes Water Quality Agreement
www.binational.net

International Joint Commission
www.ijc.org

Ontario Ministry of the Environment Great Lakes Strategy
https://www.ontario.ca/environment-and-energy/ontarios-great-lakes-strategy

Ontario Ministry of Natural Resources (Water)
www.mnr.gov.on.ca/en/STEL02_168326.html

Visualizing the Great Lakes
www.epa.gov/glnpo/image

Additional Reading

Anin, Peter. *The Great Lakes Water Wars*. Washington: Island Press, 2006.

Bakker, K., ed. *Eau Canada: The Future of Canada's Water*. Vancouver: University of British Columbia Press, 2007.

Botts, L., and P. Muldoon. *Evolution of the Great Lakes Water Quality Agreement*. East Lansing: Michigan State University Press, 2005.

Sproule-Jones, M.H. *Restoration of the Great Lakes: Promises, Practices, Performances*. Vancouver: University of British Columbia Press, 2002.

Sproule-Jones, M., C. Johns, and B.T. Heinmiller, eds. *Water Politics in Canada: Conflicts and Institutions*. Montreal and Kingston: McGill-Queen's University Press, 2008.

Notes

1. Pacific Institute, *Water Conflict Chronology*, http://worldwater.org/water-conflict/; P.H. Gleick, "Water and Conflict," in Gleick, *The World's Water 1998–1999* (Washington: Island Press, 1998), 105–35.

2. Royal Bank of Canada, *Canadian Water Attitudes Study*, 2014, http://www.rbc.com/community-sustainability/environment/rbc-blue-water/water-attitude-study.html.

3. E. Maack et al., *Environmental Policy in the Great Lakes Region: Current Issues and Public Opinion*, CLOSUP and GLPRN, 2014, http://www.greatlakespolicyresearch.org/wp-content/uploads/2014/05/Public-Opinion-and-Enviromental-Policy-in-the-Great-Lakes-Region.pdf.

4. US Environmental Protection Agency (EPA), "The Great Lakes: An Environmental Atlas and Resource Book," 2015, http://www.epa.gov/greatlakes/atlas/glat-ch1.html.

5. EPA, Great Lakes National Program Office, 2007, www.epa.gov.

6. Bank of Montreal, "Great Lakes Region: North America's Economic Engine," 2013, http://www.bmonesbittburns.com/economics/reports/20130411/greatlakes1304a.pdf.

7. S. Brooks, "Water Policy," in Brooks and L. Miljan, eds, *Public Policy in Canada: An Introduction*, 4th edn (Toronto: Oxford University Press, 2003), 262–79; M. Sproule-Jones, C. Johns, and B.T. Heinmiller, eds, *Canadian Water Politics: Conflicts and Institutions* (Montreal and Kingston: McGill-Queen's University Press, 2008).

8. Canada, Inquiry on Federal Water Policy, *Currents of Change: Final Report of the Inquiry on Federal Water Policy* (Ottawa: Environment Canada, 1985); Canada, *Freshwater Management in Canada*, 3 vols (Ottawa: Library of Parliament, 2004).

9. J. Benidickson, *The Development of Water Supply and Sewage Infrastructure in Ontario 1880–1990s: Legal and Institutional Aspects of Public Health and Environmental History*. Paper commissioned for the Walkerton Inquiry (Toronto: Ministry of the Attorney General, 2002).

10. EPA, *EPA Progress Report* (Washington, 1995); EPA, *The Great Lakes Atlas: An Environmental Atlas and Resource Book*, 3rd edn, www.epa.gov.

11. P. McCulloch and P. Muldoon, *A Sustainable Water Strategy for Ontario* (Toronto: Canadian Environmental Law Association, 1999), 29, www.cela.ca.

12. L. Botts and P. Muldoon, *Evolution of the Great Lakes Water Quality Agreement* (East Lansing: Michigan State University Press, 2005), 43.

13. T. Colborn, A. Davidson, S. Green, R.A. Hodge, C.I. Jackson, and R.A. Liroff. *Great Lakes, Great Legacy?* (Washington and Ottawa: Conservation Foundation and Institute for Research on Public Policy, 1990), 64.

14. Brooks, "Water Policy," 264.

15. A.M. Schwartz, "The Management of Shared Waters: Watershed Boards Past and Future," in P. Le Prestre and P. Stoett, eds, *Bilateral Ecopolitics: Continuity and Change in Canadian–American Environmental Relations* (Burlington, Vermont: Ashgate, 2006), 133–44.

16. *State of the Lakes Ecosystem Report*, 2011, http://binational.net/solec/sogl2011/sogl-2011-technical-report-en.pdf.

17. Botts and Muldoon, *Evolution of the Great Lakes Water Quality Agreement*, 101.

18. M.H. Sproule-Jones, *Restoration of the Great Lakes: Promises, Practices, Performances* (Vancouver: University of British Columbia Press, 2002).

19. J.H. Hartig and Z. Zarrell, *Under RAPs* (Ann Arbor: University of Michigan Press, 1992); Sproule-Jones, *Restoration of the Great Lakes*.

20. W.A. Rosenbaum, *Environmental Politics and Policy*, 2nd edn (Washington: Congressional Quarterly Press, 1991).

21. Organisation for Economic Co-operation and Development, *Environmental Performance Reviews: Progress in the 1990s* (Paris: OECD, 1996).

22. EPA, *EPA Progress Report* (Washington: EPA, 1995).

23. D. Savoie, *Towards a Different Shade of Green: Program Review and Environment Canada*. Working paper for Canadian Centre for Management Development, 1997.

24. C. Johns, "Nonpoint Source Water Pollution Management in Canada and the US: A Comparative Analysis of Institutional Arrangements and Policy Instruments," Ph.D. dissertation (McMaster University, 2000); Botts and Muldoon, *Evolution of the Great Lakes Water Quality Agreement*.

25. G.B. Doern and T. Conway, *The Greening of Canada: Federal Institutions and Decisions* (Toronto: University of Toronto Press, 1994).

26. L. Boothe and F. Quinn, "Twenty-five Years of the Canada Water Act," *Canadian Water Resources Journal* 20, 2 (1995): 65–90.

27. Botts and Muldoon, *Evolution of the Great Lakes Water Quality Agreement*, 161.

28. B.G. Rabe, "Beyond Kyoto: Climate Change Policy in Multilevel Governance Systems," *Governance* 20, 3 (2007): 423–44.

29. Botts and Muldoon, *Evolution of the Great Lakes Water Quality Agreement*, 141.

30. M. Winfield and G. Jenish, *Troubled Waters? A Review of the Performance of the Governments of Canada and Ontario under the 1994 Canada–Ontario Agreement Respecting the Great Lakes Basin Ecosystem* (Toronto: Canadian Institute of Environmental Law and Policy, 1999), www.cielap.org/pub/pub_troubledwaters.html.

31. Ontario Ministry of the Environment, *The Great Lakes: Clean Water Act, 2006*, 2007, at:www.ene.gov.on.ca/en/water/greatlakes.

32. G. Hoberg, "Comparing Canadian Performance in Environmental Policy," in R. Boardman, ed., *Canadian Environmental Policy: Ecosystems, Politics, and Process* (Toronto: Oxford University Press, 1992), 246–62; Johns, "Nonpoint Source Water Pollution"; E. Montpetit, "Sound Science and Moral Suasion, Not Regulation: Facing Difficult Decisions on Agricultural Non-Point-Source Pollution," in D. VanNijnatten and R. Boardman, eds, *Canadian Environmental Policy: Context and Cases*, 2nd edn (Toronto: Oxford University Press, 2002), 274–85; C. Johns, "Water Pollution in the Great Lakes Basin: The Global–Local Dynamic," in Christopher Gore and Peter Stoett, eds, *Environmental Challenges and Opportunities: Local–Global Perspectives on Canadian Issues* (Toronto: Emond Montgomery, 2009), 95–129.

33. Commissioner of Environment and Sustainable Development (CESD), *Annual Report* (Ottawa: Office of the Auditor General, 2001), 307.

34. Ibid, 312.

35. Botts and Muldoon, *Evolution of the Great Lakes Water Quality Agreement*, 149.

36. Canada, Standing Senate Committee on Energy, the Environment and Natural Resources, 2005, 16.

37. Botts and Muldoon, *Evolution of the Great Lakes Water Quality Agreement*, 163.

38. Great Lakes Regional Collaboration, http://www.glrc.us.

39. John Austin, *Healthy Waters, Strong Economy: The Economic Benefits of Restoring the Great Lakes Ecosystem* (Washington: Brookings Institution, 2007).

40. Great Lakes United, *The Great Lakes Blueprint: A Canadian Vision for Protecting and Restoring the Great Lakes and the St. Lawrence River Ecosystem*, 2007, www.glu.org.

41. Canada, Policy Research Initiative, *Freshwater for the Future: Policies for Sustainable Water Management in Canada*. Conference Proceedings, Gatineau, Que., 8–10 May 2006, www.policyresearch.gc.ca.

42. EPA, "Great Lakes Restoration Initiative,"http://www.epa.gov/greatlakes/glri/.

43. International Joint Commission, *Great Lakes Water Quality Agreement—2012*,http://www.ijc.org/en_/Great_Lakes_Water_Quality.

44. Great Lakes United, *Great Lakes Blueprint*.

45. J.H. Hartig, M.A. Zarull, J.J. Ciborowski, J.E. Gannon, E. Wilke, and A.N. Vincent, "Long-term Ecosystem Monitoring and Assessment of the Detroit River and Western Lake Erie," *Environmental Monitoring and Assessment* 158 (2009): 87–104; EPA, *Great Lakes Factsheet*.

46. T. Shulte, "Emerging Routes to Environmental Activism: Lake Erie Sportsmen and the League of Women Voters," *Excursions Journal* 3, 1 (2011): 7.

47. Ibid, 1–20.

48. R. Sweeney, "Rejuvenation of Lake Erie," *GeoJournal* 35, 1 (1995): 65–6.

49. International Joint Commission, "Lake Erie Ecosystem Priority Report," 2014, http://ijc.org/en_/leep.

50. L.E. Allinger and E.D. Reavie, "The Ecological History of Lake Erie as Recorded by the Phytoplankton Community," *Journal of Great Lakes Research* 39 (2013): 365–82.

51. Hartig et al., "Long-term Ecosystem Monitoring and Assessment."

52. J.C. Makarewicz and P. Bertram, "Evidence for the Restoration of the Lake Erie Ecosystem,"*BioScience* 41, 4 (1991): 216–23.

53. S. Painter et al., "Sediment Contamination in Lake Erie: A 25-Year Retrospective Analysis," *Journal of Great Lakes Research* 27, 4 (2001): 434–48.

54. EPA, "Lake Erie Dead Zone," 2002, www.epa.gov.

55. Johns, "Nonpoint Source Water Pollution."

56. EPA, "Lake Erie Dead Zone."

57. J. Pelley, "Multiple Stressors behind Lake Erie Decline,"*Environmental Science and Technology* 37, 21 (2003): 383–4.

58. International Joint Commission, *A Balanced Diet for Lake Erie: Lake Erie Ecosystem Priority Report*, 2014, http://www.ijc.org/files/publications/2014%20IJC%20LEEP%20REPORT.pdf.

59. Z. Yuntao et al.,"Record Breaking Lake Erie Hypoxia during 2012 Drought," *Environmental Science and Technology* 49, 2 (2015): 800–7.

60. IJC, *A Balanced Diet for Lake Erie*.

61. Michael Wines, "Behind Toledo's Water Crisis, a Long-Troubled Lake Erie," *New York Times*, 4 Aug. 2014.

62. The evidence in this case is culled from a number of works of the International Joint Commission, plus some secondary sources. See IJC, *Upper Great Lakes Connecting Channels Study* (Windsor, Ont., 1989); IJC, "Protection of the Waters of the Great Lakes" and "Lake Superior Regulation: Addressing Uncertainty in Upper Great Lakes Water Levels" (Washington and Ottawa, 2000). See also John Grant, "Governance of the Stock and Flow of Water in the Great Lakes Basin," Ph.D. dissertation (McMaster University, 2010); Sproule-Jones,

Restoration of the Great Lakes; George Francis, *Governance and Institutional Arrangements under the Great Lakes Water Quality Agreement* (Windsor, Ont.: IJC Science Advisory Board, 2005).

63. Mowat Centre, *Low Water Blues: An Economic Impact Assessment of Future Low Water Levels in the Great Lakes and St. Lawrence River*, 2014, http://mowatcentre.ca/low-water-blues/.

64. Ibid.

65. D. MacFarlane, "The St. Lawrence Seaway and Subnational Environmental Diplomacy," draft paper presented as part of special issue workshop of the *Canadian Foreign Policy Journal*, Toronto, 27 Mar. 2014.

66. Great Lakes–St Lawrence Seaway System, http://www.greatlakes-seaway.com/en/management/index.htm.

67. Environment Canada, "Water Withdrawal and Consumption by Sector," https://www.ec.gc.ca/indicateurs-indicators/default.asp?lang=en&n=5736C951-1.

68. Great Lakes Integrated Sciences and Assessment, *Synthesis of the Third National Climate Assessment for the Great Lakes Region*, 2014, http://glisa.umich.edu/media/files/Great_Lakes_NCA_Synthesis.pdf.

16 The West and Water Scarcity

B. Timothy Heinmiller

Chapter Summary

Canada is generally known as having an abundance of water, but in some parts of western Canada, specifically southern Alberta, southern Saskatchewan, and the British Columbia Interior, water scarcity is the norm. In these regions, water has long been allocated and managed using a system known as prior allocation. This chapter explains the origins of the prior allocation system as well as recent attempts by the provinces to adapt the prior allocation system to the challenges of modern water governance.

Chapter Outline

- When irrigation was King
  - Understanding "first in time, first in right," prior allocation, and the iron triangle
- Prior allocation comes under pressure from cities, environmentalists, and new industries
- The politics of dam construction
- Prior allocation in the twenty-first century
  - Saskatchewan: the highly centralized, discretionary approach to allocation
  - Alberta: the adoption of a cap-and-trade system
  - British Columbia: the minimalist approach to reform
- Looking ahead—the prospects for environmental considerations in water allocation decision-making

Introduction

Although Canada is generally thought to have an abundant supply of water, in some regions water scarcity is the overriding reality. These areas are found mostly in western Canada, specifically in southern Alberta, southern Saskatchewan, and the BC Interior. Average annual precipitation in these areas ranges from 300 to 500 mm and precipitation levels can vary widely from one year to the next, ranging from droughts in some years to floods in others. Because precipitation in these regions is so scarce and variable, residents rely heavily on surface water to support their economies and communities. However, supplies of surface water are finite and difficult decisions have to be made regarding water allocation, determining who gets water and who does not. Responsibility for water allocation lies mostly with the provincial governments. Until the 1980s the governments of BC, Alberta, and Saskatchewan took a very similar approach to allocating their scarce water resources, an approach known as **prior allocation**.

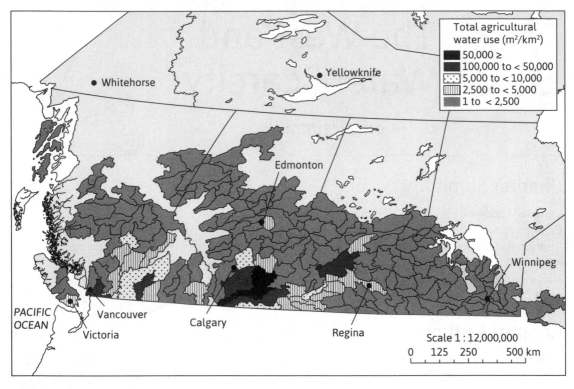

FIGURE 16.1 | Irrigation Intensity in Western Canada

Source: Martin Beaulieu, Caroline Fric, and Francois Soulard, "Agricultural Water Use by Sub-Sub Drainage Area – Western Canada, 2001." Available at http://www.statcan.gc.ca/pub/16-002-x/2008001/maps/5008077-eng.htm (accessed 21 August 2013).

Prior allocation was explicitly designed to facilitate the development and expansion of irrigation agriculture and it, combined with extensive government assistance for irrigation infrastructure, ensured that irrigation became the dominant water use in the dry areas of western Canada. Today, irrigation still accounts for 70 per cent of water use in BC's Okanagan Valley and about 72 per cent of water use in southern Alberta.[1] The most intensive irrigation areas in western Canada are shown in Figure 16.1.

Since the 1980s, the prior allocation system has come under increasing pressure. By this time, much of the available surface waters in the western dry areas had become fully allocated or over-allocated, leaving little water to support the environment or new water users. Accordingly, pressures mounted for water allocation reform driven by environmentalists, growing cities, and emerging industries not well served by the prior allocation system. The result has been a period of reform and policy divergence, with each province taking a different approach to updating its water allocation policy. This chapter explores the politics of water allocation in Canada's water-scarce regions, documenting the entrenchment of prior allocation as well as more recent efforts to reform this nineteenth-century policy to deal with twenty-first-century water governance challenges.

When Irrigation Was King

When Captain John Palliser explored the southern Canadian Prairies in 1857, he saw a dry, desolate semi-desert. In his report, Palliser surmised that the region might support a cattle ranching industry someday, but that it was too dry and its soil quality too poor to support agriculture.[2] Early assessments of the Okanagan Valley were much the same, and early ranching operations were set up in both areas, the ranches comprising vast tracts of virgin land and the cattle feeding largely on natural grasses.[3] Although these areas were well suited to ranching, the governments of western Canada had greater ambitions. Ranching provided only sparse rural settlement and did not produce nearly the economic returns that intensive agriculture did. In such dry areas the only viable means of achieving intensive agriculture was through irrigation, so, in the late nineteenth century, governments set out to devise a water allocation system that would provide farmers with all of the water they would need to undertake large-scale irrigation.

While BC had become a province in 1871 and had the power to govern most of the water resources within its borders, until 1905 Alberta and Saskatchewan were still part of a federal territory (the North-West Territories) and water use on the Prairies was governed by Ottawa. This meant that the BC government and the federal government were grappling simultaneously with the problem of how to allocate scarce surface waters in their dry areas in order to stimulate irrigation development. Remarkably, the two governments came to the same policy solution—the prior allocation system—based on independent investigations of irrigation policies in Australia and the western US.[4] Prior allocation was instituted in BC through a series of laws beginning in 1892, while it was introduced on the Prairies through the landmark Northwest Irrigation Act of 1894. When Alberta and Saskatchewan, which became provinces in 1905, took over ownership of the natural resources within their borders through the 1930 Natural Resources Transfer Agreement, their governments maintained the prior allocation system in their own water legislation.[5]

Prior allocation is a distinctly Canadian policy innovation, borrowing elements from water allocation policies in both the western US and Australia, where efforts at irrigation development preceded those in western Canada by a few decades. From the western US, Canadians borrowed the principle of **first in time, first in right** (FITFIR) water allocation. The

BOX 16.1 | Irrigation and Irrigation Methods

Irrigation is the practice of applying water to land in order to grow crops. It is generally undertaken in dry areas where land is plentiful but water is scarce. There are various irrigation methods, including **flood irrigation** (controlled flooding of entire fields); **row irrigation** (controlled flooding between rows of crops); **sprinkler irrigation** (the spraying of crops with pressurized sprinklers); and **drip irrigation** (the application of water directly to plants' roots). About 40 per cent of the world's crops are grown using irrigation and this figure is expected to rise.[6] The world's three largest irrigating states are China, India, and the United States; Canada does not even rank in the top 20.[7]

FITFIR principle allowed farmers to claim water and use it for irrigation wherever they could put it to use, even on land that does not border on a river. Irrigators could continue to claim water until supplies were exhausted. In dry years, when river flows were low, water was allocated based on the seniority of entitlements: the oldest entitlement holder got water first, followed by the next oldest, and so on. This had the potential to leave more recent entitlement holders without water in dry years, but it also provided incentive for irrigators to stake their entitlements early, thereby encouraging irrigation development.[8] From Australia, Canadians borrowed the idea of government-administered water licensing. Although the Americans' FITFIR approach had its advantages, its implementation was often disorderly and conflict-ridden.[9] The Australians, in contrast, vested ownership of all water resources in the Crown and allocated water through government licences, an orderly approach much more to the Canadians' liking.[10] Accordingly, under prior allocation, all water rights were vested in the Crown, and water use was licensed by government—the provincial government in BC and the federal government, until 1930, on the Prairies—according to the FITFIR principle.[11]

The introduction of prior allocation was enough to entice some private corporations and land speculators to undertake irrigation projects in the first two decades of the twentieth century, but irrigation did not really take off until governments began funding it. Government irrigation assistance came in two forms. One was direct assistance to expand irrigation projects. The Alberta government began assisting its irrigation projects as early as 1920; and, between 1935 and 1978, the Prairie Farm Rehabilitation Administration (PFRA)—the federal agency tasked with irrigation development—spent nearly $600 million on water control infrastructure on the Canadian Prairies.[12] Irrigation assistance also came in the form of dam construction. These dams were very important for irrigation expansion because they allowed more river water to be controlled, storing it in the spring months when water is relatively plentiful and releasing it in the summer months when water is scarce and crops are thirsty. The rivers and lakes of the Okanagan Valley, for example, were extensively dammed to control river flows and support irrigation expansion on the dry table lands. In Saskatchewan, the Gardiner Dam, completed in 1967 by the PFRA, created a 225-km-long artificial lake (Lake Diefenbaker) that provides water to most of the irrigation districts in the province. In southern Alberta, the most significant—and most controversial—dam was the Oldman River Dam, completed by the province in 1992 with the express purpose of expanding irrigation in downstream areas.

From the early 1950s to the late 1970s, at the height of government irrigation assistance, the total irrigated area in BC, Alberta, and Saskatchewan more than doubled, from 252,100 hectares to 573,760 hectares.[13] As Figure 16.2 shows, the rate of irrigation growth since the late 1970s has slowed considerably and virtually levelled off in Saskatchewan and BC, with annual fluctuations depending on the amount of rainfall during the growing season. Moderate growth occurred in southern Alberta through the 1990s, mostly due to the completion of the Oldman Dam, but it, too, has levelled off in the last 10 years or so.[14]

Throughout the period of irrigation expansion, a triad of political interests was responsible for directing the massive amounts of water and public money devoted to irrigation development. Government administrators in the provincial agricultural departments and the federal PFRA believed in the potential of irrigation to turn semi-desert into lush farmland, and benefited from irrigation expansion by increasing their profiles within government and securing resources to grow their organizations. MLAs and MPs from the dry areas of western Canada were only too happy to team up with these bureaucrats in pushing for

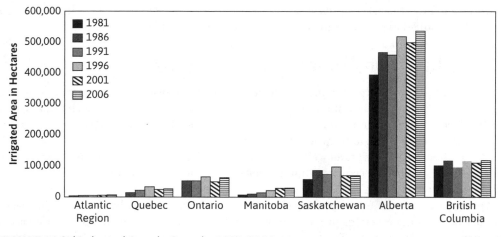

FIGURE 16.2 | Irrigated Area in Canada, 1981–2006

Source: Marie-Eve Poirier, Agricultural Water Use Survey 2007. http://www.statcan.gc.ca/pub/16-001-m/16-001-m2009008-eng.htm

new projects and new money for irrigation. Irrigators, of course, were happy to accept this state largesse and lobbied hard to secure it.

For much of the twentieth century, this triad of political interests had a virtual lock on the water policy communities of western Canada. Glenn describes water policy-making in Alberta as controlled by an **iron triangle**, the three sides of the triangle constituting the

BOX 16.2 | The Irrigation Economies of British Columbia, Alberta, and Saskatchewan

BC, Alberta, and Saskatchewan have the largest irrigation economies in Canada, yet each is distinctive (Table 16.1). In Alberta and Saskatchewan, irrigation is used to grow field crops such as wheat, barley, and hay and there are few fruits and vegetables grown. In the BC Interior, where the climate is warmer, fruits and vegetables are much more prominent and the area is famous as one of Canada's grape- and wine-producing regions. In BC and Alberta, irrigation districts constitute the vast majority of irrigation, but in Saskatchewan private irrigators are far more prevalent.

TABLE 16.1 Crops and Irrigation: British Columbia, Alberta, and Saskatchewan

Province	Field Crops (%)	Fruits (%)	Vegetables (%)	Hay (%)	Pasture (%)	Total Irrigated Area (hectares)
British Columbia	18.8	11.9	8.4	53.3	7.7	76,570
Alberta	73.8	0.0	0.9	18.2	7.1	356,500
Saskatchewan	64.3	0.0	0.0	33.3	1.9	40,810

Source: Avani Babooram et al., *Agricultural Water Use in Canada*, accessed 21 Aug. 2013, http://www.statcan.gc.ca/pub/16-402-x/16-402-x2011001-eng.htm.

government administrators, politicians, and farmers described above.[15] As long as this iron triangle remained in place, the prior allocation system was under little threat.

Prior Allocation Comes Under Pressure

By the 1980s, there was a growing ambivalence about the prior allocation system in the water-scarce areas of the Canadian West. While irrigators continued to champion this entrenched system, other actors began to challenge it, leaving provincial policy-makers in the middle, struggling to make prior allocation work for all parties.

Prior allocation had worked well in encouraging irrigation development and expansion, but as the limits of western water supplies began to be reached its continued efficacy came into question. By the late 1970s and early 1980s, some rivers in western Canada reached or surpassed the point of **full allocation**. The construction of dams had postponed this eventuality by allowing a greater proportion of available water to be controlled and allocated, but now the physical limits of water supplies loomed large. Many of the good dam construction sites in western Canada had already been exploited, so further dam construction was not much of an option. As another option, the Alberta government studied the possibility of diverting northern rivers into the South Saskatchewan River Basin to augment water supplies and support further irrigation development, as had been done in California, Australia, and a number of other water-scarce places. While technically possible, such inter-basin diversion projects were prohibitively expensive and environmentally destructive, and they found little support outside of the irrigation supporters whose political influence was in decline.[16] Without new sources of water to allocate, the prior allocation system struggled to meet the needs of emerging water users, and political pressures for water allocation reform began to mount.

The biggest change in western water policy communities was the emergence of environmental groups who demanded that riverine environments receive a fair share of the water available in western rivers. The environmental movement emerged in Canada in the 1960s, but it was not until the second wave of environmentalism, from the mid-1980s to the early 1990s, that they became a political force in western water policy communities.[17] The environmentalists were highly critical of the ecological toll placed on western rivers by large-scale irrigation. Massive water allocations to support irrigation had significantly reduced stream flows, impaired fish stocks, dried up wetlands, and degraded water quality. Moreover, the dams constructed to support irrigation had inundated some riverine environments, channellized others, and interrupted natural streamflow patterns. The environmentalists' solutions were to stop building new dams, to start operating existing dams so that they mimicked natural stream flows, and to introduce environmental flow allocations to support the plethora of environmental services provided by western rivers.

The conflict over the Oldman Dam in southern Alberta is illustrative of the environmentalists' new influence. In 1984, the Alberta government announced its intention to construct a dam on the upper reaches of the Oldman River, primarily to support irrigation expansion in downstream areas.[18] In an unprecedented show of resistance, environmentalists mobilized in opposition. Forming an umbrella organization known as Friends of the Oldman River, environmentalists engaged in public protests, lobbying, and court action, all the way to the Supreme Court.[19] Though their efforts to stop the dam were ultimately unsuccessful, the environmentalists generated considerable public sympathy and forced their way into the

TABLE 16.2 The Changing Economies and Demographics of Western Canada

	Crop and Animal Production (% of Provincial GDP)		Urban Population (% of Provincial Population)	
	1927	1984	1931	1981
Saskatchewan	83	11	32	58
Alberta	70	3	38	77
British Columbia	11	1	57	78

Sources: Government of Canada, *Canada Year Book, 1930* (Ottawa, 1931), 186, 207; Statistics Canada, "Population, Urban and Rural, by Province and Territory," accessed 4 Sept. 2013, http://www.statcan.gc.ca/tables-tableaux/ sum-som/l01/cst01/demo62a-eng.htm; Statistics Canada, "Gross Domestic Product (GDP) at Basic Prices, by North American Industry Classification (NAICS) and Province, Annual," accessed 21 June 2012, http://www5.statcan. gc.ca/cansim/home-accueil?lang=eng&tz=120308.

Alberta water policy community. They also threw into question the prevailing prior allocation system, setting the stage for future reforms.[20]

In addition to growing political pressure from environmentalists, western Canada was also experiencing an economic and demographic transformation that did not work in the irrigators' favour. In the early decades of the twentieth century, Saskatchewan, Alberta, and the BC Interior were predominantly rural societies and agricultural economies (see Table 16.2). In such societies, where agriculture was the dominant industry, substantial government investments in irrigation development and expansion seemed to make sense. By the early 1980s, however, the dry areas of western Canada had become demographically and economically transformed. Vast majorities of their populations now lived in cities, and most of these people had little connection to agriculture, having taken jobs in the growing oil, potash, manufacturing, financial, or service sectors. Agriculture's relative economic importance had declined considerably, and although farmers remained an influential interest group, their arguments about the social and economic importance of irrigation had lost much of their resonance.

Demographic and economic change also brought with it new water demands from growing cities and emerging industries. The Okanagan Valley, for instance, experienced tremendous population growth starting in the 1960s, most of it in urban areas such as Kelowna, Penticton, Vernon, and Osoyoos. During this period it became a popular retirement destination and developed a thriving tourism industry that "during the 1970s and 1980s came to rival agriculture for economic dominance."[21] With most of the available water in the Okanagan already allocated to irrigation, cities, suburbs, and the newer service industries began to pressure for water allocation reforms. Similar pressures were experienced in southern Alberta as a result of the oil boom and the massive growth of Calgary and its suburbs.

While pressures for water allocation reform mounted, the irrigators remained a formidable political force. The irrigation districts, in particular, had evolved from fragile state-funded projects into powerful economic interests with impressive technical and financial resources at their disposal. Under prior allocation, the irrigators already held the largest and most senior water licences in their respective provinces, so they merely had to defend an entrenched status quo while their opponents had the much more difficult task of trying to introduce major water allocation reforms. Furthermore, governments had invested hundreds of millions of dollars in dams and irrigation infrastructure throughout the twentieth century, and they were unlikely to abandon these investments willingly without the promised economic returns.

The countervailing pressures for and against prior allocation created a new water politics in western Canada's dry areas from the 1980s onward. Environmentalists, cities, and emerging industries broke into western water policy communities and agitated for water allocation reforms. These efforts were met with staunch resistance by irrigators and their MLAs, powerful vested interests determined to preserve their way of life. The result was a tumultuous period of water politics as the old prior allocation systems collided with new political economic realities, and provincial policy-makers searched for ways to reconcile the two.

Prior Allocation in the Twenty-First Century

While the prior allocation systems of BC, Alberta, and Saskatchewan were remarkably similar up to the 1980s, they have diverged significantly since. Saskatchewan, the first to undertake water allocation reforms, abandoned the prior allocation system in favour of a highly centralized approach that affords a lot of discretion to government water managers. Alberta, in contrast, has maintained its prior allocation system but superimposed a cap-and-trade system on top of it that limits the number of water licences available and allows licences to be bought and sold. BC has taken a minimalist approach to reform, choosing to tweak various aspects of the prior allocation system but leaving it largely untouched. Despite this recent policy divergence, one fundamental commonality remains: the water licences given to irrigators under the pre-reform systems, as well as the seniority of these licences, have been preserved and carried forward into the post-reform era.

Saskatchewan

Saskatchewan's water reforms have preserved the water-licensing aspect of the prior allocation system, but moved away from the FITFIR approach to prioritizing licences. Water users in Saskatchewan are still required to have a government licence for their water use. However, starting with the Water Corporation Act of 1984, Saskatchewan ended its use of the FITFIR approach to the allocation of new water licences. Instead, it vested all water allocation decisions in a centralized water management agency and gave this agency unprecedented discretionary authority to issue new water licences, including any terms and conditions related to prioritization. This, in effect, displaced the FITFIR principle with **administrative discretion**, resulting in a highly centralized approach to water allocation.[22]

Given the increased reliance on administrative discretion, the agencies given this discretion are central to water allocation in Saskatchewan. Since the first reforms in 1984, the province has had three successive water management agencies: the Saskatchewan Water Corporation from 1984 to 2002, the Saskatchewan Watershed Authority from 2002 to 2012, and the Saskatchewan Water Security Agency from 2012 to today. All three agencies were created as Crown corporations operating at arm's length from the government.

The water allocation discretion afforded to administrators in Saskatchewan's water agencies is unprecedented in North America. Reliance on administrative discretion was intended to involve the government's water experts more directly in the province's water management challenges, including the management of water scarcity in the southern part of the province. It was also intended to break away from the inflexibility of the old FITFIR approach to water allocation by giving administrators a free hand in allocating scarce resources. However, because water allocation decisions now rest in the hands of government administrators with no clear water allocation principle guiding them, the new approach has been sharply criticized as arbitrary and lacking transparency, exacerbating rather than reducing the uncertainties of water allocation in a water-scarce region.[23]

There is now also a crucial distinction in Saskatchewan between pre-reform water licences and post-reform licences, and the two coexist rather awkwardly. When reforms were introduced in 1984, the pre-reform licences granted under the old prior allocation system did not disappear. These licences were preserved and carried forward through all of Saskatchewan's water reforms, and their seniority is still recognized.[24] The discretion afforded to government administrators only applies to post-reform licences, those issued after 1984. Initially, the Saskatchewan Water Corporation had the power to cancel pre-reform water licences at its discretion, but this power was used very sparingly because "licensees in water-short regions in western Canada tend to view their water rights as entitlements. Any attempt by an administrator to remove or limit those rights is met with a degree of outrage that makes it politically difficult or impossible to exercise the statutory powers."[25] Subsequently, this licence cancellation power disappeared with the creation of the Saskatchewan Watershed Authority in 2002.[26]

This has made the prior allocation system something of a policy zombie in the dry areas of Saskatchewan. Legislators killed it in 1984 and no longer use it in post-reform licensing. But it is "undead" in the sense that pre-reform water licences based on prior allocation continue to live on, and constitute the vast majority of water use in the province, particularly in the dry areas. Thus, although government administrators have a lot of discretion over post-reform licences, they seem to have much less discretion over pre-reform licences.

Just as post-reform water licensing is left largely to the discretion of government administrators, so too is the preservation of river flows for environmental protection purposes. Although no legislation requires the maintenance of minimum stream flows, environmental protection and sustainability have been part of the water agencies' mandates.[27] In their water licensing decisions, they have used their discretion to limit the number of new licences in areas already heavily allocated, thereby preventing heavily used rivers from being depleted even further. The agencies have also had the power to suspend or revoke any water licence in the name of the "public interest," though in practice this power has been used sparingly.[28] Thus, environmental protection has a more prominent place in Saskatchewan water governance than in the pre-reform era, but largely at the discretion of provincial administrators.

To give its water management decisions greater legitimacy, Saskatchewan's water management agencies have increasingly relied on public participation and consultation processes, particularly in the past decade. The Saskatchewan Watershed Authority, for instance, created local watershed advisory committees to ensure its decisions were accepted and implemented by local stakeholders.[29] More recently, the Saskatchewan Water Security Agency undertook a two-phase public consultation process in developing its 25 Year Saskatchewan Water Security Plan. The Plan outlines seven broad goals and many specific action areas that are to shape the future of Saskatchewan's water policy. Notably, one of these goals is to "develop modern and comprehensive water legislation," but this remains to be done.[30] So, water allocation remains a work in progress in Saskatchewan, and it is unclear whether the province will maintain its uniquely centralized approach in the future.

Alberta

Alberta's water reforms have preserved the prior allocation system, but have overlaid it with a new cap-and-trade system for water licences. The furor over the Oldman Dam in the late 1980s and early 1990s sparked a review of Alberta's water policy that culminated in the passage of a new Water Act in 1996.[31] The Water Act introduced the two basic policy instruments necessary for a cap-and-trade system: (1) the authority to impose moratoriums on the issuance of new water licences on heavily allocated rivers (the "capping" instrument); and (2) the authority to introduce the buying and selling of water licences, separate from land, in designated basins (the "trading" instrument).[32] These two instruments were put into effect throughout much of southern Alberta with the creation of the South Saskatchewan River Basin Water Management Plan in 2006. The Plan was developed through extensive stakeholder and public consultations, and its introduction fundamentally changed water allocation in the dry areas of the province.

In the Water Act, environmentalists succeeded in securing a number of new policy instruments that can be used for environmental protection and restoration. The Water Act empowered its director to impose moratoriums on the issuance of new water licences in heavily allocated streams and empowered the Environment Minister to reserve unallocated water for any purpose, including environmental protection. The Water Act also permitted both temporary and permanent transfers of water licences, but subject to authorization in a basin water management plan (discussed below) or, in the absence of such a plan, cabinet approval.[33] When trades occur, the director is empowered to withhold up to 10 per cent of the volume of any water licence traded in order "to protect the aquatic environment or to implement a water conservation objective."[34] Although the amounts of water reallocated through conservation holdbacks have thus far been small, the conservation holdback mechanism is notable as the only instrument in western Canada allowing any amount of water to be moved from economic to environmental uses.

For their part, irrigators succeeded in ensuring that the prior allocation system was maintained and that pre-reform water licences were afforded near-absolute protection by the Water Act. Pre-reform licences are those held prior to the introduction of the Water Act, a category dominated by irrigators that accounts for most of the water diversions in southern Alberta. The Act provides that pre-reform licensees "can continue to divert water in accordance with their original priority, the terms and conditions of their original licence and the new Act. However, if there is a conflict between a term of a deemed licence and the new Act, the term of the licence prevails over the Act."[35] This, in effect, allowed irrigators to continue their water use practices under the Water Act almost exactly as before.

The Water Act also recognized the diversity of Alberta's water governance challenges—from scarcity in the south to oil sands pollution in the north—and the importance of stakeholder participation in water governance. It provided for the creation of basin-level water management planning processes in which stakeholders would be heavily involved.[36] The resulting water management plans, negotiated at the basin level and then approved by cabinet, would create specific rules and regulations relating to licensing moratoriums, licence trading, and conservation holdbacks, allowing the general provisions of the Water Act to be adapted to different basins' needs and challenges. It is through the South Saskatchewan River Basin Water Management Plan that the policy instruments of the Water Act were eventually put into action in southern Alberta and that the cap-and-trade system was introduced.

So far, this is the only water management plan put in place in the province; the oil sands-related pollution issues in Alberta's northern basins have yet to be addressed in basin plans.

The South Saskatchewan River Basin Water Management Plan was developed between 2000 and 2006 over two phases. Phase I, dealing with water trading issues, was expedient and, by most accounts, relatively uncontroversial. Few stakeholders were ideologically opposed to the introduction of water trading, and the idea was championed by Environment Minister Lorne Taylor. Consequently, phase I lasted little more than nine months and a Water Management Plan to introduce water licence trading and conservation holdbacks was approved by the Alberta cabinet in June 2002. Phase II dealt with water capping issues, and because these issues were more complex and controversial it lasted nearly four years.[37] Ultimately, it was agreed that licensing moratoriums would be imposed in the heavily allocated Oldman, Bow, and South Saskatchewan sub-basins, and that a ceiling on future licences would be imposed on the less heavily allocated Red Deer sub-basin.[38] By combining the earlier trading provisions with the new capping provisions, a cap-and-trade system was effectively superimposed on the long-standing prior allocation system.

For water users in southern Alberta, the introduction of cap-and-trade has been a major change in a number of ways. The introduction of licensing caps draws a clear regulatory line between water for human uses and water for environmental uses. The recognition and designation of water for environmental purposes is a major change in southern Alberta, though serious questions remain about the adequacy of current cap levels for protecting or restoring riverine environments, particularly in the southernmost rivers. Nevertheless, the imposition of caps is at least a major first step. The caps also mean that prospective water users in much of southern Alberta must now look at buying existing water licences rather than simply applying for new ones. This is a major cognitive and cultural shift for water users in the region and, as Box 16.3 shows, the transition has been awkward, at times.

BOX 16.3 | Cap-and-Trade in Southern Alberta

In 2004, plans were announced to construct a 1.4 million square foot shopping centre in the Municipal District of Rocky View, just west of Calgary. However, Rocky View did not have enough water to support the development, could not get a new water licence (because of the licensing moratoriums), and was forced into the new water licence market. Rocky View tried unsuccessfully to get water from the city of Calgary and the town of Drumheller before striking a deal with the Western Irrigation District in 2007. Rocky View obtained a licence for just over 2,220 million litres of water in exchange for $15 million, which the Western Irrigation District would use to convert 50 km of its open canal into pipeline. The irrigators estimated that the amount of water saved from seepage and evaporation from the old canal would more than make up for the amount of water traded away, leaving it with a net water gain. The shopping centre opened for business in August 2009, about two years behind schedule.

Source: Renata D'Aliesio, "Tapped Out: Water Woes," *Calgary Herald*, 1 Dec. 2007.

British Columbia

While Saskatchewan and Alberta have taken major departures from the prior allocation system, BC has not—at least not yet. Prior allocation persists in BC much as it has for decades, notwithstanding a number of recent reforms to adapt it to modern water governance challenges. BC's reticence in water allocation reform may be due to a number of factors. Tightly regulated water licence trading has been allowed in BC since 1939, and this may have provided sufficient flexibility for accommodating new water demands so as to dampen pressures for fundamental water allocation reform. It should also be noted that the dry areas of the BC Interior constitute only a small portion of the province in terms of both territory and population, so it was probably difficult for dry-area water allocation issues to reach the provincial policy agenda. It may also be that BC is just a few years behind Alberta and Saskatchewan in introducing fundamental water allocation reforms, as the province has just recently passed new water legislation.

BC's water allocation reform measures may, thus far, be properly characterized as tinkering with the margins of the prior allocation system. In 1979, authority over water licence distribution was decentralized from the provincial Comptroller of Water Rights to a number of regional water managers, though no changes were introduced in the criteria for distributing or prioritizing licences.[39] In 1997, the BC legislature passed the Fish Protection Act "to strengthen the protection of fish and fish habitat from water allocations."[40] Subsequent regulations gave the minister the authority to reduce water use temporarily during droughts, but powers to revoke existing licences for general environmental protection purposes were not included.[41] Following Alberta's lead, the BC Water Act was amended in 2004 to allow for basin-level water management planning processes.[42] These processes were designed to bring stakeholders together to manage conflicts between competing water demands and to mitigate the negative impacts of heavy water use on aquatic environments, but no changes were made to the underlying prior allocation system.

In May 2014, BC proclaimed into law a new Water Sustainability Act that could have huge implications for water governance in the dry areas of the BC Interior. The legislation was developed through an extensive public and stakeholder consultation process, initiated in 2008. The Water Sustainability Act preserves the prior allocation system and the water licences granted under this system, but also calls for greater use of watershed governance, the regulation of groundwater withdrawals, and the use of full-cost water pricing. These and other reforms in the new legislation could add significant constraints to how irrigators use and manage water in BC, but much remains to be determined. Regulations pursuant to the Act are still in development, and the envisioned shift to watershed governance is still a few years away.[43]

Looking Ahead

The dry areas of the BC Interior and the southern Prairies are naturally water-scarce regions. However, as many surface water sources in these regions have become fully allocated (or over-allocated) and new water demands have emerged, water in these areas has become scarcer still. The provincial governments have responded by introducing a variety of water allocation reforms, but it is unlikely that these will be enough, as the ongoing water reform processes in BC and Saskatchewan already attest.

Most trends indicate that water will become even scarcer in the future. Cities in the dry areas of all three provinces are still growing—some are among the fastest-growing cities in Canada—and this growth is projected to continue in the near future. Finding water to support these cities, and the industries in and around them, will be a considerable challenge. There are also a number of unresolved First Nations water rights claims in all three provinces and, should these claims succeed, they could result in additional water demands. Also looming over all water users in western Canada's dry areas is the prospect of climate change. Climate change threatens to melt the mountain glaciers at the source of many western Canadian rivers, it threatens to make precipitation patterns even more erratic than they already are, and it threatens to bring hotter, drier summers that will increase demands from all water users.

In combination, these demand and supply-side pressures are likely to result in increased water scarcity and further pressure for water allocation reforms. As the holders of the largest and most senior water licences, the irrigators are the linchpin of water allocation reform, and recent reform processes show that they continue to have a lot of political influence. Finding a "win-win" solution for the irrigators who have the water and the new users who want the water—whether through water licence trading or some other means of water reallocation—will be the key to effective water allocation reform.

Key Terms

administrative discretion

drip irrigation

first in time, first in right

flood irrigation

full allocation

iron triangle

prior allocation

row irrigation

sprinkler irrigation

Questions for Review

1. Why did western Canadian governments adopt the prior allocation system?
2. Which province has most effectively adapted the prior allocation system to meet the challenges of modern water governance, BC, Alberta, or Saskatchewan?
3. What are some of the advantages and disadvantages of buying and selling water licences, as is done in BC and Alberta?
4. What role does the federal government play in governing western water resources? Should it have a larger role?
5. Do the existing water allocation regimes provide enough capacity for governing western water in the context of climate change?

Internet Resources

Alberta Environment and Sustainable Resource Development
http://esrd.alberta.ca/

British Columbia Ministry of the Environment, Water Stewardship Division
http://www.env.gov.bc.ca/wsd/

International Joint Commission, Accredited Officers for the St Mary–Milk Rivers
http://ijc.org/en_/aosmmr/home

Prairie Provinces Water Board
http://www.ppwb.ca/

Saskatchewan Water Security Agency
https://www.wsask.ca/

Additional Reading

Glenn, Jack. *Once Upon an Oldman: Special Interest Politics and the Oldman River Dam*. Vancouver: University of British Columbia Press, 1999.

Heinmiller, B. Timothy. "Advocacy Coalitions and the Alberta Water Act." *Canadian Journal of Political Science* 46, 3 (2013): 525–47.

Heinmiller, B. Timothy. "From Expansion to Conservation: Federalism and Irrigated Agriculture in Alberta, New South Wales, and California." In Inger Weibust and James Meadowcroft, eds, *Multilevel Environmental Governance: Water and Climate Change Policies in Europe and North America*. Northampton, UK: Edward Elgar, 2014.

Hood, George N. *Against the Flow—Rafferty–Alameda and the Politics of the Environment*. Saskatoon: Fifth House, 1994.

Hurlbert, Margot. "Comparative Water Governance in the Four Western Provinces." *Prairie Forum* 43, 1 (2009): 45–77.

Percy, David. R. "Responding to Water Scarcity in Western Canada." *Texas Law Review* 83 (2005): 2091–2107.

Prairie Farm Rehabilitation Administration. *History of Irrigation in Western Canada*. Ottawa: Government of Canada, 1982.

Schreier, Hans. "Agricultural Water Policy Challenges in BC." *Policy Options* (July–Aug. 2009): 56–60.

Notes

1. Hans Schreier, "Agricultural Water Policy Challenges in BC," *Policy Options* (July–Aug. 2009): 57; Alberta Environment and Sustainable Resource Development, "Sectoral Water Allocations—South Saskatchewan River Basin," accessed 18 Sept. 2013, http://environment.alberta.ca/01734.html.

2. James H. Gray, *Men against the Desert* (Calgary: Fifth House, 1996), 15.

3. John R. Wagner, "Landscape Aesthetics, Water, and Settler Colonialism in the Okanagan Valley of British Columbia," *Journal of Ecological Anthropology* 12, 22 (2008): 25–6.

4. David R. Percy, *The Framework of Water Rights Legislation in Canada* (Calgary: Canadian Institute of Resources Law, 1988), 7–8.

5. Ibid, 5–11.

6. United Nations Food and Agricultural Organization, "UN World Water Day," accessed 23 Aug. 2013, http://www.unwater.org/worldwaterday/faqs.html.

7. United Nations Food and Agricultural Organization, "FAO Statistical Yearbook 2013: World Food and Agriculture," accessed 23 Aug. 2013, http://www.fao.org/statistics/en/.

8. A. Daniel Tarlock, "The Future of Prior Appropriation in the New West," *Natural Resources Journal* 41 (2001): 769–93.

9. Ibid.

10. Percy, *Framework of Water Rights Legislation*, 7–8.

11. Ibid, 9.

12. Prairie Farm Rehabilitation Administration, *History of Irrigation in Western Canada* (Ottawa: Government of Canada, 1982), 13.

13. Ibid, 5.

14. Marie-Eve Poirier, *Agricultural Water Use Survey 2007, Methodology Report* (Ottawa: Statistics Canada, 2009).

15. Jack Glenn, *Once Upon an Oldman: Special Interest Politics and the Oldman River Dam* (Vancouver: University of British Columbia Press, 1999), 130–40.

16. Ed Struzik and Hanneke Brooymans, "Is Alberta Ready for PRIME Time?" *Edmonton Journal*, 13 Jan. 2002.

17. Robert Paehlke, "Environmentalism in One Country: Canadian Environmental Policy in an Era of Globalization," *Policy Studies Journal* 28, 1 (2000): 160–75.

18. Glenn, *Once Upon an Oldman*, 130–40.

19. Robert C. de Loë, "Dam the News: Newspapers and the Oldman River Dam Project in Alberta," *Journal of Environmental Management* 55, 4 (1999): 219–37.

20. B. Timothy Heinmiller, "Advocacy Coalitions and the Alberta Water Act," *Canadian Journal of Political Science* 46, 3 (2013): 525–47.

21. John R. Wagner and Cassondra White, "Water and Development in the Okanagan Valley of British Columbia," *Journal of Enterprising Communities* 3, 4 (2009): 380.

22. Percy, *Framework of Water Rights Legislation*, 36–7.

23. Margot Hurlbert, "Comparative Water Governance in the Four Western Provinces," *Prairie Forum* 31, 1 (2009): 65; David R. Percy, "Responding to Water Scarcity in Western Canada," *Texas Law Review* 83 (2005): 2099–2100.

24. Percy, *Framework of Water Rights Legislation*, 39.
25. Percy, "Responding to Water Scarcity," 2100.
26. Ibid, 2099.
27. Hurlbert, "Comparative Water Governance," 60–1.
28. Ibid.
29. Ibid.
30. Saskatchewan Water Security Agency, *25 Year Saskatchewan Water Security Plan*, accessed 18 Sept. 2013, https://www.wsask.ca/About-WSA/25-Year-Water-Security-Plan/.
31. Heinmiller, "Advocacy Coalitions and the Alberta Water Act."
32. Percy, "Responding to Water Scarcity," 2101–5.
33. David R. Percy, "Seventy-Five Years of Alberta Water Law: Maturity, Demise and Rebirth," *Alberta Law Review* 35 (1996): 221–41.
34. Ibid, 239.
35. Ibid, 229.
36. Hurlbert, "Comparative Water Governance."
37. This account of the development of the SSRB Water Management Plan is based on confidential interviews with participants conducted by the author in July 2010.
38. Government of Alberta, "Approved Water Management Plan for the South Saskatchewan River Basin," accessed 6 Feb. 2014, http://environment.alberta.ca/01233.html.
39. Government of British Columbia, "British Columbia's Water Law Framework," accessed 23 Aug. 2013,http://livingwatersmart.ca/water-act/framework.html.
40. Ibid.
41. Hurlbert, "Comparative Water Governance," 59.
42. Government of British Columbia, "British Columbia's Water Law Framework."
43. Laura Brandes and Oliver Brandes, "BC Floats New Water Law," accessed 4 Feb. 2015, http://www.alternativesjournal.ca/policy-and-politics/bc-floats-new-water-law.

17 Environmental Policy and Politics: The Case of Oil

Angela V. Carter

Chapter Summary

This chapter discusses how the government (primarily the federal government, with brief examples drawn from provincial cases) has supported oil development, with emphasis on the weakening of environmental policy around the industry. It first considers the environmental impact of oil, focusing on emissions causing climate change. Next, the chapter provides an overview of Canadian oil production, reserves, and economic dependence, with reference to the "oil curse." The third section explores how the federal and provincial governments actively facilitate the growth of Canada's oil economy. Four notable trends include: government support for, and defence of, oil development; the obstruction of environmental research; environmental policy retrenchment; and the suppression of public debate. Together, these trends show how Canada's dependence on oil is becoming entrenched at the expense of the environment through political and policy choices. However, the chapter concludes by noting alternatives to the current oil-centred economy and the burgeoning of civil society dissent.

Chapter Outline

- Overview of the tension between oil and environment
- Canada's oil production, reserves, and economic dependence
  - Summary of the "oil curse" concept
- Trends in how the government (primarily federal, with brief provincial examples) has supported oil development in Canada:
  - Government support for the oil industry (financial subsidies and political lobbying to defend oil developments)
  - Obstruction of environmental research on the impact of the oil industry
  - Environment policy retrenchment to remove obstructions to the industry
  - Suppressing dissent against policy changes and the oil industry
- Alternatives and sources of change

Introduction

As Canadian oil production grows, the country is increasingly caught in the tension between economic dependence on oil and the steep environmental costs of the industry. Yet even as the environmental repercussions of the country's growing oil economy become more apparent, over the past decade the Canadian government (along with oil-rich provinces) has become more and more supportive of the expansion of the industry. This chapter focuses on the major trends in government support for oil development, with emphasis on how environmental policy around the industry has been substantively reformed or withdrawn. These trends show how Canada's politically chosen dependence on oil is becoming entrenched at the expense of the environment. However, as noted briefly in the chapter's conclusion, these changes are being met by strong and growing civil society dissent that is challenging the oil economy and advocating for alternatives.

The Environmental Challenge of Oil

Perhaps the most pressing environmental challenge that Canada and other industrial countries face today is a dependence on **fossil fuels**, particularly oil. Oil has powered the global production and distribution that have become fundamental to economic expansion.[1] However, this growth has come at a steep environmental cost, in particular rising greenhouse gas emissions (GHGs) causing global climate change. The Intergovernmental Panel on Climate Change (IPCC), a panel of over 1,200 international scientific experts, continues to stress that without substantial GHG reductions, the world's temperature will cross a threshold setting off dramatic and dangerous changes to the climate. Importantly, the IPCC notes that fossil fuels are the largest contributors to global emissions.[2]

Canada, regrettably, ranks high in global emissions standings. The United States Energy Information Agency data places Canada as the ninth largest emitter of GHGs in the world, and in the top three per capita emitters among rich-world democracies. The intensity of these emissions is due to the expansion of Canada's fossil fuel industries. According to the Canadian government's most recent submission to the UN Framework Convention on Climate Change, over the 1990 to 2011 period, "[b]y far the largest portion of Canada's total emission growth is observed in the Energy Sector."[3] Canada's increase in GHGs was caused primarily by fossil fuel industries (oil, gas, and coal and associated production, refining, and pipeline transportation), followed by transportation (in particular, trucks powered by gasoline and diesel). In 2011, the energy sector accounted for 81 per cent of total emissions in Canada (see Figure 17.1).

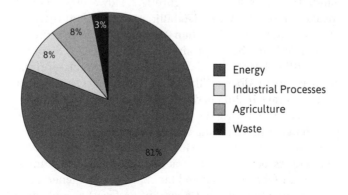

FIGURE 17.1 | Canada's 2011 GHG Emissions by IPCC Sector

Source: Based on Environment Canada, "National Inventory Report 1990–2011," 2013, Table S-2.

Within the oil and gas industries, a sub-category of the energy sector, the vast majority of emissions—88 per cent—comes from **upstream** activities, that is, from the production, processing, and transportation of gas and oil (conventional and oil sands), not the **downstream** refining activities. In particular, the growth of oil- and gas-related emissions since 1990 has been driven by the 393 per cent increase in **tar sands** production. Unsurprisingly, Alberta is the province with the largest jump in emissions.[4] Given this, Canada is far from reaching its 2020 emissions reduction targets, even after continually readjusting these targets upward. The best-case scenario predicts that Canada will get only halfway to meeting its 2020 emission reduction target of 607 megatonnes of carbon dioxide equivalent, with Alberta and Saskatchewan leading the country in per capita emissions.[5]

The Politics of Oil Dependence

Over the past 40 years, the global demand for oil has grown rapidly, often raising fears of shortages. Since 1971, oil consumption has nearly doubled, driven in great part by the need for transportation fuels in the economies of the developed world. Roughly one-fifth of the world's wealthiest populations consume nearly two-thirds of global oil, and the US has historically consumed the greatest share, over 20 per cent. Yet new growing demand has come from rapidly industrializing countries—nearly half of this demand from China, which now surpasses total American oil consumption.[6] Uncertainty over whether global oil supply could match rising demand resulted in a surge in exploration of secondary fields at the margins of major **conventional oil** fields, as well as new attempts to squeeze the last drops out of old fields using enhanced oil recovery technologies. But it has also led governments and large oil companies to explore and develop new supplies from "frontier" regions, including ultra-deep offshore wells and in the Arctic, as well as to develop **unconventional oil** reserves, primarily tar sands and shale oil (the latter using hydraulic fracturing, or "fracking").

Canada has become a globally important supplier of oil, particularly unconventional oil. According to the International Energy Agency, Canada was the world's fifth largest global oil producer in 2014,[7] with production primarily coming from Alberta and Saskatchewan as well as from Newfoundland and Labrador's offshore. Further, there is a lot of room for production to grow given Canada's extensive oil reserves, which are surpassed only by Venezuela and Saudi Arabia, as shown in Figure 17.2. However, Canadian conventional oil production has peaked: 170 of Canada's 175 billion barrels of oil reserves—a whopping 97 per cent—are in the tar sands.[8] The Canadian Association of Petroleum Producers has forecasted total Canadian daily per barrel production to increase by 55 per cent between 2013 and 2030—from 3.5 million barrels per day to 6.4 million barrels—primarily from western Canada's tar sands deposits in Alberta.[9] These long-term projections were thrown into question during the oil price crash in 2014 (a decline due in part to the rapid growth of US shale oil production); however, even during the price decline, the industry association continued to anticipate a growth in tar sands production given prior investments in the industry.[10]

The economic impact of Canada's growing oil sector is substantial. In a report commissioned by the Canadian Association of Petroleum Producers, the study authors estimated that by 2015 the oil sector (conventional and tar sands) would generate over $100 billion in sales per year (far exceeding the value of Canadian car, forestry, and agricultural sales) and over $22 billion in payments to federal and provincial governments in the form of taxes, royalties, and land sales, and this boom in the oil sector would result in nearly $60 billion in new

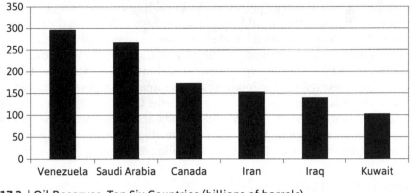

FIGURE 17.2 | Oil Reserves, Top Six Countries (billions of barrels)

Source: Based on US Energy Information Administration, 2014 International Energy Statistics at http://www.eia.gov/cfapps/ipdbproject/IEDIndex3.cfm.

investment.[11] (Declines in oil prices in 2014 resulted in reduced gains from and lower investment in the oil sector. Yet this may prove to be short-lived—oil prices appeared to rebound in early 2015.) Further, fossil energy, oil in particular, has become Canada's most valuable export, with virtually all destined for the US market (Canada surpassed Saudi Arabia as the leading foreign supplier of oil to the US in 2004). In 2013, oil and gas accounted for over one-quarter of total exports, far surpassing the mining, forestry, and automotive sectors.[12]

Of course, the economic impacts of oil are particularly concentrated in the three major oil-producing provinces, Alberta, Newfoundland and Labrador, and Saskatchewan. Over the last decade, the Alberta government's revenues from non-renewable resources (direct impacts only, not including "spinoff" secondary economic impacts) have accounted for as high as 42 per cent of all provincial revenue.[13] In Newfoundland and Labrador, 35 per cent of total revenues came directly from oil in 2011. And while Saskatchewan has not seen its total revenues dominated to the same degree by the oil sector, the direct impacts of the oil and gas industry have accounted for approximately one-quarter of that province's GDP.[14]

How might Canada's reliance on oil impact policy and politics, particularly environmental policy? Researchers have attempted to make sense of the trends by examining the resource or **oil curse**. According to this theory, heightened economic dependence on oil often leaves governments vulnerable to economic volatility due to the boom-and-bust cycles of oil production and the industry's eventual decline as reserves are depleted. Hence, in early 2015 the federal Conservative government, in a highly unusual move, delayed the release of its budget so that government number-crunchers could rationalize the precipitous drop in oil prices over the previous months. Oil-rich governments also tend towards democratic stagnation or deterioration due to growing political conservatism and authoritarianism associated with oil. Further, the costs and benefits of oil extraction are frequently unfairly distributed, leading to increased regional, sector, class, ethnic, and gender inequality.

Research on the oil curse highlights how resource-rich governments are often internally motivated to support the industry that provides the most direct economic benefits. Oil wealth generates political power that governing political parties seek to continue. Therefore, oil-rich governments tend to govern in a biased way, supporting and protecting the oil industry by offering preferential access to land and resources; providing infrastructure, education, research, and financial subsidies; and avoiding regulations protecting human rights and the environment that would restrict the industry. Yet, in so doing, governments dependent on oil face economic, social, and environmental repercussions.[15]

This pattern appears to be present in the case of Canada. The Canadian economy is obviously strongly, and increasingly, reliant on the oil industry. Further, the federal government has actively supported oil development across Canada, and has attempted to remove impediments to such development, particularly since the Conservative Party of Canada won a majority government in 2011.[16] Four notable trends are discussed below: financial support as well as lobbying to defend the industry; hollowing and withholding environmental research; curtailing environmental policies; and stifling criticism of oil development.

Government Support for the Oil Industry

One important way in which government has facilitated oil development in Canada is through multiple direct and indirect subsidies as well as lobbying campaigns to defend the industry at home and abroad. Studies on **subsidies** to the fossil fuel industry have found that the annual support to the industry remains substantial, estimated at $2.8 billion in 2010. Subsidies include government spending (such as research programs associated with the oil industry, low-cost loans and insurance), as well as government revenue not collected due to tax breaks for the industry. The Global Subsidies Initiative found over 60 programs supporting the oil industry at the federal level and in Alberta, Newfoundland and Labrador, and Saskatchewan. It concluded that "[m]ost of these subsidies seek to increase exploration and development activity, with a focus on reducing the costs of exploration, drilling and development through a mix of tax breaks and royalty reductions."[17] Alberta got the "vast share"—73 per cent—of these subsidies.

Alberta's tar sands industry would not have been possible without early and substantial provincial and federal support.[18] This support continues today with new government spending to help the oil industry overcome challenges with millions of provincial and federal dollars invested to help industry develop, for example, in-situ and carbon capture technology.[19] Similarly, in Newfoundland and Labrador, government support for offshore oil development began in the 1960s, with the federal government allocating east coast offshore exploration permits to major oil companies for over 400,000 square kilometres. These permits were "exceedingly liberal in their terms."[20] In addition, the federal government provided extensive support to the Hibernia offshore oil project. Today, the provincial government directly supports the expansion of the oil industry through Nalcor Energy, a provincial energy company that is a partner in offshore projects and an operator of onshore exploration and infrastructure projects, as well as the major player in new hydropower developments in Labrador. The provincial government also has invested in geological mapping and marketing to support the oil development and has invested in reorienting post-secondary programs around the industry.[21]

Another set of policy reforms that Canada's federal and provincial governments have used to ensure the growth of the oil industry has been the lowering of royalties and taxation. For example, due to Alberta's Oil Sands Generic Royalty Regime, which had the province collecting only 1 per cent until "project payout," government royalties were slow or stagnating even as oil sands production was ramping up over the late 2000s.[22] Today, the Parkland Institute's analysis shows that since 1997, the government of Alberta has received an average of 9 per cent of the value of tar sands production (after production costs and a "normal" 10 per cent profit rate), a paltry sum in comparison to the industry's take. As Campanella notes, "[s]ince 1997, the public's share of rent in the tar sands has consistently been dwarfed by that of the oil companies, regularly by a factor of ten or more," and yet "it was the public who, over decades, paid for the bulk of the research necessary to make the tar sands industry possible, including developing the technologies at the centre of mining and in-situ extraction."[23]

In addition to direct financial support of the oil industry, the federal government has implemented a substantial public relations and lobbying strategy to protect and promote Canadian oil projects within Canada and in the US and Europe. In contrast to the deep cuts to federal environmental programs, funding for government advertising programs promoting economic development based on fossil fuel production was increased. For example, Natural Resources Canada was allocated $9 million for advertising in 2012–13 and over $16 million for 2013–14.[24] One striking instance of this strategy at work within Canada is the advertising campaign led by Natural Resources Canada in fall 2012 and spring 2013 to inform Canadians about the importance of the country's natural resource sector, in particular energy projects and infrastructure such as the tar sands, pipelines, offshore oil, and tanker shipping. The marketing firm hired for the campaign explained that its aim was to "promote and encourage" Canadians to "become better informed about the importance and impact of Canada's energy sector on Canada's economy and quality of life." Television advertisements stressed that Canada "has a plan to develop our natural resources responsibly WHILE protecting our environment . . . Let's do both."[25]

The federal government has also undertaken lobbying in the US to counter criticisms of the tar sands and opposition to the proposed Keystone XL pipeline. Campaigns directed south of the border have focused on reminding Americans that Canada could be the solution to American oil insecurity. Gary Doer, the Canadian Ambassador to the US, claimed that the Keystone XL pipeline was an "opportunity" for the US to "establish energy independence in North America through oil from Canada."[26] Of course, this message has lost its relevance given the recent surge in US domestic shale oil production.

Canadian lobbying efforts in the US were heightened during Barack Obama's 2008 presidential campaign when a close aide of the candidate expressed reluctance to import oil derived from tar sands due to its "unacceptably high carbon emissions," which fit with Obama's commitment to use less emissions-intensive fuels.[27] Soon thereafter, senior Canadian government officials, including Tony Clement, then chair of the Environment and Energy Security Committee of cabinet, as well as oil industry representatives such as Nexen Inc., met with Obama's representatives. Clement was quoted as stating that the Canadian government was lobbying in the US at all levels of government, with senior leaders of both the Republican and Democratic parties, congressional members, state legislators and governors, and mayors of major cities, to build a "sophisticated full-court press on Canada's issues with the United States of America."[28] Then, upon Obama's election and assumption of office in 2009, Prime Minister Stephen Harper moved quickly to promote the oil sands to the new President. During Obama's first visit to Canada in February 2009, Harper specifically emphasized the importance of the oil sands to American energy security, arguing that the Alberta deposits are a conveniently close and stable replacement for Middle Eastern oil.

In more recent years, the federal government has focused on convincing American policy-makers to approve the Keystone XL pipeline, again by emphasizing the energy security implications. As explained by Prime Minister Harper, "this project will bring in enough oil to reduce American offshore dependence by 40 per cent. This is an enormous benefit to the United States in terms of long-term energy security."[29] The public relations effort was most evident in the spring of 2013 when, as one journalist described it, "[a] steady flow of Canadian political leaders from Ottawa, Alberta and Saskatchewan" went to Washington "to lobby lawmakers for the pipeline's approval,"[30] including Prime Minister Harper, ministers of environment and natural resources, provincial premiers, and senior policy-makers. These visits were paired with another public relations campaign targeted in Washington to counter environmental criticisms and remind US policy-makers that Canada is "America's best energy partner," stressing that Canada provides more oil to the US than any other country: "America's best friend is America's best energy solution," the advertisements read.

Obstructing Environmental Research and Monitoring

In addition to directly subsidizing the oil industry and defending it at home and abroad, the federal government has sought to reshape environmental policy by limiting or blocking basic environmental research and monitoring through cutbacks at environmental departments or government-funded research centres, or through withholding information on the environmental impacts of the oil industry from the public.

Effective environmental policy-making depends on knowledge about environmental impacts. However, policy-making surrounding the oil industry in Canada is plagued by the problems of missing ecosystem **baseline data**, a poor understanding of **cumulative environmental impacts**, and inadequate monitoring. This is particularly evident in Alberta's tar sands. As tar sands projects have grown exponentially, federal departments repeatedly raise concerns about missing information on projects' impacts on water pollution and withdrawal rates, air pollution, and wildlife and fish. In 2011, the Commissioner of the Environment and Sustainable Development reported that federal government departments were simply unable to assess cumulative impacts of tar sands projects due to "incomplete environmental baselines and environmental data monitoring systems." "For over a decade," the report noted, "Environment Canada and Fisheries and Oceans Canada have warned that key environmental information regarding the effects of oil sands projects has been missing."[31] Appropriate environmental monitoring in the tar sands has also been lacking. The federal government and the government of Alberta have repeatedly committed to implementing a "world-class" monitoring system. But, to date, independent scientific panels have found the monitoring system to be inadequate.[32] Since the late 1990s, a series of plans has been developed to monitor the oil sands to ascertain the environmental impacts of the industry, but these plans have been unfulfilled for years.

The lack of environmental knowledge and monitoring is due in great part to the rolling back of environmental departments. For example, federal spending for 2015–16 for environment-related departments and programs was cut by more than $1.5 billion compared to 2010–11 spending. Natural Resources Canada's environmental programs and the Canadian Environmental Assessment Agency (CEAA) experienced the steepest budget cuts, at 64 per cent and 41 per cent, respectively. Consequently, CEAA and Fisheries and Oceans Canada's environment-related programs lost over a quarter of their full-time staff.[33]

Federal research institutes critical of oil development saw similar cuts. The National Round Table on the Environment and the Economy (NRTEE) was shut down in 2013, just after delivering a report that showed the impossibility of the federal government meeting its emissions reduction targets, primarily because of the oil and gas sector. One journalist compared the termination of the NRTEE to the federal government "kill[ing] the emissions messenger."[34] Likewise, the Canadian Foundation for Climate and Atmospheric Sciences, which supported university climate research, was eliminated in 2012, as was the Hazardous Materials Information Review Commission, an independent agency responsible for regulating information disclosure about hazardous materials used in the oil industry. The Experimental Lakes Area (ELA) was also defunded by the federal government in 2012. As noted by Barlow and Schindler, the ELA "was conducting research into the effects on freshwater of endocrine disrupters, mercury and other byproducts of extractive industries the government promotes, and its findings were beginning to show serious, but preventable, damage to Canada's freshwater heritage."[35] Cuts to environmental departments contribute to dwindling environmental research, monitoring, and enforcement capacity in the regulation of Canada's oil industry—all during a period of steep growth in oil development.

Policy Retrenchment

While in-house capacity has been cut, the federal government has remade the environmental policy landscape surrounding oil by weakening or withdrawing government's role in regulating the industry. Several examples are particularly relevant to oil extraction, perhaps the most obvious instance being the continued delay in regulations to reduce the oil and gas industry's GHGs.[36] At the same time, after years of undermining global negotiations on emissions reductions, the federal government withdrew from the Kyoto Protocol in 2011 (see Chapter 13 of this volume). Canada reneged on its international commitments to reduce GHGs in great part due to the country's inability to meet reduction targets given the growth of the oil industry.

The delay of policy on oil industry emissions has been paired with very active measures to withdraw environmental policies surrounding oil development within Canada. Since 2006, and primarily through two "omnibus" budget bills in 2012, efforts to streamline environmental policy have dismantled major environmental legislation in the country, with one clear result being the facilitation of oil development. A prominent example of these changes is the Canadian Environmental Assessment Act, 2012, which repealed and replaced the 1992 Act, weakening it substantively (as discussed in detail by Valiante in Chapter 4).[37] The original Act was a central piece of environmental legislation because it institutionalized environmental assessment to ensure projects' negative environmental impacts would be prevented. Yet CEAA 2012 dramatically reduced the number of projects that require federal environmental assessment—and, therefore, public consultation—and accelerated review timelines. Following its enactment, *nearly 3,000* environmental assessments were terminated,[38] and 678 of these were related to fossil fuel projects.[39]

The Fisheries Act, another major piece of Canadian environmental legislation, was also narrowed substantively in 2012 to protect only commercial, recreational, or Aboriginal fisheries. It was further weakened to allow the Minister of Fisheries and Oceans or cabinet the discretion to permit harm to fish habitat previously prohibited under the Act. The Fisheries Act had been one of a very few pieces of legislation that required environmental protection from oil extraction and pipeline projects. With the changes, however, proposed oil and gas projects may be exempted from the requirement to protect fish habitat. Concern over these changes was widespread, notably expressed even by former Conservative

ministers of Fisheries and Oceans Canada. Tom Siddon, minister under former Conservative Prime Minister Brian Mulroney, was quoted as describing the changes to the Fisheries
Act as "taking the guts out."[40]

Other examples of active policy retrenchment include the new Navigation Protection
Act, which exempted developments, including pipeline projects potentially impacting
lakes and rivers, from needing federal approval and public consultation in the vast majority
of Canada's waterways.[41] The National Energy Board Act, which directs Canada's primary
pipeline regulator of oil and gas activities in federal land and waters, was also altered in
2012 with the effect of limiting public participation and the range of discussion in energy
project consultations, thus allowing the transfer of decisions on major projects from the
NEB to cabinet.[42]

Suppressing Dissent

The federal government has attempted to limit public debate on these major reductions to
government capacity and the significant policy changes. Civil society groups have become
vocal participants in the debate on oil projects, expressing concern about the expansion of
oil developments in Canada and the stagnation or retreat of environmental policy surrounding them. However, rather than accept these actors as part of a broad debate on Canada's
energy future, the federal government has acted defensively by limiting participation in
public hearings, denouncing environmental groups, and attempting to criminalize dissent.
Together, these trends are part of a building "advocacy chill"[43] that has threatened to hinder
public debate on Canada's oil economy.

First, the federal government has restricted public participation in hearings on oil
developments, as evidenced by the implementation of 2012 changes to the National Energy
Board Act. The amendment to the Act was first applied to hearings in the summer of 2013
on Enbridge's proposal to reverse its Line 9 pipeline, now running from Montreal to Sarnia,
to deliver tar sands oil from Alberta to Quebec refineries. Given the NEB Act changes, citizens wishing to participate in the hearings were required to complete a nine-page "Application to Participate" form and provide supporting documents, for example, a curriculum
vitae or reference letter, that would be reviewed by the NEB to determine if the applicant
was either "directly affected" or deemed to have relevant expertise. The Board also provided
a very restricted "List of Issues" that would be considered valid for discussion at the hearings; significantly, the form noted that, "[t]he Board will not consider the environmental
and socio-economic effects associated with upstream activities, the development of oil
sands, or the downstream use of the oil transported by the pipeline."[44] These new restrictions angered many interested citizens and environmental organizations that were blocked
from participating in the hearings by what they felt were undemocratic constraints on the
process. ForestEthics Advocacy launched a lawsuit at the Federal Court of Appeal claiming
the limits on participation were a violation of Canadians' right to free expression protected
in the Canadian Charter of Rights and Freedoms, and demanding the application form be
withdrawn and all participants' submissions be accepted.[45]

Similar scenarios of limiting environmental organizations' participation in hearings
on oil developments have played out in Alberta.[46] In 2012, the Alberta Energy Regulator
blocked environmental organizations from submitting Statements of Concern during hearings on a tar sands project proposed by Southern Pacific Resource Corporation because

the regulator did not deem the groups to be "directly affected." The Pembina Institute and Fort McMurray Environmental Association appealed the decision. During the legal proceedings, a 2009 "briefing note" to the deputy minister of Alberta Environment relating to a hearing on another tar sands project came to light, indicating that Pembina was blocked from participating in this and other hearings in part because the Alberta government considered the Institute "now less inclined to work cooperatively" given their "publication of negative media on the oil sands." The court ruled the process of excluding Pembina and other environmental organizations was "tainted" by the briefing note and based on "improper and irrelevant considerations."[47]

A second way in which the federal government has attempted to stifle dissent is by becoming much more active in publicly criticizing environmental organizations as well as scientists who have questioned the oil industry and its environmental impacts. The clearest examples are found in comments made by Minister of Natural Resources Joe Oliver prior to the Northern Gateway Project Joint Review Panel community hearings, which were to consider Enbridge's proposal to transport diluted bitumen by pipeline from Alberta to Kitimat, BC. Oliver's open letter criticized "environmentalists and other radical groups" that "threaten to hijack our regulatory system to achieve their radical ideological agenda." He asserted that, "[t]hey use funding from foreign special interest groups to undermine Canada's national economic interest."[48] Similarly, documents released to Greenpeace Canada and Climate Action Network showed that the federal government had listed environmentalists as "adversaries" in strategy documents on marketing tar sands oil in Europe.[49]

The federal government has also attempted to discredit scientists presenting research on the challenges of Canada's oil economy. For example, in a visit to Washington to defend the Keystone XL pipeline, Oliver accused former NASA climatologist James Hansen of "exaggerated" claims, "crying wolf," and making statements about the emissions impact of the tar sands that were "nonsense," stating Hansen should be "ashamed" of these comments.[50] Similar incidents have occurred in Alberta. For example, after the release of a new study on the scientific evidence on tar sands pollution,[51] a senior scientist in Alberta's Environment Department accused the authors of lying and omitting data contrary to their conclusions. An apology was issued after the scientists advised they would take legal action for defamation.[52]

Finally, environmental activism against oil has frequently been recast by federal agencies as linked to terrorism and other criminal activity, with the effect of raising suspicion about dissenting organizations and marginalizing their concerns and participation in public policy debates. Violence is very seldom used in the opposition to oil developments in Canada: dissent is typically characterized by standard interventions in the public debate (letters to the editor, petitions, and participation in public hearings), as well as, more recently, acts of civil disobedience (disrupting meetings, hanging banners from bridges, and road blockades). Yet, as Monaghan and Walby observe, federal intelligence agencies have "blurred the categories of terrorism, extremism and activism" by comparing environmental and social activists concerned about oil developments with extremists or terrorists. This, then, serves to justify the expansion of federal surveillance of these groups.[53]

Suggesting civil disobedience against oil projects is comparable to terrorism or extremism is a powerful part of the **criminalization of dissent**[54] by federal government agencies. Media reports based on documents released through Access to Information requests show that environmental groups were flagged in RCMP and CSIS documents on terrorist and extremist risks.[55] The risk to oil projects is at the forefront of these concerns. As Monaghan and Walby note, Canada's security and intelligence agencies are concerned about acts of civil disobedience involving "critical infrastructure," which is taken to include pipelines and tar sands sites. Journalists have reported evidence of "classified" meetings held by Natural Resources Canada, CSIS, and the RCMP on "National Security and Criminal Risks to Critical Energy Infrastructure" (sponsored in part by Enbridge).[56] In addition, Public Safety Canada's counter-terrorism strategy warned that "low-level violence by domestic issue-based groups remains a reality in Canada. Such extremism tends to be based on grievances—real or perceived—revolving around the promotion of various causes such as animal rights, white supremacy, environmentalism and anti-capitalism."[57]

The creation of an RCMP-led counter-terrorism unit in Alberta is evidence of the perceived threat to energy projects: the unit was described as "prompted by factors" that included "a strong economy supported by the province's natural resources and the need to protect critical infrastructure."[58] This threat is used to justify enhanced monitoring of civil society groups opposed to oil developments. For example, media reports based on information from freedom of information requests noted that prior to hearings on Enbridge's proposed Northern Gateway pipeline, the National Energy Board led an effort involving CSIS, the RCMP, Enbridge, and TransCanada Corporation to gather information on civil society organizations groups opposing the tar sands, specifically listing ForestEthics, the Sierra Club, and the Council of Canadians.[59]

Challenging Oil?

Canada has become a globally important supplier of oil, and the economy—particularly that of the major producing provinces—has become very dependent on the oil industry. And as oil production has grown, so too have the environmental impacts of the industry, in particular Canadian emissions that cause climate change. Yet, rather than intervening to limit the environmental impacts of the oil sector, the Canadian government has constrained scientific knowledge and stepped back from regulating the environmental impacts of the oil industry, all while actively supporting and defending the industry, on the one hand, and quelling dissent against the industry, on the other. In this way, the Canadian government is exhibiting political tendencies noted by the literature on the oil curse. Like other governments highly dependent on oil-fuelled economic growth, the federal government has facilitated the oil industry, recasting policy to support the industry or to remove obstructions to it.

Together, the trends discussed in this chapter contribute to Canada's becoming more deeply entrenched in oil dependence and "locked" into carbon emissions.[60] Yet, other policy options for longer-term environmental, economic, and community sustainability go much further than "greening" the oil industry by reducing per-barrel emissions (while absolute emissions rise), or burying waste through carbon capture and sequestration projects. These include ending subsidies to the oil industry and instead supporting the transition to renewable, sustainable energy sources, and bringing down demand for oil by improving energy efficiency (primarily through national public transportation infrastructure and the mass retrofitting of buildings and industrial processes). These policy alternatives might also involve implementing a fossil fuel **emissions budget**,[61] setting a fair price on carbon emissions, and committing to leave oil reserves in the ground.

This new dialogue on Canada's oil economy is being built through broad-based coalitions of First Nations communities and religious, labour, social justice, and environmental organizations that connect local concerned citizens with international activists to build cross-border alliances. The burgeoning movement has articulated concern and alternatives using tools ranging from petitions to municipal governments and website "blackout" days to road blockades at exploration sites and civil disobedience on Parliament Hill.[62] It is rooted in the activism of Indigenous people—encouraged by the international reach of the Idle No More movement and emboldened by the 2014 Supreme Court of Canada decision granting Aboriginal title to the Tsilhqot'in Nation in British Columbia—who challenge oil development as part of their broader demands for social and environmental justice. It also stems from the actions of young people, like the Canadian Youth Delegation to the UN Framework Convention on Climate Change who named the tar sands industry as the "(un)official sponsor of Canada's climate policy" as the federal government withdrew from the Kyoto Protocol. Today, the challenge to oil spans from legal challenges to the Northern Gateway pipeline development in British Columbia to grassroots political lobbying against fracking for oil in western Newfoundland; from resolutions against offshore seismic exploration off Baffin Island, Nunavut, to sit-ins against pipelines carrying tar sands oil in southwestern Ontario. Even as the federal government has attempted to discredit those opposing the status quo oil economy as "terrorists," public pressure for alternatives is strong and growing.

Acknowledgements

Social Sciences and Humanities Research Council funding supported this research. I thank John Peters, Debora VanNijnatten, and editors at OUP for helpful comments and revisions.

Key Terms

baseline data

conventional oil

criminalization of dissent

cumulative environmental impacts

downstream

emissions budget

fossil fuels

oil curse

subsidies

tar sands

unconventional oil

upstream

Questions for Review

1. What is the fundamental tension between global economic growth and climate?
2. How has oil dependence reshaped the Canadian economy?
3. How has environmental policy been altered to facilitate the expansion of oil expansion in Canada?
4. What are the new constraints on public participation in debates on oil in Canada?
5. What policy alternatives might permit a more sustainable approach to energy development in Canada? Which groups are advocating for these alternatives?

Internet Resources

Canadian Association of Petroleum Producers
http://www.capp.ca

Canadian Centre for Policy Alternatives, Climate Justice Project
https://www.policyalternatives.ca/projects/climate-justice-project

Climate Action Network Canada
http://climateactionnetwork.ca

Ecojustice, Climate Protection Campaign
https://www.ecojustice.ca/issues/climate-energy/

Greenpeace Canada, Climate and Energy Campaign
http://www.greenpeace.org/canada/en/campaigns/Energy/

National Round Table on the Environment and the Economy (Government of Canada Web Archive)
http://collectionscanada.gc.ca/webarchives2/20130322140948/http:/nrtee-trnee.ca/

Natural Resources Canada, Energy Sector
https://www.nrcan.gc.ca/energy

Pembina Institute
http://www.pembina.org

Additional Reading

Adkin, Laurie, ed. *First World Petro-Politics: The Political Ecology and Governance of Alberta.* Toronto: University of Toronto Press, forthcoming.

Bowden, M.A. "Environmental Assessment Reform in Saskatchewan: Taking Care of Business." *Journal of Environmental Law and Practice* 21 (2010): 261.

Clarke, Tony. *Tar Sands Showdown: Canada and the New Politics of Oil in an Age of Climate Change.* Ottawa: CCPA, 2008.

D'Arcy, Stephen, Toban Black, Tony Weis, and Joshua Kahn Russell, eds. *A Line in the Tar Sands: Struggles for Environmental Justice.* Toronto: Between the Lines, 2014.

Fraser, G.S., and J. Ellis. "The Canada–Newfoundland Atlantic Accord Implementation Act: Transparency of the Environmental Management of the Offshore Oil and Gas Industry." *Marine Policy* 33 (2009): 312–16.

Hughes, Larry. "Eastern Canadian Crude Oil Supply and Its Implications for Regional Energy Security." *Energy Policy* 28 (2010): 2692–9.

Nikiforuk, Andrew. *The Energy of Slaves: Oil and the New Servitude.* Vancouver: Greystone Books, 2012. Also his series in *The Tyee*: http://thetyee.ca/Bios/Andrew_Nikiforuk/.

Sinclair, Peter R. *Energy in Canada.* Toronto: Oxford University Press, 2011.

Stephenson, Eleanor, Alexander Doukas, and Karena Shaw. "Greenwashing Gas: Might a 'Transition Fuel' Label Legitimize Carbon-Intensive Natural Gas Development?" *Energy Policy* 46 (2012): 452–9.

Winfield, Mark. "The Environment, 'Responsible Resource Development,' and Evidence-Based Policy-Making in Canada." In Shaun Young, ed., *Evidence-Based Policy-Making in Canada,* 196–221. Toronto: Oxford University Press, 2014.

Notes

1. Elmar Altvater, "The Social and Natural Environment of Fossil Capitalism," in Leo Panitch, Colin Leys, Barbara Harriss-White, Elmar Altvater, and Greg Albo, eds, *Socialist Register 2007: Coming to Terms with Nature* (London: Merlin Press, 2006); Matthew T. Huber, "Energizing Historical Materialism: Fossil Fuels, Space and the Capitalist Mode of Production," *Geoforum* 40, 1 (2009): 105–15.

2. "IPCC, 2013: Summary for Policymakers," in T.F. Stocker, D. Qin, G.-K. Plattner, M. Tignor, S.K. Allen, J. Boschung, A. Nauels, et al., eds, *Climate Change 2013: The Physical Science Basis. Contribution of Working Group I to the Fifth Assessment Report of the Intergovernmental Panel on Climate Change* (Cambridge: Cambridge University Press, 2013).

3. Environment Canada, "National Inventory Report 1990–2011: Greenhouse Gas Sources and Sinks in Canada, Part 1," 2013, accessed 19 Mar. 2013, http://unfccc.int/files/national_reports/annex_i_ghg_inventories/national_inventories_submissions/application/zip/can-2013-nir-15apr.zip, p. 26.

4. Ibid, 22–8, 50–1.

5. National Round Table on the Environment and the Economy, *Reality Check: The State of Climate Progress in Canada* (Ottawa, 2012), accessed 20 Feb. 2014, http://collectionscanada.gc.ca/webarchives2/20130322165457/http://nrtee-trnee.ca/wp-content/uploads/2012/06/reality-check-report-eng.pdf.

6. International Energy Agency (IEA), World Energy Outlook 2010 (Paris, 2010); IEA, World Energy Outlook 2013 (Paris, 2013).

7. IEA, *Oil Market Report* (Paris, 2015).

8. IEA, *Energy Policies of IEA Countries: Canada 2009 Review* (Paris, 2009), 25.

9. Canadian Association of Petroleum Producers, "Crude Oil: Forecast, Markets and Transportation" (Calgary, 2014), accessed 14 Feb. 2015, http://www.capp.ca/getdoc.aspx?DocId5247759&DT5NTV, pp. i, 3–4.

10. Canadian Association of Petroleum Producers, "Increased Access to Markets Remains Critical Despite Recent Oil Price Decline" (Calgary, 2015), accessed 14 Feb. 2015, http://www.capp.ca/aboutUs/mediaCentre/NewsReleases/Pages/access-to-markets-remains-critical.aspx.

11. Peter Tertzakian and Kara Baynton, *Turmoil and Renewal: The Fiscal Pulse of the Canadian Upstream Oil and Gas Industry*, 2011, accessed 10 Mar. 2014, http://www.capp.ca/getdoc.aspx?DocId5188164&DT5NTV, pp. 56–7.

12. Lusine Lusinyan, Julien Reynaud, Tim Mahedy, Dirk Muir, Ivo Krznar, and Soma Patra, *Canada: Selected Issues* (Washington: IMF, 2014), accessed 7 Mar. 2014, http://www.imf.org/external/pubs/ft/scr/2014/cr1428.pdf, p. 4.

13. Angela V. Carter, "Environmental Policy in a Petro-State: The Resource Curse and Political Ecology in Canada's Oil Frontier," doctoral dissertation (Cornell University, 2011).

14. Analysis based on Statistics Canada's CANSIM data.

15. On the resource curse, see, e.g., Ellis Goldberg, Erik Wibbels, and Eric Mvukiyehe, "Lessons from Strange Cases: Democracy, Development, and the Resource Curse in the U.S. States," *Comparative Political Studies* 41, 4–5 (2008): 477–514; Macartan Humphreys, Jeffrey Sachs, and Joseph Stiglitz, eds, *Escaping the Resource Curse* (New York: Columbia University Press, 2007); Terry Lynn Karl, *The Paradox of Plenty: Oil Booms and Petro-States* (Berkeley: University of California Press, 1997); Michael Ross, *The Oil Curse: How Petroleum Wealth Shapes the Development of Nations* (Princeton, NJ: Princeton University Press, 2012); Jeffrey D. Sachs and Andrew M. Warner, "The Curse of Natural Resources," *European Economic Review* 45 (2001): 827–38; Meenal Shrivastava and Lorna Stefanick, "Do Oil and Democracy Only Clash in the Global South? Petro Politics in Alberta, Canada," *New Global Studies* 6, 1 (2012): Article 5.

16. Robert MacNeil, "Canadian Environmental Policy under Conservative Majority Rule," *Environmental Politics* 23, 1 (2014): 174–8.

17. EnviroEconomics Inc., Dave Sawyer, and Seton Stiebert, "Fossil Fuels—At What Cost? Government Support for Upstream Oil Activities in Three Canadian Provinces: Alberta, Saskatchewan, and Newfoundland and Labrador," Global Subsidies Initiative and International Institute for Sustainable Development (Geneva, 2010), 15.

18. Paul Chastko, *Developing Alberta's Oil Sands: From Karl Clark to Kyoto* (Calgary: University of Calgary Press, 2004); Andrew Nikiforuk, *Tar Sands: Dirty Oil and the Future of a Continent* (Vancouver: Douglas & McIntyre, 2008).

19. Angela Carter and Anna Zalik, "Fossil Capitalism and the Rentier State: Towards a Political Ecology of Alberta's Oil Economy," in Laurie Adkin, ed., *First World Petro-Politics:*

20. J.D. House, *The Challenge of Oil: Newfoundland's Quest for Controlled Development* (St John's: ISER Books, 1985), 55, 104.

21. Carter, "Environmental Policy in a Petro-State."

22. Dan Woynillowicz, Chris Severson-Baker, and Marlo Raynolds, *Oil Sands Fever: The Environmental Implications of Canada's Oil Sands Rush* (Drayton Valley, Alta: Pembina Institute, 2005), accessed 21 Apr. 2014, http://pubs.pembina.org/reports/OilSands72.pdf.

23. David Campanella, "Misplaced Generosity: Update 2012" (Edmonton: Parkland Institute, 2012), 8–9.

24. Treasury Board Secretariat, Supplementary Estimates (C), 2012–13, accessed 22 Apr. 2014, http://www.tbs-sct.gc.ca/ems-sgd/sups/c/20122013/index-eng.pdf, p. 17; Treasury Board Secretariat, 2013–14 Estimates: Parts I and II: The Government Expenditure Plan and Main Estimates, accessed 22 Apr. 2014, http://www.tbs-sct.gc.ca/ems-sgd/20132014/me-bpd/me-bpd-eng.pdf, p. 238; Treasury Board Secretariat, Supplementary Estimates (C), 2013–14, accessed 22 Apr. 2014, http://www.tbs-sct.gc.ca/ems-sgd/sups/c/20132014/sec-bsdc-eng.pdf, pp. 1–17. See also "Ottawa Ramps Up Ad Spending for U.S. Pipeline Fight," CBC News, 14 May 2013, accessed 22 Apr. 2014, http://www.cbc.ca/news/politics/ottawa-ramps-up-ad-spending-for-u-s-pipeline-fight-1.1307723.

25. Léger Marketing, *Pre- and Post-Testing of the Responsible Resource Development Advertising Campaign 2012–2013 and 2013–2014*, 2013, accessed 3 Mar. 2014, http://epe.lac-bac.gc.ca/100/200/301/pwgsc-tpsgc/por-ef/natural_resources/2013/007-12/report.pdf, pp. 4, 76.

26. Jonathan Kay, "United at Last," *National Post*, 15 Dec. 2011, A20.

27. Sheldon Alberts, "Obama's Oil Vow Threatens Alberta," *Edmonton Journal*, 25 June 2008, A4.

28. Tonda MacCharles, "Canada to Hard Sell Obama, McCain on Tar Sands," *Toronto Star*, 27 Aug. 2008, B1.

29. Council on Foreign Relations, "A Conversation with Stephen Harper," accessed 9 Mar. 2014, http://www.cfr.org/canada/conversation-stephen-harper/p30723.

30. Jason Fekete, "Ad Campaign Aims to Gain Pipeline Support," *Vancouver Sun*, 14 May 2013.

31. Commissioner of the Environment and Sustainable Development, *Report of the Commissioner of the Environment and Sustainable Development to the House of Commons* (Ottawa: Office of the Auditor General of Canada, 2011), accessed 9 Feb. 2014, http://www.oag-bvg.gc.ca/internet/English/parl_cesd_201110_02_e_35761.html, pp. 5, 79.

32. See, e.g., Environment Canada, *An Integrated Oil Sands Environment Monitoring Plan*, 2011, accessed 20 Feb. 2014, http://www.ec.gc.ca/pollution/EACB8951-1ED0-4CBB-A6C9-84EE3467B211/Integrated%20Oil%20Sands_low_e.pdf.

33. Based on data from Public Service Alliance of Canada, "Environmental Cutbacks: 2010 to 2016," accessed 10

Feb. 2014, http://www.psac-ncr.com/sites/ncr-rcn.psa-cadmin.ca/files/user-uploads/cuts-2010-2016.en_.xlsx.

34. Jeffrey Simpson, "Ottawa Kills the Emissions Messenger," *Globe and Mail*, 20 June 2012.

35. Maude Barlow and David Schindler, "Gov't Attack on Water Safeguards Regrettable," *Saskatoon Star-Phoenix*, 15 Mar. 2013.

36. P.J. Partington and Clare Demerse, "Context for Climate Action in Canada," Pembina Institute, 2013, accessed 5 Feb. 2014, http://pubs.pembina.org/reports/climate-context-20131009.pdf.

37. Meinhard Doelle, "CEAA 2012: The End of Federal EA as We Know It?" *Journal of Environmental Law and Practice* 24 (2012): 1–17.

38. Based on CEAA archival search at http://www.ceaa.gc.ca/052/plus-eng.cfm?canada51.

39. Mike De Souza, "Harper Government Scraps 3,000 Environmental Reviews on Pipelines and Other Projects," accessed 25 Feb. 2014, http://o.canada.com/news/politics-and-the-nation/parliament/harper-government-kills-3000-environmental-reviews-on-pipelines-and-other-projects/.

40. Mark Hume, "Don't Gut the Fisheries Act, Ex-Ministers Warn," *Globe and Mail*, 29 May 2012.

41. Ecojustice, "Legal Backgrounder: Bill C-45 and the Navigable Waters Protection Act (RSC 1985, C N-22)," 2012, accessed 5 Feb. 2014, http://www.ecojustice.ca/files/nwpa_legal_backgrounder_october-2012.

42. Ecojustice, "Legal Backgrounder: The National Energy Board Act (1985)," 2012, accessed 17 Feb. 2014, http://www.ecojustice.ca/files/neba-backgrounder-may-2012/at_download/file.

43. Susan Phillips, "Restructuring Civil Society: Muting the Politics of Redistribution," in Keith Banting and John Myles, eds, *Inequality and the Fading of Redistributive Politics* (Vancouver: University of British Columbia Press, 2014).

44. National Energy Board, "Application to Participate Form," accessed 3 Mar. 2014, https://docs.neb-one.gc.ca/ll-eng/llisapi.dll/941615/A5%2D3_%2D_Application_Form_to_Participate_in_a_Hearing_%2D_A3G6L3_.pdf?func5doc.Fetch&nodeid5941615.

45. Clayton Ruby, "Public Has a Right to Full Debate on Pipeline," *Toronto Star*, 18 Aug. 2013, A11.

46. See Evan Bowness and Mark Hudson, "Sand in the Cogs? Power and Public Participation in the Alberta Tar Sands," *Environmental Politics* 23, 1 (2014): 59–76; George Hoberg and Jeffrey Phillips, "Playing Defence: Early Responses to Conflict Expansion in the Oil Sands Policy Subsystem," *Canadian Journal of Political Science* 44, 3 (2011): 507–27.

47. *Pembina Institute v. Alberta (Environment and Sustainable Resources Development)*, 2013 ABQB 567, pp. 10, 12.

48. Joe Oliver, "An open letter from the Honourable Joe Oliver, Minister of Natural Resources, on Canada's commitment to diversify our energy markets and the need to further streamline the regulatory process in order to advance Canada's national economic interest," accessed 28 Feb. 2014, http://www.nrcan.gc.ca/media-room/news-release/2012/1/1909.

49. Meagan Fitzpatrick, "Oilsands 'Allies' and 'Adversaries' Named in Federal Documents," CBC News, accessed 28 Feb. 2014, http://www.cbc.ca/news/politics/oilsands-allies-and-adversaries-named-in-federal-documents-1.1156539.

50. Suzanne Goldenberg, "Canadian Oil Minister Joe Oliver Condemns Climatologist James Hansen," guardian.co.uk, accessed 3 Mar. 2014, http://www.theguardian.com/environment/2013/apr/24/canada-joe-oliver-attack-james-hansen.

51. Kevin P. Timoney and Peter Lee, "Does the Alberta Tar Sands Industry Pollute? The Scientific Evidence," *Open Conservation Biology Journal* 3 (2009): 65–81.

52. Alexandra Zabjek, "Gov't Scientist Apologizes for Saying Researchers 'Lied'," *Edmonton Journal*, 22 June 2010.

53. Jeffrey Monaghan and Kevin Walby, "Making Up 'Terror Identities': Security Intelligence, Canada's Integrated Threat Assessment Centre and Social Movement Suppression," *Policing and Society* 22, 2 (2012): 134.

54. Philippe Le Billon and Angela Carter, "Securing Alberta's Tar Sands: Resistance and Criminalization on a New Energy Frontier," in Matthew Schnurr and Larry Swatuk, eds, *Natural Resources and Social Conflict: Towards Critical Environmental Security* (London: Palgrave Macmillan, 2012).

55. Shawn McCarthy, "Security Services Deem Environmental, Animal-Rights Groups 'Extremist' Threats," *Globe and Mail*, 16 Feb. 2012.

56. Matthew Millar, "Harper Government's Extensive Spying on Anti-Oilsands Groups Revealed in FOIs," *Vancouver Observer*, 19 Nov. 2013.

57. Public Safety Canada, *Building Resilience against Terrorism: Canada's Counter-Terrorism Strategy*, 2013, accessed 12 Feb. 2014, http://www.publicsafety.gc.ca/cnt/rsrcs/pblctns/rslnc-gnst-trrrsm/rslnc-gnst-trrrsm-eng.pdf, p. 9.

58. Royal Canadian Mounted Police, "Creation of an RCMP-led INSET in Alberta," accessed 28 Feb. 2014, http://www.rcmp-grc.gc.ca/news-nouvelles/2012/06-06-inset-eisn-eng.htm.

59. Millar, "Harper Government's Extensive Spying."

60. Brendan Haley, "From Staples Trap to Carbon Trap: Canada's Peculiar Form of Carbon Lock-In," *Studies in Political Economy* 88 (Autumn 2011): 97–132.

61. Minqi Li, "The 21st Century Crisis: Climate Catastrophe or Socialism," *Review of Radical Political Economics* 43, 3 (2011): 289–301.

62. Randolph Haluza-DeLay and Angela Carter, "Social Movements Scaling Up: Strategies and Opportunities in Opposing the Oil Sands Status Quo," in Laurie Adkin, ed., *First World Petro-Politics: The Political Ecology and Governance of Alberta* (Toronto: University of Toronto Press, forthcoming).

18 Conserving Canada's Biodiversity in the Twenty-First Century: Challenges at the Science–Policy Interface

Christopher J. Lemieux

Chapter Summary

Despite increasing international and national commitments to protect and sustainably use biodiversity in Canada, ecosystem degradation continues and endangered species lists continue to grow. This chapter reviews a number of events that have shaped biodiversity conservation policy and management in Canada, and explores some emerging science–policy challenges including climate change, endangered species management, and the Biodiversity Convention's new Strategic Plan for the Convention on Biological Diversity, including the 2011–20 Aichi Biodiversity Targets. It also assesses Canada's ability to meet formal conservation commitments given the government of the day's science policy agenda and related austerity challenges. The chapter concludes with a discussion of a number of integrative propositions that may help Canadians and their governments respond to the novel policy and management challenges associated with twenty-first-century biodiversity conservation.

Chapter Outline

- The state of Canada's ecosystem: degradation continues and endangered species lists grow
- The Canadian response: actions have been inadequate to address pressures on biodiversity
- Challenges of government austerity and related management capacity
  - Have paralyzed the ability of agencies to effectively implement biodiversity conservation policies and programs

- Enhancing biodiversity in Canada
  - o Unprecedented and immediate financial investments in biodiversity conservation required
  - o Rapid and widespread expansion of Canada's protected areas network an immediate policy priority
  - o New governance innovations on protecting, connecting, and restoring ecosystems required to safeguard biodiversity
  - o The necessity of (re)connecting Canadians to nature and integrating the value of biodiversity in broader policies and incentive structures

Introduction

At the Rio Earth Summit on 11 June 1992, Canada was the first nation to sign the United Nations (UN) Convention on Biological Diversity (known informally as the Biodiversity Convention), a landmark treaty to aid in the conservation of biodiversity.[1] The Biodiversity Convention was inspired by public concern about the ongoing loss of species and their habitats, and a growing commitment to sustainable development in countries around the world. At that time, less than 69,000 protected areas (called for under Article 8 of the Biodiversity Convention), representing a mere 7 per cent of Earth's terrestrial area and less than 1 per cent of Earth's marine area, had been set aside.[2] However, in the last two decades, many countries have added thousands of new protected areas to the global network (there are now 160,000 terrestrial and 7,000 marine protected areas), encompassing 15.4 per cent and 3.4 per cent of Earth's total terrestrial and marine areas, respectively.[3]

This significant achievement resulted from a widespread shift in the philosophy, policy, and practice of biodiversity conservation in Canada and many other countries. For example, in the early 1990s, the plight of endangered species in Canada was poorly understood and not reflected in government policy. Then, in 1995, federal, provincial, and territorial wildlife agencies collaboratively developed a national approach to protecting endangered species. Subsequently, the National Strategy for the Protection of Species at Risk (NSPSR) committed federal, provincial, and territorial ministers responsible for wildlife to prevent species in Canada from becoming extinct as a consequence of human activity. The adoption of the Species at Risk Act (SARA) in 2002 provided the legal context for commitments outlined in the NSPSR.[4] Furthermore, since Canada ratified the Biodiversity Convention in 1992, a number of provinces and territories have completed biodiversity strategies and enacted endangered species legislation. Significantly, federal, provincial, and territorial governments have doubled the number of terrestrial and marine protected areas over this period.[5] Despite these significant accomplishments, in 2013, the Committee on the Status of Endangered Wildlife in Canada (COSEWIC) identified 691 species as extinct, extirpated (i.e., no longer found in the wild or in what had been a specific natural local habitat), endangered, threatened, or of special concern. Alarmingly, this represents an increase of nearly 20 per cent in the total number of species allocated to these categories in just five years.[6]

This chapter explores some of the key contemporary factors as well as emerging forces that affect biodiversity in Canada. The first part sets the context by reviewing the current status and trends in terrestrial, marine, and freshwater biodiversity, and highlights the contribution of biodiversity to the maintenance of human health and well-being. The second part describes a number of events that have shaped Canadian biodiversity policy, and assesses emerging science–policy challenges affecting commitments to mitigate the effects of human activity on endangered species and achieve the Biodiversity Convention's new 2011–20 Aichi Biodiversity Targets, established at the tenth Conference of the Parties in Nagoya, Aichi Prefecture, Japan. The third part examines Canada's ability to meet commitments and desired conservation outcomes in light of the current science–policy agenda and the austerity context. The chapter concludes by introducing a number of integrative propositions that may help society respond to the novel policy and management challenges associated with biodiversity conservation in the twenty-first century.

Biodiversity in Canada: Status, Trends, and Threats

The word "biodiversity," a contraction of **biological diversity**, refers to the variety of life inhabiting the ecosphere and is expressed as the diversity within and between populations of a species (e.g., genetic diversity), among species generally, and within ecosystems.[7] There are about 8.7 billion species on Earth, of which 2.1 billion inhabit marine ecosystems.[8] About 70,000 terrestrial, freshwater, and marine species inhabit Canada's diverse ecosystems, and many thousands more have not yet been identified.[9]

While much of Canada's terrestrial, freshwater, and marine ecosystems remain healthy, including large tracts of undisturbed wilderness, internationally significant wetlands, and estuaries situated in Canada's sparsely populated and less accessible North, some worrisome signs justify attention by Canadians and their governments (Table 18.1). Of particular concern is the continuing loss of old forest and wildlife habitat in agricultural landscapes, the declining numbers of birds, and the increasing numbers of invasive species.[10] In addition to these common stressors, of growing concern to scientists in recent years have been the documented effects of climate change. Climate is an important environmental influence on ecosystems, and climate change–induced effects—such as changes to species' geographic ranges and changes in the timing of seasonal life-cycle events—have been detected across Canada's ecozones and have accelerated over the past 20 years.[11] These conditions have been found to directly and indirectly alter access to habitat and species relationships, and while scientists know that many changes are occurring, description and understanding of the many community-level effects of climate change remain largely unknown.

Overall, the true value of biodiversity has been ignored or grossly underestimated for most of human history. Indeed, for many Canadians, biodiversity is a source of emotional and spiritual inspiration, good social relations, and cultural identity.[12] Aside from the many inherent, personal, and spiritual reasons to conserve nature, economists have recently attempted to monetize the direct and indirect values of biodiversity,[13] estimating multiple trillions of dollars worth of benefits from a healthy balance of biodiversity: clean air and water, productive soils and wetlands, recreation, and insurance savings. The estimated total value of **non-market ecosystem goods** (products derived from natural systems that are harvested or used by people) and **ecosystem services** (ecological processes that form the subset of ecosystem functions that benefit people) in Ontario's Greenbelt region alone is estimated to be approximately $2.6 billion annually.[14] However, this estimate is likely low due to an incomplete understanding of all the ecosystem services provided by the Greenbelt (e.g., the role of the area in providing spaces for stress relief, relaxation, and other benefits that reduce costs on the health-care system) and the difficulty of incorporating personal importance of the area into economic estimates. Overall, loss of biodiversity affects the ability of

TABLE 18.1 A Summary of Key Findings from the *Canadian Biodiversity: Ecosystem Status and Trends 2010 Report*—The First Assessment of Canada's Biodiversity from an Ecosystem Perspective

Theme	Indicator	Trend	Observations
Biomes	Forests	↓	About 0.01–0.02% of Canada's forest is lost annually; at a regional level, loss of forest extent is significant in some places.
	Grasslands	↓	Native grasslands have been reduced to a fraction of their original extent (e.g., 70% loss of prairie grasslands, Canada's largest grassland type). Decline continues in some areas.
	Wetlands	↓	High loss in southern Canada (80–98% near Canada's large urban centres); loss and degradation continues; some restoration occurring.
	Lakes/Rivers	↓	Increases in river and lake temperatures, decreases in lake levels, habitat loss and fragmentation.
	Coastal	↓	Coastal ecosystems remain healthy in less-developed areas; in developed areas, extent and quality is declining due to habitat modification, erosion, sea-level rise.
	Marine	↓	A combination of physical and human factors has affected populations; some marine mammal recovery from past overharvesting; many commercial fisheries have not recovered.
	Ice	↓↑	Declining ice extent and thickness, thawing of permafrost, impacts on species and species interactions (e.g., range expansion of killer whales into ice-free areas).
Human/Ecosystem Interactions	Protected areas	↑	Increased extent and representativeness in recent years. Establishment in developed areas and oceans remains a challenge.
	Stewardship	↑	Activity is increasing in Canada, both in number of initiatives and participation rates.
	Non-native species	↓	A significant and increasing stressor on all terrestrial, freshwater, and marine ecosystems. Economic and ecological losses estimated at $5.7 billion annually in Great Lakes alone.
	Contaminants	↓↑	Reduction in some legacy contaminants (e.g., DDT/PCBs); increases in emerging contaminants in wildlife (e.g., PBDEs).
	Nutrient loading	↓↑	Nutrient inputs increasing in some places, decreasing in others.
	Acid deposition	↓↑	Thresholds exceeded in some areas; biological recovery has not kept pace with emission reductions in some places.
	Climate change	↓	Rising temperatures across Canada with direct and indirect impacts on terrestrial, marine and freshwater systems.
	Ecosystem services	?	Cost of maintaining ecosystem services is high in areas where stressors have impaired ecosystem function.
Habitat, Wildlife & Ecosystem Services	Agriculture landscapes/ habitat	↓	Capacity to support wildlife has declined due to intensification and loss/fragmentation of natural habitat.
	Species of special interest	↓↑	Species of economic, cultural, or ecological interest are declining, stable, or healthy/recovering depending on location (e.g., caribou range contraction and northern population declines).
	Primary productivity	?	Has increased on land area as well as in some freshwater ecosystems.
	Natural disturbances	?	Natural disturbance regimes, such as fire and native insect outbreaks (e.g., mountain pine beetle), are reshaping the landscape. Direction and degree vary by region.
	Food webs	↓	Loss or reduction of important components of food webs has greatly altered some ecosystems.

TABLE 18.1 *Continued*

Theme	Indicator	Trend	Observations
Science/Policy Interface	Monitoring/ Research/ Reporting	↓ ↑	Lack of information to support decision-making has hindered biodiversity conservation initiatives.
	Rapid changes & thresholds	Insufficient data	Growing understanding of rapid and unexpected changes, interactions, and thresholds, especially in relation to climate change, points to a need for policy that responds and adapts quickly to environment change in order to avoid major and irreversible impacts on biodiversity.

↓   Trend shows improvement
↑   Trend shows decline
↓ ↑ Trend shows both improvements and declines
?   Unknown

Source: J.C. Day, J.G. Nelson, and L.M. Sportza, eds, *Protected Areas and the Regional Planning Imperative in North America: Integrating Nature Conservation and Sustainable Development* (Calgary: University of Calgary Press, 2003).

ecosystems to deliver ecosystem services, and reduces the **resilience** of both social and ecological systems to adapt to rapidly changing environmental conditions.

Contemporary and Emerging Policy Influences

The statistics noted above provide us with an understanding of the current relationship between humans and nature, help to identify some of the underlying causes leading to biodiversity loss, and ultimately provide the information upon which more effective policies can be developed to resolve contemporary and emerging challenges to the conservation of biodiversity. Canada has a rather ambiguous history of biodiversity conservation (Figure 18.1). Virtually all provincial and territorial governments have integrated biodiversity into strategies, policies, legislation, management plans, and partnerships with landowners, the private sector, and Aboriginal peoples. Some of these diverse initiatives have been discussed in other topical essays.[15] This chapter is focused in particular on the strengths and weaknesses of the *Canadian Biodiversity Strategy* (CBS), protected areas programs, SARA, and COSEWIC. Interspersed within these discussions are case studies to provide real-world examples of contemporary and emerging science policy challenges in the Canadian biodiversity conservation context.

The UN Convention on Biological Diversity and Canada's Response

The United Nations oversees more than 500 environmental agreements and treaties, 155 of which are biodiversity-related. The best known is the iconic 1992 Convention on Biological Diversity, with objectives focused on the conservation of biodiversity, sustainable use of biological resources, and fair and equitable sharing of benefits resulting from the use of genetic resources.[16] These objectives reflect the philosophy and recommendations advanced in *Our Common Future* (the Brundtland Report, 1987) and the World Conservation Strategy (1980), including sustainable development (development that meets the needs of the present without compromising the ability of future generations to meet their own needs).[17] Unlike the US, which did not ratify the treaty, Canada played an important role in the negotiations. In 1992, Prime Minister Brian Mulroney signed the Convention at the Earth Summit and Canada became the first industrialized country to ratify.

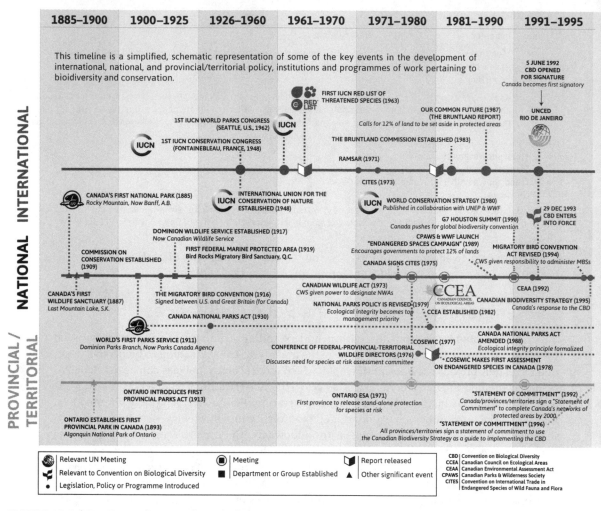

FIGURE 18.1 | Key Events in Canadian Biodiversity Policy and Practice, 1885–2014

Although the Biodiversity Convention is legally binding, states have sovereign rights over their biodiversity. Accordingly, one of the key obligations for parties that have ratified the Convention is to prepare national plans and policies for priority species or habitats at national to local levels. Canada's official response to the Biodiversity Convention, the 1995 *Canadian Biodiversity Strategy*, was prepared jointly by federal, provincial, and territorial governments, and sets out a spectrum of strategic directions for the conservation and sustainable use of Canada's biodiversity.[18] The CBS reaffirms government commitment to create policy conditions (and associated research, monitoring, and reporting mechanisms) in support of biodiversity conservation and the sustainable use of biological resources. The CBS also emphasizes that biodiversity conservation is a multi-scale, multi-jurisdictional, and

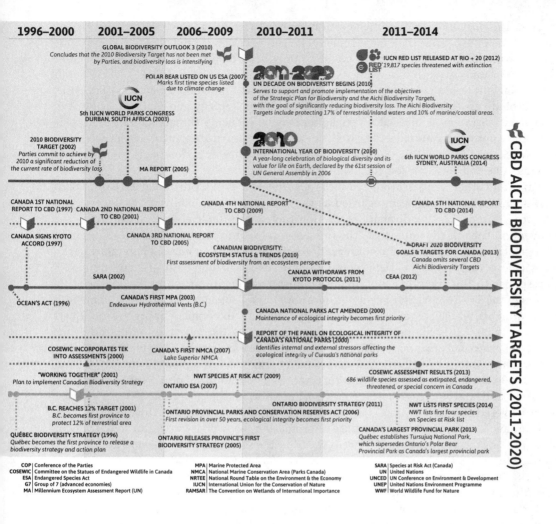

cross-sectoral issue requiring co-operation with stakeholders and the public. Specifically, direction is expressed in five goals:

1. To conserve biodiversity and sustainably use biological resources.
2. To enhance both our understanding of ecosystems and our resource management capability.
3. To promote an understanding of the need to conserve biodiversity and sustainably use biological resources.
4. To provide incentives and legislation that support the conservation of biodiversity and the sustainable use of biological resources.
5. To work with other countries to conserve biodiversity, use biological resources sustainably, and share equitably the benefits that arise from the utilization of genetic resources.

Since the early 1990s, many provinces and territories have used the Biodiversity Convention and the CBS to guide their management and conservation of biodiversity. For example, Quebec was the first province to formulate a provincial biodiversity strategy and action plan in 1996, and currently is devising its third iteration of the strategy.[19] Developed through public consultation and inter-ministerial collaborations and commitments, its priorities include biodiversity in wildlife, forests, urban areas, biotechnology, and education. Ontario's Biodiversity Strategy is focused on engaging people, reducing threats, enhancing resilience, and improving knowledge.[20] As well, the Northwest Territories, British Columbia, New Brunswick, and Nova Scotia sponsor biodiversity strategies or action plans in support of Canada's CBS and, by extension, the Biodiversity Convention.

Parks and other forms of **protected areas** (e.g., national parks, provincial parks, national wildlife areas) have long been regarded as the cornerstones of biodiversity conservation and are an important biodiversity protection tool in the Biodiversity Convention.[21] The Convention specifically notes that "the fundamental requirement for the conservation of biological diversity is the **in-situ conservation** of ecosystems and natural habitats and the maintenance and recovery of viable populations of species in their natural surroundings."[22] In response to this requirement, Canada's ministers of environment, parks, and wildlife endorsed the Tri-Council Statement of Commitment on Protected Areas (the Statement of Commitment), which committed Canadian jurisdictions to complete protected area networks by 2000.[23] This commitment was echoed in the CBS and reflected in the significant growth of protected areas across Canada. Provinces such as British Columbia, Nova Scotia, Ontario, and Manitoba in particular made steady progress throughout the late 1990s and early 2000s. British Columbia and Ontario established hundreds of protected areas during this time, and land claim agreements between First Nations and governments have increasingly delivered new national parks and protected areas in Yukon, the Northwest Territories, and Nunavut, many of which contribute to protecting biodiversity with the added benefit of supporting traditional ways of life.[24] At the time, the view that protected areas should be managed in ways that sustain both biodiversity and local livelihoods sharply contrasted with the "fortress conservation" thinking that informed much of protected area management during the past century.[25]

Today, most federal, provincial, and territorial agencies have policy frameworks that guide management of their protected areas (e.g., management planning guides, management policies, guiding principles, and program and operational policies).[26] Since the release of the CBS and the Statement of Commitment, Canada's protected areas network has nearly doubled both in the total number of sites and in total area protected, and the diversity of ecosystems represented has increased (although significant differences in progress between jurisdictions is evident). As of 2014, 7,605 protected areas encompass approximately 10 per cent of Canada's terrestrial area and 1 per cent of the marine area (Canadian Council on Ecological Areas, 2015) (Figure 18.2).[27] Furthermore, all 17 government agencies responsible for terrestrial and/or marine protected areas in Canada have enabling legislation in place for the establishment of protected areas.

In April 2002, Canada committed itself to the global Strategic Plan for the Convention on Biological Diversity.[28] In the Plan's mission statement, parties committed themselves to a more effective and coherent implementation of the three objectives of the Biodiversity Convention: "to achieve by 2010 a significant reduction of the current rate of biodiversity loss at the global, regional and national level as a contribution to poverty alleviation and

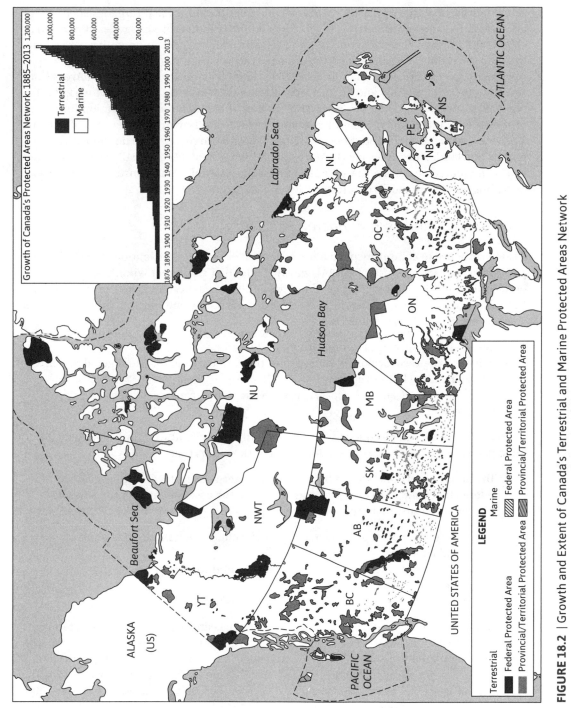

FIGURE 18.2 | Growth and Extent of Canada's Terrestrial and Marine Protected Areas Network

Source: Canadian Council on Ecological Areas, Conservation Areas and Reporting System (CARTS) v. 2014.12.31 (Ottawa, 2015).

to the benefit of all life on Earth."[29] This so-called "2010 Biodiversity Target" helped stimulate action to safeguard biodiversity globally and in Canada at many levels. In particular, significant advancements were made in the establishment of new co-operative agreements between government agencies and private land conservation organizations. For example, the Canadian government announced a $225 million investment in the Natural Areas Conservation Program in 2007 and introduced the National Conservation Plan in June 2014. The National Conservation Plan proposes $252 million of funding for conservation initiatives over five years, including a $100 million commitment to the Nature Conservancy of Canada, a private organization that protects ecologically sensitive areas, often in developed areas, by purchasing land. Since 2007, nearly 4,000 square kilometres of ecologically significant land has been secured across southern Canada under the Natural Areas Conservation Program, providing habitat for more than 160 species at risk.

Protecting Canada's Endangered Species

Also in response to commitments made under the Biodiversity Convention, in 2002 Canada passed the Species at Risk Act (SARA), which is intended to protect wildlife species at risk on federal lands, including plants and animals, their residence, and their critical habitat. In SARA, species are listed under four "risk levels": extirpated, endangered, threatened, or of special concern. SARA is intended to:

1. Prevent wildlife species in Canada from disappearing.
2. Provide for the recovery of wildlife species that are extirpated, endangered, or threatened as a result of human activity.
3. Manage species of special concern to prevent them from becoming endangered or threatened.

Before a species can be added to the List of Wildlife Species at Risk under SARA, COSEWIC must determine that it is at risk. Section 15(1) of SARA states that:

> The functions of COSEWIC are to (a) assess the status of each wildlife species considered by COSEWIC to be at risk and, as part of the assessment, identify existing and potential threats to the species and
>
> • Classify the species as extinct, extirpated, endangered, threatened or of special concern;
> • Indicate that COSEWIC does not have sufficient information to classify the species; or
> • Indicate that the species is not currently at risk.

While COSEWIC was created in 1977, it wasn't until the passing of SARA that it was established as an official advisory body to better ensure the incorporation of both scientific and Aboriginal traditional knowledge in species assessments. Under SARA, the federal government is only responsible for taking COSEWIC's assessments into consideration when establishing the List of Wildlife Species at Risk under the Act. As discussed below, this has resulted in some considerable science–policy conflict in Canada.

Most species assessed to date are considered secure (77 per cent); 12 per cent are designated as "at Risk" or "May be at Risk."[30] The status of approximately 11 per cent of Canada's known species is unknown, and substantial caveats and limitations with respect to the status of the large majority of Canada's terrestrial, marine, and freshwater species remain.[31] Between 2000 and 2010, the proportion of species ranked "secure" has varied between 70 and 77 per cent.

Under SARA, three federal departments—Environment Canada, Fisheries and Oceans Canada, and Parks Canada—are responsible for preparing recovery strategies, action plans, and management plans for the species at risk on federal lands that each organization is mandated to protect. The organizations have one to five years to develop these strategies and plans, depending on when a species is listed under SARA and the degree of the threat to the species. The recovery strategies, action plans, and management plans set out the steps needed to stop (and ultimately reverse) the decline of the species of concern. As a result, these documents are considered a critical element in managing the preservation and recovery of species at risk.

Beyond SARA, other significant achievements with respect to the protection of endangered species have also been made since the release of the CBS, including provincial/territorial statutes for New Brunswick (1996), Nova Scotia (1999), Newfoundland and Labrador (2002), Ontario (2007), and the Northwest Territories (2009). Today, British Columbia and Alberta remain the only two provinces in Canada without stand-alone legislation pertaining to endangered species.

Emerging Challenges at the Science–Policy Interface

Protected Areas, the UN Aichi Biodiversity Targets, and "Other Effective Area-based Conservation Measures"

Global Biodiversity Outlook 3, the flagship publication of the Biodiversity Convention, concluded that the "2010 Biodiversity Target" to achieve a significant reduction in the rate of biodiversity loss was, ultimately, not achieved.[32] This included Canada, which stated in its *4th National Report* to the Convention that it had achieved "mixed" results in meeting the 2010 Biodiversity Convention target of "significantly reducing the rate of biodiversity loss."[33] Given the failure of nations to meet the target, it was determined that a new global commitment and action plan to address biodiversity loss was needed. Parties to the Biodiversity Convention, including Canada, responded by adopting a revised and updated Strategic Plan for Biodiversity, including 20 "Aichi Biodiversity Targets" for the 2011–20 period (decision X/2) in 2010. Parties also agreed to translate this overarching framework into revised and updated national biodiversity strategies and action plans within two years.

The goals of the new Strategic Plan for Biodiversity 2011–20 are to:

- Address the underlying causes of biodiversity loss by mainstreaming biodiversity across government and society (Strategic Goal A).
- Reduce the direct pressures on biodiversity and promote sustainable use (Strategic Goal B).
- Improve the status of biodiversity by safeguarding ecosystems, species, and genetic diversity (Strategic Goal C).
- Enhance the benefits to all from biodiversity and ecosystem services (Strategic Goal D).
- Enhance implementation through participatory planning, knowledge management, and capacity-building (Strategic Goal E).

The Aichi Biodiversity Targets are organized under the five strategic goals listed above.[34] Because parties were invited to set their own targets within this framework, taking into account national conditions and priorities, the Aichi targets are considered more aspirational than binding. As of June 2014, nearly two years overdue, Canada's goals and targets were still in draft form and, after a very brief public comment period, a number of Aichi targets remain completely omitted from Canada's draft plan. Furthermore, some national concern has been raised specifically over the wording of Aichi Target 11, which calls on parties to set aside 17 per cent of terrestrial area and 10 per cent of marine area "through effectively and equitably managed, ecologically representative and well-connected systems of protected areas and other effective area-based conservation measures" (Target 1 in Canada's draft plan) (Box 18.1).[35] For example, the Canadian Council on Ecological Areas (CCEA) raised concerns over the "other effective area-based conservation measures" qualifier, noting that without a standardized, science-based approach to reporting on Target 11, area-based measures of limited conservation value could find their way into national reporting mechanisms, giving false or misleading impressions of national conservation progress.[36] Indeed, significantly broadening the scope of areas counted under Target 11 by including areas of limited conservation effectiveness in national protected areas reporting will not necessarily lead to real gains in biodiversity conservation as envisioned in the Biodiversity Convention's Strategic Plan for Biodiversity for 2011–20.

Climate Change and Managing Species at Risk

The biodiversity crisis was already acute before recent manifestations of climate change, and many endangered species in Canada may be among the most vulnerable and the least capable of adapting naturally, particularly in cases where populations are small, suitable habitat is limited, and there are external stressors resulting from habitat loss and fragmentation, pollution, and other human activities. Climate change is anticipated to have many implications for biodiversity policy in Canada. For example, SARA defines a "wildlife species" as a species that either is "native" to Canada or has been present in Canada for at least 50 years (S.C.2002, c. 29). Furthermore, SARA explicitly states that a wildlife species is one that has extended its range into Canada "without human intervention."[37] A literal interpretation of this temporally qualified definition would mean that a species classified as endangered in the US that naturally expands its range into Canada under changing climatic conditions, or a species requiring human assistance to facilitate its relocation to new, more suitable habitat under changing climatic and habitat conditions, would not qualify for protection as a species at risk under SARA until it has been established for 50 years.[38] SARA does not address the issue of climate change (e.g., how future habitat is to be interpreted and protected in the context of a changing climate), and an examination of provincial and territorial endangered species legislation reveals similar policy deficiencies. However, species endangered by and highly vulnerable to changes in climate will require increasing conservation policy and management attention in the future in order to mitigate current threats, and wildlife managers will need to plan for future climate change adaptation interventions (Box 18.2).

BOX 18.1 | What Should Be Counted towards Canada's Biodiversity Conservation Goals and Targets?

FIGURE 18.3 | Taku River/T'akuTeix' Conservancy, British Columbia.

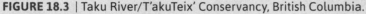

Credit: Taku River Tlingit First Nation

While well-governed and effectively managed protected areas are proven methods for safe-guarding species and for delivering important ecosystem services, the inclusion of "other effective area-based conservation measures" in international and national biodiversity targets add an additional qualifier that may have significant implications for biodiversity conservation policy and reporting in Canada.[39] For example, while some of Canada's Indigenous Peoples' and Community Conserved Areas (ICCAs) (such as newly established "conservancies" and "tribal parks" in British Columbia; see Figure 18.3) and privately owned protected areas may qualify as protected areas in certain circumstances, there has been some debate on whether and to what extent other types of area-based measures, such as fisheries closures, municipal water supply protection areas, and watercourse setbacks, should be considered to contribute to Target 11 of the Biodiversity Convention's Strategic Plan for Biodiversity 2011–20 and Target 1 of the Draft 2020 Biodiversity Goals and Targets for Canada. Specifically, such areas may have limited conservation benefit if they do not ensure a long-term conservation purpose and contain effective legal and other policy arrangements to prevent development threats within their boundaries.

BOX 18.2 | Climate Change and Polar Bears

FIGURE 18.4 | Churchill Wildlife Management Area, Manitoba.

Credit: Jackie P. Dawson, University of Ottawa

Climate change effects, including earlier ice breakup in spring and later autumn ice freeze-up, are impacting the ability of polar bears to access seals and build up body mass to ensure survival during the summer ice-free season.[40] While the US listed the polar bear as a threatened species in 2008, specifically citing loss of sea ice due to climate change, the listing of the polar bear as a species at risk in Canada has been a subject of considerable scientific, political, and public debate.[41] In 2011, Canada listed the polar bear as a species of "special concern" under SARA—one level below "threatened" and two levels below "endangered." The listing of the polar bear as a species of "special concern" meant that the federal government was *not* required to protect sea ice—the most critical habitat for polar bear survival. Furthermore, according to the COSEWIC assessment, the majority of northern communities consulted through the assessment process were not in favour of listing the polar bear. While many people in the northern communities perceived climate change to be affecting the species, they also claimed that polar bears are very adaptable to changing environmental conditions, populations were increasing in some areas, and that research on polar bear populations was not conclusive. However, in the Western Arctic, unanimous support was received for the decision to list the polar bear as a species of special concern from all Inuvialuit communities consulted. In the southern part of Canada, the vast majority of comments received indicated support for listing.[42]

Furthermore, the implications of the failure in SARA and similar provincial/territorial endangered species legislation to account for climate change means that these statutes should be revised. Such revision could provide more effective scientific guidance on how to develop management and recovery plans for species requiring assistance adapting to rapidly changing climatic and habitat conditions. For example, **assisted migration**, also known as assisted colonization, refers to the act of deliberately helping plant and animal species colonize new habitats when driven out of their historical habitats due to rapid environmental change.[43] Despite the potential of assisted migration as an active management tool that could facilitate species responses to climate change, and the fact that some Canadian jurisdictions are already conducting assisted migration experiments on private and municipal lands with some success, neither SARA nor other federal or provincial/territorial conservation-oriented legislation provides strategic or operational guidance on the issue.[44] Indeed, assisted migration raises a number of socio-economic, ethical, and biological concerns in the context of Canada's conservation initiatives. In this context, and given limited conservation resources, how will species be prioritized for assistance under rapidly changing climatic and ecological conditions? This issue will require discussion and debate among scientists, conservation managers, other stakeholders, and the Canadian public.[45]

Is Canada Living Up to Its Biodiversity Obligations?

The global decline of biodiversity is now recognized as one of the most serious environmental issues facing humanity. In Canada, many ecosystems continue to deteriorate rapidly and endangered species lists continue to grow. Furthermore, findings of independent audits at multiple levels of government reveal an alarmingly consistent finding: the wide and growing gap between biodiversity commitments and the results achieved.

Overall, Canada's actions towards the objectives of the Biodiversity Convention, the CBS, and related provincial and territorial mandates have not been at a level and scale sufficient to address the many increasing pressures on biodiversity. Four interrelated issues with respect to this failure are of particular concern. First, and perhaps most importantly, while there is now some understanding of the linkages between biodiversity, ecosystem services, and human health and well-being, the value of biodiversity is not adequately reflected in broader policies and incentive structures in Canada. While biodiversity, or natural capital, is actually the foundation of much of the other capital that society presently acknowledges (financial, built, and human), it is not presented on an equal level with these other forms of capital in economic growth strategies.

Second, despite significant advancements in conservation science, a disconcerting disconnect exists between science and policy when it comes to listing species at risk and establishing effective protected areas networks in Canada. For example, the Canadian federal government elected not to list 23 per cent of the wildlife species recommended by COSEWIC between SARA's enactment in 2002 and 2007.[46] Furthermore, a recent study by Favaro et al., which assessed the recovery status of species at risk in Canada, found that only 14 per cent of 369 species listed by COSEWIC had improved in status, while 31 per cent had deteriorated and 54 per cent remain unchanged.[47] Relatedly, despite enhanced knowledge of effective protected areas design and management, the quality of protection afforded to marine protected areas in particular is suspect and characterized by poor compliance, a lack of conservation commitment in policy, politically expedient programs that fail to protect significant assets (i.e., established in locations of little resource development interest), and conflicting regulatory responsibilities (i.e., conservation and resource extraction).[48] In fact, a recent study revealed that 59 per cent of the world's marine protected areas were "not ecologically distinguishable from fished sites."[49] The weak legal mechanisms and management effectiveness exhibited by many marine protected areas policies in Canada trigger the critical question: Should such areas be acknowledged as protected areas at all?

Third, government austerity at all levels has resulted in a lack of adequate human and financial resources, which has paralyzed the ability of agencies to implement effectively their respective biodiversity conservation-related policies and programs (Table 18.2). For example, staffing for conservation has declined by 23 per cent in Parks Canada Agency, and the scientific staff complement has been reduced by more than one-third.[50] Furthermore, Environment Canada, Fisheries and Oceans Canada, and Parks Canada Agency have not been able to meet their legal requirements for establishing species at risk strategies under

TABLE 18.2 A Summary of Assessed Performance on Various International, National, and Provincial/Territorial Biodiversity Conservation-Related Initiatives in Canada

Biodiversity Program or Objective	Significant Findings
Meeting the Goals of the *Biodiversity Convention*[i]	• Canada's draft targets are not sufficiently specific and key actions for achieving the targets have not been developed. • Without details on key actions that need to be taken, it is not clear how Canada will meet its biodiversity targets by 2020.
Recovery Planning for Species at Risk[ii]	• Environment Canada, Fisheries and Oceans Canada, and Parks Canada have not met their legal requirements for establishing recovery strategies, action plans, and management plans under the Species at Risk Act.
Protected Areas for Wildlife[iii]	• More than 70 per cent of national wildlife areas and about 55 per cent of migratory bird sanctuaries are considered to have less than adequate ecological integrity. • Environment Canada has made little progress in monitoring activities, conditions, and threats for the protected areas it manages. • Environment Canada is operating with outdated management plans for most of its 54 national wildlife areas.
Ecological Integrity in National Parks[iv]	• Canada Agency has been slow to implement systems for monitoring and reporting on ecological integrity. • Ecological integrity decline experienced in 34 per cent of park ecosystems reported. • Significant risk that Parks Canada Agency could fall further behind in efforts to maintain and restore ecological integrity.
Species at Risk Legislation in Ontario[v]	• Ontario Ministry of Natural Resources has failed to ensure the preparation of nearly half of the recovery strategies for the 155 endangered and threatened species in Ontario.
Ecological Integrity in British Columbia[vi]	• Despite declared intentions, British Columbia's parks and protected areas program plans are incomplete, the parks and protected area system has not been designed to ensure ecological integrity, and management plans are dated and incomplete.

[i] Office of the Auditor General of Canada, 2013. See note 50.
[ii] Ibid.
[iii] Ibid.
[iv] Ibid.
[v] Office of the Environmental Commissioner of Ontario, 2013. See note 52.
[vi] British Columbia Office of the Auditor General, 2013. See note 52.

SARA: 146 species recovery strategies remain to be completed and, of the 97 that required action plans, only seven are presently in place.[51] Similar capacity challenges have been observed at the provincial level, where the Environmental Commissioner of Ontario (ECO) and the BC Auditor General observed that ministries responsible for species at risk and protected areas have not been able to meet their legislated responsibilities.[52]

Finally, despite the evidence of acceleration in anthropogenic pressures, the lack of data on the status of Canada's biodiversity is disturbing. To manage something effectively, you must understand it first. Targets, or goals, are indeed the desired outcomes of a policy framework—they show where Canada (and the provinces/territories) wants to be and represent the successful implementation of policy. Good targets need good indicators with adequate data to measure progress. The lack of resources and information for decision-making in many regions has hampered policy-level assessments, including the *Ecosystems Status and Trends Report (ESTR)*, and the implementation of timely and effective recovery strategies pertaining to species at risk.[53] Long-term, standardized, spatially complete, and readily accessible monitoring information is lacking for most indicators and for most ecosystems in Canada. In fact, shortly after releasing the first ESTR (see Table 18.1), Environment Canada decided that it would no longer be responsible for such assessments.[54] Furthermore, given the projected consequences for both biodiversity and human health and well-being, there is a growing need for information on responses of ecosystems to climate change to support adaptation policy development at national, provincial, and local levels.[55] Overall, a lack of scientific information for policy and decision-making has proven to be a major obstacle for the effective implementation of the Biodiversity Convention, national and national biodiversity strategies including the CBS, and related programs.

Enhancing Biodiversity Conservation in the Twenty-First Century: Some Concluding Remarks

Canada was once considered a global leader in biodiversity conservation and environmental conservation more broadly. According to recent Ipsos Reid surveys, 97 per cent of Canadians agree that natural areas are important for well-being and 62 per cent believe that the current federal government is doing too little to protect species at risk.[56] However, these attitudes have not translated into results, a finding echoed in Chapter 1 by Cameron and Stephenson. Despite being a relatively rich nation, Canada ranks twenty-sixth out of 34 Organisation for Economic Co-operation and Development (OECD) countries in terms of the percentage of terrestrial area protected, and national annual growth rates of protected areas establishment are slowing dramatically (by more than 50 per cent between 2001 to 2005 and 2006 to 2011).[57] As well, it has been nearly 20 years since the federal government committed to leading and co-ordinating the development and implementation of a national network of marine protected areas under the Oceans Act (S.C. 1996, c. 31). Yet, there remains no national network of marine protected areas.

Over the remainder of the twenty-first century, threats to biodiversity will continue to grow more pervasive and solutions will become less attainable without more decisive action on Canada's various biodiversity conservation commitments. Considering that it took over 125 years for Canada to protect approximately 10 per cent of its terrestrial area and only 1 per cent of its marine area, if we assume "business as usual" it will take many decades for Canada to achieve the Biodiversity Conservation's Aichi Biodiversity Target to protect 17 per cent of terrestrial area and 10 per cent of marine area. Canada's withdrawal from the Kyoto Protocol in 2011, the weakening of provisions within the Canadian Environmental Assessment Act in 2012, and changes to the Fisheries Act in 2013 (the Act ironically no longer protects most fish habitat) are further indicators that the federal government of the day is focused on economic growth and more rapid resource exploitation and less so on environmental conservation.[58]

Without unprecedented and immediate financial investments in biodiversity conservation and new governance innovations in land-use planning, it is virtually certain that Canada will not achieve its biodiversity goals and targets without major compromises to the legitimacy, quality, and management effectiveness of sites included in Canada's national reporting on protected areas. Protected areas are proven governance systems to effectively care for terrestrial, freshwater, and marine ecosystems, and they should remain a primary conservation tool in Canada's efforts to protect biodiversity. Concomitantly, governments will need to value biodiversity in new ways and initiate new research initiatives to support scientific advice to decision-makers. For example, protected areas should become recognized for their inherently valuable repositories of ecological goods and services that keep humans healthy, such as through water credits, carbon sequestration, "biodiversity banking," and supporting ecosystem-based adaptation to climate change.[59]

The development and implementation of a national, cross-jurisdictional landscape-scale strategic conservation plan focused on protecting, connecting, and restoring ecosystems will also be fundamental to ensuring the persistence of biodiversity over the twenty-first century and beyond. Primarily, various levels of government and other stakeholders will need to manage Canada's biodiversity in a more co-ordinated and collaborative way. Recent research concludes that although protected areas will play an important role in conserving endangered species that occur within them, reducing species extinction rates will ultimately require integrating conservation strategies in areas outside formally protected areas on the intervening landscapes and waterscapes (e.g., agricultural/urban lands).[60]

Significant progress has been made in recent years in this regard, especially with respect to the types of partnerships and more integrated approaches now being employed in conservation planning and management. New management paradigms, such as **adaptive co-management**, might be ideal for biodiversity and policy-making related to climate change. Adaptive co-management, after all, involves stakeholders and recognizes the dynamic nature of ecosystems and climate change management.[61] Indeed, governments may not be the most influential source of biodiversity and climate change policy over the twenty-first century, and a departure from traditional top-down management may help to deal with policy conflicts that result from this form of management.[62] In times of limited resources for conservation, co-managing parks and protected areas and including relevant stakeholders provide a clear way to reduce conflict and increase ownership over biodiversity-related issues. The protected areas fraternity will need to collaborate with a full range of partners and stakeholders, including Aboriginal peoples, local communities, academic institutions, non-governmental organizations, the private sector, all levels of government, and interested individuals, in order to protect more areas, build well-connected networks of healthy ecosystems, and restore the integrity of Canada's ecosystems.

While this chapter largely concludes that current policy and organizational capacity in Canada is inadequate to fulfill international and national biodiversity conservation commitments, there are reasons to be optimistic. Canada has doubled its network of national parks and protected areas over the past 20 years, and in the process has gained a tremendous amount of insight, expertise, and practice in the art of establishing new protected areas. The range of stakeholders involved in the negotiation, establishment, and management of such areas has also diversified and is representative of a much more collaborative and equitable approach to biodiversity conservation and, more broadly, land-use planning. Finally, despite increasing natural resource development pressures, Canada is one of the few remaining countries in the world that maintains large, relatively unfragmented ecosystems, such as major segments of the boreal forest and the Arctic, which still contain large-scale functioning natural processes. As such, Canada has a unique opportunity to protect natural values that are of regional, national, and global significance. To realize this potential, however, the social and ecological benefits of biodiversity must be understood and supported by Canadians; otherwise, the will to support and invest in biodiversity conservation may diminish. Accordingly, greater commitment and determined action to connect people to nature, especially children, and to communicate how biodiversity benefits Canadians in many ways, including through better human health and well-being, is urgently required.

Key Terms

adaptive co-management

assisted migration

biological diversity

ecosystem services

in-situ conservation

non-market ecosystem goods

protected areas

resilience

species at risk

Questions for Review

1. How would you describe the current status of Canada's biodiversity?
2. How do humans benefit from biodiversity and healthy, functioning ecosystems?
3. What are the objectives of the UN Convention on Biological Diversity?
4. What are the objectives of the Canadian Biodiversity Strategy?
5. What is the role of COSEWIC?
6. In your opinion, what are the most significant and pervasive capacity issues facing agencies working to conserve biodiversity?
7. How can Canada better achieve its international and national biodiversity obligations, including those associated with the Biodiversity Convention's Aichi Biodiversity Targets?
8. What strategies could be pursued to (re)connect Canadians to biodiversity?

Internet Resources

Committee on the Status of Endangered Wildlife in Canada
http://www.cosewic.gc.ca/eng/sct5/index_e.cfm

Convention on Biological Diversity
http://www.cbd.int/

Discover the World's Protected Areas
http://www.protectedplanet.net/

Federal, Provincial, and Territorial Working Group on Biodiversity
http://www.biodivcanada.ca/default.
asp?lang=En&n=DABC84B3-1

IUCN Red List of Threatened Species
http://www.iucnredlist.org/

Additional Reading

Bocking, S., ed. *Biodiversity in Canada: Ecology, Ideas, and Action*. Toronto: University of Toronto Press, 2000.

Convention on Biological Diversity. *Strategic Plan for Biodiversity 2011–2020, including Aichi Biodiversity Targets*. http://www.cbd.int/sp/default.shtml.

Government of Canada. *Canadian Biodiversity Strategy: Canada's Response to the Convention on Biological Diversity 1995*. Ottawa: Minister of Supply and Services

Canada, 1995. http://www.biodivcanada.ca/560ED58E-0A7A-43D8-8754-C7DD12761EFA/CBS_e.pdf.

Lemieux, C.J., T.J. Beechey, and P.A. Gray. "Prospects for Canada's Protected Areas in an Era of Rapid Climate Change." *Land Use Policy* 28, 4 (2011): 928–41.

Lovejoy, T., and L. Hannah, eds. *Climate Change and Biodiversity*. New Haven: Yale University Press, 2005.

Notes

1. Convention on Biological Diversity, opened for signature 5 June 1992, 1760 U.N.T.S. 79, 31 I.L.M. 818 (hereafter Biodiversity Convention).

2. According to the International Union for the Conservation of Nature (IUCN), "A protected area is a clearly defined geographical space, recognised, dedicated and managed, through legal or other effective means, to achieve the long term conservation of nature with associated ecosystem services and cultural values." See N. Dudley, ed., *Guidelines for Applying Protected Area Management Categories* (Gland, Switzerland: IUCN, 2008).

3. D. Juffe-Bignoli et al., *Protected Planet Report 2014* (Cambridge: UNEP-WCMC, 2014).

4. Species at Risk Act, S.C. 2002, c. 29.

5. Canadian Council on Ecological Areas (CCEA), *Conservation Areas and Reporting System (CARTS)* v. 2014.12.31 (Ottawa: CCEA, 2015), http://www.ccea.org/?page_id=233.

6. Committee on the Status of Endangered Wildlife in Canada (COSEWIC), *COSEWIC Annual Report 2012–2013* (Ottawa: COSEWIC, 2013), http://publications.gc.ca/collections/collection_2013/ec/CW70-18-2013-eng.pdf. It should be emphasized that changes between years are due to an improved knowledge of wild species and the assessment of new species groups, in addition to the realized declining condition of species.

7. Biodiversity Convention, Article 2.

8. C. Mora, D.P. Tittensor, S. Adl, A.G.B. Simpson, and B. Worm, "How Many Species Are There on Earth and in the Ocean?" *PLoSBiol* 9, 8 (2011): e1001127.

9. Government of Canada, *Canada's 4th National Report to the Convention on Biological Diversity* (Ottawa, 2009), http://www.cbd.int/doc/world/ca/ca-nr-04-en.pdf.

10. Federal, Provincial, and Territorial Governments of Canada, *Canadian Biodiversity: Ecosystem Status and Trends 2010* (Ottawa: Canadian Council of Resource Ministers, 2010).

11. D.S. Lemmen and F.J. Warren, eds, *Canada in a Changing Climate: Sector Perspectives on Impacts and Adaptation* (Ottawa: Natural Resources Canada, 2014);

Federal, Provincial, and Territorial Governments of Canada, *Canadian Biodiversity*; Government of Canada, *Canada's 5th National Report to the Convention on Biological Diversity* (draft version, 2014).

12. C.J. Lemieux, P.F.J. Eagles, D.S. Slocombe, S.T. Doherty, S.J. Elliott, and S. Mock, "Human Health and Well-being Motivations and Benefits Associated with Protected Area Experiences: An Opportunity for Transforming Policy and Management in Canada," *Parks: The International Journal of Protected Areas and Conservation* 18, 1 (2012): 71–86; Millennium Ecosystem Assessment, *Ecosystems and Human Well-being: Biodiversity Synthesis* (Washington: World Resources Institute, 2005).

13. R. Costanza, "The Value of Ecosystem Services," *Ecological Economics* 25, 1 (1997): 1–2; The Economics of Ecosystems and Biodiversity (TEEB), *The Economics of Ecosystems and Biodiversity (TEEB) Ecological and Economic Foundations*, ed. P. Kumar (London and Washington: Earthscan, 2010).

14. The Greenbelt is a permanently protected area of green space, farmland, forests, wetlands, and watersheds located in southern Ontario. It surrounds a significant portion of Canada's most populated and fastest-growing area—the Golden Horseshoe, which lies at the western end of Lake Ontario with outer boundaries stretching south to Lake Erie and north to Georgian Bay and is home to 8.7 million people, approximately 68 per cent of Ontario's population. S.J. Wilson, *Ontario's Wealth, Canada's Future: Appreciating the Value of the Greenbelt's Eco-Services* (Vancouver: David Suzuki Foundation, 2008).

15. See S. Bocking, ed., *Biodiversity in Canada: Ecology, Ideas, and Action* (Toronto: University of Toronto Press, 2000).

16. Biodiversity Convention, Article 1.

17. UN World Commission on Environment and Development (WCED), *Our Common Future: Report of the World Commission on Environment and Development* (Oxford: Oxford University Press, 1987).

18. Government of Canada, *Canadian Biodiversity Strategy: Canada's Response to the Convention on Biological*

Diversity (Hull, Que.: Biodiversity Convention Office, Environment Canada, 1995).

19. See http://www.mddep.gouv.qc.ca/biodiversite/2004-2007/enbref-en.htm.

20. Ontario Biodiversity Council, *Ontario's Biodiversity Strategy, 2011: Renewing Our Commitment to Protecting What Sustains Us* (Peterborough, Ont.: Ontario Biodiversity Council, 2011).

21. Biodiversity Convention, Article 8.

22. Ibid, Preamble.

23. This document was signed by federal and provincial governments confirming Canada's commitment to establish a network of national protected areas representing each of Canada's 39 ecological regions.

24. For example, in March 1999, the Ontario provincial government announced "Ontario's Living Legacy," a strategy for expanding Ontario's system of parks and protected areas. The strategy added 378 new parks and protected areas, increasing the amount of land protected in the province by a third.

25. "Fortress conservation" commonly refers to an approach that seeks to preserve wildlife and their habitat through forceful exclusion of local people who have traditionally relied on the environment in question for their livelihoods.

26. More specifically, 12 of 17 federal, provincial, and territorial organizations have protected areas programs in place (federal: Parks Canada Agency, Fisheries and Oceans Canada, Environment Canada, Agriculture and Agri-Food Canada; provincial/territorial: Yukon, British Columbia, Saskatchewan, Manitoba, Ontario, Quebec, New Brunswick, and Nova Scotia).

27. Environment Canada, *Canada Protected Areas Status Report, 2006–2011* (Gatineau, Que.: Environment Canada, 2015).

28. COP 6 Decision VI/26, *Strategic Plan for the Convention on Biological Diversity*, April 2002, http://www.cbd.int/decision/cop/default.shtml?id57200.

29. Ibid.

30. Government of Canada, *Canada's 5th National Report*.

31. While the number of species assessed in Canada has increased from 1,670 in 2000 to 11,950 in 2010, with an estimated 70,000+ species found in Canada, many species remain to be assessed, the vast majority of these insects and other invertebrates. See Canadian Endangered Species Conservation Council, *Wild Species 2010: The General Status of Species in Canada* (National General Status Working Group, 2011), http://www.wildspecies.ca/reports.cfm?lang=e.

32. Secretariat of the Convention on Biological Diversity, *Global Biodiversity Outlook 3*, (Montreal, 2010).

33. Government of Canada, *Canada's 4th National Report*.

34. See http://www.cbd.int/sp/targets/ for the full list of targets.

35. For a useful clause-by-clause analysis of Target 11, see S. Woodley, B. Bettzky, N. Crawhall, N. Dudley, J.M. Londono, K. MacKinnon, K. Redford, and T. Sandwith, "Meeting Aichi Target 11: What Does Success Look Like for Protected Area Systems?" *Parks: The International Journal of Protected Areas and Conservation* 18, 1 (2012): 23–36, https://cmsdata.iucn.org/downloads/parks_woodley_1.pdf.

36. Canadian Council on Ecological Areas (CCEA), "Interpreting Aichi Biodiversity Target 11 in the Canadian Context: Towards Consensus on "Other Effective Area-based Conservation Measures," Summary and Results of a CCEA National Workshop, 5–7 Feb. 2013 (Ottawa: CCEA, 2013).

37. Refer to definitions provided under section 2.

38. C.J. Lemieux and D.J. Scott, "Climate Change, Biodiversity Conservation and Protected Area Planning in Canada," *Canadian Geographer* 49, 4 (2005): 384–97.

39. J. Geldmann, M. Barnes, L. Coad, I.D. Craigie, M. Hockings, and N.D. Burgess, "Effectiveness of Terrestrial Protected Areas in Reducing Habitat Loss and Population Declines," *Biological Conservation* 161 (2013): 230–8; B.S. Halpern, "Conservation: Making Marine Protected Areas Work," *Nature* 506, 7487 (2014): 167–8.

40. I. Stirling and A.E. Derocher, "Effects of Climate Warming on Polar Bears: A Review of the Evidence," *Global Change Biology* 18, 9 (2012): 2694–706. doi: 10.1111/j.1365-2486.2012.02753.x.

41. In the US, a species can be listed under the Endangered Species Act of 1973 under one of two categories: endangered or threatened. An endangered species is likely to go extinct within all or a significant portion of its range in the foreseeable future. The polar bear was petitioned to be listed as a threatened species, defined as a species likely to become endangered in the foreseeable future. See http://www.fws.gov/alaska/fisheries/mmm/polarbear/pdf/Polar_Bear_Final_Rule.pdf.

42. See *Canada Gazette*, "Order Amending Schedule 1 to the Species at Risk Act, (P.C. 2011-1264 October 27, 2011)," http://www.gazette.gc.ca/rp-pr/p2/2011/2011-11-09/html/sor-dors233-eng.html.

43. O. Hoegh-Guldberg, L. Hughes, S. McIntyre, D.B. Lindenmayer, C. Parmesan, H.P. Possingham, and C.D. Thomas, "Assisted Colonization and Rapid Climate Change," *Science* 321 (5887) (2008): 345–6.

44. In 2006, the BC Ministry of Forests' Research Branch established a large-scale assisted migration adaptation trial (AMAT) to inform the use of assisted migration as a climate change adaptation strategy. Seedlings from populations of 15 species from British Columbia and neighbouring US states were planted at 48 reforestation sites from southern Yukon to northern California. See http://www.for.gov.bc.ca/hre/forgen/interior/AMAT.htm.

45. For a useful review, see I. Aubin et al., "Why We Disagree about Assisted Migration: Ethical Implications of a Key Debate Regarding the Future of Canada's Forests," *Forestry Chronicle* 87 (2011): 755–65.

46. C.S. Findlay, S. Elgie, B. Giles, and L. Burr, "Species Listing under Canada's Species at Risk Act," *Conservation Biology* 23, 6 (2009): 1609–17.

47. B. Favaro, D.C. Claar, C.H. Fox, C. Freshwater, J.J. Holden, and A. Roberts, "Trends in Extinction Risk for Imperiled Species in Canada," *PloS One* 9, 11 (2014): e113118.

48. J.A. Hutchings et al., "Is Canada Fulfilling Its Obligations to Sustain Marine Biodiversity? A Summary Review, Conclusions, and Recommendations," *Environmental Reviews* 20, 4 (2012): 353–61; R. Devillers, R.L. Pressey, A. Grech, J.N. Kittinger, G.J. Edgar, T. Ward, and R. Watson, "Reinventing Residual Reserves in the Sea: Are We Favouring Ease of Establishment over Need for Protection?" *Aquatic Conservation: Marine and Freshwater Ecosystems* (2014), doi: 10.1002/aqc.2445.

49. Graham J. Edgar et al., "Global Conservation Outcomes Depend on Marine Protected Areas with Five Key Features," *Nature* 506 (2014): 216–20.

50. Office of the Auditor General of Canada, *2013 Fall Report of the Commissioner of the Environment and Sustainable Development* (Ottawa: Office of the Auditor General of Canada, 2013).

51. Ibid.

52. Office of the Environmental Commissioner of Ontario, *Laying Siege to the Last Line of Defence: A Review of Ontario's Weakened Protections for Species at Risk* (Toronto: Office of the Environmental Commissioner of Ontario, 2013), http://www.eco.on.ca/uploads/Reports-special/2013%20Laying%20Siege%20to%20the%20ESA/Laying%20Siege.pdf; British Columbia Office of the Auditor General, *Conservation of Ecological Integrity in B.C. Parks and Protected Areas* (Victoria: British Columbia Office of the Auditor General, 2010), file:///Users/cjlemieu/Downloads/OAGBC_Parks%20Report_OUT2.pdf.

53. Federal, Provincial, and Territorial Governments of Canada, *Canadian Biodiversity: Ecosystem Status and Trends 2010*; A.O. Mooers et al., "Science and Policy and Species at Risk in Canada," *BioScience* 60 (2010): 843–9.

54. Environment Canada, *Canada Protected Areas Status Report, 2006–2011*.

55. C.J. Lemieux, T.J. Beechey, and P.A. Gray, "Prospects for Canada's Protected Areas in an Era of Rapid Climate Change," *Land Use Policy* 28, 4 (2011): 928–41.

56. See http://www.ipsos-na.com/news-polls/pressrelease.aspx?id=5926.

57. Environment Canada, *Canada Protected Areas Status Report, 2006–2011*.

58. Canadian Environmental Assessment Act, 2012 S.C. 2012, c. 19, s. 52). For a useful review of recent changes to the Canadian Environmental Assessment Act, see R.B. Gibson, "In Full Retreat: The Canadian Government's New Environmental Assessment Law Undoes Decades of Progress," *Impact Assessment and Project Appraisal* 30, 3 (2012): 179–88. Changes to the Fisheries Act, passed by Parliament in 2012 and supported by new regulations in 2013, stipulate that habitat will now be protected only for fish considered part of a fishery or that support a fishery. The habitats of most freshwater fish species in Canada, including the majority of threatened and endangered fishes, will no longer be protected. See J.A. Hutchings and J.R. Post, "Gutting Canada's Fisheries Act: No Fishery, No Fish Habitat Protection," *Fisheries* 38 (2013): 497–501; Government of Canada, *The Road to Balance: Creating Jobs and Opportunities* (Ottawa, 2014), http://actionplan.gc.ca/en/blog/economic-action-plan-2014.

59. See http://cmsdata.iucn.org/downloads/iucn_eba_brochure.pdf; Lemieux et al., "Prospects for Canada's Protected Areas."

60. I.E. Deguise and J.T. Kerr, "Protected Areas and Prospects for Endangered Species Conservation in Canada," *Conservation Biology* 20, 1 (2006): 48–55.

61. R. Plummer, B. Crona, D.R. Armitage, P. Olsson, M. Tengo, and O. Yudina, "Adaptive Co-management: A Systematic Review and Analysis," *Ecology and Society* 17, 3 (2012): 290–306.

62. D. Armitage, R. de Loë, and R. Plummer, "Environmental Governance and Its Implications for Conservation Practice," *Conservation Letters* 5 (2012): 245–55.

19 Air Pollution Policy in Canada: Government Leadership or Smoke and Mirrors?

Owen Temby, Don Munton, and Inger Weibust

Chapter Summary

This chapter examines the problem of air pollution in Canada, and argues that pollution abatement tends to be highly episodic, implemented through technological controls, and symbolic, often promising more than it delivers. In Canada, this has resulted in laws that do not constrain, regulations that make little or no difference, bilateral treaties that appear to promise more than they actually do, and a redundancy of standards across multiple scales of government. In 2014, the Harper government proposed revised air pollution regulations, something the federal government has rarely done in the past. This chapter asks whether this represents leadership by the current government, or whether these policies are "smoke and mirrors," aimed at creating the appearance of progress while actually achieving little. As we show, the new federal–provincial Air Quality Management System and the Harper government's coal-fired power plant program actually represent a continuation of long-standing tendencies. The ambivalence noted elsewhere in this book is reflected in federal clean air regulations that, while unprecedented, are nevertheless so lax that they will likely have little influence on polluting industrial practices. At the same time, due to its technological dependence and the role of the private sector in developing abatement technology, clean air policy is not an issue area that tends to be affected by government austerity.

Chapter Outline

- Air pollution as a political challenge in Canada
  - The evolution of this issue, alongside changing chemical content and intensity, technology, and economy
- Air chemistry
  - Understanding the various manifestations of air pollution, and their impacts on human health and ecosystems
- Tendencies in clean air policy
  - Episodic

ο Reliant on technology
ο Symbolic
- The Canadian federal approach to air pollution policy
  ο Non-binding air quality standards
  ο Lists of federally unregulated pollutants
  ο Harmonization of automobile standards with those in the United States
  ο International treaties with loose commitments
- Current actions: new, but lax, regulations

Introduction

Air pollution has been a political issue in Canada for more than a century, changing and evolving along with the structure of our economy and our understanding of air chemistry. As in other countries, air pollution first emerged as a local problem, an issue for cities to address. Initially, the challenge was related to the close proximity of farmland to industrializing urban areas; for example, in the 1910s, Canada's World War I industrial mobilization pitted metal producers in Sudbury, Ontario, against farmers whose crops (and livelihoods) were destroyed by fumes from the industrial firms.[1] During the decades that followed, as cities such as Montreal and Toronto grew, urban air pollution offices and bylaws were established to target the most egregious offenders.[2] The air pollution problems of this period consisted mostly of visible smoke and particulates that often contained corrosive acids, and the main sources were garbage incineration and coal combustion from locomotives and lake freighters. These were serious problems. In London, England, which had experienced serious air pollution for centuries, an infamous 1952 "killer fog" claimed some 4,000 casualties.[3] The following year, an air pollution emergency in New York City took hundreds of lives. During the mid-1950s Torontonians saw their air quality reach similar levels of pollution as in London and New York, and they worried about roaming killer smogs. Autopsied children who lived in Toronto were found to have black lungs at only five years of age.[4] While municipal government responses no doubt relieved the problem somewhat, the transition from coal to liquid fuel during the late 1950s and early 1960s (for reasons unrelated to government efforts to limit pollution) brought about the most substantial reductions during this era.

However, these early improvements in air quality were limited both geographically and in terms of the pollutants addressed. They did little to improve the quality of air in smaller, less economically diversified towns; they did not address the emerging air quality problem related to increased automobile usage; and they did not tackle the (then little-understood) problem of long-distance air pollutant transport. In November and December of 1962, the combination of automobile fumes and aggravating climatic conditions led to an especially severe 11-day smog across southwestern Ontario that resulted in a delay of the Canadian Football League's Grey Cup game in Toronto (an event that became known as the "Fog Bowl"). Sarnia, Ontario, home of Chemical Valley (a group of petrochemical companies that dominated the town economically), experienced some of the most severe air pollution in the country but had no regulations in place to limit emissions.[5] Provinces responded to these and similar problems by creating clean air statutes in the late 1960s, regulating pollution under these new authorities, and applying the more stringent automobile emissions regulations already in place in the United States.[6]

While the cleaner automobiles coming out of Detroit made a clear contribution to improved urban air quality, the utility of early provincial statutes—which were not aggressively enforced—was less obvious. In fact, it took a crisis to stir the Canadian government into action. In the late 1970s, air pollution in the form of "acid rain" was found to be destroying lakes and forests throughout Ontario and Quebec.[7] As policy-makers soon came to understand, air pollution can travel longer distances than previously known, and in this case it was coming from metal smelters in Ontario as well as coal-fired power plants in Ontario and the American Midwest. In response to the severe economic and environmental damage caused by this pollution, the Canadian federal and provincial governments reduced coal use, regulated smelters more stringently, and, in 1991, struck a deal with the United States to lessen emissions on both sides of the border.[8]

Today, Canada's air is much cleaner than it was before the 1990s. Cities still experience smog, and plants and ecosystems continue to suffer from acid rain, but with less intensity. Automobiles run cleaner, buildings pollute less, and coal-fired power plants have in many instances been replaced with less-emitting or non-emitting natural gas, nuclear, and solar energy sources. Yet our cities continue to grow, Canadians drive more than in the past, and, thanks to epidemiological studies, we now know more about the long-term dangerous health effects of air pollution. There is much to be gained, health-wise and economically, from tighter restrictions on the release of air pollution. Fortunately, in both Canada and the United States, air pollution remains an area of government concern and efforts continue to be made to tighten standards. But, as with the other cases examined in this volume, understanding what is happening is difficult since divided powers between federal and provincial governments mean that it is not clear who is presently taking the most substantive actions in this policy space. The federal government claims to regulate air pollution, yet—as this chapter clearly shows—this task has historically been undertaken by the provinces. Adding to the complexity of the issue is the highly symbolic nature of clean air policy, as discussed below. Everybody wants clean air, so paying it "lip service" is a winner politically.

In this chapter, we provide an overview of the political problem of air pollution in Canada. We discuss the features that make it unique as an environmental policy challenge for governments, and examine the ways in which the Canadian federal government has worked with the provinces in crafting a response. In particular, we investigate the extent to which Canada's recent and ongoing programs and policies represent leadership (that is, proactive and substantive response by government) in the area of air pollution abatement or, alternatively, are "smoke and mirrors" aimed more at satisfying public demand for action than at taking substantive measures to address the problem they are ostensibly designed to ameliorate. In other words, we are probing one of the primary themes of this volume, namely, the degree to which ambivalence is an accurate descriptor in this policy area.

We examine air quality policy on several fronts. Following an introduction to Canadian domestic air pollution policy, we assess Canada's binational relations with the United States as they relate to air pollution. Given Canada's economic integration with the US and also the fact that air pollutants flow in both directions across the border (but more from the US to Canada), the binational relationship is critical in terms of understanding Canadian air pollution policy since the 1980s. Afterwards, we analyze two domestic air pollution programs under the Harper government: (1) the federal–provincial Air Quality Management System, and (2) the coal-fired power plant control program. These programs are of considerable political importance because they enable the government to claim that it is active in climate-related policy-making. However, as we argue below, in their present form they do not represent aggressive attempts to improve air quality much beyond what is achievable through technological and political processes already underway. While Ottawa is poised to regulate air pollution from industry for the first time, the rules are very lax and unlikely to bring about much of a change of behaviour on the part of polluters. "Smoke and mirrors"? Quite possibly.

Before we proceed, a brief note on the scope of how we define the environmental issue at hand. Air pollution comprises a diverse set of phenomena, too many to cover in this chapter. To make the topic manageable, we will focus on three interrelated air pollution problems in Canada: acid rain, ground-level ozone/smog, and particulate matter. There are linkages among these issues in terms of their precursors or sources. All are both local and transboundary or international; they involve both domestic sources and flows of pollutants across national boundaries. To be sure, there is substantial overlap between the chemicals underlying these air pollution problems and the chemicals causing climate change. Most air pollutants are *also* greenhouse gases (GHGs) that cause climate change. And many air pollutants that are not GHGs result from the same combustion processes that also release GHGs. With policy-makers now regulating the sources of air pollutants under the rationale of GHG abatement, it is no longer possible to completely disentangle the two. However, the high-profile issues of climate change abatement/adaptation and also ozone layer depletion differ qualitatively from the issues we discuss here. In addition, this chapter will not cover the problem of persistent organic pollutants (POPs) transported from other continents to Canada's Arctic.[9]

Types of Air Pollution: Smoke, Acid Rain, Ozone, and Particulates

The age-old problems of smoke and fumes continue to resurface in modern air quality issues. In fact, what we have come to call *acid rain* is actually a contemporary manifestation of a century-long problem with industrial emissions. In terms of its sources and transport patterns, acid rain closely relates to smog and airborne particulate matter (though they differ in terms of ecosystem and human impacts).

Acid rain was the most prominent environmental issue in Canada in the 1980s. It is the popular name now given to a complex set of physical and chemical phenomena by which gases—especially sulphur dioxide (SO_2) and nitrogen oxides (NO_x)—emitted mostly from industrial processes are transported through the atmosphere, transformed into acidic compounds, and deposited on land and water surfaces. This often has serious negative effects for aquatic and terrestrial ecosystems that lack the natural alkalinity to neutralize the acid rain. Acidified lakes and streams cannot sustain fish and other aquatic species. Acidification also has ill effects on various crops and on the growth of certain types of trees, particularly in high altitudes, and can cause long-term damage to soils lacking the capacity to buffer the acidity. We can smell pulp mill emissions and see marine oil pollution, but human senses cannot detect acidification.

The major sources of acid rain in North America as a whole are sulphur dioxide emissions from coal-burning electrical generation and non-ferrous metal smelting. In the US, the bulk of SO_2 comes from power plants, particularly those concentrated in the American

Midwest. In the late twentieth century, Canada's major sources of SO_2 were a small number of large metal smelters. Like coal, metal ores often contain significant amounts of sulphur as an impurity; smelting the ore burns off the sulphur and produces SO_2. A handful of coal-fired power plants also contribute SO_2, but in western Canada the oil and gas industry is the primary source of SO_2.

Since 2000, two related issues have come to dominate Canada's air pollution scene: ground-level ozone and particulate matter.[10] **Ground-level ozone** is known as a secondary pollutant because it results from the interaction of other substances, specifically nitrogen oxides (NO_x) and volatile organic compounds (VOCs). Ozone (O_3) forms in the lower atmosphere, or troposphere, where its growth is promoted by sunlight and warm temperatures. Ground-level ozone should not be confused with the stratospheric ozone layer. People exposed to ozone over a long period can develop various health conditions, particularly asthma, reduced lung function, and cardiovascular disease.[11] High ambient ozone concentrations also harm vegetation and synthetic materials and textiles.

Particulate matter (PM) comprises airborne particles in both solid and liquid form. PM can be either a primary air pollutant, when sources such as coal-burning power plants directly release the particles, or a secondary pollutant, when gaseous SO_2, NO_x, and ammonia react in the atmosphere to create sulphate, nitrate, and ammonia particulates. What is colloquially known as *smog* results when particulate matter combines with ground-level ozone. Although we tend to view smog as an urban problem, it can also affect rural and wilderness areas (where we most often describe it as a visibility problem).

Airborne particulates are themselves a serious air pollutant and "an important [human] health concern."[12] Humans can breathe in the smaller particles, which lodge in our lungs. Exposure to smog and particulate matter can lead to respiratory conditions, including asthma, emphysema, and pulmonary disease, as well as cardiovascular and neurological conditions. Elderly people and young children are particularly vulnerable. Long-term exposure can cause serious health disorders, especially exposure to the finer particulates (airborne matter smaller than 2.5 micrometres, referred to as $PM_{2.5}$). The Canadian Medical Association estimates that between 20,000 and 25,000 Canadians die prematurely every year from complications resulting from particulates and other air pollutants.[13] Air pollution incidents also raise hospital admissions and increase health costs. To put a human face on these statistics, Prime Minister Stephen Harper entered hospital shortly after his election victory in January 2006, a result of his being a lifelong sufferer from asthma.[14]

The atmospheric chemistry of particulates is more complex than that of acid rain, but the two issues are similar in terms of their sources and transport. The major sources of $PM_{2.5}$ are motor vehicles (particularly diesel engines) and the coal-fired power stations that produce much of our acid rain. Other sources include road dust and, on a periodic basis, forest fires. Total US emissions of particulate matter precursors are approximately 10 times the Canadian emissions, reflecting the larger US population and greater industrial output.

Air Pollution as a Policy Issue

Air pollution is perhaps unique among policy challenges. Sufferers represent different segments of society from the polluters, and the former are often located great distances away from the latter. And while it overlaps with the problem of climate change abatement in important ways, air pollution is not entirely subsumed by climate change because some pollutants are not greenhouse gases, and even those that *are* GHGs (such as O_3 from automobile emissions) double as urban air pollutants.

This essential property of air pollution—as an airborne, travelling, **negative externality** of economic activity—has numerous implications for how political responses are developed and implemented. To understand air pollution policy in Canada, it is important to acknowledge several persistent features of air pollution politics and policy. First, air pollution policy is highly episodic, with progress happening in fits and bursts in response to occasionally peaking anxiety over the problem. This is due both to the inherently political process of actors mobilizing to lobby the government and convince polluters to bear the costs of modernizing, and to the role of science in clarifying previously unrecognized weather patterns, chemical interactions among airborne pollutants, and consequences such as health and economic costs. Environmental "goods" like fisheries or forests, by contrast, tend more towards technocratic management on an ongoing basis with the institutionalized input of mature science and a well-defined set of stakeholders. Political advocacy aimed at clarifying the causes and costs of air pollution, as well as formulating economically feasible solutions, has been a particularly important means through which breakthroughs in pollution abatement occur.[15] Conversely, approaching air pollution abatement from a depoliticized technocratic management perspective (as in the Canada–US Air Quality Agreement, discussed below) rarely brings about substantial reductions because such processes are ill-suited for securing costly reductions from polluters.

Second, the primary means through which air pollution is addressed is through the technological modernization of sources.[16] This includes making production techniques at factories and smelters more efficient, capturing pollution at the stack, replacing dirty forms of combustion with cleaner types, and modifying automobiles so that they emit less pollution. Generally, all actors implicated in the policy process prefer modernization because it does not require reductions in production or consumption that would hinder economic growth. During the 1980s, for example, when a coalition of economic elites and environmental interests concerned about the effects of acid rain on Ontario's economy and environment negotiated with polluters and federal officials for reductions in sulphur dioxide, the challenge was defined by all as a "smelter modernization problem" and federal funds were offered for this purpose.[17] Throughout the twentieth century and today in Canada and the United States, the availability of technology to limit pollution has been the most important factor in whether air quality could be improved.[18] During periods when such technology did not credibly exist (as in Sudbury, Ontario, a century ago), relief was not possible and those affected simply suffered.[19]

Third, the long-distance transport of air pollutants leads to a state of affairs in which regions on the downwind (receiving) side are environmentally dependent on upwind sources and their jurisdictions.[20] In North America, the region that has most frequently invoked the ire of downwind recipients is the Ohio River Valley of the US (including portions of Indiana, Kentucky, Ohio, and other states), which has a large number of dirty coal–fired power plants. Prevailing winds transport acids and other pollutants from this region northeast, to Ontario, Quebec, the Maritime provinces, and the American Northeast (including New York State). In the US, institutional mechanisms available through the Clean Air Act (most notably, litigation) have enabled the northeastern states to force substantial reductions from Ohio River Valley polluters, and this, in turn, has improved air quality in Canada. However,

Canada's lack of access to these mechanisms has been an important factor in this country's response to American-sourced pollution.

Air pollution has one more feature that adds another layer of complexity: it is highly symbolic. As Matthew Cahn explains:

> Clean air is a special concern for most people. In addition to the inherently life-giving quality of oxygen, clean air provides an aesthetic element necessary for a high quality of life. For centuries fresh air has been recognized for its invigorating appeal. Urban vacationers have always sought to get out into "the country." Parents push their children to get out and play in the fresh air. In a sense, access to clean air is inherently symbolic.[21]

The nature of air pollution suggests a fourth implication for policy-making; namely, that clean air policy is itself often more symbolic than substantive. It responds to public anxiety with promises to achieve great things, and then quietly fails to deliver. Cahn contends that, in the US, "clean air legislation has consistently been marketed deceptively."[22] And what has been true of the United States has also been true in Canada. A noteworthy example was Ontario's 1967 Air Pollution Control Act (APCA), a statute passed during a time in Canada and elsewhere when citizens were becoming increasingly aware of and concerned about environmental degradation. The 1967 APCA promised, for the first time, to regulate air quality on a provincial basis and control polluters in municipalities that had not yet passed bylaws. Ostensibly it did this. In reality, it dismantled the aggressive control program already in place in Toronto and issued control orders on polluters in other areas that, for the most part, either were no different from what the polluters were planning to do otherwise or were simply not enforced.[23] The province did not substantively regulate air pollution sources again until 10–15 years later, when acid rain threatened Ontario's seasonal tourism industry.

An implication of the prevalence of symbolic clean air policy-making in Canada (and in the United States) is that we must distinguish between efforts to address the problem that are substantive and those that are symbolic. Do existing programs and policies represent leadership by the Canadian government in improving air quality, or do they purport to do so while actually achieving very little? This includes not only pollution generated in Canada, but also that flowing from the US. The federal government has put substantial resources into negotiating a bilateral treaty and maintaining a binational organization whose task is to facilitate co-operation on policies reducing the transboundary flow of pollution. Is it effective in doing so and, in general, how has Canada engaged its neighbour to the south on this issue?

Canada's Air Pollution Policy: Domestic and Foreign

"Canadian air pollution policy" is a bit of a misnomer. Domestic regulation is undertaken mostly by the provinces, which have authority over stationary/point sources (i.e., not cars and trucks), with the federal government providing assistance in the form of research, co-ordination, and financing for abatement projects on heavy polluters. This paucity of national regulation is not a matter of legal restrictions. Thanks to the "national concern" doctrine carved out of the "peace, order, and good government" clause of the 1867 Constitution Act, Ottawa arguably has jurisdiction over airborne pollutants that cross provincial or international boundaries (something that pollution often does).[24] But federal governments have opted to allow provinces to regulate air pollution, instead identifying non-binding benchmarks for provincial governments to consider integrating into their programs.

One task undertaken by the federal government has been negotiating bilateral pollution reductions with the United States and participating in organizations that include air pollution as one of their areas of concern (e.g., the Canada–US Air Quality Committee, the North American Commission for Environmental Cooperation, and the Convention on Long-Range Transboundary Air Pollution, or LRTAP). Canada's environmental dependence on the US in regard to air pollution makes bilateral engagement an important consideration in developing clean air policy. However, as we explain below, bilateral co-operation has been of notably limited effectiveness in terms of securing mutually dependent pollution reductions and enforcing compliance.

Domestic Air Pollution Regulation

There is no "Clean Air Act" in Canada as there is in other industrialized countries. Strictly speaking, there used to be one (it passed in 1971, but then was integrated into subsequent legislation) (see Table 19.1). It was never employed to create actual regulations.[25] Instead, it established a pattern, continued in its descendent statutes until recently, whereby the federal government identifies priority pollutants, sets objectives for air quality, and then negotiates non-binding agreements with the provinces to implement programs to attain these objectives.

Under the 1971 Clean Air Act, a federal–provincial advisory committee in 1974 established National Ambient Air Quality Objectives (NAAQOs) for SO_2, particulates, carbon monoxide (a VOC), O_3, and NO_2.[26] The 1971 Clean Air Act was replaced in 1988 by the Canadian Environmental Protection Act (CEPA, which was amended in 1999), but the NAAQOs remained mostly unchanged for decades. This was of little importance because Canada's ambient standards have no regulatory significance anyway, unlike in the US, where they are enforced by the federal government. Under CEPA, Environment Canada began identifying

TABLE 19.1 Selected Domestic Federal Air Pollution Statutes and Programs

Year	Statute	Program	Sets Regulations?
1971	Clean Air Act	NAAQOs	No
1971	Motor Vehicle Safety Act	Automobile regulations	Following US standards
1988	Canadian Environmental Protection Act	Same programs as above, plus a "toxic substances" list	Occasionally for toxic substances; otherwise, same as above
1999	Canadian Environmental Protection Act (updated)	Same as above, with expanded "toxic substances" list	Same as above
2000		Canada Wide Standards (replacing NAAQOs)	No
2012		Coal-fired power plant program	Yes
2014		CAAQS (replacing Canada Wide Standards)	No
2014		BLIERs	Occasionally

toxic substances as those that should receive some sort of regulatory control. This list has grown over time—under CEPA 1988 the original list was 26, and now the number stands at 132.[27] Among those currently listed are all of the standard air pollution forms discussed in this chapter, though the federal government is almost never the regulator.[28] CEPA's usage can generously be described as "filling in small gaps" in select domains where the provinces have not pursued aggressive regulation. For example, Environment Canada regulates dry cleaners, which use a toxic substance called perchloroethylene (a VOC) to clean clothes.[29] Heavy industrial sources appeared on the federal regulatory radar only recently (see below).

Beginning with the 1971 Motor Vehicle Safety Act (and subsequently through CEPA), the Canadian federal government has *technically* regulated emissions standards for new automobiles in the country. In reality it does not and has not; the North American automobile industry is too integrated (with cars and trucks made and sold in both Canada and the United States) for manufacturers to make different products for each national market.[30] The US government determines automobile regulations and Canadian regulations are occasionally updated to reflect new, tighter standards.[31]

In the absence of federal leadership, the provinces have created and implemented their own programs. Through the mid-1960s, clean air policy consisted of municipal bylaws passed by city councils. While this worked well in Toronto and other cities with the technical capacity to implement these programs, it led to a spotty approach whereby some cities had no regulations and, among those that did, there was considerable variation. In addition to this being harmful for the people who lived in highly polluted areas with insufficient or no regulation, it did not work well for industrial firms either, which value regulatory predictability and homogeneity. Thus, in the late 1960s, at the request of representatives of the Canadian manufacturing industry, the provinces took over control.[32]

Ontario, which has Canada's largest population and also releases the most air pollution, developed an air pollution control program based on a concept known as the **point of impingement**.[33] Basically, air pollution limits are assessed only when the pollution comes in contact with people and property it might harm. Otherwise, polluters can release as much as they please. Throughout its first decade, this approach was mildly effective at reducing air pollution from refineries and some smelters and power plants. Yet it was not enough to prevent considerable acid rain damage to tourist destinations in Ontario. In response to substantial political pressure during the 1980s from tourism and tourism-allied interests, the province created an acid rain program ("Countdown Acid Rain") to reduce emissions from coal-fired power plants and smelters for which the existing regulations had been insufficient or simply not enforced.[34]

This dynamic was representative of the broader tendencies in air pollution policy identified above, namely, that air pollution policy is highly episodic and addressed through technology. And it is a pattern that has persisted in Ontario. For the past 30 years, Ontario's primary approach to managing its air pollution is not through clean air legislation, but by managing its sources of electricity (in addition to the one-time reductions from metal smelters mentioned above). In the 1980s, the province switched a substantial portion of its electricity generation capacity from coal to nuclear. During the late 1990s, when problems with the stability of these nuclear plants required the province to lean more heavily on coal, causing a severe smog problem in Toronto, it launched the "Ontario Smog Plan" and installed "selective catalytic reduction" units on several coal plants to remove NO_x at the stack.[35] Most recently, the province has transitioned away from coal in favour of natural gas and renewables.

The forum through which the provinces collectively agree on air pollution objectives is the Canadian Council of Ministers of the Environment (CCME), discussed by Simmons in Chapter 8. For air pollution, the Council's main task has been to set ambient standards for concentrations of pollutants in outdoor air. In 2000, to reflect commitments under the Ozone Annex to the Canada–US Air Quality Agreement, they set non-binding Canada-Wide Standards for PM and O_3, effectively replacing the NAAQOs for those pollutants. While the CCME has not been an important driver of interprovincial clean air policy (because such a thing hardly exists in Canada), it is possible that it is presently taking on increased importance due to renewed enthusiasm by the federal government to regulate air pollution (discussed below).

Since forming a government in 2006, Harper's federal Conservative Party has sought to deflect criticism that it was failing to act on climate change by instead regulating air pollution. Early in its first mandate, the federal government proposed a new Clean Air Act intended to address smog, though it failed to garner support on the grounds that sufficient statutory authority already existed under CEPA to address air pollution and that it did not do enough to limit GHGs.[36] The following year, undeterred, the Conservative Party released details of its proposed "Turning the Corner Plan." It, too, proposed air pollution and GHG regulations on industries that had never been regulated by the federal government, but rather than a new law it would use existing authorities available under CEPA. "Turning the Corner" has undergone several changes since 2007, but implementation is underway. Might this represent a new era for Canadian leadership in air pollution policy? We return to this question in the final section.

Air Pollution and Canada–US Relations

The problem of transboundary environmental dependence, whereby air pollution travels from regions of the US to Canada, coupled with a lack of bilateral mechanisms with the capacity to influence domestic regulations, makes air pollution a challenging problem in terms of Canada–US relations. Despite participating in several international treaties and organizations that somehow claim air pollution within their mandates, Canada and the United States conduct little air pollution research in concert.[37] And under their existing bilateral treaty, the two countries only agree to bilateral commitments to reduce pollutants when it is clear that the programs to bring about the reductions are already in place or the commitments are themselves non-binding.

The Canadian government's desire to negotiate a bilateral air pollution treaty with the US arose in the late 1970s when SO_2 and NO_X from the Ohio River Valley contributed to considerable damage in the form of acid rain to lakes and forests in parts of Ontario and Quebec. In 1979, Canada joined the US as signatory to the European Convention on Long-Range Transboundary Air Pollution as a way of embarrassing its neighbour, in an international forum, over acid rain because this was one of several air pollution issues addressed in a series of discrete Protocols (see Table 19.2). However, it was not until 1991 that the two countries were able to agree on a bilateral treaty, the Canada–US Air Quality Agreement (AQA), under which they committed to specific reductions in acid rain precursor pollutants. This treaty contained several mechanisms to facilitate regular bilateral co-operation, notably the creation of a secretariat (the Air Quality Committee) and two subcommittees tasked with conducting research on transboundary air pollution, monitoring emissions,

TABLE 19.2 Selected International Air Pollution Treaties with Canada Participating

Year	Treaty	Protocol/Annex	Commitments
1979	Convention on Long-Range Transboundary Air Pollution (LRTAP)		Contained in subsequent protocols
1984		Protocol for financing LRTAP research program	None; Canada committed only to "voluntary" funding
1985		SO_2 Protocol	Specific reductions in overall SO_x emissions
1988		NO_x Protocol	Specific reductions in overall NO_x emissions
1994		2nd SO_2 Protocol	Specific reductions in SO_2 emissions (overall and in a specific region)
1991	Canada–United States Air Quality Agreement	Annex 1: Acid Rain	Specific reductions in overall SO_2 and NO_x emissions
1991		Annex 2: Research and Monitoring	Conduct research and publish biennial progress reports
2000		Ozone Annex	Non-specific regional reductions in NO_x and VOCs

and producing biennial progress reports. It also created a mechanism whereby each country is required to formally notify the other of each new source or modification of an existing source, built within 100 kilometres of the border, that may potentially result in transboundary air pollution. Formal air pollution abatement commitments have been contained in "annexes" to the treaty. In the 1991 Acid Rain Annex, each country agreed to specific reductions in SO_2 and NO_x emissions.

In 2000, Canada and the US signed the Ozone Annex, requiring reductions in NO_x and VOCs. However, in the case of each of these annexes, the policy formulation process can best be described as "parallel unilateral." For the Acid Rain Annex, the programs and policies expected to bring about the agreed-to reductions were already in place when the agreement was signed. The same was true for the Ozone Annex on the US side. On the Canadian side the commitments (albeit, loosely specified and non-binding) were a function of federal–provincial inter-party dynamics; the Liberal federal government used the Ozone Annex as a means of signalling intent to Ontario's Progressive Conservative government. Placing Ontario's reductions in a treaty indicated that the federal government might regulate the province's coal-fired power plants under CEPA in the absence of provincial action reducing NO_x emissions.[38] This dialectical federal–provincial–bilateral instance aside, for the AQA, domestic policy and politics drive international commitments, not the other way around.

Furthermore, both countries have underutilized the mechanisms intended to facilitate co-operation—in some instances in ways that clearly violate the treaty.[39] To give one example, in 1998 the United States did not inform Canada about the refurbishment and restarting of a mothballed coal-fired power plant in Detroit, as required by Article 5 of the AQA.[40] This particular power plant also violated the US Clean Air Act. After considerable public outcry in Michigan and litigation initiated by the US Environmental Protection Agency, DTE Energy (the plant owners) agreed to convert it to natural gas.[41] The Air Quality Committee's

2000 biennial report makes no mention of the US violation of the AQA, and instead touts the mutually acceptable outcome.[42] This sort of whitewashing of the countries' treaty violations has become so common that Don Munton labels the relationship one of "collusion."[43] "Symbolic" would be another apt description of this bilateral regime.

The next phase for the AQA will likely be an annex on particulate matter. The Air Quality Committee expressed an interest in this more than a decade ago and, in 2004, completed a scientific assessment recommending the commencement of negotiations. These negotiations began in 2007 and were still ongoing as of 2014.[44] Given that the US has taken considerable steps on PM during the last decade (tightening regulations in 2006 and again in 2012), it appears on track to make attainable bilateral commitments. With Canada's planned and continuing closure of numerous coal-fired power plants (which produce PM precursors) and the ongoing retirement of automobiles with laxer tailpipe standards, it likely is too. However, based on the AQA's record, it would be unreasonable to expect a PM annex to accomplish much more than affirm already existing programs and expected reductions for the pollutant or, more ambitious yet, non-binding commitments.

A presently more salient area for a consideration of bilateral dynamics—GHG abatement policy—is outside the scope of existing Canada–US treaties. Insofar as GHG policy entails reducing emissions from automobiles and power plants, air pollution and GHG abatement converge as a policy problem. Replacing coal-fired power plants or improving automobile fuel economy would reduce every criteria air pollutant in addition to carbon dioxide (CO_2). A GHG cap-and-trade program with the participation of both Canadian and US jurisdictions would potentially represent a significant and effective bilateral clean air program.

Given the interconnected status of the Canadian and American economies, and their well-established history of institutionalized responses to transboundary air pollution issues, it would seem plausible and reasonable that Canadian GHG policy would be linked to that of the United States. Canadian Environmental Minister Jim Prentice expressed this sentiment repeatedly throughout 2009 and 2010, during a time when the US Congress was considering a cap-and-trade law that would require substantial reductions in CO_2 (see Winfield's discussion of emissions trading in Chapter 5). Prentice claimed that Canada "is on the same page" on GHG policy, that "given the integration of our two economies it is essential our targets remain in line—not more, not less."[45] And when the American legislation failed to pass the US Senate in late 2010, Prentice cited Canada's policy of following the United States as the reason why Canada would not move forward with GHG cuts, saying, "we've been clear that we will not go it alone with cap-and-trade legislation."[46]

Yet, aside from new legislation, the US government has other options for GHG reductions by using existing authority under the 45-year-old US Clean Air Act to limit GHG emissions from automobiles, trucks, and large stationary sources such as power plants. On 2 June 2014, the details of the Obama administration's GHG program were announced. They promise 30 per cent reductions in carbon dioxide from 2005 levels by 2030, by forcing the retirement of dirty power plants and giving states a degree of flexibility in how to achieve these GHG reductions (such as participating in multi-state carbon-pricing systems). Is the Canadian government following suit, pursuing a reduction in emissions from mobile and stationary sources that also delivers benefits in terms of various forms of air pollution? Given that the Harper government has consciously linked the two—climate and air quality policy—in the past, and that the Conservatives continue to tout the benefits of co-ordinated bilateral action, is the Canadian government taking action similar to that in the US?

A National Air Pollution Strategy?

Canadian air pollution policy is presently undergoing rapid changes—at least on the surface. The Harper government has ostensibly made clean air policy one of its main environmental priorities and has decided to regulate industrial sources for the first time. This effort, initiated with the shelved Clean Air Act bill in 2006 and in the following year with the "Turning the Corner Plan," has morphed into two distinct programs: the federal–provincial Air Quality Management System (AQMS) and the Reduction of Carbon Dioxide Emissions from Coal-Fired Generation of Electricity Regulations (i.e., the "coal program").

The federal government and the CCME announced the AQMS in October 2012. It consists of two main policy instruments. The first involves non-binding **aspirational targets**, known as Canadian Ambient Air Quality Standards (CAAQS).[47] CAAQS were issued for O_3 and $PM_{2.5}$ in May 2013 and are presently under development for SO_2 and NO_2. They are essentially NAAQOs and Canada-Wide Standards under a new name. The O_3 and $PM_{2.5}$ CAAQS are slightly more stringent than their predecessors, but this is irrelevant since the vast majority of regions have already attained the targets and, in any case, there are no mandatory mechanisms to ensure compliance.

The second instrument is known as **base-level industrial emission requirements** (BLIERs). The purpose of BLIERs is to enable the Canadian government to "impose less stringent federal standards on industry" than it might otherwise, based on political pressure.[48] They are intended to specify "a consistent base-level of performance" for certain industrial polluters and thus serve as a "backstop" against extremely high emissions.[49] Environment Canada issued the first set of BLIERs regulations under CEPA in June 2014. Known as "Multi-sector Air Pollutants Regulations," they enforce lenient performance standards limiting the release of SO_2 and NO_X from engines used for tasks such as compression and pumping in industrial facilities, boilers and heaters generating steam for industrial purposes, and the country's 15 cement factories.[50] Environment Canada reports that future BLIERs will be non-regulatory "alternative instruments such as pollution prevention notices, codes of practice, release guidelines, and performance agreements."[51] It is fair to say that these new regulations are no substitute for anything resembling a modern national air pollution regime. Nevertheless, along with the coal program, they represent Ottawa's first-ever attempt to regulate air pollution from industry.[52]

The coal program's regulations also fall under CEPA. This program, announced in September 2012, caps CO_2 emissions from coal-fired power plants at 420 metric tons per gigawatt hour of electricity.[53] This is roughly equivalent to the coal plant emissions under the Obama administration's climate change program. Because no cost-effective technology exists to reduce CO_2 emissions sufficiently to comply with this regulation, it is now effectively illegal to construct a coal-fired plant in Canada. Existing coal plants are regulated on paper, although in practice the program allows them to continue to operate until the end of their effective lives. Coal-fired plants typically last for 50 years and continuing to use them beyond this normal lifespan requires refurbishment. The coal program's cutoff for the use of these plants is 2019 for those commissioned anytime before 1975 and 2029 for those commissioned between 1975 and 1986.[54] Thus, it enables utilities owning the plants to continue using them to recoup their investments while signalling that new types of plants will be required as replacements in the future.

Although this level of federal intervention on heavy industrial air pollution sources is unprecedented in Canada, there are at least two reasons for skepticism over whether the coal program represents substantive political leadership on the issues it purports to priori-tize. First, as a GHG reduction strategy, it does not target Canada's main emitters. Unlike in the United States, where coal is a heavily used source of electricity generation, Canada relies more on nuclear and hydro. Coal-fired power plants release less than 11 per cent of Canada's GHG emissions; in the US they release about 24 per cent.[55] Thus, even though the US and Can-adian regulations are comparable on a per-plant emissions basis, they are not comparable in scale. The oil and gas sector (including Alberta's oil sands), by comparison, is responsible for a quarter of Canada's GHG emissions.[56] This figure is expected to rise substantially in the coming decades, yet the Harper government has not released long-promised regulations for these sources.[57]

Second, and relatedly, the coal program places a federal government stamp on a process already underway. As mentioned above, Ontario has already shuttered all of its coal plants. Few have been built in Canada during the past three decades. This is representative of coal's decline in status while other sources of energy have gained prominence. With nuclear and hydropower providing most of the country's "baseload" electricity needs, coal's niche has narrowed towards fulfilling peak-hour demand. Yet natural gas and solar energy can also provide electricity at peak hours. Natural gas is relatively inexpensive and plants that use it cost less to build than coal plants. Solar capacity costs continue to fall and, already in Ontario, solar contributes to "peak-hour shaving" (see Rowlands, Chapter 14). As well, time-of-use pricing reduces peak-hour demand. With this expanding set of choices for generating electricity and reducing peak demand, the coal program appears on the surface more strin-gent than it is. Furthermore, the coal program allows provinces preferring to refurbish exist-ing plants to reach **equivalency agreements** with the federal government to reduce GHGs by the same amount as closing the plants, but in other ways. This regulatory provision may still result in lower GHG emissions, but it will likely keep coal plants open in Nova Scotia and Sas-katchewan that will continue to emit air pollution in large amounts and harm ecosystems and human health.

Conclusion

While air pollution policy exhibits signs of ambivalence in origins, intent, and implemen-tation, it is somewhat different from other cases in this book because it is unlikely that this particular policy regime will be dismantled or weakened appreciably. Despite austerity measures, the federal government has shown *heightened* interest in the problem, and is for the first time regulating industrial polluters. While the discussion above casts some doubt as to whether these new federal programs represent political leadership on clean air policy, at the same time, it is hard to argue they are victims of austerity.

For an understanding of Ottawa's actions on this issue, and why clean air policy is unlikely to be a victim of austerity, let us consider the four features of air pollution as a policy issue discussed above. Canada's environmental dependence due to long-distance transboundary emissions from the US seems less relevant here, since US pollution is not presently at issue in debates over Canadian clean air policy. However, recall that air pollution policy tends to be highly episodic and relies on technology (rather than, say, changes in consumption) for achieving reductions in emissions. Policy tends to be formulated at specific points in time when, for one reason or another, it rises on the political agenda. Long periods of time often occur with little in the way of new policy formulation. But because air pollution is not a public good needing active management, technology-based reductions *can* happen in fits and bursts and still be effective. Once automobiles, power plants, and cement kilns are designed with cleaner technology, the budget cuts associated with austerity do not turn back the clock. The areas of government expenditure on air pollution that might end up on the chopping block under austerity, such as compliance enforcement and research funding, are of marginal importance by comparison.

However, plenty of air pollution policy requires neither the use of modern abatement technology *nor* changes in consumption behaviour. This is because, as mentioned above, plenty of air pollution policy is symbolic. Policy-makers have consistently used it for nearly five decades to respond to public anxiety by manipulating Canadians into thinking that government is accomplishing more than it actually is. It appears the same is happening in the present context of deep ambivalence. Clear air policy and climate change abatement share enough commonalities that policy action in one domain appears as action in the other. Consider, for example, the 2006 Clean Air Act bill, the 2007 proposed "Turning the Corner" regulations, the AQMS, and the coal program. The promised substantial reductions make it appear as if the Harper government is concerned about cleaning up our atmosphere, but the federal regulations do not live up to the promises. It perhaps would be too cynical to consider the government's actions as a concerted effort at deceptively engineering consensus about its record of "political leadership" in this realm in order to facilitate continued natural resource exploitation. "Smoke and mirrors" seems more appropriate.

Key Terms

acid rain

aspirational targets

base-level industrial emission requirements

equivalency agreements

ground-level ozone

negative externality

particulate matter

point of impingement

toxic substances

Questions for Review

1. What are the main sources of air pollution and how do they differ in terms of the problems caused and in terms of how they are regulated?

2. How does air pollution abatement differ as a policy challenge compared to the management of natural resources such as fisheries and forests?

3. Describe the role of technology in bringing about improvements in air quality.

4. What are the overlaps between air pollution policy and climate and energy policy?

5. Why are Canadian federal standards, regulations, and international commitments generally non-binding or reflective of abatement processes already underway?

6. What is the significance of the United States for Canadian air pollution policy?

Internet Resources

Canada–United States Air Quality Committee, *Canada–United States Air Quality Agreement Progress Report 2012.*

https://ec.gc.ca/Publications/default.asp?lang=En&xml=D9D6380B-4834-41C4-9D36-B6E3348F1A39

Canadian Council of Ministers of the Environment, "Air Quality Management System"
http://www.ccme.ca/ourwork/air.html?category_id=146h

Environment Canada, "Canadian Smog Science Assessment Highlights and Key Messages"
http://www.ec.gc.ca/Air/default.asp?lang=En&n=72F82C27-1h

International Air Quality Advisory Board, *Report on Air Quality Issues Related to the Northern Boundary Region between Canada and the United States (2012)*.
http://ijc.org/php/publications/pdf/IAQAB-Report-to-IJC-Northern-Air-Quality-April-2012.pdf

Pollution Probe, *The Acid Rain Primer* (2006)
http://www.pollutionprobe.org/publications/the-acid-rain-primer/

Additional Reading

Cahn, Matthew A. *Environmental Deceptions: The Tension between Liberalism and Environmental Policymaking in the United States*. Albany, NY: SUNY Press, 1995.

Crenson, Matthew A. *The Un-Politics of Air Pollution: A Study of Non-Decisionmaking in the Cities*. Baltimore: Johns Hopkins University Press, 1971.

Gonzalez, George A. *The Politics of Air Pollution: Urban Growth, Ecological Modernization, and Symbolic Inclusion*. Albany, NY: SUNY Press, 2005.

Munton, Don. "Using Science, Ignoring Science: Lake Acidification in Ontario." In Neil E. Harrison and Gary C. Bryner, eds, *Science and Politics in the International Environment*, 143–72. Lanham, Md: Rowman & Littlefield, 2004.

Munton, Don. "Acid Rain Politics in North America: Conflict to Cooperation to Collusion." In Gerald R. Visgilio and Diana M. Whitelaw, eds, *Acid in the Environment: Lessons Learned and Future Prospects*, 175–201. New York: Springer, 2007.

Temby, Owen. "Trouble in Smogville: The Politics of Toronto's Air Pollution during the 1950s." *Journal of Urban History* 39, 4 (2013): 669–89.

VanNijnatten, Debora L., and W. Henry Lambright. "Canadian Smog Policy in Continental Context: Looking South for Stringency." In Debora L. VanNijnatten and Robert Boardman, eds, *Canadian Environmental Policy: Context and Cases*, 2nd edn, 253–73. Toronto: Oxford University Press, 2002.

Wirth, John D. *Smelter Smoke in North America: The Politics of Transborder Pollution*. Lawrence: University Press of Kansas, 2000.

Notes

1. Matthew Bray, "The Province of Ontario and the Problem of Sulphur Fumes Emissions in the Sudbury District," *Laurentian University Review* 16, 2 (1984): 81–90.
2. Owen Temby, "Trouble in Smogville: The Politics of Toronto's Air Pollution during the 1950s," *Journal of Urban History* 39, 4 (2013): 669–89.
3. D.L. Davis, "A Look Back at the London Smog of 1952 and the Half Century Since," *Environmental Health Perspectives* 110, 12 (2002): A734–5.
4. Gary Dunford, "Air Pollution in Metro: Even Five-Year-Olds Have Black Lungs," *Toronto Daily Star*, 3 Nov. 1967, 7.
5. Owen Temby, "Policy Symbolism and Air Pollution in Toronto and Ontario, 1963–1967," *Planning Perspectives* 30, 2(2015): 271–84. doi: 10.1080/02665433.2014.956782.
6. Ibid.
7. Don Munton, "Using Science, Ignoring Science: Lake Acidification in Ontario," in Neil E. Harrison and Gary C. Bryner, eds, *Science and Politics in the International Environment* (Lanham, Md: Rowman & Littlefield, 2004), 143–72.
8. Don Munton, "Acid Rain and Transboundary Air Quality in Canadian–American Relations," *American Review of Canadian Studies* 27, 3 (1997): 327–58; Don Munton, "Acid Rain Politics in North America: Conflict to Cooperation to Collusion," in Gerald R. Visgilio and Diana M. Whitelaw, eds, *Acid in the Environment: Lessons Learned and Future Prospects* (New York: Springer, 2007), 175–201.
9. Henrik Selin and Olof Hjelm, "The Role of Environmental Science and Politics in Identifying Persistent Organic Pollutants for International Regulatory Actions," *Environmental Reviews* 7, 2 (1999): 61–8.
10. Debora L. VanNijnatten, "Ground-Level Ozone: A Multi-Faceted Approach," in Philippe Le Prestre and Peter Stoett, eds, *Bilateral Ecopolitics: Continuity and Change in Canadian-American Environmental Relations* (Burlington, Vt: Ashgate, 2006), 51–72.
11. Canadian Medical Association, *No Breathing Room: National Illness Costs of Air Pollution* (2008), accessed 14 July 2014, http://www.cma.ca/multimedia/CMA/Content_Images/Inside_cma/Office_Public_Health/ICAP/CMA_ICAP_sum_e.pdf.
12. Canada–US Air Quality Committee, Subcommittee on Scientific Cooperation, *Canada–United States Transboundary Particulate Matter Science Assessment* (2004), accessed 14 July 2014, http://www.epa.gov/particles/pdfs/us_canada_pmscience_dec2004.pdf, p. 3.
13. Canadian Medical Association, *No Breathing Room*.

14. "Harper Treated in Ottawa Hospital," CBC News, 27 Jan. 2006, accessed 14 July 2014, http://www.cbc.ca/news/canada/harper-treated-in-ottawa-hospital-1.610576.
15. Radoslav S. Dimitrov, *Science and International Environmental Policy: Regimes and Nonregimes in Global Governance* (Lanham, Md: Rowman & Littlefield, 2009).
16. George A. Gonzalez, *The Politics of Air Pollution: Urban Growth, Ecological Modernization, and Symbolic Inclusion* (Albany, NY: SUNY Press, 2005); Owen Temby and Ryan O'Connor, "Property, Technology, and Environmental Policy: The Politics of Acid Rain in Ontario, 1978–1985," unpublished manuscript.
17. Temby and O'Connor, "Property, Technology, and Environmental Policy."
18. Gonzalez, *The Politics of Air Pollution*; Scott Hamilton Dewey, *Don't Breathe the Air: Air Pollution and U.S. Environmental Politics, 1945–1970* (College Station: Texas A&M University Press, 2000).
19. Gonzalez, *The Politics of Air Pollution*; Don Munton and Owen Temby, "From Sudbury to Trail to Sudbury: Smelter 'Fume' Damage and Canadian Environmentalism," unpublished manuscript.
20. Don Munton, "Transboundary Air Pollution: Dependence and Interdependence," in Philippe Le Prestre and Peter Stoett, eds, *Bilateral Ecopolitics: Continuity and Change in Canadian–American Environmental Relations* (Burlington, Vt: Ashgate, 2006), 73–92.
21. Matthew A. Cahn, *Environmental Deceptions: The Tension between Liberalism and Environmental Policymaking in the United States* (Albany, NY: SUNY Press, 1995), 41.
22. Ibid, 50.
23. Temby, "Policy Symbolism."
24. F.L. Morton, "The Constitutional Division of Powers with Respect to the Environment in Canada," in Kenneth M. Holland, F.L. Morton, and Brian Galligan, eds, *Federalism and the Environment: Environmental Policymaking in Australia, Canada, and the United States* (Westport, Conn.: Greenwood Press, 1996), 37–54; Marcia Valiante, "Legal Foundations of Canadian Environmental Policy: Underlining Our Values in a Shifting Landscape," in Debora L. VanNijnatten and Robert Boardman, eds, *Canadian Environmental Policy: Context and Cases*, 2nd edn (Toronto: Oxford University Press, 2002), 3–24.
25. David Estrin and John Swaigen, *Environment on Trial: A Citizen's Guide to Ontario Environmental Law* (Don Mills, Ont.: New Press, 1974), 43–5; Grace Skogstad, "Intergovernmental Relations and the Politics of Environmental Protection in Canada," in Kenneth M. Holland, F.L. Morton, and Brian Galligan, eds, *Federalism and the Environment: Environmental Policymaking in Australia, Canada, and the United States* (Westport, Conn.: Greenwood Press, 1996), 108; Edward R. Wells and Alan M. Schwartz, eds, *Historical Dictionary of North American Environmentalism* (Lanham, Md:
Scarecrow Press, 1997). Wells and Schwartz (p. 50) refer to the Clean Air Act as an "enabling rather than a regulatory piece of legislation."
26. Nancy Olewiler, "Environmental Policy in Canada: Harmonized at the Bottom?" in Kathryn Harrison, ed., *Racing to the Bottom? Provincial Interdependence in the Canadian Federation* (Vancouver: University of British Columbia Press, 2006), 113–56.
27. Environment Canada, "Schedule 1 Substances Inherited from CEPA 1988," accessed 7 July 2014, http://www.ec.gc.ca/lcpe-cepa/default.asp?lang=En&n=0DA2924D-1&wsdoc=57270C65-EFD8-CC05-AEF7-B94DB47D6F92; Environment Canada, "Toxic Substances List—Schedule 1," accessed 7 July 2014, http://www.ec.gc.ca/lcpe-cepa/default.asp?lang=En&n=0DA2924D-1&wsdoc=4ABEFFC8-5BEC-B57A-F4BF-11069545E434.
28. In a proposed regulation published 7 June 2014 called Multi-sector Pollutants Regulations, Environment Canada claims that the federal plan resulting in the new regulations "marked the first federal effort to address air pollution from industrial sources." http://www.gazette.gc.ca/rp-pr/p1/2014/2014-06-07/html/reg2-eng.html.
29. Environment Canada, "2014-2015 Report on Plans and Priorities," accessed 27 June 2014, https://www.ec.gc.ca/default.asp?lang=En&n=024B8406-1&offset=4&toc=show#s3.2.1. See also Andy Blatchford, "Local Dry Cleaners Top Target for Environment Canada Inspections," *Toronto Star*, 13 Feb. 2011.
30. Canada's federal automobile regulations were actually *laxer* than those of the US before the 1988 model year because the Canadian government did not require the installation of catalytic converters. Dimitry Anastakis, "A 'War on Pollution'? Canadian Responses to the Automotive Emissions Problem, 1970–1980," *Canadian Historical Review* 90, 1 (2009): 99–136.
31. Typically the process has taken the form of a "memorandum of understanding" (MOU) between the Canadian government and the automobile industry. More recently, Canada has issued regulations under CEPA mirroring those in the United States. For example, see the proposed Regulations Amending the Passenger Automobile and Light Truck Greenhouse Gas Emission Regulations (2017–2025), 12–49, http://www.gazette.gc.ca/rp-pr/p1/2012/2012-12-08/html/reg1-eng.html.
32. Temby, "Policy Symbolism."
33. Estrin and Swaigen, *Environment on Trial*, 45–51.
34. Temby and O'Connor, "Property, Technology, and Environmental Policy."
35. Mark Winfield, *Blue-Green Province: The Environment and the Political Economy of Ontario* (Vancouver: University of British Columbia Press, 2012), ch. 5; Owen Temby, "Environmental Policy and Property Based Interests," Ph.D. dissertation (Carleton University, 2012).
36. Environment Canada, "Canada's Clean Air Act Delivered to Canadians," press release, 19 Oct. 2006.

37. The four main treaties and matching organizations are: (1) the 1909 Boundary Waters Treaty and the International Joint Commission; (2) the 1979 Convention on Long-Range Transboundary Air Pollution (LRTAP) and its secretariat; (3) the 1991 Air Quality Agreement and the Canada–US Air Quality Committee; and (4) the 1994 North American Agreement on Environmental Cooperation and the Commission for Environmental Conservation. LRTAP is by far the most active of these in conducting and framing scientific research, but for the past decade its resources have been directed largely to intercontinental air pollution, not North American.

38. VanNijnatten, "Ground-Level Ozone"; Winfield, *Blue-Green Province*.

39. Munton, "Transboundary Air Pollution."

40. Temby, "Environmental Policy and Property-Based Interests."

41. Sally A. Talberg, "The Clean Air Act and Grandfathered Power Plants," *Journal of Public Affairs* 12 (Spring 2000): 19–31.

42. Temby, "Environmental Policy and Property-Based Interests."

43. Munton, "Acid Rain Politics in North America."

44. Canada–United States Air Quality Committee, *Canada–United States Air Quality Agreement Progress Report 2012*, http://ec.gc.ca/Publications/default. asp?lang=En&xml=D9D6380B-4834-41C4-9D36-B6E3348F1A39.

45. "Canada to Follow U.S. Lead at Climate Summit," CBC News, 4 Dec. 2009; Mitch Potter, "Canada, U.S. Share Climate Goals, Prentice Says," *Toronto Star*, 3 Mar. 2009.

46. "Cap-and-Trade Likely on Hold: Prentice," CBC News, 2 Nov. 2010, accessed 10 July 2014, http://www.cbc.ca/news/canada/cap-and-trade-likely-on-hold-prentice-1.926221.

47. http://www.gazette.gc.ca/rp-pr/p1/2014/2014-06-07/html/reg2-eng.html.

48. Ibid.

49. CCME, "The Air Quality Management System: Federal, Provincial and Territorial Roles and Responsibilities,"

3–4, updated 11 Oct. 2012, accessed 29 June 2014, http://www.ccme.ca/assets/pdf/pn_1475_roles_and_respn_final_e.pdf.

50. http://www.gazette.gc.ca/rp-pr/p1/2014/2014-06-07/html/reg2-eng.html.

51. Ibid.

52. A notable exception is the regulation of Consolidating Mining and Smelting Company's lead and zinc smelter in Trail, British Columbia, in response to a 1941 arbitration settlement with the US government.

53. Environment Canada, "Harper Government Moves Forward on Tough Rules for Coal-Fired Electricity Sector," press release, 5 Sept. 2012; Shawn McCarthy, "Ottawa Unveils New Coal-fired Power Plant Emissions Rules," *Globe and Mail*, 5 Sept. 2012.

54. Environment Canada, "Backgrounder: Reduction of Carbon Dioxide Emissions from Coal-Fired Generation of Electricity Regulations," accessed 7 July 2014, http://www.ec.gc.ca/default.asp?lang=En&n=5C4438BC-1&news=D375183E-0016-4145-A20B-272BDB94580A.

55. Environment Canada, "Questions and Answers: Reduction of Carbon Dioxide from Coal-Fired Generation," modified 5 July 2013, accessed 29 June 2014, http://ec.gc.ca/cc/default.asp?lang=En&n=E907D4D5-1; US EPA, "Sources of Greenhouse Gas Emissions: Electricity Sector Emissions," accessed 29 June 2014, http://www.epa.gov/climatechange/ghgemissions/sources/electricity.html.

56. Jennifer Ditchburn, "Harper on U.S. Climate-Change Coal Crackdown: Been There, Done That," *Vancouver Sun*, 2 June 2014; Amber Hildebrandt, "Obama's Aggressive Climate-Change Move and Canada's Response," CBC News, 3 June 2014.

57. National Round Table on the Environment and the Economy, *Reality Check: The State of Climate Progress in Canada*, 2013, http://collectionscanada.gc.ca/webarchives2/20130322165455/http:/nrtee-trnee.ca/reality-check-the-state-of-climate-progress-in-canada.

Index